THE HISTORY OF ENGLISH POETRY.

THOMAS WARTON

History of English Poetry from the Twelfth to the Close of the Sixteenth Century

Edited by W. Carew Hazlitt

(1871)

Vol. II

HASKELL HOUSE PUBLISHERS Ltd.
Publishers of Scarce Scholarly Books
NEW YORK. N. Y. 10012
1970

First Published 1871

HASKELL HOUSE PUBLISHERS LTD.
Publishers of Scarce Scholarly Books
280 LAFAYETTE STREET
NEW YORK, N. Y. 10012

Library of Congress Catalog Card Number: 68-26371

Standard Book Number 8383-0187-8

Printed in the United States of America

HISTORY OF

ENGLISH POETRY

FROM THE TWELFTH TO THE CLOSE

OF THE SIXTEENTH

CENTURY.

BY THOMAS WARTON, B.D.

FELLOW OF TRIN. COLL., OXFORD ; F.S.A.; PROFESSOR OF
POETRY IN THE UNIVERSITY OF OXFORD.

WITH A PREFACE BY RICHARD PRICE, AND NOTES VARIORUM.

EDITED BY W. CAREW HAZLITT.

WITH NEW NOTES AND OTHER ADDITIONS BY SIR FREDERIC MADDEN, K.H., F.R.S. ;
THOMAS WRIGHT, M.A., F.S.A. ; W. ALDIS WRIGHT, M.A. ; REV.
WALTER W. SKEAT, M.A. ; RICHARD MORRIS, LL.D. ;
F. J. FURNIVALL, M.A. ; AND THE EDITOR.

WITH INDEXES OF NAMES AND SUBJECTS.

IN FOUR VOLUMES.

VOL. II.

LONDON:

REEVES AND TURNER, 196, STRAND.

1871.

SKETCH OF THE HISTORY OF
ANGLO-SAXON POETRY.

[The hiſtory of Engliſh poetry begins in lands where the name of England was not known. Not in our " iſland home " was our mother tongue in its earlieſt ſtage firſt ſpoken, but in parts of the Daniſh land, the Angliſh and Saxiſh provinces, in Frieſland, Jutland, and the neighbouring iſles, whence the firſt Teutonic ſettlers and invaders came, to people our England. They brought with them the legends of their continental homes; and the one weird poem which has come to us from them whole, though much meddled with by later hands, is our national epic. But before we give an account of it, and the reſt of our forefathers' poetry, we muſt ſay ſomewhat of the forms of Anglo-Saxon verſe, and muſt note that, for convenience of claſſification, the continuous changes in our language have been ſeparated into the following ſtages:

I. Anglo-Saxon or Old Engliſh, with regular inflexions, up to 1100 A.D.
II. Semi-Saxon or Tranſition Engliſh, in two ſtages, (1) when the inflexion ſigns were ſtruggling for ſuperiority, from 1100 to 1500 A.D.;[1] (2) when the final _e_ had gained the victory, but the vocabulary was almoſt wholly Anglo-Saxon, as in Laʒamon, 1150-1250 A.D.
III. Early Engliſh, 1250-1500 A.D. when the vocabulary received large French importations, and the final _e_ gradually became grammatically valueleſs.
IV. Middle Engliſh, 1500-1620 A.D.—_F._]

---

[1] [See the preface to Dr. Richard Morris's _Old Engliſh Homilies_, I. Early Engliſh Text Society, 1868; and his ſketch of the characteriſtics of the Tranſition Period of our language in Section 1 below.]

[Sketch of the Hiſtory of Anglo-Saxon Poetry.

BY HENRY SWEET, OF BALIOL COLLEGE, OXFORD.

THE forms and traditions of Anglo-Saxon poetry[1] are thoſe which are common to all the old Germanic nations. The eſſential elements of Anglo-Saxon verſification are accent and alliteration. Each long verſe has *four* accented ſyllables, while the number of unaccented ſyllables is indifferent, and is divided by the cæſura into two ſhort verſes, bound together by alliteration : *two* accented ſyllables in the firſt ſhort line, and *one* in the ſecond, beginning with any vowel or the ſame conſonant. Inſtead of two there is often only *one* alliterative letter in the firſt ſhort verſe. The alliterative letter of the ſecond ſhort verſe muſt belong to the firſt of the two accented ſyllables. Of this metre in its ſtricteſt and ſimpleſt form the following line of Beowulf is an example :—

ríce to rúne | rǽdes eáhtedon.

---

[1] The ſtandard work for the ſtudy of Anglo-Saxon poetry is the collection of Grein, publiſhed under the title of *Bibliothek der Angelſächſiſchen Poeſie*, in four vols., the firſt two containing critical texts of all known poems, the third and fourth a complete poetical dictionary. In his *Dichtungen der Angelſachſen* Grein has given a literal tranſlation of nearly all the poems. In the *Bibliothek* will be found a complete liſt of all previous editions and tranſlations, nearly all of which, it may be added, are entirely ſuperſeded by Grein's work. It will therefore be neceſſary only to mention thoſe works which have appeared ſince the publication of Grein's *Bibliothek*. Theſe are the edition of the fragments of Waldhere by Profeſſor Stephens and by Grein, as an appendix to his edition of Beowulf and Finneſburg, and Heyne's edition and tranſlation of Beowulf, the former of which has appeared in two editions. A volume of *Metrical Homilies, or Lives of Saints* is preparing for the Early Engliſh Text Society, under Mr. Skeat's editorſhip.

Here are two accents in each fhort verfe, both accented fyllables in the firft fhort verfe, and the firft in the fecond beginning with the letter *r*. In the line

eórmenláfe | æðelan cýnnes

there are only two alliterative letters, *eo* and *æ*, which, being vowels, are allowed to be different.

As remarked above, the number of unaccented fyllables is indifferent; the fame remark applies, within certain limits, to an excefs of *accented* fyllables alfo. The moft important of thefe limitations is that all additional accents in the fecond fhort verfe muft come *before* the alliterative fyllable. Generally fpeaking, the number of accents in an ordinary long line does not exceed *five :*

mícel mórgenfwég | mǽre þeóden.
fǽder on láfte | fíððan fórð gewát.

Such is the general ftructure of the great majority of Anglo-Saxon verfes. More elaborate modifications are, however, occafionally introduced, generally in folemn, lyrical paffages. The moft important characteriftic of thefe metres is the regular introduction of unaccented fyllables, each accented fyllable being followed by one or more unaccented, the laft foot but one of the line (containing the alliterative letter) efpecially being often a dactyl. This kind of verfe often refembles the ancient hexameter, when read accentually. The comparifon of the two following lines will at once fhow how much of the character of Anglo-Saxon verfe depends on the ufe of unaccented fyllables :

mícel mórgenfwég | mǽre þeóden.
rínca to rúne gegángan | hi ða on réfte gebróhton.

This kind of verfe is alfo generally characterifed by an increafed number of accented fyllables, generally not lefs than fix, often more :

ðónne hi mǽft mid him | mǽrða gefrémedon.
geófian mid góda gehwílcum | ðeáh he his gíngran ne fénde.
geheáwan ðífne mórðres brýttan | geúnne me mínra gefýnta.
fíra beárn on ðíffum fǽftum clómmum | ongínnað nu ymb ða fýrde þéncean.

More rarely we meet with an increafed number of accented, without unaccented fyllables ; the effect is peculiar, and quite different from that of the hexameter-like lines quoted above ; two lines of the *Wanderer* afford a good example :

hwǽr cwóm meárg ? hwǽr cwóm mágo ? | hwǽr cwóm máððumgífa ?
hwǽr cwóm fímbla gefétu ? | hwǽr fíndon féledreámas ?

Different as thefe metres are, they all belong to the fame type, which is reprefented in the fimpleft form in the verfe of Beowulf firft quoted. All the variations reduce themfelves to :—

(1.) Infertion of additional feet before the alliterative fyllable of the fecond fhort line.

(2.) Regular ufe of unaccented fyllables.

(3.) Increafe in the number of accents in the firft fhort verfe.

So that the only really arbitrary feature is the varying number of accents in the firft fhort verfe ; although this licenfe, like all others in Anglo-Saxon poetry, is always regulated by the metrical feeling of the poet, and often depends on the more or lefs regular ufe of unaccented fyllables. The ftricteft part of the line is the fecond fhort verfe : only one alliterative letter is allowed, and its pofition and that of the inferted fyllables are fixed (compare alfo the remark about the dactylic feet). This tendency to metrical concentration and ftrictnefs at the end of the line is common to all metres ; it is alike evident in the ftructure of the claffical hexameter and of the modern rhyming metres. The alliteration, though not the effence of the Anglo-Saxon verfification, is a neceffary element of it, being indiffolubly connected with the accentuation. It cannot therefore, like modern rhyme, be omitted or modified at pleafure. There are alfo traces of rhyme, and one poem, commonly called the *Rhyming Poem,* is compofed throughout of very elaborate rhymes.

An effential feature of Anglo-Saxon poetry is the ufe of poetic words and phrafes : words being employed in poetry which do not occur in profe, or profe words and phrafes being ufed in a peculiar fenfe. There is alfo a ftrong tendency to appofition, which in fome cafes almoft amounts to parallelifm, as in Hebrew poetry : " dæt ic *fæneffas* gefeon mihte, *windige weallas,*" fo that I could fee the feaheadlands, the windy walls ; " dæt du us gebrohte *brante ceole,* hea hornfcipe, ofer hwæles edel," that thou mighteft bring us in a fteep veffel, a high-prowed fhip, over the whale's country (the fea). In this laft example the two adjectives are exactly parallel, and have practically the fame meaning. This tendency is ftrikingly fhown in the frequent ufe of an adjective in appofition to a fubftantive, inftead of attributively : " hæfdon fwurd nacod, heard on handa," we held in our hands keen fwords unfheathed.

This fimplicity and freedom of form, which is characteriftic of the earlieft poetry of all the Teutonic nations, has led narrowminded and fuperficial writers to defcribe Anglo-Saxon poetry as lines of bad profe, joined together by alliteration ; forgetting that the higheft artiftic excellence is attainable in many ways, and that the metrical laws which fuit one language, are totally out of place in another of different ftructure. A ftrict and unvarying fyftem of verfification, like the Homeric hexameter, in which a battle and a cooking operation are defcribed in the fame metre, would have feemed intolerable to a Northern poet : he required one which would adapt itfelf to every phafe of emotion and change of action, which in defcribing profaic incidents, fuch as will occur in every narrative poem of any length, could be let down nearly to the level of ordinary profe, with an effective tranfition to the more concentrated paffages. The leading principle in Anglo-Saxon poetry is to fubordinate form to matter. No brilliancy of language or metre is accepted as a fubftitute for poverty of thought or feeling ; purely technical poetry, with a few trifling exceptions, is not known. This tendency is clearly brought out by a comparifon of the clofely allied poetry of the Scandinavians, as carried to its higheft point of development in Norway and Iceland. Here the original metrical fyftem, eſſentially the ſame as the Anglo-Saxon, was at an early period brought to a high degree of perfection. The number of ſyllables was made invariable, the alliteration was refined and regulated, and rhymes, both initial and final, were introduced, the original alliteration being ſtill preſerved. But theſe technical advantages were counterbalanced by an almoſt total ſtagnation of any higher artiſtic development. Lyric and dramatic poetry, traces of which are found in the earlieſt poems of Edda, remain undeveloped, and at laſt poetry degenerates into a purely mechanical art, valued only in proportion to the difficulty of its execution. The Anglo-Saxons, on the other hand, whilſt preſerving the utmoſt technical ſimplicity, developed not only an elaborate epic ſtyle, but what is more remarkable, produced lyric and didactic poetry of high merit, and this at a very early period, certainly at leaſt as early as the beginning of the eighth century.

Important characteriſtics of Anglo-Saxon poetry are conciſeneſs and directneſs. Everything that retards the action or obſcures the main ſentiment of the poem is avoided, hence all ſimiles are extremely rare. In the whole poem of Beowulf there are ſcarcely half a dozen of them, and theſe of the ſimpleſt character, ſuch as comparing a ſhip to a bird. Indeed, ſuch a ſimple compariſon as this is almoſt equivalent to the more uſual " kenning " (as it is called in Icelandic), ſuch as " brimfugol," where, inſtead of comparing the ſhip to a bird, the poet ſimply calls it a ſea-bird, preferring the direct aſſertion to the indirect compariſon. Such elaborate compariſons as are found in Homer and his Roman imitator are quite foreign to the ſpirit of Northern poetry.

A marked feature of Anglo-Saxon poetry is a tendency to melancholy and pathos, which tinges the whole literature : even the ſong of victory ſhows it, and joined to the heathen fataliſm of the oldeſt poems, it produces a deep gloom, which would be painful were it not relieved by that high moral idealiſm which is never wanting in Anglo-Saxon poetry. This tendency was, no doubt, ſtrengthened by the great political calamities of the Anglo-Saxons, their precarious hold upon Britain, their civil and foreign wars, which ultimately brought about their national extinction. Deſcriptions of nature are not unfrequent in Anglo-Saxon poetry, and form one of its moſt characteriſtic features ; for deſcriptions of natural ſcenery are generally unknown in early literature, and are often rare in many, which are otherwiſe highly developed. Elaborate deſcriptions of gardens may be found in Homer and the Italian poets, but hardly any of wild nature. In the lyrical German poetry of the thirteenth century, there is evidence enough of a ſtrong feeling for nature, but there is no diſtinctneſs or individuality—nothing but general alluſions to the brightneſs of the flowers and the ſong of the birds, which ſoon petrify to mere formulæ. In Anglo-Saxon poetry, on the other hand, ſuch paſſages as the deſcriptions of Grendel's abode in Beowulf (p. 11 below), have a vividneſs and individuality which make them not inferior to the moſt perfect examples of descriptive poetry in modern English literature,—perhaps the highest praise that can be given. This characteristic forms a strong bond of union between the two literatures, so different in many other respects, and it is not impossible that some of the higher qualities of modern English poetry are to be assigned to traditions of the old Anglo-Saxon literature, obscured for a time by those didactic, political, and allegorical tendencies which almost extinguished genuine poetry in the Early English period. The bulk of the poetical literature that has come down to us is considerable, but the pieces are of various degrees of value, and some of them are totally destitute of poetical merit. There can be no doubt that the works we possess do not fairly represent the actual literature. They have not been handed down to us from generation to generation, and preserved in many MSS., as is the case with the literatures of ancient Greece and Rome; where, if a work is lost, we are to a great extent justified in assuming it to have been of inferior merit. We know that for many centuries after the Conquest books written in the old language were considered as waste parchment, and utilized accordingly; and that great havoc was made among the monastic libraries at the Reformation. The consequence is that many of the finest poems are mere fragments, and those that are preserved have escaped total destruction by a series of lucky chances, and, with a few trifling exceptions, are preserved only in single manuscripts.

The chronology and authorship of the poems are in most cases very uncertain. Several of them were certainly composed before the German colonization of Britain, however much they may have been altered and interpolated in later times. It is equally certain that by far the greater number of the other poems were composed in Northumbria. Cædmon we know to have been a Northumbrian, both from the express testimony of Bede, and from the fact of a few lines of his being preserved in the original northern dialect. The name of Cynewulf is introduced into several poems contained in the Exeter and Vercelli MSS., three times in a kind of acrostic in Runic letters, once in a riddle or rather charade on his own name. As all these poems are written in the ordinary West-Saxon dialect, it was at first supposed that Cynewulf was a native of the south of England; but when the Runic inscription of the Ruthwell cross in Dumfriesshire was deciphered, and shown to be a fragment of a poem of Cynewulf's, which is preserved entire in the Vercelli MS., it became at once evident that the poems of Cædmon and Cynewulf in their present shape are copies of Northumbrian originals, altered to suit the southern dialect. How far the analogy holds good for the remaining poems of unascertained authorship is uncertain. As we know that literature was first cultivated in the north, there is an *à priori* probability in the case of all the older poems that they were either composed by Northumbrians, or at least were first written down in Northumbria. Indeed, there are only two poems of any merit to which we can assign with any certainty a southern origin. These are the ode on the battle of Brunanburg, and the narrative of the battle of Maldon, which were, no doubt, compofed immediately after the events they record. King Alfred's tranflation of the metres of Boethius is almoft entirely deftitute of poetical merit.

It is probable that the earlieft poetry of the Anglo-Saxons confifted of fingle ftrophes, each narrating, or rather alluding to, fome exploit of a hero or god, or expreffing fome fingle fentiment, generally of a proverbial or gnomic character. Such is the poetry of favage nations. The next ftage is to combine thefe ftrophes into connected groups. The third is to abandon the ftrophic arrangement altogether. With regard to the poetical form, it is tolerably certain that in the earlieft ftage there was no difference between poetry and profe; in fact, poetry was entirely unformal—fimply a concentrated profe. Of all civilized poetical literatures, the moft primitive is that of the ancient Hebrew, which is only diftinguifhed from profe by the fymmetry and mutual correfpondence of its fentences. This parallelifm we have recognized as a frequent, though not effential, ingredient of Anglo-Saxon verfe; it is alfo ftrongly developed in the earlieft Scandinavian poetry. It feems, therefore, not improbable that the Anglo-Saxon poetry in its earlieft ftage confifted of lines of profe connected only by parallelifm. When alliteration had developed itfelf and become a conftant element of the poetic form, the parallelifm would gradually fall into difufe, as in Latin literature the regular alliteration of Nævius becomes fporadic in Virgil.

Almoft the only example of ftrophic poetry in Anglo-Saxon is the poem known as *Deor's Complaint.* The poem is obfcure, and has been handed down to us in a corrupt and mutilated ftate, but its ftrophic character is unmiftakeable. The firft and laft two ftrophes confift of fix lines each, and all fix ftrophes end with the fame refrain. All the old Scandinavian epic and mythological fongs are ftrophic; and the connection between the ftrophes is often fo little evident that it is a work of difficulty to arrange them in proper order; in fhort, the regular epos is hardly developed at all. It is not impoffible that *Deor's Complaint* is a folitary remnant of the fame ftage of Anglo-Saxon poetry; the poem deals exclufively with the hiftorical and mythological traditions common to all the Teutonic nations, and may eafily have been compofed before the migration to England. It muft, however, be borne in mind that the ufe of a primitive form is quite compatible with a comparatively recent origin of a poem, efpecially one of a half lyric character, like *Deor's Complaint.* The other epic pieces feem to be quite deftitute of ftrophic arrangement, moft of them exhibit the epos in its moft advanced and artiftic form, although the greater bulk of the epic poetry being preferved only in fragments, it is difficult to determine whether thefe fragments form part of a regular epos, or are merely epic fongs like thofe of the *Edda.* It is probable that fome of them may belong to this latter clafs, of which we have an undoubted fpecimen, compofed in hiftorical times, the *Battle of Maldon.* Every genuine

national epos prefuppofes a ftage of literature, in which thefe fhort
hiftorical fongs were the only narrative poems exifting; for the
genuine epic, which is regarded by thofe for whom it is compofed as
hiftory, and nothing elfe, is never invented, but has to draw on the
common national ftock of hiftorical and mythological tradition.
How far the original fubftruĉture of feparate fongs is ftill vifible in
the finifhed epos, depends entirely on the genius of the manipulator,
and his command of his materials. If he is deftitute of invention
and combination, he will leave the feparate poems unaltered, except,
perhaps, in cafes of repetition and very obvious contradiĉtion, and
merely cement them together by a few lines of his own. Many of
the Eddaic poems are in this ftage : they are patchwork, evidently
executed long after the true epic fpirit had died. Very often the
conneĉting and complementary paffages are written in profe, fo that
the genius of a Lachmann is hardly needed to cut out the interpola-
tion. But if the traditions contained in thefe fongs are handled by
a poet, that is to fay, a man of invention, combination, and judgment, they are liable to undergo confiderable modifications. There
will be room for original work in conneĉting the various incidents
and introducing epifodes, in removing incongruities and repetitions,
and in fufing together two or more different renderings of the fame
tradition. In fhort, the ufe of traditional material does not in the
flighteft degree preclude originality. This has often been overlooked
by critics who have endeavoured to analyfe fuch poems as the *Iliad*
or *Nibelungenlied* into their original fongs ; the refult in the cafe of
the *Nibelungenlied* is that the diffeĉtor, after employing an elaborate
apparatus of brackets, parenthefes, and italics, is obliged to confefs
that the excifed paffages not only mar by their abfence the fymmetry
of the whole, but are often fuperior to thofe which are allowed to
remain. We know that Shakefpeare founded his *Julius Cæfar* on
Plutarch, but we do not wifh to fee his play cut up according to the
chapters of North's Plutarch.

The only national epic which has been preferved entire is Beowulf.
Its argument is briefly as follows :

The poem opens with a few verfes in praife of the Danifh kings,
efpecially Scild, the fon of Sceaf. His death is related, and his
defcendants briefly traced down to Hroðgar. Hroðgar, elated
with his profperity and fuccefs in war, builds a magnificent hall,
which he calls Heorot. In this hall Hroðgar and his retainers live
in joy and feftivity, until a malignant fiend, called Grendel, jealous
of their happinefs, carries off by night thirty of Hroðgar's men, and
devours them in his moorland retreat. Thefe ravages go on for
twelve years. Beowulf, a thane of Hygelac, king of the Goths,
hearing of Hroðgar's calamities, fails from Sweden with fourteen
warriors to help him. They reach the Danifh coaft in fafety, and,
after an animated parley with Hroðgar's coaft-guard, who at firft
takes them for pirates, they are allowed to proceed to the royal hall,
where they are well received by Hroðgar. A banquet enfues, during
which Beowulf is taunted by the envious Hunferhð about his

swimming-match with Breca, king of the Brondings. Beowulf gives the true account of the contest, and silences Hunferhð. At nightfall the king departs, leaving Beowulf in charge of the hall. Grendel soon breaks in, seizes and devours one of Beowulf's companions, is attacked by Beowulf, and after losing an arm, which is torn off by Beowulf, escapes to the fens. The joy of Hroðgar and the Danes, and their festivities, are described, various episodes are introduced, and Beowulf and his companions receive splendid gifts. The next night Grendel's mother revenges her son by carrying off Æschere, the friend and councillor of Hroðgar, during the absence of Beowulf. Hroðgar appeals to Beowulf for vengeance, and describes the haunts of Grendel and his mother. They all proceed thither; the scenery of the lake, and the monsters that dwell in it are described. Beowulf plunges into the water, and attacks Grendel's mother in her dwelling at the bottom of the lake. He at length overcomes her, and cuts off her head, together with that of Grendel, and brings the heads to Hroðgar. He then takes leave of Hroðgar, sails back to Sweden, and relates his adventures to Hygelac. Here the first half of the poem ends. The second begins with the accession of Beowulf to the throne after the fall of Hygelac and his son Heardred. He rules prosperously for fifty years, till a dragon, brooding over a hidden treasure, begins to ravage the country, and destroys Beowulf's palace with fire. Beowulf sets out in quest of its hiding place with twelve men. Having a presentiment of his approaching end, he pauses and recalls to mind his past life and exploits. He then takes leave of his followers one by one, and advances alone to attack the dragon. Unable from the heat to enter the cavern, he shouts aloud, and the dragon comes forth. The dragon's scaly hide is proof against Beowulf's sword, and he is reduced to great straits, when Wiglaf, one of his followers, advances to help him. Wiglaf's shield is consumed by the dragon's fiery breath, and he is compelled to seek shelter under Beowulf's shield of iron. Beowulf's sword snaps asunder, and he is seized by the dragon. Wiglaf stabs the dragon from underneath, and Beowulf cuts it in two with his dagger. Feeling that his end is near, he bids Wiglaf bring out the treasures from the cavern, that he may see them before he dies. Wiglaf enters the dragon's den, which is described, returns to Beowulf, and receives his last commands. Beowulf dies, and Wiglaf bitterly reproaches his companions for their cowardice. The disastrous consequences of Beowulf's death are then foretold, and the poem ends with his funeral.

It is evident that the poem as we have it, has undergone considerable alterations. In the first place there is a distinctly Christian element, contrasting strongly with the general heathen colouring of the whole. Many of these passages are so incorporated into the poem, that it is impossible to remove them without violent alterations of the text; others again are palpable interpolations. Such are the passages where Grendel is described as a descendant of Cain. Perhaps the strongest instance is one where we have a christian commentary on a heathen fuperftition. We are told that the Danes, in order to avert the miferies brought on them by Grendel, began to offer facrifices to their idols. Then follow fome verfes beginning : "Such was their cuftom, the hope of heathens ; they thought of hell, but knew not the Lord, the Judge of deeds, &c."

Without thefe additions and alterations, it is certain that we have in Beowulf a poem compofed before the Teutonic conqueft of Britain. The localities are purely continental : the fcenery is laid among the Goths of Sweden and the Danes ; in the epifodes, the Swedes, Frifians, and other continental tribes appear, while there is no mention of England, or the adjoining countries and nations. It is evident that the poem, as a whole, cannot have been compofed directly from the current traditions of the period : the variety of incidents, their artiftic treatment, and the epifodes introduced, fhow that the poet had fome foundation to work upon, that there muft have been fhort epic fongs about the exploits of Beowulf current among the people, which he combined into a whole. In the poem as it ftands, we can eafily diftinguifh four elements : the prologue, the two chief exploits of Beowulf againft Grendel, the dragon, and the epifodes.

The attempt to eliminate thefe elements in their original form would be loft labour, as we have no means of determining the degree of alteration they have undergone ; an alteration which, however, to judge from the remarkable unity and homogeneoufnefs of the whole work, muft have been confiderable ; otherwife we fhould hardly fail to perceive fome traces of the incongruity and abrupt tranfition which betray a clumfy piece of compilation. The epifodes would be lefs liable to alteration than thofe paffages which form part of the main narrative, and it is highly probable that among them the oldeft parts of the poem are to be found. Many of thefe epifodes are extremely obfcure, partly from the corrupt and defective ftate of the text, partly from the elliptical way in which they are told, evidently leaving a good deal to be filled up by the hearer, to whom the traditions on which they are founded were naturally familiar.

The following literal tranflations will give fome idea of the ftyle of Beowulf. The firft is the defcription of Grendel's abode ; the fecond is part of Hrodgar's farewell addrefs to Beowulf ; the third is part of the defcription of Beowulf's funeral, with which the poem ends :

"They hold a hidden land : where wolves lurk, windy neffes, perilous fen-tracts, where the mountain-ftream fhrouded in mift pours down the cliffs, deep in earth. Not far from here ftands the lake overfhadowed with groves of ancient trees, faft by their roots. There a dread fire may be feen every night fhining wondroufly in the water. The wifeft of the fons of men knows not the bottom. When the heath-ftalker, the ftrong-horned ftag, hard-preffed by the hounds, courfed from afar, feeks fhelter in the wood, he will yield up his life on the fhore fooner than plunge in and hide his head. That is an accurfed place : the ftrife of waves rifes black to the clouds, when the wind ftirs hoftile ftorms, until the air darkens, the heavens fhed tears."

"Strange it is to say how mighty God generously dispenses wisdom, riches, and virtue among men: he has power over all! Sometimes he at will allows to wander the thoughts of the mighty race of man : grants him in his country worldly joys, a man-shelter-ing city to hold, lands and wide empire, so that for his folly he thinks not of his end. He lives in revelry; neither sickness nor age afflict him, gloomy care besets not his heart, nor does strife assail him from any side with hostile sword, but the whole world follows his will. He knows not misfortune, until pride begins to grow and blossom within him, when the guardian of the soul sleeps. The sleep is too heavy, bound with sorrows, the murderer near at hand, who shoots with cruel bow. Then he is wounded in the heart through the sheltering breast by the bitter shaft. He cannot ward off the strange influence of the accursed spirit. The riches he held so long seem to him now too little, greed hardens his heart, he seeks not fame with gifts of rings (of gold), but forgets and neglects the future, because of the honour which the Lord of glory formerly granted him. Then comes the end : the worn-out body falls, doomed to death. Another succeeds, who distributes the hoarded gold without stint, heeds not the former owner. Shun this baleful vice, dear Beowulf, best of men ! Choose what is better, eternal wisdom ! Cherish not pride, illustrious champion ! Now is the flower of thy might for a time : soon will sickness or sword part thee from thy strength, or fire's embrace, or the sea's flood, or sword's gripe, or flight of spear, or sad old age assail thee, and veil in darkness the glance of thine eyes. Soon, prince, will death overpower thee !"

"Then the men of the Goths wrought a mound on the hill, high and broad, easily seen from afar by all wave-farers, and built in ten days the warrior's beacon : they raised a wall round his ashes, as honourably as the wisest men could devise it. They placed in the mound rings and gems, all the treasures, of which hostile men had spoiled the hoard. They let the earth hold the treasure, the heritage of earls, where it still remains, as useless to men as it was before. Then round the mound rode a troop of nobles, twelve in all; they wished to mourn the king with fitting words : they praised his courage and deeds of valour, as is right for a man to praise his dear lord with words, and love him in his heart, when his soul has de-parted from his body. So the Goths mourned their lord's fall, his hearth-companions said that he was the mildest and most humane of world-kings, the gentlest to his people, and most eager for glory."

Most of the other national epic pieces are mere fragments. Two of them, Widsid and Finnesburg, are of special importance, on ac-count of their intimate connection with Beowulf. The greater part of the first of these poems is taken up by a long list of kings and nations, which Widsid, a minstrel of noble Myrging family, professes to have visited. The only passages of the poem which have any poetical worth are those in which the wandering life of the minstrel is described with considerable picturesqueness and power ; the main interest of the poem is historical and geographical. An allusion of the poet in the introductory verſes to a viſit he had made to Eormenric, king of the Goths, who died A. D. 375, has been aſſumed as a criterion for determining the age of the poem, but there ſeems reaſon to doubt whether Widſid himſelf ever exiſted at all. The name Widſid, literally the "wide wanderer," is ſuſpicious, and a com- pariſon with many names of Odin of like ſignificance in the Scandi- navian mythology, makes it probable that Widſid is a purely mytho- logical perſon, probably Odin himſelf. This does not diminiſh the value of the liſts of kings and nations put into his mouth, many of which are found alſo in Beowulf. There can be no doubt, from the want of any mention of England and the intimate knowledge diſ- played of the continental tribes, that this poem was compoſed before the conqueſt of Britain. The ſubject of the other poem is the attack on Fin's palace in Frieſland, which is alſo alluded to in Beowulf. The poem is a mere fragment. Two inconſiderable fragments of the epic of Waldhere have alſo been preſerved.

Laſtly, there remains one poem, which although not ſtrictly epic in form, yet has a certain connection with the poems treated of above, being founded on the common traditions of the north. This is the piece called *Deor's Complaint*, mentioned above as remarkable for its ſtrophic form. It is indeed almoſt lyric in its character. Deor, the court-poet of the Heodenings, complains that he is ſup- planted by his rival Heorrenda, but conſoles himſelf by the reflection that as Weland and other heroes ſurvived their misfortunes, ſo may he alſo regain his former proſperity.

Next in importance to theſe legendary poems are the two hiſtorical pieces Byrhtnod and Brunanburg, the former purely narrative, the latter ſhowing a decided lyrical tinge. Byrhtnod (otherwiſe known as the "Battle of Maldon"), is meagre in form, being in fact little better than alliterative proſe, yet ſhows conſiderable dramatic power, and is animated throughout by a ſtrong patriotic feeling. The lan- guage and general tone of the poem ſhow that it muſt have been compoſed immediately after the battle it celebrates (A. D. 993); it is even poſſible that the poet himſelf took an active part in it. This hiſtorical character gives the poem its ſpecial intereſt; in it we re- cogniſe the epic ſong in its moſt primitive ſtage, unaltered and un- adorned by tradition. The beginning and end of the poem are loſt, but the context ſhows that there cannot be many lines miſſing. The argument of the poem is as follows :—The "ealdorman" Byrhtnod aſſembles a body of men to oppoſe the landing of a body of Daniſh pirates at Maldon in Eſſex. They offer to return to their ſhips in peace, if Byrhtnod will agree to pay them any ſum of money they may fix. Byrhtnod rejects all terms, and prepares to oppoſe their landing. The bridge over the Pant is ſucceſsfully defended, but as the tide ebbs, the Danes ford the ſtream higher up, and attack the Engliſh on their own ground. Byrhtnod falls, and a general flight enſues. Many of the beſt men however rally and the fight is renewed.

The Brunanburg battle ſong commemorates the great victory of

Ædelftan over the Danes and Scotch at Brunanburg.   This piece is
inferted in the Saxon Chronicle under the year 938 inftead of the
ufual profe entry.   This deliberate fubftitution, together with the
general ftyle of the poem, fhows that it is not a popular fong, but was
compofed expreffly for the Chronicle.   This piece is inferior in intereft to Byrhtnod.   The language and metre are dignified and harmonious, but there is a perceptible tendency to bombaft and over-
charging with epithets, while the fineft paffages have rather the
charaéter of reminifcences from the common poetical traditions than
of original invention.   Neverthelefs as a whole it is a noble poem,
and ftands alone in our literature.   Its fubftance is as follows :—
King Ædelftan and his brother gained life-long glory at Brunanburg.
From early dawn till funfet the Northmen and Scotch fell   Two
kings, eight earls were flain, and a countlefs hoft befides.   Anlaf,
the Northern king, fled over the dark fea with a fad remnant, and
Conftantine, the King of Scotland, left his fon on the battle-field ;
nor had they caufe to boaft of their meeting with the fons of
Edward.   Then the brothers returned to the land of the Weft-
Saxons, leaving behind them the wolf and raven to tear the flain.
Never was a greater flaughter in this ifland, fince firft thofe proud
warriors the Englifh and Saxons croffed the broad fea, overcame the
Welfh, and won their lands !

There are feveral other poems of inferior merit incorporated into
the *Chronicle*.   The beft perhaps is the fhort piece commemorating
the releafe of five cities from the Danifh yoke by Edmund (A. D. 942):
it fhows fomething of that fkilful command of proper names, which
forms fo effential an element of Roman poetry.

Befides the national epics there are a large number of narrative
poems founded on religious fubjeéts.   Thefe poems are entirely national in treatment : the language, coftume and habits are purely
Englifh ; there is no attempt at local or antiquarian colouring.   The
moft important of thefe poems are thofe of Cædmon, of whofe life
and compofitions an interefting account is given by Bede in his
ecclefiaftical hiftory.   The fubftance of his account is this :—Attached to the monaftery of the Abbefs Hild at Whitby was a certain
man named Cædmon.   Cædmon, never having learned any poems,
often ufed to fteal out of the houfe, when the harp was paffed round
at feftive meetings.   On one of thefe occafions he retired to the
cattle-ftall, and there fell afleep.   A man appeared to him in a
dream, and commanded him to fing fomething.   He excufed himfelf
at firft, but finally when afked to fing of the beginning of things, he
began a poem, which he had never heard before.   When he awoke,
he remembered the words, and added many more in the fame metre.
The abbefs then perfuaded him to forfake worldly life, and become
a monk.   He learnt the whole of the Bible hiftory, and all that he
remembered he ruminated, like a pure animal, and turned it into the
fweeteft poetry, and his teachers wrote it down from his mouth.
He fang of the creation of the world, and the origin of the human
race, the whole hiftory contained in Genefis, the departure of the

Iſraelites from Egypt and their entering into the promiſed land, and
many other ſcripture narratives,—of the incarnation, paſſion, reſurrection and aſcenſion of Chriſt, of the coming of the Holy Ghoſt and
the apoſtolic doctrine, alſo of the terror of the day of judgment, the
torments of hell and delights of heaven, and he compoſed many other
poems about the beneficence and juſtice of God, and never would
make any poems on ſecular or frivolous ſubjects. Hild was abbeſs
from 657 to 680. The firſt lines of Cædmon are preſerved at the
end of a MS. of Bede's *Eccleſiaſtical Hiſtory* of the early part of the
eighth century. They agree very cloſely with Bede's tranſlation of
them in the hiſtory, and as they are in the old Northumbrian dialect
we may conclude that in them we have the exact words of the poet.
The great bulk of his poetry is contained in a much later MS. written
in the uſual ſouthern dialect. The beginning of this MS. correſponds
in matter to the firſt lines of Cædmon in their oldeſt form, but there
is ſuch diſcrepancy in the actual words and expreſſions, that the au-
thenticy of the later MS. has been denied. However, the compariſon of the analogous diſcrepancies between the two verſions of Cynewulf's poem of the *Croſs*, alſo preſerved both in the original northern
form and in a ſouthern MS., ſhows that either the original poems
were liable to conſiderable variations or that the ſouthern tranſcribers
took great liberties with their originals ; probably both cauſes worked
together. In the caſe of theſe lines of Cædmon ſuch variations are
quite conceivable. Their poetical merit is not high; they form merely
an introduction to a longer poem, and as ſuch might eaſily have been
altered afterwards by the poet himſelf. We may have in the earlier
lines the rough draft, which appears in the later MS. in a reviſed and
expanded form. The contents of the later MS. agree alſo with
Bede's enumeration, although it contains only a part of his poems.
Cædmon's poetry naturally falls into four diviſions. The firſt conſiſts of the poems founded on the book of Geneſis, which ſeem to be
preſerved entire, with the exception of a few leaves cut out in the
MS., down to the intended ſacrifice of Iſaac. Then follows the departure of the Iſraelites from Egypt. All the other Old Teſtament
narratives are loſt except that founded on the adventures of Daniel.
The New Teſtament pieces are chiefly repreſented by Chriſt's deſcent into hell. This poem is not mentioned by Bede, probably
becauſe it is not ſtrictly a ſcripture narrative. There are beſides
ſeveral ſmaller pieces founded on New Teſtament narratives, ſome
of doubtful authenticity.

It has exerciſed an unfortunate influence on the due appreciation
of Anglo-Saxon poetry that Cædmon has always been held up as its
moſt important repreſentative. Although his poetry contains many
fine paſſages and always ſhows conſiderable metrical power, it is as a
whole inferior to that of the other religious poets. The moſt
ſerious fault of his poetry is the almoſt total want of conſtructive
power and command of his material, which often reduced his
poems to mere paraphraſes. Thus, to the narrative of the creation
and fall is appended a circumſtantial and tedious liſt of the de-

fcendants of Adam, and the length of their lives, followed by the remaining hiftory contained in the Book of *Genefis*. This feature of Cædmon's poetry is the more ftriking as it contrafts remarkably with the perfect ftructure of *Judith* and the religious epics of Cynewulf. The beft portions of his poetry are thofe which narrate the creation and fall of the rebellious angels. Thefe paffages have all the grandeur of Milton, without his bombaftic pedantry.

Of the poem of *Judith* only the laft three cantos are preferved ; the firft nine, with the exception of a few lines of the laft, are entirely loft. The fragment opens with the defcription of a banquet, to which Holofernes invites his chiefs. Then follows the death of Holofernes at the hands of Judith, the attack on the Affyrian camp at daybreak, and flaughter of the Affyrians. Mutilated as it is, this poem is one of the fineft in the whole range of Anglo-Saxon literature. The language is of the moft polifhed and brilliant character ; the metre harmonious, and varied with admirable fkill. The action is dramatic and energetic, culminating impreffively in the cataftrophe of Holofernes' death ; but there is none of that pathos which gives Beowulf fo much of its power : the whole poem breathes only of triumph and warlike enthufiafm. In conftructive fkill and perfect command of his foreign fubject, the unknown author of *Judith* furpaffes both Cædmon and Cynewulf, while he is certainly not inferior to either of them in command of language and metre.

The name of Cynewulf has already been mentioned as contained in feveral poems. Thefe are the cycle of hymns on the threefold coming of Chrift, commonly known as Cynewulf's Crift, the Paffion of St. Juliana, both in the Exeter MS., and the Elene or Finding of the Crofs in the Vercelli MS. His name is alfo contained in a charade prefixed to the collection of riddles in the Exeter MS. The poem of Elene is immediately preceded in the MS. by a work of a fimilar character, relating the adventures of St. Andrew among the cannibal Marmedonians, ending, like the Elene and Juliana, with an epilogue, wherein the poet, after briefly alluding to the fates of the other apoftles, expreffes penitence for his fins. There is every reafon for believing that the conclufion of this piece, which is unfortunately cut out, contained an acroftic fimilar to that in the Elene, and from their marked refemblance of language and ftyle, that the two poems are by the fame author. The poem of Elene is preceded by a fhort piece called the Dream of the Crofs, evidently compofed by Cynewulf as an introduction to the longer poem, and expreffly alluded to in the epilogue of the Elene. There are feveral other pieces contained in the Exeter book, which from evidence of ftyle feem alfo to be Cynewulf's. Thefe are the Life of St. Gudlac, and the defcriptive poem of the Phœnix, and feveral fmaller lyric pieces, the moft important of which are the Wanderer and the Seafarer.

Thefe paffages in which the poet introduces his name, are alfo of value, as affording fome biographical data. They tend to fhow that in his youth Cynewulf held the poft of minftrel at the court of one of the Northumbrian kings, and that in one of thofe civil wars which defolated Northumbria in the 8th century, he was driven into exile. In his old age a total change came over Cynewulf, which he himfelf attributes to the miraculous vifion of the crofs. Up to this time he confeffes that he was a frivolous and finful man, given over to worldly purfuits; but after being commanded by the crofs to reveal his vifion to men, he devoted himfelf entirely to religious poetry. To this period of his life belong, therefore, the longer narrative poems, all of which are founded on religious fubjects. The internal evidence, on which thefe refults depend, may not be altogether truftworthy; but the main refult, viz, that Cynewulf was a minftrel by profeffion, and not, as formerly fuppofed, a churchman, feems incontrovertible. The moft valuable and characteriftic of Cynewulf's poems are the early lyric pieces; the longer poems, although always diftinguifhed by grace of diction and metre, pathos, and delicacy of feeling, are inferior to *Beowulf* and *Judith* in the fpecially epic qualities.

The fhorter poems of Cynewulf fhow lyric poetry in its earlieft ftage, in which the narrative and defcriptive element is ftill to a great degree predominant: the lyric idea is enclofed, as it were, in an epic frame. The *Wanderer* and the *Wife's Complaint* both turn on the miferies of exile and folitude. In the former of thefe poems, which is the more important, the Wanderer bewails the flaughter of his lord and kinfmen, the deftruction of their burg, and the hardfhips of his wanderings. Into this half-epic matter are woven reflections on the excellence of conftancy and filent endurance, and on the tranfitory nature of earthly things: the ruins which cover the face of the earth are but prefages of that general deftruction to which all things are tending; the world grows old and decrepit day by day. The *Seafarer* is fragmentary, and therefore fomewhat obfcure. Its general fubject is the dangers and hardfhips of the fea, and the fafcinations of a failor's roving life, with a purely lyrical undercurrent of ideas fimilar to thofe of the *Wanderer*. Thefe poems have a wonderful harmony of language and metre, which is of courfe quite loft in a tranflation. The following piece is a literal rendering of a few lines of the *Seafarer* :—

"He cares not for harp, or gifts of gold; his joy is not in woman, nor are his thoughts of the world, or of aught elfe except the rolling waves; but he yearns ever to venture on the fea. The groves refume their flowers, the hills grow fair, the heath brightens, the world fhakes off floth. All this only reminds him to ftart on his journey, eager to depart on the diftant tracts of ocean. The cuckoo alfo reminds him with his fad voice, when the guardian of fummer fings, and bodes bitter heart-forrow. (The cuckoo's fong is here taken in the double fenfe of a bad omen and harbinger of fummer— *Rieger*.) The man who lives in luxury knows not what they endure who wander far in exile! Therefore now my mind wanders out of my breaft over the fea-floods, where the whale dwells, returns again to me, fierce and eager, fcreams in its folitary flight,. impels me irrefiftibly on the path of death over the ocean waters."

The *Ruin* is, unhappily, a very mutilated fragment. It defcribes a ruined caftle, whofe builders have long fince paffed away. This poem, together with the *Wanderer* and *Seafarer*, are the fineft lyric pieces we poffefs. *The Complaint of the Soul to the Body*, and *The Bleffed Soul's addrefs to the Body*, treat of a favourite fubject of the middle ages. Other fhort poems of a lyrical and didactic character have for their fubjects the various fortunes of men, the various arts of men, the falfehood of men, the pride of men. Thefe pieces are of no great literary merit, but their antiquarian value, as illuftrations of life and manners, is confiderable. *The Father's Advice to his Son*, is, as the title fhows, purely didactic. The Gnomic poems confift of a ftring of aphorifms and proverbs ftrung together, often in a fomewhat difconnected manner. Many of the paffages are extremely poetical, and the poems generally bear a ftriking refemblance to the Norfe Hávamál, and like them, belong no doubt to the earlieft ftage of poetry, however much they may have been altered in later times. The curious poem, *Salomon and Saturn*, confifts alfo of a variety of gnomic fentences, mixed, however, with a variety of other matter, in the form of a dialogue. Much of the poem is of foreign origin, and often wildly extravagant, but many paffages have a ftrongly heathen character, and are probably fragments of fome older piece refembling the Eddaic Vafþrúdnifmál. *Salomon and Saturn* treats of the divine virtue, perfonified under the myftic name of "Pater-nofter," of "vafa mortis," the bird of death, of the fall of the angels, of the good and evil fpirits that watch over men to en-courage them to virtue or tempt to evil, of fate, old age, and various moral and religious fubjects. Many paffages of the poem are of high poetic beauty. The *Riddles* of Cynewulf are very pleafing. Many of them are true poems, containing beautiful defcriptions of nature ; and all of them have the charm of harmonious language and metre.

The religious lyric poetry is chiefly reprefented by the metrical pfalms. The tranflation is a very fine one, far fuperior to any modern verfion. The language and ftyle fhow that it was origi-nally compofed in the Northern dialect. The imperfect fcholarfhip of the tranflator makes it doubtful whether the work is to be afcribed to Aldhelm, as fuggefted by Dietrich. Several metrical hymns and prayers, of little value, have alfo been preferved. The moft valuable of the religious lyrics is the "Dream of the Crofs," compofed by Cynewulf, as an introduction to the *Elene*. The following is an abridged tranflation of the poem :—

"Lo! I will tell of the beft of vifions, which I dreamed at mid-night. I thought I faw a noble tree raifed aloft, encircled with light, bright with gems and molten gold. On it gazed all the angels of God, men, and all this fair creation; for it was no felon's gallows, but a noble victorious tree, and I was ftained with fins. My mind was fad, aweftruck at the fair fight, as I watched its changing hues:

now it was wet with blood, now bright with gold. I lay there a long while, gazing sorrowfully on the Saviour's tree, till I heard a voice : the best of woods began then to speak : ' It was long ago (I remember it still), when I was hewn on the borders of a forest, torn from my roots. Strong foes seized me, bore me on their shoulders, and fixed me on a hill. There they bade me raise aloft their felons. Then I saw the Lord of mankind hasten courageously, ready to ascend me. The young hero girded himself, he was God Almighty, resolute and stern of mood ; he ascended the lofty gallows, proudly in the sight of many, eager to redeem mankind. I trembled, when the King embraced me, yet I durst not bow to earth ; I could easily have felled all my foes, yet I stood firm. They pierced me with dark nails, the wounds are still visible on me, open gashes of malice. I durst not harm any of them, and they reviled us both together. I was all stained with blood ; it poured from the hero's side, when he had yielded up his spirit. Many cruel fates have I endured on that hill ! The Lord's body was shrouded in black clouds ; deep shade oppressed the sun's rays. All creation wept, mourned the king's fall : Christ was on the rood. Nobles came, hastening from afar ; I beheld it all. I was sorely oppressed with sorrow, yet I bowed humbly before those men, yielded myself readily into their hands. They took Almighty God, and raised him from the cruel torment. They laid him down weary in his limbs, stood around at the head of the corpse, gazing on the Lord of heaven, and he rested there a while, weary after the great toil. They began then to work an earth-house, cutting it in white stone, and placed in it the victorious king. They sang then a lay of sorrow, disconsolate at eventide, when they departed weary from the noble prince. He rested there with a scanty retinue. The corpse grew cold, the fair lifedwelling. They began then to fell us all to the ground : that was a terrible fate ! They buried us in a deep pit, but the Lord's disciples found me, and adorned me with gold and silver. Now thou hast heard, dear friend, what sorrows I have endured. On me the Son of God suffered, therefore I now tower gloriously under the heavens, and I can heal all who revere me. Once I was the hardest of tortures, the most hateful to men, until I cleared for them the way of life.' "]

The History of English Poetry.

SECTION I.

N the foregoing account of Anglo-Saxon poetry, Mr. Sweet has intentionally passed over several Saints' Lives and other like productions which are hardly to be distinguished from alliterative prose in short lines, and are not really metrical. The Percy Society's Anglo-Saxon *Passion of St. George* (1850), Mr. Earle's *Saint Swiđun*, &c., are of this class; and the third series of Ælfric's *Homilies* (mainly lives of saints), on which Mr. Skeat is now engaged for the Early English Text Society,[1] will probably prove to be so.

We now pass on to the Second or Transition stage of English, which is generally called Semi-Saxon. Its first stage,—1100-1150, A.D.—contains no very striking specimens in any species of composition Its substance was Anglo-Saxon, with degrading forms, and slightly mixed with Norman-French. The Saxon, a language subsisting on uniform principles, and polished by poets and theologists, however corrupted by the Danes, had much perspicuity, strength, and harmony: while the Norman-French imported by the Conqueror and his people—though of mixed origin (principally Latin, with a slight admixture of Teutonic and Celtic),—was a tongue of great beauty and power.

[Norman and Saxon struggled for the mastery, and] in this fluctuating state of our national speech, the French predominated [for a time]. Even before the Conquest the Saxon language began to fall into contempt, and the French, or Frankish, to be substituted in its stead: a circumstance which at once facilitated and foretold the Norman accession. In the year 652, [if we may trust the spurious History of Ingulphus] it was the common practice of the Anglo-Saxons to send their youth to the monasteries of France for educa-

---

[1] [This society has undertaken to print all our unedited Anglo-Saxon MSS. Those of the time of Alfred are under Mr. Sweet's charge; the later ones will be edited by Dr. R. Morris, Mr. Skeat, and Mr. Lumby.]

tion :[1] and not only the language but the manners of the [Franks] were esteemed the most polite accomplishments.[2] In the reign of Edward the Confessor, the resort of Normans to the English court was so frequent, that the affectation of imitating the Frankish customs became almost universal ; and the nobility were ambitious of catching the Frankish idiom. It was no difficult task for the Norman lords to banish that language, of which the natives began to be absurdly ashamed. The new invaders [are said, but probably in error, to have] commanded the laws to be administered in French.[3] Many charters of monasteries were forged in Latin by the Saxon monks for the present security of their possessions, in consequence of that aversion which the Normans professed to the Saxon tongue.[4] Even children at school were forbidden [says the spurious Ingulphus] to read in their native language, and instructed in a knowledge of the Norman only.[5] In the meantime we should have some regard to the general and political state of the nation. The natives were so universally reduced to the lowest condition of neglect and indigence, that the English name became a term of reproach : and several generations elapsed before one family of Saxon pedigree was raised to any distinguished honours or could so much as attain the rank of baronage.[6] Among other instances of that absolute and voluntary submission with which our Saxon ancestors received a foreign yoke, it is said [in the spurious Ingulphus] that they suffered their hand-writing to fall into discredit and disuse ;[7] which by degrees became so difficult and obsolete, that few beside the oldest men could understand the characters.[8] In the year 1095, Wolstan bishop of Worcester was deposed by the arbitrary Normans : it was objected against him, that he was " a superannuated English idiot, who could not speak French."[9] It is true that in some of the monasteries, particularly at Croyland and Tavistock, founded by Saxon princes, there were regular preceptors in the Saxon language : but this institution was suffered to remain after the Conquest as a matter only of interest and necessity. The religious could not otherwise have understood their original charters. William's successor, Henry I., gave an instrument of con-

---

[1] Dugd. *Mon.* i. 89.

[2] Ingulph. *Hist.* p. 62, *sub ann.* 1043.

[3] But there is a precept in Saxon from William I. to the sheriff of Somersetshire. Hickes, *Thes.* i. Par. i. p. 106. See also Præfat. *ibid.* p. xv.

[4] The Normans, who practised every specious expedient to plunder the monks, demanded a sight of the written evidences of their lands. The monks well knew that it would have been useless or impolitic to have produced these evidences, or charters, in the original Saxon ; as the Normans not only did not understand, but would have received with contempt, instruments written in that language. Therefore the monks were compelled to the pious fraud of forging them in Latin ; and great numbers of these forged Latin charters, till lately supposed original, are still extant. See Spelman, in *Not. ad Concil. Anglic.* p. 125 ; Stillingfl. *Orig. Eccles. Britann.* p. 14; Marsham, Præfat. ad Dugd. *Monast.* ; and Wharton, *Angl. Sacr.* vol. ii. Præfat. pp. ii. iii. iv. See also Ingulph. p. 512. Launoy and Mabillon have treated this subject with great learning and penetration.

[5] Ingulph. p. 71, *sub ann.* 1066.

[6] See Brompt. *Chron.* p. 1026 ; Abb. Rieval, p. 339.

[7] Ingulph. p. 85.   [8] *Ibid.* p. 98, *sub ann.* 1091.   [9] Matt. Paris. *sub ann.*

firmation to William archbifhop of Canterbury, which was written
in the Saxon language and letters.[1] That monarch's motive was
perhaps political : and he feems to have practifed this expedient with
a view of obliging his queen who was of Saxon lineage, or with a
defign of flattering his Englifh fubjects, and of fecuring his title
already ftrengthened by a Saxon match, in confequence of fo fpecious
and popular an artifice. It was a common and indeed a very natural
practice, for the tranfcribers of Saxon books to change the Saxon
orthography for the Norman, and to fubftitute in the place of the
original Saxon Norman words and phrafes. A remarkable inftance
of this liberty, which fometimes perplexes and mifleads the critics in
Anglo-Saxon literature, appears in a voluminous collection of Saxon
homilies preferved in the Bodleian library, and written about the
time of Henry II.[2] It was with the Saxon characters, as with the
fignature of the crofs in public deeds, which were changed into the
Norman mode of feals and fubfcriptions.[3] The Saxon was [of courfe]
fpoken in the country, yet not without various adulterations from the
French : the courtly language was [Norman-] French, yet perhaps
with fome veftiges of the vernacular Saxon. But the nobles in the
reign of Henry II. conftantly fent their children into France, left
they fhould contract habits of barbarifm in their fpeech, which could
not have been avoided in an Englifh education.[4] Robert Holcot, a
learned Dominican friar, confeffes that in the beginning of the reign
of Edward III. there was no inftitution of children in the old
Englifh : he complains that they firft learned the French, and from
the French the Latin language. This he obferves to have been a
practice introduced by the Conqueror, and to have remained ever
fince."[5] There is a curious paffage relating to this fubject in Trevifa's
tranflation of Hygden's *Polychronicon.*[6] "Chyldern in fcoles, aʒenes
þe ufage and manere of al oþere nacions, buþ compelled for to leve
here oune longage, and for to conftrue here leffons and here þingis
a Freynfch ; and habbeþ fuþe þe Normans come furft into Engelond. Alfo gentilmen children buþ ytauʒt for to fpeke Freynfch
fram tyme that a buþ yrokked in here cradel, and conneþ fpeke
and pleye wiþ a child his brouch : and uplondyfch[7] men wol lykne
hamfylf to gentile men, and fondeþ[8] with gret byfynes for to fpeke

---

[1] Wharton, *Auctor. Hiftor. Dogmat.* p. 388. The learned Mabillon is miftaken
in afferting, that the Saxon way of writing was entirely abolifhed in England at the
time of the Norman Conqueft. See Mabillon, *De Re Diplomat.* p. 52. The French
antiquaries are fond of this notion. There are Saxon characters in Herbert Lo-
finga's charter for founding the church of Norwich, temp. Will. Ruf. A.D. 1110.
See Lambarde's *Diction.* v. NORWICH. See alfo Hickes, *Thefaur.* i. Par. i. p. 149.
And Præfat. p. xvi. An intermixture of the Saxon *w* is common in Englifh
MSS. [up to 1200, A.D.; the ð was ufed ftill later, and the þ after 1500 ; indeed,
the latter is ftill feen in our *ye* for *the.*]

[2] MSS. Bodl. NE. F. 4. 12.   [3] Yet fome Norman charters have the crofs.

[4] Gervas. Tilbur. *de Otiis Imperial.* MSS. Bibl. Bodl. lib. iii. See Du Chefne, iii.
p. 363.

[5] *Lect. in Libr. Sapient.* Lect. ii. 1518.

[6] Lib. i. cap. 59, MSS. Coll. S. Johan. Cantabr. Robert of Gloucefter, who
wrote about 1280, fays much the fame : edit. Hearne, p. 364.

[7] upland, country.   [8] try.

Freynſch for to be more ytold of. Thys manere was moche yuſed tofore þet furſte moreyn ; and ys ſeþe ſomdel ychaunged. For John Cornwall, a mayſtere of gramere chaungede þe lore in gramere ſcole, and conſtruccion of Freynſch into Englyſch : and Richard Pen-cryche lernede þat manere techynge of hym, and oþere men of Pen-cryche. So þat þe ʒer of oure Lord *a thouſand thre hon.red foure ſcore and fyve*, [and] of þe ſecunde Kyng Richard after þe conqueſt nyne, in al þe grammere ſcoles of Engelond childern leueth Freynſch and conſtrueþ and lurneþ an Englyſch,"¹ &c. About the ſame time, or rather before, the ſtudents of our univerſities were ordered to converſe in French or Latin.² The latter was much affeſted by the Normans. All the Norman accounts were in Latin. The plan of the great royal revenue-rolls, now called the pipe-rolls, was of their conſtruction and in that language. Among the Records of the Tower, a great revenue-roll on many ſheets of vellum, or *Magnus Rotulus*, of the Duchy of Normandy for the year 1083, is ſtill pre-ſerved indorſed in a coæval hand ANNO AB ICARNATIONE DNI Mᵒ LXXXᵒ IIIᵒ APUD CADOMUM [Caen] WILLIELMO FILIO RADULFI SENESCALLO NORMANNIE.³ This moſt exaſtly and minutely re-ſembles the pipe-rolls of our exchequer belonging to the ſame age in form, method, and charaſter.⁴ But from the declenſion of the barons and prevalence of the commons, moſt of whom were of Engliſh an-ceſtry, the native language of England gradually gained ground ; till at length the intereſt of the commons ſo far ſucceeded with Edward III., that an aſt of parliament was paſſed [in 1362], appointing all pleas and proceedings of law to be carried on in Engliſh ;⁵ although the ſame ſtatute decrees, in the true Norman ſpirit, that all ſuch pleas and proceedings ſhould be enrolled in Latin.⁶ Yet this change did not reſtore either the Saxon alphabet or language. It aboliſhed a

---

[¹ From the contemporary MS. Cotton. Tiberius, D. vii., collated with Harl. MS. 1900, in Dr. R. Morris's handy book for ſtudents, *Specimens of Early Engliſh*, 1250-1400, A.D. p. 338-9.—*F.*]

² In the ſtatutes in Oriel College in Oxford, it is ordered that the ſcholars or fel-lows, "ſiqua inter ſe proferant, colloquio Latino, vel ſaltem Gallico, perfruantur." See Hearne's *Trokelowe*, p. 298. Theſe ſtatutes were given 23 Maii, A.D. 1328. I find much the ſame injunſtion in the ſtatutes of Exeter College, Oxford, given about 1330 ; where they are ordered to uſe " Romano aut Gallico ſaltem ſermone." Hearne's MSS. Colleſt. No. 132, p. 73, Bibl. Bodl. But in Merton College ſtatutes mention is made of the Latin only (cap. x.). They were given 1271. This was alſo common in the greater monaſteries. In the regiſter of Wykeham biſhop of Wincheſter, the domicellus of the prior of St. Swythin's at Wincheſter is ordered to addreſs the biſhop on a certain occaſion in French. A.D. 1398. Regiſtr. Par. iii. fol. 177.

[³ Privately printed by Petrie, 1830, 4ᵒ. Two other rolls of the Norman era have been publiſhed by Stapleton, 1848, 2 vols. 8ᵒ.]

⁴ Ayloffe's *Calendar of Ant. Chart.* Pref. p. xxiv. edit. 1774.

⁵ But the French formularies and terms of law, and particularly the French feudal phraſeology, had taken too deep root to be thus haſtily aboliſhed. Hence, long after the reign of Edward III., many of our lawyers compoſed their traſts in French. And reports and ſome ſtatutes were made in that language. See For-teſcut. *De Laud. Leg. Angl.* c. xlviii.

⁶ Pulton's Statut. 36 Edw. III. This was A.D. 1363. The firſt Engliſh inſtru-ment in Rymer is dated 1368. *Fæd.* vii. p. 526.

token of fubjection and difgrace, and in fome degree contributed to prevent further French innovations in the language then ufed, which yet remained in a compound ftate, and retained a confiderable mixture of foreign phrafeology. In the meantime, it muft be remembered that this corruption of the Saxon was not only owing to the admiffion of new words, occafioned by the new alliance, but to changes of its own forms and terminations, arifing from reafons which we cannot inveftigate or explain.[1]

[The Tranfition Period of the Englifh language, between 1100 and 1250 A. D., may be divided into two ftages, 1100-1150, 1150-1250. The characteriftics of the language of each of thefe ftages are its fucceffive changes from Anglo-Saxon, principally in inflexions; and of thefe changes, between 1100 and 1300 A. D., we are enabled to prefent[2] the following fketch :—

Changes from 1100 *to* 1150.

(This period includes part of the *A.-Sax. Chronicle*, and fome profe pieces as yet inedited. No poetical compofitions of this period have, as yet, been found.)

The changes are moftly *orthographical* ones.

1. The older vowel endings, *a*, *o*, *u*, were reduced to *e*. This change affected the oblique cafes of nouns and adjectives, as well as the nominative, caufing great confufion in the grammatical inflexions, fo that the termination

an	became	en.
um	,,	en.
ena	,,	en.
on	,,	en.
as	,,	es.
ath	,,	eth.
ra, ru	,,	re.
od, ode	,,	ed, ede.

The older endings were not wholly loft, but co-exift along with the modified forms.

2. C is fometimes foftened to *ch*, and *g* to *y* or *i*, but *fc* remains intact.

3. An *n* is often added to a final *e*, and *n* often falls off, efpecially in the endings of nouns of the *n* declenfion and in the definite declenfion of adjectives.

Changes from 1150 *to* 1250,
(Including pieces in Dr. R. Morris's *Old Englifh Homilies*,
Laʒamon, &c.)

Great grammatical changes take place, and orthographical ones become fully eftablifhed.

---

[1] This fubject will be further illuftrated in the next Section.]
[2] By the kindnefs of Dr. Richard Morris, who drew up the prefent infertion.]

1. The indefinite article *an* (*a*), is developed out of the numeral *an* (one). It retains moſt of the older inflexions.

2. The definite article becomes *the, theo, thet* (*that*), inſtead of *ſe, ſeo, thæt.*

There is a tendency to drop ſuffixes, and to uſe an uninflected *the.* *The* occurs as a plural inſtead of *tha* or *tho.*

3. Plurals of nouns end in — *en* or — *e* inſtead of the older *a* or *u*, thus conforming to the *n* declenſion.

4. The plural ending — *es* is often ſubſtituted for — *en.*

5. Genitive plural — *es*, is occaſionally found for — *e* or — *ene.*

6. Confuſion in the genders of nouns, ſhowing a tendency to aboliſh the older diſtinction of maſculine, feminine and neuter nouns.

7. Adjectives ſhow a tendency to drop certain caſe endings :
     (1.) The gen. ſing. maſc. indef. declenſion.
     (2.) The gen. and dat. fem. of indef. declenſion.

8. Dual forms are ſtill in uſe, but are leſs frequently employed.

9. New pronominal forms come into uſe :
     ha, a = he, ſhe, they ; *is* (*hiſe*) = *hire* = her ;
     his, is = *hi, heo* = them ; *me* = *men* = *man* = Fr. *on.*

That is uſed as an indeclinable relative (1) for the indeclinable *the :* (2) for *ſe* and *ſeo. Which, whoſe, whom, what,* come in as relatives.

10. The *n* of *min, thin,* drops off before conſonants, but is retained in the oblique caſes.

11. The genitive caſes of the pronouns are becoming mere poſſeſſives.

Mi-ſelf, thi-ſelf, for *me ſelf, the ſelf.*

12. The infinitive frequently omits the final *n*, as *ſmelle* = *ſmellen.* The infinitive often takes *to*, as in the earlier text of Laȝamon.

13. The gerundial or dative infinitive ends in — *en* or — *e*, inſtead of — *ene* (= *enne, anne*).

14. The *n* of the paſſive participle is often dropped, as *icume* = *icumen* = come.

15. The preſent participle ends in — *inde* (for *ende*). The participle in *inde* often does duty for the dative infinitive in — *ene*, as *to ſwimende* = *to ſwimene* = to ſwim.

This corruption is found before 1066.

Shall and *will*, are uſed as auxiliaries of the future tenſe.

16. The above remarks are baſed on the Southern dialect, but the Ormulum has a general diſregard for nearly all inflexions.

     (1.) The article is uninflected in the ſingular, and for the pl. we only find the nom. *tha.*

That is a demonſtrative, and not the neuter of the article.

     (2.) The gender of nouns is much the ſame as in modern Engliſh.

     (3.) The genitive *s* is uſed for maſc. and fem. nouns.

     (4.) *Theȝȝ, theȝȝre, theȝȝm,* are uſed for *hi, heore, heom.*

Ȝ*ho* = ſhe, for *heo.*

     (5.) Verbal plurals end in *en* inſtead of *eth* (except imper. pl.)

     (6.) The particle *i* (or *ge*) is dropt before the paſſive participle.

(7.) Inflexion is often loſt in the 2nd perſ. pret. of ſtrong verbs.

(8.) The *Ancren Riwle, St. Marharete, &c.* have *ſch* for *ſc,* which change ſeems to have taken place after 1200.

There is a mixture of dialeƈt in theſe latter works, and there is more ſimplicity of grammatical ſtruƈture than in *Laȝamon,* &c.

(9.) *Arn* occurs, as in the Ormulum, for *beoth* or *ſind.*

Changes from 1250 *to* 1300.

(1.) The def. article has not wholly loſt in the Southern dialeƈt the gen. ſing. fem. and acc. maſc. inflexions : *tho* is the plural in all caſes.

(2.) The gender of nouns is much ſimplified, owing to loſs of adjeƈtive inflexions.

(3.) Plurals of nouns in *en* and *es* are uſed indiſcriminately.

(4.) The genitive *es* becomes more general, and often takes the place

(1.) Of the older —*en* or —*e.* (n. decl.)

(2.) Of *e* (fem. nouns).

(3.) Of the plural —*ene* or —*e.*

(5.) Dative *e* (ſing. and pl.) is often dropt.

(6.) Dual forms rare ; and loſt before 1300.

(7.) Adjeƈtive inflexions are reduced to *e.*

The gen. pl. —*re* is retained in a few caſes, as *al-re,* as well as the gen. ſing. —*es*·in a few pronominal forms, as *eaches, otheres.*

(8.) The gerundial infinitive in *e* or *en* is more common than in —*ene.*

(9.) Some ſtrong verbs become weak.

(10.) Freſent participles in —*inge* make their appearance in the ſecond text of Laȝamon, ſay 1270 A. D.

All theſe points are ſubjeƈt to occaſional exceptions cauſed by dialeƈtal differences. Thus, the Kentiſh of the thirteenth century, as far as we know it, has older forms than the weſtern, as exhibited in *Laȝamon,* as *ſe* = the (m.) *si,* f. &c., while the *Ayenbite* of the fourteenth century is more infleƈtional in many reſpeƈts than the *Ancren Riwle* and *St. Marharete.*

Having thus ſtated the charaƈteriſtics of the two ſtages of the Tranſition Period, in the firſt of which we have, as above noted, no poetry, we proceed to give a liſt of the principal poetical works known to us in manuſcript in the ſecond ſtage of the Tranſition Period, and the Early Engliſh Period—with ſome extenſion,—only warning our readers that our dates are in many caſes hypothetical ones, as it is very difficult to ſettle the date of an old romance or poem known to us only through a late and often altered copy. Of the MS. of the latter we know the date, but it would be abſurd to give that date to the early original.

As it would be impoſſible, under exiſting circumſtances, to notice in detail all the Early Engliſh Poems that have been printed, or made known in modern times, we truſt that the reader will be content with our liſt of the principal ones, and the volumes containing moſt of the minor ones, fo that he may examine for himfelf thofe that he does not find defcribed in the courfe of the *Hiftory:*

Before 1200 A.D.
>   Poetical pieces from the Lambeth MS. 487.

From 1200 to 1250, A.D.
>   Dr. R. Morris's Old Englifh Homilies (Early Englifh Text Society), pp. 1 —182.
>   ? The Grave, in Thorpe's Analecta.
>   Ormulum (ed. White).
>   Laȝamon, the 1ft text (ed. Madden).
>   St. Marharete, the 1ft text (ed. Cockayne).
>   St. Katherine (ed. Morton, Abbotsford Club).
>   St. Juliana (ed. Cockayne).
>   The Poetical Pieces in Dr. R. Morris's Eng. Homilies (pp. 182—287).
>   Later verfions of the Moral Ode.

From 1250 to 1300 A.D.
>   Genefis and Exodus (ed. Dr. R. Morris).
>   Beftiary (ed. by T. Wright in Reliq. Antiq., and·by Dr. R. Morris in Old Englifh Beftiary, &c., Early Englifh Text Society, 1871).
>   Laȝamon, 2nd text (ed. Madden).
>   Cuckoo Song and Prifoners' Prayer (ed. A. J. Ellis, Philolog. Soc., 1868).
>   The Owl and Nightingale (eds. Stevenfon and T. Wright ; Stratmann, beft edition).
>   The Religious Pieces from the Jefus MS., in Old Englifh Beftiary, 1871.
>   Havelok the Dane (eds. Madden and Skeat).
>   O. E. Northern Pfalter (ed. Stevenfon, for Surtees Society).
>   Athanafian Creed (Hickes's Thefaurus).

1264-1327. Political Songs (ed. T. Wright, Camden Society).
1280-1300. Hendyng's Proverbs (ed. T. Wright and R. Morris).
>   Lyric Poetry, Harl. 2253 (ed. T. Wright, Percy Society).
>   Harrowing of Hell, Maximon &c., Harl. 2253 (ed. Halliwell, &c.)
>   Horn (ed. Michel, Roxburghe Club ; ed. Lumby, Early Englifh Text Society ; ed. Mätzner and Goldbeck in their Sprachproben, beft edition).

Clofe upon 1300 A.D., but probably after, to judge by *ou* for *u*.
>   Romance of Alexander (in Weber's Metrical Romances, vol. i.).
>   Robert of Gloucefter (Cotton MS.—*not* the verfion printed by Hearne).
>   Lives of Saints (ed. Furnivall[1]) ; SS. Brandan and Beket (Percy Society) ; Popular Science (ed. T. Wright) ; and the reft in the Harleian MS. 2277.

1303.
>   Robert Manning of Brunne's Handlyng Synne, MS. about 1370 (ed. Furnivall, Roxburghe Club).
>   ———— (?) Meditations on the Lord's Supper.
>   Curfor Mundi, or Curfur o Worlde[2] (in hand for the Early Englifh Text Society, 2 parallel texts).

1310-20 ? Metrical Homilies (ed. Small).
1310-20 ? Pieces in Digby MS. 86.   Maximian, Dame Siriz, Vox and Wolf, &c. (*Rel. Ant.*, Mätzner, Hazlitt, &c.) Harrowing of Hell, &c.
1320 ?   Poem on the times of Edward II. (ed. Hardwicke, Percy Society).
1320-30 ? All the Romances and pieces in the Auchinleck MS. in the Advocates' Library, Edinburgh, of which a lift is given in Sir Walter Scott's edition of Sir Triftram, and Mr. D. Laing's Penniworthe of Wit, &c. (Abbotsford Club, 1857).   The principal are:—Bevis of Hampton (Maitland Club) ; Guy of Warwick (Abbotsford Club) ; Sir Triftram (ed. Scott) ;

---

[1] The contraction iᵉ was by miftake printed *ic* inftead of *ich*, in this edition.—*F.*]
[2] There are a great many *u*'s for *ou*'s in *Curfor Mundi* (Cotton MS.), and Dr. R. Morris is inclined to think that the *oldeft* text, from which many dialectal copies have been made, was written before 1300 ; but this original has not yet been found.]

Otuel (Abbotsford Club); Roland and Vernagu (Abbotsford Club); Orfeo and Heurodis (ed. Laing); Arthour & Merlin (Abbotsford Club); Seven Sages (Weber); Syr Degore (Abbotsford Club); Guy and Alquine; Lai le Freine, King of Tars, and Horn Child (Ritſon); Liber Regum Anglie; Aſſumption of the Virgin; Joachim, our Lady's Mother; Amis and Amiloun (Weber); Owayn Miles; Harrowing of Hell; Body and Soul; Pope Gregory; Adam; St. Margaret; St. Katherine.

1325 ?   Shoreham's Poems (ed. T. Wright, Percy Society).

1338.   Robert Manning of Brunne's Chronicle (Part I. ed. Furnivall; Part II. ed. Hearne).

1340 ?   The Pſalms wrongly called Shoreham's (Brit. Mus. Addit. MS. 17,376).

1340 ?   Aliſaunder, a fragment, with William of Palerne (Skeat's ed.).

1340-8.   Hampole's Pricke of Conſcience (ed. R. Morris, Philological Society) and Minor Poems.

1350.   William of Palerne, or William and the Werwolf (ed. Madden, Rox-burghe Club; Skeat, Early Engliſh Text Society).

1352.   Minot's Poems (ed. Ritſon).

1360 ?   Early Engliſh Alliterative Poems (ed. R. Morris, Early Engliſh Text Society), and

Gawayne & the Green Knight, Cotton MS. Nero, A. x. (ed. Madden, Roxburghe Club; R. Morris, Early Engliſh Text Society; See too Percy Folio, ii. 56). The coarſe paintings in the cotton MS. are later than the text.

Reſpecting the age of the Cotton MS., however, Sir F. Madden obſerves (*Sir Gawayne*, 1839, 301) : " It will not be difficult, from a careful inſpection of the manuſcript itſelf, in regard to the writing and illuminations, to aſſign it to the reign of Richard the Second; and the internal evidence, ariſing from the peculiarities of coſtume, armour, and architecture, would lead us to aſſign the romance to the ſame period, or a little earlier."

1360 ?   Morte Arthure (eds. Halliwell, Perry, and Brock, the two latter for the Early Engliſh Text Society, from the Thornton MS. about 1440 A.D.).

?   The Geſt Hyſtoriale of the Deſtruction of Troy (ed. Donaldſon and Panton, Early Engliſh Text Society).

1362.   Piers Plowman, Text A (ed. Skeat, Early Engliſh Text Society).

1366 ?   Chaucer's Romaunt of the Roſe.[1]

1369.   Chaucer's Boke of the Ducheſſe.

Rewle of St. Benet (Northern).

1373 ?   Chaucer's Life of St. Cecile.

Chaucer's Aſſemble of Foules, and Palamon and Arcite.

1375.   Barbour's Brus (ed. Hart, Anderſon, &c.; Pinkerton, Jamieſon, James; beſt ed. Skeat, 1870).

About 1375. All the pieces in the (Southern) Vernon MS.,[2] of which Mr. Halli-well printed an incomplete and incorrect liſt.[3] The chief are :

*Old and New Teſtament, abridged.

Saints' Lives, &c. (Other Brit. Mus. MSS. are Harl. 2277, 4196

[[1] Mr. Henry Bradſhaw diſputes the Glaſgow MS., the only one known of any Engliſh tranſlation of the Roſe, being Chaucer's verſion.]

[[2] A very imperfect duplicate of this MS., the Simeon or Additional MS. 22,283, is in the Britiſh Muſeum.]

[[3] The Vernon MS. has theſe Lives, &c , which are not in the earlier Harl. MS. 2277. (The numbers are thoſe of Mr. Halliwell's liſt). How the Martyrs be God's Knights, " Now bloweth this newe fruyt that late bigon to ſpringe," (1ſt line of Lives.) 2 New Year's Day, 3 Twelfth Day (Epiphany), 4 St. Hillare, 5 St. Wolfton, St. Edward, and William of Normandy, 6 St. Fabian, 7 St. Agnes, 8 St. Vincent, 9 St. Juliane, 10 St. Blaſe, 11 St. Agace, 12 St. Scolace, 13 St. Valentin, 14 St. Juliane, 15 St. Mathi[as], 16 St. Gregori, 17 St. Longius, 18 St. Edward the King, 19 St. Cuthberd, (20 St. Benet), 21 St. Julian, 22 St. Bride, 23 St. Oſwald, 24, St. Chadde, 40 St. Pernele, 42 St. Adboruh, 44 St. Aylbriht, 45

(Northern), Egerton, 1993 ; Additional, 10301, 10626). Mr. Earle
has printed the St. Swithin and St. Mary of Egypt.

*Barlaam and Joſaſaph.
*La Eſtorie del Evangelie tranſlated (to the Nativity).
*Goſpels illuſtrated by Stories.
 Wm. of Naſſington's Mirror of Life, from Jn. of Waldby's Speculum Vitæ.
†Hampole's Prick of Conſcience.
 The Prikke of Love.
 Bodie and Soule (ed. T. Wright, in Mapes's Poems, pp. 340-6).
 Chriſtes Paſſion ; Chriſt and the Devil, &c.
 Caſtell off Loue (ed. Weymouth, Philological Society, 1864).
*†Kyng Robert of Cicyle, &c.
 Kyng of Tars and Soudan of Dammas (ed. Ritſon, Metr. Rom.).
*Proverbs and Cato.
 Stacions of Rome (ed. Furnivall, Early Engliſh Text Socieɪy, 1867).
 Virgin and Chriſt's Croſs (ed. Morris, Early Engliſh Text Society, 1871).
*†Piſtyl of Sweet Suſan. Stimulus Amoris.
 Hampole's Perfeɛt Living. Contemplative Life.
 Mirour of St. Edmund. Abbey of the Holy Goſt, or Conſcience.
 Spiritum Guidonis.   *Life of Adam and Eve.
 Piers Plowman, Text A. (ed. Skeat, Early Engliſh Text Society).
*Joſeph of Arimathæa, or the Holy Graal (ed. Skeat, Early Engliſh Text
  Society, 1871).
 Lives of Pilate and Judas (ed. Furnivall, Philological Society).
 Minor Poems (ſome printed).
1370-80. Sir Amadas, Avowyng of Arthur, &c. (eds. Stephens and Robſon).
1377 Piers Plowman, Text B. (ed. Crowley, T. Wright ; Skeat, beſt edition,
   Early Engliſh Text Society).
1377 ? *Sir Ferumbras (Aſhmole MS. 33).
   Chaucer's Troylus and Creſſeyde.[1]
1380 ?* Piers Plowman, text C. (ed. Whitaker).
1384 ? Chaucer's Houſe of Fame.
   Chaucer's Anelida and Arcite, Complaynt of Mars and Venus, and
    minor pieces.
   Chaucer's Legend of Good Women.
1387 ? Chaucer's Canterbury Tales.[2]
   Sowdane of Babyloyne and Sir Ferumbras (Roxburghe Club).
   Barbour's Troy Book, MSS. fragments.
   Audelay's Poems (Percy Society).

   * Copied, and in hand for the Early Engliſh Text Society.
   † Of this, another MS. has been printed.

St. Aeldrede, 46 St. Botulf, 47 St. Patrik, 50 St. Athelwold, 55 St. Mildride,
58 St. Allix (different metre), 59 St. Gregory, 60 The 7 Sleepers, 61 St. Dominick,
62 King St. Oſwold, 65 St. Perpolyt, 69 St. Egwyne, 73 St. Juſtine, 74 St. Leger,
75 St. Francis. Alſo in different metre :—87 Sanɛta Paula, 89 Virgin in Antioch,
90 ditto, Miracle of a Virgin, 91 Sithia and Climonen, 92 St. Theodora, 93 St.
Bernard, 94 St. Auſtin, 95 St. Savyn. The Beket is different too.
  The earlier Harl. MS. 2277 has theſe Lives, &c. not in the Vernon :— 4 Leynte,
6 Paſcha, 7 Aſcencio, 8 Pentecoſt, 13 Letanie, 14 Rouiſons, 18 Quiriac, 19 Brendan,
24 Teoſle, 46 Denis, 47 Luc, 48. 11,000 Virgins, 49 Symon and Jude, 50 Quintin,
51 All Saints, 52 All Souls, 53 St. Leonard, 54 St. Martin, 55 Edmund Confeſſor,
56 Edmund King, 63 St. Anaſtace, 65 Invencio Stephani.
  The following are loſt from the beginning of Harl. MS. 2277 :—Hillarij,
Wolftani, Fabiani, Sebaſtiani, Agnetis, Vincencij, Juliani conf[eſſoris], Juliani
hoſp[itis], Brigide, Blaſij, Agathe, Scolaſtice, Valentini, Juliane virginis, Mathie
apoſtoli, Oſwaldi, Cedde conf[eſſoris], Gregorij, Longij, Patricij, Edwardi
Juuenis, Cutberti, and (part) Benedicti.]
 [[1] The proſe *Boece* was probably written before *Troylus.*]
 [[2] The proſe *Aſtrolabe* contains the date 1391.]

The altered verfion of Wm. of Naffington's Mirrour of Life, (from Jn. of Waldby's Speculum Vitæ).

1390 ?   Barbour's Lives of Saints (MS. in Camb. Univ. Library, about 40,000 lines).

Troy Book, Bodleian MS.

1392-3.   Gower's Confeffio Amantis (ed. Pauli, a poor text).

1394 ?   Pierce the Ploughman's Crede (ed. Wolfe, Rogers, Whitaker, T. Wright; Skeat, Early Englifh Text Society, beft ed.).

1395 ?   Plowman's Tale (ed. 1687, Wright's Polit. Poems, ii.)

1395 ?   Richard Maydenftoon's Pfalms (Rawlinfon MS. A. 389).

The Lay Folks' Mafs Book (ed. Simmons, Early Englifh Text Society, in the prefs).

1399.   Depofition of Richard II. (ed. T. Wright for the Camden Society, and in Political Poems, vol. ii.).

After 1400 A.D. *e* final rapidly loft fuch grammatical value as it had at the clofe of the 14th century. Many copies of earlier romances, &c., are preferved for us only in 15th century MSS.

?   Morte Arthure, from MS. Harl. 2252, ab. 1440-50, A.D. (ed. Panton, Roxburghe Club; ed. Furnivall).

1410.   Lydgate's Tranflation of Boethius.

1414.   Brampton's Penitential Pfalms (Percy Society).

1414-25. Poems of James I. of Scotland.

1420 ?   Mirk's Duties of a Parifh Prieft (ed. Peacock, Early Englifh Text Society).

1420 ?   Occleve's De Regimine Principum (ed. T. Wright, Roxburghe Club): Minor Poems (ed. Mafon, 1796, and thofe in MS.)

1420.   Siege of Rouen (Archæologia, xxi, xxii.).

1425 ?   Palladius on Hufbandry, tranflated (ed. Lodge, Early Englifh Text Society; in the prefs).

1426.   Lydgate's Pilgrim (from De Guileville).

1430 ?   Partonope of Blois (ed. Buckley, Roxburghe Club).

1430 ?   Minor Poems of Lydgate (ed. Halliwell, Percy Soc. Others are in MS. at Trinity College, Cambridge, &c. &c.)

1430 ?   Merlin, Douce MS. 236, 1296 lines (differs from Affleck copy).

Athelfton (and other pieces in Reliquiæ Antiquæ, ii.).

1430 ?   Poem on Freemafonry (ed. Halliwell).

1430 ?   Chevelere Affigne (ed. Utterfon, Roxburghe Club; H. H. Gibbs, Early Englifh Text Society).

1430-40. Lincoln's Inn MS. 150; Ly beaus Difconus; Merlin, &c.

1430 ?   Ancient Myfteries from the Digby MS. (Abbotsford Club).

1430.   Political, Religious, and Love Poems (ed. Furnivall, Early Englifh Text Society).

1430 ?   Englifh verfe tranflation of *Speculum Humanæ Salvationis*. Mr. Hy. Huth's MS.

1430 ?   Sir Generides (ed. Furnivall, Roxburghe Club; Lydgate's verfion is in a MS. at Trinity College, Cambridge).

Robert of Cycille (ed. Halliwell, in Nugæ Poeticæ).

The Siege of Jerufalem (2 verfions).

Jon the Gardener, and Poems on Herbs (MS. Trinity College, Cambridge, in hand for Early Englifh Text Society).

1430 ?   Hymns to the Virgin and Chrift, the Parliament of Devils, &c. (ed. Furnivall, Early Englifh Text Society).

1430-40? The poems in the Cambr. Univerfity MS. F f 2, 38. Many of the minor poems have been printed. The principal pieces are :—

Commandments, 7 Works, 5 Wits, 7 Sins and Virtues.

The Good Man and his Son, Merchant and Wife, Merchant and Son (all printed).

Erle of Tolous (ed. Ritfon, Metr. Rom., iii. 93-114).

Syr Eglamoure (ed. Halliwell, Thornton Rom. 121-176. See too Percy Folio, ii. 338.)

Syr Tryamoure (ed. Halliwell, Percy Society. See, too, Percy Folio, ii. 78.)
Octavian (ed. Halliwell, Percy Society, 1844).
Seven Ages (imperfect, differs from Affleck copy).
Guy of Warwick (12156 lines, perfect). Another copy at Caius College, Cambridge. Copies of Lydgate's tranflation are in the Bodleian, and in Harleian MS. 5243.
Le Bone Florence of Rome (ed. Ritfon, Metr. Rom. iii. 1-92).
Robert of Sicily (ed. Halliwell, 1844).
Sir Degare (imperfect. See too Percy Folio, i. 344).
†Bevife of Hampton.

1430?   Lydgate's Siege of Thebes, and other Poems.
1430, 1460, &c. The Babees Book, Ruffell's Book of Courtefy, &c. (ed. Furnivall, Early Englifh Text Society).
1430.   Two Alexander Fragments (ed. Stevenfon, Roxburghe Club).
1440?   Lyfe of Ipomydon (Harl. MS. 2252, later ed. Weber.)
1440?   Arthur (ed. Furnivall, Early Englifh Text Society).
1440?   Torrent of Portugal (ed. Halliwell).
1440?   Sir Gowther (ed. Utterfon).
1440?   Poems of Charles Duke of Orleans (Roxburghe Club).
1440?   Thofe pieces in the Thornton MS. which do not belong to a much earlier date. See a lift of the contents of the MS. in Mr. Halliwell's "Thornton Romances" for the Camden Society. The principal poems are:

Morte Arthure (ed. Halliwell, ed. Perry, and beft ed. Brock).
†Octavyane, †Syr Ifumbrace, †Erle of Tholoufe, †Syr Degravante, †Syr Eglamoure.
Tomas off Erffeldoune (ed. Laing, in Select Remains).
Syr Perecyvelle of Gales (ed. Halliwell, Thornton Rom. 1-70).
Awntyrs of Arthur at the Tarne Wathelan (ed. Laing, in Select Remains, and Madden in Syr Gawayne, 15-128).
Wm. of Naffington on the Trinity (ed. Perry, Early Englifh Text Society).
Sayne Johan, &c. (ed. Perry, Early Englifh Text Society).

1443.   Bokenam's Lives of Saints (Roxburghe Club).
1440-50? Henry Lonelich's Saynt Graal (ed. Furnivall, Roxburghe Club) and Merlin; both imperfect.

Songs and Carols (ed. Wright, Percy Society and Warton Club).
1450?   Sir Degrevvaunt (ed. Halliwell, Thornton Romances, 177-276), and many poems in Cambridge Univerfity, MS. F f 1, 6.
1450?   Chefter Plays (ed. T. Wright, Shakefpeare Society).
1455?   The Buke of the Howlat, by Sir R. de Holande (ed. Pinkerton, 1792; Bannatyne Club, 1823).
1460.   Wyntown's Chronicle (ed. Macpherfon, 1795).
1462?   The Wright's Chafte Wife (ed. Furnivall, Early Englifh Text Society).
We7's Pilgrimage to Jerufalem (Roxburghe Club, and Mr. H. Huth's MS.)
1460?   Towneley (or Widkirk) Myfteries (ed. Surtees Society).
1460?   Play of the Sacrament (ed. Stokes, Philological Soeiety).
1460?   York Myfteries (Lord Afhburnham's MS.)
1460?   Mifcellanies from the Porkington MS.
1460?   Liber Cure Cocorum (ed. R. Morris, Philological Society).
1460?   Tundale's Vifions, &c. (ed. Turnbull).
1460?   Blind Harry's Wallace (ed. Jamiefon, &c.)
1460?   Knight and his Wife, and Life of St. Katherine (ed. Halliwell).
1460?   The pieces in the Cotton MS. Caligula A ii. from older originals.
†Eglamor of Artus.
†Octavian Imperator.
Launfal Miles (ed. Ritfon, Metr. Rom.).
Ly beaus Difconus, or The Fayre Unknown (ed. Ritfon, Metric. Rom. ii.; ed. Hippeau; fee alfo another copy in the Percy Folio, ii. 415).

---

† Of thefe, other MSS. have been printed.

The Nightingale, from John of Hoveden's Latin. He wrote the *Practica Chilindri* in the Chaucer Society's Eſſay, Part 2.

Emare (ed. Ritſon, Metr. Rom.).

Ypotis (Vernon MS. ; in hand for Early Engliſh Text Society).

Stacions of Rome, St. Gregory's Trental, (ed. Furnivall, 1866, Early Engliſh Text Society).

Urbanitas (ed. Furnivall, Babees Book, Early Engliſh Text Society, 1868).

†Owayne Miles (another MS. pr. at Edinburgh).   †Tundale.

Sege of Jeruſalem (ſee Veſp. E. xvi. leaf 78).

†Iſumbras.

St. Jerome. St. Euſtache. Minor Poems.

1460 ?   The Rule of the Moon, &c. (in hand for Early Engliſh Text Society, ed. Furnivall).

1468 ?   Coventry Myſteries (ed. Halliwell, Shakeſpeare Society).

1470.   Harding's Chronicle (printed). See MS. Selden B. 26 : Harl. 661.

1460-88. Henryſon's Poems (ed. Laing).

1500 ?   Lancelot of the Laik (ed. Skeat, Early Engliſh Text Society).

1500 ?   Partenay or Luſignan (ed. Skeat, Early Engliſh Text Society).

 ?   Robert the Devyll (ed. Herbert, 1798).

1500 ?   Doctrynall of Good Servauntes, &c. (circa 1550, repr. Percy Society).

1450-   Caxton's Book of Curteſy, 3 verſions (ed. Furnivall, Early Engliſh Text
1500.   Society.)

1480-1515. Dunbar's Poems (ed. D. Laing).

1506-30. Hawes's Poetical Works (W. de Worde, &c., Percy Society, &c.).

        Death and Life (Percy Folio Ballads and Romances, iii. 56).

1508.   Golagrus and Gawayne, &c. (ed. Madden ; ed. Laing).

1513 ?   Scotiſh Field (Percy Folio Ball. and Rom. i. 199).

1520 ?   John the Reeve (Percy Folio Ball. and Rom. ii. 550).

        Sir Lambewell,   „   „   i. 142.

        Eger and Grime   „   „   i. 341.

        Merlin,   „   „   i. 417.

1520 ?   Gawin Douglas's Works.

[The reader is alſo referred to the ſection of Engliſh Poetry in the Claſs Catalogue of MSS. in the Britiſh Muſeum, now being made under Mr. E. A. Bond's direction ; to Mr. Coxe's Catalogue of the Oxford College MSS. ; Mr. Kitchin's, of the Chriſtchurch MSS. ; the Index and Catalogue of the Cambridge Univerſity Library, of Corpus Chriſti Coll. Cambridge : of the Aſhmole, and other collections in the Bodleian Library ; in Trinity College, Dublin ; in Sir Thomas Philipps's and Lord Aſhburnham's collections ; and to the Reports of the Hiſtorical Manuſcripts Commiſſion under the Maſter of the Rolls, &c. &c. Mr. W. Aldis Wright is cataloguing the MSS. in Trinity Coll. Cambridge.]

Among the Digby MSS. in the Bodleian library, we find a religious or moral Ode, conſiſting of one hundred and ninety-one ſtanzas, [the original of which[1], if it ſhould be diſcovered, may be as old as] the Conqueſt[2] ; but [it is certain that the earlieſt MS. we have of this poem, Lambeth 487, is not earlier than the latter half of the 12th century, if it is not after 1200 A. D.[3]] It exhibits a

---

† Of theſe, other MSS. have been printed.

[1] *Ling. Vett. Thes.* Part i. p. 222. There is another copy not mentioned by Hickes, in Jeſus College library at Oxford, MSS. 85, *infra citat.* This is entitled *Tractatus quidam in Anglico.* The Digby manuſcript has no title.

[2] [Morris's *Old Engliſh Homilies*, Early Engliſh Text Society, 1868, p. vi. note.]

[3] Sir F. Madden attributes the Digby MS. to the reign of Henry III. He enumerates five other MSS. of the Ode : Jeſus Coll. 29 ; Trin. Coll. Camb. B. 14, 52 ; Lambeth, 487, f. 39 b. ; and two others in the Egerton MS. 613, in the Br. Mus. ; and printed in Dr. Morris's *Old Engliſh Homilies*, p. 159. The copy

regular lyric ftrophe of four lines, the fecond and fourth of which
rhyme together : although thefe four lines may be perhaps refolved
into two Alexandrines ; a meafure concerning which more will be
faid hereafter, and of which it will be fufficient to remark at prefent
that it appears to have been ufed very early. For I cannot recollect
any ftrophes of this fort in the elder Runic or Saxon poetry ; nor of
any of the old Frankifh poems, particularly of Otfrid, a monk in
Weiffenburgh, who turned the evangelical hiftory into Frankifh
verfe about the ninth century, and has left feveral hymns in that
language ;[1] of [the Strickers,] who celebrated the achievements of
Charlemagne ;[2] and of the anonymous author of the metrical life of
Anno, archbifhop of Cologne. The following ftanza is a fpecimen
[of the Lambeth MS., but with the lines arranged as in the Digby
MS.] :[3]

> Sendeth fum god biforen eow[4]
> The hwile thet ȝe muȝen to hovene,
> For betere is an elmeffe biforen
> Thenne both efter fouene.[5]

That is, " Send fome good thing before you to heaven while you

in the Egerton MS. 613, was printed by Mr. Furnivall for the Philological Society
(*Tranfactions*, 1858, pt. II. p. 22), and partly in Morris's *Old Englifh Homilies*,
p. 288.]

  [1] See Petr. Lambec. *Commentar. de Bibl. Cæfar. Vindebon.* pp. 418, 457. [A
modern German tranflation, by Kelle, of Otfrid's poems has juft been publifhed.]

  [2] See Petr. Lambec. *ubi fupr.* lib. ii. cap. 5. There is a circumftance belonging
to the ancient Frankifh verfification which, as it greatly illuftrates the fubject of
alliteration, deferves notice here. Otfrid's dedication of his evangelical hiftory
of Lewis I., king of Eaft France, confifts of four-lined ftanzas in rhyming
couplets : but the firft and laft line of every ftanza begin and end with the fame
letter : and the letters of the title of the dedication refpectively, and the word of
the laft line of every tetraftic. Flacius Illyricus publifhed this work of Otfrid at Bafil,
1571. But I think it has been fince more correctly printed by Johannes Schilterus.
It was written about the year 880. Otfrid was the difciple of Rhabanus Maurus.
[Schilter's book was publifhed under this title : *Schilteri Thefaurus antiquitatum
Teutonicarum, exhibens monumenta veterum Francorum, Alamannorum vernacula et
Latina, cum additamentis et notis Joan. Georg. Schertzii.* Ulmæ, 1727-8. 3 vols.
in fol. The *Thefaurus* of Schilter is a real mine of Francic literature. The text
is founded on a careful collation of all the MSS. to which he could obtain accefs ;
and thefe, with one exception, perhaps—the *Life of St. Anno*—are highly valuable
for their antiquity and correctnefs. In the fubfequent editions of this happieft
effort of the Francic Mufe, by Hegewifch, Goldman, and Beffeldt, Schilter's over-
fight has been abundantly remedied. The *Strickers* (a name which fome have interpreted *the writer*), is written in the Swabian dialect; and was compofed towards
the clofe of the thirteenth century. It is a feeble amplification of an earlier
romance, which Warton probably intended to cite, when he ufed the Strickers'
name. Both poems will be found in Schilter ; but the latter, though ufually ftyled
a Francic production, exhibits a language rapidly merging into the Swabian, if it
be not in fact an early fpecimen of that dialect in a rude uncultivated ftate.—*Price*.]

  [3] St. xiv.

> [4] " Senȝe ȝoȝ biforen him man,
> þe hpile he mai ʒo heuene ;
> Foþ beʒeþe if on elmeffe biforen
> Ðanne ben afʒeþ feuene."

This is from the Trinity MS. at Cambridge, written about the [middle of the 13th
century, in Mr. Wright's opinion.] Cod. membran. 8vo. Tractat. I. See Abr.
Wheloc, *Eccles. Hift. Bed.* p. 25, 114.

  [5] MSS. Digb. A 4, membran.

can : for one alms-giving before death is of more value than seven afterwards." The verses might have been thus written, as two Alexandrines :

> Sendeth fum god biforen eow the hwile thet ȝe moȝen to hovene,
> For betere is an elmeffe biforen, thenne both after fouene.[1]

Yet alternate rhyming, applied without regularity, and as rhymes accidentally prefented themfelves, was not uncommon in our early poetry, as will appear from other examples.

In the archiepifcopal library at Lambeth, among other [Tranfition Englifh] homilies in profe, there is a homily or exhortation on the Lord's prayer in verfe,[2] which we may place with fome degree of certainty [about the year 1200] :

> Vre feder thet in heovene is
> Thet is al fothful i wis.
> Weo moten to theos weordes ifeon
> Thet to live and to faule gode beon.
> Thet weo beon fwa his funes iborene
> Thet he beo feder and we him icorene
> Thet we don alle his ibeden
> And his wille for to reden, &c.—(lines 1-8.)
> Lauerd God we biddeth thus
> Mid edmode heorte ȝif hit us.
> Thet ure foule beo to the icore
> Noht for the flefce forlore.
> Thole us to biwepen ure funne
> Thet we ne fteruen noht therinne
> And ȝif us, lauerd, thet ilke ȝifte
> Thet we hes ibeten thurh holie fcrifte.—AMEN.[3]
>
> —(Lines 298-305.)

In the valuable library of Corpus Chrifti College in Cambridge, is a fort of poetical biblical hiftory, extracted from the books of Genefis and Exodus.[4] It was probably compofed about [1250]. But I am chiefly induced to cite this piece, as it proves the exceffive attachment of our earlieft poets to rhyme : they were fond of multi-plying the fame final found to the moft tedious monotony, and with-out producing any effect of elegance, ftrength, or harmony. It begins thus :

> Man og to luuen that rimes ren.
> The wiffed wel the logede men.
> Hu man may him wel loken
> Thog he ne be lered on no boken.
> Luuen God and ferven him ay
> For he it hem wel gelden may.
> And to alle Criftenei men
> Beren pais and luue by-twen

---

[1] As I recollect, the whole poem is thus exhibited in the Trinity MS. [and in all the others except the Digby.—Sir F. Madden's information.]

[2] [The whole of this Lambeth MS. 487, written before 1200, has been edited for the Early Englifh Text Society, by Dr. R. Morris, in his *Old Englifh Homilies*, 1867-8. The verfe Lord's Prayer is on pages 55-71 of Part I.—F.]

[3] [The Story of Genefis and Exodus. An early Englifh fong, about A.D. 1250. Now firft edited from a unique MS. in the library of Corpus Chrifti College, Cambridge. With Introduction, Notes, and Gloffary. By Richard Morris. Early Englifh Text Society, 1865.]

[4] Quart. minor. 185. Cod. membran. [487,] f. 21, b.

Than fal him almighti[n] luuven.
Here by-nethen and thund abuuen,
And given him bliffe and foules refte[n],
That him fal earvermor leften.

Ut of Latin this fong is dragen
On Engleis fpeche on fothe fagen,
Criftene men ogen ben fo fagen,
So fueles arn quan he it fen dagen.
Than man hem telled fothe tale
Wid londes fpeche and wordes fmale
Of bliffes dune, of forwes dale,
Quhu Lucifer that devel dwale
And held hem fperd in helles male,
Til God frid him in manliched,
Dede mankinde bote and red.
And unfpered al the fendes fped
And halp thor he fag mikel ned.
Biddi hie fingen non other led.
Thog mad hic folgen idel-hed.

Fader god of alle thinge,
Almigtin louerd, hegeft kinge,
Thu give me feli timinge
To thaunen this werdes beginninge.
The, leuerd God, to wurthinge
Quether fo hic rede or finge.[1]

We find this accumulation of identical rhymes in the Runic odes, particularly in the ode of Egill cited above, entitled *Egill's Ranfom.* [At the end of the Cotton MS. of the *Owl and Nightingale*, are feven religious metrical pieces which are printed in one of the modern editions [2] of that poem, and alfo in Dr. Richard Morris's *Old Englifh Beftiary*, &c., (E. E. T. Soc. 1871,) together with other verfions from the Jefus Coll. MS., which give hints towards fettling the date, &c. of the poems. Among thefe is] a poem on the fubjects of death, judgment, and hell torments, where the rhymes are fingular, and deferve our attention :

Non mai longe lives thene,
Ac ofte him lieth the wrench :
Feir weder turneth ofte into reine,
An wunderliche hit maketh his blench,
Tharvore, mon, thu the bithench,
Al fchal falewi thi grene.
Weilawei ! nis kin ne quene
That ne fchal drincke of deathes drench.
Mon, er thu falle of thi bench,
Thine funne thu aquench.[3]

To the fame period of our poetry I refer a verfion of Saint Jerom's French pfalter, which occurs in the library of Corpus Chrifti College at Cambridge [and in Cotton MS. Vefp. D. vii.[4]]. The [ninety-ninth] pfalm is thus tranflated :

---

[1] [Nafmith's Cat. No. 444. It is defcribed by Dr. Morris as in the Eaft Midland dialect.]

[2] [Edited by T. Wright for the Percy Society, 1843.]

[3] Bibl. Cotton. MSS. Calig. A ix.—vi. f. 243. [Sir F. Madden pointed out that there is another copy in Jefus Coll. Oxf. 29, f. 252, b.]

[4] [Printed from this MS. by Mr. Stevenfon for the Surtees Society, 1843-7, 2 vols. 8vo.—F.]

> Mirthhes to lauerd al erthe that es
> Serues to lauerd in fainenes.
> Ingas of him in the fight,
> In gladeſchip bi dai and night.
> Wite ye that lauerd he God is thus
> And he vs made and oure ſelf noght **vs,**
> His folk and ſchepe of his fode :
> Ingas his ẏhates that ere gode :
> In ſchrift his porches that be,
> In ympnes to him ſchriue ẏhe.
> Heryes of him name ſwa fre,
> For that lauerd ſoft es he ;
> In euermore his merci eſſe,
> And in ſtrende and ſtrende his ſothneſſe.

In the Bodleian library there is [another MS. of this] tranſlation of the Pſalms, (No. 921, *olim* Arch. B. 38,) a folio on vellum, written in the fifteenth century.[2] A fourth copy written in the reign of Edward II. has been purchaſed for the Britiſh Muſeum. This verſion may be aſcribed to the period of his predeceſſor. The Bodleian MS. alſo contains the Nicene creed[3] and ſome church hymns verſified ; but it is mutilated and imperfect. The nineteenth pſalm runs thus :

> Heuenes tellen Godes blis
> And wolken ſhewes loůd werk his,
> Dai to dai worde riſe right,
> And wiſdome ſhewes niht to niht,
> And pai nare ſpeches ne ſaihes euen.
> Of whilk wat noht es herde war ſteuen.
> In al the werld out yhode war rorde
> And in ende of erþ of pame þe worde.
> In ſunne he ſette his telde to ſtande
> And bridegome he als of his boure comād.
> He gladen als eten to renne þe wai
> Fro heghiſt heuen his outcoming ai,
> And his gainrenning til heht ſete
> Ne is gwilk mai hide him fro his hete
> Lagh of louerd vnwemned iſſe
> Turnand ſaules in to bliſſe
> Witnes of louerd es euer trewe,
> Wiſdom leuand to litel newe
> Louerdes rightwiſnes riht hertes fainand
> Bode of louerd light eghen lighand
> Drede of louerd hit heli iſſe
> In werlde of werld ai ful of bliſſe,
> Domes of louerd ful ſōþe are ai
> Righted in pame ſelue are pai
> More to be yorned ouer golde
> Or ſton derwurþi pat is holde,
> Wel ſwetter to mannes wombe,
> Ouer honi ande te kombe.

This is the beginning of the eighteenth pſalm :

---

[1] [Cott. MS. Veſp. D, vii. fol. 70.]   [2] [Sir F. Madden's information.]
[3] Hickes has printed a metrical verſion of the creed of St. Athanaſius : to whom, to avoid prolix and obſolete ſpecimens already printed, I refer the reader, *Theſaur.* Par. i. p. 233. I believe it to be of the age of Henry II. [In 1835, Mr. Thorpe publiſhed his edition of the Pſalter in Anglo-Saxon from a MS. in the Bibl. Imper. at Paris.]

> I ſal loue the lou*er*d of bliſſe
> Strengh mine lou*er*d feſtnes min eſſe
> And in fleing min als ſo
> And mi leſer out of wo.

I will add another religious fragment on the crucifixion, in the ſhorter meaſure [of the middle of the thirteenth century]:

> Vyen i o the rode ſe,
> Faſt nailed to the tre,
> Jeſu mi lefman,
> Ibunden, bloc ant blodi,
> An hys moder ſtant him bi,
> Wepande, and Johan:
> Hys bac wid ſcuurge iſwungen,
> Hys ſide depe iſtungen,
> For ſinne and lowe [love] of man ;
> Weil aut [well ought] i ſinne lete
> An neb wit teres wete,
> Thif i of loue can.[1]

In the library of Jeſus College at Oxford [MS. Arch. 1. 29], I have ſeen [an early Engliſh] poem of another caſt, yet without much invention or poetry. [This Jeſus MS. is of the latter half of the thirteenth century. Another MS. of the firſt half of the ſame century is in the Britiſh Muſeum, Cotton, Caligula, A. ix.[2]] The poem[3] is a conteſt between an owl and a nightingale about ſuperiority in

---

[1] MSS. Bibl. Bodl. 57, f. 102, b. [In MS. Bodl. 42, are two ſtanzas of a metrical verſion of a paſſage in the Meditations of St. Auſtin, very ſimilar to Warton's fragment, and the ſame lines occur on a piece of vellum inſerted in a MS. in the Cath. Lib. Durh. written in the middle of the thirteenth century. Both texts are printed in Mr. Furnivall's *Political, Religious, and Love Poems*, for the Early Engliſh Text Society, p. 214.]

[2] The latter has been edited by Mr. T. Wright for the Percy Society, and very carefully by Dr. Stratmann (Krefeld, 1868), with a full collation of the Jeſus MS. The Jeſus MS. was printed by Mr. Stevenſon for the Roxburghe Club, and his Gloſſary contains ſome aſtoniſhing miſtakes.]

[3] [Nicholas de] Guldevorde is the author of the poem which immediately precedes in the manuſcript, as appears by the following entry at the end of it, in the handwriting of [Thomas Wilkins, LL.B., rector of St. Mary, Glamorganſhire. Sir F. Madden's Corr.] : " On part of a broken [fly?] leaf of this MS. I find theſe verſes written, whearby the author may be gueſt at :

> "'Mayſter Johan eu greteth of Guldworde tho,
> And ſendeth eu to ſeggen that ſynge he nul he wo,
> On thiſſe wiſe he will endy his ſonge,
> God louerde of hevene, beo us alle amonge."

The piece [which is printed in Dr. R. Morris's *Old Engliſh Beſtiary*, &c., Early Engliſh Text Society, 1871] is entitled and begins thus:

Ici commence la Puſſyun Ihu Chriſt en engleys.
" Ihereth eu one lutele tale that ich eu wille telle
As we vyndeth hit iwrite in the godſpelle :
Nis hit nouht of Karlemeyne ne of the Duzpere,
Ac of Criſtes thruwynge," &c.

It ſeems to be of equal antiquity with that mentioned in the text. The whole manuſcript, conſiſting of many detached pieces both in verſe and proſe, was perhaps written in the [thirteenth century. It is attributed to Nicholas de Guilford, who was poſſibly related to John de Guilford].

voice and finging. It is not later than [Edward] I.[1] The rhymes
are multiplied, and remarkably interchanged :

> Ich was in one fumere dale :
> In one fwithe diȝele hale,
> Iherde ich holde grete tale,
> An ule [2] and one nihtegale.
> That plaid was ftif & ftarc and ftrong,
> Sum hwile fofte and lud among.
> And either aȝen other fwal
> And let that uvele mod ut al.
> And either feide of othres cufte,
> That alre worfte that hi wufte ;
> And hure and hure of othres fonge
> Hi heolde plaiding fwithe ftronge.[3]
>
> [—*Stratmann*, p. 1.]

The earlieft love-fong which I can difcover in our language, is [in
Harl. MS. 2253]. I would place it before or about the year 1200.
It is full of alliteration, and has a burthen or chorus : [4]

> Blow northerne wynd,
> Sent thou me my fuetyng ;
> Blow northerne wynd,
> 　　Blou, blou, blou.
> Ichot a burde in boure bryht
> That fully femly is on fyht,
> Menfkful maiden of myht,
> 　　Feir ant fre to fonde.
> In al this wurhliche won,
> A burde of blod & of bon,
> Never ȝete y nufte [5] non
> 　　Luffomore in londe. *Blou, &c.*

From the fame collection I have extracted a part of another ama-
torial ditty, of equal antiquity, which exhibits a ftanza of no inelegant or unpleafing ftructure, and approaching to the octave rhyme.
It is, like the laft, formed on alliteration :

> In a fryht as y con fare fremede
> Y founde a wel feyr fenge to fere,
> Heo glyftnede afe gold when hit glemede,
> Nes ner gome fo gladly on gere,
> Y wolde wyte in world who hire kenede,
> This burde bryht, ȝef hire wil were ;
> Heo me bed go my gates, left hire gremede,
> Ne kepte heo non hevyng here.[6]

In the following lines a lover compliments his miftrefs named
Alyfoun :

---

[1] [Sir F. Madden feems inclined to identify Nicholas de Guilford with the vicar
of Portefhom, near Abbotfbury.]

[2] owl.　　　　　　　　　　　　[3] MSS. Coll. Jes. Oxon. 86, membr.

[4] [Printed in Ritfon's *Ancient Songs*, 1792, p. 26 ; 2nd ed. i. 58 ; and in T.
Wright's *Specimens of Lyric Poetry* (Percy Soc. 1842), which contains all the fongs
quoted from the MS. (about 1307 A.D.) by Warton. It was not thought defirable,
therefore, to retain Warton's very lengthy extract, and only the commencement has
been given.]

[5] knew not.

[6] MSS. *ibid.* f. 66. [*Hevyng* is hoving, ftopping. Sir F. Madden, judging from
internal evidence, fuppofes that this piece was written fhortly after 1307, to which
date he affigns the execution of the MS.]

Bytuene Merfhe ant Aueril
When fpray biginneth to fpringe,
The lutel foul hath hire wyl
On hyre lud to fynge,
Ich libbe in louelonginge
For femlokeft of alle thynge.
He may me blyffe bringe;
Icham in hire baundoun;
An hendy hap ichabbe yhent
Ichot from heuene it is me fent.
From alle wymmen mi love is lent
And lyht on Alifoun.

On heu hire her is fayre ynoʒ,
Hire browe broune, hire eye blake,
With loffum chere he on me loh:
With middel fmal and wel ymake,
Bote he me wolle to hire take, &c.[1]

The following fong, containing a defcription of the fpring, difplays glimmerings of imagination, and exhibits fome faint ideas of
poetical expreffion.　It is extracted from the fame inexhauftible repofitory.　I have tranfcribed the whole:[2]

Lenten ys come with love to toune,
With blofmen ant with briddes roune,
    That al this bliffe bryngeth;
Dayes eʒes in this dales,
Notes fuete of nyʒtegales,
    Uch foul fong fingeth.

The threftelcoc[3] him threteth oo,
Away is huere wynter wo,
    When woderoue fpringeth;
This foules fingeth ferly fele,
Ant wlyteth on huere wynter wele,
    That al the wode ryngeth.

The rofe rayleth hir rode,
The leves on the lyʒte wode
    Waxen al with wille:
The mone mandeth hire bleo
The lilie is loffum to feo;
    The fenyl and the fille.

Wowes this wilde drakes,
Miles murgeth huere makes.
    As ftreme that ftriketh ftille
Mody meneth, fo doh mo.
Ichot ycham on of tho,
    For love that likes ille.

---

[1] Harl. MSS. fol. 2253 63, b.

[2] [The following ftanza formed the opening of this fong as printed by Warton.
It appears to have been inadvertently copied from a poem in the parallel column
of the manufcript, Harl. 2253. (See Wright's *Lyric Poetry*, p. 45.)

    " In May hit muryeth when hit dawes,[1]
    In dounes with this dueres plawes,[2]
    Ant lef is lyʒt on lynde;
    Blofines bredeth on the bowes,
    Al this wylde wyʒtes wowes,
        So wel ych under-fynde."—*Price.*]

[3] throftle, thrufh.

---

[1] " it is mery at dawn."   [2] plays.

The mone mandeth hire ly3t,
[So doth the femly fonne bry3t,]
    When briddes fyngeth breme,
Deawes donketh the dounes
Deores with huere derne rounes,
    Domes forte deme.

Wormes woweth under cloude,
Wymmen waxith wounder proude,
    So wel hyt wol hem feme :
3ef me fhal wonte wille of on
This wunne weole ӯ wol forgon
    Ant wyht in wode be fleme.[1]

This fpecimen will not be improperly fucceeded by the following
elegant lines, which a contemporary poet appears to have made in a
morning walk from Peterborough, on the bleffed Virgin ; but whofe
genius feems better adapted to defcriptive than religious fubjects :

Now fkruketh rofe ant lylie flour,
That whilen ber that fuete favour
    In fomer, that fuete tyde ;
Ne is no quene fo ftark ne ftour,
Ne no leuedy fo bry'nt in bour
    That ded ne fhal by-glyde :
Whofo wol fleyfh-luft for-gon
    And hevene-bliffe abyde,

---

[1] MSS. *ibid.* ut fupr. f. 71, b.   In the fame ftyle, as it is manifeftly of the fame
antiquity, the following little defcriptive fong, on the Approach of Summer, deferves notice.—*MSS. Harl.* 978, f. 5 :

" Sumer is i-comen in,
    Lhude fing cuccu ;
Groweth fed, and bloweth med,
    And fpringeth the wde nu.
        Sing cuccu.

Awe bleteth after lomb,
    Lhouth after calve cu ;
Bulluc fterteth, bucke verteth :
    Murie fing, cuccu,
        Cuccu, cuccu :
Wel finges thu cuccu ;
Ne fwik thou nauer nu.
        Sing cuccu nu,
        Sing cuccu.

That is, " Summer is coming : Loudly fing, Cuckow ! Groweth feed, and bloweth
mead, and fpringeth the wood now.   Ewe bleateth after lamb, loweth cow after
calf ; bullock ftarteth, buck *verteth* :[1] merrily fing, Cuckow ! Well fingeft thou,
Cuckow, Nor ceafe to fing now."   This is the moft ancient Englifh fong that appears in our manufcripts, with the mufical notes annexed.   The mufic is of that
fpecies of compofition which is called *Canon in the Unifon,* and is fuppofed to be of
the fifteenth century.   [See Chappell's *Popular Mufic of the Olden Time,* 23-5, and
references there given to other fongs of the fame character ; alfo Mr. Alexander
J. Ellis's careful edition of this fong and the Prifoner's Prayer in the *Philological
Society's Tranfactions,* 1868.   Mr. Richard Taylor has drawn attention to the
fimilarity of this fong to fome of the lays of the *Minnefingers,* collected by Mr.
Edgar Taylor, 1825.]

---

[1] goes to harbour among the fern.

On Jhefu be is thoht anon,
That therled was ys fide.[1]

To which we may add a fong, probably written by the fame author, on the five joys of the bleffed Virgin, [a common topic, treated by Shoreham and other poets :]

Afe y me rod this ender day,
By grene wode, to feche play ;
Mid herte y thohte al on a May.
Suetest of alle thinge ;
Lythe, and ich ou telle may
Al of that fuete thinge.[2]

In the fame paftoral vein, a lover, perhaps of the reign of King John, thus addreffes his miftrefs, whom he fuppofes to be the moft beautiful girl, " bituene Lyncolne and Lyndefeye, Northampton and Lounde" :[3]

When the nyȝtegale finges, the wodes waxen grene ;
Lef and gras and blofme fpringes in Averyl, y wene.
Ant love iⵑ to myn herte gon with one fpere fo kene
Nyȝt and day my blod hit drynkes, myn herte deth me tene.

Ich have loved al this ȝer that y may love na more,
Ich have fiked moni fyk, lemmon, for thin ore,
Me nis love never the ner, ant that me reweth fore ;
Suete lemmon, thench on me, ich have loved the ȝore,

Suete lemmon, y preye the of love one fpeche,
While y lyve in worlde fo wyde other nulle y feche.[5]
[With thy love, my fuete leof, mi blis thou miȝtes eche,
A fuete cos of thy mouth miȝte be my leche.]

Nor are thefe verfes, in fomewhat the fame meafure, unpleafing :

My deth y love, my lyf ich hate, for a levedy fhene,
Heo is brith fo daies liȝt, that is on me wel fene.
Al y falewe, fo doth the lef in fomer when hit is grene ;
Ȝef mi thoht helpeth me noȝt, to wham fhal I me mene ?

Another, in the following little poem, enigmatically compares his miftrefs, whofe name feems to be Joan, to various gems and flowers. The writer is happy in his alliteration, and his verfes are tolerably harmonious :

Ichot a burde in a bour, afe beryl fo bryȝt,
Afe faphyr in felver femly on fyȝt,
Afe jafpe[6] the gentil that lemeth[7] with lyȝt,
Afe gernet[8] in golde and ruby wel ryȝt,
Afe onycle[9] he ys on yholden on hyȝt ;
Afe diamaund the dere in day when he is dyȝt :
He is coral y-cud with Cayfer ant knyȝt,
Afe emeraude a morewen this may haveth myȝt.
The myȝt of the margarite haveth this mai mere,
For charbocle iche hire chafe bi chyn ant bi chere.
Hire rode ys as rofe that red ys on rys,[10]

---

[1] Harl. MSS. 2253, f. 80 ; [*Lyric Poetry*, p. 87.]
[2] MS. *ibid.* f. 81, b ; *Lyric Poetry*, p. 94.   [3] London.
[4] MSS. *ibid.* f. 80, b. [The confufion, adverted to above, prevailed in the difpofition of this fong. The prefent copy follows the MS.—*Price*.] Ritfon's *Anc. Songs*, p. 30.   [5] MSS. *ibid.* f. 80, b.
[6] jafper.   [7] ftreams, fhines.   [8] garnet.   [9] onyx.   [10] branch.

> With lilye white leves loſſum he ys,
> The primroſe he paſſeth, the parvenke of prys,
> With aliſaundre thareto, ache ant anys:
> Coynte[1] as columbine ſuch hire cande[2] ys,
> Glad under gore in gro ant in grys
> He is bloſme opon bleo briȝteſt under bis
> With celydone ant ſauge aſe thou thi ſelf ſys, &c.
> From Weye he is wiſiſt into Wyrhale,
> Hire nome is in a note of the nyȝtegale;
> In an note is hire nome, nempneth hit non,
> Who ſo ryzt redeth, ronne to Johon.[3]

The curious Harleian volume, to which we are ſo largely indebted, has preſerved a moral tale, a compariſon between age and
youth, where the ſtanza is remarkably conſtructed. The various
ſorts of verſification which we have already ſeen, evidently prove that
much poetry had been written, and that the art had been greatly
cultivated before this period.

> Herkne to my ron,   }   *Of elde al hou yt ges.*
> As ich ou tell con,   }
> Of a mody mon,   }   *Soth withoute les.*
> Hihte Maximion,   }
> Clerc he was ful god,   }   *Nou herkne hou it wes*[4].
> So moni mon undirſtod.   }

For the ſame reaſon, a ſort of elegy on our Saviour's crucifixion
ſhould not be omitted. It begins thus (*Lyric Poetry*, p. 85):

> I ſyke when y ſinge,
>   For ſorewe that y ſe,
> When y with wypinge
>   Bihold upon the tre,
> Ant ſe Jheſu the ſuete
> Is hert blod for-lete,
>   For the love of me;
> Ys woundes waxen wete,
> Thei wepen ſtill and mete,
>   Marie, reweth the.[5]

Nor an alliterative ode on heaven, death, judgment, &c. (*Lyric
Poetry*, p. 22.):

> Middel-erd for mon wes mad,
> Un-mihti aren is meſte mede,
> This hedy hath on honde yhad,
> That hevene hem is heſt to hede.
> Icherde a bliſſe budel us bade,
> The dreri domeſdai to drede,
> Of ſunful ſauhting ſone be ſad,
> That derne doth this derne dede,
>   *Thah he ben derne done.*
> This wrakefall werkes under wede,
>   In ſoule ſoteleth ſone.[6]

Many of theſe meaſures were adopted from the French chanſons.[7]
I will add one or two more ſpecimens.

---

[1] quaint.   [2] [kind, nature. Sir F. Madden's corr.]   [3] MSS. *ibid.* f. 63.
[4] MSS. *ibid.* f. 82, [printed in *Reliquiæ Antiquæ*, i. 119-125. There is another
copy in the Digby MS. 86, leaf 134 back, ab. 1320 A. D.]
[5] *Ibid.* f. 80.
[6] MS. Harl. 2253, f. 62, b.   [7] See MSS. Harl. *ut ſupr.* f. 49, 76.

On our Saviour's paſſion and death :

> Jeſu for thi muchele miȝt
> Thou ȝef us of thi grace,
> That we mowe dai ant nyht
> Thenken o thi face.
> In myn herte hit doth me god,
> When y thenke on Jeſu blod,
> That ran doun bi ys ſyde ;
> From is herte doune to his fot,
> For ous he ſpradde is herte blod
> His wondes were ſo wyde.[1]

On the ſame ſubjeƈt :

> Lutel wot hit any mon
> How love hym haveth y-bounde,
> That for us o the rode ron,
> Ant bohte us with is wounde ;
> The love of him us haveth ymaked ſounde,
> And y-caſt the grimly goſt to grounde :
> Ever ant oo, nyȝt ant day, he haveth us in is thoȝte,
> He nul nout leoſe that he ſo deore boȝte.[2]

The following are on love and gallantry. The poet, named Richard, profeſſes himſelf to have been a great writer of love-ſongs :

> Weping haveth myn wonges[3] wet,
> For wikked werk ant wone of wyt,
> Unblithe y be til y ha bet,
> Bruches broken, aſe bok byt :
> Of levedis love that y ha let,
> That lemeth al with lueſly lyt,
> Ofte in ſonge y have hem ſet,
> That is unſemly ther hit ſyt.
> Hit ſyt and ſemeth noht,
> Ther hit ys ſeid in ſong
> That y have of them wroht,
> Ywis hit is al wrong.[4]

It was cuſtomary with the early ſcribes, when ſtanzas conſiſted of ſhort lines, to throw them together like proſe. As thus :

" A wayle whyt as whalles bon | a grein in golde that godly ſhon | a tortle that min herte is on | in tounes trewe | Hire gladſhip nes never gon | whil y may glewe." [5]

Sometimes they wrote three or four verſes together as one line :

With longyng y am lad | on molde y waxe mad | a maide marreth me,
Y grede, y grone un-glad | for ſelden y am ſad | that ſemly for te ſe.
Levedi, thou rewe me | to routhe thou haveſt me rad | be bote out of that y bad
   | my lyf is long on the.[6]

Again,

---

[1] MS. Harl. 2253, f. 79. Probably this ſong has been ſomewhat moderniſed by tranſcribers.

[2] *Ibid.* f. 128. Theſe lines afterwards occur, burleſqued and parodied, by a writer of the ſame age.

[3] [cheeks, A. S. panȝ, Ital. guancia.]

[4] MSS. *Ibid.* f. 66 ; [*Lyric Poetry*, p. 30-33.]

[5] *Ibid.* f. 67. [Mr. R. Taylor refers us to Hoffmann's *Fundgruben* 1830 ; *Danſke Kiæmpe Viſer*, 1787 ; and Raynouard, *Poeſies des Troubadours*, ii. Poeme ſur Boece, p. 6.]

[6] *Ibid.* f. 63, b.

Mofti ryden by Rybbes-dale | wilde wymmen for te wale | ant welde wuch ich
  wolde :
Founde were the feyreft on | that ever wes mad of blod ant bon | in boure beft with
  bolde.[1]

This mode of writing is not uncommon in ancient manufcripts of
French poetry. And fome critics may be inclined to fufpect, that
the verfes which we call Alexandrine, accidentally affumed their
form merely from the practice of abfurd tranfcribers, who frugally
chofe to fill their pages to the extremity, and violated the metrical
ftructure for the fake of faving their vellum. It is certain, that the
common ftanza of four fhort lines may be reduced into two Alexandrines, and on the contrary. I have before obferved that the
[old Englifh] poem cited by Hickes, confifting of one hundred and
ninety-one ftanzas, is written in ftanzas in the Bodleian, and in
Alexandrines in the Trinity manufcript at Cambridge. How it
came originally from the poet I will not pretend to determine.

Our early poetry often appears in fatirical pieces on the eftablifhed
and eminent profeffions; and the writers, as we have already feen,
fucceeded not amifs, when they cloathed their fatire in allegory. But
nothing can be conceived more fcurrilous and illiberal[2] than their
fatires when they defcend to mere invective. In the Britifh Mufeum,
among other examples which I could mention, we have a fatirical ballad on the [Confiftory Courts, and the vexation which they
caufed to the peafantry. The whole ballad is printed in Mr. T.
Wright's *Political Songs*, for the Camden Society, 1839, pp. 155-9,
and we quote a few lines againft the Summoners, whom we know
from Chaucer's fketch, eight years later :—]

    Hyrd-men hem hatieth, ant vch mones hyne,
    For everuch a parrofshe heo polketh in pyne,
    Ant claftreth with heore colle :
    Nou wol vch fol clerc that is fayly
    Wende to the byfshop ant bugge bayly,
    Nys no wyt in is nolle.[3]

The elder French poetry abounds in allegorical fatire; and I
doubt not that the author of the fatire on the [legal] profeffion,
cited above, copied fome French fatire on the fubject. Satire was
one fpecies of the poetry of the Provençal troubadours. Gau-
celm Faidit, a troubadour of the eleventh century, who will again
be mentioned, wrote a fort of fatirical drama called the Herefy of
the Fathers, *Heregia del Preyres*, a ridicule on the council which
condemned the Albigenfes. The papal legates often fell under the
lafh of thefe poets : whofe favour they were obliged to court, but in
vain by the promife of ample gratuities.[4] [There is a very lively
and fevere fatire (erroneoufly attributed to Hugues de Bercy,) belonging to the 12th or 13th century, which is called by the writer *Bible
Guiot de Provins*,] as containing nothing but truth.[5]

---

[1] Harl. MSS. 2253, f. 66.
[2] [I doubt whether they faid one word more than the oppreffions they fuffered
juftified.—*F.*]
[3] Harl. MS. 2253, f. 71.
[4] Fontenelle, *Hift. Theatr. Fr.* p. 18, edit. 1742.   [5] See Fauchet, *Rec.* p. 151.

In Harl. MS. 2253, I find an ancient French poem, yet refpecting England, which is a humorous panegyric on a new religious order called *Le Ordre de bel Eyfe*. This is the exordium :—

> Qui vodra a moi entendre
> Oyr purra e aprendre
> L'eftoyre de un Ordre Novel
> Qe mout eft delitous e bel. [1]

The poet ingeniouſly feigns that his new monaſtic order conſiſts of the moſt eminent nobility and gentry of both ſexes, who inhabit the monaſteries aſſigned to it promiſcuouſly; and that no perſon is excluded from this eſtabliſhment who can ſupport the rank of a gentleman. They are bound by their ſtatutes to live in perpetual idleneſs and luxury : and the ſatiriſt refers them for a pattern or rule of practice in theſe important articles, to the monaſteries of Sempringham in Lincolnſhire [where Robert Manning of Brunne dwelt for a time [2]], Beverley in Yorkſhire, the Knights Hoſpitallers, and many other religious orders then flouriſhing in England.[3]

When we conſider the feudal manners and the magnificence of our Norman anceſtors, their love of military glory, the enthuſiaſm with which they engaged in the Cruſades, and the wonders to which they muſt have been familiarized from thoſe eaſtern enterpriſes, we naturally ſuppoſe, what will hereafter be more particularly proved, that their retinues abounded with minſtrels and harpers, and that their chief entertainment was to liſten to the recital of romantic and martial adventures. But I have been much diſappointed in my ſearches after the metrical tales which muſt have prevailed in their times. Moſt of thoſe old heroic ſongs have periſhed, together with the ſtately caſtles in whoſe halls they were ſung. Yet they were not ſo totally loſt as we may be apt to imagine. Many of them ſtill partly exiſt in the old Engliſh metrical romances, which will be mentioned in their proper places ; yet diveſted of their original form, poliſhed in their ſtyle, adorned with new incidents, ſucceſſively moderniſed by repeated tranſcription and recitation, and retaining little more than the outlines of the original compoſition. This has not been the caſe with the legendary and other religious poems written ſoon after the Conqueſt, manuſcripts of which abound in our libraries. From the nature of their ſubject they were leſs popular and common, and being leſs frequently recited, became leſs liable to perpetual innovation or alteration.

In the reign of [Edward II.], a poem occurs, the date of which may be determined with ſome degree of certainty. It is a ſatirical ſong or ballad, written by one of the adherents of Simon de Mont-

---

[1] [It will be found in the ſecond volume of Barbazan's *Fabliaux*, p. 307. "La Bible au Seignor de Berze " is a more courtly compoſition, and forms a part of the ſame collection, p. 194. The earlier French antiquaries have frequently confounded theſe two productions.—*Price*. *L'Ordre de Bel Eyfe* is printed alſo by Wright, *Political Songs of England*, 1839, p. 137. Mr. Wright aſſigns it to the reign of Edward II.]

[2] [*Handlyng Synne*, Prologue, edit. Furnivall.]

[3] MSS. ibid. f. 121.

fort earl of Leicefter, a powerful baron, foon after the battle of Lewes, which was fought in the year 1264, and proved very fatal to the interefts of the king.   In this decifive action, Richard king of the Romans, his brother Henry the Third, and Prince Edward, with many others of the royal party, were taken prifoners :[1]—

> Sitteth alle ftille, ant herkneth to me :
> The kyn of Alemaigne, bi mi leaute,
> Thritti thoufent pound afkede he [2]
> For te make the pees in the countre,
>   And fo he dude more.
> Richard, thah thou be ever trichard,
>   trichen fhall thou never more.

> Richard of Alemaigne, whil that he was kyng,
> He fpende al is trefour opon fwyvyng :
> Haveth he nout of Walingford o ferlyng ;
> Let him habbe, afe he brew, bale to dryng,
>   Maugre Wyndefore.
> Richard, thah thou, &c.

Thefe popular rhymes had probably no fmall influence in encouraging Leicefter's partifans, and diffufing his faction.   There is fome humour in imagining that Richard fuppofed the windmill to which he retreated, to be a fortification ; and that he believed the fails of it to be military engines.   In the manufcript, from which this fpecimen is tranfcribed, immediately follows a fong in French, feemingly written by the fame poet, on the battle of Evefham fought the following year ; in which Leicefter was killed, and his rebellious barons defeated.[3]   Our poet looks upon his hero as a martyr, and particularly laments the lofs of Henry his fon, and Hugh le Defpenfer jufticiary of England.   He concludes with an Englifh ftanza, much in the ftyle and fpirit of thofe juft quoted.

[Daines Barrington, in his *Obfervations on the Statutes*, 1766,] has obferved, that this ballad on Richard of Alemaigne probably occafioned a ftatute againft libels in the year 1275, under the title, " Againft flanderous reports, or tales to caufe difcord betwixt king and people."[4]   That this fpirit was growing to an extravagance

---

[1] [Printed entire in *Political Songs*, ed. Wright, 1839, p. 69.   The firft and fecond ftanzas have therefore been thought a fufficient fpecimen of the production.]

[2] The barons made this offer of thirty thoufand pounds to Richard.

[3] f. 59.   It begins,

" Chaunter meftoit | mon ever le voit | en un duré langage,

Tut en pluraunt | fuft fet le chaunt | de noitre duz Baronage," &c.

[4] [Privately printed by Palgrave, 1818, with three other pieces from the fame fource.   Sir F. Madden's information.   It has alfo been included in Ritfon's *Ancient Songs*, ed. 1829.   A verfion of it was made by Sir Walter Scott, at the requeft of Ritfon, and has been reprinted in the [fecond edition] of his *Englifh Songs*, vol. ii.   Mr. Geo. Ellis made another metrical tranflation, which perifhed with many of Ritfon's MS. treafures.—*Park.*

This Norman ballad has fince been printed in the new edition of Ritfon's *Ancient Songs*.   Political fongs feem to have been common about this period : both Englifh, Norman, and Latin, the three languages then ufed in England, feem to have been enlifted into the caufe of Simon de Montfort.   I have fomewhere feen a Latin poem in his praife ; and, in the following paffage from a MS. containing his miracles (for Simon, like Harold, and Waltheof, and moft of the popular heroes of thofe days, was looked upon as a faint), and written apparently no very long time

which deferved to be checked, we fhall have occafion to bring further proofs.

I muft not pafs over the reign of Henry III. who died in the year 1272, without obferving that this monarch entertained in his court a poet with a certain falary, whofe name was Henri d'Avranches.[1] And although this poet was a Frenchman, and moft probably wrote in French, yet this firft inftance of an officer who was afterwards, yet with fufficient impropriety, denominated a *poet laureate* in the Englifh court, defervedly claims particular notice in the courfe of thefe annals. He is called *Mafter Henry the Verfifier* :[2] which appellation perhaps implies a different charaƈter from the royal *Minftrel* or *Joculator.* The king's treafurers are ordered to pay this *Mafter Henry* one hundred fhillings, which I fuppofe to have been a year's ftipend, in the year 1251.[3] And again the fame precept occurs under the year 1249.[4] Our Mafter Henry, it feems, had in fome of his verfes refleƈted on the rufticity of the Cornifh men. This infult was refented in a Latin fatire now remaining, written by Michael Blaunpayne, a native of Cornwall, and recited by the author in the prefence of Hugh, abbot of Weftminfter, Hugh de Mortimer, official of the archbifhop of Canterbury, the bifhop eleƈt of Winchefter, and the bifhop of Rochefter.[5] While we are fpeaking

---

after his death, we have apparently the fragment of a hymn addreffed to him when canonized by the popular voice. MS. Cotton. Vefp. A. VI. fol. 189. "Anno Domini m° ccᵐᵒ lx° vᵗᵒ oƈtavo Symonis Montis Fortis fociorumque ejus pridie nonas Augufti.

> "Salve Symon Montis Fortis,
>   tocius flos milicie,
> Duras penas paffus mortis,
>   proteƈtor (?) gentis Anglie.
> Sunt de fanƈtis inaudita,
> Cunƈtis paffis in hac vita
>   quemquam paffum talia : (*fic.*)
> Manus, pedes amputari ;
> Caput, corpus vulnerari ;
>   abfcidi virilia.
> Sis pro nobis interceffor
> Apud Deum, qui defenfor
>   in terris exterritas. (*fic.*)

Ora pro nobis, beate Symon, ut digni efficiamur promiffionibus Chrifti." There are found many political fongs in Latin, which fhows that the monks took much intereft in politics.—*W.*]

[1] See Carew's *Surv. Cornw.* p. 58, edit. 1602.

[2] Henry of Huntingdon fays, that Walo *Verfificator* wrote a panegyric on Henry the Firft : and that the fame Walo *Verfificator* wrote a poem on the park which that king made at Woodftock. Leland's *Colleƈtan.* vol. ii. 303, i. 197, edit. 1770. Perhaps he was in the department of Henry mentioned in the text. One Gualo, a Latin poet, v.ho flourifhed about this time, is mentioned by Bale, iii. 5, and Pits, p. 233. He is recommended in the *Policraticon.* A copy of his Latin hexametrical fatire on the monks is printed by Mathias Flacius, among mifcellaneous Latin poems *De corrupto Ecclefiæ ftatu,* 1557, p. 489.

[3] "Magiftro Henrico Verfificatori." See Madox, *Hift. Excheq.* p. 268.

[4] *Ibid.* p. 674. In MSS. Digb. Bibl. Bodl. I find, in John of Hoveden's *Salutationes quinquaginta Mariæ,* "Mag. Henricus, verfificator magnus, de B. Virgine," &c.

[5] MSS. Bibl. Bodl. Arch. Bodl. 29, viz : "Verfus magiftri Michaelis Cornu-

of the *Verſifier* of Henry III., it will not be foreign to add, that in the thirty-ſixth year of the ſame king, forty ſhillings and one pipe of wine were given to Richard the king's harper, and one pipe of wine to Beatrice his wife.[1] But why this gratuity of a pipe of wine ſhould alſo be made to the wife, as well as to the huſband who from his profeſſion was a genial charaċter, appears problematical according to our preſent ideas.[2]

The moſt ancient Engliſh metrical romance which I can diſcover, is entitled the *Geſte of King Horn.*[3] It was evidently written after the Cruſades had begun, is mentioned by Chaucer,[4] and probably ſtill remains in [ſomething near] its original ſtate. I will firſt give the ſubſtance of the ſtory, and afterwards add ſome ſpecimens of the compoſition. But I muſt premiſe, that this ſtory occurs in very old French metre in the manuſcripts of the Britiſh muſeum ;[5] [but

---

bienſis contra Mag. Henricum Abricenſem coram dom. Hugone abbate Weſtmon. et aliis." fol. 81, b. *Princ.* "Archipoeta vide quod non ſit cura tibi de." See alſo fol. 83, b. Again, fol. 85 :

> "Pendo poeta prius te diximus Archipoetam,
> Quam pro poſtico nunc dicimus eſſe poetam,
> Imo poeticulum," &c.

Archipoeta means here the *king's chief poet.*
In another place our Corniſh ſatiriſt thus attacks maſter Henry's perſon :

> " Eſt tibi gamba capri, crus paſſeris, et latus apri ;
> Os leporis, catuli naſus, dens et gena muli :
> Frons vetulæ, tauri caput, et color undique mauri."

In a blank page of the Bodleian MS., from which theſe extraċts are made, is written, "Iſte liber conſtat Fratri Johanni de Wallis monacho Rameſeye." The name is elegantly enriched with a device. This MS. contains, amongſt other things, *Planċtus de Excidio Trojæ*, by Hugo Prior de Montacino, in rhyming hexameters and pentameters, viz. fol. 89. Camden cites other Latin verſes of Michael Blaunpain, whom he calls "Merry Michael the Corniſh poet." *Rem.* p. 10. See alſo p. 489, edit. 1674. He wrote many other Latin pieces, both in proſe and verſe. Compare Tanner in *Joannes Cornubienſis*, for his other pieces. *Bibl.* p. 432, notes, f, g. [The poems of Michael Cornubienſis (in Latin) are preſerved, as Mr. Wright informs us, in MS. Cotton. Veſp. D. 5, 49. The ſame gentleman ſtates that in the Britiſh Muſeum there is more than one copy of the verſes quoted by Warton. In one (MS. Reg. 14 C. xiii. 269), they are ſaid to have been recited at Cambridge before the univerſity and maſters.]

[1] *Rot. Pip. an.* 36 *Henr.* iii. "Et in uno dolio vini empto et dato magiſtro Ricardo Cithariſtæ regis, xl. ſol. per Br. Reg. Et in uno dolio empto et dato Beatrici uxori ejuſdem Ricardi."

[2] [Beatrice may poſſibly have been a *juglereſs*, whoſe pantomimic exhibitions were accompanied by her huſband's harp, or who filled up the intervals between his performances. This union of profeſſional talents in huſband and wife was not uncommon. In a copy of the ordonnances for regulating the minſtrels, &c. reſiding at Paris, a document drawn up by themſelves in the year 1321, and ſigned by thirty-ſeven perſons on behalf of all the *meneſtreux jougleurs et jouglereſſes* of that city, we find among others the names of Iehanot Langlois et Adeline, fame de Langlois Jaucons, fils le moine et Marguerite, la fame au moine. See Raynouard, *De la Poeſie Françoiſe dans les xii. et xiii. Siècles,* p. 288.—*Price.*]

[3] See Mätzner and Goldbeck's text in their *Sprachproben.*—F.]

[4] Rim. Thop. 3402, Urr.

[5] MSS. Harl. 527, b. f. 59, Cod. membr. [*King Horn* has been edited for the Early Engliſh Text Society ; it was included (from Harl. 2253) in Ritſon's col-

it is probably not] a tranflation : a circumftance which will [affect]
an argument purfued hereafter, proving that moft of our metrical
romances are tranflated from the French.

[The] king of the Saracens lands in the kingdom of Suddene,
where he kills the king named Allof [or Mury]. The queen,
Godylt, efcapes ; but [the king] feizes on her fon Horne, a beautiful
youth aged fifteen years, and puts him into a galley, with two of his
play-fellows, Athulph and Fykenyld : the veffel being driven on the
coaft of the kingdom of Weftneffe, the young prince is found by
Aylmer king of that country, brought to court, and delivered to
Athelbrus his fteward, to be educated in hawking, harping, tilting,
and other courtly accomplifhments. Here the princefs Rymenild
falls in love with him, declares her paffion, and is betrothed. Horn,
in confequence of this engagement, leaves the princefs for feven years ;
to demonftrate, according to the ritual of chivalry, that by feeking
and accomplifhing dangerous enterprifes he deferved her affection.
He proves a moft valorous and invincible knight : and at the end of
feven years having killed King Mury, recovered his father's kingdom,
and achieved many fignal exploits, recovers the Princefs Rymenild
from the hands of his treacherous knight and companion Fykenyld,
carries her in triumph to his own country, and there reigns with her
in great fplendour and profperity. The poem itfelf begins and proceeds thus :[1]—

> Alle beon he blithe
> That to my fong lythe :
> A fang ich fchal ʒou finge
> Of Murry the kinge.
> King he was biwefte
> So long fo hit lafte.
> Godhild het his quen,
> Faire ne miʒte nou ben.
> He hadde a fone that het horn.
> Ne no rein upon birine,
> Ne fun[n]e upon bifchine.
> Faifer nis no[n] thane he was,
> He was briʒt fo the glas,
> He was whit fo the flur :
> Rofe ʒed was his colur.
> In none kinge-riche
> Nas no[n] his iliche.
> Twelf feren he had
> That alle with him ladde.
> Alle riche manes fon[n]es,
> Alle hi were faire gomes,
> With him for to pleie,

---

lection. It is fubftantially the fame ftory as *Ponthus of Galicia*, printed in 1511,
4to. In 1845, M. Francifque Michel completed for the Bannatyne club his long-
promifed volume on this fubject. It is entitled, " Horn et Rimenhild. Recueil
de tout ce qui refte des poemes, relatifs a leurs Aventures, compofés en François,
en Anglais, et en Ecoffais, dans le xiii. xiv. xv. et xvi. Siècle."]

[[1] The following extracts have now been collated with the Early Englifh Text
Society's edit. of *Horn*, 1866, from the Cambridge Univerfity MS.]

> Meſt he lu[u]ede tweie ;
> That on him het hathulf child,
> That oth[er] Fikenild.
> Athulf was the beſte,
> Fikenylde the werſte.
> Hit was upon a ſomeres day,
> Alſo ich ʒou telle may,
> Murri the gode king
> Rod on his pleing
> Bi the ſe ſide,
> Aſe he was woned ride,
> He fonde by the ſtronde,
> Ariued on his londe,
> Schipes fiftene
> With ſarazins kene :
> He axede what iſoʒte
> Other to londe broʒte.

But I haſten to that part of the ſtory where Prince Horne appears at the court of the king of Weſtneſſe :

> The kyng com in to halle,
> Among his kniʒtes alle ;
> Forth he clupede Athelbrus,
> That was ſtiward of his hus,
> Stiwarde, tak nu here
> My fundlyng for to lere,
> Of thine meſtere
> Of wude [and] of riuere,[1]
> Ant tech him to harpe
> With his nayles ſcharpe,[2]
> Thou tech him of alle the liſte
> That thee eure of wiſte,
> Biuore me to kerue,

---

[1] So Robert de Brunne, of King Marian. Hearne's *Rob. Glouc.* p. 622.

> " Marian faire in chere
> He couthe of wod and ryvere
> In alle maner of venrie," &c.

[Sir F. Madden points out that the phraſe is from the French, and inſtances the following :

> " Tant ſeit apris qu'il liſe un bref
> Car ces ne li eſt pas trop gref,
> D'eſchas, *de rivere*, et de *chace*,
> Voil que del tot apreuze e ſace."
>   —*Roman du Rou* (MS. Harl. 1717, fol. 79).]

[2] In another part of the poem he is introduced playing on his harp :

> " Horn ſette him abenche,
> Is harpe he gan clenche,
> He made Rymenild a lay,
> Ant hue ſeide weylaway," &c.

In the chamber of a biſhop of Wincheſter at Merdon caſtle, now ruined, we find mention made of benches only. *Comp. MS. J. Gerveys, Epiſcop. Winton,* 1266. " Iidem red. comp. de ii. menſis in aula ad magnum deſcum. Et de iii. menſis, et una parte, et ii. menſis ex altera parte cum treſſellis in aula. Et de i. menſa cum treſſellis in camera dom. epiſcopi. Et v. *formis* in eadem camera." *Deſcus,* in old Engliſh *dees*, is properly a canopy over the high table. See a curious account of the goods in the palace of the biſhop of Nivernois in France, in the year 1287, in Montf. *Cat. MSS.* ii. p. 984, col. 2.

And of the cupe ſerue,[1]
In his feiren thou wiſe
Into other ſeruiſe ;
Horn thu underuonge,
Tech him of harpe and ſonge
Ailbrus gan lere
Horn [and] his yfere :
Horn in herte laȝte
Al that he him taȝte,
In the curt and ute,
And elles al abute,
Luuede men horn child,
And meſt him louede Rymenhild
The kynges oȝene doſter,
He was meſt in thoȝte,
Heo louede ſo horn child,
That neȝ heo gan wexe wild :
For heo ne miȝte at borde
With him ſpeke no worde,
Ne noȝt in the halle
Among the kniȝtes alle,
Ne nowhar in non othere ſtede :
Of folk heo hadde drede :
Bi daie ne bi niȝte
With him ſpeke ne miȝte,
Hire ſoreȝe ne hire pine,
Ne miȝte neure fine.
In heorte heo hadde wo,
And thus hire bithoȝte tho :
Heo ſende hire ſonde
Athelbrus to honde,
That he come hire to,
And alſo ſcholde horn do,
Al in to bure,
For heo gan to lure,
And the ſonde ſeide,
That ſik lai that maide,
And bad him come ſwythe
For heo nas nothing blithe.
The ſtuard was in herte wo,
For he nuſte what to do,
Wat Rymenhyld byſuȝte
Gret wunder him thuȝte ;
Abute horn the ȝonge
To bure for to bringe,
He thoȝte upon his mode
Hit nas for none gode ;
He tok him another,
Athulf, hornes brother.
Athulf, he ſede, riȝt anon
Thu ſchalt with me to bure gon,
To ſpeke with Rymenhild ſtille,
To wyte hure wille,

---

[1] According to the rules of chivalry, every knight before his creation paſſed through two offices. He was firſt a page : and at fourteen years of age he was formally admitted an eſquire. The eſquires were divided into ſeveral departments ; that of the body, of the chamber, of the ſtable, and the carving eſquire. The latter ſtood in the hall at dinner, where he carved the different diſhes with proper ſkill and addreſs, and directed the diſtribution of them among the gueſts. The inferior offices had alſo their reſpective eſquires. *Mem. Anc. Cheval.* i. 16, *ſeq.*

> In hornes ilike,
> Thu fchalt hure bifwike :
> Sore ihc me ofdrede
> He wolde horn mis-rede
> Athelbrus gan Athulf lede
> And into bure with him ʒede :
> Anon upon Athulf child
> Rymenhild gan wexe wild :
> He[o] wende that Horn hit were,
> That heo hauede there.

At length the princefs finds fhe has been deceived ; the fteward is feverely reprimanded, and Prince Horn is brought to her chamber ; when, fays the poet :

> Of his feire fiʒte
> Al the bur gan liʒte.

It is the force of the ftory in thefe pieces that chiefly engages our attention. The minftrels had no idea of conducting and defcribing a delicate fituation. The general manners were grofs, and the arts of writing unknown. Yet this fimplicity fometimes pleafes more than the moft artificial touches. In the mean time, the pictures of ancient manners prefented by thefe early writers ftrongly intereft

---

[1] There is a copy, much altered and modernized, in the Advocates' library at Edinburgh, W. 4, i. Numb. xxxiv. [and another in MS. Harl. 2253, temp. Edw. II. printed in Ritfon's *Romances*, vol. 3.] The title *Horn-childe and Maiden Rimnild.* The beginning :

> " Mi leve frende dere,
> Herken and ye fhall here."

[The bifhop of Dromore confidered this production " of genuine Englifh growth;" and though his lordfhip may have been miftaken in afcribing it, in its prefent form, to fo early an æra as " within a century after the Conqueft;" yet the editor has no hefitation in expreffing his belief, that it owes its origin to a period long anterior to that event. The reafons for fuch an opinion cannot be entered upon here. They are too detailed to fall within the compafs of a note, and though fome of them will be introduced elfewhere, yet many perhaps are the refult of convictions more eafily felt than expreffed, and whofe fhades of evidence are too flight to be generally received, except in the rear of more obvious authority. However, to thofe who with Mr. Ritfon perfift in believing the French fragment of this romance to be an earlier compofition than *The Gefte of Kyng Horn*, the following paffage is fubmitted, for the purpofe of contrafting its highly wrought imagery with the fimple narrative, and natural allufion, obferved throughout the Englifh poem :

> " Lors print la harpe a fei fi commence a temprer
> Deu ki dunc lefgardaft, cum il la fot manier !
> Cum les cordes tuchot, cum les fefeit trembler,
> A quantes faire les chanz, a cuantes organer,
> *Del armonie del ciel lie pureit remembrer*
> Sur tuz ceus ke i funt fait cift à merveiller
> Kuant celes notes ot fait prent fen amunter
> E par tut autre tuns fait les cordes foner."—*Price.*

Both Mr. Wright and Sir F. Madden believe the French romance of *Horn* to be a tranflation from the Englifh *Geft*, and the former points out, as one ground for his opinion, that the French MSS. (of which there are three, all imperfect) exhibit traces of additions and embellifhments, and that many new names are interpolated. Sir F. Madden adds that the French romance of *Atla* declares that *Horn* (there called *Aelof*) was tranflated from Englifh into French.]

the imagination; especially as having the same uncommon merit with the pictures of manners in Homer, that of being founded in truth and reality, and actually painted from the life. To talk of the grossness and absurdity of such manners is little to the purpose; the poet is only concerned in the justness and faithfulness of the representation.

Hickes has printed a satire on the monastic profession; the MS. of which was written [a little before the year 1300, according to Sir F. Madden, but early in the following century, Mr. Wright inclines to believe. It is printed (the spelling modernised) by Eliis,[1] and from the Harl. MS. 913, leaf 3, &c., by Mr. Furnivall.[2]] The poet begins with describing the land of indolence or luxury:

> Fur in see, bi west Spaynge,
> Is a lond ihote Cokaygne;
> Ther nis lond under hevenriche,[3]
> Of wel of godnis hit iliche.
> Tho3 paradis be miri[4] and bri3t
> Cockaygn is of fairir si3t.
> What is ther in paradis
> Bot grasse, and flure, and grene ris?
> Tho3 ther be joy,[5] and grete dute,[6]
> Ther nis mete bote frute.
> Ther nis halle, bure,[7] no benche,
> Bot watir, manis thurs[t] to quenche, &c.

In the following lines there is a vein of satirical imagination and some talent at description. The luxury of the monks is represented under the idea of a monastery constructed of various kinds of delicious and costly viands:

> Ther is a wel fair abbei,
> Of white monkes and of grei,
> Ther beth bowris and halles:
> All of pasteiis beth the walles,
> Of fleis, of fisse, and rich[e] met,
> The likfullist that man mai et.
> Fluren cakes beth the scingles[8] alle,
> Of cherche, cloister, boure, and halle.
> The pinnes[9] beth fat podinges
> Rich met to princez and [to] kinges . . . .
> Ther is a cloister fair and li3t,
> Brod and lang, of sembli si3t.
> The pilers of that cloistre alle
> Beth iturned of cristale,
> With harlas and capitale

---

[1] *Specimens,* vol. i.

[2] [In *Poems and Lives of Saints.* Phil. Soc. Trans. 1858, part II. p. 156. The MS. was lent to Hickes by Tanner, but in 1698 it was the property of Bishop More. How it came into the Harleian Collection, Sir F. Madden professes himself unable even to guess.]

[3] Heaven. Sax.

[4] Merry, cheerful. "Although Paradise is chearful and bright, *Cokayne* is a much more beautiful place."

[5] ioi, Orig.   [6] Pleasure.   [7] [A chamber.]

[8] *Shingles.* "The tiles, or covering of the house, are of rich cakes."

[9] The pinnacles.

Of grene jaſpe and rede corale
In the praer is a tre
Swithe likful for to ſe,
The rote is gingeuir and galingale,
The ſiouns beth al ſedwale.
Trie maces beth the flure,
The rind, canel of ſwet odur :
The frute gilofre of gode ſmakke,
Of cucubes ther nis no lakke. . . . .
There beth iiii. willis[1] in the abbei
Of triacle and halwei,
Of baum and ek piement,[2]
Ever ernend[3] to riʒt rent ;[4]
Of thai ſtremis al the molde,
Stonis preciuſe[5] and golde,
Ther is ſaphir, and uniune,
Carbuncle and aſtiune,
Smaragde, lugre, and praſſiune,
Beril, onix, topoſiune,
Ametiſt and criſolite,
Calcedun and epetite.[6]
Ther beth birddes mani and fale
Throſtil, thruiſſe, and niʒtingale,
Chalandre, and wood[e]wale,
And other briddes without tale,
That ſtinteth never bi her miʒt
Miri to ſing[e] dai and niʒt. . . .
Yi[t]e I do ʒow mo to witte,
The gees iroſtid on the ſpitte,
Fleeʒ to that abbai, God hit wot,
And gredith,[7] " gees al hote, al hote," &c.

Our author then makes a pertinent tranſition to a convent of nuns, which he ſuppoſes to be very commodiouſly ſituated at no great diſtance, and in the ſame fortunate region of indolence, eaſe, and affluence :

An other abbai is therbi
For ſoth a gret fair nunnerie ;[8]
Up a river of ſwet milke
Whar is plente grete of ſilk.
When the ſomeris dai is hote,
The ʒung[e] nunnes takith a bote
And doth ham forth in that river
Both with oris and with ſtere :
Whan hi beth fur from the abbei,
Hi makith ham nakid for to plei,

---

[1] Fountains.
[2] This word will be explained at large hereafter.   [3] Running, Sax.
[4] Courſe, Sax.
[5] The Arabian philoſophy imported into Europe was full of the doctrine of precious ſtones.
[6] Our old poets are never ſo happy as when they can get into a catalogue of things or names. See *Obſervat. on the Fairy Queen,* i. p. 140.
[7] Cryeth. [Anglo-Sax.] [See Conybeare's *Illuſtr. of A.-S. Poetry,* 1826, 3-8, and Thorpe's *Cædmon,* 1832, Pref.—Madden.]
[8] [*La grange eſt pres des bateurs ;* ("Said of a Nunnerie thats neere vnto a Fryerie :) the Barne ſtands neere the Threſher's."—Cotgrave, under *Bateur.—F.*]

And lepith dune in to the brimme
And doth ham fleilich for to fwimme :
The zung[e] monkes that hi feeth,
Hi doth ham up, and forth hi fleeth,
And comith to the nunnes anon,
And euch monke him takith on,
And fnellich[1] berith forth har prei
To the mochil grei abbei,[2]
And techith the nunnes an oreifun
With jambleue[3] up and dun.[4]

---

[1] Quickly, quickly. [Anglo-Saxon.]
[2] " To the great abbey of Grey Monks."
[3] Lafcivious motions, gambols. Fr. *gambiller.*
[4] Hickes, *Thes.* i. Par. i. p. 231 *feq.* [A French fabliau, bearing a near refemblance to this poem, and poffibly the production upon which the Englifh minftrel
founded his fong, has been publifhed in Barbazan, *Fabliaux et Contes*, 1808, iv.
175.—*Price.* But Mr. Wright has pointed out that Price errs in defcribing the
fabliau as fimilar to the Englifh poem, and fpecifies, on the other hand, an old
Dutch poem which, from the fpecimen he affords, certainly exhibits a ftriking
refemblance.]

The fecular indulgences, particularly the luxury, of a female convent, are intended to be reprefented in the following paffage of an ancient poem, called *A Difputation bytwene a Cryftene mon and a Jew,* [from a MS.] written [near the end of
the 14th century.] MS. Vernon, fol. 301 :

" Till a Nonneri thei came,
But I knowe not the name ;
Ther was mony a derworthe[1] dame
    In dyapre dere :[2]
Squi3eres[3] in vche fyde,
In the wones[4] fo wyde :
Hur fchul we lenge[5] and abyde,
    Auntres[6] to heare.
Thene fwithe[7] fpekethe he,
Til a ladi fo fre,
And biddeth that he welcum be,
    ' Sire Water my feere.'[8]
Ther was bords[9] i-clothed clene
With fchire[10] clothes and fchene,
Sepþe[11] a waffchen,[12] i wene,
    And wente to the fete ;
Riche metes was forth brouht,
To all men that gode thouht :
The criften mon wolde nouht
    Drynke nor ete.
Ther was a wyn ful clere
In mony a feir mafere,[13]
And other drynkes that weore dere,
    In coupes[14] ful gret :

---

[1] Dear-worthy.   [2] Diaper fine.   [3] Squires, attendants.
[4] Rooms, apartments.   [5] Shall we tarry.   [6] Adventures.
[7] Swiftly, immediately.
[8] My companion, my love. He is called afterwards, " [Sir] Walter of Berwick."
[9] Tables.   [10] Sheer, clean.
[11] Or *fithe*, i. e. [afterwards : but perhaps we fhould read *feththe thei*, " afterwards they."—*Price.*]
[12] Wafhed.   [13] Mazer, great cup.   [14] Cups.

This poem was defigned to be fung at public feftivals :[1] a practice, of which many inftances occur in this work ; and concerning which it may be fufficient to remark at prefent, that a Joculator or bard was an officer belonging to the court of William the Conqueror.[2]

Another [Early Englifh] poem cited by the fame induftrious antiquary [and fince printed by Mr. Cockayne], is entitled *The Life of Saint Margaret.* The ftructure of its verfification confiderably differs from that in the laft-mentioned piece, and is like the French Alexandrines. But I am of opinion that a paufe, or divifion, was intended in the middle of every verfe : and in this refpect its verfification refembles alfo that of [Warner's] *Albion's England,* or Drayton's *Polyolbion,* which was a fpecies very common about the reign of Queen Elizabeth.[3] The rhymes are alfo continued to every fourth line. It appears to have been written about the time of [Henry III.]. It begins thus :[4]

> Seinte Margarete was: holi maide 't god
> Ibore heo was in Antioche : icome of cunde blod
> Terdofe hire fader het : while bi olde dawe
> Patriarch he was wel he3 : 't maifter of the lawe
> He ne bileouede on ihefu crift no3t : for he hethene was
> Margarete his 3unge dou3ter : ipaid therwith no3t has
> For hire hurte bar anon : criftene to beo
> The falfe godes heo het deuelen : that heo mi3te aldai ifeo—.

In the fequel, Olibrius, lord of Antioch, who is called a Saracen, falls in love with Margaret : but fhe being a Chriftian and a candidate for canonization, rejects his folicitations, and is thrown into prifon.[5]

> Meidan Maregrete one nitt in prifun lai
> Ho com biforn Olibrius on that other dai.

> Sihthe was fchewed him bi
> Murththe and munftralfy,[1]
> And preyed hem do gladly,
>   With ryal rechet.[2]
> Bi the bordes up thei ftode," &c.

[1] As appears from this line :
> "Lordinges gode and hende," &c.

[2] His lands are cited in Doomfday Book (*Gloucefterfhire.*) " Berdic, Joculator Regis, habet iii. villas et ibi v. car. nil redd. See Anftis, *Ord. Gart.* ii. 304.

[3] It is worthy of remark, that we find in the collection of ancient Northern monuments publifhed by M. Biorner, a poem of fome length, faid by that author to have been compofed in the twelfth or thirteenth century. This poem is profeffedly in rhyme, and the meafure like that of the heroic Alexandrine of the French poetry. See Mallet's *Introd. Dannem,* &c., ch. xiii.

[4] I direct, Fr. "I advife you, your," &c. [The writer of this Life in the Bodleian MS., who is quite as likely to have underftood the author's meaning, reads, " I preye you :" words bearing no doubt the fame fignification then as they do at prefent."—*Price.* This extract has now been taken from edit. Cockayne, 1ft text, 1866.]

[5] [Edit. Cockayne (2nd text), p. 37].

---

[1] Afterwards there was fport and minftrelfy.

[2] *i. e.* recept, reception. But fee Chaucer's *Rom. R.* v. 6509 :
> " Him woulde I comfort and *rechete.*"

[Cheer, from Fr. *rehaitier.*—Sir F. Madden's inform.] And *Tr. Crefs.* iii. 350.

Meidan Maregrete, lef up on my lay,
And Iheſu that thou leveſt on, thou do him al awey.
Lef on me, ant be my wife, ful wel the mai ſpede.
Auntioge and Aſie ſcaltou han to mede :
Ciclatoun[1] ant purpel pal ſcaltou haue to wede :
Wid all the metes of my lond ful wel I ſcal the fede.[2]

This piece was printed by Hickes from a MS. in Trinity College library at Cambridge, [and has been lately re-edited]. It ſeems to belong to the manuſcript metrical *Lives of the Saints*,[3] which form a very conſiderable volume, and were probably tranſlated or paraphraſed from Latin or French proſe into Engliſh rhyme before the year 1[3]00.[4] We are ſure that they were written after the year

---

[1] Checklaton. See *Obs. Fair. Q.* i. 194.

[2] The legend of *Saint Julian* in the Bodleian, is [in proſe, with verſes at the end, which Sir F. Madden notes, are not in MS. Reg. 17 A. xxvii. Both texts are now in type for the Early Engliſh Text Society, ed. Cockayne.] MSS. Bibl. Bodl. NE. 3 xi. membran. 8vo. iii. fol. 86. This MS. I believe to be of the age of Henry III. or King John : the compoſition much earlier. It was tranſlated from the Latin. Theſe are the laſt five lines :

"Hƿen ꝺꞃihꞇin o ꝺomeꞅ ꝺei ƿinꝺþeð hiꞅ hƿeaꞇe,
Anꝺ ƿeꞃƿeð þæꞇ ꝺuꞅꞇi cheꝼ ꞇo hellene heaꞇe,
He moꞇe beon a coꞃn i ᵹoꝺeꞅ ᵹulꝺene eꝺene,
Ðe ꞇuꞃnꝺe ðiꞅ oꝼ Laꞇin ꞇo Enᵹliꞅche leꝺenne
Anꝺ he þæꞇ her leaꞅꞇ onƿraꞇ ꞅƿa aꞅ he cuþe. AMEN."

That is, "When the judge at doomſday winnows his wheat, and drives the duſty chaff into the heat of hell; may he be a corn in God's golden Eden, who turned this book [from] Latin," &c. [Sir F. Madden points out that theſe lines are taken from an inedited proſe life of St. Hugh (MS. Digby, 165, fol. 114.) See Hume's monograph on St. Hugh, 1849, for ſome curious particulars reſpecting that ſingular tradition.]

[3] The ſame that are mentioned by Hearne, from a MS. of Ralph Sheldon. See Hearne's *Petr. Langt.* pp. 542, 607, 608, 609, 611, 628, 670. Saint Winifred's Life is printed from the ſame collection by Biſhop Fleetwood, in his *Life and Miracles of S. Winifred*, p. 125, ed. 1713.

[4] It is in fact a metrical hiſtory of the feſtivals of the whole year. The life of the reſpective ſaint is deſcribed under every ſaint's day, and the inſtitutions of ſome Sundays, and feaſts not taking their riſe from ſaints, are explained on the plan of the *Legenda Aurea* written by Jacobus de Voragine, Archbiſhop of Genoa, about the year 1290, from which Caxton, through the medium of a French verſion entitled *Legend Dorée*, tranſlated his *Golden Legend*. The *Feſtival* or *Feſtiall* by Myrk (ſee preface to Myrk's *Duties of P. Prieſts*, Early Eng. Text Society), is a book of the ſame ſort, yet with homilies intermixed. See MSS. Harl. 2247 and 2371, and 2391, and 2402 and 2800 *ſeq.* Manuſcript lives of ſaints, detached and not belonging to this collection, are frequent in libraries. The *Vitæ Patrum* were originally drawn from S. Jerome and Johannes Caſſianus. In Greſham College library are metrical lives of ten ſaints, chiefly from the *Golden Legend*, by Oſberne Bokenham, an Auguſtine canon in the abbey of Stoke-clare in Suffolk, tranſcribed by Thomas Burgh, at Cambridge, 1477. *The Life of St. Katharine* appears to have been compoſed in 1445. MSS. Coll. Greſh. 315, [but now MS. Arundel Br. Mus. 327: Printed for the Roxb. Club, 1835, 4to. Some other *Lives of Saints* have been printed by the Philological Society, ed. Furnivall (*Tranſactions*, 1858, Pt. ii.); the *Life of St. Quiriacus*, with the *Legends on the Croſs*, from a Saint's Lives' MS., is in the preſs for the Early Engliſh Text Society, under the editorſhip of Dr. Morris. The *Life of St. Katharine* is alſo in MS. Publ. Lib. Camb. Ff. ii. 38, and has been printed by Halliwell (*Contrib. to Early Engl. Lit.*, 1849).] The French tranſlation of the *Legenda Aurea* was made by Jehan de Vignay, a monk, ſoon after 1300.

1169, as they contain the *Life of Saint Thomas Becket*.[1] In the Bodleian library are three manuscript copies of these *Lives of the Saints*,[2] in which the *Life of Saint Margaret* constantly occurs;

[1] Afhmole cites this Life, *Inftit. Ord. Gart.*, p. 21. And he cites S. Brandon's *Life*, p. 507. Afhmole's MS. was in the hands of Silas Taylor. It is now in [the Bodleian]. MSS. Afhm. 50. [7001.]

[2] MSS. Bodl. 779, Laud, L 70. And they make a confiderable part of a prodigious folio volume, beautifully written on vellum [about 1400], and elegantly illuminated [of which the firft foliated text has the title] : " *Here begynnen the tytles of the book that is cald in Latyn tongue Salus Anime, and in Englyfh tonge Sowlehele.*" It was given to the Bodleian library by Edward Vernon, Efq., foon after the civil war. I fhall cite it under the title of MS. Vernon. Although pieces not abfolutely religious are fometimes introduced, the fcheme of the compiler or tranfcriber feems to have been, to form a complete body of legendary and fcriptural hiftory in verfe, or rather to collect into one view all the religious poetry he could find. Accordingly the *Lives of the Saints* a diftinct and large work of itfelf properly conftituted a part of his plan. There is another copy of the *Lives of the Saints* in the Britifh Mufeum, MSS. Harl. 2277; and in [the Bodleian] MSS. Afhm. *ut fupr.* This MS. is alfo in Bennet College library [and elfewhere : MS. Laud. 108 ; MS. Afhmole, No. 43 [6924] ; Cotton MS. Julius, D ix. and Add. MS. 10, 301, &c.] The Lives feem to be placed according to their refpective feftivals in the courfe of the year. The Bodleian copy (marked 779) is a thick folio, containing 310 leaves. The variations in thefe manufcripts feem chiefly owing to the tranfcribers. The *Life of Saint Margaret* in MS. Bodl. 779, begins much like that of Trinity Library at Cambridge.

     " Old and yonge I preye you your folyis for to lete," &c.
I muft add here, that in the Harleian library, a few Lives, from the fame collection of *Lives of the Saints*, occur, MSS. 2250, 23 f. 72, b. *feq.* chart. fol. See alfo *Ib.* 19, f. 48.
     The *Lives of the Saints* in verfe, in Bennet library, contain the martyrdom and tranflation of Becket, Num. clxv. This MS. is fuppofed to be of the fourteenth century. Archbifhop Parker, in a remark prefixed, has affigned the compofition to the reign of Henry II. But in that cafe, Becket's tranflation, which did not happen till the reign of King John, muft have been added. See a fpecimen in Nafmith's *Catalogue of the Bennet MSS.* 1777, p. 217. There is a MS. of thefe Lives in Trinity College library at Oxford, but it has not the Life of Becket, MSS. Num. lvii. In pergamine, fol. The writing is about the fourteenth century. I will tranfcribe a few lines from the *Life of St. Cuthbert*, f. 2, b :
     " Seint Cuthberd was ybore here in Engelonde,
     God dude for him meraccle, as ʒe fcholleth vnderftonde.
     And wel ʒong child he was, in his eigtethe ʒere,
     Wit children he pleyde atte balle, that his felawes were :
     That com go a lite childe, it thoʒt thre ʒer old,
     A fwete creature and a fayr, yt was myld and bold :
     To the ʒong Cuthberd he ʒede ' fene brother,' he fede,
     ' Ne ʒench than noʒt fuch ydell game for it ne oʒte noʒt be thy dede :'
     Seint Cuthberd ne tok no ʒeme to the childis rede
     And pleyde forth with his felawes, al fo they him bede.
     Tho this ʒonge child y feʒ that he is red forfok,
     A doun he fel to grounde, and gret del to him tok,
     It by gan to wepe fore, and his honden wrynge,
     This children hadde alle del of him, and bylevede hare pleyinge.
     As that they couthe hy gladede him, fore he gan to fiche,
     At even this ʒonge child made del y liche,
     ' A welaway,' qd feint Cuthbert, ' why wepes thou fo fore
     ' Sif we the haveth oʒt myfdo, we ne fcholleth na more.'
     Thanne fpake this ʒonge child, fore hy wothe beye,
     ' Cuthberd, it falleth noʒt to the with ʒonge children to pleye,

but it is not always exactly the ſame with this printed by Hickes;
and, on the whole, the Bodleian Lives ſeem inferior in point of antiquity. I will here give ſome extracts:

From the *Life of Saint Swithin :* [1]

> Seint Swithin the confeſſour : was her of Engelande,
> Biſide wyncheſtre he was ibore : as ic vndirſtonde :
> By the kinges day Egberd : this gode man was ibore,
> That tho was king of Engelond : and ſomwhat ek bifore ;
> The eiʒteothe king he was that com : after Kenewold the kynge,
> That ſeint Berin dude to Criſtendom : in Engelond furſt bringe :
> Ac ſeynt Auſtin hadde bifore : to criſtendom ibroʒt
> Athelbriʒt the gode king : ac al the londe noʒt.
> Ac ſitthe hit was that ſeint berin : her bi weſte wende,
> And turnde the king Kenewold : as our louerd him grace ſende :
> So that ſeint Egberd was kyng : tho ſeint ſwithin was ibore
> The eiʒteteothe he was : after kenewold that ſo longe was bifore, &c.
> Seint Swithin his biſchopriche : to alle gode drouʒ (line 51)
> The toun alſo of Wyncheſtre he amended enouʒ,
> For he let the ſtronge brugge : withoute the eſt ʒate arere
> And fond therto lym and ſton : to worcmen that ther were.

From the *Life of Saint Wolſtan :*

> Seynt Wolſton byſſcop of Wirceter was then in Ingelonde,
> Swithe holyman was all his lyf, as ich onderſtonde :
> The while he was a yonge childe, good lyf hi ladde ynow,
> Whenne other children orne play, toward cherche hi drow.

> ' For no ſuche idell games it ne cometh the to worche,
> ' Whanne god hath y-proveyd the an heved of holy cherche.'
> With this word, me nyſte whidder, this ʒong child wente,
> An angel it was of heven that our lord thuder ſent.''

I will exhibit the next twelve lines as they appear in that mode of writing:
together with the punctuation.

> '' Þo by-gan ſeint Cuthberd. for to wepe ſore
> [And by-leuede al þis ydel game, nolde he pleye no more.[1]]
> He made his fader and frendis. ſette him to lore
> So þat he ſervede boþe nyʒt and daẏ. to pleſe god þe more
> And in his ʒoughede nyʒt and daẏ. of ſervede godis ore
> Þo he in grettere elde was, as þe bok us hap ẏſed
> It byfel þat ſeint Aẏdan. þe biſſchop was ded
> Cuthberd was a felde with ſchep. angeles of heven he ſeʒ
> Þe biſſchopis ſoule ſeint Aẏdan. to heven bere on heʒ
> Allas ſede ſeint Cuthberd. fole ech am to longe
> I nell þis ſchep no longer kepe. afonge hem who ſo afonge[2]
> He wente to þe abbeẏe of Germans. a grey monk he þer bẏcom
> Gret joye made alle þe covent. þo he that abbẏt nom,'' &c.

The reader will obſerve the conſtant return of the hemiſtichal point, which I
have been careful to preſerve, and to repreſent with exactneſs ; as I ſuſpect that it
ſhows how theſe poems were ſung to the harp by the minſtrels. Every line was
perhaps, uniformly recited to the ſame monotonous modulation, with a pauſe in the
midſt ; juſt as we chant the pſalms in our choral ſervice. In the pſalms of our
liturgy, this pauſe is expreſſed by a colon : and often, in thoſe of the Roman miſſal,
by an aſteriſk. The ſame mark occurs in every line of this manuſcript, which is
a folio volume of conſiderable ſize, with upwards of fifty verſes in every page.

[¹ *Early Engliſh Poems and Lives of Saints,* edit. Furnivall, pp. 43-7 ; *St. Swithun,*
ed. Earle, 1861, pp. 78-81.]

[¹ Inſerted from Add. MS. 10,301.   Sir F. Madden's inform.]
[² '' Take them who will.''—*Price.*]

Seint Edward was tho vr kyng, that now in hevene is,
And the biffcoppe of Wircefter Brytthege is hette I wis, &c.
Biffcop hym made the holi man feynt Edward vre kynge
And undirfonge his dignite, and tok hym cros and ringe.
His bufhopreke he wuft wel, and eke his priorie,
And forcede him to ferve wel God and Seinte Marie.
Four 3er he hedde biffcop ibeo and not folliche fyve
Tho feynt Edward the holi kyng went out of this lyve.
To gret reuge to al Engelonde, fo welaway the ftounde,
For ftrong men that come fithen and broughte Engelonde to grounde.
Harald was fithen kynge with trefun, allas!
The crowne he bare of England which while hit was.
As William Baftard that was tho duyk of Normaundye [1]
Thouhte to winne Englonde thoru3 ftrength and felonye:
He lette hym greith foulke inou3 and gret power with him nom,
With gret ftrengthe in the fee he him dude and to Engelonde com :
He lette ordayne his oft wel and his baner up arerede,
And deftruyed all that he fond and that londe fore aferde.
Harald hereof tell kynge of Engelonde
He let garke faft his ofte agen hym for to ftonde :
His baronage of Engelonde redi was ful fone
The kyng to helpe and eke himfelf as ri3t was to done.
The warre was then in Engelonde dolefull and ftronge inou3
And heore either of othures men al to grounde flou3 :
The Normans and this Englifch men day of batayle nom
There as the abbeye is of the batayle a day togedre com,
To grounde thei fmiit and flowe alfo ; as God yaf the cas,
William Baftard was above, and Harald bi-neothe was. [2]

From the *Life of Saint Chriftopher :*

[3] Seint Criftofre was fara3in : in the lond of Canaan,
In no ftede bi him daye : ne fond me fo ftrong a man :
Four & tuentie fet he was long : & thicke & brod inou3,
Such mon bote he were ftrong me thin3th hit were wou3 :
Al a contrai where he were : for him wolde fleo,
Therfore him thou3te that no man : a3en him fcholde beo.
With no man he feide he nolde beo : bote with on that were
Hexift louerd of alle men : & vnder non, other uere.

Afterwards he is taken into the fervice of a king :

Criftofre him feruede longe ; (l. 17)
The kyng louede melodie : of harpe & of fonge ;
So that his iugelour adai : to-fore him pleide fafte,
& anemnede in his rym : the deuel atte lafte :
Tho the kyng ihurde that : he blefcede him anon, &c. [4]

From the *Life of Saint Patrick :*

Seyn Pateryk com thoru Godes grace to preche in Irelonde
To teche men ther ryt believe Jhefu Cryfte to underftonde :
So ful of wormes that londe he founde that no man ni myghte gon,
In fom ftede for worms that he nas wenemyd anon ;
Seynt Pateryk bade our lorde Cryft that the londe delyvered were,
Of thilke foul wormis that none ne com there.

---

[1] [See Small's *Metrical Homilies*, p. xvi.]   [2] MS. Vernon. fol. 76, b.
[3] MSS. Harl. *ut fupr.* fol. 101, b.

" Seint Criftofre was Sarazin in ðe lond of Canaan
In no ftede bi his daye ne fond me fo ftrong a man
Four and tuenti fet he was long and þiche and brod y-nou3, &c."

[4] [*Early Englifh Poems and Lives of Saints*, edit. Furnivall, 1862, pp. 59-60.]

From the *Life of Saint Thomas Becket* : [1]

> Gilbert was Thomas fader name : that the true was and gode
> And lovede God and holi churche : fiththe he wit underftod.
> The croice to the holie lond : in his ʒunghede he nom,
> And mid on Richard that was his man : to Jerufalem com,
> There hi dude here pelrynage : in holi ftedes fafte
> So that among the Sarazyns : ynome hi were atte lafte, &c.

[One authority[2] attributes thefe *Lives* to the clofe, and another[3] to the middle, of the thirteenth century.[4] The former remarks: " The ftyle and language of thefe Lives of Saints would lead us at once, from their fimilarity to the Chronicle afcribed to Robert of Gloucefter, to attribute them to the clofe of the thirteenth century, and perhaps to the fame writer. Had Warton[5] looked into thefe *Lives* a little more attentively, he would have found the *Legend of St. Dominic*, who died in 1221, and that of *St. Edmund of Pountney*, who was canonized in 1248. But in the latter legend we have decifive proof that thefe lives were written in the reign of Edward I."]

Thefe metrical narratives of Chriftian faith and perfeverance feem to have been chiefly compofed for the pious amufement, and perhaps edification, of the monks in their cloifters. The fumptuous volume of religious poems which I have mentioned above[6] was undoubtedly chained in the cloifter or church of fome capital monaftery. It is not improbable that the novices were exercifed in reciting portions from thefe pieces. In the Britifh Mufeum[7] there is a fet of legendary tales in rhyme, which appear to have been folemnly pronounced by the prieft to the people on Sundays and holidays. This fort of poetry[8]

---

[1] [*Life and Martyrdom of Thomas Becket*, edit. Black (Percy Soc.), p. 1.]

[2] [Madden's note in *H. E. P.* ed. 1840, i. 17. Guernes, an ecclefiaftic of Pont St. Maxence in Picardy, wrote a metrical life of Thomas à Becket, and from his anxiety to procure the moft authentic information on the fubject, came over to Canterbury in 1172, and finally projected his work in 1177. It is written in ftanzas of five Alexandrines, all ending with the fame rhymes, a mode of compofition fuppofed to have been adopted for the purpofe of being eafily chanted. A copy is preferved in MS. Harl. 270, and another in MS. Cotton, *Domit.* A. xi. See *Archæol.* vol. xiii. and Ellis's *Hift. Sketch*, &c. p. 57."—*Park.*]

[3] [*Life and Martyrdom of St. Thomas A Becket*, ed. Black, Introd.]

[4] [Warton fuppofed them written in the reign of Richard I.]

[5] In the Cotton library I find the lives of Saint Jofaphas and the Seven Sleepers: [compofed in the French of the thirteenth century, and in a hand of the time. Sir F. M.'s corr.] Brit. Mus. MSS. Cott. *Calig.* A ix. Cod. membran. 4to. ii. fol. 192 :

> Ici commence la vie ꝺe ꝩeınꞇ Ioꞃaphaꝫ.
> Ki vouꞇꞃ a nul bien æntendre
> Per effample poeꞇ mulꞇ aprenꝺre,

iii. fol. 213, b. *Ici commence la vie de* Seꞇ Dormanꝫ.

> La verꞇu ꝺeu ke tut ꞁur ꝺure
> E ꞇuꞇ ꞁurꝫ eꞃꞇ cerene e puꞁe.

Many legends and religious pieces in Norman rhyme were written about [the time of Edward I.] See MSS. Harl. 2253, f. 1, membr. fol. *fupra citat.* p. 15.

[6] Viz. MS. Vernon.

[7] MSS. Harl. 2391. 70. The dialect is perfectly Northern.

[8] That legends of Saints were fung to the harp at feafts, appears from *The Life of Saint Marine*, MSS. Harl. 2253, fol. memb. f. 64, b.

was alfo fung to the harp by the minftrels on Sundays, inftead of the romantic fubjects ufual at public entertainments.[1]

> " Herketh hideward and beoth ftille,
> Y praie ou 3if hit be or wille,
> And 3e fhule here of one virgin
> That was ycleped faint Maryne."

And from various other inftances. [But Sir F. Madden very properly doubts whether this expreffion means, in many cafes, any thing further than an invitation to the lifteners to attend to the recital.]

Some of thefe religious poems contain the ufual addrefs of the minftrel to the company. As in a poem of our Saviour's defcent into hell, and his difcourfe there with Sathanas the porter, Adam, Eve, Abraham, &c. MSS. *ibid.* f. 57.

> " Alle herkeneth to me now,
> A ftrif wolle y tellen ou :
> Of Jhefu and of Sathan,
> Tho Jhefu wes to hell y-gan."

Other proofs will occur occafionally. [The lives of St. Jofaphat and of the Seven Sleepers are attributed by the Abbé de la Rue to Chardry, an Anglo-Norman poet, who alfo wrote *le petit plebs*, a difpute between an old and a young man on human life. Stephen Langton, archbifhop of Canterbury in 1207, wrote a canticle on the paffion of Jefus Chrift in 123 ftanzas, with a theological drama, in the Duke of Norfolk's library, and Denis Pyrannus, who lived in the reign of Henry III., wrote in verfe the life and martyrdom of King St. Edmund in 3286 lines, with the miracles of the fame faint in 600 lines : a manufcript in the Cott. Library, Dom. A. xi. See *Archæologia*, vol. xiii.—*Park.*]

[1] As I collect from the following poem, MS. Vernon, fol. 229 :—

> " *The* Vifions *of Seynt Poul won he was rapt into Paradys.*
>
> " Lufteneth lordynges leof and dere,
> 3e that wolen of the Sonday here ;
> The Sonday a day hit is
> That angels and archangels joyn iwis,
> More in that ilke day
> Then any odur," &c.

[It was enjoined by the ritual of the Gallican church, that the Lives of the Saints fhould be read during mafs, on the days confecrated to their memory. On the introduction of the Roman liturgy, which forbad the admixture of any extraneous matter with the fervice of the mafs, this practice appears to have been fufpended, and the Lives of the Saints were read only at evening prayer. But even in this the inveteracy of cuftom feems fpeedily to have re-eftablifhed its rights ; and there is reafon to believe that the lives of fuch as are mentioned in the New Teftament were regularly delivered from the chancel. Of this a curious example, the " Planch de Sant Efteve," has been publifhed by M. Raynouard in his " Choix des Poefies originales des Troubadours [Paris, 1817] ;" where the paffages from the Acts of the Apoftles referring to St. Stephen are introduced between the metrical tranflations of them. From France it is probable this rite found its way into England ; and the following extract from the piece alluded to above will fhow the uniformity of ftyle adopted in the exordiums to fuch productions on both fides of the Channel :

> " Sezets, fenhors, e aiats pas ;
> Se que direm ben efcoutas ;
> Car la liffon es de vertat,
> Non hy a mot de falfetat."

" Be feated, lordings, and hold your peace (*et ayez paix*) ; liften attentively to what we fhall fay ; for it is a leffon of truth without a word of falfehood." It has been recently maintained, that the term " lording," of fuch frequent occurrence in the preludes to our old romances and legends, is a manifeft proof of their being

In that part of Vernon's manufcript entitled "Soulehele,"[1] we
have a tranflation of the Old and New Teftament into verfe, which
I believe to have been made before the year 1300 [though the MS.
is fome feventy-five years later]. The reader will obferve the fondnefs of our anceftors for the Alexandrine : at leaft, I find the lines
arranged in that meafure :—

Oure ladi and hire fuftur ftoden vndur the Roode,
And feint jon and marie magdaleyn with wel fori moode :
Vr ladi biheold hire fwete fone ; heo gon to wepe fore,
That thre teres heo let of red blod, tho heo nedde watur no more.
Vr lord feide : "Wommon, to her thi fone ibrouht in gret pyne
For monnes gultes nouthē her, and nothing for myne."
Marie weop wel fore, and bitter teres leet ;
The teres fullen uppon the fton doun at hire feet.
"Allas, my fone, for ferwe wel ofte" feide heo,
"Nabbe ich bote the one, that honguft on the treo ;
So ful icham of ferwe, as any wommon may beo,
That i fchal my deore child in al this pyne ifeo :
How fchal I, fone deore, hou haft i thou3t liuen with outen the,
Nufti neuere of ferwe nou3t, fone, what feyft thou me ?"
Thenne fpak Ihefus wordus goode tho to his modur dere,
Ther he heng vppon the roode : "here I the take a fere,
That treweliche fchal ferue the, thin owne cofin Jon,
The while that thou alyue beo among alle thi fon :"
"Ich the hote, jon," he feide, "thou wite hire bothe day and niht,
That the Gȳwes, hire fon, ne don hire non vnriht."
Seint Jon in the ftude vr ladi in to the temple nom ;
God to feruen he hire dude, fone fo he thider com ;
Hole and feeke heo duden good that heo founden thore,
Heo hire ferueden to hond and foot, the laffe and eke the more.
The Pore folk feire heo fedde there, heo fe3e that hit was neode,
And the feke heo brou3te to bedde, and mete and drinke ron heom beode.
With al heore mihte 3ong and olde hire loueden, bothe fyke and fer,
As hit was ri3t, for alle and fūme to hire feruife hedden mefter.
Jon hire was a trewe feere, and nolde nou3t fro hire go,
He loked hire as his ladi deore ; and what heo wolde, hit was ido.[2]

"compofed for the gratification of knights and nobles." There are many valid
objeĉtions to fuch a conclufion ; but one perhaps more cogent than the reft. The
term is a diminutive, and could never have been applied to the nobility as an
order, however general its ufe as an expreffion of courtefy. By way of illuftration,
let it alfo be remembered, that the "Difours" of the prefent day, who ply upon
the Mole at Naples, addrefs every ragged auditor by the title of "Eccellenza."—
Price.]

[1] [The firft foliated part of the MS. A profe tranflation of Ailred's *Regula
Inclufarum*, or *Rule of Nuns*, is on the preceding unfoliated leaves. Both treatifes
are in the hands of editors for the Early Englifh Text Society.—F.]

[2] MS. Vernon, fol. 8.

SECTION II.

HITHERTO we have been engaged in examining the ftate of our poetry from the Conqueft to the year 1[3]00, or rather afterwards. It will appear to have made no very rapid improvement from that period. Yet, as we proceed, we fhall find the language lofing much of its ancient obfcurity, and approaching more nearly to the dialeĉt of modern times.

The firft poet whofe name occurs in the reign of Edward I., and indeed in thefe annals, is Robert of Gloucefter, a monk of the abbey of Gloucefter. He has left a poem of confiderable length, which is a hiftory of England in verfe, from Brutus to the reign of Edward I. It was evidently written after the year 1278, as the poet mentions King Arthur's fumptuous tomb, erećted in that year before the high altar of Glaftonbury church [1]: and he declares himfelf a living witnefs of the remarkably difmal weather which diftinguifhed the day on which the battle of Evefham above mentioned was fought, in the year 1265. [2] From thefe and other circumftances this piece appears to have been compofed [after] the year [1297]. [3] It is exhibited in the manufcripts, is cited by many antiquaries, and printed by Hearne, in the Alexandrine meafure; but with equal probability might have been written in four-lined ftanzas. This rhyming chronicle is totally deftitute of art or imagination. The author has clothed in rhyme the fables of Geoffry of Monmouth, which have often a more poetical air in Geoffry's profe. The language is not much more eafy or intelligible than that of many of the [Early Englifh] poems quoted in the preceding fećtion: it is full of Saxonifms, which indeed abound, more or lefs, in every writer before Gower and Chaucer. But this obfcurity is perhaps owing to the weftern dialećt, in which our monk of Gloucefter was educated. Provincial barbarifms are naturally the growth of extreme counties, and of fuch as are fituated at a diftance from the metropolis; and it is probable that the Saxon heptarchy, which confifted of a clufter of feven independent ftates, contributed to produce as many different provincial dialećts. In the mean time it is to be confidered, that writers of all ages and languages have their affećtations and fingularities, which occafion in each a peculiar phrafeology.

---

[1] Pag. 224, edit. Hearne.   [2] Pag. 560.
[3] [Sir F. Madden's corr., founded on the mention in the piece of the canonization of St. Louis in 1297. Sir F. M. refers to the Cotton MS. Calig. A. xi. (from which Dr. R. Morris has printed an extraĉt in his *Specimens*) as nearly coeval with the author, and as the proper bafis of a new edition. He tells us that Waterland's annotated copy of ed. Hearne (erroneoufly taken from Harl. MS. 201 in chief meafure), is in the Bodleian. Mr. Furnivall notes that there is a MS., one of a clais, with great differences, in the library of Trinity College, Cambridge. Mr. W. Aldis Wright is preparing a new edition of Robert of Gloucefter for the Rolls Series.]

[The MSS. of Robert of Glouceſter divide themſelves naturally into two claſſes. Taking the Cotton MS. as the type of what we may call the earlier recenſion, and the MS. in Trinity College Library, Cambridge, as the type of the later, the two claſſes may be readily diſtinguiſhed by a reference to the beginning of the reign of King Stephen. Up to this point the MSS. of the two recenſions agree roughly in their contents, thoſe of the later having inſertions in various places and of various lengths, amounting altogether to between eight and nine hundred lines. From this point they differ entirely ; the reigns from Stephen to Edward I. occupying in the earlier recenſion about three thouſand lines, while in the later they are compreſſed into about ſix hundred of an entirely different character. In the Cotton MS. King Stephen's reign begins thus :

> Steuene þe bleis þat god kniʒt . & ſtalwarde was alſo
> þo þe king was ded is vncle . an oþer he þoʒte do.

In the Trinity MS. it begins :

> þo com ſtephene þe bleys ﹖ mid ſtrēgþe & quaintiſe
> & ſeide he wolde be king ﹖ in alle kūnes wyſe.

This diſtinction furniſhes a ready teſt of the claſs to which any MS. belongs. Tried by it, we find that the known MSS. of the earlier recenſion are Cotton Calig. A. xi., Harl. 201, Add. MSS. 18631 and 19677 in the Britiſh Muſeum, and MS. S. 3. 41 in the Hunterian Muſeum, Glaſgow. The MSS. of the later recenſion are Sloane 2027 in the Britiſh Muſeum ; Ee. 4. 31 in the Univerſity Library, Cambridge ; R. 4. 26 in the Library of Trinity College, Cambridge ; Bodleian, Digby 205 ; Lord Moſtyn's MS. ; and MS. 2014 in the Pepyſian Library. The MS. in the Herald's College, of which the readings are quoted in the notes to Hearne's edition, contains a mixture of proſe and verſe, and cannot be aſſigned to either recenſion. Beſides theſe there formerly exiſted two others, of which one belonged to the famous Thomas Allen of Glouceſter Hall ; the other, quoted by Camden in his *Remaines,* was in the poſſeſſion of John Stow the antiquary ; but of theſe no trace has yet been found. The paſſages from the former, given in Hearne's *Appendix,* ſhew that it probably belonged to the later recenſion.][1]

Robert of Glouceſter thus deſcribes the ſports and ſolemnities which followed King Arthur's coronation :

> The kyng was to ys paleys, tho the ſervyſe was ydo,[2]
> Ylad wyth his menye, and the quene to hire al·ſo.
> Vor hii hulde the olde vſages, that men wyth men were
> By them ſulue, and wymmen by hem ſulue al ſo there.[3]
> Tho hii were echone yſet, as yt to her ſtat bycom,
> Kay, king of Aungeo, a thouſend kynʒtes nome

---

[1] [Mr. W. Aldis Wright's addition.]
[2] "when the ſervice in the church was finiſhed."
[3] "They kept the antient cuſtom at feſtivals, of placing the men and women ſeparate. Kay, king of Anjou, brought a thouſand nobl⌐ knights clothed in ermine of one ſuit, or *ſecta.*"

Of noble men, yclothed in ermyne echone
Of on ſywete, and ſeruede at thys noble feſt a non.
Bedwer the botyler, kyng of Normandye,
Nom al ſo in ys half a uayr companye
Of on ſywyte[1] vorto ſeruy of the botelerye.
By uore the quene yt was alſo of al ſuche corteyſye,
Vorto telle al the noblye thet ther was ydo,
They my tonge were of ſtel, me ſſolde noꝣt dure therto.
Wymmen ne kepte of no kynꝣt as in druery,[2]
Bote he were in armys wel yprowed, & atte leſte thrye.[3]
That made, lo, the wymmen the chaſtore lyf lede,
And the kynꝣtes the ſtalwordore,[4] & the betere in her dede.
Sone after thys noble mete,[5] as ryꝣt was of ſuch tyde,
The kynzts atyled hem aboute in eche ſyde,
In feldes and in medys to preue her bachelerye.[6]
Somme wyth lance, ſome wyth ſuerd, wyth oute vylenye,
Wyth pleyynge at tables, other atte chekere,
Wyth caſtynge,[7] other wyth ſſettinge,[8] other in ſom oꝣyrt manere.
And wuch ſo of eny game adde the mayſtrye,
The kyng hem of ys ꝣyfteth dude large corteyſye.
Vpe the alurs of the caſtles the laydes thanne ſtode,
And byhulde thys noble game, & wyche kynꝣts were god.
All the thre hexte dawes[9] ylaſte thys nobleye
In halles and in veldes, of mete and eke of pleye.
Thys men come the verthe[10] day byuore the kynge there,
And he ꝣef hem large ꝣyftys, euere as hii wurthe were.
Byſſopryches and cherches, clerkes he ꝣef ſomme,
And caſtles and tounes, kynꝣtes that were ycome.[11]

Many of theſe lines are literally tranſlated from Geoffry of Monmouth, [and more from Wace.] In King Arthur's battle with the giant at Barbesfleet, there are no marks of Gothic painting. But there is an effort at poetry in the deſcription of the giant's fall:

Tho gryſlych ꝣal the ſſrewe tho, that griſlych was ys bere:
He vel dounꝣ as a gret ok, that bynethe ycorue were,
That yt thoꝣte that al hul myd the vallynge ſſok.[12]

That is, "Then horribly yelled the ſhrew, that fearful was his braying: he fell down like an oak cut through at the bottom, and [it ſeemed that][13] all the hill ſhook with his fall." But this ſtroke is copied from Geoffry of Monmouth, who tells the ſame miraculous ſtory, and in all the pomp with which it was perhaps dreſſed up by his favourite fablers. "Exclamavit vero inviſus ille ; et velut quercus ventorum viribus eradicata, cum maximo ſonitu corruit." It is difficult to determine which is moſt blameable, the poetical hiſtorian or the proſaic poet.

It was a tradition invented by the old fablers, that giants brought

---

[1] " brought alſo, on his part, a fair company cloathed uniformly."
[2] [gallantry.]   [3] thrice.   [4] [ſuite.]
[5] " Soon after this noble feaſt, which was proper at ſuch an occaſion, the knights accoutred themſelves."
[6] [The ſtate preparatory to knighthood.]   [7] [Caſting the ſtone.—M.]
[8] [Aiming with ſpears or javelins.]
[9] " All the three higheſt or chief days. In halls and fields, of feaſting, and turneying, &c."   [10] fourth.   [11] Pag. 191, 192 [edit. 1810.]   [12] Pag. 208 [*ibid.*]
[13] [Mr. Garnett's correction.]

the ſtones of Stonehenge from the moſt ſequeſtered deſerts of Africa, and placed them in Ireland ; that every ſtone was waſhed with juices of herbs, and contained a medical power ; and that Merlin the magician, at the requeſt of King Arthur, tranſported them from Ireland, and erected them in circles, on the plain of Ameſbury, as a ſepulchral monument for the Britons treacherouſly ſlain by Hengiſt. This fable is thus delivered, without decoration, by Robert of Glouceſter :

"Sire kyng," quoth Merlin tho, "ſuche thinges y wis
Ne beth for to ſchewe no3t, but wen gret nede ys,
For 3ef ich ſeide in biſmare, other bute yt ned were,
Sone from me he wold wende the Goſt, that doth me lere :"[1]
The kyng, tho non other nas, bod hym ſom quoyntyſe
Bi thenke aboute thilke cors, that ſo noble were and wyſe,[2]
"Sire kyng," quoth Merlyn tho, "3ef thou wolt here caſte
In the honour of hem, a werk that euer ſchal y laſte,[3]
To the hul of Kylar[4] ſend in to Yrlond
Aftur the noble ſtones that ther habbet[5] lenge y ſtonde;
That was the treche of geandes,[6] for a quoynte werk ther ys
Of ſtones al wyth art y mad, in the world ſuch non ys.
Ne ther nys nothing that me ſcholde myd ſtrengthe a doun caſte.
Stode heo here, as heo doth there, euer a wolde laſte."[7]
The kyng ſomdel to ly3he,[8] tho he herde this tale,
"How my3te," he ſeyde, "ſuche ſtones ſo grete & ſo fale[9]
Be y brort of ſo fer lond ? & 3et meſt of were,
Me wolde wene, that in this lond no ſton to worche nere."
"Syre kyng," quoth Merlyn, "ne make no3t an ydel ſuch ly3hyng.
For yt nys an ydel no3t that ich telle this tything.[10]
For in the farreſte ſtude of Affric geandes while fette[11]
Thike ſtones for medycine & in Yrlond hem ſette,
While heo woneden in Yrlond, to make here bathes there,
Ther vnder for to bathi, wen thei ſyk were.
For heo wuld the ſtones waſch, and ther inne bathe y wis.
For ys no ſton ther among, that of gret vertu nys."[12]
The kyng and ys conſeil radde[13] tho ſtones forto fette,
And with gret power of batail, 3ef any mon hem lette.
Uter the kynges brother, that Ambroſe hette al ſo
In another maner name, y choſe was ther to,

---

[1] If I ſhould ſay any thing out of wantonneſs or vanity, the ſpirit, or demon, which teaches me, would immediately leave me. "Nam ſi ea in deriſionem, ſive vanitatem, proferrem, taceret Spiritus qui me docet, et, cum opus ſuperveniret, recederet." Galfrid. Mon. viii. 10.

[2] "hade him uſe his cunning, for the ſake of the bodies of thoſe noble and wiſe Britons."

[3] "if you would build, to their honour, a laſting monument."

[4] "To the hill of Kildare." [5] have.

[6] "the dance of giants." The name of this wonderful aſſembly of immenſe ſtones.

[7] "Grandes ſunt lapides, nec eſt aliquis cujus virtuti cedant. Quod ſi eo modo, quo ibi poſiti ſunt, circa plateam locabuntur, ſtabunt in æternum." Galfrid. Mon. viii. x. 11.

[8] ſomewhat laughed. [9] ſo great and ſo many. [10] tyding.

[11] "Giants once brought them from the fartheſt part of Africa," &c.

[12] "Lavabant namque lapides et infra balnea diffundebant, unde ægroti curabantur. Miſcebant etiam cum herbarum confectionibus, unde vulnerati ſanabantur. Non eſt ibi lapis qui medicamento careat." Galfrid. Mon. ibid.

[13] [adviſed or counſelled].

And fiftene thouſant men this dede for to do
And Merlyn for his quoyntiſe thider wente al ſo.[1]

If anything engages our attention in this paſſage, it is the wildneſs of the fiction; in which, however, the poet had no ſhare. I will here add Uther's intrigue with Ygerne:

At the feſt of Eſtre tho kyng ſende ys ſonde,
That heo comen alle to London the hey men of this londe,
And the leuedys al ſo god, to his noble feſt wyde,
For he ſchulde crowne here, for the hye tyde.
Alle the noble men of this lond to the noble feſt come,
And heore wyues & heore do3tren with hem mony nome,
This feſt was noble ynow, and nobliche y do;
For mony was the faire ledy, that y come was therto.
Ygerne, Gorloys wyf, was faireſt of echon,
That was contaſſe of Cornewail, for ſo fair nas ther non.
The kyng by huld hire faſte y now, & ys herte on hire caſte,
And tho3te, thay heo were wyf, to do folye atte laſte.
He made hire ſemblant fair y now, to non other ſo gret.
The erl nas not ther with y payed, tho he yt vnder 3et.
Aftur mete he nom ys wyfe myd ſtordy med y now,
And, with oute leue of the kyng, to ys contrei drow.
The kyng ſende to hym tho, to by leue al ny3t,
For he moſte of gret conſel habbe ſom inſy3t.
That was for no3t. Nolde he no3t the kyng ſende 3et ys ſonde.
That he by leuede at ys parlemente, for nede of the londe.
Tho kyng was, tho he nolde no3t, anguyſſous & wroth.
For deſpyte he wolde a wreke be, he ſwor ys oth,
Bute he come to amendement. Ys power atte laſte
He 3arkede, and wende forth to Cornewail faſte.
Gorloys ys caſteles a ſtore al a boute.
In a ſtrong caſtel he dude ys wyf, for of hire was al ys doute.

---

[1] Pag. 145, 146, 147. That Stonehenge is a Britiſh monument, erected in memory of Hengiſt's maſſacre, reſts, I believe, on the ſole evidence of Geoffry of Monmouth, who had it from the Britiſh bards. But why ſhould not the teſtimony of the Britiſh bards be allowed on this occaſion? For they did not invent facts, ſo much as fables. In the preſent caſe, Hengiſt's maſſacre is an allowed event. Remove all the apparent fiction, and the bards only ſay, that an immenſe pile of ſtones was raiſed on the plain of Ambreſbury in memory of that event. They lived too near the time to forge this origin of Stonehenge. The whole ſtory was recent, and, from the immenſity of the work itſelf, muſt have been ſtill more notorious. Therefore their forgery would have been too glaring. It may be objected, that they were fond of referring every thing ſtupendous to their favourite hero Arthur. This I grant: but not when known authenticated facts ſtood in their way, and while the real cauſe was remembered. Even to this day, the maſſacre of Hengiſt, as I have partly hinted, is an undiſputed piece of hiſtory. Why ſhould not the other part of the ſtory be equally true? Beſides the ſilence of Nennius, I am aware that this hypotheſis is ſtill attended with many difficulties and improbabilities. And ſo are all the ſyſtems and conjectures ever yet framed about this amazing monument. It appears to me to be the work of a rude people who had ſome ideas of art: ſuch as we may ſuppoſe the Romans left behind them among the Britons. In the mean time I do not remember, that in the very controverted etymology of the word *Stonehenge,* the name of Hengiſt has been properly or ſufficiently conſidered. [The etymology referred to by Mr. Ritſon is evidently the moſt plauſible that has been ſuggeſted: Stan-henge—hanging ſtone: *Obſervations,* &c. In addition to this it is ſupported by an authority of high antiquity:

" *Stanheng* ont non en Anglois,
Pierres pendues en François."—Wace's *Brut.*—Price.]

In another hym ſelf he was, for he nolde noȝt,
Ȝef cas come, that heo were bothe to dethe y broȝt.
The caſtel, that the erl inne was, the kyng by ſegede faſte,
For he myȝte hys gynnes for ſchame to the other caſte.
The he was ther ſene nyȝt, and he ſpedde noȝt,
Igerne the conteſſe ſo muche was in ys thoȝt,
That he nuſte non other wyt, ne he ne myȝte for ſchame
Telle yt bute a pryve knyȝt, Ulfyn was ys name,
That he truſte meſt to.   And tho the knyȝt herde this,
" Syre," he ſeide, " y ne can wyte, wat red here of ys,
For the caſtel ys ſo ſtrong, that the lady ys inne,
For ich wene al the lond ne ſchulde yt myd ſtrengthe wynne.
For the ſe geth al aboute, bute entre on ther nys,
And that ys vp on harde roches, & ſo narw wei it ys,
That ther may go bote on & on, that thre men with inne
Myȝte ſle al the lond, er heo come ther inne.
And noȝt for than, ȝef Merlyn at thi conſeil were,
Ȝef any mygte, he couthe the beſt red the lere."
Merlyn was ſone of ſend, y-ſeid yt was hym ſone,
That he ſchulde the beſte red ſegge, wat were to done.
Merlyn was ſory ynow for the kynges folye,
And natheles, " Sire kyng," he ſeide, " here mot to maiſtrie,
The erl hath twey men hym next, Bryȝthoel & Jordan.
Ich wol make thi ſelf, ȝef thou wolt, thoru art that y can,
Habbe al tho fourme of the erl, as thou were ryȝt he,
And Olfyn as Jordan, and as Brithoel me."
This art was al clene y do, that al changet he were,
Heo thre in the otheres forme, the ſelve at yt were.
Aȝeyn euen he wende forth, nuſte no mon that cas,
To the caſtel heo come ryȝt as yt euene was.
The porter y ſe ys lord come, & ys meſte priuey twei,
With god herte he lette ys lord yn, & ys men beye.
The contas was glad y now, tho hire lord to hire com
And eyther other in here armes myd gret joye nom.
Tho heo to bedde com, that ſo longe a two were,
With hem was ſo gret delyt, that bitwene hem there
Bi gete was the beſte body, that euer was in this londe,
Kyng Arthure the noble mon, that euer worthe vnderſtonde.
Tho the kynges men nuſte amorwe, wer he was bi come,
Heo ferde as wodemen, and wende he were ynome.
Heo a ſaileden the caſtel, as yt ſchulde adoun a non,
Heo that with inne were, ȝarkede hem echon,
And ſmyte out in a fole wille, and foȝte myd here fon :
So that the erl was y ſlawe, and of ys men mony on,
And the caſtel was y nome, and the folk to ſprad there,
Ȝet, tho thei hadde al ydo, heo ne fonde not the kyng there.
The tything to the contas ſone was ycome,
That hire lord was y ſlawe, and the caſtel ynome.
Ac tho the meſſinger hym ſey the erl, as hym thoȝte,
That he hadde ſo foule y-low, ful ſore hym of thoȝte,
The contaſſe made ſom del deol, for no ſothneſſe heo nuſte.
The kyng, for to glade here, bi clupte hire and cuſte.
" Dame," he ſeide, " no ſixt thou wel, that les yt ys al this ?
Ne woſt thou wel ich am olyue ? Ich wole the ſegge how it ys.
Out of the caſtel ſtilleliche ych wende al in priuete,
That none of myne men yt nuſte, for to ſpeke with the.
And tho heo miſte me to day, and nuſte wer ich was,
Heo ferden riȝt as gydie men, myd wam no red nas,
And foȝte with the folk with oute, & habbeth in this manere.
Y lore the caſtel and hem ſelue, ac wel thou woſt y am here.

Ac for my caftel, that is ylore, fory ich am y now,
And for myn men, that the kyng and ys power flo3.
Ac my power is now to lute, ther fore y drede fore,
Lefte the kyng vs nyme here, & forwe that we were more.
Ther fore ich wole, how fo yt be, wende a3en the kynge,
And make my pays with hym, ar he to fchame vs brynge."
Forth he wende, & het ys men that 3ef the kyng come,
That hei fchulde hym the caftel 3elde, ar he with ftrengthe it nome.
Tho he come toward ys men, ys own forme he nom,
And leuede the erles fourme, & the kyng Uter by com.
Sore hym of tho3te the erles deth, ac in other half he fonde
Joye in hys herte, for the contaffe of fpoufhed was vnbonde,
Tho he hadde that he wolde, and payfed with ys fon,
To the contaffe he wende a3en, me let hym in a non.
Wat halt it to telle longe ? bute heo were fethth at on,
In gret loue longe y now, wan yt nolde other gon ;
And hadde to gedere this noble fone, that in tho world ys pere nas,
The kyng Arture, and a do3ter, Anne hire name was.[1]

In the latter end of the reign of Edward I. many officers of the
French king, having extorted large fums of money from the citizens
of Bruges in Flanders, were murdered : and an engagement fucceeding, the French army, commanded by the Count of Saint Pol,
was defeated ; upon which the King of France, who was Philip the
Fair, fent a ftrong body of troops, under the conduct of the Count
of Artois, againft the Flemings ; he was killed, and the French
were almoft all cut to pieces. On this occafion the following ballad
was made in the year 1301.[2]

Luftneth, lordinges, bothe 3onge ant olde,
Of the Freynfshe-men that were fo proude ant bolde,
Hou the Flemmyfshe-men bohten hem ant folde,
                    Upon a Wednefday,
Betere hem were at home in huere londe,
Then for te feche Flemmyfshe by the fee ftronde
Wharethourh moni Frenfhe wyf wryngeth hire honde,
                    Ant fyngeth, weylaway.
The Kyng of Fraunce made ftatu3 newe,
In the lond of Flaundres among falfe ant trewe,
That the commun of Bruges ful fore can a-rewe,
                    And feiden amonges hem,
Gedere we us togedere hardilyche at ene,
Take we the bailifs by twenty ant by tene,
Clappe we of the hevedes an oven o the grene,
                    Ant caft we y the fen.
The webbes ant the fullaris affembleden hem alle,
And makeden huere confail in huere commune halle,
Token Peter Conyng huere kyng to calle
                    Ant beo huere cheventeyn, &c.

Thefe verfes fhow the familiarity with which the affairs of France
were known in England, and difplay the difpofition of the Englifh
towards the French at this period. It appears from this and previous inftances, that political ballads, I mean fuch as were the

---

[1] *Chron.* p. 156[-60, *ut fupr.*]
[2] The laft battle was fought that year, July 7. [The ballad is in Harl. MS.
2253, fol. 73, and is printed entire in Wright's *Political Songs*, 1839, p. 187. A
fpecimen only has therefore been retained, from the text of 1839.]

vehicles of political fatire, prevailed much among our early anceftors. About the prefent era we meet with a ballad complaining of the exorbitant fees extorted, and the numerous taxes levied, by the king's officers.[1] There is a libel remaining, written indeed in French Alexandrines, on the commiffion of trayl-bafton,[2] or the juftices fo denominated by Edward I. during his abfence in the French and Scotifh wars about the year 1306. The author names fome of the juftices or commiffioners, now not eafily difcoverable : and fays, that he ferved the king both in peace and war in Flanders, Gafcony, and Scotland.[3] There is likewife a ballad [written in the reign of Edward II.] againft the Scots, traitors to Edward I., and taken prifoners at the battles of Dunbar and Kykenclef, in 1305 and 1306.[4] The licentioufnefs of their rude manners was perpetually breaking out in thefe popular pafquins, although this fpecies of petulance ufually belongs to more polifhed times.

Nor were they lefs dexterous than daring in publifhing their fatires to advantage, although they did not enjoy the many conveniencies which modern improvements have afforded for the circulation of public abufe. In the reign of Henry VI., to purfue the topic a little lower, we find a [fatire] ftuck on the gates of the royal palace, feverely reflecting on the king and his counfellors then fitting in parliament.[5] But the ancient ballad was often applied to better purpofes : and it appears from a valuable collection of thefe little pieces, lately publifhed by my ingenuous friend and fellow-labourer Dr. Percy, in how much more ingenuous a ftrain they have tranfmitted to pofterity the praifes of knightly heroifm, the marvels of romantic fiction, and the complaints of love.

[In] the reign[s] of [the three Edwards],[6] a poet occurs named

---

[1] MSS. Harl. 2258, f. 64. There is a fong half Latin and half French, much on the fame fubject. *Ibid.* f. 137, b.

[2] See Spelman and Dufrefne *in v.* and Rob. Brunne's Chron, ed. Hearne, p. 328.

[3] MSS. Harl. *ibid.* f. 113, b.

[4] *Ibid.* f. 59. [This will be found in Wright's *Political Songs,* 1839. The ballad againft the French is in Ritfon's *Anc. Songs,* 1792.—*Price.*}

[5] This piece is preferved in the Afhmolean Mufeum, with the following Latin title prefixed : " *Copia fcedulæ valvis domini regis exiftentis in parliamento fuo tento apud Weftmonafterium menfe marcii anno regni Henrici fexti vicefimo octavo.*" [See Hearne's *Hemingi Chartularium.*—Ritfon.

[6] " In the third Edwards time was I,
When I wrote all this ftory ;
In the houfe of Sixille I was a throwe ;
Dan Robert of Malton that ye know,
Did it write for felaws fake."

" By this paffage he feems to mean that he was born at a place called Malton ; that he had refided fome time in a houfe in the neighbourhood called Sixhill ; and that *there* he, Robert de Brunne, had compofed at leaft a part of his poem during the *reign of Edward III.*—Ellis.] MSS. Bibl. Bodl. 415. Cont. 80, pag. Pr. " Fadyr and fone and holy gofte." And MSS. Harl. 1701. [The Harleian MS., like the Bodleian, if Warton followed the Bodleian manufcript, profeffes to be a tranflation from the French of Groffetefte. But this may be a mere dictum of the

Robert Mannyng, but more commonly called Robert de Brunne. He was [born at Brunne in Lincolnſhire, and became] a Gilbertine canon in the [priory of Sempringham, where he remained fifteen years. He afterwards removed to] Sixhille, a houſe of the ſame order, and in the ſame county. He was [not] merely a tranſlator. He [turned] into Engliſh metre, or rather paraphraſed [with large omiſſions and additions] a French book, written by [William of Wadington, and falſely attributed to Biſhop Groſſeteſte], entitled *Manuel Peche*, or *Manuel de Peche*, that is, the Manual of Sins. This tranſlation was [not printed till of late years].[1] It is a long work, and treats of the decalogue and the Seven Deadly Sins, which are illuſtrated by many legendary ſtories. This is the title of the [copies of the MS.]: *Here bygynneth the boke that men clepyn in Frenſhe Manuel Peche, the which boke made yn Frenſhe Robert Grooſteſte byſhop of Lyncoln.* From the Prologue, among other circumſtances, it appears that Robert de Brunne deſigned this performance

---

tranſcriber. All we gather from the work itſelf is an acknowledgment of a French original called *Manuel Peche*, whoſe author was clearly unknown to De Brunne. Had it been written by a man of Groſſeteſte's eminence, it would hardly have been publiſhed anonymouſly; nor can we ſuppoſe this circumſtance, if really true, would have been paſſed over in ſilence by his tranſlator. Be this as it may, the French production upon which De Brunne unqueſtionably founded his poem, is claimed by a writer calling himſelf William of Wadington, and that in language too peculiar and ſelf-condemning to leave a doubt as to the juſtice of his title :

> " De le françeis vile ne del rimer,
> Ne me deit nuls hom blamer,
> Kar en Engletere fu ne,
> E norri, e ordiné, e alevé.
> De une vile ſui nomé,
> Ou ne eſt burg ne cité, &c.
> De Deu ſeit beneit cheſcun hom,
> Ke prie por Wilhelm de Wadigton."
>
> *Manuel Peche*, Harl. MSS. 4657.

De Brunne, however, is not a mere tranſlator. He generally amplifies the moral precepts of his original; introduces occaſional illuſtrations of his own (as in the caſe of Groſſeteſte cited in the text), p. 74, and ſometimes avails himſelf of Wadington's Latin authorities, where theſe are more copious or circumſtantial than their French copyiſt. Wadington's work, according to M. de la Rue (*Archæologia*, vol. xiv.), is a free tranſlation of a Latin poem called *Floretus;* by ſome aſcribed to St. Bernard, and by others to Pope Clement. But *Floretus* is ſo ſhort that it cannot fairly be taken as Wadington's original, any more than the Bible and Church Services can. The following lines in one of Manning's ſtories—

> " Equitabat Bevo per ſilvam frondoſam,
> Ducebat ſecum Merſwyndam formoſam,
> Quid ſtamus ? cur non imus ?
>
> By the leved wode rode Bevolyne,
> Wyth hym he ledde feyre Merſwyne,
> Why ſtond we ? why go we noght ?—

have been identified by Sir F. Madden as part of the unique Latin legend of St. Edith, by Goſcelin (MS. Rawl. Bodl. 1027). They are not in Wadington's French, and are only part of De Brunne's many additions to the latter.]

[1] [Edit. Furnivall, 1862 (Roxb. Club), with William of Wadington's French original, in parallel columns.]

to be fung to the harp at public entertainments, and that it was written or begun in the year 1303 :[1]

> For lewdè[2] men y undyrtoke,
> On Englyfsh tunge to make thys boke :
> For many ben of fwyche manere
> That talys and rymys wyl blethly[3] here,
> Yn gamys and feftys, and at the ale[4]
> Love men to leftene trotevale[5] : (l. 43-8) &c.
> To alle Cryftyn men undir funne,
> And to godè men of Brunne ;
> And fpeciali, alle be name
> The felaufhepe of Symprynghame,[6]
> Roberd of Brunnè greteth yow,
> In al godeneffe that may to prow.[7]
> Of Brymwake yn Keftevene[8]
> Syxe myle befyde Sympringham evene,
> Y dwelled yn the pryorye
> Fyftenè yere yn conpanye,
> In the tyme of gode Dane Jone
> Of Camelton, that now ys gone ;
> In hys tyme was Y there ten yeres,
> And knewe and herde of hys maneres ;
> Sythyn wyth Dane Jone of Clyntone
> Fyve wyntyr wyth hym gan Y wone.
> Dane Felyp was mayfter that tyme
> That y began thys Englyfsh ryme,
> The yeres of grace fyl[9] than to be
> A thoufand and thre hundred and thre.
> In that tyme turned y thys
> On Englyfshe tunge out of Frankys (l. 57-78).

From the work itfelf I am chiefly induced to give the following fpecimen ; as it contains an anecdote relating to bifhop Groffetefte, who will again be mentioned :

> Y fhall yow telle as y have herd
> Of the byfshope Seynt Roberd,
> Hys toname[10] ys Grofteft
> Of Lynkolne, fo feyth the geft.

---

[1] fol. 1, a.   [2] laymen, illiterate.   [3] gladly.
[4] So in *Pierce Ploughman*, fol. xxvi. b. edit. 1550.—
     " I am occupied every day, holy day and other,
       With idle tales *at the Ale*, &c."

Again, fol. 1, b—
     " Foughten *at the Ale*
       In glotony, godwote, &c."

And in the *Plowman's Tale*, p. 185, v. 2110—
     " And the chief chantours at the *nale*."

[5] truth and all.
[6] The name of his order.   [7] Profit.
[8] A part of Lincolnfhire. *Chron. Br.* p. 311.
     " At Lincoln the parlement was in
     Lyndefay and Keftevene."

See a ftory of three monks of Lyndefay, *ibid.* p. 80. [The county of Lincoln is divided into the hundreds of Lindfay and Kifteven.—*Park.*]   [9] Fell.
[10] Surname. See Rob. Br. *Chron.* p. 168. "Thei cald hi this tonomez," &c.
Fr. " Eft furnomez," &c. On St. Robert of Lincoln, fee p. 82 *note*.

> He lovede moche to here the harpe,
> For mannys wytte hyt makyth fharpe.
> Next hys chaumbre, befyde hys ftody,
> Hys harpers chaumbre was faft therby.
> Many tymes, be nyghtys and dayys,
> He had folace of notes and layys,
> One afked hym onys, refun why
> He hadde delyte in mynftralfy?
> He anfwered hym on thys manere,
> Why he helde the harper fo dere:
> "The vertu of the harpe, thurghe fkylle and ryght,
> Wyl deftroye the fendes[1] myght;
> And to the croys, by godè fkylle,
> Ys the harpè lykened weyle. (p. 150, l. 4742-59).
> Tharefor, gode men, ye fhul lere,
> Whan ye any glemen[2] here,
> To wurfchep God at youre powere,
> As Davyd feyth yn the fautere:[3]
> Yn harpe, yn thabour, and fymphan gle[4]
> Wurfchepe God; yn trounpes and fautre;
> In cordys, an organes, and bellys ryngyng;
> Yn all thefe, wurfhepe ye hevene kyng," &c.[5] (l. 4768-75).

But Robert de Brunne's largeft work is a metrical chronicle of England.[6] The former part, from Æneas to the death of Cadwallader, is tranflated from an old French poet called Mafter Wace or Gaffe, who manifeftly copied Geoffry of Monmouth,[7] in a poem

---

[1] the *Devil's*.   [2] harpers; minftrels.   [3] pfalter.

[4] Chaucer, R. *Sir Thop.* v. 3321:—

> Here wonnith the queene of Fairie,
> With harpe, and pipe, and *Simphonie.*

[5] Fol. 30, b. There is an old Latin fong in Burton which I find in this MS. poem. Burton's *Mel.*, part iii. § 2. Memb. iii. p. 423.

[6] The fecond part [tranflated from the French of Peter Langtoft,] was printed by Hearne in 1725. Of the firft part Hearne has given us the Prologue, Pref. p. 96; an extract, *ibid.* p. 188; and a few other paffages in his Gloffary to Robert of Gloucefter. [The whole of it will be iffued in the Rolls Series in 1871.] It appears from *Chron.* p. 337, that our author was educated and graduated at Cambridge.

[How long Mannyng was employed upon his tranflation of Langtoft does not appear; but that he had not finifhed it in 1337 is clear from a paffage on p. 243 of the printed copy (of 1725) of the Second Part; and indeed he, elfewhere, exprefsly tells us:

> "Idus that is of May left I to wryte this ryme,
> B letter & Friday bi ix. that 3ere 3ede prime."

The dominical letter, as Hearne obferves, fhould be D: fo that the poet finifhed his work, upon which he had probably been engaged for fome years, upon Friday, the 15th May, 1339."—*Ritfon.* The only perfect MS. of the Chronicle known is a vellum one in the Inner Temple library; a more modern and abridged copy of Part II. is in Lambeth, MS. 131. (Sir F. Madden's inform.) But the Lambeth copy of Part I., on the old clofe-ribbed paper of the 14th century, was judged by the experts of the Britifh Mufeum to be at leaft as early as the Temple vellum copy, while Dr. Richard Morris, our chief authority on Early Englifh dialects, judges the dialect of the Lambeth MS. to be much nearer the Eaft-Midland of Manning than the decidedly northernized Temple MS. From the Lambeth MS., therefore, Mr. Furnivall has printed his edition of Part I. for the National Series of the Mafter of the Rolls, 1871.—F.]

[7] Whether written Euftace, Euftache, Wiftace, Huiftace, Vace, Gaffe, or Gace, the name through all its difguifes is intended for one and the fame perfon, Wace of Jerfey. Mr. Tyrwhitt was the firft to refcue this ingenious writer from the

commonly entitled *Roman des Rois d'Angleterre.* It is efteemed one of the oldeft of the French romances; and was commenced under the title of *Brut d'Angleterre,* in the year 1155. Hence Robert de Brunne calls it fimply the *Brut.*[1] This romance was foon afterwards

---

errors which had gathered round his name; and M. de la Rue has fully eftablifhed his rights, by fupplying us with an authentic catalogue of his works, and exhibiting their importance both to the hiftorian and antiquary. [Wace's *Brut* was printed by Le Roux de Linçy at Rouen in 1836.] De Brunne was induced to follow the *Brut d'Angleterre* in the firft part of his Chronicle, from the copioufnefs of its details upon Britifh hiftory. But the continuation noticed in the text was the production of Geoffri Gaimar, a poet rather anterior to Wace; and is fuppofed to have formed a part of a larger work on Englifh and Norman hiftory. *Le Roman du Rou,* or the Hiftory of Rollo, firft duke of Normandy, is another of Wace's works; and *Les Vies des Ducs de Normandie,* which is brought down to the fixth year of Henry I., a third. But the reader who is defirous of further information on this fubject, is referred to the 12th, 13th, and 14th volumes of the *Archæologia,* where he will find a brief but able outline of the hiftory of Anglo-Norman poetry, by M. de la Rue.—PRICE. Εεε alfo M. Joly's comparifon of Wace with his rival chronicler of Normandy, in his *Benoit de St. More et le Roman de Troie,* Caen, 1870, and M. Edeleftand du Meril's treatife on *Wace et fes Ouvrages.*—F.]

In the Britifh Mufeum there is a fragment of a poem in very old French verfe, a romantic hiftory of England, drawn from Geoffry of Monmouth, perhaps before the year 1200. MSS. Harl. 1605, 1, f. 1. In the library of Dr. Johnfton of Pontefract, there was a MS. on vellum, containing a hiftory in old Englifh verfe from Brute to the eighteenth year of Edward II.; and in that of Lord Denbigh, a metrical hiftory in Englifh from the fame period to Henry III. Wanley fuppofed it to have been of the handwriting of the time of Edward IV.

[1] The *Brut of England,* a profe chronicle of England, fometimes continued as low as Henry VI., is a common MS. It was at firft tranflated from a French chronicle [MSS. Harl. 200], written in the beginning of the reign of Edward III. The French have a famous ancient profe romance called *Brut,* which includes the hiftory of the Sangreal. I know not whether it is exactly the fame. In an old metrical romance, the ftory of *Rollo,* there is this paffage (MS. Vernon, f. 123):—

> "Lordus ʒif ye wil leften to me,
> Of Croteye the nobile citee
> As wrytten i fynde in his ftory
> Of *Bruit* the chronicle," &c.

In the Britifh Mufeum we have *Le petit Bruit,* compiled by Meiftre Raufe de Boun, and ending with the death of Edward I. MSS. Harl. 902, f. 1. It is [a feparate compilation, made in 1310, as fhown by Sir F. Madden, in his Preface to *Havelock the Dane*]. In the fame library I find *Liber de Bruto et de geftis Anglorum metrificatus;* (that is, turned into rude Latin hexameters). It is continued to the death of Richard II. Many profe annotations are intermixed. MSS. *ibid.* 1808, 24, f. 31. In another copy of this piece, [there is at the end *qd Peckward,* which may merely mean that Peckward was the copyift]. MSS. *ib.* 2386, 23, f. 35. In another MS. the grand *Brut* [that is, as Sir F. Madden notes, *Caxton's Chronicle*] is faid to be tranflated from the French by " John Maundeuile parfon of Brunham Thorpe." MSS. *ibid.* 2279, 3.

[It was firft printed by Caxton, in 1480, under the title of *The Chronycles of England,* and under the fame title was twice republifhed. In 1483 it appeared, with a few alterations and confiderable additions, under the title of *Fructus Temporum,* and thefe are later impreffions.]

[In the *Chroniques Anglo-Normandes,* 1836, will be found part of Geoffrey Gaimar, of the continuation of the *Brut,* of the Chronicle of Benoit de Sainte More, &c. The *Roman du Rou* was printed in 1827, and a tranflation of part of it, by Mr. E. Taylor, with notes, in 1837. Laʒamon's *Brut* was publifhed from the Cotton MS., as elfewhere mentioned, in 1847.]

continued to William Rufus, by Geoffri Gaimar, in the year 1146.[1]
Thus both parts were blended, and became one work. Among the
royal MSS. in the Britiſh Muſeum it is thus entitled : *Le Brut, ke
maiſtre Wace tranſlata de Latin en Franceis de tutt les Reis de Brittaigne*.[2]
That is, from the Latin proſe hiſtory of Geoffry of Monmouth.
And that Maſter Wace aimed only at the merit of a tranſlator,
appears from his exordial verſes :—

> Maiſtre Gaſſe l'a tranſlatè
> Que en conte le veritè.

Otherwiſe we might have ſuſpeĉted that the authors drew their materials from the old fabulous Armoric MS., which is ſaid to have
been Geoffry's original.

An ingenious French antiquary ſuppoſes, that Wace took many
of his deſcriptions from that invaluable and ſingular monument,
the *Tapeſtry of the Norman Conqueſt*, preſerved in the treaſury of the cathedral of Bayeux,[3] and engraved and explained in
Ducarel's *Anglo-Norman Antiquities*. Lord Lyttelton has quoted
this romance, and ſhewn that important faĉts and curious illuſtrations of hiſtory may be drawn from ſuch obſolete but authentic
reſources.[4]

The meaſure uſed by Robert de Brunne, in his tranſlation[5] of the
former part of our French chronicle or romance, is exaĉtly like

---

[1] [*Anglo-Norman Metrical Chronicle with Notes and Appendix, &c.*, edited by T.
Wright, 1850, 8vo.] See Lenglet, *Biblioth. des Romans*, ii. pp. 226-7, and Lacombe,
Diĉtion. de la veille Lang. Fr. pref. p. xviii. And compare Montfauc. *Catal. Manuſcr.*
ii. p. 1669. See alſo M. Galland, *Mem. Lit.* iii. p. 426, 8vo.
[2] 3 A xxi. 3. [Sir F. Madden obſerves, that this is only in part the *Brut* of Wace.]
It occurs again, 4 C xi. *Hiſtoire d'Angleterre en vers, par Maiſtre Wace.* In the
Cotton library [an early Engliſh MS.] occurs twice, which ſeems to be a tranſlation
of Geoffry's Hiſtory, or very like it. Calig. A ix. and Otho. C 13. [Since
printed under the care of Sir F. Madden, 1847, 3 vols. 8vo.] The tranſlator is one
Laȝamon, a prieſt, born at Ernly on Severn. He ſays, that he had his original
from the book of a French clergyman, named *Wate* [Walter Calenius, archdeacon
of Oxford,] which book Wate the author had preſented to Eleanor, queen of
Henry II. So Laȝamon in the preface, "Bot he nom the thridde, leide ther
amidden : tha makede a frenchis clerc : Wate (Waȝe) wes ihoten," &c.
[3] *Rec.* p. 82, edit. 1581. Mons. Lancelot, *Mem. Lit.* viii. 602. And ſee *Hiſt.
Acad. Inſcript.* xiii. 41, 4to. [M. de la Rue has advanced ſome very ſatisfaĉtory
reaſons for ſuppoſing this tapeſtry to have been made by, or wrought under the
direĉtion of, the Empreſs Matilda, who died in the year 1167. (See *Archæologia*,
vol. xviii.) It was evidently ſent to Bayeux at a period ſubſequent to the death
of its projeĉtor, at whoſe demiſe it was left in an unfiniſhed ſtate. Wace probably
never ſaw it. At all events, could it be proved that he did, he diſdained to uſe it
in his *Hiſtory of the Irruption of the Normans into England*, his only work where it
could have aſſiſted him ; ſince his narrative is at variance with the repreſentations
this monument contains.—*Price.* But Mr. Bolton Corney has ſought to contro-
vert the opinion that the tapeſtry was preſented by the Empreſs Matilda, and
maintains that it was executed for the chapter of Bayeux at their own coſt.]
[4] *Hiſt. Hen. II.* vol. iii. p. 180.
[5] [The work here cited is in courſe of editing for the Maſter of the Rolls' Series
by Mr. Furnivall. See notes, p. 75.]

that of his original. Thus the Prologue, [from the northernized
Temple MS.] :

> Lordynges that be now here !
> If ye wille, liftene and lere
> All the ftory of Inglande,
> Als Robert Mannyng wryten it fand,
> And on Inglyfch has it fchewed,
> Not for the lerid, bot for the lewed ;
> For tho that in this land[e] wone
> That the Latyn no Frankys cone,
> For to half folace and gamen
> In felawfchip when thai fitt famen.
> And it is wifdom forto wytten
> The ftate of the land, and haf it wryten,
> What manere of folk firft it wan,
> And of what kynde it firft began.
> And gude it is for many thynges,
> For to here the dedis of kynges,
> Whilk were foles, and whilk were wyfe,
> And whilk of tham couthe moft quantyfe ;
> And whylk did wrong, and whilk [did] ryght,
> And whilk maynten[e]d pes and fyght.
> Of thare dedes fall be mi fawe,
> And what tyme, and of what law,
> I fall you fchewe fro gre to gre,
> Sen the tyme of Sir Noe :
> Fro Noe unto Eneas,
> And what [thynges] betwixt tham was,
> And fro Eneas till Brutus tyme,
> [That kynd he telles in this ryme.]
> Fro Brutus till Cadwaladres,
> The laft Bryton that this lande lees.
> Alle that kynd, and alle the frute
> That come of Brutus that is the Brute ;
> And the ryght Brute is told no more
> Than the Brytons tymè wore.
> After the Bretons the Inglis camen,
> The lordfchip of this lande thai namen ;
> South, and north, weft, and eaft,
> That calle men now the Inglis geft.
> When thai firft [came] amang the Bretons,
> That now ere Inglis than were Saxons :
> ' Saxons ' Inglis hight all oliche.
> Thai aryved up at Sandwyche,
> In the kynges tyme Vortogerne
> That the lande walde tham not werne, &c. (l. 1-44).
> One, mayfter Wace, the Frankes telles ;
> The Brute, all that the Latyn fpelles,
> Fro Eneas till Cadwaladre, &c.
> And ryght as mayfter Wacè fays,
> I telle myn Inglis the fame ways, (l. 57-62) &c.[1]

The fecond part of Robert de Brunne's *Chronicle*, beginning from
Cadwallader, and ending with Edward I., is tranflated in great meafure from the fecond part of a French metrical chronicle, written in five
books by Peter Langtoft, an Auguftine canon of the monaftery of

---

[1] [Furnivall's edit. pp. 1-2.]

Bridlington in Yorkſhire, who wrote not many years before his tranſlator. This is mentioned in the prologue preceding the ſecond part:

> Frankyſche ſpeche ys cald Romaunce,[1]
> So ſey this clerkes and men of Fraunce.
> Peres of Langtoft, a chanoun
> Schaven y[n] the hous of Brydlyngtoun,
> On Romaunce al thys ſtory he wrot
> Of Engliſhe kynges, &c.[2]

As Langtoft had written his French poem in Alexandrines,[3] the tranſlator, Robert de Brunne, has followed him, the prologue excepted, in uſing the double diſtich for one line, after the manner of Robert of Glouceſter, as in the firſt part he copied the metre of his author Wace. But I will exhibit a ſpecimen from both parts. In the firſt, he gives us this dialogue between Merlin's mother and King Vortigern, from Maſter Wace:

> " Dame," ſeyde the kyng, " welcom be thou :
> Nedlike at the y mot wyte how [4]
> Who than gat [5] thy ſone Merlyne,
> And on what manere was he thyne."
> His moder ſtod a throwe [6] and thought
> Er ſche to the kyng onſwered ought :
> When ſcheo had ſtande a litel wyght,[7]
> Sche ſeyde "by Marye bright,
> That I ne ſey ne nevere knew
> Hym that this child on me ſew.[8]
> Ne wiſte neuere, ne y ne herd,
> What maner wyght wyth me ſo ferde ;[9]
> Bot this thyng am y wel of graunt,[10]
> That I was of elde avenaunt :[11]
> On com to my bed, y wyſt,
> And with force me clipte and kyſt :
> Als [12] a man y hym felt,
> And als a man he me welt ;[13]

---

[1] The Latin tongue ceaſed to be ſpoken in France about the ninth century, and was ſucceeded by what was called the Romance tongue, a mixture of Frankiſh and bad Latin. Hence the firſt poems in that language are called Romans or Romants. *Eſſay on Pope*, p. 281. In the following paſſage of this chronicle, where Robert de Brunne mentions Romance, he ſometimes means Langtoft's French book, from which he tranſlated : viz. *Chron.* p. 205 :

> " This that I have ſaid it is Pers ſawe ;
> Als he in Romance laid, thereafter gan I drawe."

See Chauc. *Rom.* R. v. 2170. Alſo *Balades*, p. 554, v. 508. And Creſcembin, *Iſtor. della Volg. Poes.* vol. i. L. v. p. 316, *ſeq.*

[2] [Furnivall's edit., 579, l. 16709-14.]

[3] Some are printed by Hollinſh. *Hiſt.* iii. 469. Others by Hearne, *Chron. Langt. Pref.* p. 58, and in the margin of the pages of the Chronicle. [A portion appears in the *Chroniques Anglo-Normandes*, already referred to : it extends from William the Conqueror to Henry I.]

[4] " I muſt by all means know of you." [5] begot.
[6] awhile. [7] *white*, while. [8] begot. [9] [fared.—*Ritſon.*]
[10] aſſured. [11] [of a fit age.—*Ritſon.*] [12] as. [13] *wielded*, moved.

And als a man he fpak to me.
Bot what he was, myght y nought fe.[1]

The following, extracted from the fame part, is the fpeech of the Romans to the Britons, after the former had built a wall againft the Picts, and were leaving Britain :

We haue yow clofed ther moft nede was ;
And 3yf ye defende wel that pas
Wyth archers[2] and wyth mangeneles,[3]
And wel kepe the carneles ;
Theron ye may bothe fcheote and kafte :
Wexeth bold, and fendeþ yow fafte!
Thenk, your fadres wonne fraunchife,
Be ye na more in otheres fervife,
Bot frely lyves to your lyves ende :
We taken now leve fro you to wende (p. 239, l. 6797-6800).

---

[1] [Ed. Furnivall, pp. 282-3, l. 8039-58.]

[2] Not *bowmen*, but apertures in the wall for fhooting arrows, viz , in the repairs of Taunton Caftle, 1266, *Comp. J. Gerneys, Epifc. Wint.* "Tantonia. Expenfe domorum. In mercede Cementarii pro muro erigendo juxta turrim ex parte orientali cum Kernellis et Archeriis faciendis, xvi. s. vi. d." *Archiv. Wolves. apud Wint. Kernells* mentioned here and in the next verfe were much the fame thing : or perhaps Battlements. In repairs of the great hall at Wolvefey Palace, I find, " In kyrnillis emptis ad idem, xii. d." *Ibid.* There is a patent granted to the monks of Abingdon, in Berkfhire, in the reign of Edward III. " Pro kernellatione monafterii." Pat. an. 4, par. 1.

[3] Cotgrave has interpreted this word, an old-fafhioned fling. V. *Mangoneau.* See *Rot. Pip.* An. 4 Hen. iii. (A. D. 1219). "Nordhant. Et in expenfis regis in obfidione caftri de Rockingham, 100*l.* per Br. Reg. Et cuftodibus ingeniorum (engines) regis ad ea carianda ufque Bifham, ad caftrum illud obfidendum, 13*s.* 10*d.* per id. Br. Reg. Et pro duobus coriis, emptis apud Northampton ad fundas petrariarum et mangonellorum regis faciendas, 5*s.* 6*d.* per id. Br. Reg."—*Rot. Pip.* 9 *Hen. III.* (A. D. 1225). "Surr. Comp. de Cnareburc. Et pro vii. cablis emptis ad petrarias et mangonellos in eodem caftro, 7*s.* 11*d.*" *Rot. Pip.* 5 *Hen. III.* (A. D. 1220). " Devons. Et in cufto pofito in 1. petraria et 11, mangonellis cariatis a Nottingham ufque Bifham, et it eifdem reductis a Bifham ufque Notingham, 7*l.* 4*s.*" See *infr.* Mangonel alfo fignified what was thrown from the machine fo called. Thus Froiffart : " Et avoient les Brabançons de tres grans engins devant la ville, qui *gettoient* pierres de faix et *mangoneaux* jufques en la ville."—Liv. iii. c. 118. And in the old French *Ovide* cited by Borel, *Trefor.* in v. :

" Onques pour une tor abatre,
Ne oit on Mangoniaux defcendre
Plus briement ne du ciel deftendre
Foudre pour abatre un clocher."

Chaucer mentions both *Mangonels* and *Kyrnils*, in a caftle in the *Romaunt of the Rofe,* v. 4195, 6279. Alfo *archers, i. e. archeriæ,* v. 4191. So in the *Roman de la Rofe,* v. 3945 :

" Vous puiffiez bien les Mangonneaulx,
Veoir la par-deffus les Creneaulx.
Et aux archieres de la Tour
Sont arbaleftres tout entour."

Archieres occur often in this poem. Chaucer, in tranflating the above paffage [if we have his tranflation,] has introduced guns, which were not known when the original was written, v. 4191. The ufe of artillery, however, is proved by a curious paffage in Petrarch to be older than the period to which it has been commonly referred. The paffage is in Petrarch's book *de Remediis utriufque fortunæ,* undoubtedly written before the year 1334. " G. Habeo machinas et baliftas. R. Mirum,

Vortigern, King of the Britons, is thus defcribed meeting the beautiful Princefs Rouwen, daughter of Hengift, the Rofamond of the Saxon ages, at a feaft of waffail.   It is a curious picture of the gallantry of the times, [or, at leaft, Wace's conception of that gallantry.]

> Hengift that day dide his myght,
> That all was glad, kyng and knyght,
> And als thei were beft in gladyng,
> And wel cuppe-fchoten[1] knyght and kyng,
> Fro chaumbre cam Ronewenne fo gent,
> Byfore the kyng in halle fcheo went.
> A coupe wyth wyn fche hadde in hande
> And hure atyr[2] was wel farande.[3]
> Byfore the kyng o knes fche hir fette
> In hure langage ful faire him grette.
>   "Waffayl, my lord ! Waffail !" feyd fche.
> Then, afked the kyng, what that myght be.
> On that langage the kyng ne couthe.[4]
> Bot a knyght that fpeche had lered[5] in youthe.
> Breyth highte[6] that knyght, y-born Bretoun,
> That wel fpak langage of Saxoun.
> Thys Breth was the kynges latynier.[7]
> And what fcheo feyde teldyt Fortyger.

---

nifi et glandes æneas, quæ flammis injectis horrifono fonitu jaciuntur.—Erat hæc peftis nuper rara, ut cum ingenti miraculo cerneretur : nunc, ut rerum peffimarum dociles funt animi, ita communis eft, ut quodlibet genus armorum." Lib. i. Dial. 99. See Muratori, *Antiquitat. Med. Æv.* tom. ii. col. 514. Cannons are fuppofed to have been firft ufed by the Englifh at the battle of Creffy, in the year 1346. It is extraordinary that Froiffart, who minutely defcribes that battle, and is fond of decorating his narrative with wonders, fhould have wholly omitted this circumftance. Mufquets are recited as a weapon of the infantry fo early as the year 1475. " Quilibet peditum habeat baliftam vel bombardam." Lit. Cafimiri III. an. 1475. *Leg. Polon.* tom. i. p. 228. Thefe are generally affigned to the year 1520. I am of opinion that fome of the great military battering engines, fo frequently mentioned in the hiftories and other writings of the dark ages, were fetched from the Crufades. See a fpecies of the catapult, ufed by the Syrian army in the fiege of Mecca, about the year 680. *Mod. Univ. Hift.* b. i. c. 2, tom. ii. p. 117. Thefe expeditions into the Eaft undoubtedly much improved the European art of war. Taffo's warlike machines, which feem to be the poet's invention, are formed on defcriptions of fuch wonderful machines as he had read of in the Crufade hiftorians, particularly William of Tyre.

[1] [Drunk : *enivré.*—*Wace.*   See Cotgrave under *yvre.*]   [2] attire.
[3] [well facing, fitting, very becoming.—*Ellis.*]
[4] was not fkilled.   [5] learned.   [6] was called.
[7] Interpreter. [Formerly printed *Latimer.* Mr. Wright is quite correct in his furmife, that Latimer is a mere ignorant mifreading of the MSS. for Latinier.] Thus, in the romance of *King Richard,* Saladin's *Latimer* at the fiege of Babylon proclaims a truce to the Chriftian army from the walls of the city.   Signat. M. i.

> " The Latemere tho tourned his eye
> To that other fyde of the toune,
> And cryed trues with gret foune."

In which fenfe the French word occurs in the *Roman de Garin,* MSS. Bibl. Reg. Paris, Num. 7542. [Printed in 1833-5, 2 vols. by M. Paulin Paris, and again by Du Meril, in 1845 :]

> " Latimer fu fi fot parler Roman,
> Englois, Gallois, et Breton, et Norman."

[See Selden's *Table-Talk,* edit. 1860, p. 179.]

"Sire," Breth feyde, " Ronewenne yow gretes,
And kyng calles, and lord yow letes.[1]
Thys ys ther cuftume and ther geft,
Whan they arn at ther [ale or] feft.
Ilk man that loues, ther hym beft thynk,
Schal fey ' Waffail,' and to him drynk.
He that haldes fchal fey, ' Waffayl,'
That other fchal feye ageyn, ' Drynk hayl.'
That feys [Waffeyl] drynkes of the coppe,
Kiffing his felawe he gyveth hit uppe.
' Drynk hail,' he feyth, and drinketh ther-of,
Kyffyng hym in bourde and fcof.'[2]
The kyng feide as the knight gan kenne,[3]
" Drynk hayle," fmylynge on Rouewenne.
Ronewenne drank right as hure lyft,
And gaf the kyng, and fyn[4] hym kift.
That was the firfte waffail in dede,
That now and evere the fame yede.[5]
Of that ' waffail' men tolde grete tale,
And ufed ' waffail' when they were at th' ale.
And 'drynkhail' to them that drank,
Thus was waffail take to thank.
   Ful often thus thys mayden 3yng[6]
Waffailed and kyfte ther the kyng.
Of body fche was ful avenaunt,[7]
Of fair colour, wyth fwet femblaunt.[8]
Hure atir[9] ful wel hit byfemed,
Merveillyke[10] the kyng fcheo quemed,[11]
Out of mefure was he glad,
Opon that mayden he wax al mad.
The fend and dronkeneffe hit wrought,
Of that Payen[12] was al his thought.
As mefchaunce that tyme hym fpedde ;
He afked that Payen for to wedde ;
And Hengift wernde hym bot lyte,[13]
Bot graunted hure hym al fo tyt.

And again :—

   " Un Latinier vieil ferant et henu
   Molt fot de plet, et molt entrefnie fu."

And in the *Roman du Rou*, which will again be mentioned :—

   " L'archevefque Franches a Jumeges ala,
   A Rou, et a fa gent par Latinier parla."

We find it in Froiffart, tom. iv. c. 87, and in other ancient French writers. In the old Norman poem on the fubject of King Dermod's expulfion from his kingdom of Ireland, in the Lambeth library [and printed by M. Michel in 1837,] it feems more properly to fignify, in a limited fenfe, the *king's domeftic fecretary.*

   " Parfon demeine Latinier
   Que moi conta de luy l'hiftore," &c.

See Lyttelton's *Hift. Hen. II.* vol. iv. App. p. 270. We might here render it literally his Latinift, an officer retained by the king to draw up the public inftruments in Latin. As in *Domefdai-Book :* " Godwinus accipitrarius, Hugo Latinarius, milo portarius." *MS. Excerpt. penes me.* But in both the laft inftances the word may bear its more general and extenfive fignification. Camden explains Latimer by Interpreter. *Rem.* p. 158. See alfo p. 151, edit. 1674.

[1] efteems.   [2] fport, joke.   [3] to [fhew.]
[4] fince, afterwards.   [5] went.   [6] young.
[7] handfome, gracefully fhaped, &c.   [8] [appearance.—*Ellis.*]
[9] attire.   [10] marvelloufly.   [11] pleafed.
[12] pagan, heathen.   [13] [refufed him but little.]

> And Hors his brother confented fone.
> Hire frendes feyd alle, hit was to done.
> They afkede the kyng to gyve hure Kent,
> In dowarye, to take of rent.
> Upon that mayde his herte fo kaft,
> What-fo they afked, the kyng mad faft.
> I wene the kyng tok hure that day,
> And wedded hure on Payens lay.[1]
> Of preft was ther no benifoun,[2]
> No meffe fongen, ne oryfoun.
> In fefyn the kyng had hure that nyght.
> Of Kent he gaf Hengift the ryght.
> The Erl that tyme that Kent held,
> Sir Gorogon, that bar the fcheld,
> Of that gyft no thyng he ne wyfte,[3]
> Til he was dryuen out wyth[4] Hengift.[5]

In the fecond part, [from Langtoft] the attack of Richard I. on a caftle held by the Saracens is thus defcribed :—

> The dikes were fulle wide that clofed the caftelle about,
> & depe on ilk a fide, with bankis hie without.
> Was ther non entre that to the caftelle gan ligge,[6]
> Bot a ftreite kauce,[7] at the end a drauht brigge.
> With grete duble cheynes drauhen ouer the gate,
> And fyfti armed fueynes,[8] porters at that ʒate.
> With flenges & magneles[9] thei kaft[10] to kyng Richard ;
> Our Criften by parcelles kafted ageynward.[11]
> Ten fergeanz of the beft his targe gan him bere,
> That egre wer & preft to couere him & to were.[12]
> Himfelf as a Geant the cheynes in tuo hew,
> The targe was his warant,[13] that non tille him threw.
> Right unto the ʒate with the targe thei ʒede,
> Fightand on a ʒate, vndir him the flou his ftede.
> Ther for ne wild he feffe,[14] alone in to the caftele
> Thorgh tham alle wild preffe, on fote fauʒht he fulle wele.
> & whan he was withinne, fauʒt as a wilde leon,
> He fondred the Sarazins otuynne, & fauht as a dragon.
> Without the Criften gan crie, allas ; R[ichard] is taken,
> Tho Normans were forie, of contenance gan blaken,
> To flo doun & to ftroye neuer wild thei ftint,
> Thei ne left for dede no noye,[15] ne for no wound no dynt,
> That in went alle ther pres, maugre the Sarazins alle,
> And fond R[ichard] on des fightand, & wonne the halle.[16]

From thefe paffages it appears that Robert of Brunne has fcarcely more poetry than Robert of Gloucefter. He has, however, taken care to acquaint his readers that he avoided high defcription, and

---

[1] in pagans' law ; according to the heathenifh cuftom.
[2] benediction, bleffing.   [3] knew not.   [4] by.
[5] [ed. Furnivall, pp. 265-268. See the Temple MS. verfion in] Hearne's *Robert of Glo.* p. 695.
[6] lying.   [7] caufey.   [8] fwains, young men, fodiers.
[9] mangonels.   [10] caft.
[11] In Langtoft's French :—

> " Dis feriauntz des plus feres e de melz vanez,
> Devaunt le cors le Reis fa targe ount portez."

[12] ward, defend.   [13] guard, defence.
[14] " he could not ceafe."   [15] annoyance.   [16] *Chron.* ed. Hearne, pp. 182, 183.

that fort of phrafeology which was then ufed by the minftrels and
harpers; that he rather aimed to give information than pleafure, and
that he was more ftudious of truth than ornament. As he intended
his chronicle to be fung, at leaft by parts, at public feftivals, he
found it expedient to apologife for thefe deficiencies in the prologue;
as he had partly done before in his prologue to [his *Handlyng Synne*,
[or the *Manual of Sins*:

> I mad noght for no difours,[1]
> Ne for feggers, no harpours,
> Bot for the luf of fymple men,
> That ftrange Inglis can not ken:[2]
> For many it ere[3] that ftrange Inglis
> In ryme wate[4] never what it is (l. 75-80).
> I made it not for to be prayfed,
> Bot at[5] the lewed men were ayfed (l. 83-4).[6]

He next mentions feveral forts of verfe or profody, which were
then fafhionable among the minftrels, and have become long fince
unknown:

> If it were made in ryme *couwée*,
> Or in *ftrangere* or *enterlacè*, (l. 85-6), &c.[7]

---

[1] tale-tellers, *Narratores*, Lat.: *Conteours*, Fr.   *Segger* in the next line perhaps
means the fame thing, *i.e.* Sayers.   The writers either of metrical or of profe
romances.   See *Antholog. Fran.* p. 17, 1765, 8vo.   Or *Difours* may fignify Difcourfe, *i.e.* adventures in profe.   We have the "Devils difours," in *P. Plowman*,
fol. xxxi. b. edit. 1550.   *Difour* precifely fignifies a tale-teller at a feaft in Gower.
Conf. Amant. lib. vii. fol. 155, a, edit. 1554.   He is fpeaking of the coronation
feftival of a Roman emperor :—

> "When he was gladeft at his mete,
> And every minftrell had plaide
> And every *diffour* had faide
> Which moft was pleafaunt to his ere."

Du Cange fays, that *Difeurs* were judges of the turney.   *Diff. Joinv.* p. 179.
[2] know.   [3] *it ere*, there are.   [4] knew.   [5] that.   [6] eafed.
[7] The rhymes here called by Robert de Brunne *Couwée* [*verfus caudati*, final
rhymes, equivalent to the *coda* in mufic] and *Enterlacée*, were undoubtedly derived
from the Latin rhymers of that age, who ufed verfus *caudati* et *interlaqueati*.
Brunne here profeffes to avoid thefe elegancies of compofition, yet he has intermixed many paffages in *Rime Couwée*. See his *Chronicle*, pp. 266, 273, &c. &c.
[and Gueft's *Hiftory of Englifh Rhythms*.] Almoft all the latter part of his work from
the Conqueft is written in rhyme *interlacée*, each couplet rhyming in the middle as
well as the end.   As thus, MSS. Harl. 1002:

> "Plaufus Græcorum | lux cæcis et via claudis
> Incola cælorum | · virgo digniffima laudis."

The rhyme Bafton had its appellation from Robert Bafton, a celebrated Latin
rhymer about the year 1315.   The rhyme *ftrangere* means uncommon. See *Canterbury Tales*, vol. iv. p. 72, *feq. ut infra*.   The reader, curious on this fubject, may
receive further information from a MS. in the Bodleian library, in which are fpecimens of *Metra Leonina, criftata, cornuta, reciproca*, &c.   MSS. Laud. K 3. 4to.
In the fame library there is a very ancient MS. of Aldheim's Latin poem *De Vir-
ginitate et Laude Sanctorum*, written about the year 700, and given by Thomas
Allen, with Saxon gloffes, and the text almoft in femi-faxon characters.   Thefe are
the firft two verfes:

> "Metrica tyrones nunc promant carmina cafti,
> Et laudem capiat quadrato carmine Virgo."

[But fee Wright's *Biog. Brit. Literaria*, A-S. period, 217.] Langbaine, in reciting

He adds that the old ftories of chivalry had been fo difguifed by
foreign terms, by additions and alterations, that they were now
become unintelligible to a common audience : and particularly that
the tale of *Sir Triftram*,[1] the nobleft of all, was much changed from
the original compofition of its firft author :

> I fee in fong in fedgeyng tale[2]
> Of Erceldoun, and of Kendale,
> Non tham fays as thai tham wroght,[3]
> And in ther fay[i]ng[4] it femes noght :
> That may thou here in Sir Triftram ;[5]
> Over geftes* it has the fteem,[6]

---

this MS. thus explains the *quadratum* carmen. " Scil. prima cujufque verfus litera,
per Acroftichidem, conficit verfum illum *Metrica tyrones*. Ultima cujufque verfus
litera, ab ultimo carmine ordine retrogrado numerando, hunc verfum facit :

> " Metrica tyrones nunc promant carmina cafti."

(Langb. MSS. v. p. 126.) MSS. Digb. 146. There is a very ancient tract, by one
Mico, I believe called alfo Levita, on Profody, *De Quantitate Syllabarum*, with
examples from the Latin poets, perhaps the firft work of the kind. Bib. Bodl.
MSS. Bod. A 7. 9. See Hocker's *Catal. MSS. Bibl. Heidelb.* p. 24, who recites a
part of Mico's Preface, in which he appears to have been a grammatical teacher of
youth. See alfo Dacheri *Spicileg.* tom. ii. p. 300, b, edit. *ult.* [Mr. Wright has
obferved that the *ryme couwée* occurs both in heroic and elegiac verfe.]

[1] [Sir W. Scott and others have endeavoured to prove that the Englifh romance
of Triftram was written by Thomas of Erceldoune ; but the tranflator merely
alludes to him at the commencement in a fanciful manner ; and I think it, with
Mr. Wright, moft probable, that finding the name *Thomas* in the French original,
and not underftanding it, he was induced to take a character, then fo famous, to
add fome popularity to the fubject.—*Halliwell.* See *On the Legend of Triftan :
its origin in myth, and its development in romance.* By E. T. Leith. Bombay, 1868,
8vo.—*F.* In all the former editions of Warton, eighteen pages were occupied by
a vain difcuffion of the clearly erroneous opinion of Scott, that the romance, as he
has (not very correctly) printed it, is the original caft of the ftory from the pen of
Thomas of Erceldoune. In the edition of Warton, which appeared in 1840,
Mr. Garnett thus fums up the evidence : "Upon the whole, then, it appears :
1. That the prefent *Sir Triftram* is a modernized copy of an old Northumbrian
romance, which was probably written between A.D. 1260-1300 ; 2. That it is not,
in the proper fenfe of the word, an original compofition, but derived more or lefs
directly from a Norman or Anglo-Norman fource ; 3. That there is no direct tefti-
mony in favour of Thomas of Erceldoune's claim to the authorfhip of it, while the
internal evidence is, as far as it goes, greatly adverfe to that fuppofition. It is,
however, by no means improbable that the author availed himfelf of the previous
labours of Erceldoune on the fame theme."]

[2] " among the romances that are fung," &c.

[3] " none recite them as they were firft written."

[4] " as they tell them." [5] " this you may fee," &c. [6] efteem.

* Hearne fays that Gefts were oppofed to Romance. *Chron. Langt.* Pref. p. 37.
But this is a miftake. Thus we have the *Gefte of kyng Horne*, a very old metrical
romance. MSS. Harl. 2253, p. 70. Alfo in the Prologue of *Rychard Cuer de Lyon :*

> " King Richard is the beft
> That is found in any *jefte*."

And the paffage in the text is a proof againft his affertion. Chaucer, in the following paffage, by Jeftours, does not mean jefters in modern fignification, but
writers of adventures. *Houfe of Fame*, v. 108 :

> " And Jeftours that tellen tales
> Both of wepyng and of game."

> Over alle that is or was,
> If men it fayd, as made Thomas (l. 93-100).
> Thai fayd in fo quante Inglis
> That many one[1] wate not what it is (l. 109-110).
> And forfoth I couth[e] noght
> So ftrange Inglis as thai wroght (l. 115-116).

On this account, he fays, he was perfuaded by his friends to write his *Chronicle* in a more popular and eafy ftyle, that would be better underftood:

> And men befoght me many a tyme
> To turne in bot in light[e] ryme.
> Thai fayd if I in ftrange it turne
> To here it manyon fuld fkurne[2]
> For it ere names fulle felcouthe[3]
> That ere not ufed now in mouth (l. 117-122).
> In the hous of Sixille I was a throwe[4]
> Danz Robert of Meltone,[5] that ye knowe,
> Did it wryte for felawes fake,
> When thai wild folace make[6] (l. 141-4).

[Thomas of[7]] Erceldoune and [Thomas of[8]] Kendal are mentioned, in fome of thefe lines of Brunne, as [writers of] old romances

---

In the *Houfe of Fame* he alfo places thofe who wrote " olde geftes," v. 425.   It is however obvious to obferve from whence the prefent term *jeft* arofe.   See Fauchet, *Rec.* p. 73.   In *P. Plowman*, we have *Job's Jeftes*, fol. xlv. b :

> " Job the gentyl in his jeftes greatly wytneffeth."

That is, " Job in the account of his Life."   In the fame page we have :

> " And japers and judgelers, and jangelers of jeftes."

That is, minftrels, reciters of tales.   Other illuftrations of this word will occur in the courfe of the work.   *Chanfons de geftes* were common in France in the thirteenth century among the [trouvères].   See *Mem. concernant les principaux monumens de l'Hiftoire de France : Mem. Lit.* xv. p. 582 ; by M. de Sainte Palaye.   I add the two firft lines of a MS. entitled, *Art de Kalender par Rauf*, who lived 1256.   Bibl. Bodl. J. b. 2. Th. (Langb. MSS. 5. 439):

> " De *gefte* ne voil pas chanter,
> Ne *veilles eftoires* el canter."

There is even *Gefta Paffionis et Refurrectionis Chrifti*, in many MSS. libraries. [The *chanfons de gefte*, as Mr. Wright has fhown, do not fupport Warton here, as they were poems founded on the real or fuppofed exploits of the earlier kings of France.]

[1] many a one.   [2] fcorn.   [3] ftrange.   [4] a little while.
[5] " Sir Robert of Malton."   It appears [hence that he caufed the work to be written.—*Madden.*]
[6] Pref. *Rob. Glouc.* pp. 57, 58.
[7] [Compare " as made Thomas," l. 100 of Manning's *Chronicle*, with line 94, " tale of Erceldoun and of Kendale," and with " I was at [Erceldoune :] with Tomas fpak y there," *Sir Triftram*, l. 1, &c.:

> " When Engle hadde þe lond al þorow,
> He gaf to Scardyng Scardeburghe;
> Toward þe northe, by þe fee fide,
> An hauene hit is, fchipes in to ryde.
> fflayn highte his broþer, als feyþ þe tale
> þat Thomas made of Kendale;
> Of Scarthe & fflayn, Thomas feys,
> What þey were, how þey dide, what weys."
>
> Manning's *Chronicle*, part i. p. 514.]

or popular tales. Of the latter I can difcover no traces in our ancient literature. As to the former, Thomas of Erceldoun or Afhelington is faid to have written *Prophecies*, like thofe of Merlin. Leland, from the *Scalæ Chronicon*,[1] fays that " William Banaftre,[2] and Thomas Erceldoune, fpoke words " yn figure as were the prophecies of Merlin." In the library of Lincoln cathedral there is a [poem, which is almoft entitled to the name of a romance,] entitled, *Thomas of Erfeldown*, [flightly imperfect,] which begins with an addrefs [not found in the other MSS. of this piece] :

" Lordynges both great and fmall "—

[But feveral other MSS. copies of it are extant.[3] The Lincoln MS. has been printed.[4]] In the Bodleian library, among the theological works of John Lawern, monk of Worcefter, and ftudent in theology at Oxford about the year 1448, written with his own hand, a fragment of an Englifh poem occurs, which begins thus :

Joly chepert of Afkeldowne.[5]

[but is wholly unconnected, except in name, with Erceldoun.] In the Britifh Mufeum a MS. Englifh poem occurs, with this French title prefixed : *La Counteffe de Dunbar, demanda a Thomas Effedoune quant la guere dEfcoce prendret fyn.*[6] This was probably our pro-

---

[1] An ancient French hiftory or chronicle of England never printed, which Leland fays was tranflated out of French rhyme into French profe. *Coll.* vol. i. p. ii. pag. 59, edit. 1770. It was probably written or reduced by Thomas Gray into profe. *Londinens. Antiquitat. Cant.* lib. i. p. 38. Others affirm it to have been the work of John Gray, an eminent churchman, about the year 1212. It begins, in the ufual form, with the creation of the world, paffes on to Brutus, and clofes with Edward III.

[2] One Gilbert Baneftre was a poet and mufician. The *Prophefies of Banifter of England* are not uncommon among MSS. In the *Scotch Prophefies*, printed at Edinburgh, [1603,] Banafter is mentioned as the author of fome of them. " As Berlington's books and Banefter tell us," p. 2. Again, " Beid hath brieved in his book and Banefter alfo," p. 18. He feems to be confounded with William Banifter, a writer of the reign of Edward III. Berlington is probably John Bridlington, an Auguftine canon of Bridlington, who wrote three books of *Carmina Vaticinalia*, in which he pretends to foretell many accidents that fhould happen to England. MSS. Digb. Bibl. Bodl. 89 and 186. There are alfo *Verfus Vaticinales* under his name, MSS. Bodl. NE. E. ii. 17, f. 21. He died, aged fixty, in 1379. He was canonifed. There are many other *Prophetiæ*, which feem to have been fafhionable at this time, bound up with thofe of the canon of Bridlington in MSS. Digb. 186.

[3] [MSS. Publ. Lib. Camb. Ff. v. 48 (printed by Halliwell in 1845) ; MS. Cotton. Vitell. E, x ; MS. Lanfd. 762 ; MS. Sloane 2578. Of thefe the firft is damaged, the fecond is a copy of no great importance or antiquity, and the third and fourth are imperfect. A later tranfcript is in MS. Rawl. c. 258.]

[4] [Laing's *Remains of the Early Popular Poetry of Scotland*, 1822.]

[5] MSS. Bodl. 692, fol.

["Joly chepte of Afchell downe
Can more on love than al the town."—*Price.*

Ritfon could, of courfe, make out no more, becaufe there is no more to make out, the leaf being torn off here."—*Madden.*]

[6] MSS. Harl. 2253, f. 127. It begins thus :

" When man as mad a kingge of a capped man
When mon is lever other monnes thynge then ys owen."

phefier Thomas of Erceldown. One of his predictions is mentioned in a Scotifh poem entitled [*ane new ʒeir gift*] written in the year 1562 by Alexander Scot.[1] One Thomas [of] Leirmouth, or [the] Rhymer, was alfo a prophetic bard, and lived at Erflingtoun, fome-times perhaps pronounced Erfeldoun. This is therefore probably the fame perfon. One who perfonates him, fays :

> In Erflingtoun I dwell at hame,
> Thomas Rymer men call me.

He has left vaticinal rhymes, in which he predicted the union of Scotland with England, about the year 1279.[2] Fordun mentions feveral of his prophecies concerning the future ftate of Scotland.[3]

Robert de Brunne [perhaps] tranflated into Englifh rhymes the trea-tife of Cardinal Bonaventura, his cotemporary,[4] *De cœna et paffione domini et pœnis S. Mariæ Virginis*, with the following title : *Medy-taciuns of the Soper of our Lorde Jhefu, and alfo of hys Paffyun, and eke of the Peynes of hys fwete Modyr mayden Marye, the whiche made yn Latyn Bonaventure Cardynall.*[5] But I forbear to give further extracts from this writer, who appears to have poffeffed much more induftry than genius,[6] and cannot at prefent be read with much

---

[1] [Alex. Scot's *Poems*, ed. 1821, p. 5.]

[2] See *Scotch Prophecies*, [ed. 1680], pp. 11, 13, 18, 19, 36, viz. *The Prophefy of Thomas Rymer.* Pr. "Stille on my wayes as I went."

[3] Lib. x. cap. 43, 44. I think he is alfo mentioned by Spottifwood. See Dempft. xi. 810.

[4] He died 1272. Many of Bonaventure's tracts were at this time tranflated into Englifh. We have, "The Treatis that is kallid *Prickynge of Love*, made bi a Frere menour Bonaventure, that was Cardinall of the courte of Rome." Harl. MS. 2254, 1. f. 1. This book belonged to Dame Alys Braintwat "the worchyp-full prioras of Dartforde." This is not an uncommon MS. [Bonaventura] flourifhed in Italy, about the year 1270. The enormous magnificence of his funeral deferves notice more than any anecdote of his life; as it paints the high devotion of the times, and the attention formerly paid to theological literature. There were prefent Pope Gregory X., the emperor of Greece by feveral Greek noblemen his proxies, Baldwin II., the Latin eaftern emperor, James, king of Arragon, the patriarchs of Conftantinople and Antioch, all the cardinals, five hundred bifhops and archbifhops, fixty abbots, more than a thoufand prelates and priefts of lower rank, the ambaffadors of many kings and potentates, the deputies of the Tartars and other nations, and an innumerable concourfe of people of all orders and degrees. The fepulchral ceremonies were celebrated with the moft con-fummate pomp, and the funeral oration was pronounced by a future pope. Miræi *Auctar. Script. Eccles.* p. 72, edit. Fabric.

[5] MSS. Harl. 1701, f. 84. The firft line is, "Almighti god in trinite."

[In the two beft MSS. known to us of Manning's complete *Handlyng fynne*, the *Medytaciuns* follow it, after a break. Mr. Bowes, of Streatham caftle, Durham, has a later MS. of the *Handlyng fynne*, not yet examined.—F. Caxton printed a com-pilation from the Latin of Bonaventura under the title of *Speculum vite Crifti.* See Blades, ii. 194-7.]

[6] [Sir F. Madden and Mr. Furnivall are of opinion that Warton has done fcanty juftice to De Brunne. They confider him the beft poet before Chaucer, anterior to 1330, and very fuperior to the later Hampole and Naffyngton, though not to the writer of *The Pearl* in the Early Englifh Alliterative Poems, edited by Mr. R. Morris for the Early Englifh Text Society in 1864, or the compofer of the allitera-

pleafure. Yet it fhould be remembered, that even fuch a writer as
Robert de Brunne, uncouth and unpleafing as he naturally feems,
and [partly] employed in turning the theology of his age into rhyme,
contributed to form a ftyle, to teach expreffion, and to polifh his
native tongue. In the infancy of language and compofition, nothing
is wanted but writers: at that period even the moft artlefs have
their ufe.

Robert [Groffetefte,] bifhop of Lincoln,[1] who died in 1253, is
faid in fome verfes of Robert de Brunne, quoted above, to have
been fond of the metre and mufic of the minftrels. He was moft
attached to the French minftrels, in whofe language he [is faid to
have] left a poem of fome length. This was tranflated into Englifh
rhyme probably about the reign of Edward [II. or III.] It is called
by Leland *Chateau d'Amour*.[2] But in one of the Bodleian MSS. of
this book we have the following title : *Romance par Meftre Robert
Groffetefte*.[3] In another it is called, *Ce eft la vie de D. Jhū de fa*

---

tive *Morte Arthure* in the Thornton MS., affuming that that fpirited poem was
written fome feventy or eighty years before the date of the MS. it is in (1440 A.D.).]

[1] See Diff. ii.—The author and tranflator are often thus confounded in manufcripts. To an old Englifh religious poem on the holy Virgin, we find the following title : *Incipit quidam cantus quem compofuit frater Thomas de Hales de ordine
fratrum minorum*, &c. MSS. Coll. Jes. Oxon. [29,] *fupr. citat.* [It is hard to tell
whether this de Hales is the fame as Tanner affigns (by miftake) to the fourteenth
century, or a different perfon.] But this is the title of our friar's original, a Latin
hymn de B. Maria Virgine, improperly adopted in the tranflation. Thomas de
Hales was a Francifcan friar, a doctor of the Sorbonne, and flourifhed about the
year 1340. We fhall fee other proofs of this.

[2] *Script. Brit.* p. 285. [The Englifh verfion was printed for the Philological
Society.]

[3] MSS. Bodl. NE. D. 69. [It has been fhown in a former note, that Groffetefte's
claim to the authorfhip of the French *Manuel Peches*—at leaft to the work at prefent
known by that name—cannot be made good]. The following extract from the
Chateau d'Amour, afcribed to him by Leland and others, [fhows that the poem was
alfo afcribed to him in early times ; for in it he is called " Saint Robert de Nichole "
(the French name for Lincoln), juft as he is called "Seynt Robert," whofe furname
is " Grofteft of Lynkolne," by Robert of Brunne in the *Handlyng Synne*, l. 4743-5,
p. 64 above. Price, feemingly ignorant of *Nichole* meaning Lincoln, thought that
St. Robert de Nichole could not be Groffetefte.]

> " Ici comence un efcrit,
> Ke Seint Robert de Nichole fift.
> Romanze de romanze eft apelé,
> Tel num a dreit li eft affigné ;
> Kar de ceo livre la materie,
> Eft eftret de haut cleregie,
> E pur ceo ke il pafco (furpaffe) altre romanz
> Apelé eft romanz de romanz.
> Les chapitres ben conuz ferunt
> Par les titres ke fiverunt
> *Les titles ne voil pas rimer*
> Kar leur matiere ne volt fuffrer.
> Primis fera le prologe mis
> E puz les titles tuz affis."
>
>   MSS. Reg. 20 B. xiv.

[It is juft poffible that both the prefent poem and the *Manuel Peche* are founded
on fimilar works of Groffetefte written in the Latin language ; and that the tran-

humanite fet a ordine de Saint Robert Groſſeteſte ke fut eveque de Nichole;[1] and in this copy a very curious apology to the clergy is prefixed to the poem for the language in which it is written.[2] "Et quamvis lingua romana [romance] coram clericis ſaporem ſuavitatis non habeat, tamen pro laicis qui minus intelligunt opuſculum illud aptum eſt."[3] This piece profeſſes to treat of the creation, the redemption, the day of judgment, the joys of heaven, and the torments of hell: but the whole is a religious allegory, and under the ideas of chivalry the fundamental articles of Chriſtian belief are repreſented. It has the air of a ſyſtem of divinity written by a troubadour. The poet, in deſcribing the advent of Chriſt, ſuppoſes that he entered into a magnificent caſtle, which is the body of the immaculate virgin. The ſtructure of this caſtle is conceived with ſome imagination, and drawn with the pencil of romance. The poem begins with theſe lines:

> Ki penſe ben, ben peut dire:
> Sanz penſer ne poet ſuffiſe:
> De nul bon oure commencer
> Deu nos dont de li penſer
> De ki par ki, en ki, ſont
> Tos les biens ki font en el mond.

But I haſten to the tranſlation, which is more immediately connected with our preſent ſubject, and has this title:

> Her bygenet a tretys that ys yclept *Caſtel of Love*
> that biſcop Groſtey3t made ywis for lewde mennes by-hove.[4]

Then follows the prologue or introduction, [from which an extract may ſuffice, as the work has been printed three times:]

ſcribers, either from ignorance, or a deſire of giving a fictitious value to their own labours, have inſcribed his name upon the copies. His *Templum Domini*, a copious ſyſtem of myſtical divinity, abounding in pious raptures and ſcholaſtic ſubtleties, may have afforded the materials for the former poem; and his treatiſe, *De ſeptem vitiis et remediis*—if we except the *Contes devots*, which Wadington may have gleaned from another ſource—poſſibly ſupplied the doctrines of the latter. The title adopted by Leland and the Engliſh tranſlator has been taken from the following paſſage of the French work:

> "En un chaſtel bel e grant,
> Bien fourme et avenant,
> *Ceo eſt le chaſtel d'amour*,
> E de ſolaz e de ſocour."
>
> Harl. MSS. No. 1121.—*Price*.]

[1] F 16, Laud. The word *Nicole* is perfectly French for *Lincoln*. See likewiſe MSS. Bodl. E. 4, 14. [A parliament was held at Nicole in 1300-1. Riley's *Chronicles of Old London*, p. 245, ed. 1863.—*F*.]

[2] In the hand-writing of the poem itſelf, which is very ancient.

[3] f. 1. So alſo in MSS. C. C. C. Oxon. 232. In MSS. Harl. 1121, 5. "[Ici demouſtre] Roberd Groſſeteſte eveſque de Nichole un tretis en Franceis, del commencement du monde," &c. f. 156. Cod. membran.

[4] Bibl. Bodl. MS. Vernon, f. 292. This tranſlation [has been printed from a later copy in a MS. of the 14th century, differing greatly from the Vernon in its language and dialect, in private hands, by Mr. Halliwell, 1849, 4to. The Vernon MSS. and Add. MS. Brit. Mus. 22283, were edited for the Philological Society in 1864 by Mr. Weymouth.]

On Engliſch[1] I chul mi reſun ſchowen
For him that con not i-knowen
Nouther French ne Latyn :
On Engliſch I chulle tullen him
Wherfore the world was i-wrouht,
And aftur how he was bi-tauht,
Adam vre fader to ben his,
With al the merthe of paradys,
To wonen and welden to ſuch ende
Til that he ſcholde to heuene wende ;
And hou ſone he hit for-les
And ſeththen hou hit for-bouht wes
Thorw the hei3e kynges ſone,
That here on eorthe wolde come,
For his ſuſtren that were to-boren,
And for a priſon that was forloren ;
And hou he made as 3e ſchul heeren
That heo i-cuſte and ſauht weren ;
And to w3uche a Caſtel he alihte, &c.

The moſt poetical paſſages of this poem [are thoſe which deſcribe the caſtle. Of theſe we quote a few lines :]

This Caſtel is ſiker and feir abouten,[2]
And is al depeynted withouten
With threo heowes that wel beth ſene,[3]
So is the foundement al grene,
That to the roche faſte lith.
Wel is that ther murthe i-ſihth,
For the greneſchipe laſteth euere,
And his heuh ne leoſeth neuere,
Seththen abouten that other heu3
So is inde and eke bleu.[4]
That the midel heu3 we clepeth ariht,
And ſchyneth ſo feire and ſo bri3t.

The thridde heu3 an ouemaſt
Ouer-wri3eth al and ſo is i-caſt
That withinnen and withouten
The caſtel lihteth al abouten,
And is raddore then euere eny roſe ſchal
That thuncheth as hit barnde[5] al.[6]
Withinne the Caſtel is whit ſchinynge
So[7] the ſnow3 that is ſneuwynge,
And caſteth that li3t ſo wyde
After-long the tour and be-ſyde,
That never cometh ther wo ne wou3,
Ac ſwetneſſe ther is euer i-nou3.

---

[1] [*Caſtel off Loue*, edit. Weymouth, p. 3.]

[2] [Edit. Weymouth, p. 31.]

[3] [" Li chaſteaus eſt bel e bon
De hors depeint enuiron,
De iii. colurs diuerſement."— *Fr. Orig.*]

[4] " Si reſte ynde ſi blui."—*Fr. Orig.*   [5] burned, on fire.

[6] " Plus eſt vermaille qui neſt roſe
E piert vne ardante choſe."—*Fr. Orig.*

[7] as.

Amidde¹ the heiȝe tour is ſpringynge
A welle that euere is eornynge²
With foure ſtremes that ſtriketh wel,
And erneth vppon the grauel,
And fulleth the diches a-boute the wal ;
Muche bliſſe ther is ouer-al,
Ne dar he ſeche non other leche
That mai riht of this water cleche.

In³ thulke derworth feire tour
Ther ſtont a trone with muche honour,
Of whit iuori, and feirore of liht
Then the ſomeres day whon hee is briht,
With cumpas i-throwen, and with gin al i-do.
Seuene ſteppes ther beoth ther-to, &c.
The⁴ foure ſmale toures abouten,
That [witeth] the heiȝe tour with-outen,
Foure hed thewes that aboute hire i-ſeoth,
Foure vertues cardinals [that] beoth, &c.
And⁵ whyche beoth the threo bayles ȝet,
That with the carnels beth ſo wel i-ſet,
And i-caſt with cumpas and walled abouten,
That witeth the heiȝe tour with-outen ?
Bote the inemaſte bayle, I wot,
Bi-tokeneth hire holy maidenhod, &c.
The⁶ middel bayle, that wite ȝe,
Bi-tokeneth hire holy chaſtite
And ſeththen the [outemaſte] bayle
Bi-tokeneth hire holy ſpoſayle, &c.
The ſeue [berbicans] abouten,
That with gret gin beon i-wrouȝt withouten,
And witeth this Caſtel ſo wel,
With arwe and with qwarel,⁷
That beth the ſeuen vertues with winne
To ouercome the ſeuen dedly ſinne, &c.⁸

---

¹ " In mi la tur plus hauteine
   Eſt ſurdant une funtayne
   Dunt iſſent quater ruiſſell.
   Ki bruinet par le gravel," &c.—*Fr. Orig.*

² running.

³ " En cele bel tur a bone
   A de yvoire un trone
   Ke pluſa eiſſi blanchor
   Ci en mi eſte la beau jur
   Par engin eſt compaſſez," &c.—*Fr. Orig.*

⁴ [Edit. Weymouth, p. 37.]   ⁵ [*Ibid.* p. 38.]

   " Les treis bailles du chaſtel
   Ki ſunt overt au kernel
   Qui a compas ſunt en virun
   E defendent le dungun."—*Fr. Orig.*

⁶ [*Ibid.*]

⁷ " Les barbicanes ſeet
   Kis hors de bailles ſunt fait,
   Ki bien gardent le chaſtel,
   E de ſeete e de quarrel."—*Fr. Orig.*

⁸ [*Ibid.* 38-9.] Afterwards the fountain is explained to be God's grace: Charity is conſtable of the caſtle, &c. &c.

It was undoubtedly a great impediment to the cultivation and pro-
greffive improvement of the Englifh language at thefe early periods,
that the beft authors chofe to write in French. Many of Robert
[Groffetefte's] pieces are indeed in Latin; yet where the fubject was
popular, and not immediately addreffed to learned readers, he adopted
the Romance or French language, in preference to his native Englifh.
Of this, as we have already feen, his *Chateau d' Amour* is fufficient
proof; and his example and authority muft have had confiderable influence in encouraging the practice. Peter Langtoft not only compiled the large chronicle of England, above recited, in French, but
even tranflated Herbert Bofcam's Latin *Life of Thomas Becket* into
French rhymes.[1] John [de] Hoveden, a native of London, doctor
of divinity, and chaplain to Queen Eleanor, mother of Edward I.
wrote in French rhymes a book entitled, *Rofarium de Nativitate,
Paffione, Afcenfione, Jhefu Chrifti*.[2] Various other proofs have before
occurred. [There is in] the Lambeth library [an imperfect] poem
in [Anglo-] Norman verfe on the fubject of King Dermod's expulfion from Ireland and the recovery of his kingdom.[3] I could
mention many others. Anonymous French pieces, both in profe and
verfe, and written about this time, are innumerable in our manufcript
repofitories.[4] Yet this fafhion proceeded rather from neceffity and

---

[1] Pits, p. 890. Append. He with great probability fuppofes him to have been
an Englifhman.

[2] MSS. Bibl. C. C. C. Cant. G. 16. where it is alfo called *The Nightingale*. Pr.
" Alme feffe lit de pereffe."

In this MS. the whole title is this: *Le Roffignol, ou la penfee Jehan de Hove-
dene clerc la roine d'Engleterre mere le roi Edward, de la naiffance et de la mort et du
relievement et de lafcenfion Jefu Crift et de laffumption notre dame.* This MS. was
written in the 14th century.

Our author, John [de] Hoveden, was alfo fkilled in facred mufic, and a great
writer of Latin hymns. He died, and was buried, at Hoveden, 1275. Pits, p. 356,
Bale, v. 79.

There is an old French metrical life of Tobiah, which the author, moft probably
an Englifhman, fays he undertook at the requeft of William, Prior of Kenilworth
in Warwickfhire. MSS. Jes. Coll. Oxon. 85, *fupr. citat.*

" Le prior Gwilleyme me prie
De l'eglyfe feynte Marie
De Kenelworth an Ardenne,
Ki porte le plus haute peyne
De charite, ke nul eglyfe
Del reaume a devyfe
Ke jeo liz en romaunz le vie
De kelui ki ont nun Tobie," &c.

[3] [MS. Lamb. 96. See Todd's *Cat.* 1812, p. 94. The poem, which wants beginning and end, has been printed by Michel, 1837, 12mo. An incorrect analyfis
of it, made by Sir George Carew, to whom it once belonged, is in Harris's *Hibernica,*
1757.] It was probably written about 1190. See Ware, p. 56, and compare
Walpole's *Anecd. Paint.* i. 28, Notes. [The original Latin of this has been already
noticed as a production of the reign of Edward I., to whofe queen John de Hoveden
was chaplain. In the Obfervations on the *Lai de Lauftic,* the error of identifying
an Englifh tranflation of de Hoveden's tract with the lay is pointed out.]

[4] Among the learned Englifhmen who now wrote in French, Tyrwhitt mentions
Helis de Guinceftre, or Winchefter, a tranflator of Cato into French. (See vol. ii.

a principle of convenience, than from affectation. The vernacular English, as I have before remarked, was rough and unpolished: and although these writers possessed but few ideas of taste and elegance, they embraced a foreign tongue almost equally familiar, and in which they could convey their sentiments with greater ease, grace, and propriety. It should also be considered, that our most eminent scholars received a part of their education at the university of Paris. Another and a very material circumstance concurred to countenance this fashionable practice of composing in French. It procured them readers of rank and distinction. The English court, for more than two hundred years after the Conquest, was totally French: and our kings, either from birth, kindred, or marriage, and from a perpetual intercourse, seem to have been more closely connected with France than with England.[1] It was however fortunate that these French pieces were written, as some of them met with their translators who, perhaps, unable to aspire to the praise of original writers, at least by this means contributed to adorn their native tongue: and who very

---

sect. xxvii.) And Hue de Roteland [or rather, according to Sir F. Madden, Walter de Biblesworth] author of the Romance, in French verse, called *Ipomidon.* MSS. Cott. Vesp. A. vii. [Hugh] is supposed to have written a French Dialogue in metre, MSS. Bodl. 3904. *La pleinte par entre mis Sire Henry de Lacy Counte de Nichole, et Sire Wauter de Byblesworth pur la croiserie en la terre seinte.* And a French romantic poem on a knight called *Capanee,* perhaps Statius's Capaneus. MSS. Cott. Vesp. A vii. *ut supr.* It begins:

> " Que bons countes viel entendre."

I have before hinted that it was sometimes customary to intermix Latin with French. As thus, MSS. Harl. 2253, f. 137, b.:

> " Dieu roy de Mageste,
>   *Ob personas trinas,*
>   Nostre roy esa meyne
>   *Ne perire sinas,*" &c.

Again, ibid. f. 76, where a lover, an Englishman, addresses his mistress who was of Paris:

> " *Dum ludis floribus velut lacinia,*
>   Le dieu d'amour moi tient en tiel *Angustia,*" &c.

Sometimes their poetry was half French and half English. As in a song to the holy virgin on our Saviour's passion. *Ibid.* f. 83.

> " Mayden moder milde, oyez cel oreysoun,
>   From shome thou me shilde, e de ly mal feloun:
>   For love of thine childe me menez de tresoun,
>   Ich wes wod and wilde, ore su en prisoun," &c.

In the same MS. I find a French poem probably written by an Englishman, and in the year 1300, containing the adventures of Gilote and Johanne, two ladies of gallantry, in various parts of England and Ireland; particularly at Winchester and Pontefract, f. 66, b. The curious reader is also referred to a French poem, in which the poet supposes that a minstrel, *jugelour,* travelling from London, clothed in a rich tabard, met the king and his retinue. The king asks him many questions, particularly his lord's name and the price of his horse. The minstrel evades all the king's questions by impertinent answers; and at last presumes to give his majesty advice. *Ibid.* f. 107, b.

[1] [It is very certain that many French poems were written during this period by Englishmen; but it is probable that several were also composed by Normans.—*Douce.*]

probably would not have written at all, had not original writers, I mean their cotemporaries who wrote in French, furnifhed them with models and materials.

Hearne, to whofe diligence even the poetical antiquarian is much obliged, but whofe conjectures are generally wrong, imagines that the old Englifh metrical romance, called *Rychard cuer de Lyon*, was written by Robert de Brunne. It is at leaft probable, that the leifure of monaftic life produced many rhymers. From proofs here given we may fairly conclude, that the monks often wrote for the minftrels : and although our Gilbertine brother of Brunne chofe to relate true ftories in plain language, yet it is reafonable to fuppofe, that many of our ancient tales in verfe containing fictitious adventures were written, although not invented, in the religious houfes. The romantic hiftory of *Guy Earl of Warwick* is expreffly faid, on good authority, to have been written by Walter of Exeter, a Francifcan friar of Carocus in Cornwall, about the year 1292.[1] The libraries of the monafteries were full of romances. *Bevis of Southampton*, in French, was in the library of the abbey of Leicefter.[2] In that of the abbey of Glaftonbury, we find *Liber de Excidio Trojæ*, *Gefta Ricardi Regis*, and *Gefta Alexandri Regis*, in the year 1247.[3] Thefe were fome of the moft favourite fubjects of romance, as I fhall fhew hereafter. In a catalogue of the library of the abbey of Peterborough are recited *Amys and Amelon*,[4] *Sir Triftram*, *Guy de*

---

[1] Carew's *Surv. Cornw.* p. 59, edit. *ut fupr.* I fuppofe Carew means the metrical Romance of *Guy.* But Bale fays that Walterw rote *Vita Guidonis*, which feems to imply a profe hiftory. x. 78. [Gerard of Cornwall, a very obfcure writer, in the eleventh chapter of his loft work, *De Geftis regum Weft-Saxonium*, introduced] Guy's hiftory. Hearne has printed an *Hiftoria Guidonis de Warwik: Append. ad Annal. Dunftaple*, num. xi. It was extracted from Girald. Cambrens. *Hift. Reg. Weft-Sax.*, capit. xi. by Girardus Cornubienfis. Lydgate's *Life of Guy*, never printed, is tranflated from this Giratdus, as Lydgate himfelf informs us at the end. MSS. Bibl. Bodl. Laud. D 31, f. 64, Tit. *Here gynneth the liff of Guy of Warwyk:*
　　" Out of the Latyn made by the Chronycler
　　Called of old Girard Cornubyence :
　　Which wrote the dedis, with grete diligence,
　　Of them that were in Weftfex crowned kynges," &c.
See Wharton, *Angl. Sacr.* i. p. 89.

[2] See *Regiftrum Librorum omnium et Jocalium in monafterio S. Mariæ de Pratis prope Leyceftriam.* f. 132, b. MSS. Bibl. Bodl. Laud. I 75. This catalogue was written by Will. Charite, one of the monks, A.D. 1517, f. 139.

[3] Hearne's Joann. Glafton. *Catal. Bibl. Glafton.* p. 435. One of the books of Troy is called *bonus et magnus.* There is alfo *Liber de Captione Antiochiæ Gallice. legibilis*, ibid.

[4] The fame Romance is in MSS. Harl.
[The Harl. MS. is a bad copy of about one half of the poem. This Romance was tranflated into German verfe by Conrad of Würzburg, who flourifhed about the year 1300. He chofe to name the heroes Engelhard and Engeldrud.—*Weber.* See Du Cang. *Gloff. Lat.* i. *Ind. Auctor*, p. 193. There is an old French Morality on this fubject—" *Comment Amille tue fes deux enfans pour guerir Amis fon compagnon*," &c. Beauchamps, *Rech. Theatr. Fr.* p. 109. There is a French metrical romance, *Hiftoire d'Amys et Amilion*, MSS. Reg. 12, C xii. 9, and at Bennet College, Num. L. 1. It begins,
　　" Ki veut oir chauncoun damur."

Burgoyne, and *Gesta Osuelis* [*Otuelis*],¹ all in French : together with
Merlin's Prophecies, Turpin's Charlemagne, and the *Destruction of
Troy*.² Among the books given to Winchester college by the
founder William of Wykeham, a prelate of high rank, about the
year 1387, we have *Chronicon Trojæ*.³ In the library of Windsor
college, in the reign of Henry VIII., were discovered, in the midst
of missals, psalters and homilies, *Duo libri Gallici de Romances, de
quibus unus liber de Rose, et alius difficilis materiæ.*⁴ This is the
language of the king's commissioners, who searched the archives of
the college : the first of these two French romances is perhaps
[Guillaume de Lorris]'s *Roman de la Rose*. A friar, in *Pierce Plowman*, is said to be much better acquainted with the *Rimes of Robin
Hood* and *Randal Erle of Chester* than with his Pater-noster.⁵ The
monks, who very naturally sought all opportunities of amusement in
their retired and confined situations, were fond of admitting the
minstrels to their festivals, and were hence familiarised to romantic
stories. Seventy shillings were expended on minstrels, who accompanied their songs with the harp, at the feast of the installation
of Ralph abbot of Saint Augustin's at Canterbury, in the year 1309.
At this magnificent solemnity, six thousand guests were present in
and about the hall of the abbey.⁶ It was not deemed an occurrence
unworthy to be recorded, that when Adam de Orleton, bishop of
Winchester, visited his cathedral priory of Saint Swithin in that
city, a minstrel named Herbert was introduced, who sang the *Song*

[In the Pipe-roll, 34 and 36 Hen. III. is mentioned, "liber magnus, *Gallico
ydiomiate* scriptus, in quo continentur Gesta Antiochie et regum et etiam aliorum."
—Mr. Wright's inform. Sir F. Madden conjectures this to have been a version of
the *Antiocheis* of Joseph of Exeter. Mr. Wright also refers us to a very curious list
of romances given by Guy de Beauchamp, Earl of Warwick, to the abbey of
Bardesley, printed from the original deed in M. Michel's *Tristan*.
¹ There is a romance called *Otuel*, MSS. Bibl. Adv. Edinb. W 4, l. xxviii. I
think he is mentioned in Charlemagne's story. He is converted to Christianity,
and marries Charlemagne's daughter. [Analysed by Mr. Ellis: vol. ii. p. 324.
It has been printed entire for the Abbotsford Club, with the romance of *Rowland and Vernagu*, 1836.
But as to the signification of the word *romance* in early documents, it is extremely difficult, after all, to come to any conclusion. In a Close-roll of 6 John
(1205), *Romancium de historia Angliæ* evidently means merely a narrative of English
history.]
² Gunton's *Peterb.* p. 108, *seq.* I will give some of the titles as they stand in
the catalogue. *Dares Phrygius de Excidio Trojæ*, bis, p. 180. *Prophetiæ Merlini
versifice*, p. 182. *Gesta Caroli secundùm Turpinum*, p. 187. *Gesta Æneæ post de-
structionem Trojæ*, p. 198. *Bellum contra Runcivallum*, p. 202. There are also the
two following articles, viz., *Certamen inter regem Johannem et Barones, versifice*,
per H. de Davench, p. 188. This I have never seen, nor know anything of the
author. *Versus de ludo scaccorum*, p. 195.
³ Ex archivis Coll. Wint.
⁴ Dugd. *Mon.* iii. *Eccles. Collegiat.* p. 80.
⁵ Fol. xxvi. b, edit. 1550. [See the *Erles of Chestre* in the *Percy Folio*, Ballads
and Romances.]
⁶ *Dec. Script.* p. 2011.

of Colbrond, a Danish giant, and the tale of *Queen Emma delivered from the ploughshares,* in the hall of the prior Alexander de Herriard, in the year 1338. I will give this very curious article, as it appears in an ancient register of the priory : " Et cantabat Joculator quidam nomine Herebertus canticum Colbrondi, necnon Geftum Emme regine a judicio ignis liberate, in aula prioris."[1] In an annual accompt-roll of the Augustine priory of Bicester in Oxfordshire, for the year 1431, the following entries relating to this subject occur, which I choose to exhibit in the words of the original : " Dona Prioris. Et in datis cuidam citharizatori in die sancti Jeronimi, viii. d. Et in datis alteri citharizatori in Festo Apostolorum Simonis et Jude cognomine Hendy, xii. d. Et in datis cuidam minstrallo domini le Talbot infra natale domini, xii. d. Et in datis ministrallis domini le Straunge in die Epiphanie, xx. d. Et in datis duobus ministrallis domini Lovell in craftino S. Marci evangeliste, xvi. d. Et in datis ministrallis ducis Glocestrie in Festo nativitatis beate Marie, iii. s. iv. d." I must add, as it likewise paints the manners of the monks, " Et in datis cuidam Ursario, iiii. d."[2] In the Prior's accounts of the Augustine canons of Maxtoke in Warwickshire, of various years in the reign of Henry VI., one of the styles or general heads is *De Joculatoribus et Mimis.* I will without apology produce some of the particular articles, not distinguishing between *Mimi, Joculatores, Jocatores, Lusores,* and *Citharistæ,* who all seem alternately, and at different times, to have exercised the same arts of popular entertainment : "Joculatori in septimana S. Michaelis, iv. d. Citharifte tempore natalis domini et aliis jocatoribus, iv. d. Mimis de Solihull, vi. d. Mimis de Coventry, xx. d. Mimo domini Ferrers, vi. d. Luforibus de Eton, viii. d. Luforibus de Coventry, viii. d. Luforibus de Daventry, xii. d. Mimis de Coventry, xii. d. Mimis domini de Asteley, xii. d. Item iiii. mimis domini de Warewyck, x. d. Mimo ceco, ii. d. Sex mimis domini de Clynton. Duobus Mimis de Rugeby, x. d. Cuidam citharifte, vi. d. Mimis domini de Asteley, xx. d. Cuidam citharifte, vi. d. Citha-

---

[1] *Regiftr. Priorat. S. Swithini Winton.* MSS. Archiv. de Wolvesey Wint. These were local stories. Guy fought and conquered Colbrond, a Danish champion, just without the northern walls of the city of Winchester, in a meadow to this day called Danemarch : and Colbrond's battle-axe was kept in the treasury of St. Swithin's priory till the Diffolution. Th. Rudb. apud Wharton, *Angl. Sacr.* i. 211. This history remained in rude painting against the walls of the north transept of the cathedral till within my memory. Queen Emma was a patroness of this church, in which she underwent the trial of walking blindfold over nine red-hot ploughshares. Colbrond is mentioned in the *Squyr of Lowe Degre.* [Hazlitt's *Pop. Poetry,* ii. 26 :]

" Or els fo doughty of my hande
As was the gyaunte fyr Colbrande."

[See Turnbull's edit. of *Guy of Warwick,* 1840, Introd.]
[2] *Compotus dñi Ricardi Parentyn Prioris, et fratris Ric. Albon canonici, burfaril ibidem, de omnibus bonis per eofdem receptis et liberatis a craftino Michaelis anno Henrici Sexti poft Conqueftum octavo ufque in idem craftinum anno R. Henrici prædicti nono.* In Thefaurar. Coll. SS. Trin. Oxon. Bishop Kennet has printed a Computus of the same monastery under the same reign, in which three or four entries of the same fort occur. *Paroch. Antiq.* p. 578.

riſte de Coventry, vi. d.   Duobus cithariſtis de Coventry, viii. d.
Mimis de Rugeby, viii. d.   Mimis domini de Buckeridge, xx. d.
Mimis domini de Stafford, ii. s.   Luſoribus de Coleſhille, viii. d." [1]
Here we may obſerve, that the minſtrels of the nobility, in whoſe
families they were conſtantly retained, travelled about the county to
the neighbouring monaſteries; and that they generally received
better gratuities for theſe occaſional performances than the others.
Solihull, Rugby, Coleſhill, Eton or Nun-Eton, and Coventry, are
all towns ſituated at no great diſtance from the priory.[2] Nor muſt
I omit that two minſtrels from Coventry made part of the feſtivity
at the conſecration of John, prior of this convent, in the year 1432,
viz. "*Dat. duobus mimis de Coventry in die conſecrationis prioris*, xii. d." [3]
Nor is it improbable, that ſome of our great monaſteries kept
minſtrels of their own in regular pay. So early as the year 1180, in
the reign of Henry II., *Jeffrey the harper* received a corrody or

---

[1] *Ex orig. penes me.*

[2] In the ancient annual rolls of accompt of Wincheſter College, there are many
articles of this ſort. The few following, extracted from a great number, may ſerve
as a ſpecimen. They are chiefly in the reign of Edward IV. viz. in the year 1481 :
"Et in ſol. miniſtrallis dom. Regis venientibus ad collegium xv. die Aprilis, cum
12*d.* ſolut. miniſtralis dom. Epiſcopi Wynton. venientibus ad collegium primo die
junii, iiii *s.* iiii *d.*—Et in dat. miniſtralis dom. Arundell ven. ad Coll. cum viii *d.* dat.
miniſtrallis dom. de Lawarr, ii *s.* iii *d.*"—In the year 1483 : "Sol. miniſtrallis dom.
Regis ven. ad Coll. iii *s.* iiii *d.*"—In the year 1472 : "Et in dat. miniſtrallis dom.
Regis cum viii *d.* dat. duobus Berewardis ducis Clarentie, xx *d.* Et in dat. Johanni
Stulto quondam dom. de Warewyco, cum iiii *d.* dat. Thome Nevyle taborario.—Et
in datis duobus miniſtrallis ducis Gloceſtrie, cum iiii *d.* dat. uni miniſtrallo ducis de
Northumberlond, viii *d.* Et in datis duobus citharatoribus ad vices venient. ad col-
legium viii *d.*"—In the year 1479 : "Et in datis ſatrapis Wynton venientibus ad
coll. feſto Epiphanie, cum xii *d.* dat. miniſtrallis dom. epiſcopi venient. ad coll. infra
octavas epiphanie, iii *s.*"—In the year 1477 : "Et in dat. miniſtrallis dom. Principis venient. ad coll. feſto Aſcenſionis Domini, cum xx *d.* dat miniſtrallis dom.
Regis, v*s.*"—In the year 1464 : "Et in dat. miniſtrallis comitis Kancie venient. ad
Coll. in menſe julii, iiii *s.* iiii *d.*"—In the year 1467 : "Et in datis quatuor mimis
dom. de Arundell venient. ad Coll. xiii. die Febr. ex curialitate dom. Cuſtodis, ii *s.*"
—In the year 1466 : "Et in dat. ſatrapis, [*ut ſupr.*] cum ii *s.* dat. iiii. interludenti-
bus et J. Meke cithariſtæ eodem ffeſto, iiii *s.*"—In the year 1484 : "Et in dat. uni
miniſtrallo dom. principis, et in aliis miniſtrallis ducis Gloceſtrie v. die julii, xx *d.*"
The minſtrels of the biſhop, of lord Arundel, and the Duke of Gloceſter, occur
very frequently. In domo muniment. coll. prædict. in ciſta ex orientali latere.

In rolls of the reign of Henry VI. the counteſs of Weſtmoreland, ſiſter of cardinal Beaufort, is mentioned as being entertained in the college; and in her retinue
were the minſtrels of her houſehold, who received gratuities. *Ex Rot. Comp. orig.*

In theſe rolls there is an entry, which ſeems to prove that the *Luſores* were a ſort
of actors in dumb ſhow or maſquerade. *Rot. ann.* 1467. "Dat. luſoribus de civitate Winton. venientibus ad collegium in *apparatu* ſuo mens. julii, v *s.* vii *d.*" This
is a large reward. I will add from the ſame rolls, *ann.* 1479. "In dat. Joh. Pontiſ-
bery and ſocio ludentibus in aula in die circumciſionis, ii *s.*"

[3] *Ibid.* It appears that the Coventry-men were in high repute for their performances of this ſort. In the entertainment preſented to Queen Elizabeth at Kenilworth
caſtle in 1575, the Coventry-men exhibited "their old ſtoriall ſheaw." Laneham's
Narrative, &c. p. 32. Minſtrels were hired from Coventry to perform at Holy
Croſſe feaſt at Abingdon, Berks, 1422. Hearne's *Lib. Nig. Scacc.* ii. p. 598. See
an account of their play on Corpus Chriſti day, in Dugdale's *Monaſticon*, by Stevens, i. p. 138, and Hearne's *Fordun*, p. 1450, *ſub ann.* 1492.

annuity from the Benedictine abbey of Hide near Winchester ;[1] undoubtedly on condition that he should serve the monks in the profession of a harper on public occasions.   The abbeys of Conway and
Stratflur in Wales respectively maintained a bard :[2] and the Welsh
monasteries in general were the grand repositories of the poetry of
the British bards.[3]

In the statutes of New College at Oxford, given about the year
1380, the founder, William of Wykeham, orders his scholars, for
their recreation on festival days in the hall after dinner and supper,
to entertain themselves with songs and other diversions consistent
with decency : and to recite poems, chronicles of kingdoms, the
wonders of the world, together with the like compositions, not mis-
becoming the clerical character.[4]   The latter part of this injunction
seems to be an explication of the former : and on the whole it appears
that the *Cantilenæ*, which the scholars should sing on these occasions,
were a sort of *Poemata* or poetical Chronicles, containing general
histories of kingdoms.[5]   It is natural to conclude that they preferred
pieces of English history, [such as the *Brut* already described, of a
somewhat amplified version of which (of the reign of Edward III.)
some fragments occur among Hearne's MSS.][6]

Although we have taken our leave of Robert de Brunne, yet as
the subject is remarkable, and affords a striking portraiture of ancient
manners, I am tempted to transcribe that chronicler's description of
the presents received by King Athelstane from the king of France ;
especially as it contains some new circumstances, and supplies the

---

[1] Madox, *Hist. Exchequer*, p. 251. Where he is styled, "Galfridus citharœdus."
[2] Powel's *Cambria.   To the Reader*, pag. 1, edit. 1584.
[3] Evans's *Diss. de Bardis. Specimens of Welsh Poetry*, p. 92. Wood relates a
story of two itinerant priests coming, towards night, to a cell of Benedictines near
Oxford, where, on a supposition of their being mimes or minstrels, they gained
admittance. But the cellarer, sacrist, and others of the brethren, hoping to have
been entertained with their *gesticulatoriis ludicrisque artibus*, and finding them to be
nothing more than two indigent ecclesiastics who could only administer spiritual con-
solation, and being consequently disappointed of their mirth, beat them and turned
them out of the monastery.—*Hist. Antiq. Univ. Oxon.* i. 67. Under the year 1224.
[4] I will transcribe his words : " Quando ob dei reverentiam aut sue matris, vel
alterius sancti cujuscunque, tempore yemali, ignis in aula sociis ministratur ; tunc
scolaribus et sociis post tempus prandii aut cene liceat gracia recreationis in aula,
in Cantilenis et aliis solaciis honestis, moram facere condecentem ; et Poemata,
regnorum Chronica, et mundi hujus Mirabilia, ac cetera que statum clericalem
condecorant, seriosius pertractare."—*Rubric.* xviii.   The same thing is enjoined in
the statutes of Winchester College, *Rubr.* xv. I do not remember any such passage
in the statutes of preceding colleges in either university. But this injunction is
afterwards adopted in the statutes of Magdalene College, and thence, if I recollect
right, was copied into those of Corpus Christi, Oxford.
[5] Hearne thus understood the passage : " The wise founder of New College permitted them [metrical chronicles] to be sung by the fellows and scholars upon extraordinary days."—Heming. *Cartul.* ii. Append. Numb. ix. § vi. p. 662.
[6] Given to him by Mr. Murray. See Heming, *Chartul.* ii. p. 654. And *Rob.
Glouc.* ii. p. 731. Nunc MSS. Bibl. Bodl. Oxon. *Rawlins*, Cod. 4to. (E. Pr. 87.)
[Ritson has printed these fragments entire in his *Metrical Romances*, 1802 ; and the
editor could not perceive the advantage of quoting them to the extent that Warton,
not knowing what they were, has done.]

defects of [the *Brut*]. It is from his verfion of Peter Langtoft's chronicle above mentioned :

> At the fefte of oure lady the Affumpcion,
> Went the kyng fro London toward Abindon.
> Thider out of France, fro Charles kyng of fame,
> Com the duke of Boloyn, Adulphus was his name,
> & the duke of Burgoyn, Edmonde fonne Reynere.
> The brouht kynge Athelfton prefent withouten pere :
> Fro Charles kyng fanz faile thei brouht a gonfaynoun
> That Saynt Morice bare in batayle befor the legioun ;
> & the fcharp lance that thrilled Ihefu fide ;
> & a fuerd of golde,—in the hilte did men hide
> Tuo of tho nayles that war thorh Jhefu fete
> Tached[1] on the croyce ; the blode thei out lete ;
> & fom of the thornes that don were on his heued,
> & a fair pece that of the croyce leued,[2]
> That faynt Heleyn fonne at the batayle wan
> Of the Soudan Afkalone, his name was Madan.
> Than blewe the trumpes fulle loud & fulle fchille,
> The kyng com in to the halle that hardy was of wille.
> Than fpak Reyner, Edmunde fonne, for he was meffengere :
> ' Athelftan, my lord, the gretes, Charles that has no pere ;
> He fends the this prefent, and fais, he wille hym bynde
> To the thorh[3] Ilde thi fiftere, & tille alle thi kynde."
> Befor the meffengers was the maiden brouht,
> Of body fo gentill was non in erthe wrouht ;
> No non fo faire of face, ne non of fpech fo lufty.
> Scho granted befor tham all to Charles hir body :
> & fo did the kyng, & alle the baronage,
> Mykelle was the richeffe thei purveied [in] hir paffage.[4]

[One of Hearne's fragments is added here, becaufe it defends and explains the derivation of the name Ynglond from maiden Ynge, of whom Robert Manning declares twice[5] that he had never heard. She is the later reprefentative of Ronwen or Rowenna. This fragment] begins with the martyrdom of Saint Alban, and paffes on to the introduction of Waffail, and to the names and divifion of England :

> And now he ys alle fo hole yfonde,
> As whan he was yleyde on grounde.
> And ʒyf ʒe wille not trow[6] me,
> Goth to Weftmyftere, and ʒe mow fe.
> In that tyme Seynt Albon
> For Goddys loue tholed[7] martirdome,
> And xl. ʒere with fchame & fchonde[8]
> Was drowen[9] oute of Englond.

---

[1] Tacked, faftened.   [2] Remained.   [3] "Thee through."

[4] *Chron.* pp. 29, 30, [edit. 1810, *ut fupr.*] Afterwards follows the combat of Guy with "a hogge (huge) geant, hight Colibrant." As in our fragment, p. 31. See Will. Malms. *Geft. Angl.* ii. 6. The lance of Charlemagne is to this day fhown among the relics of St. Denis in France.—Carpentier, *Suppl. Gloff. Lat. Ducange.* tom. ii. p. 994, edit. 1766.

[5] [*Chronicle*, Part i. pp. 265, 515.

> " Bot this lewed men fey and fynge,
> And telle that hit was mayden Inge.
> Wryten of Inge, no clerk may kenne,
> Bot of Hengifte doughter, Ronewenne."]

[6] Believe.   [7] Suffered.   [8] Confufion.   [9] Driven, drawn.

In that tyme wete[1] the welle,
Cam ferſt waſſayle & drynkehayl
In to this londe, with owte wene,[2]
Thurghe a mayde brygh[3] and ſchene.[4]
Sche was cleput[5] mayde ynge.
For hur many dothe rede & ſynge,
Lordyngys gent[6] & free.
This lond hath hadde namys thre.
Ferſt hit was cleput Albyon
And ſyth,[7] for Brute, Bretayne anon,
And now ynglond clepyd hit ys,
Aftir mayde ynge ywyſſe.
Thilke ynge fro Saxone was come,
And with here many a moder ſonne,
For gret hungure y underſtonde
ynge went oute of hure londe.
And thorow leue of oure kyng
In this lande ſche hadde reſtyng.
As meche lande of the kyng ſche bade,[8]
As with a hole hyde me my ʒth[9] ſprede,
The kyng graunted [t]he bonne:[10]
A ſtrong caſtel ſche made ſone,
And when the caſtel was al made,
The kyng to the mete ſche bade.[11]
The kyng graunted here anone.
He wyſt not what thay wolde done.

*   *   *   *

And ſayde to ham[18] in this manere,
" The kyng to morrow ſchal ete here,
He and alle hys men,
Euer[13] one of vs and one of them,
To geder ſchal ſitte at the mete.
And when thay haue al moſt yete,
I wole ſay waſſayle to the kyng,
And ſle hym with oute any leſyng.[14]
And loke that ʒe in this manere
Eche of ʒow ſle his fere."[15]
And ſo ſche dede thenne,
Slowe the kyng and alle hys men.
And thus, thorowgh here queyntyſe,[16]
This londe was wonne in this wyſe.
Syth[17] anon ſone an ſwythe[18]
Was Englond deled[19] on fyue,
To fyue kynggys trewelyche,
That were nobyl and ſwythe ryche.
That one hadde alle the londe of Kente,
That ys free and ſwythe gente.
And in hys lond byſhopus tweye.
Worthy men where[20] theye.
The archebyſhop of Caunturbery,
And of Rocheſtere that ys mery.
The kyng of Eſſex of renon[21]

---

[1] know ye.	[2] doubt.	[3] bright.
[4] fair.	[5] called.	[6] gentle.
[7] [afterwards.]	[8] requeſted, deſired.	[9] men might.
[10] granted her requeſt.	[11] bid.	[12] them.
[13] every.	[14] lye.	[15] companion.
[16] ſtratagem.	[17] after.	[18] [quickly].
[19] divided.	[20] were.	[21] renown.

> He hadde to his portion
> Weftfchire, Barkfchire,
> Souffex, Southamptfhire.
> And ther-to Dorfetfhyre,
> All Cornewalle & Deuenfhire,
> All thys were of hys anpyre.[1]
> The kyng hadde on his hond
> Fyue Byfshopes ftarke & ftrong,
> Of Salufbury was that on.[2]

As to the *Mirabilia Mundi*, mentioned in the ftatutes of New College at Oxford, in conjunction with thefe *Poemata* and *Regnorum Chronica*, the immigrations of the Arabians into Europe and the Crufades produced numberlefs accounts, partly true and partly fabulous, of the wonders feen in the eaftern countries; which, falling into the hands of the monks, grew into various treatifes under the title of *Mirabilia Mundi*. There were alfo fome profeffed travellers into the Eaft in the dark ages, who furprifed the weftern world with their marvellous narratives which, could they have been contradicted, would not have been believed.[3] At the court of the grand Khan, perfons of all nations and religions, if they difcovered any diftinguifhed degree of abilities, were kindly entertained and often preferred.

In the Bodleian Library we have a fuperb vellum MS. [of Marco Polo, in French,] decorated with ancient defcriptive paintings and illuminations, entitled, *Hiftoire de Graunt Kaan et des Merveilles du Monde.*[4] The fame work is among the royal MSS.[5] A [fpurious] Latin epiftle, faid to be tranflated from the Greek by Cornelius Nepos, is an extremely common manufcript, entitled, *De fitu et Mirabilibus Indiæ.*[6]

---

[1] empire.   [2] [Robert of Gloucefter, edit. 1810, 731·3.]

[3] The firft European traveller who went far Eaftward, is Benjamin, a Jew of Tudela in Navarre. He penetrated from Conftantinople through Alexandria in Ægypt and Perfia to the frontiers of Tzin, now China. His travels end in 1173. He mentions the immenfe wealth of Conftantinople, and fays that its port fwarmed with fhips from all countries. He exaggerates in fpeaking of the prodigious number of Jews in that city. He is full of marvellous and romantic ftories. William de Rubruquis, a monk, was fent into Perfic Tartary, and by the command of S. Louis, King of France, about the year 1245; as was alfo Carpini, by Pope Innocent IV. Marco Polo, a Venetian nobleman, travelled eaftward into Syria and Perfia to the country conftantly called in the dark ages Cathay, which proves to be the northern part of China. This was about the year [1280.] His book is [fometimes] entitled *De Regionibus Orientis*. He mentions the immenfe and opulent city of Cambalu, undoubtedly Pekin. Hakluyt cites a friar, named Oderick, who tarvelled to Cambalu in Cathay, and whofe defcription of that city correfponds exactly with Pekin. Friar Bacon, about 1280, from thefe travels formed his geography of this part of the globe, as may be collected from what he relates of the Tartars. See Purchas, *Pilgr.* iii. 52, and Bac. *Op. Maj.* 228, 235.

[4] MSS. Bodl. F. 10 [264] ad calc. Cod. The handwriting is about the reign of Edward III. [1380-1400].

[5] MSS. Bibl. Reg. 19, D i. 3. [The royal MS. is a magnificent copy of the French tranflation of Marco Polo's travels, which it affirms to have been made in the year 1298.—*Price.*]

[6] [Maittaire cites an edition of the Latin tranflation as printed at Venice in 1499, but fee Brunet, *dern.* edit. i. 163. The Greek has been often printed. Sir F. Madden refers to a Saxon tranflation in Cotton. MS. Vitell. A. xv.]

It is from Alexander the Great to his preceptor Ariftotle; and the Greek original was moft probably drawn from fome of the fabulous authors of Alexander's ftory.

There is a MS. containing *La Chartre que Preftre Jehan maunda a Fredewik l' Empereur de Mervailles de fa Terre.*[1] This was Frederic Barbaroffa, emperor of Germany, or his fucceffor, both of whom were celebrated for their many fuccefsful enterprifes in the Holy Land before the year 1230. Prefter John, a Chriftian, was emperor of India. I find another tract, *De Mirabilibus Terræ Sanctæ.*[2] A book of Sir John Mandeville, a famous traveller into the Eaft about the year 1340, is under the title of *Mirabilia Mundi.*[3] His *Itinerary* might indeed have the fame title.[4] [A copy of his famous book] in the Cotton Library is, "The Voiage and Travaile of Sir John Maundevile knight, which treateth of the way to Hierufaleme and of the *Marveyles of* Inde with other ilands and countryes;"[5] [but in the edition by Wynkyn de Worde in 1499 the title is fomewhat more elaborate.][6] In the Cotton Library there is a piece with the title, *Sanctorum Loca, Mirabilia Mundi,* &c.[7] Afterwards the wonders of other countries were added : and when this fort of reading began to grow fafhionable, Gyraldus Cambrenfis compofed his book *De Mirabilibus Hiberniæ.*[8] There is alfo another *De Mirabilibus Angliæ,*[9] [a very common MS., of which a copy is attached to Hearne's edition of *Robert of Gloucefter.*] At length the fuperftitious

---

[1] MSS. Reg. 20, A xii. 3. And in Bibl. Bodl. MSS. Bodl. E 4. 3. "Literæ Joannis Prefbiteri ad Fredericum Imperatorem," &c.

[2] MSS. Reg. 14, C xiii. 3.

[3] MSS. C. C. C. Cant. A iv. 69. We find *De Mirabilibus Mundi Liber,* MSS. Reg. 13, E ix. 5. And again, *De Mirabilibus Mundi et Viris illuftribus Tractatus* 14, C vi. 3.

[4] His book is fuppofed to have been interpolated by the monks. Leland obferves that Afia and Africa were parts of the world at this time, " Anglis de fola fere nominis umbra cognitas." *Script. Br.* p. 366. He wrote his *Itinerary* in French, Englifh, and Latin. It extends to Cathay or China before mentioned. Leland fays that he gave to Becket's fhrine in Canterbury cathedral a glafs globe enclofing an apple, which he probably brought from the Eaft. Leland faw this curiofity, in which the apple remained frefh and undecayed. *Ubi fupr.* Mandeville, on returning from his travels, gave to the high altar of St. Albans abbey church a fort of patera brought from Ægypt, [formerly] in the hands of an ingenious antiquary in London. He was a native of the town of St. Albans, and a phyfician. He fays that he left many Mervayles unwritten, and refers the curious reader to [the] *Mappa Mundi,* chap. cviii, cix. A hiftory of the Tartars became popular in Europe about the year 1310, written or dictated by Aiton, [kinfman to] a king of Armenia who, having traverfed the moft remarkable countries of the Eaft, turned monk at Cyprus, and publifhed his travels which, on account of the rank of the author, and his amazing adventures, gained great efteem. [A competent and critical edition of Sir John Mandeville's *Travels* is ftill a want. It has been long on the lift of intended re-editions by the Early Englifh Text Society.]

[5] [Printed in 1725, again in 1839, and thirdly in 1866.]

[6] [See *Handb. of E. E. Lit.* art. *Mandevile.*]   [7] Galb. A xxi. 3.

[8] It is printed among the *Scriptores Hift. Angl.* 1602, 692. Written about the year 1200. It was fo favourite a title that we have even *De Mirabilibus Veteris et Novi Teftamenti.* MSS. Coll. Æn. Nas. Oxon. Cod. 12, f. 190, a.

[9] Bibl. Bodl. MSS. C 6.

curiosity of the times was gratified with compilations under the comprehensive title of *Mirabilia Hiberniæ, Angliæ, et Orientis*.[1] But enough has been said of these infatuations. Yet the history of human credulity is a necessary speculation to those who trace the gradations of human knowledge. Let me add, that a spirit of rational enquiry into the topographical state of foreign countries, the parent of commerce and of a thousand improvements, took its rise from these visions.

[There is a French elegy on the death of Edward I. in 1307, written in the succeeding reign, and also an English version, which is supposed to be taken from it, as it is substantially identical. As the whole has been printed,[2] a specimen will probably be sufficient :]

> The messager to the pope com
>   And seyde that oure kynge was ded :[3]
> Ys oune hond the lettre he nom,
>   Y-wis his herte wes ful gret :
> The Pope himself the lettre redde,
>   And spec a word of gret honour.
> Alas, he seide, is Edward ded ?
>   Of Cristendome he ber the flour.
>
> The pope to is chaumbre wende
>   For del ne mihte he speke na more ;
> Ant after cardinals he sende
>   That muche couthen of Cristes lore.
> Both the lasse ant eke the more
>   Bed hem both rede ant synge :
> Gret deol me myhte se thore,
>   Many mon is honde wrynge.
>
> The pope of Peyters stod at is masse
>   With ful gret solempnete,
> Ther me con the soule blesse :
>   Kyng Edward, honoured thou be :
> God leue thi sone come after the
>   Bringe to ende that thou hast bygonne,
> The holy crois y-mad of tre
>   So fain thou woldest hit han y-wonne, &c.[4]

---

[1] As in MSS. Reg. 13 D, i. 11. I must not forget that the *Polyhistor* of Julius Solinus appears in many MSS. under the title of Solinus *de Mirabilibus Mundi*. This was so favourite a book as to be translated into hexameters by some monk in the twelfth century, according to Voss. *Hist. Lat.* iii. p. 721.

[2] [Wright's *Political Songs*, 1839, 241-50.]

[3] He died in Scotland, July 7, 1307. The chronicles pretend that the Pope knew of his death the next day by a vision or some miraculous information. So Robert of Brunne, who recommends this tragical vent to those who " Singe and say in romance and ryme."—*Chron.* p. 340, edit. *u tsupr.* :

> " The Pope the tother day wist it in tne court of Rome.
> The Pope on the morn bifor the clergi cam
> And tolde tham biforn, the floure of Cristendam
> Was ded and lay on bere, Edward of Ingeland.
> He said with hevy chere, in spirit he it fond."

He adds, that the Pope granted five years of pardon to those who would pray for his soul.

[4] MSS. Harl. 2253, f. 73. In [Mrs. Cooper's] *Muses Library*, 1737, there is an elegy on the death of Henry I., " wrote immediately after his death, the author

That the Pope fhould here pronounce the funeral panegyric of Edward I. is by no means furprifing, if we confider the predominant ideas of the age. And in the true fpirit of thefe ideas, the poet makes this illuftrious monarch's achievements in the Holy Land his principal and leading topic. But there is a particular circumftance alluded to in thefe ftanzas, relating to the crufading character of Edward,[1] together with its confequences, which needs explanation. Edward, in the decline of life, had vowed a fecond expedition to Jerufalem; but finding his end approach, in his laft moments he devoted the prodigious fum of thirty thoufand pounds to provide one hundred and forty knights,[2] who fhould carry his heart into Paleftine. But this appointment of the dying king was never executed. Our elegift and the chroniclers impute the crime of withholding fo pious a legacy to the advice of the king of France, whofe daughter Ifabel was married to the fucceeding king. But it is more probable to fuppofe that Edward II. and his profligate minion Piers Gavefton diffipated the money in their luxurious and expenfive pleafures.

SECTION III.

E have feen, in the preceding fection, that the character of our poetical compofition began to be changed about the reign of the firft [or fecond] Edward: that either fictitious adventures were fubftituted by the minftrels in the place of hiftorical and traditionary facts, or reality difguifed by the mifreprefentations of invention; and that a tafte for ornamental and even exotic expreffion gradually prevailed over the rude fimplicity of the native Englifh phrafeology. This change, which with our language affected our poetry, had been growing for fome time, and among other caufes was occafioned by the introduction and increafe of the tales of chivalry.

The ideas of chivalry, in an imperfect degree, had been of old eftablifhed among the Gothic tribes. The fafhion of challenging to fingle combat, the pride of feeking dangerous adventures, and the

---

unknown," p. 4. [It has been remarked by Ritfon, that the elegy printed by Mrs. Cooper was the compofition of Fabyan the chronicler, who died in 1511: but then it is a tranflation from the original Latin, preferved by Knighton, of the twelfth century.—*Park*.]

[1] It appears that King Edward I. about the year 1271, took his harper with him to the Holy Land. This officer was a clofe and conftant attendant of his mafter: for when Edward was wounded with a poifoned knife at Ptolemais, the harper, *cithareda fuus*, hearing the ftruggle, rufhed into the royal apartment, and killed the affaffin. *Chron.* Hemingford, cap. xxxv. p. 591. (*V. Hiftor. Anglic. Scriptor.* vol. ii. 1687.) [After the king himfelf had flain the affaffin his harper had the fingular courage to brain a dead man with a trivet or *tripod*, for which act of heroifm he was juftly reprimanded by Edward.— *Ritfon*.]

[2] The poet fays eighty.

spirit of avenging and protecting the fair fex, feem to have been peculiar to the Northern nations in the moft uncultivated ftate of Europe. All thefe cuftoms were afterwards encouraged and confirmed by correfponding circumftances in the feudal conftitution. At length the Crufades excited a new fpirit of enterprife, and introduced into the courts and ceremonies of European princes a higher degree of fplendour and parade, caught from the riches and magnificence of eaftern cities.[1]　Thefe oriental expeditions eftablifhed a tafte for hyperbolical defcription, and propagated an infinity of marvellous tales, which men returning from diftant countries eafily impofed on credulous and ignorant minds.　The unparalleled emulation with which the nations of Chriftendom univerfally embraced this holy caufe, the pride with which emperors, kings, barons, earls, bifhops, and knights, ftrove to excel each other on this interefting occafion, not only in prowefs and heroifm, but in fumptuous equipages, gorgeous banners, armorial cognifances, fplendid pavilions, and other expenfive articles of a fimilar nature, diffufed a love of war and a fondnefs for military pomp. Hence their very diverfions became warlike, and the martial enthufiafm of the times appeared in tilts and tournaments. Thefe practices and opinions co-operated with the kindred fuperftitions of dragons,[2] dwarfs, fairies, giants, and enchanters, which the traditions of the Gothic fcalds had already planted ; and produced that extraordinary fpecies of compofition which has been called Romance.

Before thefe expeditions into the Eaft became fafhionable, the principal and leading fubjects of the old fablers were the achievements of King Arthur with his knights of the round table, and of Charlemagne with his twelve peers. But in the romances written after the holy war, a new fet of champions, of conquefts and of countries were introduced. Trebizond took place of Roncevalles, and Godfrey of Bulloigne, Solyman, Nouraddin, the caliphs, the foldans, and the cities of Ægypt and Syria, became the favourite topics.[3]　The

---

[1] I cannot help tranfcribing here a curious paffage from old Fauchet. He is fpeaking of Louis the young king of France about the year 1150. " Le quel fut le premier roy de fa maifon, qui monftra dehors fes richeffes allant en Jerufalem. Auffi la France commença de fon temps a s'embellir de baftimens plus magnifiques: prendre plaifir a pierrieres et autres delicateffes gouftus en Levant par luy, ou les feigneurs qui avoient ja fait ce voyage. De forte qu'on peut dire qu'il a efte le premier tenant Cour de grand Roy : eftant fi magnifique, que fa femme, dedaignant la fimplicité de fes predeceffeurs, luy fit elever une fepulture d'argent, au lieu de pierre." *Recueil de la Lang. et Poes. Fr.* ch. viii. p. 76. edit. 1581. He adds, that a great number of French romances were compofed about this period.

[2] See Kircher's *Mund. Subterran.* viii. § 4. He mentions a knight of Rhodes made grand mafter of the order for killing a dragon, 1345.

[3] [Though this paffage has been the fubject of fevere animadverfion, and characterized as containing nothing but " random affertion, falfehood and impofition," there are few of its pofitions which a more temperate fpirit of criticifm might not reconcile with the truth. The popularity of Arthur's ftory, anterior to the firft Crufade, is abundantly manifefted by the language of William of Malmefbury and Alanus de Infulis, who refer to it as a fable of common notoriety and general belief among the people. Had it arifen within their own days, we may be certain

troubadours of Provence, an idle and unfettled race of men, took up
arms, and followed their barons in prodigious multitudes to the conqueft of Jerufalem. They made a confiderable part of the houfehold
of the nobility of France. Louis VII., king of France, not only
entertained them at his court very liberally, but commanded a confiderable company of them into his retinue, when he took fhip for
Paleftine, that they might folace him with their fongs during the
dangers and inconveniences of fo long a voyage.[1] The ancient chronicles of France mention *Legions de poetes* as embarking in this wonderful enterprife.[2] Here a new and more copious fource of fabling
was opened : in thefe expeditions they picked up numberlefs extravagant ftories, and at their return enriched romance with an infinite
variety of oriental fcenes and fictions. Thus thefe later wonders in
fome meafure fupplanted the former : they had the recommendation
of novelty, and gained ftill more attention, as they came from a
greater diftance.[3]

---

that Malmefbury, who rejected it as beneath the dignity of hiftory, would not have
fuffered an objection fo well founded as the novelty of its appearance to have
efcaped his cenfure ; nor can the narrative of Alanus be reconciled with the general
progrefs of traditionary faith—a plant of tardy growth—if we limit its firft publicity
to the period thus prefcribed (1096-1142). With regard to Charlemagne and his
peers, as their deeds were chaunted by Talliefer at the battle of Haftings (1066), it
would be needlefs to offer further demonftrations of their early popularity ; nor in
fact does the accuracy of this part of Warton's ftatement appear to be called in
queftion by the writer alluded to. It would be more difficult to define the degree
in which thefe romances were fuperfeded by fimilar poems on the achievements of
the Crufaders ; or, to ufe the more cautious language of the text, to ftate how far
"Trebizond took place of Roncevalles." But it will be recollected that in confequence of the Crufades, the action of feveral romances was transferred to the Holy
Land, fuch as Sir Bevis, Sir Guy, Sir Ifumbras, the King of Tars, &c. : and that
moft of thefe were "favorite topics" in high efteem, is clear from the declaration
of Chaucer, who catalogued them among the "romances of Pris." In fhort, if
we omit the names of the caliphs, and confine ourfelves to the Soldans—a generic
name ufed by our early writers for every fucceffive ruler of the Eaft—and the cities of
Egypt and Syria, this rhapfody, as it has been termed, will contain nothing which is
not ftrictly demonftrable by hiftorical evidence or the language of the old romancers.
The Life of Godfrey of Boulogne was written in French verfe by Gregory Bechada,
about the year 1130. It is ufually fuppofed to have perifhed ; unlefs, indeed, it
exift in a poem upon the fame fubject by Wolfram Von Efchenbach, who generally
founded his romances upon a French or Provençal original.—*Price.*]

[1] Velley, *Hift. Fr.* fub an. 1178.

[2] Maffieu, *Hift. Poes. Fr.* p. 105. Many of the troubadours, whofe works now
exift, and whofe names are recorded, accompanied their lords to the holy war.
Some of the French nobility of the firft rank were troubadours about the eleventh
century : and the French critics with much triumph obferve, that it is the glory of
the French poetry to number counts and dukes, that is fovereigns, among its profeffors, from its commencement. What a glory ! The worfhipfull company of
Merchant-taylors in London, if I recollect right, boaft the names of many dukes,
earls, and princes, enrolled in their community. [Herbert's *Hift. of the 12 Livery-
Companies*, ii. 384.] This is indeed an honour to that otherwife refpectable fociety.
But poets can derive no luftre from counts and dukes, or even princes, who have
been enrolled in their lifts ; only in proportion as they have adorned the art by the
excellence of their compofitions.

[3] The old French hiftorian Mezeray goes fo far as to derive the origin of the
French poetry and romances from the Crufades. *Hift.* pp. 416, 417. Geoffrey Vine-

In the mean time we fhould recollect that the Saracens or Aràbians, the fame people which were the object of the Crufades, had acquired an eftablifhment in Spain about the ninth century : and that by means of this earlier intercourfe many of their fictions and fables, together with their literature, muft have been known in Europe before the Chriftian armies invaded Afia. It is for this reafon the elder Spanifh romances have profeffedly more Arabian allufions than any other. Cervantes makes the imagined writer of Don Quixote's hiftory an Arabian. Yet, exclufively of their domeftic and more immediate connection with this eaftern people, the Spaniards from temper and conftitution were extravagantly fond of chivalrous exercifes. Some critics have fuppofed that Spain, having learned the art or fafhion of romance-writing from their naturalifed guefts the Arabians, communicated it, at an early period, to the reft of Europe.[1]

It has been imagined that the firft romances were compofed in metre, and fung to the harp by the poets of Provence at feftive folemnities : but an ingenious Frenchman, who has made deep refearches into this fort of literature, attempts to prove that this mode of reciting romantic adventures was in high reputation among the natives of Normandy above a century before the troubadours of Provence, who are generally fuppofed to have led the way to the poets of Italy, Spain and France, and that it commenced about the year 1162.[2] If the critic means to infinuate, that the French troubadours acquired their art of verfifying from thefe Norman bards, this reafoning will favour the fyftem of thofe who contend that metrical romances lineally took their rife from the hiftorical odes of the Scandinavian fcalds ; for the Normans were a branch of the Scandinavian ftock. But Fauchet, at the fame time that he allows the Normans to have been fond of chanting the praifes of their heroes in verfe, expreffly pronounces that they borrowed this practice from the Franks or French.[3]

---

fauf fays, that when King Richard I. arrived at the Chriftian camp before Ptolemais, he was received with *populares Cantiones,* which recited *Antiquorum Præclara Gefta. It. Hierofol.* cap. ii. p. 332, *ibid.*

[1] Huet in fome meafure adopts this opinion. But that learned man was a very incompetent judge of thefe matters. Under the common term Romance, he confounds romances of chivalry, romances of gallantry, and all the fables of the Provençal poets. What can we think of a writer who, having touched upon the gothic romances, at whofe fictions and barbarifms he is much fhocked, talks of the confummate degree of art and elegance to which the French are at prefent arrived in romances ? He adds, that the fuperior refinement and politeffe of the French gallantry has happily given them an advantage of fhining in this fpecies of compofition. *Hift. Rom.* p. 138. But the fophiftry and ignorance of Huet's Treatife has been already detected and expofed by a critic of another caft in the *Supplement to Jarvis's Preface,* prefixed to the Tranflation of *Don Quixote.*

[2] Mons. L'Eveque de la Ravaliere, in his *Revolutions de la Langue Françoife, à la fuite des Poefies du Roi de Navarre.* [2 vols. 12mo., Paris, 1743.]

[3] "Ce que les Normans avoyent pris des François." *Rec.* liv. i. p. 70. edit. 1581. [Mr. Wright very properly animadverts on the temerity of feeking the origin of romance in any one fource, or of tracing the progrefs of romance from one people to another, and illuftrates his pofition by pointing out that, while there

It is not my bufinefs, nor is it of much confequence, to difcufs this obfcure point, which properly belongs to the French antiquaries. I therefore proceed to obferve, that [William Bifhop of Ely, chancellor to] our Richard I., who [was] a diftinguifhed hero of the Crufades, a moft magnificent patron of chivalry, and a Provençal poet,[1] invited to his [mafter's] court many minftrels or troubadours from France, whom he loaded with honours and rewards.[2]   Thefe

---

is no nation which has not probably borrowed fome of its romantic literature from other nations, there is alfo none which has not a certain fhare of home-grown romance. He thinks that the Teutonic tribes poffeffed many of the *fabliaux*, before they were known to Weftern Europe.]

[1] See *Obfervations on Spenfer*, i. § i. pp. 28, 29.   And Mr. Walpole's *Royal and Noble Authors*, i. 5.   See alfo Rymer's *Short View of Tragedy*, ch. vii. p. 73. [Guilhem le Breton,] one of the Provençal poets, faid of Richard:—

> " Coblas a teira faire adroitement
> Pou voz oillez enten dompna gentiltz."

"He could make ftanzas on the eyes of gentle ladies." Rymer, *ibid.* p. 74.   There is a curious [but moft probably apocryphal] ftory recorded by the French chroniclers concerning Richard's fkill in the minftrel art. [Here, in all the editions, follows the abfurd ftory of Blondel, which is not worth repeating, efpecially as it is to be found in fo many books. It may, however, be worth while to refer the reader to M. de la Rue, *Effais fur les Fougleurs*, ii. 325-9, where Guillaume Blondel, an Anglo-Norman, is faid to have been the real Blondel, and to have been rewarded with eftates, which were reftored to his defcendant by Henry III. —Mr. Thoms' inform.] See alfo Fauchet, *Rec.* p. 93.   Richard lived long in Provence, where he acquired a tafte for their poetry.

[There is too much reafon to believe the ftory of Blondel and his illuftrious patron to be purely apocryphal. The poem publifhed by Walpole is written in the Provençal language, and a Norman verfion of it is given by M. Sifmondi, in his *Literature du Midi*, vol. i. p. 149.   In which of thefe languages it was originally compofed remains a matter of difpute among the French antiquaries.—*Price*.]

[2] "De regno Francorum cantores et joculatores muneribus allexerat." *Rog. Hoved.* Ric. i. p. 340.   Thefe gratuities were chiefly arms, clothes, horfes, and fometimes money.

It appears to have been William bifhop of Ely, chancellor to Richard I. who thus invited minftrels from France, whom he loaded with favours and prefents to fing his praifes in the ftreets. This paffage is in a letter of Hugh bifhop of Coventry, which fee alfo in Hearne's *Benedictus Abbas*, vol. ii. p. 704, *fub ann.* 1191. It appears from this letter, that he was totally ignorant of the Englifh language, *ibid.* p. 708. By his cotemporary Gyraldus Cambrenfis he is reprefented as a monfter of injuftice, impiety, intemperance, and luft. Gyraldus has left thefe anecdotes of his character, which fhew the fcandalous groffnefs of the times.   " Sed taceo quod ruminare folet, nunc clamitat Anglia tota, qualiter puella, matris induftria tam coma quam cultu puerum profeffa, fimulanfque virum verbis et vultu, ad cubiculum belluæ iftius eft perducta. Sed ftatim ut exofi illius fexus eft inventa, quanquam in fe pulcherrima, thalamique thorique deliciis valde idonea, repudiata tamen eft et abjecta. Unde et in craftino, matri filia, tam flagitiofi facinoris confcia, cum Petitionis effectu, terrifque non modicis eandem jure hæreditario contingentibus, virgo, ut venerat, eft reftituta. Tantæ nimirum intemperantiæ, et petulantiæ fuerat tam immoderatæ, quod quotidie in prandio circa finem, pretiofis tam potionibus quam cibariis ventre diftento, virga aliquantulum longa in capite aculeum præferente pueros nobiles ad menfam miniftrantes, eique propter multimodam qua fungebatur poteftatem in omnibus ad nutum obfequentes, pungere viciffim confueverit : ut eo indicio, quafi figno quodam fecretiore, quem fortius, inter alios, atque frequentius fic quafi ludicro pungebat," &c. &c.   *De Vit. Galfrid. Archiepifcop. Ebor.* apud Whart. *Angl.*

poets imported into England a great multitude of their tales and fongs; which before or about the reign of Edward II. became familiar and popular among our anceftors, who were fufficiently acquainted with the French language. The moft early notice of a profeffed book of chivalry in England, as it fhould feem, appears under the reign of Henry III., and is a curious and evident proof of the reputation and efteem in which this fort of compofition was held at that period. In the revenue roll of the twenty-firft year of that king, there is an

---

Sacr. vol. ii. p. 406. But Wharton endeavours to prove, that the charaĉter of this great prelate and ftatefman in many particulars had been mifreprefented through prejudice and envy. *Ibid.* vol. i. p. 632.

[Two metrical reliques by Richard I. were firft printed in *La Tour ténébreufe*, &c. 1705. The firft of thefe, in mixed *Romance* and Provençal, profeffes to be the veritable *chanfon* of Blondel; the other is a love-fong in Norman French. The fonnet cited by Mr. Walpole was exhibited with an Englifh verfion in Dr. Burney's *Hiftory of Mufic*, but has fince received a more graceful illuftration from the pen of Mr. George Ellis, in the laft edition of *Royal and Noble Authors.—Park.* The whole has been publifhed by M. Raynouard, in the fourth volume of his *Choix des Poefies originales des Troubadours*, a volume which had not reached me when the note, to which this is a fupplement, was fent to the prefs. Another poem by Richard I. will be found in the *Parnaffe Occitanien*, Touloufe, 1819, a publication from which the following remark has been thought worth extraĉting : " Crefcimbeni avait dit qu'il exiftait des poefies du roi Richard dans le manufcrit 3204; et la-deffus Horace Walpole le taxe d'inexaĉtitude. Cependant le firvente fe trouve au fol. 170, Ro. et 171 Ro. C'eft donc l'Anglois qui fe trompe en difant : there is no work of King Richard."—*Price.* Mr. Thoms adds, that there may be fome foundation for the ftatement in the preface to *La Tour Tenebreufe*, that the bafis of the work was a MS. communicated by the then poffeffor, and called *Chronique et Fabliaux de la compofition de Richard Roy d'Angleterre recueillis tot a nouvel et conjoints enfemblement, par le labour de Jean de Sorels l'an* 1308. Thefe fabliaux are the two which Richard is alleged to have written during his imprifonment in La Tour Tenebreufe.]

It feems the French minftrels, with whom the Song of Roland originated, were famous about this period. Muratori cites an old hiftory of Bologna, under the year 1288, by which it appears that they fwarmed in the ftreets of Italy. " Ut Cantatores Francigenarum in plateis comunis ad cantandum morari non poffent." On which words he obferves, " Colle quale parole fembra verifimile, che fieno difegnati i cantatori del favole romanze, che fpezialmente della Franzia erano portate in Italia." *Differt. Antichit. Ital.* tom. ii. c. xxix. p. 16. He adds, that the minftrels were fo numerous in France as to become a peft to the community, and that an ediĉt was iffued, about the year 1200, to fupprefs them in that kingdom. Muratori, in further proof of this point, quotes the above paffage from Hoveden, which he [alfo] mifapplies to our Richard I. But, in either fenfe, it equally fuits his argument. In the year 1334, at a feaft on Eafter Sunday, celebrated at Rimini, on occafion of fome noble Italians·receiving the honour of knighthood, more than one thoufand five hundred hiftriones are faid to have attended. " Triumphus quidem maximus fuit ibidem, &c.—Fuit etiam multitudo Hiftrionum circa mille quingentos et ultra." *Annal. Cæfenat.* tom. xiv. *Rer. Italic. Scriptor.* col. 1141. But their countries are not fpecified. In the year 1227, at a feaft in the palace of the archbifhop of Genoa, a fumptuous banquet and veftments without number were given to the minftrels or Joculatores then prefent, who came from Lombardy, Provence, Tufcany, and other countries. Caffari *Annal. Genuens.* lib. vi. p. 449, D. *apud* tom. vi. *ut fupr.* In the year 774, when Charlemagne entered Italy and found his paffage impeded, he was met by a minftrel of Lombardy, whofe fong promifed him fuccefs and viĉtory. " Contigit Joculatorem ex Longobardorum gente ad Carolum venire, et Cantiunculam a fe compofitam, rotando in confpeĉtu fuorum, cantare." Tom. ii. p. 2, ut fupr. *Chron. Monaft. Noval.* lib. iii. cap. x. p. 717, D.

entry of the expenſe of ſilver claſps and ſtuds for the king's great book of romances. This was in the year 1237. But I will give the article in its original dreſs: "Et in firmaculis hapſis et clavis argenteis ad magnum librum Romancis regis."[1] That this ſuperb volume was in French, may be partly collected from the title which they gave it: and it is highly probable that it contained [ſome of the *Round Table* romances or the *Brut*. An earlier inſtance may be pointed out in the Cloſe Rolls of King John, in 1205, where Reginald Cornhille is ordered to ſend to the king *Romancium de Hiſtoria Angliæ*.[2]] The victorious achievements of Richard I. were ſo famous in the reign of Henry III. as to be made the ſubject of a picture in the royal palace of Clarendon near Saliſbury. A circumſtance which likewiſe appears from the ſame ancient record, under the year 1246: "Et in camera regis ſubtus capellam regis apud Clarendon lambruſcanda, et muro ex tranſverſo illius cameræ amovendo et hyſtoria Antiochiæ in eadem depingenda cum duello regis Ricardi."[3] To theſe anecdotes we may add that in the Royal library at Paris there is, *Lancelot du Lac mis en François par [Walter Mapes,] du commandement d'Henri roi de Angleterre avec figures;*[4] and the ſame MS. occurs twice again in that library in three and in four volumes of the largeſt folio.[5] Which of our Henries it was who thus commanded the romance of *Lancelot au Lac* to be tranſlated [out of Latin, as is pretended,] into French, is indeed uncertain: but moſt probably it was Henry [II.][6]

---

[1] *Rot. Pip. an.* 21, *Hen. III.* [Although Warton has himſelf ſtated frequently enough that the word *romance* in early writers need mean nothing but French, yet he is continually arguing on the ſuppoſition that it muſt mean romance in our preſent acceptation of the term. The above-mentioned book was not neceſſarily a book of romances. However, the following entry in the Cloſe Roll of the 34th of the ſame reign (March 17) may refer to the ſame book, in which caſe it would ſeem to countenance Warton's ſuppoſition:—"De quodam libro liberato ad opus regine. Mandatum eſt fratri R. de Sanforde, magiſtro milicie Templi in Anglia, quod faciat habere Henrico de Warderoba, latori preſencium, ad opus Regine, quendam librum magnum, qui eſt in domo ſua Londoniis, Gallico ydiomate ſcriptum, in quo continentur Geſta Antiochie et regum et etiam aliorum." Teſte *ut ſupra.—Wright.*]

[2] [Sir F. Madden's correction. It by no means follows that the contents of this book were romances of chivalry. Any collection of French pieces, eſpecially in verſe, would at this time be called romances; and this from the language, not the ſubject.—*Douce.*]

[3] *Rot. Pip. an.* 36, *Henr. III.* Richard I. performed great feats at the ſiege of Antioch in the Cruſade. The Duellum was another of his exploits among the Saracens. Compare Walpole's *Anecd. Paint.* i. 10. Who mentions [the *Geſta Antiochiæ* above referred to]. He adds, that there was a chamber in the old palace of Weſtminſter painted with this hiſtory in the reign of Henry III., and therefore called the Antioch Chamber: and another in the Tower.

[4] Cod. 6783, fol. max. See Montfauc. *Cat. MSS.* p. 785 a.

[5] The old *Guiron le Courtois* is ſaid to be tranſlated by "Luce chevalier ſeigneur du chaſteau du Gal, [perhaps Sal., an abbreviation for Saliſberi,] voiſin prochain du Sablieres, par le commandement de tres noble et tres puiſſant prince M. le roy Henry jadis roy d'Angleterre."—*Bibl. Reg. Paris. Cod.* 7526.

[6] [With regard to the period when the proſe romances of the *Round Table* were compiled, and whether by order of King Henry II. or III., has long been a ſubject of diſcuſſion; but the writers on it have generally been too little acquainted with the ſubject to attempt to draw any certain or reaſonable concluſions. A recent

From an ingenious correspondent, who has not given me the honour of his name, and who appears to be well acquainted with the manners and literature of Spain, I have received the following notices relating to the Spanish Trovadores, of which other particulars may be seen in the old French history of Languedoc. "At the end of the second volume of Mayan's *Origines de la Lingua Espanola*, 1737, is an extract from a MS. entitled, *Libro de la Arte de Trovar, ò Gaya Sciencia, por Don Enrique de Villena*, said to exist in the library of the cathedral of Toledo, and perhaps to be found in other libraries of Spain. It has these particulars. The Trovadores had their origin at Toulouse, about the middle of the twelfth century. A Consistorio de la Gaya Sciencia was there founded by Ramon Vidal de Besalin, containing more than one hundred and twenty celebrated poets, and among these, princes, kings, and emperors. Their art was extended throughout Europe, and gave rise to the Italian and Spanish poetry, *servio el Garona de Hippocrene*. To Ramon Vidal de Besalin succeeded Jofre de Foxa, Monge negro, who enlarged the plan, and wrote what he called *Continuacion de trovar*. After him Belenguer de Troya came from Majorca, and compiled a treatise *de Figuras y Colores Rhetoricos*. And next Gul. Vedal of Majorca wrote *La Suma Vitulina*. To support the Gaya Sciencia at the poetical college of Toulouse, the King of France appropriated privileges and revenues: appointing seven Mantenedores, *que liciessen Leyes*. These constituted the Laws of Love, which were afterwards abridged by Guill. Moluier under the title *Tratado de las Flores*. Next Fray Ramon framed a system called Doctrinal, which was censured by Castilnon. From thence nothing was written in Spanish on the subject till the time of Don Enrique de Villena. So great was the credit of the Gay Science, that Don Juan, the first king of Arragon, who died 1393, sent an embassy to the king of France requesting that some Troubadours might be transmitted to teach this art in his kingdom. Accordingly two Mantenedores were dispatched from Toulouse, who founded a college for poetry in Barcelona, consisting of four Mantenedores, a cavalier, a master in theology, a master in laws, and an honourable citizen. Disputes about Don Juan's successor occasioned the removal of the college to Tortosa. But Don Ferdinand being elected king, Don Enrique de Villena was taken into his service; who restored the college, and was chosen principal. The subjects he proposed were sometimes the Praises of the Holy Virgin, of Arms, of Love, *y de buenas Costumbres*. An account of the ceremonies of their public acts then follows, in which

writer, however, M. Paulin Paris, in his account of the French MSS. preserved in the Bibliothèque du Roi, 8vo. Par. 1836, more critically considered the history of these remarkable compositions, and has produced a passage from the Chronicle of Helinand, (who brings down his work to the year 1204, and died in 1227,) which proves satisfactorily that the prose romance of the *Saint Graal* was composed in the twelfth century, a fact confirmed by the lines quoted by Warton from Fauchet. Now as Robert de Borron, who composed the *Saint Graal*, wrote also the romance of *Merlin* and the first part of *Lancelot*, we must necessarily refer the period of their composition to the reign of Henry II.—*M.*]

every compofition was recited, being written 'en papeles Damafquinos dediverfos colores, con letras de oro y de platau, et illuminaduras formofas, lo major qua cada una podio.' The beft performance had a crown of gold placed upon it ; and the author, being prefented with a *joya* or prize, received a licence to *cantar y decir in publico*. He was afterwards conducted home in form, efcorted among others by two Mantenedores, and preceded by minftrels and trumpets, where he gave an entertainment of confects and wine."

There feems to have been a fimilar eftablifhment at Amfterdam, called Rhederiicker camer, or the Chamber of Rhetoricians, mentioned by Ifaacus Pontanus, who adds, "Sunt autem hi rhetores viri amœni et poetici fpiritus, qui lingua vernacula, aut profa aut verfa oratione, comœdias, tragœdias, fubindeque et mutas perfonas, et facta maiorum notantes, magna fpectantium voluptate exhibent." [1] In the preceding chapter, he fays that this fraternity of rhetoricians erected a temporary theatre at the folemn entry of Prince Maurice into Amfterdam in 1594, where they exhibited in dumb fhow the hiftory of David and Goliah. [2] Meteranus, in his Belgic hiftory, fpeaks largely of the annual prizes, affemblies, and contefts of the guilds or colleges of the rhetoricians in Holland and the Low Countries. They anfwered in rhyme queftions propofed by the Dukes of Burgundy and Brabant. At Ghent, in 1539, twenty of thefe colleges met with great pomp, to difcufs an ethical queftion, and each gave a folution in a moral comedy, magnificently prefented in the public theatre. In 1561, the rhetorical guild of Antwerp, called the Violet, challenged all the neighbouring cities to a decifion of the fame fort. On this occafion, three hundred and forty rhetoricians of Bruffels appeared on horfeback, richly but fantaftically habited, accompanied with an infinite variety of pageantries, fports and fhows. Thefe had a garland, as a reward for the fuperior fplendour of their entry. Many days were fpent in determining the grand queftions : during which there were feaftings, bonfires, farces, tumbling, and every popular diverfion. [3]

In Benet College Library at Cambridge, there is [part of] an Englifh poem on the Sangreal and [Merlin], containing forty thoufand verfes. [4] The MS. is imperfect both at the beginning and at the end.

---

[1] *Rer. et Urb. Amft.* lib. ii. c. xvi. p. 118, ed. 1611, fol.
[2] *Ibid.* c. xv. p. 117.
[3] *Belg. Hiftor. Vniverfal.* fol. 1597, lib. i. pp. 31, 32.
[4 MS. lxxx. Edited by F. J. Furnivall for the Roxburghe Club, 1862-6, 2 vols. The reader, who is defirous of forming more correct opinions upon the fubject, is referred to M. Raynouard's *Poefies des Troubadours* (*Lexique Roman*, 1838, i.) a work which has done more towards forming a juft underftanding of the merits of Provençal poetry, and the extent and value of Provençal literature, than any publication which has hitherto appeared. The mafs of evidence there adduced in favour of the early efforts of the Provençal mufe muft effectually filence every theory attempting to confine fong and romantic fiction to any particular age or country.— *Price.* Mr. R. Taylor alfo refers us to M. Rochegude's *Parnaffe Occitanien*, 1819, Mr. E. Taylor's *Lays of the Minnefingers*, 1825, and to De la Rue's *Hift. of Northern French Poetry.*]

The title at the head of the firſt page is *Acta Arthuri Regis*, written probably by Joceline, chaplain and ſecretary to Archbiſhop Parker. The narrative, which appears to be on one continued ſubject, is divided into books or ſections of unequal length. It is a tranſlation made from Robert [de] Borron's French romance[s of the *Saint Graal* and *Merlin*] by Henry Lonelich, Skinner, a name which I never re-member to have ſeen among thoſe of the Engliſh poets. The diction is of the age of Henry VI. Borel, in his *Treſor de Recherches et Antiquitez Gauloiſes et Francoiſes*, ſays, "Il y'a un Roman ancien in-titule le Conqueſte de Sangreall," &c. [In the recent edition of the *Saint Graal*] Robert [de] Borron's French [proſe] romance [is printed in parallel columns with Lonelich's tranſlation]. The dili-gence and accuracy of Mr. Naſmith have furniſhed me with the following tranſcript from Lonelich's tranſlation in Benet College Library :—

> Thanne paſſeth forth this ſtorye with al,
> That is cleped of ſom men Seynt Graal;
> Alſo the Sank Ryal iclepid it is
> Of mochel peple with owten mys.
>
> .   .   .   .   .
>
> Now of al this ſtorie have I mad an ende
> That is ſchwede of Celidoygne, and now forthere to wend,
> And of anothir brawnche moſt we begynne,
> Of the ſtorye that we clepen prophet Merlynne,
> Wiche that Maiſter Robert of Borrown
> Owt of Latyn it tranſletted hol and ſoun ;
> Onlich into the langage of Frawnce
> This ſtorie he drowgh be adventure and chaunce ;
> And doth Merlynne inſten with Sank Ryal,
> For the ton ſtorie the tothir medlyth withal,
> After the ſatting of the forſeid Robert
> That ſomtym is tranſletted in Middilerd.
> And I, as an unkonneng man trewely,
> Into Engliſch have drawen this ſtorye ;
> And thowgh that to ȝow not pleſyng it be,
> ȝit that ful excuſed ȝe wolde haven me
> Of my neclegence and unkonnenge,
> On me to taken ſwich a thinge,
> Into owre modris tonge for to endite,
> The ſwettere to ſowne to more and lyte,
> And more cler to ȝoure undirſtondyng
> Thanne owthir Frenſh other Latyn to my ſuppoſing.
> And therfore atte the ende of this ſtorye
> A pater noſter ȝe wolden for me preye,
> For me that Herry Lonelich hyhte ;
> And greteth owre lady ful of myhte.
> Hartelich with an ave that ȝe hir bede,
> This proceſſe the bettere I myhte procede,
> And bringen this book to a good ende :
> Now thereto Jeſu Criſt grace me ſende,
> And than an ende there offen myhte be,
> Now good Lord graunt me for charite.
>
> .   .   .   .   .
>
> Thanne Merlyn to Blaſye cam anon,
> And there to hym he ſeide thus ſon :
> " Blaſye, thou ſchalt ſuffren gret peyne

This ſtorye to an ende to bringen certeyne ;
And ȝit ſchall I ſuffren mochel more."
How ſo, Merlyn, quod Blaſye there.
" I ſhall be ſowht," quod Merlyne tho,
" Owt from the weſt with meſſengeris mo,
And they that ſcholen comen to ſeken me,
They have maad ſewrawnce, I telle the,
Me forto ſlen for any thing,
This ſewrawnce hav they mad to her kyng.
But whanne they me ſen, and with me ſpeke,
No power they ſchol hav on me to ben awreke,
For with hem hens moſte I gon,
And thou into othir partyes ſchalt wel ſon,
To hem that hav the holy veſſel
Which that is icleped the Seynt Graal ;
And wete thow wel and ek ſorſothe,
That thow and ek this ſtorye bothe
Ful wel beherd now ſchall it be,
And alſo beloved in many contre ;
And has that will knowen in ſertaygne
What kynges that weren in grete Bretaygne
Sithan that Chriſtendom thedyr was browht,
They ſcholen hem fynde has ſo that it ſawht
In the ſtorye of Brwttes book ;
There ſcholen ȝe it fynde and ȝe weten look,
Which that Martyn de Bewre tranſlated here
From Latyn into Romaunce in his manere.
But leve me now of Brwttes book,
And aftyr this ſtorye now lete us look.

After this latter extract, which is to be found nearly in the middle of the MS., [the romance of *Merlin* begins, and] the ſcene and perſonages of the poem are changed ; and King Evalach, King Mordreins, Sir Naſciens, Joſeph of Arimathea, and the other heroes of the former part, give place to King Arthur, King Brangors, King Loth, and the monarchs and champions of the Britiſh line. In a paragraph, very ſimilar to the ſecond of theſe extracts, the following note is written in the hand of the text, " Henry Lonelich, Skynner, that tranſlated this boke out of Frenſhe into Englyſhe, at the inſtaunce of Harry Barton."

The *Queſt of the Sangreal*, as it is called, in which devotion and necromancy are equally concerned, makes a conſiderable part of King Arthur's romantic hiſtory, and was one grand object of the knights of the Round Table. He who achieved this hazardous adventure was to be placed there in the " ſiege perillous," or ſeat of danger. " When Merlyn had ordayned the rounde table, he ſaid, by them that be fellowes of the rounde table the truthe of the Sangreall ſhall be well knowne, &c.—They which heard Merlyn ſay ſoe, ſaid thus to Merlyn, Sithence there ſhall be ſuch a knight, thou ſhouldeſt ordayne by thy craft a ſiege that no man ſhould ſitte therein, but he onlie which ſhall paſſe all other knights.—Then Merlyn made the ſiege perillous," &c.[1] Sir Lancelot, " who is come but of the eighth degree from our Lord Jeſus Chriſt," is repreſented as the chief adventurer in this honourable expedition.[2] At a celebration of the

---

[1] [Maloɩy's] *Mort d'Arthur*, B. xiv. c. 2.   [2] *Ibid.* B. iii. c. 35.

feaft of Pentecoft at Camelot by King Arthur, the Sangreal fuddenly enters the hall, " but there was no man might fee it nor who bare it," and the knights, as by fome invifible power, are inftantly fupplied with a feaft of the choiceft difhes.[1] Originally *Le Brut, Lancelot, Triftan,* and the *Saint Greal* were feparate hiftories ; but they were [fubfequently brought into a certain degree of connection— perhaps at a very early date, and fome confufion may alfo have arifen from the careleffnefs or ignorance of copyifts]. The book of the *Sangreal,* a feparate work, is referred to in *Morte Arthur.* "Now after that the queft of the *Sancgreall* was fulfylled, and that all the knyghtes that were lefte alive were come agayne to the Rounde Table, as the booke of the Sancgreall makethe mencion, than was there grete joye in the courte. And efpeciallie King Arthur and quene Guenever made grete joye of the remnaunt that were come home. And paffynge glad was the kinge and quene of fyr Launcelot and fyr Bors, for they had been paffynge longe awaye in the queft of the Sancgreall. Then, as the Frenfhe booke fayeth, fyr Lancelot," &c.[2] And again, in the fame romance : " Whan fyr Bors had tolde him [Arthur] of the adventures of the Sancgreall, fuch as had befallen hym and his felawes,—all this was made in grete bookes, and put in almeryes at Salifbury."[3] The former part of this paffage is almoft literally tranflated from one in the French romance of *Triftan.*[4] " Quant Boort ot conte laventure del Saint Graal teles com eles eftoient avenues, eles furent mifes en efcrit, gardees en lamere de Salifbieres, *dont Meftre Galtier Map l'eftreft a faift fon livre du Saint Graal por lamor du roy Herri fon fengor, qui fift leftoire tralater del Latin en romanz.*"[5] In the Royal Library at Paris there is *Le Roman de Triftan et Ifeult, traduit de Latin en François, par Lucas, Chevalier du Gaft pres de Sarifberi, Anglois, avec figures.*[6] And again,[7] *Liveres de Triftan mis en François par Lucas chevalier fieur de chateau du Gat.*[8] *Almeryes* in the Englifh, and *l'Amere,* properly *aumoire* in the French, mean, I believe, *Preffes, Chefts,* or *Archives. Ambry,* in this fenfe, is not an uncommon old Englifh word. From the fecond part of the firft

---

[1] [Malory's] *Mort d'Arthur,* B. iii. c. 35.　　　[2] B. xviii. cap. 1.

[3] B. xvii. c. 23. The romance fays that King Arthur " made grete clerkes com before him that they fhould cronicle the adventures of thefe goode knygtes." [See *infra,* Section xi.]

[4] Bibl. Reg. MSS. 20 D. ii. fol. antep.

[5] See *infra,* fect. xxviii. note. [No doubt the " chaftel de Gaft-prés de Salifberi " is referred to here as well as in the next paragraph; it appears to have been in the canton of St. Severe, in the department of Calvados.—De la Rue, *Effais fur les Bardes,* &c., vol. ii. p. 231, quoted by Sir F. Madden. See efpecially M. Paulin Paris's introduction to his *Romans de la Table Ronde mis en nouveau Langage,* Paris, 1868.—*F.*]

[6] Montfauc. Catal. MSS. Cod. Reg. Paris, Cod. 6776, fol. max.

[7] Cod. 6956, fol. max.

[8] There is printed, *Le Roman du noble et vaillant Chevalier Triftan fils du noble roy Meliadus de Leonnoys, par Luce, chevalier, feigneur du chafteau de Gaft.* Rouen, 1489, fol. [But fee Brunet, *dern.* edit. v. 955. All the poems relating to this hero were collected by M. Michel, 3 vols. 12mo.]

French quotation which I have diftinguifhed by italics, it appears that Walter Mapes,[1] a learned archdeacon in England, under the reign of Henry II., wrote a French *Sangreal*, which he tranflated from Latin, by the command of that monarch. Under the idea that Walter Mapes was a writer on this fubject, and in the fabulous way, fome critics may be induced to think, that the Walter, Archdeacon of Oxford, from whom Geoffrey of Monmouth profeffes to have received the materials of his hiftory, was this Walter Mapes, and not Walter Calenius, who was alfo an eminent fcholar, and an archdeacon of Oxford. Geoffrey fays in his Dedication to Robert Earl of Gloucefter, "Finding nothing faid in Bede or Gildas of King Arthur and his fucceffors, although their actions highly deferved to be recorded in writing, and are orally celebrated by the Britifh bards, I was much furprifed at fo ftrange an omiffion. At length Walter, archdeacon of Oxford, a man of great eloquence, and learned in foreign hiftories, offered me an ancient book in the Britifh or Armorican tongue which, in one unbroken ftory and an elegant diction, related the deeds of the Britifh kings from Brutus to Cadwallader. At his requeft, although unufed to rhetorical flourifhes, and contented with the fimplicity of my own plain language, I undertook the tranflation of that book into Latin."[2] Some writers fuppofe that Geoffrey pretended to have received his materials from Archdeacon Walter, by way of authenticating his romantic hiftory. Thefe notices feem to difprove that fufpicion. In the year 1488, a French romance was publifhed, in two magnificent folio volumes, entitled *Hiftoire de Roy Artus et des Chevaliers de la Table Ronde.* The firft volume was printed at Rouen, the fecond at Paris. It contains in four detached parts the Birth and Achievements of King Arthur, the Life of Sir Launcelot, the Adventure of the Sangreal, and the Death of Arthur and his Knights. In the body of the work, this romance more than once is faid to be written by Walter Map or Mapes, and by the command of his mafter King Henry. For inftance :[3] "Cy fine Maiftre Gualtier Map fon traittie du Saint Graal." Again :[4] "Apres ce que Maiftre Gualtier Map eut tractie des avantures du Saint Graal affez foufifamment, ficomme il luy fembloit, il fut ad adviz au roy Henry fon feigneur, que ce quil avoit fait ne debuit foufrire fil ne racontoys la fin de ceulx dont il fait mention.—Et commence Maiftre Gualtier en telle manier cefte derniere partie." This derniere partie treats of the death of King Arthur and his knights. At the end of the fecond tome there is this colophon : "Cy fine le dernier volume de La Table Ronde,

---

[1] [From a paffage in the French romance of *Lancelot du Lac,* M. Roquefort is of opinion that there were two perfons of this name. In that he is ftyled "meffire Gautier Map qui fut chevalier le roi." But fo much confufion prevails upon this fubject, that it is almoft impoffible to name the author of any profe romance.—*Price.*]

[2] B. i. ch. i. See alfo B. xii. ch. xx.

[3] Tom. ii. fign. Dd i. end of *Partie du Saint Graal.*

[4] Tom. ii. ch. i. fign. D d ii. (*La derniere partie*).

faifant mencion des fais et proeffes de monfeigneur Launcelot du Lac et dautres plufieurs nobles et vaillans hommes fes compagnons. Compile et extraict precifement et au jufte des vrayes hiftoires faifantes de ce mencion par trefnotable et trefexpert hiftorien Maiftre Gualtier Map," &c. The paffage quoted above from the royal MS. in the Britifh Mufeum, where King Arthur orders the adventures of the Sangreal to be chronicled, is thus reprefented in this romance : " Et quant Boort eut compte depuis le commencement jufques a la fin les avantures du Saint Graal telles comme il les avoit veues, &c. Si fift le roy Artus rediger et mettre par efcript aus dictz clers tout ci que Boort avoit compte," &c.[1] At the end of the royal MS. at Paris,[2] entitled *Lancelot du Lac mis en François par Robert de Borron par le commandement de Henri roi d'Angleterre*, it is faid that Meffire Robert de Borron tranflated into French not only Lancelot, but alfo the ftory of the *Saint Graal:* " Li tout du Latin du Gautier Mappe." The French antiquaries in this fort of literature are of opinion that the word Latin here fignifies Italian, and that by this Latin of Gualtier Mapes we are to underftand Englifh verfions of thofe romances made from the Italian language; [but fuch a notion feems fcarcely deferving of ferious difcuffion.] The French hiftory of the *Sangreal*, printed at Paris in 1516, is faid in the title to be tranflated from Latin into French rhymes, and from thence into French profe by Robert [de] Borron. This romance was reprinted in 1523.

[Malory's] *Morte Arthur*, finifhed in the year 1469, [is an abftract of certain old French Arthur romances.][3] But the matter of the whole is fo much of the fame fort, and the heroes and adventures of one ftory are fo mutually and perpetually blended with thofe of another, that no real unity or diftinction is preferved. It confifts of twenty-one books. The firft feven books treat of King Arthur. The eighth, ninth, and tenth, of Sir Triftram. The eleventh and twelfth, of Sir Lancelot.[4] The thirteenth of the Saingral, which is alfo called Sir Lancelot's book. The fourteenth, of Sir Percival. The fifteenth, again, of Sir Launcelot. The fixteenth, of Sir Gawaine. The feventeenth, of Sir Galahad. [But all the four laft-mentioned books are alfo called the *hiftorye of the holy Sancgreall*.] The eighteenth and nineteenth, of mifcellaneous adventures. The two laft, of

---

[1] *Ibid.* tom. ii. *La Partie du Saint Graal*, ch. *ult.* Juft before it is faid, " Le roy Artus fift venir les clercs qui les aventures aux chevallieres mettoient en efcript" —as in *Mort d'Arthur*.

[2] *Cod.* 6783.

[3] [The only MS. exhibiting in French the ftory of *Balin and Balan*, which Sir Thomas Malory has in his Englifh, (printed by Caxton in 1485,) is at prefent in the poffeffion of Mr. Henry Huth. It is a folio volume on vellum, with initial letters, but no miniatures. Three or four leaves, including the firft, are deficient. It exhibits in thofe parts where it covers the fame ground as the Englifh work, marked variations from the latter. This MS. is in preparation for the prefs by Mr. Furnivall.]

[4] But at the end, this twelfth book is called " the fecond booke of *Syr Tryftram*." And it is added, " But here is no reherfall of the thyrd booke [of *Sir Triftram*."]

King Arthur and all the knights.   Lwhyd mentions a Welfh Sangreall which, he fays, contains various fables of King Arthur and
his knights, &c.[1]   *Morte Arthur* is often literally tranflated[2] from
various and very ancient detached hiftories of the heroes of the
round table, which I have examined; and on the whole, it nearly
refembles Walter Map's romance above mentioned, printed at Rouen
and Paris, both in matter and difpofition.

I take this opportunity of obferving, that a very valuable vellum
fragment of *Le Brut*, of which the writing is uncommonly beautiful
and of high antiquity, containing part of the ftory of Merlin and
King Vortigern, covers a MS. of Chaucer's *Aftrolabe*, prefented,
together with feveral Oriental MSS., to the Bodleian library by
Thomas Hedges, of Alderton in Wiltfhire; a gentleman poffeffed
of many curious MSS. and Greek and Roman coins, and moft
liberal in his communications.

But not only the pieces of the French minftrels, written in French,
were circulated in England about this time, but tranflations of thefe
pieces were made into Englifh which, containing much of the French
idiom, together with a fort of poetical phrafeology before unknown,
produced various innovations in our ftyle.   Thefe tranflations, it is
probable, were enlarged with additions, or improved with alterations
of the ftory.   Hence it was that Robert de Brunne, as we have already feen, complained of ftrange and quaint Englifh, of the changes
made in the ftory of *Sir Triftram*, and of the liberties affumed by his
cotemporary minftrels in altering facts and coining new phrafes.   Yet
thefe circumftances enriched our tongue, and extended the circle of
our poetry.   And for what reafon thefe fables were fo much admired
and encouraged, in preference to the languid poetical chronicles of
Robert of Gloucefter and Robert of Brunne, it is obvious to conjecture.   The gallantries of chivalry were exhibited with new fplendour,
and the times were growing more refined.   The Norman fafhions
were adopted even in Wales.   In the year 1176, a fplendid caroufal,
after the manner of the Normans, was given by a Welfh prince.
This was Rhees ap Gryffyth king of South Wales, who at Chriftmas made a great feaft in the caftle of Cardigan, then called Aber-
Teify, which he ordered to be proclaimed throughout all Britain; and
to " which came many ftrangers, who were honourably received and
worthily entertained, fo that no man departed difcontented.   And
among deeds of arms and other fhewes, Rhees caufed all the poets of
Wales[3] to come thither; and provided chairs for them to be fet in

---

[1] *Archæolog. Brit.* Tit. vii. p. 265, col. 2.   [It is only a tranflation of Map's
French *Quefte del Saint Graal.*]
[2] [In Hoffmann's *Horæ Belgicæ*, 1830, according to Mr. R. Taylor, is an
account of various Flemifh verfions of thefe romances.]
[3] In illuftration of the argument purfued in the text we may obferve, that about
this time the Englifh minftrels flourifhed with new honours and rewards.   At the
magnificent marriage of [Joan Plantagenet, grand-]daughter of Edward I., every
king minftrel received xl. fhillings.   See Anftis, *Ord. Gart.* ii. p. 303; and Dugd.
Mon. i. 355.   In the fame reign a multitude of minftrels attended the ceremony of
knighting Prince Edward on the Feaft of Pentecoft.   They enter·d the hall, while

his hall, where they fhould difpute together to try their cunning and gift in their feveral faculties, where great rewards and rich giftes were appointed for the overcomers.[1]" Tilts and tournaments, after a long difufe, revived with fuperior luftre in the reign of Edward I. Roger [de] Mortimer, a magnificent baron of that reign, erected in his ftately caftle of Kenilworth a Round Table, at which he reftored the rites of King Arthur. He entertained in this caftle the conftant retinue of one hundred knights and as many ladies, and invited thither adventurers in chivalry from every part of Chriftendom.[2] Thefe fables were therefore an image of the manners, cuftoms, mode of life, and favourite amufements, which now prevailed not only in France but in England, accompanied with all the decorations which fancy could invent, and recommended by the graces of romantic fiction. They complimented the ruling paffion of the times, and cherifhed in a high degree the fafhionable fentiments of ideal honour and fantaftic fortitude.

Among Richard's French minftrels, the names only of three are recorded. I have already mentioned Blondel de Nefle. Fouquet of Marfeilles[3] and [Gauç]elme Fayditt,[4] many of whofe compofitions

---

the king was fitting at dinner furrounded with the new knights. Nic. Trivet. *Annal.* p. 342, edit. Oxon. The whole number knighted was two hundred and fixty-feven. Dugd. *Bar.* i. 80, b. Robert de Brunne fays this was the greateft royal feaft fince King Arthur's at Carleon, concerning which he adds, "thereof yit men *rime*," p. 332. In the wardrobe-roll of the fame prince, under the year 1306, we have this entry: "Will. Fox et Cradoco focio fuo cantatoribus cantantibus coram Principe et aliis magnatibus in comitiva fua exiftente apud London, &c. xx *s*." Again, "Willo Ffox et Cradoco focio fuo cantantibus in præfentia principis et al. Magnatum apud London de dono ejufdem dni per manus Johis de Ringwode, &c. 8 die jan. xx *s*." Afterwards, in the fame roll, four fhillings are given, "Miniftrallo comitiffæ Marefchal. facienti meneftralciam fuam coram principe, &c. in comitiva fua exiftent. apud Penreth." *Comp. Garderob. Edw. Princip. Wall.* ann. 35 Edw .I. This I chiefly cite to fhew the greatnefs of the gratuity. Minftrels were part of the eftablifhment of the houfeholds of our nobility before the year 1307. Thomas Earl of Lancafter allows at Chriftmas cloth, or *veftis liberata*, to his houfehold minftrels at a great expence, in the year 1314. Stow's *Surv. Lond.* p. 134, edit. 1618. See *fupr.* Soon afterwards the minftrels claimed fuch privileges that it was thought neceffary to reform them by an edict in 1315. See Hearne's *Append. Leland. Collectan.* vi. 36. Yet, as I have formerly remarked in Obfervations on Spenfer's *Faerie Queene*, we find a perfon in the character of a minftrel entering Weftminfter-hall on horfeback while Edward I. was folemnizing the feaft of Pentecoft as above, and prefenting a letter to the king. See Walfing. *Hift. Angl. Franc.* p. 109.

[1] Powell's *Wales*, 237, edit. 1584. Who adds, that the bards of "Northwales won the prize, and amonge the muficians Rees's owne houfhold men were counted beft." Rhees was one of the Welfh princes who, the preceding year, attended the Parliament at Oxford, and were magnificently entertained in the caftle of that city by Henry II. Lord Lyttelton's *Hift. Hen. II.* edit. iii. p. 302. It may not be foreign to our prefent purpofe to mention here, that Henry II., in the year 1179, was entertained by Welfh bards at Pembroke caftle in Wales, in his paffage into Ireland. Powell, *ut fupr.* p. 238. The fubject of their fongs was the hiftory of King Arthur. See Selden on *Polyolb.* s. iii. p. 53.

[2] Drayton's *Heroic. Epift.* Mort. Ifabel. v. 53. And Notes *ibid.* from Walfingham.

[3] Mr. Thoms refers us to Diez (*Leben und Werke der Troubadours*, f. 234-51) for

ſtill remain, were alſo among the poets patroniſed and entertained in
England by Richard. They are both celebrated and ſometimes imitated by Dante and Petrarch. Fayditt, a native of Avignon, united
the profeſſions of muſic and verſe ; and the Provençals uſed to call
his poetry *de bon mots e de bon ſon.* Petrarch is ſuppoſed to have copied, in his *Triomfo d'Amore,* many ſtrokes of high imagination from
a poem written by Fayditt on a ſimilar ſubjeét ; particularly in his
deſcription of the Palace of Love. But Petrarch has not left Fayditt
without his due panegyric : he ſays that Fayditt's tongue was ſhield,
helmet, ſword, and ſpear.[1] He is likewiſe in Dante's *Paradiſo.* Fayditt was extremely profuſe and voluptuous. On the death of King
Richard, he travelled on foot for nearly twenty years, ſeeking his
fortune ; and during this long pilgrimage he married a nun of Aix in
Provence, who was young and lively, and could accompany her huſband's tales and ſonnets with her voice. Fouquet de Marſeilles
had a beautiful perſon, a ready wit, and a talent for ſinging ; theſe
popular accompliſhments recommended him to the courts of King
Richard, Raymond, count of Touloufe, and Beral de Baulx ; where,
as the French would ſay, *il ſit les delices de cour.* He fell in love with
Adelaſia the wife of Beral, whom he celebrated in his ſongs. One
of his poems is entitled, *Las complanchas de Beral.* On the death of
all his lords, he received abſolution for his ſin of poetry, turned monk,
and at length was made Archbiſhop of Touloufe.[2] But among the

---

an account of Fouquet. Twenty-five of his ſongs are extant, of which two are
printed in Raynouard's *Lexique Romain,* i. 341-5).]

[[4] See Raynouard, *Lexique,* ed. 1838, i. 368. Mr. Thoms remarks that the ob-
jeét of Fayditt's admiration and poetical ardour was Maria de Ventadour, daughter
of Boſo II. and wife of Ebles IV. Vicomte de Ventadour, " a lady of refined taſte
in poetry, and celebrated by the troubadours and their hiſtorians as the nobleſt of
her ſex." A confiderable number of Fayditt's pieces is extant.]

[1] Triunf. Am. c. iv.

[2] See Beauchamps, *Recherch. Theatr. Fr.* 1735, pp. 7, 9. It was Jeffrey, Richard's
brother, who patroniſed Jeffrey Rudell, a famous troubadour of Provence, who is
alſo celebrated by Petrarch. This poet had heard, from the adventurers in the Cruſades, the beauty of a Counteſs of Tripoli highly extolled. He became enamoured
from imagination ; embarked for Tripoli, fell ſick in the voyage through the fever
of expeétation, and was brought on ſhore at Tripoly half expiring. The counteſs,
having received the news of the arrival of this gallant ſtranger, haſtened to the
ſhore and took him by the hand. He opened his eyes, and, at once overpowered
by his diſeaſe and her kindneſs, had juſt time to ſay inarticulately that, having ſeen
her, he died ſatisfied. The counteſs made him a moſt ſplendid funeral, and ereéted
to his memory a tomb of porphyry, inſcribed with an epitaph in Arabian verſe.
She commanded his ſonnets to be richly copied and illuminated with letters of gold ;
was ſeized with a profound melancholy, and turned nun. I will endeavour to tranſlate one of the ſonnets which he made on his voyage. *Yrat et dolent m'en partray,*
&c. It has ſome pathos and ſentiment, " I ſhould depart penſive, but for this love
of mine *ſo far away ;* for I know not what difficulties I have to encounter, my native land being *ſo far away.* Thou who haſt made all things, and who formed this
love of mine *ſo far away,* give me ſtrength of body, and then I may hope to ſee
this love of mine *ſo far away.* Surely my love muſt be founded on true merit, as I
love one *ſo far away !* If I am eaſy for a moment, yet I feel a thouſand pains for
her who is *ſo far away.* No other love ever touched my heart than this for her *ſo*

many French minftrels invited into England by Richard, it is natural
to fuppofe, that fome of them made their magnificent and heroic
patron a principal fubjeƈt of their compofitions.¹ And this fubjeƈt,
by means of the conftant communication between both nations, probably oecame no lefs fafhionable in France; efpecially if we take
into the account the general popularity of Richard's charaƈter, his
love of chivalry, his gallantry in the Crufades, and the favours which
he fo liberally conferred on the minftrels of that country. We have
a romance now remaining in Englifh rhyme, which celebrates the
achievements of this illuftrious monarch. It is entitled *Richard Cuer
de Lyon*, and was probably tranflated from the French about the
[reign of Edward I.] That it was, at leaft, tranflated from the
French, appears from the prologue :

> In Fraunce thefe rymes were wroht,
> Every Englyfhe ne knew it not.

From which alfo we may gather the popularity of his ftory, in thefe
lines :

> King Richard is the befte
> That is found in any gefte.

[It was printed by W. de Worde in 1509 and 1528.]² That this romance, either in French or Englifh, exifted before the year 1300, is
evident from its being cited by Robert of Gloucefter, in his relation
of Richard's reign :

> In Romance of him imade me it may finde iwrite.³

This tale is alfo mentioned as a romance of fome antiquity among
other famous romances, in the prologue of a voluminous metrical
tranflation of Guido de Colonna, [wrongly] attributed to Lidgate.⁴

---

far away. A fairer than fhe never touched any heart, either near, or *far away.*"
Every fourth line ends with *du luench.* See Noftradamus, &c.
[The original poem, of which the above is only a fragment, will be found in the
third volume of M. Raynouard's *Choix des Poefies Originales des Troubadours.*
[*Lexique Roman,* 1838, i. 341.] The feeming inaccuracies of Warton's tranflation
may have arifen from the varied readings of his original text. The fragment publifhed by M. Sifmondi differs effentially from the larger poem given by M. Raynouard.—*Price.*]
¹ Fayditt is faid to have written a *Chant funèbre* on his death. Beauchamps,
ibid. p. 10.
[For fpecimens of the poetry of Fouquet de Marfeilles and Gauçelm Faidit the
reader is referred to the firft volume of M. Raynouard's excellent work already
noticed. The fecond volume of the old edition contains a profe tranflation of
Faidit's *Planh* on the death of Richard I.—*Price.*]
² There is a MS. copy of it in Caius College, Cambridge.
³ *Chron.* p. 487.
⁴ " " Many fpeken of men that romaunces rede," &c.
> " Of Bevys, Gy, and Gawayne,
> Of Kyng Rychard, and Owayne,
> Of Triftram, and Percyvayle,
> Of Rowland ris, and Aglavaule,
> Of Archeroun, and of Oƈtavian,
> Of Charles, and of Caffibelan,
> Of K[H]eveloke, Horne, and of Wade,
> In romances that of hem bi made

It is likewife frequently quoted by Robert de Brunne, who wrote much about the fame time with Robert of Gloucefter :

> Whan Philip tille Acres cam, litelle was his dede,
> The Romance fais gret fham who fo that pas[1] will rede.
> The Romancer it fais Richard did make a pele.[2]—
> The Romance of Richard fais he wan the toun.[3]—

> That geftours dos of him geftes
> At mangeres and at great feftes,
> Here dedis ben in remembraunce
> In many fair romaunce.
> But of the worthieft wyght in wede,
> That ever byftrod any ftede,
> Spekes no man, ne in romaunce redes,
> Off his battayle ne of his dedes;
> Off that battayle fpekes no man,
> There all prowes of knyghtes began,
> Thet was forfothe of the batayle
> Thet at Troye was faunfayle,
> Of fwythe a fyght as ther was one, &c.
> For ther were in thet on fide,
> Sixti kynges and dukes of pride.—
> And there was the beft bodi in dede
> That ever yit wered wede,
> Sithen the world was made fo ferre,
> That was Ector in eche werre," &c.

Laud. K 76 [595], f. 1, MSS. Bibl. Bodl. Cod. membr. [There is no authority, as Sir F. Madden has ftated, for attributing this to Lydgate.] Whether this poem was written by Lidgate, I fhall not enquire at prefent. I fhall only fay here, that it is totally different from either of Lidgate's two poems on the Theban and Trojan Wars; and that the manufcript, which is beautifully written, appears to be of the age of Henry VI.

By the way, it appears from this quotation that there was an old romance called *Wade.* Wade's *Bote* is mentioned in Chaucer's *Marchaunts Tale*, v. 940 :

> " And eke thefe olde wivis, god it wote,
> They connin fo much crafte in Wadis bote."

Again *Troil. Crefs.* iii. 615 :

> " He fonge, fhe plaide, he tolde a tale of Wade."

Where, fays the gloffarift, "A romantick ftory, famous at that time, of one Wade, who performed many ftrange exploits, and met with many wonderful adventures in his boat *Guigelot.*" Speght fays that Wade's hiftory was *long* and *fabulous.*

[The ftory of Wade is alfo alluded to in the following paffage taken from the romance of Sir Bevis :

> " Swiche bataile ded neuer non
> Criftene man of flefch and bon—
> Of a dragoun thar befide,
> That Beues flough ther in that tide,
> Saue Sire Launcelot de Lake,
> He faught with a fur-drake,
> And Wade dede alfo,
> And neuer knightes boute thai to."—*Price.*

A perfonage of fimilar name occurs in the *Vilkina Saga* and in the *Scôp, or Gleeman's Tale*, l. 46. The Englifh myth is referred to in the metrical *Morte Arthure*, edited by Halliwell, 1847, and again for the Early Englifh Text Society. M. Michel has publifhed a *brochure*, entitled *Wade : Lettre a M. Henri Ternaux-Compans, &c. fur une Tradition Angloife du Moyen Age.* Paris, 1837. 8vo.]

[1] Paffus. Compare Percy's *Reliques*, ii. 66, 398, edit. 1767.
[2] Percy's *Rel.* ii. p. 157.   [3] *Ibid.*

He tellis in the Romance fen Acres wonnen was
How God gaf him fair chance at the bataile of Caifas.[1]—
Sithen at Japhet was flayn fauelle his ftede
The Romans tellis gret pas of his douhty dede.[2]—
Soudan fo curteys never drank no wyne,
The fame the Romans fais that is of Richardyn.[3]
In prifoun was he bounden, as the Romance fais,
In cheynes and lede wonden, that hevy was of peis.[4]

I am not indeed quite certain, whether or no in fome of thefe inftances, Robert de Brunne may not mean his French original Peter
Langtoft. But in the following lines he manifeftly refers to our
romance of *Richard*, between which and Langtoft's chronicle he
exprefsly makes a diftinction. And in the conclufion of the reign:

I knowe no more to ryme of dedes of kyng Richard:
Who fo wille his dedes all the fothe fe,
The romance that men reden, ther is propirte.
This that I have faid it is Pers fawe.[5]
Als he in romance[6] lad, ther after gan I drawe.[7]

It is not improbable that both thefe rhyming chroniclers cite from
the Englifh tranflation: if fo, we may fairly fuppofe that this romance
was tranflated in the reign of Edward I. This circumftance throws
the French original to a ftill higher period.

In the Royal Library at Paris there is *Hiftoire de Richard Roi
d'Angleterre et de Maquemore d'Irlande en rime.*[8] Richard is the laft
of our monarchs whofe achievements were adorned by fiction and
fable. If not a fuperftitious belief of the times, it was an hyperbolical invention ftarted by the minftrels, which foon grew into a
tradition, and is gravely recorded by the chroniclers, that Richard
carried with him to the Crufades King Arthur's celebrated fword
Caliburn, and that he prefented it as a gift or relic of ineftimable
value, to Tancred King of Sicily, in the year 1191.[9] Robert of
Brunne calls this fword a *jewel*.[10]

And Richard at that time gaf him a faire juelle,
The gude fwerd Caliburne which Arthur luffed fo well.[11]

---

[1] p. 175. [Warton's conjecture is perfectly correct in moft of thefe inftances.
They contain allufions to circumftances which are unnoticed by Langtoft.—
Price.]

[2] Percy's *Rel.* ii. p. 175.   [3] *Ibid.* p. 188.   [4] p. 198.
[5] "The words of my original *Peter Langtoft.*"   [6] In French.
[7] p. 205. Du Cange recites an old French MS. profe romance, entitled *Hiftoire
de la Mort de Richard Roy d'Angleterre. Glofs. Lat. Ind. Auct.* i. p. cxci. [But this
is upon the depofition of Richard II.] There was one, perhaps the fame, among
the MSS. of Martin of Palgrave.

[8] Num. 7532. [An account of this hiftorical poem will be found in Mr.
Strutt's *Regal Antiquities.* It relates entirely to the Irifh wars of Richard II. and
the latter part of the reign of that unfortunate monarch.—*Price.* The poem is
printed entire in *Archæologia*, xx.]

[9] In return for feveral veffels of gold and filver, horfes, bales of filk, four great
fhips, and fifteen galleys, given by Tancred. Benedict. Abb. p. 642, edit. Hearne.

[10] *Jocale.* In the general and true fenfe of the word. Robert de Brunne, in
another place, calls a rich pavilion a *jowelle*, p. 152.

[11] *Chron.* p. 153. [Sir F. Madden refers for an account of *Caliburne* to M.
Michel's *Triftan*, lxxxv.]

Indeed the Arabian writer of the life of the Sultan Saladin mentions some exploits of Richard almoſt incredible. But, as Lord Lyttelton juſtly obſerves, this hiſtorian is highly valuable on account of the knowledge he had of the faĉts which he relates. It is from this writer we learn, in the moſt authentic manner, the aĉtions and negotiations of Richard in the courſe of the enterpriſe for the recovery of the Holy Land, and all the particulars of that memorable war.[1]

But before I produce a ſpecimen of Richard's Engliſh romance, I ſtand ſtill to give ſome more extraĉts from its prologues, which contain matter much to our preſent purpoſe : as they have very fortunately preſerved the ſubjeĉts of many romances, perhaps metrical, then faſhionable both in France and England. And on theſe therefore, and their origin, I ſhall take this opportunity of offering ſome remarks :

> Fele romanſes men make newe
> Of good knyghtes ſtrong and trewe :
> Of hey dedys men rede romance,
> Bothe in England and in Fraunce ;
> Of Rowelond and of Olyver,
> And of everie Doſeper,[2]
> Of Alyſander and Charlemain,
> Of Kyng Arthor and of Gawayn ;
> How they wer knyghtes good and curteys,
> Of Turpyn and of Ocier Daneys.
> Of Troye men rede in ryme,
> What werre ther was in olde tyme ;
> Of Eĉtor and of Achylles,
> What folk they ſlewe in that pres, &c.[3]

And again, in a ſecond prologue, after a pauſe has been made by the minſtrel in the courſe of ſinging the poem :

> Now hearkenes to my tale ſothe,
> Though I ſwere yow an othe
> I wole reden romaunces non
> Of Paris,[4] ne of Ypomydone,
> Of Aliſaundre, ne Charlemagne,
> Of Arthour, ne of ſere Gawain,
> Nor of ſere Launcelot the Lake,
> Of Beffs, ne Guy, ne ſere Sydrake,
> Ne of Ury, ne of Oĉtavian,
> Ne of Heĉtor the ſtrong man,
> Ne of Jaſon, neither of Hercules,
> Ne of Eneas, neither Achilles.[5]

---

[1] See *Hiſt. of Hen. II.* vol. iv. p. 361, App.

[2] Charlemagne's twelve peers. *Douze Pairs.* Fr.

[3] [The text has been correĉted by Mr. Weber's edition of this romance, in his *Metrical Romances*, 1810.—*Price.*]

[4] [The old printed copy reads Pertonape,] perhaps Parthenope, or Parthenopeus.

[5] Line 6657. To ſome of theſe romances the author of the MSS. *Lives of the Saints*, written about the year 1[3]00, and cited above at large, alludes in a ſort of prologue. See ſeĉt. i. *ſupr.*

> " Wel auht we loug Criſtendom that is ſo dere y bouȝt,
> With oure lordes herte blode that the ſpere hath y-ſouȝt.

Here, among others, some of the most capital and favourite stories of romance are mentioned, Arthur, Charlemagne, the Siege of Troy with its appendages, and Alexander the Great: and there are four authors of high esteem in the dark ages, Geoffry of Monmouth, Turpin, Guido di Colonna, and Callisthenes, whose books were the grand repositories of these subjects, and contained most of the traditionary fictions, whether of Arabian or classical origin, which constantly supplied materials to the writers of romance.

> Men wilnethe more yhere of batayle of kyngis,
> And of kny3tis hardy, that mochel is lesyngis.
> Of Roulond and of Olyvere, and Gy of Warwyk,
> Of Wawayen and Triftram that ne foundde here y-like.
> Who fo loveth to here tales of fuche thinge,
> Here he may y-here thyng that nys no lesynge,
> Of poftoles and marteres that hardi kny3ttes were,
> And ftedfaft were in bataile and fledde no3t for no fere,' &c.

The anonymous author of *The boke of Stories called Curfor Mundi*, tranflated from the French, feems to have been of the fame opinion. His work [is a hiftory of the two Teftaments] : but in the prologue he takes occafion to mention many tales of another kind, which were more agreeable to the generality of readers. MSS. Laud, K 53, f. 177, Bibl. Bodl.

> " Men lykyn Jeftis for to here
> And romans rede in divers manere :
> Of Alexandre the conquerour,
> Of Julius Cefar the emperour,
> Of Greece and Troy the ftrong ftryf,
> Ther many a man loft his lyf :
> Of Brut, that baron bold of hand,
> The firft conquerour of Englond ;
> Of kyng Artour that was fo ryche,
> Was non in hys tyme fo ilyche :
> Of wonders that among his knyghts felle,
> And auntyrs dedyn, as men her telle,
> As Gaweyn and othir full abylle,
> Which that kept the round tabyll.
> How kyng Charles and Rowland fawght
> With Sarazins, nold thei be cawght ;
> Of Tryftram and Yfoude the fwete,
> How thei with love firft gan mete.
> Of kyng John and Ifenbras,
> Of Ydoyne and Amadas.
> Stories of divers thynges,
> Of princes, prelates and kynges :
> Many fongs of divers ryme,
> As Englifh, French, and Latyne, &c.
> This ylke boke is tranflate
> Into Englifh tong to rede
> For the love of Englifh lede,
> For comyn folk of England, &c.
> Syldyn yt ys for any chaunce
> Englifh tong preched is in Fraunce," &c.

See Montf. Par. MSS. 7540, and p. 123, *fupr.* [Sir F. Madden cites other MSS. of the *Curfor Mundi* in the Bodleian, Adv. Lib. Edinb., at Göttingen, *et alibi.* The work is to be printed from MSS. in the Br. Mus. and at Cambridge by the Early Englifh Text Society. Mr. Furnivall notes, that the MS. Cotton Vefp. A. iii. is the beft in the Northern dialect : that at Trinity College, in a Midland one.]

But I do not mean to repeat here what has been already obſerved[1] concerning the writings of Geoffrey of Monmouth and Turpin. It will be ſufficient to ſay at preſent, that theſe two fabulous hiſtorians recorded the achievements of Charlemagne and of Arthur : and that Turpin's hiſtory was artfully forged under the name of that arch-biſhop about the year 1110, with a deſign of giving countenance to the Cruſades from the example of ſo high an authority as Charlemagne, whoſe pretended viſit to the holy ſepulchre is deſcribed in the twentieth chapter.

As to the ſiege of Troy, it appears that both Homer's poems were unknown, at leaſt not underſtood, in Europe from the abolition of literature by the Goths in the fourth century to the fourteenth. Geoffrey of Monmouth indeed, who wrote about the year 11[28], a man of learning for that age, produces Homer in atteſtation of a fact aſſerted in his hiſtory : but in ſuch a manner as ſhows that he knew little more than Homer's name, and was but imperfectly acquainted with Homer's ſubject. Geoffrey ſays that Brutus, having ravaged the province of Aquitaine with fire and ſword, came to a place where the city of Tours now ſtands, as Homer teſtifies.[2] But the Trojan ſtory was ſtill kept alive in two Latin pieces, which paſſed under the names of Dares Phrygius and Dictys Cretenſis. Dares' hiſtory of the deſtruction of Troy, as it was called, which purports to have been tranſlated from the Greek of Dares Phrygius into Latin proſe by Cornelius Nepos, is a wretched performance, and was forged under thoſe ſpecious names in the decline of Latin literature.[3] Dictys Cretenſis is a proſe Latin hiſtory of the Trojan war, in ſix books, paraphraſed about the reign of Diocleſian or Conſtantine by one Septimius from ſome Grecian hiſtory on the ſame ſubject, ſaid to be diſcovered under a ſepulchre by means of an earthquake in the city of Cnoſſus about the time of Nero, and to have been compoſed by Dictys, a Cretan and a ſoldier in the Trojan war. The fraud ſo frequently practiſed, of diſcovering copies of books in this extraordinary manner, in order to infer thence their high and indubitable antiquity, betrays itſelf. But that the preſent Latin Dictys had a Greek original, now loſt, appears from the numerous greciſms with which it abounds, and from the literal correſpondence of many paſſages with the Greek fragments of one Dictys cited by ancient authors. The Greek original was very probably forged under the

---

[1] See Diſs. i.   [2] L. i. ch. 14.

[3] In the Epiſtle prefixed, the pretended tranſlator Nepos ſays, that he found this work at Athens in the handwriting of Dares. He adds, ſpeaking of the controverted authenticity of Homer, " De ea re Athenis judicium fuit, cum pro infano Homerus haberetur, quod deos cum hominibus belligeraſſe deſcripſit." In which words he does not refer to any public decree of the Athenian judges, but to Plato's opinion in his *Republic.* Dares, with Dictys Cretenſis next mentioned in the text, was firſt printed at Milan in 1477. Mabillon ſays, that a manuſcript of the Pſeudo-Dares occurs in the Laurentian library at Florence, upwards of eight hundred years old. *Mus. Ital.* i. p. 169. This work was abridged by Vincentius Bellova-cenſis, a friar of Burgundy, about the year 1244. See his *Specul. Hiſtor.* lib. iii. 63.

name of Dictys, a traditionary writer on the subject, in the reign of Nero, who is said to have been fond of the Trojan story.[1] On the whole, the work appears to have been an arbitrary metaphrase of Homer, with many fabulous interpolations. At length Guido di Colonna, a native of Messina in Sicily, a learned civilian, and no contemptible Italian poet, about the year 1260, engrafting on Dares and Dictys many new romantic inventions, which the taste of his age dictated, and which the connection between Grecian and Gothic fiction easily admitted, at the same time comprehending in his plan the Theban and Argonautic stories from Ovid, Statius, and Valerius Flaccus,[2] compiled a grand prose romance in Latin, containing fifteen books, and entitled in most manuscripts *Historia de Bello Trojano*.[3] It was written at the request of Matteo di Porta, Archbishop of Salerno. Dares Phrygius and Dictys Cretensis seem to have been in some measure superseded by this improved and comprehensive history of the Grecian heroes, [for, of course, Colonna cannot be regarded as the first popularizer of the subject;] and from this period Achilles, Jason and Hercules were adopted into romance, and celebrated in common with Lancelot, Rowland, Gawain, Oliver, and other Christian champions, whom they so nearly resembled in the extravagance of their adventures.[4] This work abounds with Ori-

---

[1] See Perizon. *Dissertat. de Dict. Cretens.* sect. xxix. Constantinus Lascaris, a learned monk of Constantinople, one of the restorers of Grecian literature in Europe near four hundred years ago, says that Dictys Cretensis in Greek was lost. This writer is not once mentioned by Eustathius, who lived about the year 1170, in his elaborate and extensive commentary on Homer.

[2] The *Argonautics* of Valerius Flaccus are cited in Chaucer's *Hypsipile and Medea*. " Let him reade the boke Argonauticon," v. 90. But Guido is afterwards cited as a writer on that subject, *ibid.* 97. [Only two MSS. appear to be known : in Queen's Coll. Oxford, and at Holkham. It seems to be almost open to question, whether Chaucer refers to Valerius Flaccus.]

[3] It was first printed [at Cologne, 1477, and there are many later edits.] The work was finished, as appears by a note at the end, in 1287. It was translated into Italian by Philip or Christopher Ceffio, a Florentine, and this translation was first printed at Venice in 1481, 4to. It has also been translated into German. See Lambec. ii. 948. The purity of our author's Italian style has been much commended. For his Italian poetry, see Mongitor, *ubi. infra*, p. 167. Compare also, *Diar. Eruditor. Ital.* xiii. 258. Montfaucon mentions, in the royal library at Paris, Le Roman de Thebes qui futracine de Troye la grande. *Catal. MSS.* ii. p. 923—198. [This *Roman de Thebes* is in reality one of those works on the story of the siege of Troy, engrafted either on that of Columna or on his materials.—*Douce.*]

[4] Bale says, that Edward I. having met with our author in Sicily, in returning from Asia, invited him into England, xiii. 36. This prince was interested in the Trojan story, as we shall see below. Our historians relate, that he wintered in Sicily in the year 1270. *Chron. Rob. Brun.* p. 227. A writer quoted by Hearne, supposed to be John Stow the chronicler, says that " Guido de Columpna arriving in England at the commaundement of king Edward the Firste, made scholies and annotations upon Dictys Cretensis and Dares Phrigius. Besides these, he writ at large the Battayle of Troye." Heming. *Cartul.* ii. 649. Among his works is recited *Historia de Regibus Rebusque Angliæ*. It is quoted by many writers under the title of *Chronicum Britannorum*. He is said also to have written *Chronicum Magnum libris* xxxvi. See Mongitor. *Bibl. Sic.* i. 265.

[Eichhorn has stated these " Scholies" of Guido to have been published in the year 1216 ; a manifest mistake,—since it leaves seventy-one years between this

ental imagery, of which the subject was extremely susceptible. It has also some traits of Arabian literature. The Trojan horse is a horse of brass; and Hercules is taught astronomy and the seven liberal sciences. But I forbear to enter at present into a more par-

---

date and the period to which he assigns the first appearance of the *Historia Trojana*. But whatever may have been Guido's merit in thus affording a common text-book for subsequent writers, his work could have contained little of novelty, either in matter or manner, for his contemporaries; and it may be reasonably doubted, whether his labours extended beyond the humble task of reducing into prose the metrical compilations of his predecessors. It is true, this circumstance will not admit of absolute proof, till the several poems upon the Trojan story extant in our own and various continental libraries shall be given to the world; but the following notices of some of these productions, though scanty and imperfect, will perhaps justify the opinion which has been expressed. The history of the Anglo-Saxon kings by Geoffri Gaimar, a poet antecedent to Wace (1155), is but a fragment of a larger work, which the author assures us commenced with an account of Jason and the Argonautic expedition. This was doubtless continued through the whole cycle of Grecian fabulous history, till the siege of Troy connected Brutus, the founder of the British dynasty, with the heroes of the ancient world. The voluminous work of Benoit de Saint More (noticed by Warton below) is confessedly taken from Dares Phrygius and Dictys Cretensis, and is adorned with all those fictions of romance and chivalric costume, which these writers are supposed to have received from the interpolations of Guido. Among the romances enumerated by Melis Stoke, as the productions of earlier writers in Holland, and still (1300) held in general esteem, we find "The Conflict of Troy" (*De Stryd van Troyen*); and we know upon the authority of Jakob van Maerlant (1270), the translator of Vincent de Beauvais' *Speculum Historiale*, that this was a version of Benoit's poem. It is not so certain whence Conrad of Wurzburg, a contemporary of Guido, derived his German Ilias; but he professes to have taken it from a French original, and his poem, like Gaimar's, commences with Jason and the Argonautic expedition. Upon the same principle that Conrad conceived it necessary to preface his Ilias with the story of the Golden Fleece, his countryman Henry von Veldeck embraced the whole of the Trojan war, its origin and consequences, in his version of the Æneis. This, however, is usually believed to be a translation from the *Enide* of Chretien de Troyes; and, if the date (*ante* 1186) assumed for its appearance by Von der Hagen be correct, would place the French original in an earlier period than is given it by the French antiquaries. In the year 1210, Albrecht von Halberstadt published a metrical version of Ovid's *Metamorphoses*. See Von der Hagen's *Grundriss zur Geschichte der Deutschen Poesie*, Berlin, 1812; and Henrik van Wyn's *Historische Avondstonden*, Amsterdam, 1800.—*Price.*]

[Sir F. Madden refers us to Hoffmann's *Horæ Belgicæ*, 1830, p. 30. Mr. Wright speaks of a history of the siege of Troy in Latin prose, attributed to the eleventh century, and executed in France (Arundel MSS. Br. Mus. No. 375).]

[The popularity of the *Historia Trojana* in Britain is well attested by the number of versions of it in English that have come down to us. Besides Lydgate's *Troy Book* and the metrical version in the Bodleian Library, noticed by Warton, there is an Alliterative version in the Hunterian Museum, University of Glasgow, which the Early English Text Society is now publishing; and in a MS. copy of Lydgate in the University Library, Cambridge, there are two considerable fragments of another version by Barbour, author of the *Brus*, discovered by Mr. Bradshaw in 1866. These versions are independent translations from Guido de Colonna, belong to the end of the fourteenth and beginning of the fifteenth century, and must have been made within a period of fifty years. Probably the earliest was that by Barbour, then the Alliterative, then Lydgate's, and last of all, the Bodleian. Yet there is abundant evidence that Lydgate had read the Alliterative version, for many of his interpolations and renderings are the same as, or expansions of those given in that version; the same may be affirmed of the author of the Bodleian version. Indeed, it may be to the Alliterative version that the author refers as the

ticular examination of this hiſtory, as it muſt often occaſionally be cited hereafter. I ſhall here only further obſerve in general, that this work is the chief ſource from which Chaucer derived his ideas about the Trojan ſtory; that it was profeſſedly paraphraſed by Lydgate [between the years 1414 and 1420] into a prolix Engliſh poem, called the *Boke of Troye*,[1] at the command of Henry V.; that it became the ground-work of a new compilation in French on the ſame ſubjeĉt [" out of dyuerce bookes of latyn"] by Raoul le Feure, chaplain to the Duke of Burgundy, in the year 1464 and partly tranſlated into Engliſh proſe in the year 1471 by Caxton, under the title of the [recuyell of the hiſtoryes of Troye,] at the requeſt of Margaret, ducheſs of Burgundy: and that from Caxton's book, afterwards moderniſed, Shakeſpeare [may have] borrowed his drama of *Troilus and Creſſida*.[2]

Romana that the " ſothe telles,"—a phraſe that occurs very frequently in the Alliterative verſion.

Beſides theſe metrical renderings, the third book of Caxton's *Recuyell of the Hiſtoryes of Troye*, is a proſe tranſlation of the greater portion of the *Hiſtoria Trojana*, omitting the ſtory of Jaſon and Medea.

That the Bodleian MS. is probably a popular rendering of the Alliterative, compare the paſſages given by Warton with thoſe in the Early Engliſh Text Society, vol. i. pp. 12*-15. All the paſſages from the Bodleian MS. that I have compared, and they were many, ſhow the ſame peculiarities : ſome of them are even more ſtriking.—*Donaldſon.*]

[1] Who mentions it in a French as well as Latin romance : edit. 1555, ſignat. B i. pag. 2 :

" As in the latyn and the frenſhe yt is."

It occurs in French, MSS. Bibl. Reg. Brit. Mus. 16 F. ix. This MS. was probably written not long after the year 1300. In Lincoln's-inn Library there is a poem entitled *Bellum Trojanum*. Num. 150. Pr.

" Sithen god hade this worlde wroght."

[2] The weſtern nations, in early times, have been fond of deducing their origin from Troy. This tradition ſeems to be couched under Odin's original emigration from that part of Aſia which is conneĉted with Phrygia. Aſgard, or Aſia's fortreſs, was the city from which Odin led his colony; and by ſome it is called Troy. To this place alſo they ſuppoſed Odin to return after his death, where he was to receive thoſe who died in battle, in a hall roofed with glittering ſhields. See Bartholin. l. ii. cap. 8, pp. 402, 403. *ſeq.* This hall, ſays the Edda, is in the city of Aſgard, which is called the Field of Ida. Bartholin. *ibid.* In the very ſublime ode on the Diſſolution of the World, cited by Bartholinus, it is ſaid, that after the twilight of the gods ſhould be ended, and the new world appear, " the Aſæ ſhall meet in the field of Ida, and tell of the deſtroyed habitations." Barthol. l. ii. cap. 14, p. 597. Compare Arngrim. Jon. Crymog. l. i. c. 4, pp. 45, 46. See alſo Edda, fab. 5. In the proem to Reſenius's Edda it is ſaid, " Odin appointed twelve judges or princes at Sigtune in Scandinavia, as at Troy; and eſtabliſhed there all the laws of Troy and the cuſtoms of the Trojans." See Hickes, *Theſaur.* i. Diſſertat. Epiſt. p. 39. See alſo Mallet's *Hiſt. Dannem.* ii. p. 34. Bartholinus thinks that the compiler of the Eddic mythology, who lived A.D. 1070, finding that the Britons and Franks drew their deſcent from Troy, was ambitious of aſſigning the ſame boaſted origin to Odin. But this tradition appears to have been older than the Edda. And it is more probable that the Britons and Franks borrowed it from the Scandinavian Goths, and adapted it to themſelves; unleſs we ſuppoſe that theſe nations, I mean the former, were branches of the Gothic ſtem, which gave them a ſort of inherent right to the claim. This reaſoning

Proofs have been given in the two prologues juſt cited of the general popularity of Alexander's ſtory, another branch of Grecian hiſtory famous in the dark ages. To theſe we may add the evidence of Chaucer :

> Aliſaundres ſtorie is ſo commune,
> That everie wight that hath diſcrecioune
> Hath herde ſomewhat or al of his fortune.

In the *Houſe of Fame*, Alexander is placed with Hercules.[2] I have already remarked that he was celebrated in a Latin poem by Gualtier de Chatillon, in the year 1212.[3] Other proofs will occur in their proper places.[4] The truth is, Alexander was the moſt eminent knight errant of Grecian antiquity. He could not therefore be long without his romance. Calliſthenes, an Olynthian, educated under Ariſtotle with Alexander, wrote an authentic life of Alexander.[5] This hiſtory,

---

may perhaps account for the early exiſtence and extraordinary popularity of the Trojan ſtory among nations ignorant and illiterate, who could only have received it by tradition. Geoffrey of Monmouth took this deſcent of the Britons from Troy from the Welſh or Armoric bards, and they perhaps had it in common with the Scandinavian ſcalds. There is not a ſyllable of it in the authentic hiſtorians of England, who wrote before him ; particularly thoſe ancient ones, Bede, Gildas, and the uninterpolated Nennius. Henry of Huntingdon began his hiſtory from Cæſar ; and it was only on further information that he added Brute. But this information was from a manuſcript found by him in his way to Rome in the abbey of Bec in Normandy, [which, ſays Sir F. Madden, is, however, merely a copy of Geoffrey of Monmouth's Latin work.] H. Hunt. *Epiſtol. ad Warin.* MSS. Cantabr. Bibl. publ. cod. 251. I have mentioned in another place, that Witlaf, a king of the Weſt Saxons, grants in his charter, dated A.D. 833, among other things to Croyland-abbey his robe of tiſſue, on which was embroidered " The deſtruction of Troy." *Obs. on Spenſer's Fairy Queen,* i. ſect. v. p. 176. This proves the ſtory to have been in high veneration even long before that period : and it ſhould at the ſame time be remembered, that the Saxons came from Scandinavia.

This fable of the deſcent of the Britons from the Trojans was ſolemnly alleged as an authentic and undeniable proof in a controverſy of great national importance, by Edward I. and his nobility, without the leaſt objection from the oppoſite party. It was in the famous diſpute concerning the ſubjection of the crown of England to that of Scotland, about the year 1301. The allegations are in a letter to Pope Boniface, ſigned and ſealed by the king and his lords. *Ypodigm. Neuſtr.* apud Camd. *Angl. Norman.* p. 492. Here is a curious inſtance of the implicit faith with which this tradition continued to be believed even in a more enlightened age, and an evidence that it was equally credited in Scotland.

[1] V. 656.   [2] V. 323.   [3] See Second Diſſertation.

[4] In the reign of Henry I. the ſheriff of Nottinghamſhire is ordered to procure the queen's chamber at Nottingham to be painted with the Hiſtory of Alexander. Madox, *Hiſt. Exch.* pp. 249-259. " Depingi facias hiſtoriam Alexandri undiquaque." In the Romance of Richard, the minſtrel ſays of an army aſſembled at a ſiege in the Holy Land, ſign. Q iii :

> " Covered is both mount and playne
> Kvng Alyſaunder and Charlemayne
> He never had halfe the route
> As is the city now aboute."

By the way, this is much like a paſſage in Milton, *Par. Reg.* iii. 337 :

> " Such forces met not, nor ſo wide a camp,
> When Agrican," &c.

[5] See *Recherch. ſur la Vie et les Ouvrages de Calliſthene.* Par M. l'Abbe Sevin.

which is frequently referred to by ancient writers, has been long since lost. But a Greek life of this hero, under the adopted name of Callisthenes, at present exists, and is no uncommon manuscript in good libraries.[1] It is entitled, Βιος Αλεξανδρου του Μακεδονος και Πραξεις. That is, *The Life and Actions of Alexander the Macedonian.*[2] This piece was written in Greek, being a translation from the Persic, by Simeon Seth, styled *Magister*, and protovestiary or wardrobe keeper of the Palace of Antiochus at Constantinople[3] about the year 1070 under the Emperor Michael Ducas.[4] It was most probably very

Mem. de Lit. viii. p. 126, 4to. But many very ancient Greek writers had corrupted Alexander's history with fabulous narratives, such as Orthagoras, Oneficritus, &c.

[Julian Africanus, who lived in the third century, records the fable of Nectanabus, king of Egypt, the presumptive father of Alexander, who figures so conspicuously in the later romances. It is also presumed, that similar fictions were introduced into the poems of Arrian, Hadrian, and Soterichus. See *Görres Volksbücher*, p. 58, a translation of whose observations upon this subject will be found in the *Retrospective Review*, No. vi. For an account of Arabic, Turkish, and Persian versions of this story, see Herbelot, i. 144, and Weber's *Metrical Romances*, vol. i. xx.— Price.]

[1] Particularly Bibl. Bodl. Oxon. MSS. Barocc. Cod. xvii. And Bibl. Reg. Paris. Cod. 2064. See Montfauc. *Catal. MSS.* p. 733. See passages cited from this manuscript, in Steph. Byzant. Abr. Berckel. V. Βουκεφαλεια. Cæfar Bulenger de Circo, c. xiii. 30, &c. and Fabric. *Bibl. Gr.* xiv. 148, 149, 150. It is adduced by Du Cange, *Glossar. Gr.* ubi vid. tom. ii. *Catal. Scriptor.* p. 24.

[2] Undoubtedly many smaller histories now in our libraries were formed from this greater work.

[3] Πρωτοβεςιαριος, *Protovestiarius*. See Du Cange, *Constantinop. Chrift.* lib. ii. § 16. n. 5. Et ad Zonar. p. 46.

[4] Allat. de Simeonibus, p. 181. And Labb. *Bibl. nov. MSS.* p. 115. Simeon Seth translated many Persic and Arabic books into Greek. Allat. *ubi fupr.* p. 182, *seq.* Among them he translated from Arabic into Greek, about the year 1100, for the use of or at the request of the Emperor Alexius Comnenus, the celebrated Indian Fables now commonly called the *Fables of Bidpay.* This work he entitled, Στεφανιτης και Ιχνηλατης, and divided it into fifteen books. It was printed at Berlin, A.D. 1697, under the title, Συμεων Μαγιςρυ και φιλοσοφυ του Σηθ Κυλιλε και Διμνη. These are the names of two African or Asiatic animals, called in Latin *Thoes*, a sort of [jackall,] the principal interlocutors in the fables. Sect. i-ii. This curious monument of a species of instruction peculiar to the Orientals is upwards of two thousand years old. It has passed under a great variety of names. Khosru a king of Persia, in whose reign Mahomet was born, sent his physician named Burzvisch into India, on purpose to obtain this book, which was carefully preserved among the treasures of the kings of India, and commanded it to be translated out of the Indian language into the ancient Persic. Herbelot. *Dict. Oriental.* p. 456. It was soon afterwards turned into Syriac, under the title *Calaileg* and *Damnag.* Fabric. *Bibl. Gr.* vi. p. 461. About the year of Christ 750, one of the caliphs ordered it to be translated from the ancient Persic into Arabic, under the name *Kalila ve Damna.* Herbel. *ubi fupr.* In the year 920, the Sultan Ahmed, of the dynasty of the Samanides, procured a translation into more modern Persic: which was soon afterwards put into verse by a celebrated Persian poet named Roudeki. Herbel. *ibid.* Fabric. *ibid.* p. 462. About the year 1130, the Sultan Bahram, not satisfied with this Persian version, ordered another to be executed by Nasrallah, the most eloquent man of his age, from the Arabic text of Mocanna: and this Persian version is what is now extant under the title *Kalila ve Damna.* Herbel. *ibid.* See also Herbel. p. 118. But as even this last-mentioned version had too many Arabic idioms and obsolete phrases, in the reign of Sultan Hosein Mirza, it was thrown into a more modern and intelligible style, under the name of *Anuar Soheli.* Fraser's *Hift. Nadir-Shah. Catal. MSS.* pp. 19, 20. Nor must it

foon afterwards tranflated from the Greek into Latin, and at length from thence into French, Italian, and German.[1] The Latin tranf-

be forgotten, that about the year 1100, the Emir Sohail, general of the armies of Huffain, Sultan of Khoraffan of the pofterity of Timur, caufed a new tranflation to be made by the Dr. Huffien Vaez, which exceeded all others in elegance and per-fpicuity. It was named *Anwair Sohaili*, Splendor *Canopi*, from the Emir who was called after the name of that ftar. Herbel. pp. 118, 245. It would be tedious to mention every new title and improvement which it has paffed through among the eaftern people. It has been tranflated into the Turkifh language both in profe and verfe: particularly for the ufe of Bajazet II. and Solyman II. Herbel. p. 118. It has been alfo tranflated into Hebrew by Rabbi Joel: and into Latin, under the title *Directorium Vitæ humanæ*, by Johannes of Capua [about 1480.] From thence [in 1498] it got into Caftilian: and from the Spanifh was made an Italian verfion, printed at Ferrara, A.D. 1583, viz. *Lelo Damno* [for *Calilah u Damnah*] *del Governo de regni, fotto morali*, &c. A fecond edition appeared at Ferrara in 1610, viz. *Philofophia morale del doni*, &c. But there was an Italian edition at Venice, under the laft-mentioned title, with old rude cuts, 1552. From the Latin verfion [alfo] it was tranflated into German, by the command of Ebelhard firft Duke of Wirtenberg: and this tranflation was printed at Ulm [1485. There are feveral later editions by David Sahid d'Ifpahan which appeared at Paris in 1644, of which Gilbert Gaulmin is believed to have been in great part the author.] But this is rather a paraphrafe, and was reprinted in Holland. See Starchius, *ubi fupr.* præf. § 19, 20, 22. Fabric. *ubi fupr.* p. 463, *feq.* Another tranflation was printed at Paris, viz. *Contes et Fables Indiennes de Bidpai et De Lokman traduits d'Ali Tchelchi-Bengalek auteur Turc, par M. Galland* [1724, and again, 1778.] Fabricius fays, that Mons. Galland had procured a Turkifh copy of this book four times larger than the printed copies, being a verfion from the original Perfic, and entitled *Hu-magoun Nameh*, that is, *The royal* or *imperial book*, fo called by the Orientals, who are of opinion that it contains the whole art of government. See Fabric. *ubi fupr.* p. 465. Herbel. p. 456. A tranflation into Englifh from the French of the four firft books was printed at London in 1747, under the title of *Pilpay's Fables;* [but all the earlier Englifh verfions are fingularly indifferent. The beft tranflation is that by Eaftwick in 1854.] As to the name of the author of this book, Herbelot fays that Bidpai was an Indian philofopher, and that his name fignifies the merciful phy-fician. See Herbelot, pp. 206, 456, and *Bibl. Lugdun. Catal.* p. 301. [Sir Wm. Jones, who derives this name from a Sanfcrit word, interprets it the beloved or favourite phyfician.—*Price.*] Others relate, that it was compofed by the Brahmins of India, under the title *Kurtuk Dumnik*. Frafer, *ubi fupr.* p. 19. It is alfo faid to have been written by Ifame fifth king of the Indians, and tranflated into Arabic from the Indian tongue three hundred years before Alexander the Macedonian. Abraham Ecchelens, *Not. ad Catal. Ebed Jefu*, p. 87.—The Indians reckon this book among the three things in which they furpafs all other nations, *viz.* "Liber Culila et Dimna, ludus Shatangri, et novem figuræ numerariæ." Saphad. *Comment. ad Carm. Tograi.* apud Hyde, *prolegom. ad lib. de lud. Oriental.* d. 3. Hyde intended an edition of the Arabic verfion. *Præfat. ad lib. de lud. Oriental.* vol. ii. 1767, edit. ad calc. I cannot forfake this fubject without remarking, that the Perfians have another book, which they efteem older than any writings of Zoroafter, entitled *Javidan Chrad*, that is, *æterna Sapientia*. Hyde *Præfat. Relig. Vet. Perfarum*. This has been alfo one of the titles of Bidpai's Fables.

See Wolfii *Bibl. Hebr.* i. 468, ii. 931, iii. 350, iv. 934.

[The Indian origin of thefe fables is now placed beyond the poffibility of dif-pute. Mr. Colebrooke has publifhed a Sanfcrit verfion of them, under the title of *Hitopadefa*, and they have been tranflated, from the fame language, by Sir Wm. Jones and Dr. Wilkins.—*Price.* See *fupra*.]

[1] Cafaub. *Epift. ad Jos. Scaliger.* 402, 413. Scalig. *Epift. ad Cafaubon*, 113, 115; who mentions alfo a tranflation of this work from the Latin into Hebrew, by one who adopted the name of Jos. Gorionides, called Pfeudo-Gorionides. This Latin hiftory was tranflated into German by John Hartlieb Moller, a German

lation was printed at Cologne in 1489.[1] [Among Rawlinſon's books at Oxford is a MS. copy of the *Geſta Alexandri Metricé Compoſita*, which once belonged to Hearne.] It is ſaid to have been [written in Greek by Æſopus, and to have been thence turned into Latin] by Julius Valerius :[2] ſuppoſititious names, which ſeem to have been forged by the artifice, or introduced through the ignorance, of ſcribes and librarians. This Latin tranſlation, however, is of high antiquity in the middle age of learning : for it is quoted by Giraldus Cambrenſis, who flouriſhed about the year 1190.[3] About the year 1236, the ſubſtance of it was thrown into a long Latin poem, written in elegiac verſe[4] by Aretinus Quilichinus.[5] This fabulous narrative of Alexander's life and achievements is full of prodigies and extravagances.[6] But we ſhould remember its origin. The Arabian books

---

phyſician, at the command of Albert Duke of Bavaria, and publiſhed Auguſt. Vindel. A.D. 1478, fol. [This edition was preceded by two others from the preſs of Bämler, dated 1472 and 1473. Theſe and the Straſburg edition of 1488 call the tranſlator Dr. John Hartlieb of Munich.—*Price.*] See Lambecc. lib. ii. *de Bibl. Vindobon,* p. 949. Labbe mentions a fabulous hiſtory of Alexander, written, as he ſays, in 1217, and tranſcribed in 1455. Undoubtedly this in the text. Londinenſis quotes "pervetuſtum quendam librum manuſcriptum de actibus Alexandri." Hearne's T. Caius *ut infr.* p. 82. See alſo pp. 86, 258.

[1] Lenglet mentions *Hiſtoria fabuloſa incerti authoris de Alexandri Magni præliis,* 1494. He adds, that it is printed in the laſt edition of Cæſar's Commentaries by Grævius in octavo. *Bibl. des Romans,* ii. pp. 228, 229, edit. Amſt. Compare Vogt's *Catalogus librorum rarior,* p. 24, edit. 1753. Montfaucon ſays this hiſtory of Calliſthenes occurs often in the royal library at Paris, both in Greek and Latin : but that he never ſaw either of them printed. *Cat. MSS.* ii. p. 733, 2543. I think a life of Alexander is ſubjoined to an edition of Quintus Curtius in 1584 by Joannes Monachus.

[2] Du Cange *Gloſſar. Gr.* v. Εβελλινος. Jurat. ad Symmach. iv. 33. Barth. Adverſar. ii. 10, v. 14. [Sir F. Madden has ſhown that the work of Julius Valerius, which is ſaid to have been taken from the Greek of Æſopus, is entirely different from the ordinary Latin proſe narratives of the Life of Alexander. It was publiſhed by Mai, Frankf. 1818, 8vo., with a ſecond piece called *Itinerarium Alexandri,* from MSS. in the Ambroſian library, at Milan, of the twelfth century.]

[3] Hearne, T. Caii *Vindic. Antiquit. Acad. Oxon.* tom. ii. Not. p. 802, who thinks it a work of the monks. "Nec dubium quin monachus quiſpiam Latine, ut potuit, ſcripſerit. Eo modo, quo et alios id genus fœtus parturiebant ſcriptores aliquot monaſtici, e fabulis quas vulgo admodum placere ſciebant."—*Ibid.*

[4] A Greek poem on this ſubject will be mentioned below, written in politic verſes, entitled Αλεξανδρευς ὁ Μακεδων.

[5] Labb. *Bibl. Nov. MSS.* p. 68. Ol. Borrich. *Diſſertat. de Poet.* p. 89.

[6] The writer relates that Alexander, incloſed in a veſſel of glaſs, dived to the bottom of the ocean for the ſake of getting a knowledge of fiſhes and ſea monſters. He is alſo repreſented as ſoaring in the air by the help of gryphons. At the end, the opinions of different philoſophers are recited concerning the ſepulchre of Alexander. Nectabanos, a magician and aſtrologer, king of Egypt, is a very ſignificant character in this romance. He transforms himſelf into a dragon, &c. Compare Herbelot. *Bibl. Oriental.* p. 319, b. *ſeq.* In ſome of the MSS. of this piece which I have ſeen, there is an account of Alexander's viſit to the trees of the ſun and moon : but I do not recollect this in the printed copies. Undoubtedly the original has had both interpolations and omiſſions. Pſeudo-Gorionides above mentioned ſeems to hint at the groundwork of this hiſtory of Alexander in the following paſſage : "Cæteras autem res ab Alexandro geſtas, et egregia ejus facinora ac quæcunque demum perpetravit, ea in libris Medorum et Perſarum,

abound with the moſt incredible fictions and traditions concerning
Alexander the Great, which they probably borrowed and improved
from the Perſians.   They call him Eſcander.   If I recollect right,
one of the miracles of this romance is our hero's horn.   It is ſaid,
that Alexander gave the ſignal to his whole army by a wonderful
horn of immenſe magnitude, which might be heard at the diſtance
of ſixty miles, and that it was blown or ſounded by ſixty men at
once.[1]   This is the horn which Orlando won from the giant Jat-
mund, and which, as Turpin and the Iſlandic bards report, was
endued with magical power, and might be heard at the diſtance of
twenty miles.   Cervantes ſays, that it was bigger than a maſſy
beam.[2]   Boiardo, Berni and Arioſto have all ſuch a horn: and
the fiction is here traced to its original ſource.   But in ſpeaking
of the books which furniſhed the ſtory of Alexander, I muſt not
forget that Quintus Curtius was an admired hiſtorian of the romantic
ages.   He is quoted in the *Policraticon* of John of Saliſbury, who
died in the year 1181.[3]   Eneas Sylvius relates, that Alphonſus IX.,
king of Spain in the thirteenth century and a great aſtronomer, endeavoured to relieve himſelf from a tedious malady by reading the
Bible over fourteen times, with all the gloſſes ; but not meeting with
the expected ſucceſs, he was cured by the conſolation he received
from once reading Quintus Curtius.[4]   Peter Bleſenſis, [or Peter of
Blois,] Archdeacon of London, a ſtudent at Paris about the year 1150,
mentioning the books moſt common in the ſchools, declares that he
profited much by frequently looking into this author.[5]   Vincentius
Bellovacenſis, cited above, a writer of the thirteenth century, often
quotes Curtius in his *Speculum Hiſtoriale*.[6]   He was alſo early tranſlated into French.   Among the royal MSS. in the Britiſh Muſeum,
there is a fine copy of a French tranſlation of this claſſic, adorned
with elegant old paintings and illuminations, entitled, *Quinte Curſe
Ruf, des faiz d'Alexandre,* ix. *liv. tranſlate par Vaſque de Lucene
Portugalois.   Eſcript par la main de Jehan du Cheſne, a Lille.*[7]   It

---

atque apud Nicolaum, Titum, et Strabonem ; et in libris nativitatis Alexandri,
rerumque ab ipſo geſtarum, quos Magi ac Ægyptii eo anno quo Alexander deceſſit,
compoſuerunt, ſcripta reperies." Lib. ii. c. 12-22, [Lat. Vers.] p. 152, edit. Jo.
Frid. Briethaupt.

[1] It is alſo in a MS. entitled *Secreta Secretorum Ariſtotelis*, lib. 5. MSS. Bodl.
D. 1, 5.   This treatiſe, aſcribed to Ariſtotle, was anciently in high repute.   It is
pretended to have been tranſlated out of Greek into Arabic or Chaldee by one
John, a Spaniard; thence into Latin by Philip, a Frenchman; at length into
Engliſh verſe by Lydgate : under whom more will be ſaid of it. [The Latin is
dedicated to Guido Vere de Valentia, Biſhop of Tripoli.—*Madden.*]

[2] See *Obſervat. Fair. Qu.* i. § v. p. 202.

[3] viii. 18.   [4] Op. p. 476.

[5] Epiſt. 101.   *Frequenter inſpicere hiſtorias Q. Curtii,* &c.

[6] iv. 61, &c.   Montfaucon, I think, mentions a MS. of Q. Curtius in the Col-
bertine library at Paris 800 years old.   See Barth. ad Claudian. p. 1165.   Alexander Benedictus, in his hiſtory of Venice, tranſcribes whole pages from this
hiſtorian.   I could give other proofs.

[7] 17 F i. Brit. Mus.   And again, 20 C. iii. and 15 D. iv.   [Sir F. Madden
refers to M. Paris's Cat. of the MSS. of the Bibl. Imper. 1836, Noes, 6727-9.]

was made in 1468.   But I believe the Latin tranſlations of Simeon
Seth's romance on this ſubjeƈt were beſt known and moſt eſteemed
for ſome centuries.

The French, to reſume the main tenor of our argument, had
written metrical romances on moſt of theſe ſubjeƈts before or about
the year 1200.   Some of theſe ſeem to have been formed from proſe
hiſtories, enlarged and improved with new adventures and embelliſhments from earlier and more ſimple tales in verſe on the ſame ſubjeƈt.   Chreſtien of Troyes wrote *Le Romans du Graal*, or the adventures of the Sangraal, which included the deeds of King Arthur,
Sir Triſtram, Lancelot du Lac, and the reſt of the knights of the
round table, before 1191.   There is a paſſage in a coeval romance,
relating to Chreſtien, which proves what I have juſt advanced, that
ſome of theſe hiſtories previouſly exiſted in proſe :—

> Chriſtians qui entent et paine
> A rimoyer le meillor conte,
> Par le commandement le Conte,
> Qu'il ſoit contez in cort royal
> Ce eſt li contes del Graal
> Dont li quens li bailla le livre.[1]

Chreſtien alſo wrote the romance of *Sir Percival*, which belongs to
the ſame hiſtory.[2]   Godfrey de Ligny, a cotemporary, finiſhed a
romance begun by Chreſtien, entitled *La Charette* [or Du Chevalier a
la Charette], containing the adventures of Launcelot.   [This has been
printed of late years.]   Fauchet affirms, that Chreſtien abounds with

---

[1] *Apud* Fauchet, *Rec.* liv. ii. x. p. 99, who adds, " Je croy bien que Romans que
nous avons ajourdhuy imprimez, tels que Lancelot du Lac, Triſtan, et autres, ſont
refondus ſus les vielles proſes et rymes et puis refraichis de language."
[The *Roman du Saint Graal* is aſcribed to an anonymous *Trouvere* by M. Roquefort, who denies that it was written by Chretien de Troyes.   On the authority
of the *Cat. de la Valliere*, he alſo attributes the firſt part of the proſe verſion of this
romance to Luces du Gaſt, and the continuation only to Robert de Borron.   Of de
Borron's work entitled *Enſierrement de Merlin ou Roman de St. Graal*, there is a metrical verſion MS. no. 1987 fonds de l'abbaye St. Germain.   See *Poeſie Françaiſe dans
les xii. et xiii. Siècles.*—Price.]
The oldeſt MSS. of romances on theſe ſubjeƈts which I have ſeen are the following.   They are in the royal MSS. of the Britiſh Muſeum.   *Le Romanz de Triſtran,*
20 D. ii.   This was probably tranſcribed not long after the year 1200.—*Hiſtoire
du Lancelot ou S. Graal*, ibid. iii.   Perhaps older than the year 1200.   Again,
Hiſtoire du S. Graal, ou Lancelot, 20 C. vi. 1.   Tranſcribed ſoon after 1200.   This
is imperfeƈt at the beginning.   The ſubjeƈt of Joſeph of Arimathea bringing a veſſel of the Sangral, that is [the holy diſh or veſſel] into England, is of high antiquity.   It is thus mentioned in *Morte Arthur.*   " And then the old man had an
harpe, and he ſung *an olde ſonge* how Joſeph of Arimathy came into this lande."
B. iii. c. 5.
[2] Fauchet, p. 103. [*Perceval le galloys, le qui acheua les aduētures du Saƈt Graal,
auec aulchuns faiƈz belliqueulz du noble cheualier Gauuaï, &c.*], *tranſlatees de rime de
l'ancien auteur.*—[Chretien de Troyes.   Printed at Paris, 1530, folio.   This writer
at his death left the ſtory unfiniſhed.   It was reſumed by Gautier de Denet, and
concluded by Meſſenier.   See Roquefort *ut ſup.* p. 194.—Price.]
In the royal library at Paris is *Le Roman de Perſeval le Galois, par Creſtien de
Troyes*.   In verſe, fol.   Mons. Galland thinks there is another romance under this
title, *Mem. de Lit.* iii. p. 427, ſeq. 433, 8vo.   The author of which he ſuppoſes may
be Rauol de Biavais, mentioned by Fauchet, p. 142.   Compare Lenglet, *Bibl. Rom.*

beautiful inventions.[1] But no ſtory is ſo common among the earlieſt
French poets as Charlemagne and his Twelve peers. In the Britiſh
Muſeum we have an old French MS. containing the hiſtory of
Charlemagne, tranſlated into proſe from Turpin's Latin. The
writer declares, that he preferred a ſober proſe tranſlation of this
authentic hiſtorian, as hiſtories in rhyme, undoubtedly very numerous
on this ſubject, looked ſo much like lies.[2] His title is extremely
curious : *Ci comence l'Eſtoire que Turpin le Ercevefque de Reins
fit del bon roy Charlemayne, coment il conquiſt Eſpaigne, e delivera
des Paens. Et pur ceo qe Eſtoire rimee ſemble menſunge, eſt ceſte mis
in proſe, ſolun le Latin qe Turpin meſmes fiſt, tut enſi cume il le viſt
et viſt.*[3]

Ogier the Dane makes a part of Charlemagne's hiſtory, and, I
believe, is mentioned by Archbiſhop Turpin. But his exploits have
been recorded in verſe by Adenez, an old French poet, not mentioned by Fauchet, author of the two metrical romances of
[Berthe] and *Cleomades*, under the name of *Ogier le Danois*, in the
year 1270. This author was maſter of the muſicians, or, as others
ſay, heralds at arms, to the Duke of Brabant. Among the royal

---

p. 250. The author of this laſt-mentioned Percevall, in the exordium, ſays that he
wrote, among others, the romances of Eneas, Roy Marc, and Uſelt le Blonde : and
that he tranſlated into French, Ovid's *Art of Love*. [The French romance of *Perceval* is preſerved in a MS. in the College of Arms, No. 14.—*Madden*. The
Engliſh tranſlation is preſerved in a MS. in Lincoln Cathedral Library, and is included in Mr. Halliwell's *Thornton Romances*, 1844.]

[1] P. 105, *ibid.* [Perhaps the ſame, ſays Ritſon, with *Les romans de Chevalier
à l'épée, ou L'Hiſtoire de Lancelot du Lac*. To the ſame romance-writer are attributed, *Du Chevalier à Lion, du prince Alexandre, d'Erec*, with others that are now
loſt.—*Park*. M. Roquefort's catalogue of Chretien's works ſtill extant contains :
Perceval, le Chevalier au Lion, Lancelot du Lac, Cliget (Cleges ?), *Guillaume d'Angleterre*, and *Erec et Enide*. The latter probably gave riſe to the opinion, that Chretien
tranſlated the Æneid, and which has been adopted from Von der Hagen.—*Price*.]

[2] There is a curious paſſage to this purpoſe in an old French proſe romance
of *Charlemagne*, written before the year 1200. " Baudouin Comte de Hainau
trouva a Sens en Bourgongne le vie de Charlemagne : et mourant la donna a ſa
four Yolond Comteſſe de S. Pol, qui m'a prie que je la mette en *Roman ſans ryme*.
Parce que tel ſe delitera el Roman qui del Latin n'ent cure ; et par le Roman ſera
mielx gardee. Maintes gens en ont ouy conter et chanter, mais n'eſt ce *menſonge*
non ce qu'ils en diſent et chantent cil conteour ne cil jugleor. Nuz contes rymes
n'en eſt vrais : tot menſonge ce qu'ils dient." Liv. quatr. [Sir F. Madden notes that
this is the ſame as that of Turpin, and refers to M. Paris's Cat. of the MSS.
in the national library at Paris, pp. 211-20. There is certainly no concluſive
teſtimony in favour of the compoſition of the tranſlation between 1178 and 1205,
though Sir F. M. poſitively declares, that it " muſt be limited between theſe dates."
He mentions that it was Yoland Counteſs of St. Pol, who cauſed the metrical ſtory
of Guillaume de Palerme to be tranſlated into French. This is our *William and the
Werwolf*, edited by Sir F. M. 1832, and more recently by the Early Text Society.]

[3] MSS. Harl. 273, f. 86. There is a very old metrical romance on this ſubject,
ibid. MSS. Harl. 527, l. f. 1. [*Ogier le Dannois duc de Dannemarche* was printed
at Paris about 1498 ; and at Troyes in 1608, were printed, *Hiſtoire de Morgant
le geant*, and *Hiſtoire des nobles Proveſſes et Vaillances de Gallien reſtauré*.—*Park*.
See alſo M. Michel's edit. of *Charlemagne*, 1836, from Royal MS. 16 E. viii. 7,
written in the twelfth century.]

MSS. in the Museum we have a poem, *Le Livre de Ogeir de Danne-marche*.[1] The French have likewise illustrated this champion in Leonine rhyme. And I cannot help mentioning that they have in verse *Visions of Oddegir the Dane in the kingdom of Fairy*, "Visions d'Ogeir le Danois au Royaume de Faerie en vers François," printed at Paris in 1548.[2]

On the Trojan story the French have an ancient poem, at least not posterior to the thirteenth century, entitled *Roman de Troye*, written by Benoit de Sainct More. As this author appears not to have been known to the accurate Fauchet, nor la Croix du Maine, I will cite the exordium, especially as it records his name, and implies that the piece [was] translated from the Latin, and that the subject was not then common in French :

> Cette estoire n'est pas usée,
> N'en gaires livres n'est trouvée :
> La retraite ne fut encore
> Mais Beneoit de sainte More,
> L'a translaté, et fait et dit,
> Et a sa main les mots ecrit.

He mentions his own name again in the body of the work, and at the end :—

> Je n'en fait plus ne plus en dit ;
> Beneoit qui c'est Roman fit.[3]

Du Cange enumerates a metrical MS. romance on this subject by Jaques Millet, entitled *De la Destruction de Troie*.[4] Montfaucon, whose extensive inquiries nothing could escape, mentions Dares Phrigius translated into French verse, at Milan, about the twelfth century.[5] We find also, among the royal MSS. at Paris, Dictys Cretensis translated into French verse.[6] To this subject, although almost equally belonging to that of Charlemagne, we may also refer a French romance in verse, written by Philipes Mousques, canon and chancellor of the church of Tournay. It is, in fact, a chronicle of France : but the author, who does not choose to begin quite so high as Adam and Eve, nor yet later than the Trojan war, opens his history with the rape of Helen, passes on to an ample description of the siege of

---

[1] 15 E. vi. 4.

[The title of Adenez' poem is *Les Enfances d'Ogier-le-Danois*, a copy of which is preserved among the Harl. MSS. No. 4404. His other poem, noticed in the text, is called *Le Roman de Pepin et de Berthe*. See *Cat. Valliere*, No. 2734. The life of Ogier contained in the royal MS. embraces the whole career of this illustrious hero ; and is evidently a distinct work from that of Adenez. Whether it be the same version alluded to in the French romance of *Alexander*, where the author is distinguished from the " conteurs batards " of his day, is left to more competent judges.—*Price*. For an account of the modern printed edition of these and other romances of the same cycle, see Brunet, *dern.* edit. art. *Roman*.]

[2] There is also *L'Histoire du preux Meurvin fils d'Ogier le Danois*, Paris, 1539 and 1540. [Of this there is an English version, Lond. 1612, 4to.]

[3] See Galland *ut supr.* p. 425. [For an account of Benoit de Saint More's poem, the reader is referred to the 12th vol. of the *Archæologia*, and to the modern edition of the original.]

[4] Gloss. *Lat. Ind. Aut.* p. cxiii.   [5] *Monum. Fr.* i. 374.

[6] See Montf. *Catal. MSS.* ii. p. 1669.

Troy, and through an exact detail of all the great events which succeeded conducts his reader to the year 1240. This work comprehends all the fictions of Turpin's Charlemagne, with a variety of other extravagant stories difperfed in many profeffed romances. But it preferves numberlefs curious particulars, which throw confiderable light on hiftorical facts. Du Cange has collected from it all that concerns the French emperors of Conftantinople, which he has printed at the end of his entertaining hiftory of that city.

It was indeed the fafhion for the hiftorians of thefe times to form fuch a general plan as would admit all the abfurdities of popular tradition. Connection of parts and uniformity of fubject were as little ftudied as truth. Ages of ignorance and fuperftition are more affected by the marvellous than by plain facts, and believe what they find written without difcernment or examination. No man before the fixteenth century prefumed to doubt that the Francs derived their origin from Francus, a fon of Hector ; that the Spaniards were defcended from Japhet, the Britons from Brutus, and the Scots from Fergus. Vincent de Beauvais, who lived under Louis IX. of France, and who, on account of his extraordinary erudition, was appointed preceptor to that king's fons, very gravely claffes archbifhop Turpin's Charlemagne among the real hiftories, and places it on a level with Suetonius and Cæfar. He was himfelf an hiftorian, and has left a large hiftory of the world, fraught with a variety of reading, and of high repute in the middle ages ; but edifying and entertaining as this work might have been to his cotemporaries, at prefent it ferves only to record their prejudices, and to characterife their credulity.[1]

Hercules and Jafon, as I have before hinted, were involved in the Trojan ftory by Guido di Colonna, and hence became familiar to the romance writers.[2] The Hercules, the Thefeus, and the Amazons of Boccaccio, hereafter more particularly mentioned, came from this fource. I do not at prefent recollect any old French metrical romances on thefe fubjects, but prefume that there are many. Jafon feems to have vied with Arthur and Charlemagne ; and fo popular was his expedition to Colchos, or rather fo firmly believed, that in honour of fo refpectable an adventure a duke of Burgundy inftituted the order of the Golden Fleece in the year 1468. At the fame time his chaplain Raoul le Feure illuftrated the ftory which gave rife to this magnificent inftitution, in a prolix and elaborate hiftory, afterwards tranflated by Caxton.[3] But I muft not forget, that

---

[1] He flourifhed about 1260.

[2] The Trojomanna Saga, a Scandic manufcript at Stockholm, feems to be pofterior to Guido's publication. It begins with Jafon and Hercules, and their voyage to Colchos : proceeds to the rape of Helen, and ends with the fiege and deftruction of Troy. It celebrates all the Grecian and Afiatic heroes concerned in that war. Wanl. *Antiquit. Septentr.* p. 315, col. 1.

[3] See *Obfervat. on Spenfer's Fairy Queen,* i. § v. p. 176, *feq.* Montfaucon mentions *Medeæ et Jafonis Hiftoria a Guidone de Columna.* Catal. MSS. Bibl. Coiflin. ii. p. 1109.—818.

among the royal manuscripts in the Museum, the French romance of *Hercules* occurs in two books, enriched with numerous ancient paintings.[1] [It was, at a later date, reduced into a chap-book. *Parthenope* is, of course, the hero of the romance of that name, inserted in Le Grand's collection, and of which the English versions have been lately printed.][2] *Ypomedon* has also christened a tale of chivalry, to be noticed hereafter.

The conquests of Alexander the Great were celebrated by one Simon, in old [French], about the twelfth century. This piece thus begins:

> Chanson voil dis per ryme et per Leoin
> Del fil Filippe lo roy de Macedoin.

An Italian poem on Alexander, called *Trionfo Magno*, was presented to Leo X. by Dominicho Falugi Anciseno, in the year 1521. Crescimbeni says it was copied from a Provençal romance.[3] But one of the most valuable pieces of the old French poetry is on the subject of this victorious monarch, entitled *Roman d' Alexandre*. It has been called the second poem now remaining in the French language, and was written about the year 1200. It was confessedly translated from the Latin; but it bears a nearer resemblance to Simeon Seth's romance than to Quintus Curtius. It was the confederated performance of four writers who, as Fauchet expresses himself, were *associez en leur jouglerie*.[4] Lambert li Cors, a learned

---

[1] 17 E. ii. [This romance of *Hercules* commences with an account of Uranus or Cælum, and terminates with the death of Ulysses by his son Telegonus. The mythological fables with which the first part abounds, are taken from Boccaccio's *Genealogia Deorum*; and the third part, embracing the destruction of Troy by the Greeks under Agamemnon, professes to be a translation from *Dictys of Greece and Dares of Troy*. The Pertonape of the text is evidently Partonopex de Blois (see Le Grand, *Fabliaux*, tom. iv. p. 261, and *Notices des Manuscrits*, tom ix.), and Ypomedon the hero whom Warton dignifies with the epithet of Childe Ippomedone.—*Price*.]

[2] [*The Old English Versions of Partenope of Blois*. Edited by the Rev. W. E. Buckley. Roxburghe Club, 1862. There is a modern paraphase in verse by Mr. W. S. Rose.]

[3] *Istor. Volg. Poes.* i. iv. p. 332. In the royal manuscripts there is a French poem entitled *La Vengeaunce du graunt Alexandre*, 19 D. i. 2, Brit. Mus. I am not sure whether it is not a portion of the French *Alexander*, mentioned below, written by Jehan li Nivelois [Venelais].

[4] Fauchet, Rec. p. 83. [The order in which Fauchet has classed Lambert li Cors and Alexander of Paris, and which has also been adopted by M. Le Grand, is founded on the following passage of the original poem:

> " La verité d l'istoire si com li roys la fist
> Un clers de Chastiaudun Lambers li Cors li mist
> Qui du Latin la trait et en roman la fist. . . . .
> Alexandre nous dit qui de Bernay fu nez
> Et de Paris refu se surnoms appelles
> Qui or a les siens vers o les Lambert melles."

MM. de la Ravalliere and Roquefort have considered Alexander as the elder writer; apparently referring (*Alexandre nous dit*) to Lambert li Cors. But the last line in this extract clearly confirms M. Le Grand's arrangement. The date assigned by M. Roquefort for its publication is 1184. Jehan li Venelais wrote *Le Testament d'Alexandre*; and Perot de Saint Cloot, *La Vengeaunce d'Alexandre*. Mr. Douce has enumerated eleven French poets, who have written on the subject

civilian, began the poem; and it was continued and completed by
Alexandre de Paris, Jean le [Venelais], and [Perot] de Saint [Cloot],[1]
The poem is clofed with Alexander's will. This is no imagination
of any of our three poets, although one of them was a civil lawyer.
Alexander's will, in which he nominates fucceffors to his provinces
and kingdoms, was a tradition commonly received, and is mentioned
by Diodorus Siculus and Ammianus Marcellinus.[2] [This work has
never been edited.][3] It is voluminous; and in the Bodleian library
at Oxford is a vaft folio MS. of it in vellum, which is of great
antiquity, richly decorated, and in high prefervation.[4] The margins
and initials exhibit not only fantaftic ornaments and illuminations
exquifitely finifhed, but alfo pictures executed with fingular elegance,
expreffing the incidents of the ftory, and difplaying the fafhion of
buildings, armour, drefs, mufical inftruments,[5] and other particulars
appropriated to the times. At the end we read this hexameter,
which points out the name of the fcribe [of that portion, which
contains a Scotifh metrical romance of Alexander, an addition of the
fifteenth century]:[6]

Nomen fcriptoris eft Thomas plenus amoris.

Then follows the date of the year in which the tranfcript was completed, viz. 1338. Afterwards there is the name and date of the
illuminator, in the following colophon, written in golden letters:
*Che livre fu perfais de la enluminiere an xviii°. jour davryl par Jehan
de grife l'an de grace m.ccc.xliiii.*[7] Hence it may be concluded, that
the illuminations and paintings of this fuperb manufcript, which
were moft probably begun as foon as the fcribe had finifhed his part,
took up fix years: no long time, if we confider the attention of
an artift to ornaments fo numerous, fo various, fo minute, and fo
laborioufly touched. It has been fuppofed that before the appearance

---

of Alexander or his family: and Mr. Weber obferves, that feveral others might be
added to the lift. See Weber's *Metrical Romances* (who notices various European
verfions), *Notices des Manufcrits du Roi*, t. v.; *Catalogue de la Valliere*, t. ii.—*Price.*
Sir F. Madden refers us alfo to De la Rue, *Effais*, &c. ii. 341-56, and fupplies us
with the name of Thomas of Kent, an Anglo-Norman (not mentioned by Mr.
Price or by Mr. Wright) as one of the continuators of the romance of *Alexander.*]

[1] Fauchet, *ibid.* Mons. Galland mentions a French romance in verfe, unknown
to Fauchet, and entitled *Roman d'Athys et de Prophylias*, written by one Alexander,
whom he fuppofes to be this Alexander of Paris. *Mem. Lit.* iii. p. 429, edit.
Amft. [This conjecture is confirmed by M. Roquefort, *ubi fupr.* p. 118.—*Price.*]
It is often cited by Carpentier, Suppl. Cang.

[2] See Fabric. *Bibl. Gr.* c. iii. l. viii. p. 205.   [3] [Sir F. Madden's inform.]

[4] MSS. Bodl. B 264, fol.

[5] The moft frequent of thefe are organs, bagpipes, lutes, and trumpets.

[6] [Sir F. Madden's inform. He adds, that another portion of the *Alexander*
is in MS. Afhmole, 44. The Rev. J. S. Stevenfon edited the Alliterative Romances
of Alexander for the Roxburghe Club in 1849. In it he printed the alliterative
fragments from Bodl. MS. 264, and Afhmole 44 (ab. 1450 A.D.) The far earlier
alliterative fragment in MS. Greaves 60 was printed by Mr. Skeat in his edit. of
William of Palerne, Early Englifh Text Society, 1867.]

[7] [Bifhop Warburton had] a moft beautiful French manufcript on vellum or
Mort d'Arthur, ornamented in the fame manner. It was a prefent from Vertue
the engraver.

of this poem, the *Romans*, or thofe pieces which celebrated Gefts, were conftantly compofed in fhort verfes of fix or eight fyllables: and that in this *Roman d' Alexandre* verfes of twelve fyllables were firft ufed. It has therefore been imagined, that the verfes called *Alexandrines*, the prefent French heroic meafure, took their rife from this poem; Alexander being the hero, and Alexander the chief of the four poets concerned in the work. That the name, fome centuries afterwards, might take place in honour of this celebrated and early effort of French poetry, I think very probable; but that verfes of twelve fyllables made their firft appearance in this poem, is a doctrine which, to fay no more, from examples already produced and examined is at leaft ambiguous.[1] In this poem Gadifer, hereafter mentioned, of Arabian lineage, is a very confpicuous champion:

> Gadifer fu moult preus, d'un Arrabi lignage.

A rubric or title of one of the chapters is, " Comment Alexander fuit mys en un vefal de vooire pour veoir le merveiles," &c. This is a paffage already quoted from Simeon Seth's romance, relating Alexander's expedition to the bottom of the ocean, in a veffel of glafs, for the purpofe of infpecting fifhes and fea monfters. In another place from the fame romance, he turns aftronomer, and foars to the moon by the help of four gryphons. The caliph is frequently mentioned in this piece; and Alexander, like Charlemagne, has his twelve peers.

Thefe were the four reigning ftories of romance: on which perhaps Englifh pieces, tranflated from the French, exifted before or about the year 1300. But there are fome other Englifh romances mentioned in the prologue of *Richard Cuer du Lyon*, which we likewife probably received from the French in that period, and on which I fhall here alfo enlarge.

Beuves de Hanton, or *Sir Bevis de Southampton*, is a French romance of confiderable antiquity, although the hero is not older than the Norman conqueft. It is alluded to in our Englifh romance on this ftory, which will again be cited, and at large:

> Forth thei yode, *fo faith the boke*.[2]

And again more exprefsly,

> Under the bridge wer fixty belles,
> Right as the *Romans* telles.[3]

The *Romans* is the French original. It is called the Romance of *Beuves de Hanton*, by Pere Labbe.[4] The very ingenious Monfieur de la Curne de fainte Palaye mentions an ancient French romance in profe, entitled *Beufres de Hanton*.[5] Chaucer mentions Bevis, with other famous romances, but whether in French or Englifh is uncer-

---

[1] See Pref. *Le Roman de la Rofe*, par Mons. L'Abbé Lenglet, i. p. xxxvi.

[2] Signat. P ii. [*Bevis of Hamton* was edited from the Auchinleck MS. for the Maitland Club, 1838, 4to.]

[3] Signat. E iv.　　[4] *Nov. Bibl.* p. 334, edit. 1652.

[5] *Mém. Lit.* xv. 582, 4to.

tain.[1] *Beuves of Hantonne* was printed at [Troyes as early as 1489].[2]
Afcapart was one of his giants, a character[3] in very old French
romances. Bevis lived at Downton in Wiltfhire. Near Southampton
is an artificial hill called Bevis Mount, on which was probably a
fortrefs ; [and within the town there is a gate which ftill retains his
name].[4] It is pretended that he was Earl of Southampton. His
fword is fhown in Arundel caftle. This piece was evidently written
after the Crufades ; as Bevis is knighted by the King of Armenia,
and is one of the generals at the fiege of Damafcus.

Guy Earl of Warwick is recited as a French romance by Labbe.[5]
In the Britifh Mufeum a metrical hiftory in very old French appears,
in which Felicia, or Felice, is called the daughter of an earl of
Warwick, and Guido, or Guy, of Warwick is the fon of Seguart
the earl's fteward. The manufcript is at prefent imperfect.[6] Montfaucon mentions among the royal manufcripts at Paris, *Roman de
Guy et Beuves de Hanton.* The latter is the romance laft mentioned.
Again, *Le Livre de Guy de Warwick et de Harold d'Ardenne.*[7] This
Harold d'Arden is a diftinguifhed warrior of Guy's hiftory, and
therefore his achievements fometimes form a feparate romance : as
in the royal MSS. of the Britifh Mufeum, where we find *Le Romant
de Herolt Dardenne.*[8] In the Englifh romance of Guy, mentioned

---

[1] *Rim. Thop.* [Mr. Wright refers to a good MS. of Bevis, in Caius Coll.
Camb.; but the editor does not obferve any fuch MS. in Smith's Cat. 1849.]

[2] [The earlieft printed copy of this romance that I have met with, is in Italian,
and printed at Venice, 1489, 4to. Other editions in the fame language are,
Venice, 1562, 1580, 12mo.; Milan, 1584, 4to.; Piacenza, 1599, 12mo.; French
editions, Paris, folio, no date, by Verard; *Ibid.* 4to., no date, by Bonfons. I have
been informed from refpectable authority, that this romance is to be found in Provençal poetry, among the MSS. of Chriftina, queen of Sweden, now in the Vatican
library, and that it appears to have been written in 1380. See likewife *Bibl. de du
Verdier*, tom. iii. p. 266.—*Douce.* For an account of the Englifh editions, fee
Handb. of E. E. Lit., art. Bevis and Additions, *ibid.*]

[3] Selden's Drayton, *Polyolb.* s. iii. p. 37.

[4] [*Bevis* feems long to have retained its popularity, fince Wither thus complained
of the fale it had about the year 1627. "The ftationers have fo peftered their
printing houfes and fhopps with fruitleffe volumes, that the auncient and renowned
authors are almoft buried among them as forgotten ; and at laft you fhall fee nothing
to be fould amongft us, but Currantos, Beavis of Hampton. or fuch trumpery."
Scholler's Purgatory, (circa 1625).—*Park.* Sir F. Madden and fome other gentlemen, in the year 1833, opened the tumulus at the bottom of the vale of Pugh Dean,
about a mile from Arundel caftle, but found no remains of the hero. The tradition
is, that Bevis threw his fword, fix feet long, from the walls of the caftle into the
valley, and there appointed to be buried.]

[5] *Ubi fupr.*

[6] MSS. Harl. 3775, 2. [Other copies are in Corpus Chrifti Coll. Camb. and
in the College of Arms.—*Madden.*]

[7] Catal. MSS. p. 792. Among the Benet manufcripts there is *Romanz de Gui
de Warwyk*, Num. l. It begins,

" Puis cel tems ke deus fu nez."

This book belonged to Saint Auguftin's abbey at Canterbury. With regard to
the preceding romance of Bevis, the Italians had *Buovo d'Antona*, undoubtedly
from the French, before 1348. And Lhuyd recites in Welfh, *Yftori Boun o Hamtun.
Archæol.* p. 264.

[8] 15 E. vi. 8. [This romance might be called with more propriety an epifode in

at large in its proper place, this champion is called, *Syr Heraude of Arderne*.[1] At length this favourite subject formed a large profe romance, entitled *Guy de Warwick, Chevalier d' Angleterre, et de la belle fille Felix famie*, and printed at Paris [March 12, 1525-6]. Chaucer mentions Guy's ftory among the *Romaunces of Pris*:[2] and it is alluded to in the Spanifh romance of *Tirant lo Blanch*, or *Tirante the White*, fuppofed to have been written not long after the year 1430.[3] This romance was compofed, or perhaps enlarged, after the Crufades, as we find that Guy's redoubted encounters with Colbrond the Danifh giant, with the monfter of Dunfmore-heath, and the dragon of Northumberland, are by no means equal to fome of his achievements in the Holy Land, and the trophies which he won from the Soldan under the command of the Emperor Frederick.

The romance of *Sidrac*, entitled in the French verfion [*La fontaine de toutes fcièces du philofophe Sydrach*], appears to have been very popular, from the prefent frequency of its MSS. [both in French and Englifh.] But it is rather a romance of Arabian philofophy than of chivalry. It is a fyftem of natural knowledge, and particularly treats of the virtues of plants. Sidrac, the philofopher of this fyftem, was aftronomer to an eaftern king. He lived eight hundred and fortyfeven years after Noah, of whofe book of aftronomy he was poffeffed.

He converts Bocchus, an idolatrous king of India, to the Chriftian faith, by whom he is invited to build a mighty tower againft the invafions of a rival king of India. But the hiftory, no lefs than the fubject of this piece, difplays the ftate, nature and migrations of literature in the dark ages. After the death of Bocchus, Sidrac's book fell into the hands of a Chaldean renowned for piety. It then fuccefsively becomes the property of King Madian, Naaman the Affyrian, and Grypho, archbifhop of Samaria. The latter had a prieft named Demetrius, who brought it into Spain, and here it was tranflated from the Greek into Latin. This tranflation is faid to be made at Toledo by Roger of Palermo, a minorite friar, in the 13th century. A king of Spain then commanded it to be tranflated from Latin into Arabic, and fent it as a moft valuable prefent to Emir Elmomenim, lord of Tunis. It was next given to Frederick II., emperor of Germany, famous in the Crufades. This work, which is of confiderable length, was tranflated into Englifh verfe, and will be mentioned on that account again. Sidrac is recited as an eminent philofopher, with Seneca and King Solomon, in the *Marchaunts Second tale*, afcribed to Chaucer.[4]

It is natural to conclude that moft of thefe French romances were

---

the life of Raynbrun, Guy's fon. It recounts the manner in which he releafed Herolt d'Ardenne from prifon, and the return of both to their native country. It has the merit of being exceedingly fhort, and ftates, among other matter, that Herolt was born at Walmforth in England.—*Price*.]

[1] Sign. L ii. *vers*.   [2] *Rim. Thop.*   [3] Percy's *Ball.* iii. 100.

[4] v. 1932. There is an old tranflation of *Sidrac* into Dutch, MSS. Marfhall, Bibl. Bodl. 31, fol. [King Bocchus or Boccus feems to have been rather a popular character in our own early literature. See *Handb. of E. E. Lit.* p. 43.]

current in England, either in the French originals, which were well
underſtood at leaſt by the more polite readers, or elſe by tranſlation
or imitation, as I have before hinted, when the romance of *Richard
Cuer de Lyon*, in whoſe prologue they are recited, was tranſlated into
Engliſh.   That the latter was the caſe as to ſome of them, at leaſt,
we ſhall ſoon produce actual proofs.   A writer, who has conſidered
theſe matters with much penetration and judgment, obſerves, that
probably from the reign of our Richard I. we are to date that remarkable intercommunication and mutual exchange of compoſitions,
which we diſcover to have taken place at ſome early period between
the French and Engliſh minſtrels ; the ſame ſet of phraſes, the ſame
ſpecies of characters, incidents, and adventures, and often the identical
ſtories, being found in the metrical romances of both nations.[1] From
cloſe connection and conſtant intercourſe, the traditions and the
champions of one kingdom were equally known in the other : and
although Bevis and Guy were Engliſh heroes, yet on theſe principles
this circumſtance by no means deſtroys the ſuppoſition, that their
achievements, although perhaps already celebrated in rude Engliſh
ſongs, might be firſt wrought into romance by the French ;[2] and it
ſeems probable, that we continued for ſome time this practice of bor-
rowing from our neighbours.   Even the titles of our oldeſt romances,
ſuch as [*Sir Pleyndamour*, mentioned by Chaucer in the *Rime of Sir
Thopas*, but not at preſent known under ſuch a title],[3] *Sir Triamour*,[4]

---

[1] Percy's *Eſſ. on Anc. Eng. Minſtr.* p. 12, [attached to his edit. of the *Reliques.*]

[2] Dugdale relates, that in the reign of Henry IV., about the year 1410, a lord
Beauchamp, travelling into the Eaſt, was hoſpitably received at Jeruſalem by the
Soldan's lieutenant : " Who hearing that he was deſcended from the famous Guy
of Warwick, *whoſe ſtory they had in books of their own language,* invited him to his
palace and, royally feaſting him, preſented aim with three precious ſtones of great
value, beſides divers cloaths of ſilk and gold given to his ſervants." Baron. i. p. 243,
col. 1.   This ſtory is delivered on the credit of John Rouſe, the traveller's cotemporary.   Yet it is not ſo very improbable that Guy's hiſtory ſhould be a book
among the Saracens, if we conſider, that Conſtantinople was not only a central and
connecting point between the eaſtern and weſtern world, but that the French in the
thirteenth century had acquired an eſtabliſhment there under Baldwin earl of
Flanders : that the French language muſt have been known in Sicily, Jeruſalem,
Cyprus, and Antioch, in conſequence of the conqueſts of Robert Guiſcard, Hugo
le Grand, and Godfrey of Bulloigne : and that pilgrimages into the Holy Land
were exceſſively frequent.   It is hence eaſy to ſuppoſe, that the French imported
many of their ſtories or books of this ſort into the Eaſt ; which being thus underſtood there, and ſuiting the genius of the Orientals, were at length tranſlated into
their language.   It is remarkable, that the Greeks at Conſtantinople, in the twelfth
century and ſince, called all the Europeans by the name of Franks, as the Turks
do to this day.   See Seld. [Note on Drayton's] *Polyolb.* § viii. p. 130. [Buſbec, in
the third letter of his Embaſſy into Turkey, mentions that the Georgians in their
ſongs make frequent mention of Roland, whoſe name he ſuppoſes to have paſſed
over with Godfrey of Bulloigne.—*Douce.*]

[3] [The editor merely throws out the ſuggeſtion that *Pleyndamour* is merely another
form of *Plenus Amoris*, and that Thomas Plenus Amoris purports to have been the
writer or tranſcriber of an early Scotiſh romance on the ſubject of Alexander, above
mentioned.   *Sir Blandamour* is one of the characters in the *Faerie Queene*.]

[4] [Edited by Mr. Halliwell for the Percy Society, 1846.]

Sir Eglamour of Artois,[1] *La Mort d'Arthur*, with many more, betray their French extraction. It is likewife a prefumptive argument in favour of this affertion, that we find no profe romances in our language before Caxton tranflated from the French the Hiftory of Troy, the Life of Charlemagne, the Hiftories of Jafon, Paris and Vyenne,[2] [Morte d'Arthur,] and other profe pieces of chivalry : by which, as the profeffion of minftrelfy decayed and gradually gave way to a change of manners and cuftoms, romances in metre were at length imperceptibly fuperfeded, or at leaft grew lefs in ufe as a mode of entertainment at public feftivities.

Various caufes concurred, in the mean time, to multiply books of

---

[1] In our Englifh *Syr Eglamour of Artoys*, there is this reference to the French, from which it was tranflated. Sign. E. i.

> " His own mother there he wedde,
> In Romaunce as we rede."

Again, fol. ult.

> " In Romaunce this cronycle ys."

The authors of thefe pieces often refer to their original. Juft as Ariofto mentions Turpin for his voucher. [Halliwell's *Thornton Romances*, Camd. Soc. 1844.]

[2] [A fhort profe tale of chivalry, an Englifh verfion of which was printed by Caxton in 1485. See Roxburghe Library reprint, 1868, Pref. But to what is there faid may now be added that in the French language there are no fewer than three independent verfions of this ftory, all derived from an at prefent undifcovered Provençal original. 1. The MS. No. 7534 in the Bibliothèque Imperiale, at Paris, printed in 1835. 2. A MS. in large 4to. on paper, with the prologue of Pierre de la Sippade dated, not 1459, as in the Paris copy, but 1432, a very important variation, fince in the Paris MS. Sippade is made (as it would feem falfely) to reprefent that he did not tranflate the work out of the Provençal till 1459. 3. An abridged verfion, of which there were feveral early-printed editions in 4to., of which one, now before me, has thirty-two leaves, with woodcuts, and is in two columns. This laft was Caxton's original; and he has followed the French text very clofely. There muft have been impreffions of the fhorter ftory in type before 1485, therefore ; but the earlieft editions cited by Brunet are without note of the year. The copy, mentioned above as having the date 1432 to the Prologue, differs likewife materially in the arrangement of the text, and, to a certain extent, in the conduct of the ftory. In the old library of the Dukes of Burgundy,[1] according to an inventory taken about 1467, No. 2291 of the MSS. was *Le Roman de Paris et de la belle Vienne traduit de provençal en françois, par Pierre de la Ceppède Marfeillois*, fur papier, avec miniatures.

Mr. Price obferves : Its early and extenfive popularity is manifefted by the prologue to the Swedifh verfion, made by order of Queen Euphemia, in the fecond month of the year 1308. This refers to a German original, executed at the command of the Emperor Otho (1197-1208) ; but this again was taken from a foreign (Wälfche) fource.]

But I muft not omit here that Du Cange recites a metrical French romance in MS., *Le Roman de Girard de Vienne*, written by Bertrand le Clerc. *Glofs. Lat.* i. *Ind. Auct.* p. cxciii. Madox has printed the names of feveral French romances found in the reign of Edward III., among which one on this fubject occurs. *Formul. Anglic.* p. 12. Compare *Obfervations on Spenfer's Fairy Queen*, vol. ii. § viii. p. 43. Among the royal MSS. in the Britifh Mufeum, there is in verfe *Hiftoire de Gyrart de Vienne et de fes freres*, 20 D. xi. 2. This MS. was perhaps written before the year 1300. [It is on vellum, in two columns. It appears to be the romance quoted by Du Cange.]

---

[1] [Blades, *Life and Typogr. of W. Caxton*, i. 278.]

chivalry among the French, and to give them a superiority over the English, not only in the number but in the excellence of those compositions. Their barons lived in greater magnificence. Their feudal system flourished on a more sumptuous, extensive, and lasting establishment. Schools were instituted in their castles for initiating the young nobility in the rules and practice of chivalry. Their tilts and tournaments were celebrated with a higher degree of pomp; and their ideas of honour and gallantry were more exaggerated and refined.

We may add, what indeed has been before incidentally remarked, that their troubadours were the first writers of metrical romances. But by what has been here advanced, I do not mean to insinuate without any restrictions, that the French entirely led the way in these compositions. Undoubtedly the Provençal bards contributed much to the progress of Italian literature. Raimond IV. of Arragon, count of Provence, a lover and a judge of letters, about the year 1220, invited to his court the most celebrated of the songsters who professed to polish and adorn the Provençal language by various sorts of poetry.[1] Charles I., his son-in-law, and the inheritor of his virtues and dignities, conquered Naples, and carried into Italy a taste for the Provençal literature. This taste prevailed at Florence especially, where Charles reigned many years with great splendour, and where his successors resided. Soon afterwards the Roman court was removed to Provence.[2] Hitherto the Latin language had only been in use. The Provençal writers established a common dialect ; and their example convinced other nations that the modern languages were no less adapted to composition than those of antiquity.[3] They introduced a love of reading, and diffused a general and popular taste for poetry, by writing in a language intelligible to the ladies and the people. Their verses, being conveyed in a familiar tongue, became the chief amusement of princes and feudal lords, whose courts had now begun to assume an air of greater brilliancy ; a circumstance which necessarily gave great encouragement to their profession, and by rendering these arts of ingenious entertainment universally fashionable, imper-

---

[1] Giovan. Villani, *Istor.* l. vi. c. 92.

[2] Villani acquaints us, that Brunetti Latini, Dante's master, was the first who attempted to polish the Florentines by improving their taste and style. He died in 1294. See Villan. *ibid.* l. ix. c. 135. [That Brunetti did not write his *Tesoro* in Provençal we have his own authority, and the evidence of the work itself:—Et se aucuns demandoit pourquoi chis livre est escrit en roumans selon la raison de France, pour chou que nous sommes Ytalien je diroie que ch'est pour chou que nous sommes en France ; l'autre pour chou que la parleure en est plus delitable et plus commune a toutes gens. Notices des Manuscripts, t. v. p. 270.--*Price.*]

[3] Dante designed at first that his *Inferno* should appear in Latin. But finding that he could not so effectually in that language impress his satirical strokes and political maxims on the laity or illiterate, he altered his mind, and published that piece in Italian. Had Petrarch written his *Africa*, his Eclogues, and his prose compositions in Italian, the literature of his country would much sooner have arrived at perfection. [Mr. R. Taylor refers to Rossetti's *Spirito Antipapale*, 1832.]

ceptibly laid the foundation of polite literature. From thefe be-
ginnings it were eafy to trace the progrefs of poetry to its perfection,
through John de Meun in France, Dante in Italy, and Chaucer in
England.

This praife muft undoubtedly be granted to the Provençal poets.
But in the mean time, to recur to our original argument, we fhould
be cautious of afferting, in general and undifcriminating terms, that
the Provençal poets were the firft writers of metrical romance : at
leaft we fhould afcertain, with rather more precifion than has been
commonly ufed on this fubject, how far they may claim this merit.
I am of opinion that there were two forts of French troubadours, who
have not hitherto been fufficiently diftinguifhed. If we diligently
examine their hiftory, we fhall find that the poetry of the firft troubadours confifted in fatires, moral fables, allegories, and fentimental
fonnets. So early as the year 1180, a tribunal, called the Court of
Love, was inftituted both in Provence and Picardy, at which queftions in gallantry were decided. This inftitution furnifhed eternal
matter for the poets, who threw the claims and arguments of the
different parties into verfe, in a ftyle that afterwards led the way to
the fpiritual converfations of Cyrus and Clelia.[1] Fontenelle does not
fcruple to acknowledge, that gallantry was the parent of French
poetry.[2] But to fing romantic and chivalrous adventures was a very
different tafk, and required very different talents. The troubadours,
therefore, who compofed metrical romances, form a different fpecies,
and ought always to be confidered feparately. And this latter clafs
feems to have commenced at a later period, not till after the Crufades
had effected a great change in the manners and ideas of the weftern
world. In the meantime I hazard a conjecture. Giraldi Cinthio
fuppofes that the art of the troubadours, commonly called the Gay
Science, was firft communicated from France to the Italians, and
afterwards to the Spaniards.[3] This, perhaps, may be true; but at
the fame time it is highly probable, as the Spaniards had their
Juglares or convivial bards very early, as from long connection they
were immediately and intimately acquainted with the fictions of the
Arabians, and as they were naturally fond of chivalry, that the troubadours of Provence in great meafure caught this turn of fabling
from Spain. To mention no other obvious means of intercourfe in
an affair of this nature, the communication was eafy through the
ports of Toulon and Marfeilles, by which the two nations carried on
from early times a conftant commerce. Even the French critics
themfelves univerfally allow that the Spaniards, having learned
rhyme from the Arabians, through this very channel conveyed it to
Provence. Taffo preferred *Amadis de Gaul*, a romance originally
written in [Portugal] by Vafco Lobeyra before the year 1300,[4] to

---

[1] This part of their character will be infifted upon more at large when we come
to fpeak of Chaucer.
[2] *Theatr. Fr.* p. 13.   [3] *Apud* Huet. *Orig. Rom.* p. 108.
[4] Nic. Antonius, *Bibl. Hifpan. Vet.* tom. ii. l. viii. c. 7, num. 291.

the moft celebrated pieces of the Provençal poets.[1] But this fubject
[has received illuftration from feveral writers to whom we may refer,
Sainte Palaye,[2] Millot,[3] Fauriel,[4] Paulin Paris,[5] Paul Meyer, Gafton
Paris, &c.]

SECTION IV.

ARIOUS matters fuggefted by the Prologue of *Richard
cuer de Lyon*, cited in the laft fection, have betrayed us
into a long digreffion, and interrupted the regularity of
our annals. But I could not neglect fo fair an opportunity of preparing the reader for thofe metrical tales
which, having acquired a new caft of fiction from the Crufades and
a magnificence of manners from the increafe of chivalry, now began
to be greatly multiplied, and as it were profeffedly to form a feparate
fpecies of poetry. I now therefore refume the feries, and proceed
to give fome fpecimens of the Englifh metrical romances which
appeared before or about the reign of Edward II.: and although
moft of thefe pieces continued to be fung by the minftrels in the
halls of our magnificent anceftors for fome [time] afterwards, yet,
as their firft appearance may moft probably be dated at this period,
they properly coincide in this place with the tenor of our hiftory.
In the mean time, it is natural to fuppofe, that by frequent repetition
and fucceffive changes of language during many generations, their
original fimplicity muft have been in fome degree corrupted. Yet
fome of the fpecimens are extracted from manufcripts written in the
reign of Edward III. Others indeed from printed copies, where
the editors took great liberties in accommodating the language to
the times. However, in fuch as may be fuppofed to have fuffered
moft from depravations of this fort, the fubftance of the ancient ftyle
ftill remains, and at leaft the ftructure of the ftory. On the whole,
we mean to give the reader an idea of thofe popular heroic tales in
verfe, profeffedly written for the harp, which began to be multiplied
among us about the beginning of the fourteenth century. We will
begin with the romance of *Richard cuer de Lyon*, already mentioned.

The poem opens with the marriage of Richard's father, Henry
II. with the daughter of Carbarryne, a king of Antioch. But this
is only a lady of romance. Henry married Eleanor, the divorced

---

[1] *Difc. del Poem. Eroic.* l. ii. pp. 45, 46.

[2] [*Memoires fur l'ancienne Chevalerie*, 1781, 3 vols. 12mo.]

[3] [*Hiftoire Litteraire des Troubadours*, 1774, 3 vols. 12mo. An abridged Englifh
verfion appeared in 1807. See Brunet, *dern. edit.* v. 65.]

[4] [*Hiftoire de la Poefie Provençale*, 1847-8, 3 vols. 8vo.]

[5] *Li Romans de Garin le Loherain, publié pour la première fois, et precedé de l'exa-
men du fyftème de M. Fauriel fur les romans Carlovingiens*, 1833-5, 2 vols. 12mo. It
may be worth while to add Bifhop Hurd's *Letters on Chivalry and Romance*, 1762,
8vo.]

queen of Louis of France. The minſtrels could not conceive any
thing leſs than an Eaſtern princeſs to be the mother of this magna-
nimous hero :

> His barons hym ſedde[1]
> That he graunted a wyff to wedde.
> Haſtely he ſente hys ſondes
> Into many dyuerſe londes,
> The feyreſte wyman that wore on liff
> Men wolde[2] bringe hym to wyff.[3]

The meſſengers or ambaſſadors, in their voyage, meet a ſhip adorned
like Cleopatra's galley :

> Swylk on ne ſeygh they never non ;
> All it was whyt of huel-bon,
> And every nayl with gold begrave :
> Off pure gold was the ſtave ;[4]
> Her maſt was [of] yvory ;
> Off ſamyte the ſayl wytterly.
> Her ropes wer off tuely ſylk,
> Al ſo whyt as ony mylk.
> That noble ſchyp was al withoute
> With clothys of golde ſprede aboute ;
> And her loof[5] and her wyndas[6]
> Off aſure forſothe it was.
> In that ſchyp ther wes i-dyght
> Knyghts and ladyys of mekyll myght ;
> And a lady therinne was,
> Bryght as the ſunne thorugh the glas.
> Her men aborde gunne to ſtonde,
> And ſeſyd that other with her honde,
> And prayde hem for to dwelle
> And her counſayl for to telle :
> And they graunted with all ſkylle
> For to telle al at her wylle :
> " Swo wyde landes we have went[7]
> For kyng Henry us has ſent,

---

[1] [redde, *adviſed.*]   [2] [ſholde.]

[3] [The preſent text has been taken from the edition of this romance by Mr.
Weber, who followed a manuſcript of no very early date in Caius College library,
Cambridge. The variations between this and the early printed editions conſiſt
principally in the uſe of a more antiquated phraſeology, with ſome trifling changes
of the ſenſe. The moſt important of theſe are given in the notes below. Mr.
Ellis, who has analyſed this romance (vol. ii. p. 186), conceives the fable in its
preſent form to have originated with the reign of Edward I.; and that the extravagant fictions it contains were grafted by ſome Norman minſtrel upon an earlier
narrative, more in uniſon with Richard's real hiſtory. Of the ſtory in its uncor-
rupted ſtate, he conſiders a fragment occurring in the Auchinlech MS. to be an
Engliſh tranſlation ; and as this document was "tranſcribed in the minority of
Edward III." the following declaration of Mr. Weber may not exceed the truth :
—"There is no doubt that our romance exiſted before the year 1300, as it is
referred to in the Chronicles of Robert of Glouceſter and Robert de Brunne ; and
as theſe rhymeſters wrote for mere Engliſh readers, it is not to be ſuppoſed that
they would refer them to a French original."—*Price.*]

[4] [ſklave, *rudder : clavus.*]

[5] [loft, *deck.* Sir F. Madden refers for an explanation of this word to Michel's
Triſtan, Gloſſ. under *Lof.* and to his own edit. of Laʒamon's *Brut*, 1847, i. 335,
where the word is tranſlated *luff.*]

[6] [wyndlace.]   [7] [" To dyverſe londes do we wende."]

For to feke hym a qwene
The fayrefte that myghte fonde bene."
Upros a kyng off a chayer
With that word they fpoke ther.
The chayer was [of] charboncle fton,
Swylk on ne fawgh they never non :
And tuo dukes hym befyde,
Noble men and mekyl off pryde,
And welcomed the meffangers ylkone.
Into that fchyp they gunne gone. . . .
They fette trefteles and layde a borde;
Cloth of fylk theron was fprad,
And the kyng hymfelve bad,
That his doughter were forth fette,
And in a chayer before hym fette.
Trumpes begonne for to blowe;
Sche was fette forth in a throwe [1]
With twenty knyghtes her aboute
And moo off ladyes that wer ftoute. . .
Whenne they had nygh i-eete,
Adventures to fpeke they nought forgeete.
The kyng ham tolde, in hys refoun
It com hym thorugh a vyfyoun,
In his land that he cam froo,
Into Yngelond for to goo;
And his doughtyr that was fo dere
For to wende bothe in fere,[2]
"In this manere we have us dyght
Into that lande to wende ryght."
Thenne aunfweryd a meffanger,
Hys name was callyd Bernager,
"Forther wole we feke nought
To my lord fhe fchal be brought."

They foon arrive in England, and the lady is lodged in the Tower
of London, one of the royal caftles :

The meffangers the kyng have tolde
Of that ladye fayr and bold,
Ther he lay in the Tour
Off that lady whyt fo flour.
Kyng Henry gan hym fon dyght,
With erls, barons, and manye a knyght.
Agayn the lady for to wende :
For he was curteys and hende.
The damyfele on lond was led,
And clothes of gold before her fpred,
And her fadyr her beforn
With a coron off gold icorn ;
The meffangers be ylk a fyde
And menftralles with mekyl pryde
Kyng Henry lyght in hyyng
And grette fayr that uncouth kyng. . .

---

[1] immediately. [In an ancient Provençal poem, of which M. de Sainte Palaye
has given fome account in his *Mémoires fur l'ancienne Chevalerie*, tom. ii. p. 160,
a mafter gives the following inftructions to his pupil, "Ouvrez a votre cheval par
des coupes redoublés, la route qu'il doit tenir, et que fon portrail foit garni de
beaux grelots ou fonnettes bien rangées; car ces fonnettes reveillent merveilleufe-
ment le courage de celui qui le monte, et repandent devant lui la terreur."—*Douce.*]

[2] company.

> To Weftemenftre they wente in fere
> Lordyngs and ladys that ther were.
> Trumpes begonne for to blowe,
> To mete ¹ they wente in a throwe, &c.²

The firft of our hero's achievements in chivalry is at a fplendid tournament held at Salifbury. Clarendon, near Salifbury, was one of the king's palaces : ³

> Kyng Rychard gan hym dyfguyfe
> In a ful ftrange queyntyfe.⁴
> He cam out of a valaye
> For to fe of theyr playe,
> As a knyght aventurous :
> Hys atyre was orgolous :⁵
> Al togyder cole black
> Was hys horfe withoute lacke ;
> Upon hys creft a raven ftode,
> That yaned ⁶ as he wer wode.
> He bare a fchafte that was grete and ftrong,
> It was fourtene foot long ;
> And it was grete and ftout,
> One and twenty ynches about.⁷
> The fyrft knyght that he there mette,
> Ful egyrly he hym grette
> With a dente amyd the fchelde ;
> His hors he bar doun in the felde, &c.⁸

A battle-axe which Richard carried with him from England into the Holy Land is thus defcribed :

> King Richard, I underftond,
> Or he went out of Englond,

---

¹ to dinner.   ² line 135.

³ In the pipe-rolls of this king's reign I find the following articles relating to this ancient palace, which has been already mentioned incidentally. *Rot. Pip.* 1 *Ric. I.* "Wiltes.—Et in cariagio vini Regis a Clarendon ufque Woodeftoke, 34s. 4d. per Br. Reg. Et pro ducendis 200 m. [marcis] a Sarefburia ufque Briftow, 7s. 4d. per Br. Reg. Et pro ducendis 2500 libris a Sarefburia ufque Glocef-triam, 26s. 10d. per Br. Reg. Et pro tonellis et clavis ad eofdem denarios. Et in cariagio de 4000 marcis a Sarum ufque Suthanton, et pro tonellis et aliis neceffariis, 8s. et 1d. per Br. Reg." And again in *Rot. Pip.* 30 *Hen. III.* "Wilte-fcire.—Et in una marcelfia ad opus regis et reginæ apud Clarendon cum duobus intercluforiis et duabus cameris privatis, hoftio veteris aulæ amovendo in porticu, et de eadem aula camera facienda cum camino et feneftris, et camera privata, et quadam magna coquina coquina quadrata, et aliis operationibus, contentis in Brevi, inceptis per eundem Nicolaum et non perfectis, 526l. 16s. 5d. ob. per Br. Reg." Again, *Rot. Pip.* 39 *Hen. III.* "Sudhamt.—*Comp. Novæ foreftæ.* Et in triginta miliaribus fcindularum [fhingles] faciend. in eadem forefta et cariand. eafdem ufque Clarendon ad domum regis ibidem cooperiandam, 6l. et 1 marc. per Br. Reg. Et in 30 mill. fcindularum faciend. in eadem, et cariand. ufque Clarendon, 11l. 10s." And again, in the fame reign, the canons of Ivy-church receive penfions for celebrating in the royal chapel there. *Rot. Pip.* 7 *Hen. III.* "Wiltes.—Et canonicis de monafterio ederofo miniftrantibus in Capella de Clarendon. 35l. 7d. ob." Stukeley is miftaken in faying this palace was built by King John.

⁴ See Du Cange, *Gl. Lat.* Cointife.

⁵ proud, pompous.   ⁶ yawned.

⁷ It is "One and twenti inches aboute." So Dr. Farmer's MS., purchafed from Mr. Martin's library. See *fupr.* This is in Englifh.

⁸ line 267.

Let him make an axe[1] for the nones,
To breke therwith the Saraſyns[2] bones.
The head was wrought right wele ;
Therin was twenty pounde of ſtele ;
And when he came into Cyprus lond,
The ax he tok in his hond.
All that he hit, he all to-frapped ;
The griffons[3] away faſt rapped ;
Natheles many he cleaved,
And their unthanks ther by-lived ;
And the priſoun when he cam to,
With his ax he ſmot right tho,
Dores, barres, and iron chains, &c.[4]

This formidable axe is again mentioned at the ſiege of Acon or Acre, the ancient Ptolemais :

Kyng Rychard aftyr, anon ryght,
Toward Acres gan hym dyght ;
And as he ſaylyd toward Surreye,[5]
He was warnyd off a ſpye,
Howe the folk off the hethene lawe
A gret cheyne hadden i-drawe
Ovei the havene of Acres ſers,
And was feſtnyd to two pelèrs,
That noo ſchyp ne ſcholde in-wynne,[6]
Ne they nought out that wer withynne.
Therfore ſevene yer and more
Alle Cryſtene kynges leyen thore,
And with gret hongyr ſuffryd payne,
For lettyng off that ilke chayne.
Kyng Richard herd that tydyng ;
For joye hys herte beganne to ſprynge,
And ſwor and ſayde in his thought,
That ylke chayne ſcholde helpe hem nought
A ſwythe ſtrong galeye he took,
And[7] Trenchemer,[8] ſo ſays the book,

---

[1] Richard's battle-axe is alſo mentioned by [de] Brunne, and on this occaſion, *Chron.* p. 159.

[2] The Cruſades imported the phraſe Jeu Sarrazionois, for any ſharp engagement, into the old French romances.—Thus in the *Roman d'Alexandre*, MSS. Bibl. Bodl. *ut ſupr.* P. 1.

    " Tholomer le regrette et le plaint en Grijois,
      Et diſt que s'il cuſſent o culz telz vingt et trois,
      Il nous euſſent fet un Jeu Sarrazionois."

[3] The Byzantine Greeks are often called Griffones by the hiſtorians of the middle ages. See Du Cange *Gloſſ. Ville-Hard.* p. 363. See alſo Rob. [de] Brun. *Chron.* pp. 151, 157, 159, 160, 165, 171, 173. Wanley ſuppoſes that the Griffin in heraldry was intended to ſignify a Greek or Saracen, whom they thus repreſented under the figure of an imaginary eaſtern monſter, which never exiſted but as an armorial badge.

[4] line 2196.   [5] Syria.

[6] So Fabyan, of Roſamond's bower : " that no creature, man or woman, myght *wynne* to her," *i. e.* go in, by contraction, Wih. *Chron.* vol. i. p. 320, col. i. edit. 1533. [þinnan A.-S. to labour, ſtrive at, and hence attain to by labour.—*Price.*]

[7] Rob. [de] Brun. *Chron.* p. 170.

    " The kynge's owne galeie he cald it *Trencthemere.*"

    [8] [" *Trenchemere*, ſo ſaith the boke.—
      The galey yede as ſwift
      As ony fowle by the lyfte."]

Steryd the galey ryght ful evene,
Ryght in the myddes off the havene.
Wer the maryners faughte or wrothe,
He made hem fayle and rowe bothe ;
And kynge Rychard, that was fo good,
With hys axe in forefchyp ftood.
And whenne he com the cheyne too,
With hys ax he fmot it in two,[1]
That all the barouns, verrayment,
Sayde it was a noble dent ;
And for joye off this dede
The cuppes faft abouten yede,[2]
With good wyn, pyement and clarré ;
And faylyd toward Acres cyté.
Kyng Richard, oute of hys galye,
Cafte wylde-fyr into the fkeye,
And fyr Gregeys into the fee,
And al on fyr wer thê.
Trumpes yede in hys galeye,
Men mighte it here into the fkye,
Taboures and hornes Sarezyneys,[3]
The fee brent all off fyr Gregeys.[4]

This *fyr Gregeys*, or Grecian fire, feems to be a compofition belonging to the Arabian chemiftry. It is frequently mentioned by the
Byzantine hiftorians, and was very much ufed in the wars of the
middle ages, both by fea and land. It was a fort of wild-fire, faid to
be inextinguifhable by water, [but innocuous againft vinegar prepared
in a certain manner,] and chiefly ufed for burning fhips, againft which
it was thrown in pots or phials by the hand. In land engagements
it feems to have been difcharged by machines conftructed on purpofe.
The oriental Greeks pretended that this artificial fire was invented
by Callinicus, an architect of Heliopolis, under Conftantine ; and
that Conftantine prohibited them from communicating the manner
of making it to any foreign people. It was, however, in common ufe
among the nations confederated with the Byzantines ; and Anna
Comnena has given an account of its ingredients,[5] which were bitu-
men, fulphur, and naphtha. It is called *feu gregois* in the French
chronicles and romances. Our minftrel, I believe, is fingular in
faying that Richard fcattered this fire on Saladin's fhips : many
monkifh hiftorians of the holy war, in defcribing the fiege of Acon,
relate that it was employed on that occafion and many others by the
Saracens againft the Chriftians.[6] Procopius, in his hiftory of the
Goths, calls it *Medea's Oil*, as if it had been a preparation ufed in the
forceries of that enchantrefs.[7]

---

[1] Thus R. de Brunne fays, " he fondred the Sarazyns otuynne." p. 574. [But *fondred* feems to be a mif-reading for *fondred*, parted or clove.]
[2] went. [3] [fhalmys, *fhawms*.] [4] line 2593.
[5] See Du Cange, *Not. ad. Joinvil.* p. 71. And *Gl. Lat.*, V. *Ignis Græcus*.
[6] See more particularly *Chron.* Rob. [de] Brun. p. 170. And Benedict. Abb. p.
652. And Joinv. *Hift.* L. pp. 39, 46, 52, 53, 62, 70.
[7] iv. 11.

The quantity of huge battering rams and other military engines, now unknown, which Richard is faid to have tranfported into the Holy Land, was prodigious. The names of fome of them are given in another part of this romance.[1] It is an hiftorical fact, that Richard was killed by the French from the fhot of an arcubalift, a machine which he often worked fkilfully with his own hands : and Guillaume le Breton, a Frenchman, in his Latin poem called *Philippeis*, introduces Atropos making a decree that Richard fhould die by no other means than by a wound from this deftructive inftrument, the ufe of which, after it had been interdicted by the Pope in the year 1139, he revived, and is fuppofed to have fhown the French in the Crufades :[2]

> [Ginnes ?] he hadde on wondyr wyfe ;
> Mang[o]neles[3] off gret queintyfe ;[4]
> Arwblaft bowe, and[5] with gynne
> The Holy Lond[e] for to wynne.
> Ovyr al othyr wyttyrly,
> A melle[6] he hadde off gret mayftry ;

---

[1] " Twenty grete gynnes for the nones
Kynge Richard fent for to caft ftones," &c.

Among thefe were the Mategriffon and the Robynet. Sign. N. iii. The former of thefe is thus defcribed. Sign. E. iiii. :

> " I have a caftell I underftonde
> Is made of tembre of Englonde
> With fyxe ftages full of tourelles
> Well flouryfhed with cornelles," &c.

See Du Cange *Not. Joinv.* p. 68, Mategryffon is the Terror or plague of the Greeks. Du Cange, in his [*Hiftoire de Conftantinople fous les empereurs Français,*] mentions a caftle of this name in Peloponefus. Benedict fays that Richard erected a ftrong caftle, which he called Mate-gryffon, on the brow of a fteep mountain without the walls of the city of Meffina in Sicily. Benedict. Abb. p. 621, ed. Hearn. fub. ann. 1190. Robert de Brunne mentions this engine from our romance. *Chron.* p. 157 :

> " The romancer it fais Richarde did make a pele,
> On kaftelle wife allwais wrought of tre ful wele.—
> In fchip he ded it lede, &c. . . . . .
> His pele from that dai forward he cald it Mate-griffon."

Pele is a houfe [a caftle, fortification]. Archbifhop Turpin mentions Charlemagne's wooden caftles at the fiege of a city in France, cap. ix.

[2] See Carpentier's *Suppl. Du Cange*, Lat. Gl. tom. i. p. 434. And Du Cange, *ad Ann. Alex* p. 357.

[3] See *fupr.* It is obfervable that *Manganum*, Mangonell, was not known among the Roman military machines, but exifted firft in the Byzantine Greek Μαγγανον, a circumftance which feems to point out its inventors, at leaft to fhew that it belonged to the oriental art of war. It occurs often in the Byzantine Tactics, although at the fame time it was perhaps derived from the Latin *Machina :* yet the Romans do not appear to have ufed in their wars fo formidable and complicated an engine, as this is defcribed to have been in the writers of the dark ages. It was the capital machine of the wars of thofe ages. Du Cange, in his [*Conftantinople fous les empereurs Français*] mentions a vaft area at Conftantinople in which the machines of war were kept. p. 155.

[4] See *fupr.*   [5] [made.]   [6] mill.

In myddys a fchyp for to ftand ;
Swylke on fawgh nevyr man in land :
Four[e] fayles wer theretoo,
Yelew and grene, red and bloo.
With canevas layd wel al about,
Ful fchyr withinne and eke without ;
Al withinne ful off feer,
Of torches maad with wex ful cleer ;
Ovyrtwart and endelang,
With ftrenges of wyr the ftones hang ;[1]
Stones that deden never note,
Grounde they never whete, no grote,
But rubbyd as they wer wood.
Out of the eye ran red blood.[2]
Beffore the trowgh there ftood on ;
Al in blood he was begon,
And hornes grete upon his hede ;
Sarezynes theroff hadde gret drede.[3]

The laft circumftance recalls a fiend-like appearance drawn by Shakefpeare ; in which, exclufive of the application, he has converted ideas of deformity into the true fublime, and rendered an image terrible, which in other hands would have probably been ridiculous :—

Methought his eyes
Were two full moons ; he had a thoufand nofes,
Horns whelk'd and wav'd like the enridged fea,
It was fome fiend——[4]

---

[1] [With fpryngelles of fyre they dyde honde.]—Efpringalles, Fr. Engines. See Du Cange, *Gl. Lat.* Spingarda, Quadrellus. And Not. Joinv. p. 78. Perhaps he means pellets of tow dipped in the Grecian fire, which fometimes were thrown from a fort of mortar. Joinville fays, that the Greek fire thrown from a mortar looked like a huge dragon flying through the air, and that at midnight the flashes of it illuminated the Chriftian camp, as if it had been broad day. When Louis's army was encamped on the banks of the Thanis in Ægypt, fays the fame curious hiftorian, about the year 1249, they erected two *chats chateils*, or covered galleries, to fhelter their workmen, and at the end of them two *befrois*, or vaft moveable wooden towers, full of crofsbow men, who kept a continual difcharge on the oppofite fhore. Befides eighteen other new-invented engines for throwing ftones and bolts. But in one night, the deluge of Greek fire ejected from the Saracen camp utterly deftroyed thefe enormous machines. This was a common difafter; but Joinville fays, that his pious monarch fometimes averted the danger, by proftrating himfelf on the ground, and invoking our Saviour with the appellation of *Beau Sire*, pp. 37, 39.

[2] This device is thus related by Robert of Brunne, *Chron.* pp. 175-176:

" Richard als fuithe did raife his engyns
The Inglis wer than blythe, Normans and Petevyns :
In bargeis and galeis he fet mylnes to go,
The failes, as men fais, fom were blak and blo,
Som were rede and grene, the wynde about them blewe.
The ftones were of Rynes, the noyfe dreadfull and grete ;
It affraied the Sarazins ; as leven the fyre out fchete.
The noyfe was unride," &c.

Rynes is the river Rhine, whofe fhores or bottom fupplied the ftones fhot from their military engines. The Normans, a barbarous people, appear to have ufed machines of immenfe and very artificial conftruction at the fiege of Paris in 885. See the laft note. And *Vit. Saladin.* per Schultens, pp. 135, 141, 167, &c.

[3] Line 2631.   [4] King Lear, iv. vi. [Dyce's edit. 1868, vii. 324.]

At the touch of this powerful magician, to fpeak in Milton's language, "The griefly terror grows tenfold more dreadful and deform."

The moving caftles defcribed by our minftrel, which feem to be fo many fabrics of romance, but are founded in real hiftory, afforded fuitable materials for poets who deal in the marvellous. Accordingly they could not efcape the fabling genius of Taffo, who has made them inftruments of enchantment, and accommodated them with great propriety to the operations of infernal fpirits.

At the fiege of Babylon, the foldan Saladin fends King Richard a horfe. The meffenger fays :

> Thou fayeft thy God is ful of myght :
> Wylt thou graunt, with fpere and fcheeld,
> Deraye the ryghte in the feeld,
> With helm, hawberk and brondes bryght
> On ftrong[e] ftedes, good and lyght,
> Whether is off more powèr
> Jefu or Jubyter ?
> And he fente thè to fay this,
> Yiff thou wilt have an hors [of] hys ?
> In alle the landes ther thou haft gon,
> Swylk on fay thou nevyr non !
> Favel off Cypre, ne Lyard off Prys,[1]
> Are nought at nede as that he is ;
> And, yiff thou wylt, this felve day
> It fhall be brought thè to afay.'
> Quoth kyng Richard : "Thou fayeft wel ;
> Swylke an hors, by Seynt Mychel,

---

[1] Horfes belonging to Richard, "Favel of Cyprus and Lyard of Paris." Robert de Brunne mentions one of thefe horfes, which he calls [Fauuel]. *Chron.* p. 175 :

> "Sithen at Japhet was flayn [Fauuel] his ftede,
> The Romans telles gret pas ther of his douhty dede."

This is our romance, viz. Sign. Q. iii. :

> "To hym gadered every chone
> And flewe Favell under hym,
> Tho was Richard wroth and grym."

This was at the fiege of Jaffa, as it is here called. Favell of Cyprus is again mentioned, Sign. O. ii. :

> "Favell of Cyprus is forth fet
> And in the fadell he hym fett."

Robert of Brunne fays that Saladin's brother fent King Richard a horfe. *Chron.* p. 194 :

> "He fent to King Richard a ftede for curteifie
> On of the beft reward that was in paemie."

In the wardrobe-roll of Prince Edward, afterwards Edward II., under the year 1272, the mafters of the horfe render their accounts for horfes purchafed, fpecifying the colours and prices with the greateft accuracy. One of them is called "Unus equus *favellus* cum ftella in fronte," &c. Hearne's *Joann. de Trokelowe.* Præf. p. xxvi. Here *favellus* is interpreted by Hearne to be *honeycomb.* I fuppofe he underftands a dappled or roan horfe. But *favellus*, evidently an adjective, is barbarous Latin for *falvus* or *fulvus*, a dun or light yellow, a word often ufed to exprefs the colour of horfes and hawks. See Carpentier, Suppl. Du Cange, *Lat. Glos.* V. *Favellus*, tom. ii. p. 370. It is hence that King Richard's horfe is called Favel. From which word [Fauvel] in Robert de Brunne is a corruption.

I wolde have to ryde upon.
Bydde hym fende that hors to me ;
I fchal afaye, what that he be.
Yiff he be trufty, withoute fayle
I kepe non othir in batayle."
The meffanger thenne home wente,
And tolde the Sawdon in presènte,
Hou kyng Richard wolde hym mete.
The rych[e] Sawdon, al fo fkete,
A noble clerk he fente for thenne
A maftyr negromacien,[1]
That conjuryd as [I] you telle,
Thorwgh the feendes craft off helle,
Twoo ftrongè feendes off the eyr
In lykneffe off twoo ftedes fevr,
Lykè bothe of hewe and here ;
As they faydè that wer there,
Never was ther feen non flyke.
That on was a merè lyke,
That other a colt, a noble ftede,
Wher he wer in ony nede,
Was nevyr kyng ne knyght[2] fo bolde,
That, whenne the damè neyghè[3] wolde,
Scholde hym holde agayn hys wylle,
That he ne woldè renne her tylle,[4]
And knele adoun, and foukè[5] hys dame :
That whyle, the Sawdon [thought] with fchame,
Scholde Kyng Richard foone aquelle.
All thus an aungyl gan hym telle,
That cam to hym aftyr mydnyght ;
And fayd " Awake, thou Goddes knyght !
My lord[6] dos thè to undyrftande,
Thè fchal com an hors to hande ;
Fayr he is off body pyght ;
Betraye thè yiff the Sawdon myght.
On hym to ryde have thou no drede,
He fchal thè help[en] at thy nede."

The angel then gives King Richard feveral directions about managing this infernal horfe, and a general engagement enfuing, between the Chriftian and Saracen armies :—[7]

To lepe to hors thenne was he dyght ;
Into the fadyl or he leep,
Off many thynge he took keep.
Hys men him brought al that he badde.
A quarry tree off fourty foote
Before hys fadyl anon dyd hote

---

[1] necromancer.   [2] his rider.   [3] neigh.
[4] go to her.   [5] fuck.   [6] God.
[7] In which the Saracen line extended twelve miles in length, and
         " The grounde myght unnethe be fene
         For bryght armure and fperes kene."
Again
         " Lyke as fnowe lyeth on the mountaynes
         So were fulfylled hylles and playnes
         With hauberkes bryght and harneys clere
         Of trompettes, and tabourere."

Faſte that men ſcholde it brace, &c.
Hymſelf was rychely begoo
From the creſt unto the too.[1]
He was armyd wondyr weel,
And al with plates off good ſteel;
And ther aboven, an hawberk;
A ſchafft wrought off truſty werk;
On his ſchuldre a ſcheeld off ſteel,
With three lupardes[2] wrought ful weel.
An helme he hadde off ryche entayle;
Truſty and trewè hys ventayle;
On hys creſt a douvè whyte
Sygnyfycacioun off the Holy Spryte:
Upon a croys the douvè ſtood,
Off goldè wrought ryche and good.
God[3] hymſelf, Mary and Jhon,
As he was naylyd the roode upon,[4]
In ſygne off hym for whom he faught,
The ſperè-hed forgatt he naught:
Upon hys ſpere he wolde it have,
Goddes hygh name theron was grave.
Now herkenes what oth they ſwore,
Ar they to the batayle wore:
Yiff it were ſoo, that Richard myght
Sloo the Sawdon in feeld with fyght,
Hee and alle hys ſcholde gon,
At her wylle everilkon,
Into the cytè off Babylone;
And the kyngdom of Maſſidoyne
He ſcholde have undyr his hand:
And yiff the Sawdon off that land
Myghte ſloo Richard in that feeld
With ſwerd or ſpere undyr ſcheeld,
That Criſtene men ſcholde goo
Out off that land for ever moo,
And Sarezynes have her wylle in wolde.
Quod kyng Richard: " Thertoo I holde!
Thertoo my glove, as I am knyght!"
They ben armyd and wel i-dyght.
Kyng Richard into the ſadyl leep;
Who that wolde, theroff took keep.
To ſee, that ſyght was ful fayr.
The ſtede[s] ran ryght with gret ayr,[5]
Al ſo harde as they myght dure,
Aftyr her feet ſprong the fure,
Tabours beten, and trumpes blowe;
Ther myghte men ſee in a throwe,
How kyng Richard, the noble man,
Encounteryd with the Sawdan,
That cheef was told off Damas.[6]
Hys truſt upon hys merè was.
Therfoore, as the booke[7] telles,

---

[1] from head to foot.   [2] leopards.   [3] Our Saviour.
[4] " As he died upon the cross."   So in [the fragmentary verſion of the *Brut.*]
cited by Hearne, *Gloſſ. Rob. Br.* p. 634.

" Pyned under Ponce Pilat,
Don on the rod after that."

[5] ire.   [6] See Du Cange, *Joinv.* p. 87.   [7] The French romance.

Hys crouper heeng al ful off belles,[1]
And his peytrel [2] and his arſoun [3]
Three myle myghte men here the ſoun.
The mere gan nygh, her belles to ryng
For grete pryde, withoute leſyng,
A brod fawchoun to hym he bar,
For he thought that he wolde thar
Have ſlayn kyng Richard with treſoun,
Whenne hys hors had knelyd doun,
As a colt that ſcholde ſouke.
And he was war off that pouke : [4]
Hys [5] eeres with wax wer ſtoppyd faſt,
Therfore was he nought agaſt.
He ſtrook the feend that undyr hym yede,
And gaff the Sawdon a dynt off dede.
In his blaſoun, verrayment,
Was i-paynted a ſerpent.
With the ſpere, that Richard heeld,
He beor him thorwgh and undyr the ſcheeld,
None off hys armes myghtè laſte ;
Brydyl and peytrel al to-braſt ;
Hys gerth and hys ſteropes alſoo ;
The merè to the grounde gan goo.
Mawgry him, he garte hym ſtaupe [6]
Bakward ovyr hys meres croupe ;
The feet toward the fyrmament.
Behynd the Sawdon the ſpere out went.
He leet hym lye upon the grene ; [7]
He prekyd the feend with ſpores [8] kene ;
In the name off the Holy Goſt,
He dryves into the hethene hooſt,

---

[1] Anciently no perſon ſeems to have been gallantly equipped on horſeback, unleſs the horſe's bridle or ſome other part of the furniture was ſtuck full of ſmall bells. Vincent of Beauvais, who wrote about 1264, cenſures this piece of pride in the knights-templars. They have, he ſays, bridles embroidered, or gilded, or adorned with ſilver, " Atque in pectoralibus campanulas infixas magnum emittentes ſonitum, ad gloriam eorum et decorem." Hiſt. lib. xxx. cap. 85. Wicliffe, in his *Trialoge,* inveighs againſt the prieſts for their "fair hors, and jolly and gay ſadeles, and bridles ringing by the way," &c. Lewis's *Wickliffe,* p. 121. Hence Chaucer may be illuſtrated, who thus deſcribes the ſtate of a monk on horſeback. *Prol. Cant. Tales,* v. 170:

> " And when he rode, men might his bridell here
> Gingling in a whiſtling wind as clere,
> And eke as lowde, as doth the chapell bell."

That is, becauſe his horſe's bridle or trappings were ſtrung with bells.
[2] The breaſt-plate, or breaſt-band of a horſe. *Poitral,* Fr. *Pectorale,* Lat. Thus Chaucer, of the Chanones Yemans horſe. *Chan. Yem. Prol.* v. 575:

> " About the paytrell ſtoode the fome ful hie."

[3] The ſaddle-bow. "Arcenarium extencellatum cum argento," occurs in the wardrobe rolls, ab an. 21 ad an. 23 Edw. III. Membr. xi. This word is not in Du Cange or his *Supplement.*
[4] [And he was ware of that ſhame.]   [5] The colt's ears.
[6] [Maugre her heed, he made her ſeche
The grounde, withoute more ſpeche.]
[7] [Ther he fell dede on the grene.]   [8] ſpurs.

And al fo foone as he was come,
He brak afunder the fcheltrome ;
For al that ever before hym ftode
Hors and man to erthe yode,
Twenty foot on every fyde, &c.
Whenne they of Fraunce wyfte,
That the mayftry hadde the Chryfte,
They wer bolde, her herte they tooke ;
Stedes prekyd, fchaufftes fchooke.[2]

Richard arming himfelf is a curious Gothic picture. It is certainly
a genuine picture, and drawn with fome fpirit : as is the fhock of
the two necromantic fteeds, and other parts of this defcription.
The combat of Richard and the Soldan, on the event of which the
Chriftian army got poffeffion of the city of Babylon, is probably the
Duel of King Richard, painted on the walls of a chamber in the
royal palace of Clarendon. The foldan is reprefented as meeting
Richard with ["A faucon brode," or a broad falchion,] in his hand.
Tabour, a drum, a common accompaniment of war, is mentioned
as one of the inftruments of martial mufic in this battle with characteriftical propriety. It was imported into the European armies from
the Saracens in the holy war. The word is conftantly written tabour,
not tambour, in Joinville's *Hiftory of Saint Louis,* and all the elder
French romances. Joinville defcribes a fuperb bark or galley belonging to a Saracen chief, which he fays was filled with fymbols,
tabours, and Saracen horns.[3] Jean d'Orronville, an old French
chronicler of the life of Louis, duke of Bourbon, relates that the
king of France, the king of Thrafimere, and the king of Bugie,
landed in Africa according to their cuftom with cymbals, kettle-
drums, tabours,[4] and whiftles.[5] Babylon, here faid to be befieged
by King Richard, and fo frequently mentioned by the romance
writers and the chroniclers of the Crufades, is Cairo or Bagdat.
Cairo and Bagdat, cities of recent foundation, were perpetually confounded with Babylon, which had been deftroyed many centuries
before, and was fituated at a confiderable diftance from either. Not
the leaft enquiry was made in the dark ages concerning the true
fituation of places, or the difpofition of the country in Paleftine,

---

[1] *Schiltron.* I believe, foldiers drawn up in a circle. Rob. de Brunne ufes it in
defcribing the battle of Fowkirke, *Chron.* p. 305 :
    " Ther Scheltron fone was fhad with Inglis that wer gode."
Shad is *feparated.* [Scheltron, *turma clipeata,* a troop armed with fhields. See
Jamiefon's *Etymol. Scott. Dict.—Price.*]
[2] Line 5642.
[3] *Hiftoire de S. Loys,* p. 30. The original has " Cors Sarazinois." See alfo
pp. 52, 56. And Du Cange's Notes, p. 61.
[4] [Roquefort, who cites the fame paffage, calls Glais a mufical inftrument, without defining its peculiar nature.—*Price.*]
[5] Cap. 76. Nacaires is here the word for kettle-drums. See Du Cange, *ubi
fupr.* p. 59. Who alfo from an old roll "de la chambre des Comptes de Paris"
recites, among the houfehold muficians of a French nobleman, " Meneftrel du
Cor Sarazinois," *ib.* p. 60. This inftrument is not uncommon in the French
romances.

although the theatre of fo important a war; and to this neglect were owing, in a great meafure, the fignal defeats and calamitous diftreffes of the Chriftian adventurers, whofe numerous armies, deftitute of information, and cut off from every refource, perifhed amidft unknown mountains and impracticable waftes. Geography at this time had been but little cultivated. It had been ftudied only from the ancients: as if the face of the earth and the political ftate of nations had not, fince the time of thofe writers, undergone any changes or revolutions.

So formidable a champion was King Richard againft the infidels, and fo terrible the remembrance of his valour in the holy war, that the Saracens and Turks ufed to quiet their froward children only by repeating his name. Joinville is the only writer who records this anecdote. He adds another of the fame fort. When the Saracens were riding, and their horfes ftarted at any unufual object, "ils difoient a leurs chevaulx en les picquant de l'efperon: et cuides tu que ce foit le Roy Richart?"[1] It is extraordinary that thefe circumftances fhould have efcaped Malmefbury, Matthew Paris, [Benedictus Abbas], Langtoft, and the reft of our old hiftorians, who have exaggerated the character of this redoubted hero by relating many particulars more likely to be fabulous, and certainly lefs expreffive of his prowefs.

SECTION V.

HE romance of *Sir Guy* which [probably in one of its earlier casts, as exhibited in the Auchinleck MS.] is enumerated by Chaucer among the " Romances of pris," affords a feries of fictions cuftomary in pieces of this fort, concerning the [adventures of the hero both in England and abroad.[2] The following is the defcription of the firft meeting of Guy and Felice, his future wife:[3]

---

[1] *Hift. de S. Loys*, pp. 16, 104. Who had it from a French MS. chronicle of the holy war. See Du Cange's Notes, p. 45.

[2] [See *The Romances of Sir Guy of Warwick, and Rembrun his Son. Now firft edited from the Auchinleck MS.* (by W. B. D. D. Turnbull). Edinburgh: Printed for the Abbotsford Club. MDCCCXL. In the Preface the Editor has given an account of the various MSS. and printed editions of the romance, and has printed at length a fragment of an otherwife unknown Englifh verfion in the poffeffion of Sir Thomas Philipps.] The [old printed] copy of Sir Guy is a confiderable volume in quarto. My edition is without date, " Imprynted at London in Lothbury by Wylliam Copland," with rude wooden cuts. It runs to Sign. Ll. iii. [An imperfect copy is in Garrick's Collection, vol. K, 9, and a perfect one was in Heber's library, Cat. pt. iv. 961. A fragment of this romance belonged to Dr. Farmer, and afterwards to Mr. Douce, which Ritfon in his MS. Cat. of Engl. Romances, ftates to have been printed by W. de Worde, about 1495. In the poffeffion of Mr. Staunton of Longbridge Houfe, co. Warw. is a larger fragment of thirty-fix leaves, printed in a thinner letter than W. de Worde's, with wood-cuts, which I

" It was opon a Pentecoſt day y-teld
Therl a gret feſt held
At Warwike in that cite
That than was y-won to be
Thider cam men of miche might
Erls and barouns bothe aplight
Leuedis and maidens of gret mounde
That in the lond wer y-founde
Eueriche maiden ches hir loue
Of knightes that wer thider y-come
And euerich knight his leman
Of that gentil maiden wiman
When thai were fro chirche y-come
Ther alight mani a noble gome
Therl to the mete was ſett
Gij ſtode forn him in that ſlett
That was the ſteward ſone
Therl to ſerue it was his wone
To him he cleped Gij
And him hete and comandi
That he in to chaumber went

ſhould feel inclined to aſcribe to Pynſon. Ritſon mentions alſo an edition by John Cawood.—*Madden.*

It ſeems to be older than the *Squyr of lowe degree,* in which it is quoted. Sign. a. iii.:

" Or els ſo bolde in chivalrie
As was ſyr Gawayne or ſyr Gie."

The two beſt MSS. are at Cambridge, MSS. Bibl. Publ. Mor. 690, 33, and MSS. Coll. Caii, A 8, from which text it has now been given.

An analyſis of this romance will be found in the " Specimens " of Mr. Ellis, who is of opinion that " the tale in its preſent ſtate has been compoſed from the materials of at leaſt two or three if not more romances. The firſt is a moſt tireſome love ſtory which, it may be preſumed, originally ended with the marriage of the fond couple. To this it ſhould ſeem was afterwards tacked on a ſeries of freſh adventures, invented or compiled by ſome pilgrim from the Holy Land ; and the hero of this legend was then brought home for the defence of Athelſtan and the deſtruction of Colbrand." Mr. Ritſon, in oppoſition to Dugdale, who regarded Guy as an undeniably hiſtorical perſonage, has laboured to prove that " no hero of this name is to be found in real hiſtory," and that he was " no more an Engliſh hero than Amadis de Gaul or Perceforeſt." Mr. Ellis, on the other hand, con-ceives the tale " may poſſibly be founded on ſome Saxon tradition," and that though the name in its preſent form be undoubtedly French, yet as it bears ſome reſemblance to Egil, the name of an Icelandic warrior, who " contributed very materially to the important victory gained by Athelſtan over the Danes and their allies at Brunanburgh," he thinks " it is not impoſſible that this warlike foreigner may have been transformed by ſome Norman monk into the pious and amorous Guy of Warwick." This at beſt is but conjecture, nor can it be conſidered a very happy one. Egil himſelf (or his nameleſs biographer) makes no mention of a ſingle combat on the occaſion in which he had been engaged ; and the fact, had it occurred, would have been far too intereſting, and too much in uniſon with the ſpirit of the times, to have been paſſed over in ſilence. In addition to this, the ſubſtitution of Guy for Egil is againſt all analogy, on the transformation of a Northern into a French appellation. The initial letters in Guy, Guyon, and Guido, are the repreſentatives of the Teutonic W, and clearly point to ſome cognomen beginning with the Saxon Wig, *bellum.*—*Price.*]

[3] [In the preſent edition extracts from the Auchinleck MS., as printed in 1840, have been ſubſtituted for Warton's quotations from Copland's modernized and altered text.]

And grete wele that maiden gent
And that he fchuld that ich day
Serue wele that feir may
 Gij him anfwerd freliche
Sir Ichil wel bletheliche
In a kirtel of filk he gan him fchrede
Into chaumber wel fone he zede
The kirtel bicom him fwithe wel
To amenden theron was neuer a del
The maidens biheld him feir an wel
For that he was fo gentil
Gij on his knes fone him fett
And on hir fader half he hir grett
And feyd he was thider fent
To ferue hir to hir talent
Felice anfwerd than to Gij
Bieus amis molt gramerci
And feththe fche afked him in the plas
Whennes he cam and what he was
Mi fader he feyd hat Suward
That is thi fader fteward
That with him me hath y-held
And forth y-brought God him foryeld
Artow fche feyd Suward fone
That of al godenes hath the wone
Gij ftode ftille and feyd nought
With that was the water forth brought
Thai fett hem to mete anon
Erl baroun fweyn and grom[1]

We fhall next give the account of the knighthood of our hero:[2]

It was at the holy Trinite
Therl dubbed Sir Gij the fre
And with him tventi god gomis
Knightes and riche baroun fonis
Of cloth of Tars and riche cendel
Was he dobbeing euerich adel
The pauis al of fow and griis
The mantels weren of michel priis
With riche armour and gode ftedes
The beft that wer in lond at nedis
Alder beft was Gij y-dight
Thei he wer an emperour fone aplight
So richeliche dubbed was he
Nas no fwiche in this cuntre
With riche ftedes wel erninde
Palfreys courfours wele bereinde
No was ther noither fweyn no knaue
That ought failed that he fchuld haue
 How is Sir Gij dobbed to knight
Feir he was and michel of might
To Felice went Sir Gij
And gret her wel curteyflie
And feyd Ichaue don aftow feydeft me to
For the Ichaue fuffred miche wo
Arme for the Ichaue vnderfong
The to fe me thought long

[1] [Ed. 1840, pp. 3-5.] [2] [*Ibid.* p. 22.]

> Thou art me bothe leue and dere
> Ich am y-comen thi wille to here.

A knight, who goes under the name of Amis of the Mountain, is introduced into this romance, and in the fequel, where the later adventures of Guy's fon, Rembrun, are related, the fame character is defcribed as fuffering a captivity in a myfterious and inacceffible caftle, from which, however, Rembrun fucceeds in delivering him. Here is a picture of Rembrun's journey in fearch of the caftle:

> Amorwe Rembroun aros erly
> And armede him ful haftely
>   For to winne pris
> A gode ftede he beftrod
> And forth a wente withoute abod
>   To the foreft Y wis
>
> Heraud with him go wolde
> Ac he feide that he ne fcholde
>   For non fkines nede
> And he dradde of him ftrangliche
> And betaughte him God in heuen riche
>   And in is wey a yede
> Heraud blefte and he gan gon
> The merkes ftake a pafed anon
>   That was wel vnrede
> Al the dai a tok the pas
> Til it noun apafed was
>   Ridand vpon is ftede
>
> An hille he fegh before him there
> Gates theron maked were
>   Forth right he rod in
> The gate agen anon was fpered
> Tho was Rembroun fore afered
>   And fafte bleffede him
> Nought he ne fegh boute the fterneffe
> Half a mile a rod Y wiffe
>   The wai was therk and dim
> He rod afe fafte afe a mighte
> Thanne he fegh more lighte
>   Be a water is brim
>
> To the water he com fone thas
> A riuer be a launde ther was
>   Thar he gan to lighte
> Faire hit was y-growe with gras
> A fairer place neuer nas
>   That he fegh with fighte
> On that place was a paleis on
> Swich ne fegh he neuer non
>   Ne of fo meche mighte
> The walles were of criftal
> The heling was of fin ruwal
>   That fchon fwithe brighte
>
> The reftes al cipres be
> That fwote fmal caften he
>   Ouer al aboute
> The refins wer of fin coral
> Togedre iuned with metal
>   Withinne and ek withoute
> On the front ftod a charbokel fton

Ouer al the contre it fchon
Withouten eni doute
Poftes and laces that ther were
Of iafpe gentil that was dere
Al of one foute

The paleis was beloken al
Aboute with a marbel wal
Of noble entaile
Upon eueriche kernal
Was ful of fperes and of fpringal
And ftoutliche enbataile
Withoute the gate ftod a tre
With foules of mani kines gle
Singande withoute faile
The water was fo fterne and grim
Mighte no man come therin
Boute he hadde fchip to faile

Rembroun dorfte nought pafy
With is fpere a gan it prouy
How dep hit was befide
He thoughte on is fader fot hot
The ftede in the fide a fmot
And in he gan to ride
Ouer is helm the water is gon
He nolde haue be ther for eighte non
Swich aunter him gan betide
Er he vp of the water ferde
A fond it was thretti mete yerde
Se dep he gan doun glide

Thanne he thoughte on Ihefu Crift
His hors was wel fwithe trift
And quikliche fwam to londe
His fet faftnede on the grounde
Rembroun was glad in that ftounde
And thankede Gode fonde
In to the pales he him dede
He helde the eftes of that ftede
For no man a nolde wonde
Ac wimman ne man fand he non there
That with him fpeke or confort bere
Naither fitte ne ftonde

And tharof war a is
Into a chaumber a goth Y wis
A knight a fe alone
A-grette him with wordes fre
And feide fire God with the be
That fit an hegh in trone
Sire a fede tel thow me
Gif this pales thin owen be
Ich bidde the a bone
And gif thow ert her in prifoun dight
Tel hit me fo wel thow might
To me now make the mone]

Afterwards, the knight of the mountain directs Raynburne to find a wonderful fword which hung in the hall of the palace. With this weapon Raynburne attacks and conquers the Elvifh knight; who buys his life, on condition of conducting his conqueror over the perilous ford, or lake, above defcribed, and of delivering all the captives confined in his fecret and impregnable dungeon.

[A] romance of the *Squire of Low Degree*[1] is alluded to by Chaucer in the *Rime of Sir Topas;*[2] [and it is probably the fame as that which was inferted by Ritfon in his *Ancient Romancees*, and more recently in a new collection of a fomewhat fimilar character. What feems to be the original edition, and from the appearance of the types, was printed by W. de Worde, is entitled oddly enough : " Here begynneth Undo your Dore," which correfponds exactly with the reading in the colophon of a later impreffion by W. Copland : " Thus endeth vndo your doore ; otherwife called the fquyer of lowe degre." But only a fragment of the former has yet been found.] The princefs is thus reprefented, in her clofet adorned with painted glafs, liftening to the fquire's complaint.[3]

> That lady herde his mournyng alle,
> Ryght vnder the chambre wall :
> In her oryall[4] there fhe was,
> Clofed well with royall glas,

---

[1] [Printed twice. firft, as it is fuppofed, by W. de Worde, under a different title (fee *Handb. of E. E. Lit.* art. SQUYR OF LOWE DEGRE), and fecondly by W. Copland. Warton's extracts were, in all the preceding editions, moft inaccurate. See the romance in *Remains of E. Pop. Poetr. of England*, 1864-6, ii.] I have never feen it in MS. [Ritfon characterizes it as a " ftrange and whimfical but genuine Englifh performance." On Warton's opinion, " that it is alluded to by Chaucer in the *Rime of Sir Topas*," he remarks : " as Lybeaus Difconus [Le Bel Inconnu] one of the romancees enumeratëed by Chaucer, is alluded to in the Squyr of lowe degre, it is not probablely, allfo, of his age." But the Lybeaus Difconus, referred to in this romance, is evidently a different verfion of the ftory from that printed by Mr. Ritfon [and from a different text by the Early Englifh Text Society] ; and the quotation, if it prove anything, would rather fpeak for the exiftence of a more ancient tranflation now unknown. Befides, Mr. Ritfon himfelf has fupplied us with an argument ftrongly favouring Warton's conjecture. For if, as he obferves, the Squyr of lowe degre be the only inftance of a romance containing any fuch impertinent digreffions or affected enumerations of trees, birds, &c. as are manifeftly the object of Chaucer's fatire, the natural inference would be—in the abfence of any evidence for its more recent compofition—that this identical romance was intended to be expofed and ridiculed by the poet. At all events, Copland's editions with their modern phrafeology are no ftandard for determining the age of any compofition ; and until fome better arguments can be adduced than thofe already noticed, the ingenious fuppofition of Dr. Percy—for by him it was communicated to Warton—may be permitted to remain in full force.—*Price.*]

[2] See *Obfervations on the Fairy Queen*, i. § iv. p. 139.

[3] Sign. a. iii.

[4] An Oriel feems to have been a recefs in a chamber, or hall, formed by the projection of a fpacious bow-window from top to bottom. *Rot. Pip.* an. 18. Hen. III. [A.D. 1234.] " Et in quadam capella pulchra et decenti facienda ad caput Orioli camere regis in caftro Herefordie, de longitudine xx. pedum." This Oriel was at the end of the king's chamber, from which the new chapel was to begin. Again, in the caftle of Kenilworth. *Rot. Pip.* an. 19. Hen. III. [A.D. 1235.] " Et in uno magno Oriollo pulchro et competenti, ante oftium magne camere regis in caftro de Kenilworth faciendo, *vil.* xvis. ivd. per Brev. regis."

The etymologifts have been puzzled to find the derivation of an oriel-window. A learned correfpondent fuggefts, that Oriel is Hebrew for Lux mea, or Dominus illuminatio mea. [See a note to the *Squyr of Low Degre* (R. *of the E. P. Poetry of England* ii. 27, *ad finem*).]

> Fulfylled it was with ymagery,
> Euery wyndowe by and by
> On eche fyde had there a gynne,
> Sperde[1] with many a dyuers pynne.
> A none that lady fayre and fre
> Undyd a pynne of yueré,
> And wyd the windowes fhe open fet,
> The funne fhone in at her clofet.
> In that arber fayre and gaye
> She faw where that fqyre lay, &c.

I am perfuaded to tranfcribe the following paffage, becaufe it de-
lineates in lively colours the fafhionable diverfions and ufages of
ancient times. The king of Hungary endeavours to comfort his
daughter with thefe promifes, after fhe had fallen into a deep and
incurable melancholy from the fuppofed lofs of her paramour :

> To morowe ye fhall on hunting fare ;
> And ryde, my doughter, in a chare,
> It fhalbe couered with veluet reede
> And clothes of fyne golde al about your heid,
> With damfke, white and afure blewe
> Well dyapred[2] with lyllyes newe ;

---

[1] Clofed, fhut. In *P. Plowman*, of a blind man, " unfparryd his eine, *i. e.*
opened his eyes.

[2] Embroidered, diverfified. So Chaucer, of a bow, *Rom. R.* v. 934.

> " And it was painted wel and thwitten
> And ore all diapred, and written," &c.

Thwitten is twifted, wreathed. The following inftance from Chaucer is more to
our purpofe. *Knight's Tale*, v. 2160:

> " Upon a ftede bay, trappid in ftele,
> Coverid with cloth of gold diaprid wele."

This term, which is partly heraldic, occurs in the Provifor's rolls of the Great-
wardrobe, containing deliveries for furnifhing rich habiliments at tilts and tournaments, and other ceremonies. " Et ad faciendum tria harnefia pro Rege, quorum
duo de velvetto albo operato cum garteriis de blu et diafprez per totam campedinem
cum wodehoufes." *Ex comp. J. Coke Clerici, Provifor Magn. Garderob.* ab ann.
xxi. Edw. III. de 23 membranis. ad ann. xxiii. memb. x. I believe it properly
fignifies embroidering on a rich ground, as tiffue, cloth of gold, &c. This is confirmed by Peacham. " Diapering is a term in drawing.—It chiefly ferveth to
counterfeit cloth of gold, filver, damafk, brancht velvet, camblet, &c." *Compl.
Gent.* p. 345. Anderfon, in his *Hiftory of Commerce*, conjectures that Diaper, a
fpecies of printed linen, took its name from the city of Ypres in Flanders, where
it was firft made, being originally called *d'ipre*. But that city and others in
Flanders were no lefs famous for rich manufactures of ftuff; and the word in
queftion has better pretenfions to fuch a derivation. Thus, " rich cloth embroidered
with raifed work" we called *d'ipre*, and from thence Diaper ; and to do this, or any
work like it, was called to diaper, whence the participle. Satin of Bruges,
another city of Flanders, often occurs in inventories of monaftic veftments, in the
reign of Henry VIII : and the cities of Arras and Tours are celebrated for their
tapeftry in Spenfer. All thefe cities, and others in their neighbourhood, became
famous for this fort of workmanfhip before 1200. The Armator of Edward III.,
who finifhes all the coftly apparatus for the fhows above mentioned, confifting,
among other things, of a variety of the moft fumptuous and ornamented embroi-
deries on velvet, fatin, tiffue, &c. is John of Cologn. Unlefs it be Colonia in Italy,
Rotul prædict. memb. viii. memb. xiii. " Quæ omnia ordinata fuerunt per gar-

Your pomelles fhalbe ended with gold,
Your chaynes enameled many a folde;
Your mantel of ryche degre,
Purpyl palle and armyne fre;
Jennettes of fpayne that ben fo wyght
Trapped to the ground with veluet bright;
Ye fhall have harp, fautry, and fonge,
And other myrthés you amonge;
Ye fhal haue rumney and malmefyne,
Both ypocraffe and vernage wyne,
Mountrofe and wyne of greke,
Both algrade and refpice eke,
Antioche and baftarde,
Pyment[1] alfo and garnarde;

---

derobarium competentem, de precepto ipfius Regis: et facta et parata per manus
Johis de Colonia, Armatoris ipfius domini noftri Regis." Johannes de Strawef-
burgh [Strafburgh] is mentioned as *broudator regis*, i.e. of Richard II. in Anftis,
Ord. Gart. i. 55. See alfo ii. 42. I will add a paffage from Chaucer's *Wife of
Bath*, v. 450:

" Of cloth-making fhe had fuch a haunt,
She paffid them of *Ipre* and of *Gaunt*."

" Cloth of Gaunt," *i.e.* Ghent, is mentioned in the *Romaunt of the Rofe*, v. 574.
Bruges was the chief mart for Italian commodities, about the thirteenth century.
In the year 1318, five Venetian galeaffes, laden with Indian goods, arrived at this
city in order to difpofe of their cargoes at the fair. L. Guic. *Defcr. di Paefi Baff.*
p. 174. Silk manufactures were introduced from the Eaft into Italy, before 1130.
Giannon. *Hift. Napl.* xi. 7. The crufades much improved the commerce of the
Italian ftates with the Eaft in this article, and produced new artificers of their own.
But to recur to the fubject of this note. Diaper occurs among the rich filks and
ftuffs in the French *Roman de la Rofe*, where it feems to fignify Damafk, v. 21867:

"Samites, *dyaprés*, camelots."

I find it likewife in the *Roman d'Alexandre*, written about 1200. MSS. Bodl.
fol. i. b. col. 2:

" *Dyapres* d'Antioch, famis de Romanie."

Here is alfo a proof that the Afiatic ftuffs were at that time famous; and probably
Romanie is Romania. The word often occurs in old accounts of rich ecclefiaftical
veftments. Du Cange derives this word from the Italian *diafpro*, a jafper, a precious ftone which fhifts its colours. V. Diafprus. In Dugdale's *Monafticon* we
have *diafperatus*, diapered. "Sandalia cum caligis de rubeo fameto *diafperato*
breudata cum imaginibus regum," tom. iii. 314 and 321.

[1] Sometimes written *pimeate*. In the romance of *Syr Bevys*, a knight juft going
to repofe takes the ufual draught of *pimeate;* which mixed with fpices is what the
French romances call *vin du coucher*, and for which an officer, called Efpicier, was
appointed in the old royal houfehold of France. Sig. m. iii. :

" The knight and fhe to chamber went:
With *pimeate* and with fpifery,
When they had dronken the wyne."

See Carpentier, *Suppl. Glofs. Lat. du Cange*, tom. iii. p. 842. So Chaucer, *Leg.
Dido.* v. 185:

" The fpicis parted, and the wine agon,
Unto his chamber he is lad anon."

Froiffart fays, among the delights of his youth, that he was happy to tafte:

" Au couchier, pour mieulx dormir,
Efpeces, clairet, et rocelle."

Mem. Lit. x. 665. Lidgate, of Tideus and Polimite in the palace of Adraftus at
Thebes. *Stor. Theb.* p. 634, edit. Chauc. 1687:

Wyne of Greke and muſcadell,
Both claré, pyment, and rochell,
The reed your ſtomake to defye
And pottes of oſey ſett you by.
You ſhall haue veniſon ybake,[1]
The beſt wylde foule y[t] may be take.
A leſe of grehound[2] with you to ſtreke,
And hert and hynde and other lyke,
Ye ſhalbe ſet at ſuch a tryſt
That hert and hynde ſhall come to your fyſt.
Your dyſeaſe to dryue you fro,
To here the bugles there yblow.
Homward thus ſhall ye ryde,
On haukyng by the ryuers ſyde,
With Goſhauke and with gentyll fawcon,
With Egle horne and merlyon.
Whan you come home your men amonge,
Ye ſhall haue reuell, daunces and ſonge :
Lytle chyldren, great and ſmale,
Shall ſyng, as doth the nyghtyngale,
Than ſhal ye go to your euenſong
With tenours and trebles a mong,
Threſcore of copes of damaſke bryght
Full of perles th[e]y ſhalbe pyght :—

" gan anon repaire
To her lodging in a ful ſtately toure ;
Aſſigned to hem by the herbeiour.
And aftir ſpicis plenty and the wine
In cuppis grete wrought of gold ful fyne,
Without tarrying to bedde ſtraightes they gone," &c.

Chaucer has it again, *Squ. T.* v. 311, p. 62, and *Mill. T.* v. 270, p. 26 :

" He ſent her *piment*, methe, and ſpicid ale."

Some orders of monks are enjoined to abſtain from drinking *pigmentum*, or *piment*.
Yet it was a common refeſtion in the monaſteries. It is a drink made of wine,
honey, and ſpices. " Thei ne could not medell the geſte of Bacchus to the clere
honie ; that is to ſay, they could not make ne *piment* ne *clarè.*" Chaucer's *Boeth.*
p. 371, a. Urr. *Clarre* is clarified wine. In French *Clarey.* Perhaps the ſame
as piment, or hypocraſs. See *Mem. Lit.* viii. p. 674, 4to. Compare Chauc. *Sh. T.*
v. 2579. Du Cange, *Gloſs. Lat.* v. Pigmentum. Species. and *Suppl. Carp.*
and *Mem. ſur l'anc. Chevalerie,* i. pp. 19, 48. I muſt add, that πιγμεντάριος, or
πιμεντάριος, ſignified an Apothecary among the middle and lower Greeks. See Du
Cange, *Gl. Gr.* in voc. i. 1167, and ii. *Append. Etymolog. Vocab. Ling. Gall.* p. 301,
col. 1. In the regiſter of the Biſhop of Nivernois, under the year 1287, it is cove-
nanted, that whenever the biſhop ſhall celebrate maſs in St. Mary's abbey, the
abbeſs ſhall preſent him with a peacock and a cup of piment. Carpentier, *ubi
ſupr.* vol. iii. p. 277. [Sir F. Madden refers us alſo to Weber's *Met. Rom.* note
on Aliſaunder, l. 4178, and Roquefort, *Hiſtoire de la vie priveè des François,* iii.
pp. 65-8.]

[1] Chaucer ſays of the Frankelein, *Prol.* v. 345 :

" Withoutin *bake mete* never was his houſe."

And in this poem, ſignat. B. iii :

" With birds in *bread ybake,*
The tele, the duck and drake."

[2] In a MS. of Froiſſart full of paintings and illuminations, there is a repreſentation of the grand entrance of Queen Iſabel of England into Paris, in the year
1324. She is attended by a greyhound who has a flag, powdered with fleurs de
lys, bound to his neck. Montf. *Monum. Fr.* ii. p. 234.

Your fenfours fhalbe of Golde,
Endent with afure many a folde :
Your quere nor organ fonge fhall wante
With countre note and dyfcant.
The other halfe on orgayns playeng,
With yonge chyldren full fayre fyngyng.
Then fhall ye go to your fuppere,
And fytte in tentes in grene arbere,
With clothes of aras pyght to the grounde,
With faphyres fet and dyamonde.—
An hundreth knyghtes truly tolde
Shall play with bowles in alayes colde,
Your difeafe to driue awaie :
To fe the fifhes in poles plaie ;—
To a draw brydge than fhall ye,
The one halfe of ftone, the other of tre,
A barge fhall mete you full ryght,
With xxiiii ores full bryght,
With trompettes and with claryowne,
The frefhe water to rowe vp and downe.—
Than fhal ye, doughter, afke the wyne,
With fpices that be good and fyne :
Gentyll pottes, with genger grene,
With dates and deynties you betwene.
Forty torches brenynge bryght
At your brydges to brynge you lyght.
Into your chambre they fhall you brynge
With muche myrthe and more lykyng.—
Your blankettes fhall be of fuftyane,
Your fhetes fhall be of clothe of rayne :[1]
Your head fhete fhall be of pery pyght,[2]
With dyamondes fet and rubyes bryght.

---

[1] cloth, or linen, of Rennes, a city in Brittany.   Chaucer, *Dr.* v. 255.

     " And many a pilowe, and every bere
       Of clothe of raynes to flepe on fofte,
       Him thare not nede to turnin ofte.''

Tela de Raynes is mentioned among habits delivered to knights of the garter, 2
Rich. ii. Anftis, *Ord. Gart.* i. 55.

     Cloth of Rennes feems to have been the fineft fort of linen.   In [one of the
Coventry Myfteries, edited by Mr. Halliwell, 1841, there is a paffage, fuppofed by Mr.
Collier to have been interpolated towards the clofe of the 15th century, in which]
a Galant, one of the retainers to the group of the Seven Deadly Sins, is introduced
with the following fpeech :

     " Hof, Hof, Hof, a fryfch new galaunt !
     Ware of thryft, ley that a doune :
     What mene ye, fyrrys, that I were a marchaunt,
     Becaufe that I am new com to toun ?
     With praty . . . . wold I fayne round,
     I have a *fhert* of *reyns* with fleves peneaunt,
     A lafe of fylke for my lady Conftant—
     I woll, or even, be fhaven for to feme yong," &c.

So alfo in Skelton's *Magnificence,* a Morality written [about 1500], f. xx. b :

     " Your fkynne, that was wrapped in *fhertes of raynes,*
     Nowe muft be ftorm ybeten.''

[2] " Inlaid with jewels."   Chaucer, *Kn. T.* v. 2938 :

     " And then with cloth of gold and with *perie.*''

And in numberlefs other places.

Whan you are layde in bedde fo fofte,
A cage of Golde fhal hange a lofte
With longe peper fayre burnning,
And cloues that be fwete fmellyng,
Frankenfence and olibanum,
That whan ye flepe the tafte may come,
And yf ye no reft may take,
All night minftrelles for you fhall wake.[1]

Syr Degoré, [or *L'Egaré, the Strayed One,*] is a romance perhaps belonging to the fame period.[2] After his education under a hermit, Sir Degore's firft adventure is againft a dragon. This horrible monfter is marked with the hand of a mafter :"[3]

Degore went furth his waye,
Through a foreft halfe a daye :
He herd no man, nor fawe none,
Tyll yt paft the hygh none,
Then herde he grete ftrokes falle,
That yt made grete noyfe with alle,
Full fone he thoght that to fe,
To wete what the ftrokes myght be:
There was an erle, both ftout and gaye,
He was com ther that fame daye,
For to hunt for a dere or a do,
But hys houndes were gone hym fro.
Then was ther a dragon grete and grymme,
Full of fyre and alfo venymme,
Wyth a wyde throte and tufkes grete,
Uppon that knygte faft gan he bete.
And as a lyon then was hys feete,
Hys tayle was long, and full unmeete :
Betwene hys head and hys tayle
Was xxii fote withouten fayle ;
Hys body was lyke a wyne tonne,
He fhone ful bryght agaynft the funne :
Hys eyen were bright as any glaffe,

---

[1] Sign. D ii. *feq.* [In Warton's original text, fcarcely a line, which he quoted, was without feveral blunders in orthography and fenfe, and the obfervation applies equally to the editions of 1824 and 1840.] At the clofe of the romance it is faid that the king, in the midft of a great feaft which lafted forty days, created the fquire king in his room ; in the prefence of his twelve lords. See what I have obferved concerning the number twelve, Introd. Difs. i.

[2] [There are three old printed editions ; See *Handb. of E. E. Lit. Art.* DEGORÉ. The Auchinleck copy, noticed below by Mr. Price, has been printed three times, once in 1817, by Mr. Utterfon ; for the Abbotsford Club, with the cuts from De Worde's ed. 1849 ; and in Mr. Laing's *Antient Englifh Poetry*, 1857.] There is a manufcript of it among Bifhop More's at Cambridge, Bibl. Publ. 690, 36.

[This romance is analyfed by Mr. Ellis in his " Specimens.''' From a fragment of it preferved in the Auchinleck MS. it is clear that the poem in its prefent form is an unfkilful *rifacimento* of an earlier verfion, fince the writer was even ignorant of the true mode of pronouncing the hero's name. Throughout Copland's edition— with one exception—it is a word of two fyllables, rhyming with " before ;" but in p. 135 of the reprint we obtain its true accentuation as exhibited in the Auchinleck MS. :

" As was the yonge knyght Syr Degoré,
But none wyft what man was he."

The name is intended to exprefs, as the author tells us (line 230), " a thing (or perfon) almoft loft," *Dégaré* or *Lígaré.*—PRICE.]

[3] Sign. B. ii.

His fcales were hard as any braffe ;
And therto he was necked lyke a horfe,
He bare hys hed up wyth grete force :
The breth of hys mouth that did out blow
As yt had been a fyre on lowe.
He was to loke on, as I you telle,
As yt had bene a fiende of helle.
Many a man he had fhent,
And many a horfe he had rente.

As the minftrel profeffion became a fcience, and the audience grew more civilized, refinements began to be ftudied, and the romantic poet fought to gain new attention, and to recommend his ftory, by giving it the advantage of a plan. Moft of the old metrical romances are, from their nature, fuppofed to be incoherent rhapfodies. Yet many of them have a regular integrity, in which every part contributes to produce an intended end. Through various obftacles and difficulties one point is kept in view, till the final and general cataftrophe is brought about by a pleafing and unexpected furprife. As a fpecimen of the reft, and as it lies in a narrow compafs, I will develop the plan of the fable now before us, which preferves at leaft a coincidence of events, and an uniformity of defign.

[A king of England has a beautiful daughter, who is wooed by many fuitors; but none can win her, becaufe none can perform the neceffary condition by unhorfing her father in a jouft. At laft, when fhe has accompanied her father to an abbey near a foreft to attend mafs, on the anniverfary of his wife's death, fhe feparates herfelf unintentionally from her companions, lofes her way in the foreft, and is met by a knight, who deflowers her. He leaves in her charge, as a token, his fword. The princefs has a fon, who is fecretly carried by one of her attendants to a hermit's cottage, and left at the door in a cradle with £30 under his head, a pair of gloves, which muft fit the girl whom he marries, and a requeft that whoever finds him, will have him chriftened. The foundling is chriftened Sir Degoré [L'Egaré] by the hermit, and educated by him. When he is twenty years of age he is allowed to return to his mother, and takes the gloves, which were difcovered in his cradle. Having refcued an earl from a dragon, armed with nothing but an oak-fapling, he is invited to his deliverer's houfe. The earl offers him his daughter in marriage, but Degoré, mindful of the gloves, afks to fee all the ladies. The gloves fit none of them.

His next adventure is with a king, who has offered his daughter and half his lands to any knight who can unhorfe him at the tournament. Degoré fucceeds, and marries the princefs, without calling to mind the gloves, which ought to have been tried firft. His wife

---

¹ Gloves were anciently a coftly article of drefs, and richly decorated. They were fometimes adorned with precious ftones. *Rot. Pip. an.* 53. *Henr.* iii. [A. D. 1267.] "Et de i. pectine auri cum lapidibus pretiofis ponderant. xliiis. et iiid. ob. Et de ii. paribus chirothecarum cum lapidibus." This golden comb, fet with jewels, realifes the wonders of romance.

turns out to be his own mother; but neither is aware of the fact until it is time to retire, when Degoré mentions his cafe, and infifts on trying the gloves as a preliminary.[1] The princefs puts on the gloves, and then declares herfelf to be his mother. There is hereupon great rejoicing. Degoré is made known to the king as his daughter's fon; and when the knight demands who and where his father is, fhe can only give him the pointlefs fword fhe had received as a token from her feducer. He fwears that he will not fleep till he has found the perfon. He meets with an extraordinary adventure at a caftle, and afterwards fallying forth, he encounters a knight richly armed, with whom he fights, till the knight, feeing that his fword has no point, difcovers Degoré to be his fon by that fign, and the conteft ceafes. His father and mother are married, and Degoré efpoufes the lady whom he had met at the caftle, and whom he had delivered from a giant. The incident of the mother marrying her fon alfo occurs in *Sir Eglamore of Artois*.]

The romance of *King Robert of Sicily* begins and proceeds thus:[2]

> Pryncis, that be prowde in prefe,
> I wylle [telle] that that ys no lees.
> Yn Cyfylle was a nobulle kynge,
> Fayre and ftronge, and fome dele ʒinge;
> He had a brodur in grete Rome,
> That was pope of alle Cryftendome;
> Of Almayne hys odur brodur was emperowre,
> Thorow Cryftendome he had honowre.
> The kynge was calde kynge Roberd,
> Never man in hys tyme wyfte hym aferde.
> He was kynge of grete valowre,
> And alfo callyd conquerowre;
> Nowhere in no lande was hys pere,
> Kynge nor dewke, ferre nor nere,
> And alfo he was of chevalrye the flowre:
> And hys odur brodur was emperowre.
> Hys own brodur in ʒorthe Godes generalle vykere,
> Pope of Rome, as ye may here;
> Thys pope was callyd pope Urbane:
> For hym lovyd bothe God and man;
> The emperowre was callyd Valamownde,
> A ftrawnger warreowre was none founde
> After hys brodur, the kyng of Cyfyle,
> Of whome y thynke to fpeke a whyle.
> The kynge thoght he had no pere
> For to acownte, nodur far nor nere,
> And thorow hys thoght he had a pryde,
> For he had no pere, he thoʒt, on no fyde.

---

[1] All the romances have fuch an obftacle as this. They have all an enchantrefs, who detains the knight from his queft by objects of pleafure; and who is nothing more than the Calypfo of Homer, the Dido of Virgil, and the Armida of Taffo.

[2] MS. Vernon, *ut fupr*. Bibl. Bodl. f. 299. It is alfo in Caius College Camb. MSS. Clafs. E 174. 4. and Bibl. Publ. Cambr. MSS. More, 690. 35 [printed in Halliwell's *Nugæ Poeticæ*, 1844, 8vo.] and Brit. Mus. MSS. Harl. 525. 2. f. 35. [Printed privately by Utterfon, 1839, 8vo. The extracts in this edition have been copied from the text given from a collation of the Publ. Lib. Camb. and Harl. MSS. in *Remains of the Early Popular Poetry of England*, 1864-6, i.]

And on a nyght of ſeynt Johan,
Thys kynge to the churche come,
For to here hys evynſonge ;
Hys dwellynge thoƷt he there to longe,
He thoght more of worldys horowre,
Then of Cryſte hys ſaveowre.
In *magnificat* he harde a vers,
He made a clerke hym hyt reherſe
In the langage of hys owne tonge :
For in Laten wyte he not what they ſonge.
The verſe was thys, as y telle the,
Depoſuit potentes de ſede,
Et exaltavit humiles.
Thys was the verſe withowten lees :
The clerke ſeyde anon ryght :
Syr, ſoche ys Godys myght,
That he make may hye lowe,
And lowe hye in a lytylle throwe.
God may do, withowten lye,
Hys wylle in the twynkelyng of an ye,
The kyng ſeyde than with thoƷt unſtabulle :
Ye ſynge thys ofte, and alle ys a fabulle,
What man hath that powere
To make me lowear and in dawngere ?
I am flowre of chevalrye ;
Alle myn enmyes y may dyſtroye.
Ther levyth no man in no lande,
That my myght may withſtande ;
Then ys yowre ſonge a ſonge of noght.
Thys arrowre had he in hys thoght,
And in hys thoght a ſlepe hym toke
In hys cloſet, ſo ſeyth the boke.
When evynſonge was alle done,
A kynge, hym lyke, owte can come,
And alle men with hym can wende,
And kynge Roberd lefte behynde.
The newe kynge was, y yow telle,
Godys aungelle, hys pryde to felle ;
The aungelle in the halle yoye made,
And alle men of hym were glade.
Kynge Roberd wakenyd that was in the kyrke :
Hys men he thoƷt now for to wyrke,
For he was lefte there allone,
And merke nyght felle hym upon.
He began to crye upon hys men,
But there was none that anſweryd then,
But the ſexten at the ende
Of the kyrke, and to hym can wende,
And ſeyde : lurden, what doyſt thou here ?
Thou art a theſe or theſeys fere ;
Thou art here ſykerlye
Thys churche to robbe with felonye.
He ſeyde : fals theſe and fowle gadlyng,
Thou lyeſt falſely ; y am thy Kynge.
Opyn the churche dore anon,
That y may to my paleys gone.
The ſexten went welle than,
That he had be a wode man,
And of hym he had farlye,
And wolde delyver the churche in hye.

And openyd the dore ry3t ſone in haſte.
The kyng began to reaue owte faſte,
As a man that was nere wode,
And at hys pales 3ate he ſtode,
And callyd the porter : gadlyng, begone,
And bad hym come faſte, and hye hym ſoone.

When admitted, he is brought into the hall, where the angel, who had aſſumed his place, makes him *the fool of the hall*, and clothes him in a fool's coat. He is then ſent out to lie with the dogs ; in which ſituation he envies the condition of thoſe dogs, which in great multitudes were permitted to remain in the royal hall. At length the Emperor Valemounde ſends letters to his brother King Robert, inviting him to viſit, with himſelf, their brother the pope at Rome. The angel, who perſonates King Robert, welcomes the meſſengers, and clothes them in the richeſt apparel, ſuch as could not be made in the world :

The aungelle welcomyd the meſſengerys,
And clad them alle in clothys of pryſe,
And furryd them with armyne ;
Ther was never 3yt pellere half ſo fyne ;
And alle was ſet with perrye,
Ther was never no better in cryſtyante' ;
Soche clothyng and hyt were to dyght,
Alle cryſten men hyt make ne myght,
Where ſoche clothys were to ſelle,
Nor who them made, no man can telle.
On that wondyrd alle that bande,
Who wro3t thoſe clothys with any hande.
The meſſengerys went with the kynge
To grete Rome, withowte leſynge ;
The fole Roberd with hym went
Clad in a fulle ſympulle garmente,
With foxe tayles riven alle abowte ;
Men myght hym knowe in alle the rowte.
A babulle he bare agenſte hys wylle,
The aungelles heſte to fulfylle.

Afterwards they return in the ſame pomp to Sicily, where the angel, after ſo long and ignominious a penance, reſtores King Robert to his royalty.

Sicily was conquered by the French in the eleventh century,[1] and

---

[1] There is an old French romance, *Robert le Diable*, often quoted by Carpentier in his *Supplement to Du Cange*, and a French Morality, without date or name of the author : [" Cy commence un miracle de Noſtre dame, de Robert le dyable, fils du duc de Normandie, a qui il fut enjoint pour ſes mesfaiz quil feiſt le fol ſans parler, et depuis or Noſtre Seignor mercy de li, et eſpouſa la fille de lempereur."] Beauchamp's *Rech. Theat. Fr.* p. 109. [Printed at Rouen, 1836, 8vo.]

The French proſe romance of *Robert le Diable*, printed in 1496, is extant in the collection called *Bibliothèque Bleue*. It has been tranſlated into other languages : among the reſt into Engliſh. The Engliſh verſion was [twice] printed by Wynkyn de Worde, [and is reprinted in Thom's *Early Proſe Romances*, 1828 and 1858]. The title of one of the chapters is, " How God ſent an aungell to the hermyte to ſhewe him the penaunce that he ſholde gyve to Robert for his ſynnes."—" Yf that Robert wyll be ſhryven of his ſynnes, he muſt kepe and counterfeite the wayes of a fole and be as he were dombe," &c. There is an old Engliſh Morality on this tale.

this tale might have been originally got or written during their poffeffion of that ifland, which continued through many monarchies.[1] But Sicily, from its fituation, became a familiar country to all the weftern continent at the time of the Crufades, and confequently foon found its way into romance, as did many others of the Mediterranean iflands and coafts, for the fame reafon. Another of them, Cilicia, has accordingly given title to an ancient tale called *The King of Tars,* touched with a rude but expreffive pencil, from which I fhall give fome extracts: " Her bigenneth of the Kyng of Tars, and of the

---

under the very corrupt title of *Robert Cicyll,* which was reprefented at the High-Crofs in Chefter in 1529. There is a MS. of the poem on vellum in Trinity College library at Oxford (MSS. Num. lvii.).

[*Robert of Cicyle* and *Robert the Devil,* though not identical, are clearly members of the fame family, and this poetic embodiment of their lives is evidently the off-fpring of that tortuous opinion fo prevalent in the middle ages, and which time has mellowed into a vulgar adage, that " the greater the finner the greater the faint." The fubject of the latter poem was doubtlefsly Robert the fixth duke of Normandy, who became an early object of legendary fcandal; and the tranfition to the fame line of potentates in Sicily was an eafy effort when thus fupported. The romantic legend of " Sir Gowther" publifhed in the *Select Pieces of Early Popular Poetry,* [1817], is only a different verfion of Robert the Devil with a change of fcene, names, &c.—*Price.*

That the fubject of the legend of Robert the Devil was Robert the fixth duke of Normandy, is treated by fome writers as a matter of much uncertainty, although Mr. Price appears to have entertained no doubt of it. In the *Revue de Rouen* for March, 1836, M. Pothier obferves: " Setting out with the fcarcely plaufible opinion, that all the perfonages of femi-hiftoric romance muft have their type and reprefentative in hiftory, they have fet themfelves to inveftigate what real pattern the fabulous Robert the Devil could have been modelled after. As the chronicle [of Normandy], the drama, and the romance agree in making him the fon of a duke of Normandy, it has been thence concluded that he muft himfelf have been duke of Normandy; and comparifons have been inftituted of his legend with the hiftory of the two or three Roberts that the whole ducal lineage furnifhes. Yet neither chroniclers nor poets had ever dreamt of creating, of their own mere authority, Robert the Devil duke of Normandy: the chronicle makes him die at Jerufalem; the romance, in a hermitage near Rome; and the miracle makes him marry the emperor's daughter, and then of courfe fucceed his father-in-law, agreeably to the external law of all feekers of adventures, from the paladins of the round table down to the renowned Knight of the Sorrowful Countenance." According to the later verfion of the Bibliotheque Bleue, Robert brings his wife into Normandy, afcends the ducal throne, and having lived a good prince, dies laden with honours and with years, leaving the duchy to *his fon Richard-fans-Peur,* whofe marvellous hiftory has alfo been recounted by the writers of romance."—*Taylor.*

See alfo remarks on this fubject in *Remains of the Early Popular Poetry of England,* 1864-6, i. 264-9.]

[1] A paffage in Fauchet, fpeaking of rhyme, may perhaps deferve attention here. " Pour le regard de *Siciliens,* je me tiens prefque affeure, que Guillaume Ferrabrach frère de Robert Guifchard et autres feigneurs de Calabre et Pouille enfans de Tancred François-Normand, l'ont portee aux pais de leur conquefte, eftant une couftume des gens de deça chanter, avant que combattre, les beaux faits de leurs anceftres, compofez en vers." *Rec.* p. 70. Boccaccio's *Tancred,* in his beautiful tale of *Tancred and Sigifmunda,* was one of thefe Franco-Norman kings of Sicily. Compare *Nouv. Abreg. Chronol. Hift. Fr.* pag. 102, edit. 1752. [Alfo Gibbon, ch. lvi.—*Anon.*]

Soudan of Dammias,[1] how the Soudan of Dammias was criftened thoru Godis gras :"[2]

> Herkeneth now, bothe olde and ȝyng,
> For Maries love, that fwete thyng :
>   How a werre bigan
> Bitwene a god Criftene kyng,
> And an hethene heyȝe lordyng,
>   Of Damas the Soudan.
> The kyng of Taars hedde a wyf,
> The feirefte that mighte bere lyf,
>   That eny mon telle can :
> A doughter thei hadde hem bitwen,
> That heore[3] riȝte heir fcholde ben ;
>   White fo[4] fether of fwan :
> Chaaft heo[5] was, and feir of chere,
> With rode[6] red fo blofme on brere,
>   Evyen[7] ftepe and gray,
> With lowe fchuldres and whyte fwere ;[8]
> Hire to feo[9] was gret preyere
>   Of princes pert in play.
> The word[10] of nire fprong ful wyde
> Feor and ner, bi vche a fyde :
>   The Soudan herde fay ;
> Him thoughte his herte wolde breke on five
> Bot he mihte have hire to wyve,
>   That was fo feir a may ;
> The Soudan ther he fat in halle ;
> He fente his meffagers fafte withalle,
>   To hire fader the kyng.
> And feide, hou fo hit ever bifalle,
> That mayde he wolde clothe in palle
>   And fpoufen hire with his ryng.
> " And elles[11] I fwere withouten fayle
> I fchull[12] hire winnen in pleyn battayle
>   With mony an heiȝ lordyng," &c.

The Soldan, on application to the King of Tarfus for his daughter, is refufed ; and the meffengers return without fuccefs. The Soldan's anger is painted with great charaƈteriftical fpirit :

> The Soudan fat at his des,
> I-ferved of his furfte mes ;
>   Thei comen into the halle
> To fore the prince proud in pres :
> Heore tale thei tolden withouten lees,
>   And on heore knees gunne falle :

---

[1] Damafcus.

[2] MS. Vernon. Bibl. Bodl. f. 304. It is alfo in Bibl. Adv. Edinb. W 4, 1, Num. iv. In five leaves and a half.

[This romance will be found in Mr. Ritfon's Colleƈtion, vol. ii. from whofe tranfcript the prefent text has been correƈted. On the authority of Douglas's verfion of the *Æneid* and Ruddiman's Gloffary, he interprets " Tars " to mean Thrace, but as the ftory is one of pure invention, and at beft but a romantic legend, why not refer the Damas and Tars of the text to the Damafcus and Tarfus of Scripture ? —*Price.*]

[3] their.   [4] as.   [5] fhe.   [6] [complexion.]

[7] eyes.   [8] neck.   [9] fee.   [10] The report of her.

[11] [elfe.]   [12] fhall.

And feide, "Sire, the king of Tars
Of wikked wordes nis not fears,
 Hethene hound [1] he doth the [2] calle;
And er his doughtur he give the tille, [3]
Thyn herte blode he wol fpille
 And thi barouns alle."
Whon the Soudan this iherde,
As a wod man he ferde:
 His robe he rente adoun;
He tar the her [4] of hed and berd,
And feide he wold her wiue with fwerd,
 Beo his lord feynt Mahoun.
The table adoon ri3t he fmot,
In to the floore foot hot, [5]
 He lokede as a wylde lyoun;
Al that he hitte he fmot doun ri3t,
Bothe fergaunt and kni3t,
 Erl and eke baroun.
So he ferde forfothe a pli3t,
Al a day and al a ni3t,
 That no man mi3te him chafte: [6]
A morwen whon hit was day li3t,
He fent his meffagers ful ri3t,
 After his barouns in hafte:
[That thai com to his parlement,
For to heren his jugement
 Bothe left and maft.
When the parlement was pleyner,
Tho bifpac the Soudan fer,
 And feyd to hem in haft.] [7]
"Lordynges," he feith, "what to rede? [8]
Me is don a grete myfdede,
 Of Taars the Criften kyng;
I bed him bothe lond and lede
To have his douhter in worthli wede,
 And fpoufe hire with my ryng
And he feide withouten fayle.
Arft he wolde me fle in batayle
 And mony a gret lordynge.
Ac fertes [9] he fchal be forfwore,
Or to wrothe hele [10] that he was bore.

---

[1] A phrafe often applied to the Saracens. So, in *Syr Bevys,* fig. C ii b:
  "To fpeke with an *hethene hounde."*
[2] thee.   [3] "Before his daughter is given to thee."
[4] "tore the hair."
[5] ftruck, ftamped. [Sir F. Madden fays, that this is ftill in ufe in Ireland to
denote *anger* or *hafte.*]
[6] check.
[7] [The lines within brackets were inferted by Mr. Ritfon from the Auchinleck
MS.— *Price.*]
[8] "what counfel fhall we take?"
[9] But certainly.
[10] Lofs of health or fafety. Malediction. So R. of Brunne, *Chron.* apud Hearne's
Rob. Glouc. pp. 737, 738:
  "Morgan did after confeile,
  And wrought him felfe to *wrotherheile."*
Again:
  "To zow al was a wikke confeile,
  That ze felle fe full *wrotherheile."*

Bote he hit therto [1] bryng.
Therefore, lordynges, I have after ow fent
For to come to my parliment,
　　To wite of ȝow counfayle.
And alle onfwerde with gode entent
Thei wolde be at his comaundement
　　Withouten eny fayle.
And whon thei were alle at his hefte,
The Soudan made a wel gret fefte
　　For love of his batayle ;
The Soudan gedred an ofte unryde [2]
With Sarazyns of muchel pryde,
　　The kyng of Taars to affayle.
Whon the kyng hit herde that tyde,
He fent about on vche a fyde,
　　Alle that he miȝte of feende ;
Gret werre tho bigan to wrake
For the mariage ne moft be take
　　Of that mayden heende.[3]
Batayle thei fette uppon a day,
Withinne the thridde day of May,[4]
　　Ne longer nolde thei leende.[5]
The Soudan com with gret power,
With helm briȝt and feir baneer,
　　Uppon that kyng to wende.
The Soudan ladde an huge oft,
And com with much pruyde and coft,
　　With the kyng of Tars to fiȝte.
With him mony a Sarazyn feer :[6]
Alle the feldes feor and neer,
　　Of helmes leomede [7] liȝte.
The kyng of Tars com alfo
The Soudan batayle for to do
　　With mony a Criftene kniȝe ;
Either oft gon othur affayle :
Ther bigon a ftrong batayle,
　　That griflych was of fiȝt.
Threo hethene ayein twey Criftene men,
And falde hem doun in the fen,
　　With wepnes ftif and goode :
The fteorne Sarazyns in that fiȝt,
Slowe vr Criften men doun riȝt,
　　Thei fouhte as heo weore woode.
The Soudan oft in that ftounde
Feolde the Criftene to the grounde,
　　Mony a freoly foode ;
The Sarazyns withouten fayle
The Criftens culde [8] in that battayle,
　　Nas non that hem withftoode.
Whon the king of Tars fauȝ that fiȝt
Wodde he was for wrathe [9] apliȝt ;
　　In honde he hent a fpere,

---

[1] to that iffue.　　　　　　　　　[2] [numerous.]

[3] [courteous. A general term expreffive of perfonal and mental accomplifhments.
—*Price.*]

[4] [Refpecting the felection of this period for a conteft, fee a fuggeftion in *Rem.
of the E. P. Poetr. of Engl.* 1864-6, ii. 109.]

[5] tarry.　　　　　　　　[6] companion.　　　　　　　　[7] fhone.

[8] killed.　　　　　　　　[9] wraþþe. *Orig.*

And to the Soudan he rode ful ri3t
With a dunt[1] of much mi3t,
 Adoun he gon him bere :
The Soudan neigh he hedde i-lawe,
But thritti thoufent of hethene lawe
 Coomen him for to were ;
And broughten him ayeyn upon his ftede,
And holpe him wel in that nede,
 That no mon mi3t him dere.[2]
Whon he was brou3t uppon his ftede,
He sprong, as fparkle doth of glede,[3]
 For wrathe and for envye.
Alle that he hutte he made hem blede,
He ferde as he wolde a wede,[4]
 Mahoun help, he gan crye.
Mony an helm ther was unweved,
And mony a bacinet[5] to-cleved,
 And fadeles mony emptye ;
Men mi3te fe uppon the feld
Moni a kni3t ded under fcheld
 Of the Criften cumpagnie.
Whon the kyng of Taars faugh hem fo ryde,
No lengor there he nolde abyde,
 Bote fley[6] to his oune citè :
The Sarazyns that ilke tyde
Slough adoun bi vche fyde
 Vr Criftene folk fo fre.
The Sarazyns that tyme fauns fayle
Slowe vre Criftene in battayle,
 That reuthe hit was to fe ;
And on the morwe for heore[7] fake
Truwes thei gunne togidere take,[8]
 A moneth and dayes thre.
As the kyng of Tars fat in his halle,
He made ful gret deol[9] withalle,
 For the folk that he hedde i-lore :[10]
His dou3ter com in riche palle.
On kneos heo[11] gon biforen him falle,
 And feide with fyking fore :
Fader, heo feide, let me beo his wyf,
That ther be no more ftryf, &c.

To prevent future bloodfhed, the princefs voluntarily declares fhe
is willing to be married to the Soldan, although a Pagan : and notwithftanding the king her father peremptorily refufes his confent,
and refolves to continue the war, with much difficulty fhe finds
means to fly to the Soldan's court, in order to produce a fpeedy and
lafting reconciliation by marrying him :

  To the Soudan heo[11] is i-fare ;
He com with mony an hei3 lordyng,
For to welcom that fwete thyng,
 Ther heo com in hire chare :[12]
He cufte[13] hire wel mony a fithe,
His joye couthe no man kithe,[14]

---

[1] *dint,* wound, ftroke.   [2] hurt.   [3] coal, fire-brand.
[4] as if he was mad.   [5] helmet.   [6] flew.
[7] their.   [8] They began to make a truce together.
[9] dole, grief.   [10] loft.   [11] fhe.   [12] chariot.   [13] kift.   [14] know.

> Awei was al hire care.
> Into chambre heo was led,
> With riche clothes heo was cled,
>   Hethene as thauȝ heo were.[1]
> The Soudan ther he fat in halle,
> He comaundede his kniȝtes alle
>   That mayden for to fette,
> In cloth of riche purpil palle,
> And on hire hed a comeli calle:
>   Bi the Soudan heo was fette.
> Unfemli was hit for to fe
> Heo that was fo bright of ble,
>   To habbe [2] fo foule a mette,[3] &c.

They are then married, and the wedding is folemnized with a grand tournament, which they both view from a high tower. She is afterwards delivered of a fon, which is fo deformed as to be almoft a monfter. But at length fhe perfuades the Soldan to turn Chriftian ; and the young prince is baptized, after which ceremony he fuddenly becomes a child of moft extraordinary beauty. The Soldan next proceeds to deftroy his Saracen idols :

> He hente a ftaf with herte grete,
> And al his goddes he gan to bete,
>   And drouȝ hem alle adoun ;
> And leyde on, til that he con fwete,
> With fterne ftrokes and with grete,
>   On Jovyn [4] and Plotoun,
> On Aftrot and fire Jovin,
> On Tirmagaunt and Apollin,
>   He brak hem fcolle and croun ;
> On Tirmagaunt, that was heore brother,
> He lafte no lym hole with other,
>   Ne on his lord feynt Mahoun, &c.

The Soldan then releafes thirty thoufand Chriftians, whom he had long detained prifoners. As an apoftate from the pagan religion, he is powerfully attacked by feveral neighbouring Saracen nations : but he folicits the affiftance of his father-in-law, the king of Tars ; and they, joining their armies, in a pitched battle defeat five Saracen kings, Kenedoch, Lefyas, king of Taborie, Merkel, Cleomadas, and Membrok. There is a warmth of defcription in fome paffages of this poem, not unlike the manner of Chaucer. The reader muft have already obferved that the ftanza refembles that of Chaucer's *Rime of Sir Topas.*[5]

---

[1] as if fhe had been a heathen, one of that country.   [2] have.   [3] mate.
[4] I know not if by *fire Jovyn* he means Jupiter, or the Roman emperor called Jovinian, againft whom Saint Jerom wrote, and whofe hiftory is in the *Gefta Romanorum*, c. 59. He is mentioned by Chaucer as an example of pride, luxury, and luft. *Somp. T.* v. 7511. Verdier (in v.) recites a *Moralité* on Jovinian, with nineteen characters, printed at Lyons, from an ancient copy in 1584, 8vo, with the title *L'Orgueil et prefomption de l'Empereur Jovinian.* [Compare *fupra*, vol. i. p. 255, and fee Brunet, *dern.* edit. iii. 1885.] But Jovyn being mentioned here with Plotoun and Apollin, feems to mean Jove or Jupiter ; and the appellation *fire* perhaps implies father, or chief, of the heathen gods.
[5] The romance of *Sir Libeaux* or *Lybius Difconius* [printed by Ritfon], is in this

[Of the romance of *Ypotis*,[1] mentioned by Chaucer, there are four copies preferved in the Britifh Mufeum,[2] and three at Oxford.[3]

Though mentioned by Chaucer along with *Horn Child*, *Sir Bevis*, and *Sir Guy*, it has but little in common with thofe romances of Price. It profeffes to be " a tale of holy writ," and the work of St. John the Evangelift. The fcene is Rome. A child, named Ypotis, appears before the Emperor Adrian, faying that he is come to teach men God's law ; whereupon the emperor proceeds to interrogate him as to what is God's law, and then of many other matters, not in any captious fpirit, but with the utmoft reverence and faith. He afks queftions about heaven, Adam's fin, the Trinity, the creation, Sins, why men fhould faft on Fridav, and other fubjects ; and at laft he afks the wondrous child who has folved all his queries whether he is a wicked angel or a good :

> þe child onfwerde with milde mood :
> " I am he þat þe wrouhte
> And alfo þat þe deore abougte."
> þe child wente to heuene þo
> To þe ftude þat he com fro
> þe Emperour kneled on þe grounde
> And þonked God, þat blifsful ftounde
> He bi com good. In alle wyfe
> Lyuede & diyede in Godes feruife.

And fo, with a fecond afcription of itfelf to Saint John as its author, the work ends. There is a little tract in profe on the fame legend from the prefs of Wynkyn de Worde.

The editor of the *Catalogue of the Afhmolean MSS.* fuggefts that the origin of this curious dialogue is to be found in thofe fpurious pieces relating to the philofopher Secundus, &c, which are defcribed by Fabricius.[4] What little is known of Secundus is given by Philoftratus, in his *Vitæ Sophiftarum.* He was an Armenian fophift, who flourifhed about A.D. 100. Suidas confounds him with the younger Pliny ; his words are, ὃς ἐχρημάτισε πλήνιος. Vincent of Beauvais made him known to the Middle Ages, or at leaft extended the knowledge of him, by recording the wonderful taciturnity he was faid to have preferved, and alfo certain anfwers in writing given to the Emperor Hadrian.[5] Befides this converfation between the Emperor Hadrian and Secundus, Fabricius gives a fimilar altercation

---

ftanza. MSS. Cott. Cal. A 2, f. 40. [The *Beau Difconu, Bel Inconnu*, or rather *Li Biaus Defconneus* was written by Renals de Biauju, and a MS. of the original French is in the poffeffion of the Duc d'Aumale. But the Englifh verfions are not a literal tranflation of the Duc d'Aumale's French copy, and therefore there muft have been formerly a fomewhat different text, or the Englifh author took unacknowledged liberties with the poem. The title of the original French is : " Le Bel Inconnu, ou Giglain fils de Meffire Gauvain et de la Fee aux Blanches Mains, Poeme de la Table Ronde, par Renauld de Beaujeu, Poete du XIIIᵉ. fiecle. Publié d'après le MS. unique, par C. Hippeau. Paris, 1860, 8vo.]

[1] [Communicated by Mr. J. W. Hales.]
[2] Arundel MSS. No. 140, addit. MSS. No. 22283 ; Cott. MSS. Calig. A. ii. and Titus A. xxvi.
[3] Vernon MS. 140 ; Afhm. Nos. 61 and 750.
[4] *Bibl Græc.* tom. xiii.   [5] See *Spec. Hift.* x. 70, 71.

between that fame emperor and Epictetus. But indeed between thefe pieces and *Ypotis* there is no likenefs whatever, except that the form is catechetical, and that the queftions are put in the mouth of the fame imperial figure. Secundus's anfwers are not anfwers, but mere accumulations of epigrams, mere rhetorical bouquets. He is afked what are κόσμος, ὠκεανός, θεός, ἡμέρα, ἥλιος, &c., and replies in each cafe with a feries of elaborate metaphors. Thus, to the queftion, τί ἐστι γυνη; the refponfe of the oracle is, ἀνδρὸς ἐπιθύμιον, συνεστιώμενον θηρίον, συγκοιμω μένη λέαινα . . . . . ἀνθρωπόποιον ὑπούργημα, ζῶον πονηρον, ἀναγκαῖον κακόν. Whereas in *Ypotis* the queftions are all anfwered with the wifh, not to air tropes and fimiles, but to convey information. In fact, *Ypotis* is a very curious medieval catechifm. It is evidently the work of fome fober-minded ecclefiaftical inftructor—of fome monaftic Pinnock of the thirteenth or fourteenth century. The ftatements contained in it concerning the feven elements of which Adam was compofed, the lift of the fins committed by him, the defcription of the feven heavens and the nine celeftial orders, the thirteen reafons for fafting on Friday—all thefe things formed part of what was once held to be highly important knowledge, to impart which in a form eafy to remember, and to inveft with a certain perfonal intereft, was the object of the verfifier, who produced *Ypotis*.

For the name I venture to fuggeft that it is a corruption of the Greek Ὑπόστασις, or rather, perhaps, Ὑποστάτης. The former was a common word with the Greek ecclefiaftical writers for a perfon of the Trinity ; the latter is ufed by them for a creator.]

Ipomydon is mentioned among the romances in the Prologue of *Richard Cuer de Lyon*; in an ancient copy of the Britifh Mufeum, it is called *Syr Ipomydon*, a name borrowed from the Theban war, and transferred here to a tale of the feudal times.[1] This piece is derived from a French original. Our hero Ippomedon is fon of Ermones king of Apulia, and his miftrefs is the fair heirefs of Calabria. About the year 1230, William Ferrabras[2] and his brethren, fons of Tancred the Norman, and well known in the hiftory of the Paladins, acquired the fignories of Apulia and Calabria. But our Englifh romance feems to be immediately tranflated from the French ; for Ermones is called king of *Poyle* or Apulia, which in French is *Pouille*. I have tranfcribed fome of the moft interefting paffages.[3]

Ipomydon, although the fon of a king, is introduced waiting in his father's hall, at a grand feftival. This fervitude was fo far from being difhonourable, that it was always required as a preparatory ftep to knighthood :

> Every yere the kyng wold
> At Whytfontyde a feft hold

MSS. Harl. 2252, 44, f. 54. [In Heber's library was a printed copy deficient of fheet A, which had been part of the collection bequeathed to Lincoln Cathedral by Dean Honeywood. It was from the prefs of W. de Worde.]

[Printed in Mr. Weber's collection of Metrical Romances, whofe text has been fubftituted for Warton's. It has alfo been analyfed by Mr. Ellis.—*Price.*]

[2] *Bras de fer.* Iron arm.　　　　[3] MSS. f. 55.

Off dukis, erlis, and barons,
Many there come frome dyvers townes,
Ladyes, maydens, gentill and fre,
Come thedyr from ferre contrè :
And grette lordis of ferre lond
Thedyr were prayd by fore the hond.[1]
When all were come togedyr than
There was joy of mani a man ;
Full riche I wote were hyr feruice,
For better might no man devyfe.
Ipomydon that day feruyd in halle,
All fpake of hym bothe grete and fmalle,
Ladies and maydens by helde hym on,
So godely a man they had fene none :
Hys feyre chere in halle theym fmert
That mony a lady fmote throw the hert.
And in there hertis they made mone
That there lordis ne were fuche one.
After mete they went to pley,
All the peple, as I you fey ;
Some to chambre, and fome to boure,
And fome to the hye towre ;[2]
And fome in the halle ftode
And fpake what hem thought gode :
Men that were of that cite[3]
Enquered of men of other cuntrè, &c.

Here a converfation commences concerning the heirefs of Calabria :
and the young Prince Ipomydon immediately forms a refolution to
vifit and to win her.   He fets out in difguife :

Now they go furth on her way,
Ipomydon to hys men gan fay,
That ther be none of hem alle,
So hardy by his name hym calle,
Whereto thei wend ferre or nere,
Or over the ftrange ryvere ;
" Ne man telle what I am,
What I fchall be, ne whens I cam."
All they granted hys commandement,
And forthe they went with one affent.
Ipomydon and Tholomew
Robys had on and mantillis new,
Of the richeft that myght bee,
Ther nas ne fuche in that cuntrèe :
For many was the ryche ftone
That the mantillis were uppon.
So longe there weys they have nome[4]
That to Calabre they ar come :
They come to the caftelle yate
The porter was redy there at,
The porter to theme they can calle
And prayd hym go into the halle

---

[1] before-hand.
[2] In the feudal caftles, where many perfons of both fexes were affembled, who
did not know how to fpend the time, it is natural to fuppofe that different parties
were formed, and different fchemes of amufement invented.   One of thefe was to
mount to the top of one of the higheft towers in the caftle.
[3] The Apulians.   [4] [taken.]

And fay thy lady[1] gent and fre,
That come ar men of ferre contrèe,
And if it plefe hyr we wold hyr prey,
That we might ete with hyr to day.
The porter feyd full cortefsly
" Your errand to do I am redy."
The lady to hyr mete was fette,
The porter come and feyre hyr grette,
" Madame," he fayd, " God you fave,"
Atte your gate geftis ye have,
Strange men all for to fee
Thei afke mete for charytè."
The lady comaundith fone anon
That the gates were undone,
" And bryng theym all byfore me
For wele at efe fhall they bee."
They toke hyr pagis hors and alle,
Thefe two men went into the halle.
Ipomydon on knees hym fette,
And the lady feyre he grette:
" I am a man of ftrange contrè
And pray you yff your will to [fo] be
That I myght dwelle with you to-yere
Of your norture for to lere,[2]
I am come frome ferre lond ;
For fpeche I here bi fore the hand
That your norture and your fervyfe
Ys holden of fo grete empryfe.
I pray you that I may dwelle here
Some of your fervyfe to lere."
The lady by held Ipomydon,
Hym femyd wele a gentilmon,
She knew non fuche in hyr lande,
So goodly a man and wele farand ;[3]
She faw alfo by his norture
He was a man of grete valure :
She caft full fone in hyr thoght
That for no fervyfe come he noght ;
But it was worfhip hyr unto
In feir fervyfe hym to do.
She fayd, Syr, welcome ye be,
And all that comyn be with the ;
Sithe ye have had fo grete travayle,
Of a fervife ye fhall not fayle :

---

[1] She was lady, by inheritance, of the fignory. The female feudatories exercifed all the duties and honours of their feudal jurifdiction in perfon. In Spenfer, where we read of the *Lady of the Caftle*, we are to underftand fuch a character. See a ftory of a *Comteffe*, who entertains a knight in her caftle with much gallantry. *Mem. fur l'Anc. Chev.* ii. 69. It is well known that anciently in England ladies were fheriffs of counties. [Margaret, countefs of Richmond, was a juftice of peace. Sir W. Dugdale tells us that Ela, widow of William, earl of Salifbury, executed the fheriff's office for the county of Wilts in different parts of the reign of Henry III. (See *Baronage*, vol. i. 177.) From Fuller's *Worthies* we find that Elizabeth, widow of Thomas Lord Clifford, was fheriffefs of Weftmoreland for many years, and from Pennant's *Scottifh Tour* we learn that for the fame county Anne, the celebrated Countefs of Dorfet, Pembroke and Montgomery, often fat in perfon as fheriffefs.—*Park.*]
[2] learn.   [3] handfome.

In thys contre ye may dwelle here
And at your will for to lere,
Of the cuppe ye fhall ferve me
And all your men with you fhal be,
Ye may dwelle here at youre wille,
But¹ your beryng be full ylle.
Madame, he fayd, grantmercy,
He thankid the lady cortefly.
She comandyth hym to the mete,
But or he fatte in ony fete,
He faluted theym grete and fmalle,
As a gentillman fhuld in halle;
All they fayd fone anone,
They faw nevyr fo goodli a mon,
Ne fo light, ne fo glad,
Ne non that fo ryche atyre had :
There was non that fat nor yede,²
But they had marvelle of hys dede,³
And fayd, he was no lytell fyre,
That myght fhew fuche atyre.
Whan they had ete, and grace fayd,
And the tabyll away was leyd ;
Upp than aroos Ipomydon,
And to the botery he went anon,
Ant [dyde] hys mantille hym aboute ;
On hym lokyd all the route,
Ant every man fayd to other there,
" Will ye fe the proude fqueer
Shall ferve⁴ my ladye of the wyne,
In hys mantell that is fo fyne ?"
That they hym fcornyd wift he noght :
On othyr thyng he had his thoght.
He toke the cuppe of the botelere,
And drewe a lace of fylke ful clere,
Adowne than felle hys mantylle by,
He prayd hym for hys curtefly,
That lytelle yifte⁵ that he wolde nome
Tille efte fone a better come ;
Up it toke the botelere.
Byfore the lady he gan it bere,
And prayd the lady hertely
To thanke hym of his corteffye ;
All that was tho in the halle
Grete honowre they fpake hym alle.
And fayd he was no lytelle man
That fuch yiftys yiffe kan.
There he dwellyd many a day,
And fervid the lady wele to pay.
He bare hym on fo feyre manere
To knyghtes, ladyes, and fquyere,
All lovyd hym that com hym by,
For he bare hym fo cortefly.
The lady had a cofyne that hight Jafon,
Full well he lovyd Ipomydon ;
Where that he yede in or oute,
Jafon went with hym aboute.

---

¹ unlefs.   ² walked.   ³ behaviour.
⁴ " who is to ferve."   ⁵ *i. e.* his mantle.

The lady lay, but ſhe ſlept noght,
For of the ſquyere ſhe had grete thoght;
How he was feyre and ſhapè wele,
Body and armes, and every dele:
Ther was non in al hir land
So wel beſemyd dougty of hand.
But ſhe kowde wete for no caſe,
Whens he come ne what he was,
Ne of no man cowde enquere
Other than the ſtrange ſquyere.
She hyr bythought on a quentyſe,
If ſhe myght know in ony wyſe,
To wete whereof he were come.
Thys was hyr thoght all and ſome:
She thought to wode hyr men to tame[1]
That ſhe myght knowe hym by his game.
On the morow, whan it was day,
To hyr men than gan ſhe ſay,
" To morrow whan it is day lyght,
Loke ye be all redy dight,
With youre houndis more and leſſe,
In the forreſt to take my greſe,
And there I will myſelf be
Youre game to byhold and ſee."
Ipomydon had houndis thre
That he broght frome his contrè;
When they were to the wode gone,
This lady and hyr men ichone,
And with hem her houndis ladde,
All that ever any howndis hadde.
Sir Tholomew foryate he noght,
His maiſtres howndis thedyr he broght,
That many a day ne had ronne ere,
Full wele he thoght to note hem there.
Whan they come to the laund on hight,
The quenys pavylon there was pight,
That ſhe myght ſe of the beſt
All the game of the forèſt,
The wandleſſours went throw the forèſt,
And to the lady broght many a beſt,[2]
Herte and hynde, buk and doo,
And othir beſtis many moo.
The howndis that were of gret priſe
Pluckid downe dere all at a tryſe;
Ipomydon with his houndis thoo
Drew downe bothe buk and doo;
More he tok with houndis thre
Than all that othyr compaigne.
There ſquyres undyd hyr dere,
Iche man on his owne manere:
Ipomydon a dere yede unto,
Full konnyngly gan he it undo;
So feyre that venyſon he gan to dight,
That bothe hym byheld ſquyer and knight:
The lady lokyd oute of her pavyloun,
And ſaw hym dight the venyſon.
There ſhe had grete deyntè
And ſo had all that dyd hym ſee:

---

[1] [tane or tan, A.-S. to *lure* or *entice*.]   [2] beaſt.

> She faw all that he downe droughe
> Of huntyng fhe witt he cowde ynoughe
> And thoght in hyr herte then
> That he was come of gentillmen :
> She bad Jafon hyr men to calle:
> Home they paffyd grete and fmalle :
> Home they come fone anone,
> This lady to hyr mete gan gone,
> And of venery [1] had hyr fille
> For they had take game at wille.

He is afterwards knighted with great folemnity :

> The heraudes gaff the child [2] the gree,
> A m. pownde he had to fee,
> Mynftrellys had yiftes of golde
> And fourty dayes thys feft was holde.[3]

The metrical romance entitled *La Mort Arthure,* preferved in the fame repofitory, is fuppofed by the learned and accurate Wanley to be a tranflation from the French : he adds, that it is not perhaps older than the times of Henry VII.[4]   But as it abounds with many Saxon words, and feems to be quoted in *Syr Bevys,* I have given it a place here.[5]   Notwithftanding the title and the exordium which promife the hiftory of Arthur and the Sangreal, the exploits of Sir Lancelot du Lak, king of Benwike, his intrigues with Arthur's queen Geneura, and his refufal of the beautiful daughter of the Earl of Afcalot, form the greateft part of the poem.   At the clofe, the repentance of Lancelot and Geneura, who both affume the habit of religion, is introduced.   The writer mentions the Tower of London. The following is a defcription of a tournament performed by fome of the knights of the Round Table : [6]

> Tho to the caftelle gon they fare,
> To the ladye fayre and bryht :
> Blithe was the ladye thare,
> That they wold dwelle with hyr that nyght.
> Haftely was there foper yare [7]
> Off mete and drinke rychely dight ;
> On the morow gon they dine and fare
> Both Launcelott and that other knight.

---

[1] [hunting, game.]   [2] Ipomydon.   [3] MS. f. 61. b.
[4] MSS. Harl. 2252. 49. f. 86.   Pr. "Lordinges that are leffe and deare."
[Edited by F. J. Furnivall for the Roxburghe Club, 1864.   The late Mr. Ritfon was of opinion that [this romance] was verfified from the profe work of the fame name written by Malory and printed by Caxton ; in proof of which he contended that the ftyle is marked by an evident affectation of antiquity.   But in truth it differs moft effentially from Malory's work, which was a mere compilation, whilft this follows with tolerable exactnefs the French romance of *Lancelot* ; and its phrafeology, which perfectly refembles that of Cheftre and other authors of the fifteenth century, betrays no marks of affectation.—*Ellis.*   A new edition of Caxton's *Morte Arthur* has fince been publifhed by Mr. Southey.—*Price.*   The Early Englifh Text Society alfo propofes to republifh Caxton's edit.   Southey's fo-called edition, 1817, was a mere bookfeller's fpeculation, with a very elaborate, but fomewhat difcurfive introduction by the nominal editor.   An imperfect copy feems to have been employed, and the deficiencies fupplied from a later text.]
[5] Signat. K ii b.   [6] MS. f. 89. b.   [7] re dy.

Whan they come in to the feld
　　Myche there was of game and play,
Awhile they hovid[1] and byheld
　　How Arthurs knightis rode that day,
Galehodis[2] party bygan to held[3]
　　On fote his knightis ar led away.
Launcelott ftiff was undyr fcheld,
　　Thinkis to helpe yif that he may.
Befyde hym come than fir Ewayne,
　　Breme[4] as eny wilde bore;
Launcellott fpringis hym ageyne,[5]
　　In rede armys that he bore:
A dynte he yaff with mekill mayne,
　　Sir Ewayne was unhorfid thare,
That alle men wente[6] he had ben flayne
　　So was he woundyd wondyr fare.[7]
Sir Boerte thoughte no thinge good,
　　When Syr Ewaine unhorfid was;
Forthe he fpringis, as he were wode,
　　To Launcelot withouten lees:
Launcellot hyte hym on the hode,
　　The nexte way to grounde he chefe:
Was none fo ftiff agayne hym ftode
　　Ffule thynne he made the thikkeft prees.[8]
Sir Lyonelle beganne to tene,[9]
　　And haftely he made hym bowne,[10]
To Launcellott, with herte kene,
　　He rode with helme and fword browne;
Launcellott hitte hym as I wene,
　　Throughe the helme in to the crowne:
That evyr after it was fene
　　Bothe hors and man there yod adoune.
The knightis gadrid to gedir thare
　　And gan with crafte, &c.

I could give many more ample fpecimens of the romantic poems
of thefe namelefs minftrels, who probably flourifhed before or about
the reign of Edward II.[11]　But it is neither my inclination nor inten-

---

[1] tarried.—Sir F. Madden's corr.]　　　　　　[2] Sir Galahad's.
[3] [heel, *i. e.* give way.—Sir F. Madden's note.]　　[4] fierce.
[5] againft.　　　[6] weened.　　　[7] fore.　　　[8] crowd.
[9] be troubled.　　[10] ready.

[11] *Octavian* is one of the romances mentioned in the Prologue to *Richard Cuer de
Lyon,* above cited. [An imperfect copy of an early printed edition, fuppofed to be
from W. Copland's prefs, was fold amongft Mr. Heber's books.]　In the Cotton
MSS. there is the metrical romance of *Octavian imperator,* but it has nothing of
the hiftory of the Roman emperors. Pr. "Jhefu pat was with fpere yftonge."
Calig. A. 12. f. 20. It is a very fingular ftanza.　In Bifhop More's manufcripts at
Cambridge, there is a poem with the fame title, but a very different beginning, viz.
"Lytyll and mykyll olde and younge." Bibl. Publ. 690. 30.—[This romance has
been edited by Mr. Halliwell for the Percy Society.]　The Emperor *Octavyen,* perhaps the fame, is mentioned in Chaucer's *Dreme,* v. 368.　Among Hatton's MSS.
in Bibl. Bodl. we have a French poem, *Romaunce de Otheuien Empereur de Rome.*
Hyper. Bodl. 4046. 21. [Of which Conybeare printed an Englifh epitomized verfion,
1809, 8vo.]

In the fame line of the aforefaid Prologue, we have the romance of *Ury.*　This
is probably the father of the celebrated Sir Ewaine or Yvain, mentioned in the
Court Mantel. (*Mem. Anc. Cheval.* ii p. 62).

tion to write a catalogue, or compile a miscellany. It is not to be expected that this work should be a general repository of our ancient poetry. I cannot however help observing, that English literature and English poetry suffer[ed], while so many pieces of this kind still remain[ed] concealed and forgotten in our manuscript libraries. They contain in common with the prose-romances, to most of which indeed

---

> " Li rois pris par la deftre main
> L'amiz monfeignor Yvain
> Qui au roi Urien fu filz,
> Et bons chevaliers et hardiz,
> Qui tant ama chiens et oifiaux."

Specimens of the English *Syr Bevys* may be feen in Percy's *Reliques*, iii. 216, 217, 297, edit. 1767, and *Obfervations on the Fairy Queen*, § ii. p. 50. It is in manufcript at Cambridge, Bibl. Publ. 690. 30, and Coll. Caii. A 9. 5. And MSS. Bibl. Adv. Edinb. W 4. 1. Num. xxii.

It is in this romance of *Syr Bevys*, that the knight paffes over a bridge, the arches of which are hung round with fmall bells. Signat. E iv. This is an oriental idea. In the *Alcoran* it is faid, that one of the felicities in Mahomet's paradife will be to liften to the ravifhing mufic of an infinite number of bells, hanging on the trees, which will be put in motion by the wind proceeding from the throne of God. Sale's *Koran*, Prelim. Difc. p. 100. In the enchanted horn, as we fhall fee hereafter, in *le Lai du Corn*, the rim of the horn is hung round with a hundred bells of a moft mufical found.

We fhall have occafion, in the progrefs of our poetry, to bring other fpecimens of thefe compofitions. See *Obs. on Spenfer's Fairy Queen*, ii. 42, 43.

I muft not forget here, that Sir Gawaine, one of Arthur's champions, is celebrated in a feparate romance. [In MS. Rawlinfon, C. 86, is *The Wedding of Sir Gawayne*, a later copy of which, mutilated, occurs in the Percy MS. Sir F. Madden, who included the Rawlinfon copy in his *Sir Gawayne*, 1839, obferves: "It is, unqueftionably, the original of the mutilated poem in the Percy folio, and is fufficiently curious to render its infertion in the Appendix an object of intereft." It is called *The weddynge of Sr Gawen & Dame Ragnell*, and begins:

> " Lythe and liftenyth the lif of a lord riche
> The while that he lyvid was none hym̄ liche."]

Dr. Percy has printed the *Marriage of Sir Gawayne*, which he believes to have furnifhed Chaucer with his *Wife of Bath*, *Reliques*, i. 11. It begins, "Kinge Arthur liues in merry Carliele." [This is printed in Sir F. Madden's *Sir Gawayne*, 1839.] I think I have fomewhere feen a romance in verfe entitled, *The Turke and Gawaine*. [This romance occurs in the recently edited *Percy MS*. Many important romances altogether omitted and probably unfeen by Warton and his editors, might be mentioned here, fuch as *Blonde of Oxford and Jehan of Dammartin*, edited for the Camden Society, 1858; *Sir Generides*, recently edited for the Roxburghe Club by Mr. Furnivall (a ballad-poem on the fame fubject is in a MS. in the library of Trinity College, Cambridge; and of the longer narrative fragments printed with the types of W. de Worde are extant); *The Romans of Partenay or Melufine*, Early Englifh Text Society, 1866; and *Torrent of Portugal*, printed from the Chetham MS. 1842, 8vo. *Torrent of Portugal*, which, from a fmall fragment with his types remaining, feems to have been printed by Pynfon in the early part of the fixteenth century, is a very dull and puerile performance. It appears to be in heroic fiction what *Jack the Giant Killer* is in the romance of the nurfery. How far Jack may have owed his exiftence to his grander and more impofing prototype, it is not eafy to fay. We fee in *Torrent of Portugal* a curioufly vague ufe of geographical terms connected with America; poffibly the ftory, in its prefent fhape, was not compofed long before it came from Pynfon's prefs.]

they gave rife, amufing images of ancient cuftoms and inftitutions not
elfewhere to be found, or at leaft not otherwife fo ftrikingly delineated:
and they preferve, pure and unmixed, thofe fables of chivalry which
formed the tafte, and awakened the imagination, of our elder Englifh
claffics. The antiquaries of former times overlooked or rejected
thefe valuable remains, which they defpifed as falfe and frivolous, and
employed their induftry in reviving obfcure fragments of uninftructive
morality or uninterefting hiftory. But in the prefent age we are
beginning to make ample amends: in which the curiofity of the antiquarian is connected with tafte and genius, and his refearches tend
to difplay the progrefs of human manners, and to illuftrate the hiftory
of fociety.

As a further illuftration of the general fubject and many particulars of this fection and the three laft, I will add a new proof of
the reverence in which fuch ftories were held, and of the familiarity
with which they muft have been known, by our anceftors. Thefe
fables were not only perpetually repeated at their feftivals, but were
the conftant objects of their eyes. The very walls of their apartments were clothed with romantic hiftory. Tapeftry was anciently
the fafhionable furniture of our houfes, and it was chiefly filled with
lively reprefentations of this fort. The ftories are ftill preferved of
the tapeftry in the royal palaces of Henry VIII.;[1] which I will here
give without referve, including other fubjects, as they happen to
occur, equally defcriptive of the times. In the tapeftry of the Tower
of London, the original and moft ancient feat of our monarchs, there
are recited "Godfrey of Bulloign, the three kings of Cologne, the
emperor Conftantine, faint George, king Erkenwald,[2] the hiftory of
Hercules, Fame and Honour, the Triumph of Divinity, Efther and
Ahafuerus, Jupiter and Juno, faint George, the eight Kings, the ten
Kings of France, the Birth of our Lord, Duke Jofhua, the rich
hiftory of king David, the feven Deadly Sins, the rich hiftory of the
Paffion, the Stem of Jeffe,[3] our Lady and Son, king Solomon, the

---

[1] "The feconde part of the Inventorye of our late fovereigne lord kyng Henry
the Eighth, conteynynge his guardrobes, houfhold ftuff," &c. &c. MSS. Harl. 1419,
fol. The original. [The account which followed here in all the former edits. of
the furniture in Henry VIII.'s palace at Greenwich, did not feem to be any part
of the fubject; but at any rate it is to be found much more full and accurate in
the *Retrofpective Review*, fecond feries, i. 132-6]
[2] So in the record. But he was the third bifhop of St. Paul's, London, fon of
King Offa, and a great benefactor to St. Paul's church, in which he had a moft
fuperb fhrine. He was canonifed. Dugdale, among many other curious particulars
relating to his fhrine, fays that in the year 1339 it was decorated anew, when three
goldfmiths, two at the wages of five fhillings by the week, and one at eight,
worked upon it for a whole year. *Hift. St. Paul's*, p. 21. See alfo p. 233.
[3] This was a favourite fubject for a large gothic window. This fubject alfo
compofed a branch of candleftics thence called a *jeffe*. not unufual in the ancient
churches. In the year 1097, Hugo de Flori, abbot of St. Auft. Canterb., bought
for the choir of his church a great branch-candleftick. "Candelabrum magnum
in choroæneum quod *jeffe* vocatur in partibus emit tranfmarinis." Thorn. *Dec.
Script*. col. 1796. About the year 1330, Adam de Sodbury, abbot of Glaftonbury,

Woman of Canony, Meleager, and the Dance of Maccabre."[1] At Durham-place we find the " Citie of Ladies,[2] the tapeſtrie of Thebes and of Troy, the City of Peace, the Prodigal Son,[3] Eſther, and other pieces of Scripture." At Windſor caſtle the "ſiege of Jeruſalem, Ahaſuerus, Charlemagne, the ſiege of Troy, and *hawking and hunting.*"[4] At Nottingham caſtle, "Amys and Amelion."[5] At Woodſtock manor, the "tapeſtrie of Charlemagne."[6] At the More, a palace in Hertfordſhire, "king Arthur, Hercules, Aſtyages, and Cyrus." At Richmond, the "arras of Sir Bevis, and Virtue and Vice fighting."[7] Many of theſe ſubjects are repeated at Weſtminſter, Greenwich, Oatlands, Bedington in Surrey, and other royal ſeats, ſome of which are now unknown as ſuch.[8] Among the reſt we have alſo Hannibal, Holofernes, Romulus and Remus, Æneas, and Suſannah.[9] I have mentioned romances written on many of theſe

gave to his convent "Unum dorſale laneum *le Jeſſe.*" Joan. Glaſton, edit. Hearne, p. 265. That is, a piece of tapeſtry embroidered with the *ſtem of Jeſſe*, to be hung round the choir, or other parts of the church, on high feſtivals. He alſo gave a tapeſtry of this ſubject for the abbot's hall. *Ibid.* And I cannot help adding, what indeed is not immediately connected with the ſubject of this note, that he gave his monaſtery, among other coſtly preſents, a great clock, "proceſſionibus et ſpectaculis inſignitum," an organ of prodigious ſize, and eleven bells, ſix for the tower of the church, and five for the clock tower. He alſo new-vaulted the nave of the church, and adorned the new roof with beautiful paintings. *Ibid.*

[1] f. 6. In many churches of France there was an ancient ſhew of mimicry, in which all ranks of life were perſonated by the eccleſiaſtics, who all danced together, and diſappeared one after another. It was called *Dance Maccabre*, and ſeems to have been often performed in St. Innocent's at Paris, where was a famous painting on this ſubject, which gave riſe to Lydgate's poem under the ſame title. See Carpent. *Suppl. du Cange*, Lat. Gl. ii. p. 1103. More will be ſaid of it when we come to Lydgate.

[2] A famous French allegorical romance [by Chriſtine de Piſe. An Engliſh tranſlation appeared in 1521].

[3] A picture on this favourite ſubject is mentioned in Shakeſpeare. And in Randolph's *Muſes Looking-glaſs.* "In painted cloth the ſtory of the Prodigal." *Dodſl. Old Pl.* vi. 260.

[4] f. 298.   [5] f. 364.   [6] f. 318.   [7] f. 346.

[8] Some of the tapeſtry at Hampton-court, deſcribed in this inventory, is to be ſeen ſtill in a fine old room, now remaining in its original ſtate, called the Exchequer. [In an inventory of the effects of King Henry V. ſeveral pieces of tapeſtry are mentioned, with the ſubjects of the following romances, viz. Bevis of Hampton, Octavian, Gyngebras (?) Hawkyn namtelet, l'arbre de jeoneſſe, Farman (*i. e.* Pharamond), Charlemayn, Duke Glorian, Elkanus le noble, Renaut, Trovis roys de Coleyn, &c. See Rolls of Parl. *ſub anno* 1423.—*Douce.* Theſe *Rolls* are not very correctly printed, and the editor ſuſpects ſome errors in the preceding liſt.]

[9] Montfaucon, among the tapeſtry of Charles V. king of France, in the year 1370, mentions, *Le tappis de la vie du ſaint Theſeus.* Here the officer who made the entry calls Theſeus a ſaint. *The ſeven Deadly Sins, Le ſaint Graal, Le graunt tappis de Neuf Preux, Reyne d'Ireland*, and *Godfrey of Bulloign. Monum. Fr.* iii. 64. The *neuf preux* are the Nine Worthies. Among the ſtores of Henry VIII. we have, "two old ſtayned clothes of the ix worthies for the greate chamber," at Newhall in Eſſex, f. 362. Theſe were pictures. Again, at the palace of Weſtminſter in "the little ſtudy called the Newe Librarye," which I believe was in Holbein's elegant Gothic gatehouſe, there is, " Item, xii pictures of men on horſebacke of enamelled ſtuffe of the Nyne Worthies, and others upon ſquare tables." f. 188. MSS. Harl. 1419, *ut ſupr.*

ſubjeĉts, and ſhall mention others. In the romance of Syr Guy, that hero's combat with the dragon in Northumberland is ſaid to be repreſented in tapeſtry in Warwick caſtle :

> In Warwike the truth ſhall ye ſee
> In arras wrought ful craftely.[1]

This piece of tapeſtry appears to have been in Warwick caſtle before the year 1398. It was then ſo diſtinguiſhed and valued a piece of furniture, that a ſpecial grant was made of it by Richard II. in that year, conveying " that ſuit of arras hangings in Warwick caſtle, which contained the ſtory of the famous Guy earl of Warwick," together with the caſtle of Warwick, and other poſſeſſions, to Thomas Holland, earl of Kent;[2] and in the reſtoration of forfeited property to this lord after his impriſonment, theſe hangings are particularly ſpecified in the patent of Henry IV., dated 1399. When Margaret, daughter of Henry VII., was married to James IV. of Scotland in 1503, Holyrood Houſe at Edinburgh was ſplendidly decorated on that occaſion ; and we are told in an ancient record, that the " hanginge of the queenes grett chammer repreſented the yſtory of Troye toune." Again, " the king's grett chammer had one table, wer was ſatt hys chammerlayn, the grett ſqyer, and many others, well ſerved ; the which chammer was haunged about with the ſtory of Hercules, together with other yſtorys."[3] And at the ſame ſolemnity, " in the hall wher the qwenes company wer ſatt in lyke as in the other, an wich was haunged of the hiſtory of Hercules," &c.[4] A ſtately chamber in the caſtle of Heſdin in Artois was furniſhed by a duke of Burgundy with the ſtory of Jaſon and the Golden Fleece, about the year 1468.[5] The affecting ſtory of Coucy's Heart, which [may have given] riſe to an old metrical Engliſh romance entitled, the *Knight of Courteſy and the Lady of Faguel*, was woven in tapeſtry in Coucy caſtle in France.[6] I have ſeen an ancient ſuite of arras, containing Arioſto's Orlando and Angelica, where at every group the ſtory was all along illuſtrated with ſhort rhymes in romance or old French. Spenſer ſometimes dreſſes the ſuperb bowers of his fairy caſtles with this ſort of hiſtorical drapery.

---

[1] Signat. Ca 1. Some, perhaps, may think this circumſtance an innovation or addition of later minſtrels. A praĉtice not uncommon.

[2] Dugd. *Bar.* i. p. 237.

[3] Leland. *Coll.* vol. iii. p. 295, 296. *Opuſcul.* edit. 1770. [4] *Ibid.*

[5] See *Obs. Fair. Qu.* i. p. 177.

[6] Howell's *Letters*, xx. § vi. B. i. This is a true ſtory, about the year 1180. Fauchet relates it at large from an old authentic French chronicle ; and then adds, " Ainſi finerint les amours du Chaſtelain du Couci et de la dame de Faiel." Our Caſtellan, whoſe name is [Raoul] de Couci, was famous for his *chanſons* and chivalry, but more ſo for his unfortunate love, which became proverbial in the old French romances. See Fauch. *Rec.* pp. 124, 128. [The Knight of Curteſy and the Fair Lady of Faguel has been reprinted by Mr. Ritſon, vol. iii. p. 193. See *Memoires Hiſtoriques ſur Raoul de Courcy.* Paris, 1781.—*Price.* See *Remains of the E. P. Poetry of Engl.* ii. 65·6 ; the romance is alſo included in that colleĉtion. Ritſon's text is not accurate. The French ſtory of *Le Chatelain de Coucy et la dame de Fayel* was printed at Paris, 1829, 8vo. ; but it has very little in common with the Engliſh romance.]

In Hawes's *Paſtime of Pleaſure* [1517,] the hero of the piece ſees all his future adventures diſplayed at large in the ſumptuous tapeſtry of the hall of a caſtle. I have before mentioned the moſt valuable and perhaps the moſt ancient work of this ſort now exiſting, the entire ſeries of Duke William's deſcent on England, preſerved in the church of Bayeux in Normandy, and intended as an ornament of the choir on high feſtivals. Bartholinus relates that it was an art much cultivated among the ancient Iſlanders, to weave the hiſtories of their giants and champions in tapeſtry.[1] The ſame thing is recorded of the old Perſians ; and this furniture is ſtill in high requeſt among many Oriental nations, particularly in Japan and China.[2] It is well known, that to frame pictures of heroic adventures in needle-work was a favourite practice of claſſical antiquity.

[The following liſt compriſes all the known Engliſh Romances relating to Charlemagne.[3]

1. *Roland.* All that remains of this is a fragment[4] of a poem, probably written in the thirteenth century. It is not ſtrictly alliterative, but abounds with alliteration. An analyſis and ſome extracts furniſhed by Mr. Thos. Wright are printed at the end of M. Michel's edition of *La Chanſon de Roland.* The whole of the fragment will probably be publiſhed by the Early Engliſh Text Society. It relates the treachery of Gwynylon (the French *Ganelon* or *Guenelon*), and the beginning of the fight at Roncevaux. In deſcribing Gwynylon's treachery the poet has derived one remarkable circumſtance, not from the French *Roland*, but from the Chronicle of the pſeudo-Turpin. M. Paris is miſtaken, however, in ſuppoſing that he does not include Turpin in the number of the combatants at Roncevaux.[5] He ſays expreſſly (leaf 384) :

> vnto Roulond then 'vent the princ*is* xij
> Olyu*er* and Rog*er* and Aubry hym-ſelue
> Richard and Rayn*er* that redy was eu*er*
> tirry and turpyn all redy wer.

The following deſcription of the " ſtrange weather" that happened in France while the battle was going on may ſerve as a ſpecimen of the ſtyle of the poem, which is remarkably vigorous :

> — while our folk fought to-gedur
> ther fell in Fraunce A ſtrau*n*g wedur
> A gret derk myſt in the myd-day-tym
> thik and clowdy and euyll wedur thene
> and thiknes of ſterris and thonder light
> the erthe dynnyd doillfully to wet

---

[1] *Antiquit. Dan.* lib. i. 9, p. 51.

[2] In the royal palace of Jeddo, which overflows with a profuſion of the moſt exquiſite and ſuperb eaſtern embelliſhments, the tapeſtry of the emperor's audience-hall is of the fineſt ſilk, wrought by the moſt ſkilful artificers of that country, and adorned with pearls, gold, and ſilver. *Mod. Univ. Hiſt.* B. xiii. c. ii. vol. ix. p. 83. (Not. G.) edit. 1759.

[3] [Communicated by Mr. Shelly, of Plymouth.]

[4] [Lanſd. MS. 388, leaf 381 to 395.]

[5] [*Hiſt. Poét de Charlemagne,* p 155, note.]

Foulis fled for fere it was gret wond*er*
bowes of trees *th*en breftyn afond*er*
beft ran to bank*is* And cried full fore
they durft not abid in the mor
ther was no man but he hid his hed
And thought not but to dy in *th*at fted
the wekid wedur laftid full long
from the mornying to the euynfong
then Rofe a clowd euyn in the weft
as red as blod wi*th*-outon reft
It fhewid doun on the erthe & *th*er did thyn
So many doughty men as died *th*at tym.

2. *Otuwel.* This is alfo incomplete. Ellis has given an analyfis of it;[1] and the poem was printed from the Auchinleck MS. for the Abbotsford Club in 1836. Its date is fuppofed to be not later than 1330. Ellis has completed the ftory, as he fays, from another MS. then in the poffeffion of Mr. Fillingham, in which, however, M. Gafton Paris has recognized a portion of a cyclic poem, to which he gives the title of *Charlemagne and Roland*, and which I will next defcribe. Our Otuwel is the French *Otinel*.[2] Otuwel or Otinel, the hero of the poem, comes as the ambaffador of the Saracen king Garfie (Garfile), to fummon Charles to pay homage to his mafter, and to abjure the Chriftian faith; but by a miracle he is himfelf converted, and " forfakes all his gods." He is then betrothed to Belecent, the daughter of Charles, and marches with Charles and his " duzze peres" (douze pairs) to fight againft Garfie in Lombardy. Garfie is taken prifoner, and led to Charles by Otuwel, who is rewarded—according to the French Romances, for here our fragment ends—with the hand of Belecent and the crown of Lombardy.

3. *Charlemagne and Roland.* This is the title which, according to M. Paris,[3] ought to be given to a poem which we poffefs only in fcattered fragments. The poem belongs probably to the beginning of the fourteenth century. M. Paris divides it into four parts. 1ft. Charlemagne's Journey to the Holy Land according to the Latin legend. 2nd. The beginning of the war in Spain after the firft chapters of Turpin's *Chronicle*. 3rd. Otuwel, but a different verfion from that defcribed above. 4th. The end of Turpin's hiftory. The firft and fecond parts confift of the poem in the Auchinleck MS., printed for the Abbotsford Club under the title of *Roland and Vernagu*, and analyfed by Ellis as *Roland and Ferragus*.[4] The ftory of the firft part, as related in this poem, fhould rather be defcribed as Charles's vifit to the emperor " Conftanfious," and that of the fecond part, which begins on page 15 of the Abbotsford [Club] edition, as the combat of Roland and Vernagu. The concluding lines of this fecond part connect it with the third:

To Otuel alfo yern
That was a farrazin ftern
Ful fone this word fprong.

---

[1] *Specimens of Early Engl. Metr Romances* (ed. 1811), vol. ii. p. 324.]
[2] *Les Anciens Poetes de la France*, tom. i.]
[3] *Hift. Poét. de Charlem.* liv. 1, ch. viii.]   [4] Vol. ii. 302.]

This third and the fourth part are comprised in Mr. Fillingham's MS., which we know only from Ellis's analysis. It contains, according to Ellis, about 11,000 lines, and relates not only the story of Otuwel (the third part of the poem), but also the conquest of Spain, the deceit of Ganelon, the fight at Roncevaux, the defeat of the Saracens by Charles,[1] and the punishment of Ganelon, which form the fourth part. The poem concludes as follows :—

> Here endeth Otuel, Roland, and Olyuere,
> And of the twelve duffypere.

It is worth while remarking how entirely the meaning of the title given to the peers has been lost by the English poets. Here we read of " the *twelve duffypere* " (les douze pairs), and in other places we find each single knight called " a dozeper," while in the Ashmole MS. of Sir Ferumbras the word becomes " doth*the*per."

4. *Ferumbras.* We have two versions of this romance ; one of them the Farmer MS. analyzed by Ellis,[2] and now in the library

---

[1] [*La Conqueste que fit le grand roi Charlemaigne es Espaignes* ne doit pas être confondue avec la compilation de David Aubert. Ce livre est le même que celui qui porte le nom de *Fierabras* . . . . . . Sous le nom de *Fierabras* M. Brunet indique une édition de 1478 ; sous le titre de la *Conquête de Charlemagne* il n'en connaît pas avant 1501, mais la Bibliothèque Impériale en possède une de 1486. Cy finist Fierabras. Imprimée a Lyon par Pierre de Saincte Lucye dict le Prince. Lan de grace MCCCCLXXXVI. Le vii jour de Septembre. Toutefois le titre au moins et les trois feuillets qui suivent cet explicit sont postérieurs. Au reste l'ouvrage est divisé en trois livres, et la traduction en prose de *Fierabras* ne forme que le second ; l'ensemble a la prétention d'être une histoire de Charlemagne. Elle y est même précédée d'un abrégé de l'histoire de France depuis Clovis, grossièrement conforme aux chroniques. Puis vient l'éloge de Charlemagne et un sommaire de son règne ; on raconte ensuite le voyage à Jérusalem d'après la légende latine—tel est le contenu du premier livre. Le troisième comprend le récit de la guerre d'Espagne d'après Turpin. L'auteur nous a donné lui-même des renseignements sur ses sources. Il nous apprend d'abord qu'il a écrit sur la demande de messire Henry Bolomier, chanoine de Lausanne, grand admirateur de Charlemagne. " Selon les matières que j'ay peu amasser, j'ay ordonné cestuy livre ; car je n'ay eu intencion de déduyre la matière que je ne aye esté informé par plusieurs livres et principallement par ung qui est intitulé le *Mirouer hystorial*, et aussi par les cronicques qui font mention de l'oeuvre suyvante." Il est fort probable que ces *cronicques*, vaguement désignées, n'ont jamais été consultées par notre auteur, qui trouvait dans le *Speculum historiale* de Vincent de Beauvais tout ce dont il parle, sauf le *Fierabras;* aussi dit-il au début du second livre: " Ce que j'ay dessus escript, je l'ay prins en ung moult autentique livre, lequel se nomme le Mirouer hystorial, et aussi es croniques anciennes, et l'ay translaté de latin en françoys ; et la matière suyvante que fera le second livre est d'ung romant faict en l'ancienne façon, sans grande ordonnance, dont j'ay esté incité à le réduyre en prose par chapitres ordonnez. Et est appellé celluy livre selon aulcuns *Fierabras*." On voit que le travail auquel le compilateur s'est livré, " selon la capacité de son petict engin," n'etait pas fort difficile : il a simplement mis en mauvaise prose française le latin de Vincent de Beauvais et les vers de *Fierabras*. Son ouvrage n'en a pas moins eu dès son apparition un succès immense, qui d'ailleurs n'est pas épuisé ; car on le réimprime encore à Epinal et à Montbéliard, de plus en plus défiguré dans chaque édition successive, et de temps à autre un peu rajeuni.—Gaston Paris (*Hist. Poët de Charlemagne*, livre i. chap. iv. § iv. pp. 97-8-9).]

[2] [Vol. ii. p. 369.]

of Sir Thomas Phillipps; the other a fragment[1] of great length, which will ſhortly be printed by the Early Engliſh Text Society. They both belong probably to the end of the fourteenth century. The original of the romance is the French Fierabras.[2] I give parallel extracts from the French and the two Engliſh verſions. There is a Provençal as well as a French verſion of the romance, and I would ſuggeſt the enquiry whether the poem analyzed by Ellis does not follow this Provençal verſion, or rather perhaps the loſt French original of which the French editors have ſhown the Provençal verſion to be a tranſlation. They agree at any rate in brevity, though they both give a long introduction, which the exiſting French verſion omits. The Aſhmole MS. is imperfect at the beginning and at the end; but it appears generally to follow very nearly the ſtory of the exiſting French verſion, though it is much more diffuſe, the remaining fragment containing about 10,450 lines, while the entire French poem contains only 6219. Both the Engliſh verſions agree, however, in ſome little particulars which the French omits; *e. g.* the mention of Richard bleſſing himſelf in the extracts I give. Our fragment begins, like the French poem, with the relation of a long combat between Oliver and Ferumbras (Fierabras, *ferri brachium*), the ſon of the admiral (anirans, *Arab.* amir) Balan, who in the Farmer MS. is ſtrangely called Laban. Ferumbras is vanquiſhed, and embraces the Chriſtian faith; but Oliver is ſurpriſed by the Saracens, and made priſoner, with four other peers. The reſt of the peers are ſent by Charles to demand the ſurrender of their companions, but are thrown into the ſame dungeon. They are, however, protected by Florippe, the daughter of Balan, and after many battles are at length delivered by Charlemagne. Balan refuſes baptiſm, but Florippe is baptized, and here the Aſhmole MS. ends, being imperfect; but the other verſions relate the marriage of Florippe to Guy de Bourgoyne, and the diviſion of the kingdom of Spain between him and Ferumbras.

With the Aſhmole MS. is preſerved its ancient vellum cover, made out of portions of two Latin documents, one relating to the Vicarage of Columpton, and the other to the chapel of Holne and pariſh of "Bukfaſtleghe." This cover, however, is chiefly remarkable, becauſe it contains what is evidently part of the firſt draft of the poem, written in the ſame hand as the MS. itſelf. The following extracts from both will ſhow how the poet corrected his verſes:

DRAFT.

So ſturne ſtrokes thay araȝte
 eyther til other the whyle
That al the erthe about quaȝte
 men miȝt hure a myle
They wer ſo fers on hure mod
 And eger on hure fiȝte
That eyther of hem thoȝte god
 to ſlen other if he miȝt.

[Aſhm. MS. 33.]   [2] [*Les Anciens Poetes de la France*, tom. iv.]

MS.

So fterne ftrokes thay arauȝte
eyther til other with ftrenghthe
That al the erthe ther ofte quaȝte
a myle and more on lenghthe
They weren fo eger bothe of mod
And eke fo fers to fiȝte
That eyther of hem than thoȝte god
to fle other if he miȝte.[1]

The poem is written in the Southern dialect, but it contains a remarkably large admixture of Northern forms, words occurring fometimes in two forms in lines clofe together, if not in the fame line. Thus we find *ich* and *I*, *a* and *he*, *heo* and *fche*, *hy* and *thay* (the latter moft frequently), and *thilke* and *this*, *to* and *til*, *prykyng* and *prykande*, *vafte* and *fafte*, and fo forth, the former being the Southern, the latter the Northern form. The Southern infinitive in *y* (ftill ufed occafionally in Devonfhire) continually occurs: *e. g.* *maky*, *afky*, *graunty*, *robby*, *wivy* (to wed), &c. On the whole one would be inclined to fuppofe that the poem was written in the South (perhaps in the diocefe of Exeter) by a fouthern man, who had, however, lived in the North fufficiently long to become familiar with northern forms. But a more careful examination (in preparation for the Early Englifh Text Society's edition) will very likely lead to our being better informed concerning the character and hiftory of this moft interefting MS.

From *Fierabras*, *Chanfon de Gefte*, edited from MSS. of the xiv. and xv. centuries by MM. A. Krœber and G. Servois (Paris, 1860). The extract begins with line 4354, p. 132 of this edition:

RICHARS refgarde l'yaue, qui moult fait à douter;
Se eft grande et hideufe que il n'i offe entrer.
Plus toft cuert que fajete, quaint on le lait aler;
Ne barge ne galie n'i puent abiter;
La rive en eft moult haute, bien fait à redouter.
Richars de Normendie fe prinft à refgarder,
Efcortrement commence Jhefu à reclamer:
" Glorieus fire pere, qui te laifas pener

---

[1] [Refpecting the early Englifh profe life of Charles the Great, from the prefs of Caxton, M. Gafton Paris remarks: "Au quinzième fiècle, le célèbre imprimeur Caxton publia un livre intitulé, 'The lyf of Charles the Great,' &c. Cette *Vie de Charles le Grand*, qui eft à préfent d'une rareté exceffive, a été généralement regardée comme une compilation faite par Caxton; on a loué le difcernement qu'il avait montré dans la choix de fes fources, et on a remarqué qu'il avait donné un beau rôle au duc de Normandie, Richard fans peur, évidemment par patriotifme. Voy. *Revue britannique* [Britifh Review?] Mars, 1844. On lui a fait honneur furtout des fentiments exprimés dans la préface, adreffée *à un de fes amis particuliers*, Henri Bolomyer, chanoine de Laufanne. Mais ce nom fuffit pour nous faire voir que Caxton avait fimplement traduit, et, comme il le dit lui-même, *réduit en anglais* le livre des *Conqueftes de Charlemagne* ou de *Fierabras*. . . . Quant au rôle de Richard fans peur, il fe trouvait auffi développé dans le livre français, qui l'avait pris lui-même dans le poëme de *Fierabras*."—*Hiftoire Poétique de Charlemagne*, livre i. chap. viii. p. 157.]

" En la crois benéoite pour ton pule fauver,
" Garifiés hui mon cors de mort et d'afoler,
" Que je puiffe Karlon mon meffage conter."
Or oiés quel vertu Diex i vaut demonftrer
Por le roi Karlemaine, qui tant fait à douter.
Ançois que on éuft une liuée alé,
Véiffiés fi Flagot engroifier et enfler,
Que par defous la rive commence à feronder.
Atant es vous . 1 . cerf, que Diex i fift aler,
Et fu blans comme nois, biaus fu à refgarder.
Devant le ber Richart fe prent à demonftrer,
Devant lui eft tantoft eus en Flagot entrés.
Li dus voit Sarrazins après lui aroutés;
S'il ot paour de mort ne fait à demander.
Après le blance biffe comme[n] cha à errer,
Tout ainfi com ele vait, lait le ceval aler;
Et li ciers vait devant, qui bien f'i fot garder,
D'autre part à la rive fe prent à ariver.

From the *Romance of Ferumbras*, analyzed by Ellis, who has
modernized the fpelling :

When Richard faw there was no gate
　　But by Flagote the flood,
His meffage would he not let ;
　　His horfe was both big and good.
He kneeled, befeeching God, of His grace,
　　To fave him fro mifchief :
A white hind he faw anon in that place,
　　That fwam over to the cliff.
He bleffed him in Goddis name,
　　And followed the fame way,
The gentil hind that was fo tame,
　　That on that other fide gan play.

From the *Romance of Ferumbras* (Afhmole MSS. 33).   The following paffage begins on fol. 52 :

¶ Now y-come ys he to *th*e ryuere
　By fyde a treo *and* a ftod him *th*ere
　　　*Th*at water to by holde
　And faw *th*e ryuer was dup *and* brod
　And ran away as he were wod
　　　Ys herte gan waxe colde
¶ Richard tok herte *and th*enche gan
　*Th*at nedelich a moft entrye *than*
　　　In *and* paffe *th*at ryuere
　Ou*th*er he mofte turn agee
　And figte agayn al *th*at maygne
　　　*Th*at after him come there
　To ihe*f*u *tha*nne he had a bone
　Lord *th*at madeft funne mone
　　　Lond *and* water cler
　Kep me *th*ys day fram my fone
　And if y *th*ys ryuer potte me one
　　　*Th*at y ne a-drenche her
　And fuch grace *th*ow me fende
　*Th*at y may fafe to Charlis wende
　　　And telle hy*m* my porpos
　So *th*at he may come wy*th* focour

And delyuery ys barons of hono*ur*   [Fol. 523.]
    *Th*at ligge*th* among *th*y fos
¶ Nad he nogt *th*at word ful fpeke
Er *th*at *th*ar cam an hert for*th* reke
    As wyt afe melkys fom
Rygt euene by-fore duk Rychard
*Th*e hert hym wente to watre-ward
    And fayre by-fore hym fwom
W*a*nne *th*e duk *th*at wonder y-feg
And *th*e farfyns *th*at *th*o wer come wel neg
    W*ith* boft *and* noyfe gret
W*ith* is rigt honde *th*an bleffede he hym
And *th*og *th*e ryuere were ftyf *and* grym
    Wy*th* bo*th*e hors in a fchet
Ys ftede was an hors of prys
And bar *th*e knigt at al dyuys
    Swymmynge wi*th* ys felawe
*Th*e hert *th*at was fo fair of figt
Ouer *th*e Ryuer fwam ful rigt
    And Ry*ch*ard do*th* after-drawe.

SECTION VI.

LTHOUGH much poetry began to be written about the reign of Edward II., yet I have found only [two] Englifh poet[s] of that reign whofe name[s] ha[ve] defcended to pofterity.[1] [One] is Adam Davy or Davie. He may be placed about the year 1312. I can collect no circumftances of his life, but that he was marfhal of Stratford-le-bow near London.[2] He has left feveral poems never printed, which are almoft as forgotten as his name. Only one manufcript of thefe pieces now remains, which feems to be coeval with its author.[3] They are, *Vifions, The Battell of Jerufalem, The Legend of Saint Alexius, Scripture hiftories, of fifteen toknes before the day of Judgement,* [and] *Lamentations of Souls.*[4]

In the *Vifions,* which are of the religious kind, Adam Davie draws this picture of Edward II. ftanding before the fhrine of Edward the Confeffor in Weftminfter Abbey at his coronation. The lines have a ftrength arifing from fimplicity :

---

[1] Robert de Brunne, above mentioned, lived, and wrote fome of his pieces, in this reign ; but he more properly belongs to the laft.

[2] This will appear from citations which follow.

[3] MSS. Bibl. Bodl. Laud. 622 *olim* I 74, fol. 26 *b*. It has been much damaged. [All the extracts have now been collated with the original MS.—a procefs which was found highly neceffary.]

[4] In the MS. there is alfo a piece in profe, entitled, *The Pylgrymages of the holi land*, f. 65, 66. It begins : " Qwerr foever a cros ftandyth ther is a forgivenes of payne." I think it is a defcription of the holy places, and it appears at leaft to be of the hand-writing of the reft.

To oure lorde Ihesu crist in heuene
Ich to day shawe myne sweuene,[1]
þat ich mette[2] in one niȝth,
Of a kniȝth of mychel miȝth :
His name is ihote[3] sir Edward þe kynge,
Prince of Wales Engelonde the faire þinge ;
Me mette þat he was armed wel,
Boþe wiþ yrne *and* wiþ stel,
And on his helme that was of stel,
A Coroune of golde bicom hym wel.
Bifore þe shryne of Seint Edward he stoode,
Myd glad chere *and* mylde of mood.[4]

Most of thefe Vifions are compliments to the king.   Our poet then
proceeds thus :

ANoþer sweuene me mette on a tiwes niȝth[5]
Bifore the feste of Allehalewen of þat ilke kniȝth,
His name is nempned[3] here bifore,
Blissed be þe tyme þat he was bore, [&c.]
Of sir Edward oure derworþ[6] kynge
Ich mette of hym anoþere fair metynge, [&c.]
Me þouȝth he rood vpon an Asse,
And þat ich take god to witnesse ;
Y-wonden he was in a Mantel gray,
Toward Rome he nom[7] his way,
Vpon his heuede sate an gray hure,
It semed hym wel a mesure ;
He rood wiþouten hose *and* sho,
His wone was nouȝth so forto do ;
His shankes semeden al blood-rede,
Myne herte wop[8] for grete drede ;
Als a pilgryme he rood to Rome,
And þider he com wel swiþe sone.
þe þrid sweuene me mette a niȝth
Rigth of þat derworþe kniȝth :
þe Wedenysday a niȝth it was
Nexte þe day of seint lucie bifore cristenmesse, [&c.]
Me þouȝth þat ich was at Rome,
And þider ich com swiþe sone,
The Pope *and* sir Edward oure kynge
Boþe hij[9] hadden a newe dubbynge, [&c.]
Ihesus crist ful of grace
Graunte oure kynge in euery place
Maistrie of his wiþerwynes
And of alle wicked Sarasynes.
Me met a sweuene on worþinge[10] niȝth
Of þat ilche derworþe kniȝth,
God ich it shewe *and* to witnesse take
And so shilde me fro synne *and* sake.
In-to an chapel ich com of oure lefdy,[11]
Ihesus crist hire leue[12] son stood by,

---

[1] dream.
[2] thought, dreamed.   In the first sense, we have *me mette* in Chaucer, *Non. Pr*
T. v. 1013.   And below.
[3] named.   [4] fol. 26 *b.*   [5] twelfth-night.
[6] dear-worthy.   [7] took.   [8] wept.
[9] they.   [10] [on worthing nyth.—*Park.*]   [11] lady.
[12] dear.

On rode[1] he was an louelich Man,
Als þilk*e* þat on rode was don
He vnneiled[2] his honden two, [&c.]
Adam þe marchal of stretford*e* atte bowe
Wel swiþe wide his name is yknowe
He hymself*e* mette þis metyng*e*,
To witnesse he takeþ Ihe*s*u heuene kyng*e*,
On wedenysday[3] in clene leinte[4]
A voice me bede I ne shulde nouȝth feinte,
Of þe sweuenes þat her ben write
I shulde swiþe don[5] my lorde kyng*e* to wite, [&c.]
Þe þursday next þe berynge[6] of our*e* lefdy
Me þouȝth an Aungel com sir Edwa*r*d by, [&c.]
Ich telle ȝou forsoþe wiþouten les,[7]
Als god of heuene maide marie to moder ches,[8]
Þe Aungel com to me Adam Dauy *and* sede
Bot þou Adam shewe þis þee worþe wel yuel mede, [&c.]
Who-so wil speke myd me Adam þe marchal
In stretforþe bowe he is yknowe *and* ouere al,
Ich ne shewe nouȝth þis forto haue mede
Bot for god Almiȝtties drede.

There is a very old prose romance, both in French and Italian, on the subject of the *Destruction of Jerusalem*.[9] It is translated from a Latin work in five books, very popular in the middle ages, entitled, *Hegesippus de Bello Judaico et Excidio Urbis Hierosolymitanæ Libri quinque.* This is a licentious paraphrase of a part of Josephus's Jewish history, made about the fourth century: and the name Hegesippus is most probably corrupted from Josephus, perhaps also called Josippus. The paraphrast is supposed to be Ambrose of Milan, who flourished in the reign of Theodosius.[10] On the subject of Vespasian's siege of Jerusalem, as related in this book, our poet Adam

---

[1] cross.   [2] unnailed.
[3] Wodenis day. Woden's day, *i.e. Wednesday.*   [4] Lent.
[5] [Swithe don to wite, *quickly let him know.—Ritson.*]
[6] Christmas-day.   [7] lies.
[8] "As sure as God chose the Virgin Mary to be Christ's mother."
[9] In an ancient inventory of books, all French romances, made in England in the reign of Edward III., I find the romance of *Titus and Vespasian.* Madox, *Formul. Anglican.* p. 12. See also Scipio Maffei's *Traduttori Italiani,* p. 48. Crescimbeni (*Volg. Poes.* vol. i. l. 5, p. 317), does not seem to have known of this romance in Italian. Du Cange mentions *Le Roman de la Prise de Jerusalem par Titus,* in verse, *Gloss. Lat.* i. *Ind. Auct.* p. cxciv. A metrical romance on this subject is in Royal MS. 16 E viii. 2, Brit. Mus. [and has been printed by M. Michel, as already mentioned, 1836, 12mo. But it merely relates to the mythical expedition of Charlemagne to Jerusalem]. There is an old French play on this subject, acted in 1437. It was printed in 1491, fol. Beauchamps, *Rech. Fr. Theat.* p. 134. [This is probably the same as Le Vengeance et Destruction de Iherusalem par personages executée par Vespasien et son filz Titus, contenant en soy plusieurs chroniques Rommaines tant du regne de Neron Empereur que de plusieurs aultres belles hystoires. Printed at Paris, 1510, 4to, for Jehan Trepparel.—*Douce. The Dystruccyon of Iherusalem by Waspazyan and Tytus,* of which there are two old printed edits. appears to be a paraphrase of the French.]
[10] He mentions Constantinople and New Rome: and the provinces of Scotia and Saxonia. From this work the Maccabees seem to have got into romance. It was first printed at Paris, fol. 1511. Among the Bodleian MSS. there is a most beautiful copy of this book, believed to be written in the Saxon times.

Davie has left a poem entitled the *Battell of Jeruſalem.*[1] It begins thus :

> ÞE BATAILE OF JERUſALEM.
>
> Liſtneþ alle þat beþ alyue,
> boþe criſten Men *and* wyne :
> I wil ȝou telle a wonder cas,
> hou Iheſus criſt bihated *was,*
> Of þe Iewes felle *and* kene,
> Þat *was on* hem ſiþþe iſene,
> Goſpelles I dr*awe* to witneſſe
> of þis mat*ere* more *and* leſſe, &c.[2]

In the courſe of the ſtory, Pilate challenges our Lord to ſingle combat. This ſubjeᴄt will occur again.

Davie's *Legend of ſaint Alexius the confeſſor, ſon of Euphemius,* is tranſlated from Latin, and begins thus :

[The line preceding is this :

> *Here endeþ the vengeaunce of goddes deth.*]

> Alle þat willen here in ryme,
> Hou gode Men in olde tyme,
>   Loueden god Almiȝth ;
> Þat weren riche, of grete valoure,
> Kynges ſones and Emperoure
>   Of bodies ſtronge *and* liȝth ;
> Ȝee habbeþ yherde ofte in geſte,
> Of holy men maken feſte
>   Boþe day *and* niȝth,
> Forto haue þe ioye in heuene
> (Wiþ Aungels ſonge, *and* mery ſteuene,)
>   Þere blis is brode *and* briȝth :
> To ȝou alle heiȝe *and* lowe
> Þe riȝth ſoþe to biknowe
>   Ȝoure ſoules forto ſaue, [&c.]³

Our author's *Scripture Hiſtories* want the beginning. Here they begin with Joſeph, and end with Daniel :

> For þritty pens[4] þai ſolde*n* þat childe
>   Þe ſeller hiȝth Judas,
> Þo[5] Ruben com hom *and* myſſed hy*m*
>   Sori ynoȝ he was.[6]

His *Fifteen Toknes*[7] *before the Day of Judgment* are taken from the prophet Jeremiah :

---

[1] The latter part of this poem appears detached, in a former part of our MS. with the title *The Vengeaunce of Goddes Death,* viz. fol. 1. This latter part begins with theſe lines :

> " And at þe fourty dayes ende,
> Whider I wolde he bad me wende,
> Vpon þe mount of Olyuete," [&c.

An imperfeᴄt copy, ſays Mr. Furnivall, is in Addit. MS. Brit. Mus. 10,036, and another, wanting only one ſheet, is in the poſſeſſion of the Earl of Cardigan. See alſo Addit. MS. 10,269.]

[2] MS. *ut ſupr.* f. 71 b.
[3] *Ibid.* f. 21 b.   [4] Thirty pence.
[5] [The capital "Þ" in this MS. is always written thus : " IÞ".]
[6] MS. *ut ſupr.* f. 65.   [7] Tokens.

ÞE firſt ſigne þer aȝeins, as oure lord hym-ſelf ſede,
Hungere ſchal on erþe be, treccherie, *and* falſhede,
Batailes, *and* litel loue, ſekeneſſe *and* haterede,
And þe erþe ſchal quaken, þat vche man ſchal drede:
Þe mone ſchal turne to blood, þe ſunne to derkhede, &c.[1]

Another of Davie's poems may be called the *Lamentation of Souls.*
But the ſubjeƈt is properly a congratulation of Chriſt's advent, and
the lamentation of the ſouls of the fathers remaining in limbo, for
his delay:

OF ioye *and* bliſſe is my ſonge, care to bileue,[2]
And to herie hym amonge þat al oure ſorouȝ ſchal reue,
Ycome he is þat ſwete dew, þat ſwete hony drope,
Iheſus kynge of alle kynges, to whom is al oure hope:
Bicome he is oure broþer, whare was he ſo longe?
He it is *and* non oþer, þat bouȝth vs ſo ſtronge:
Oure broþer we mowe[3] hym clepe wel, ſo ſeiþ hym-ſelf ilome.[4]

My readers will be perhaps ſurpriſed to find our language improve
ſo ſlowly, and will probably think, that Adam Davie writes in a leſs
intelligible phraſe than many more ancient bards already cited. His
obſcurity, however, ariſes in great meaſure from obſolete ſpelling, a
mark of antiquity which I have here obſerved in exaƈt conformity
to a manuſcript of the age of Edward II., and which in the poetry
of his predeceſſors, eſpecially the minſtrel-pieces, has been often
effaced by multiplication of copies and other cauſes. In the meantime it ſhould be remarked, that the capricious peculiarities and even
ignorance of tranſcribers often occaſion an obſcurity, which is not
to be imputed either to the author or his age.[5]

[The ſame volume with Adam Davie's poems (fol. 27 *b*), and
therefore ſometimes, but wrongly aſcribed to him, has a produƈtion
without any author's name, of the ſame period, entitled] the *Life of
Alexander*, which deſerves to be publiſhed entire on many accounts.
It ſeems to be founded chiefly on Simeon Seth's romance above
mentioned ; but many paſſages are alſo copied from the French
Roman d'Alexandre, a poem in our author's age perhaps equally
popular both in England and France. It is a work of conſiderable
length.[6] I will firſt give ſome extraƈts from the Prologue:

---

[1] MS. *ut ſupr.* f. 70 b.   [2] Leave.   [3] May.   [4] MS. *ut ſupr.* f. 71.
[5] Chaucer in *Troilus and Creſſida* mentions "the grete diverſite in Engliſh, and
in writing of our tongue." He therefore prays God, that no perſon would *miſwrite*,
or *miſſe-metre* his poem. Lib. *ult.* v. 1792, *ſeq.*
[6] [In attributing this romance to Davie [in his original edition] Warton has
followed the authority of Tanner, who was probably led into the miſtake by
finding it bound up with the remaining works of this "poetic marſhall." We are
indebted to Mr. Ellis for deteƈting—upon the force of internal evidence—this miſ-
appropriation of a very ſpirited compoſition to the inſipid author of the Legend of
Saint Alexius. It has ſince been publiſhed from a tranſcript of the Lincoln's-Inn
MS. made by Mr. Park, and forms the firſt volume in Mr. Weber's colleƈtion.—
Price. The text, conformably with Price's own opinion, has now been taken from
the Laud MS. in preference to that preſerved at Lincoln's-Inn, and printed by
Weber.]

Diuers is þis middellerrde
To lewed Men *and* to lerede,[1]
Byſyneſſe, care and ſorouȝ
Is myd Man vche morowȝe [&c.]
Naþeles, wel fele *and* fulle
Boeþ y-founde in herte *and* ſhulle
þat hadden leuer a Ribaudye
þan here of god, oiþer ſeint Marie;
Oiþer to drynke a Copful ale,
þan to heron any gode tale:
Swiche ich wolde were oute-biſhett;
For certeyn lich, it were nett.
For hire ne haeþ wille ich woot welbb
Bot in þe gute *and* in þe barel.[2]

[The writer] thus deſcribes a ſplendid proceſſion made by Olympias:

In þis tyme faire *and* Iolyfe[3]
Olympyas, þat faire wȳfe
Wolde make a riche feſte
Of kniȝttes *and* leſdyes honeſte,
Of Burgeys *and* of Iugelers
And of Men of vche meſters,[4]
For Men ſeiþ by north *and* ſouth
Wymmen beeþ, euere ſelcouþ;
Mychel ſhe deſireþ to ſhewe hire body
Her faire here, her face rody,
To haue loos[5] *and* ek praiſynge:
And al is folye by heuene kynge
So dude þe dame Olympyas
Forto ſhowe hire gentyl face.
She hete Marſhales, *and* kniȝhtes
Greiþe hem to ryde onon riȝttes
And leuedyes *and* damoyſele
Quyk hem greiþed þouſandes fele,
In faire atyre, in dyuers queyntiſe
Many þere roode on riche wiſe.
A Mule, alſo whyte ſo mylke
Wiþ ſadel of gold, ſambu of ſylke
Was y-brouȝth to þe quene
Myd many belle of ſyluer ſhene
Yfaſtned on Orfreys[6] of mounde
þat hengen doune to neiȝ grounde.
Forþ ſhe ferdeu[7] myd her rote
A þouſande leſdyes of riche ſoute.

---

[1] Leg. *lerd.* learned.
[2] The work begins thus:

Wнilom clerkes wel ylerede
On þre diztten þis Middel erde,
And clepid hit in here maiſtrie,
Europe, Affryke, and Aſyghe:
At Aſyghe al ſo muchul ys
As Europe, and Affryk, I wis, &c.

And ends with this diſtich:

Aliſaunder! me reowith thyn endyng
That thou n'adeſt dyghed in criſtenyng.

[3] Jolly. [4] Of each, or every, profeſſion, trade, ſort. [5] Praiſe.
[6] Er.broidered work, cloth of gold. *Aurifrigium*, Lat. [7] Fared: went.

A ſperuer[1] þat was honeſt*e*
So ſat on þe leſdyes fyſt*e* :
Foure trumpes toforne[2] hir*e* belew :
Many Man þat day hire knew :
An hundreþ houſande *and* ek moo
Alle alouten hire vnto.
Al þe tou*n* by-honged was[3]
Azeins[4] þe leſdy Olympyas.[5]
Orgues, Chymbes, vche man*ere* glee[6]
Was dryuen azein þat leuedy free.
Wiþouten þees tounes Murey :
Was arered vche man*er* pley ;[7]
Þere was knizttes tourneying*e*
Þere was maydens Carolyng*e*
Þere was Champions ſkirmyng*e*,[8]
Of hem of oþer alſo wreſtlyng*e*
Of lyons chace, of bere baitynge.
A bay of bore[9] of bole ſlatynge.[10]
Al þe Cite was by-honge
Wiþ Riche Samytes *and* pelles[11] longe
Dame Olympias amonge this pres[12]
Sengle rood,[13] al Mantel-les.—
And naked heued in one coroune
She rood þorouz out*e* al þe tou*n*.
Here zelewe her[14] was faire atired*e*
Mid riche ſtrenges of golde wyred*e*
It helyd her*e* abouten al[15]
To her*e* gentale Myddel ſmal
Brizth *and* ſhene was her face[16]
Eu*er*y fairehede[17] in hir was.[18]

---

[1] ſparrow-hawk ; a hawk.   [2] before.

[3] "hung with tapeſtry." We find this ceremony practiſed at the entrance of Lady Elizabeth, queen of Henry VII. into the city of London.—"Al the ſtrets ther whiche ſhe ſhulde paſſe by wer clenly dreſſed and beſene with cloth, of tappeſtrye and arras, and ſome ſtreetes as Chepe, hanged with riche clothes of golde, velvettes and ſilkes." This was in the year 1481. Leland. *Coll.* iv. *Opuſcul.* p. 220, edit. 1770.

[4] "againſt her coming."

[5] See the deſcription of the tournament in Chaucer, *Knight's Tale*, where the city is hanged with cloth of gold. v. 2570.

[6] "organs, timbrels, all manner of muſic."

[7] "all ſorts of ſports."   [8] ſkirmiſhing.

[9] "baying or bayting of the boar."

[10] *ſlaying bulls*, bull-feaſts. [Sir F. Madden ſays, bull-*baiting*.] Chaucer ſays that the chamber of Venus was painted with "white *bolis* grete." *Compl. of Mars and Ven.* v. 86.

[11] ſkins.   [12] crowd ; company.   [13] rode ſingle.

[14] yellow hair.   [15] "covered her all over."

[16] line 155.   [17] beauty.

[18] John Gower, who lived an hundred years after our author, hath deſcribed the ſame proceſſion. *Confeſs. Amant.* lib. vi. [ed. 1857, iii. 62-3.]

> " But in that citee thanne was
> The quene, whiche Olimpias
> Was hote, and with ſolempnite
> The feſte of her nativite
> As it befell, was than holde ;
> And for her luſt to be beholde,
> And preiſed of the people about,
> She ſhop her for to riden out,

Much in the fame ftrain the marriage of Cleopatra is deſcribed :

> Þhoo þis meſſage was hom y-come
> Þere was many a bliþe gome
> Of Olyue *and* of muge floures
> Weren ſtrywed halle *and* boures :
> Wiþ Samytes *and* Baudekyns
> Weren curtyned þe gardyns.
> Alle þe Innes of þe tou*n*
> Hadden litel foyſou*n*,[1]
> Þat day þat com Cleopatras ;
> So mychel poeple wiþ hir was.
> She rood on a Mule, white ſo mylk*e* ;
> Her herneys was gold beten ſylk*e*
> Þe prince hire led*e* of Candas,
> And of Sydoyne Sir Ionathas,
> Ten þouſande barons hir co*m*me myde,
> And to chirche wiþ hire ryde.
> Yſpouſed ſhe is *and* ſet on deys :
> Nov gynneþ geſt of gret nobléys :
> Aт þe feſt was harpynge,
> And pipyng*e and* tabourynge,
> And ſitelynge *an*d tru*m*pynge.[2]

We have frequent opportunities of obſerving, how the poets of theſe times engraft the manners of chivalry on ancient claſſical hiſtory. In the following lines Alexander's education is like that of Sir Triſtram. He is taught tilting, hunting, and hawking :

> Now can Aliſaundre of ſkirmyng*e*
> As of ſtedes derayeyng*e*,

> At after-mete all openly.
> Anone were alle men redy,
> And that was in the month of may
> This luſty quene in good array
> Was ſet upon a mule white
> To ſene it was a great delite
> The joie that the citee made.
> With freſhe thinges and with glade
> The noble town was al behonged ;
> And every wight was ſore alonged
> To ſe this luſty ladie ride.
> There was great merth on alle ſide,
> Where as ſhe paſſeth by the ſtrete
> There was ful many a tymbre bete,
> And many a maide carolende.
> And thus through out the town pleinde
> This quene unto the pleine rode
> Where that ſhe hoved and abode
> To ſe diverſe games pley,
> The luſty folk jouſt and tourney.
> And ſo foıth every other man
> Which pleie couth, his pley began,
> To pleſe with this noble quene."

Gower continues this ſtory, from a romance mentioned above, to fol. 140.

[1] proviſion.
[2] line 1023 ; f. 32 of MS. Laud.

> Vpon ſtedes of Juſtuynge,
> And wiþ ſwerdes turneyeinge,
> Of aſſailynge and defendynge.
> Jn grene woode *and* of huntynge
> And of Ryuer of haukynge :[1]
> Of bataile *and* of alle þinge. [2]

In another place Alexander is mounted on a ſteed of Narbonne,[3] and, amid the ſolemnities of a great feaſt, rides through the hall to the high table. This was no uncommon practice in the ages of chivalry : [4]

> He lepeþ vp myd ydone
> On a ſtede of Nerebone ;
> He daſsheth forþ vpon þe londe
> Þe riche coroune on his honde,
> Of Nicholas þat he wan :
> Biſide hym rideþ many a gentil man.
> To þe paleys he comeþ ryde
> And fyndeþ þis feſte *and* al þis pride
> Forþ gooþ Aliſaundre, ſaunȝ fable
> Riȝth vnto þe heiȝe table.[5]

His horſe Bucephalus, who even in claſſical fiction is a horſe of romance, is thus deſcribed :

> An horne in the forhed amydwarde
> Þat wolde perce a ſhelde harde.[6]

To which theſe lines may be added :

> ALiſaunder ariſen is
> And ſitteþ on his deys I wys
> His dukes *and* his barouns ſaunȝ doute
> Stondeþ *and* ſitteþ hym aboute.[7]

The two following extracts are in a ſofter ſtrain, and not inelegant for the rude ſimplicity of the times :

> MEry is þe blaſt of þe ſtyuoure[8]
> Mery is þe touchynge of þe harpoure ; [9]

---

[1] Chaucer, *R. of Sir Thop.* v. 3245 :
  "He couth hunt al the wild dere,
    And ride an *hawkyng by the rivere.*"
And in the *Squyr of low degree* [*Rem. of the E. P. Poet. of Engl.* ii. 52] :
      "—— Shall ye *ryde*
    On haukyng by the ryuers ſide.*"
Chaucer, *Frankleins Tale,* v. 1752 :
    "Theſe fauconers upon a faire rivere
    That with the hawkis han the *heron* ſlaine."

[2] f. 30 *b.* MS. Laud.

[3] [The Lincoln's Inn MS. reads " faire bone," which is probably the correcter verſion.—*Price.*]

[4] See *Obſervations on the Fairy Queen,* i. § v. p. 146.

[5] line 1075, (ll. 1074-83 Laud. MS. f. 32.)   [6] ll. 692, 3 ; f 30 *b.*

[7] line 3966 ; (ll. 3954-7, f. 45 *b.*)

[8] [The editor thinks that Mr. Halliwell is ſcarcely correct in defining this to be a kind of bagpipe. Mr. Herbert Coleridge (*Gloſſary,* 1859, *in voce*) is ſurely nearer the truth in deſcribing it as a ſort of *trumpet,* Fr. *eſtive.* In the preſent paſſage it ſtands for a trumpeter, or, at leaſt, a perſon blowing a *ſtive.*]

[9] This poem has likewiſe, in the ſame vein, the following well-known old rhyme, which paints the manners, and is perhaps the true reading, line 1163 :

> Swete is þe fmellynge of þe floure
> Swete yit is in maydens boure
> Appel fwete bereþ fair[1] coloure
> Of trewe loue is fwe (*fic*) amoure.

Again:

> IN tyme of May, þe niȝttyngale
> In wood makeþ mery gale;
> So don þe foules grete *and* fmale
> Summe on hylles, *and* fumme in dale.[2]

Much the fame vernal delights, clothed in a fimilar ftyle, with the addition of knights turneying and maidens dancing, invite King Philip on a progrefs; he is entertained on the road with hearing tales of ancient heroes:

> MEry tyme it is in may
> þe foules fyngeþ her lay;
> þe kniȝttes loueþ þe turnay
> Maydens fo dauncen *and* þay play.
> þe kynge forþ rideþ his Iournay
> Now hereþ gefte of grete noblay.[3]

Our author thus defcribes a battle:[4]

> ALifaunder tofore is ride
> And many a gentil kniȝth hym myde
> Ac, forto gadre his meignè free
> He abideþ vnder a tree.
> Fourty þoufande of fhyualerie
> He takeþ in his compaignye.
> He dafsheþ hym forþ þan faftwarde:
> And þe oþer comen afterwarde:
> He feeþ his kniȝttes, in Mefchief
> He takeþ it gretlich a greef.
> He taked Bulcyphal[5] by þe fide;
> So a fwalewe he gynneþ forþ glide.
> A duke of Perce fone he mette
> And wiþ his launce he hym grette;
> He perceþ his breny and cleueþ his fhelde,
> þe herte tokerneþ þe yrne chelde:
> þe duke fel doune to þe grounde
> And ftarf quykly in þat ftounde.
> Alifaunder aloude þan feiede,

> " Swithe mury hit is in halle
> When the *burdes wawen alle*."

And in another place we have:

> " Mury hit is in halle to here the harpe;
> The mynftrall fyngith, theo jogolour carpith."—l. 5990.

Here, by the way, it appears, that the minftrels and juglers were diftinct characters. So Robert de Brunne, in defcribing the coronation of King Arthur, apud Anftis, *Ord. Gart.* i. p. 304:

> " *Jogeleurs* wer ther inouȝ
> That wer queitife for the drouȝ,
> *Mynftrels* many with dyvers glew," &c.

And Chaucer mentions " *minftrels* and *eke joglours.*"—*Rom. R.* v. 764. But they are often confounded or made the fame.

    line 2571; (ll. 2566-71, f. 39.)
[2] line 2546; (ll. 2542-5, f. 39).   [3] line 5210; (ll. 5194-9, f. 51).
[4] line 3776; (ll. 3764-3853, ff. 44 b, 45).   [5] Bucephalus.

Oþere tol neuere ich ne paiede :
Ʒute ʒee ſhullen of myne paie
Or ich gon more Aſſaie !
Anoþer launce in honde he hente ;
Aʒein þe prince of Tyre he wente,
He ſmoote hym þorouʒ þe breeſte þare
And out of ſadel ouere croupe hym bare ;
And I ſigge forſoþe þinge
He braake his nek in þe fallynge.
Oxeatre, wiþ mychel wonder
Antiochum hadde hym vnder,
And wiþ ſwerd wolde his heuede
From his body habbe yreuede.
He ſeiz Aliſaunder þe gode gome
Towardes hym ſwiþe come
He lete his pray *and* fleiz on hors
Forto ſaue his owen cors.
Antiochus on ſtede lep
Of none woundes ne tooke he kep ;
And eke he hade foure forde
Alle ymade wiþ ſperes orde.[1]
Þolomeus *and* alle hiſe felawen[2]
Of þis ſocour ſo weren wel fawen.
Aliſaunder made a cry hardy
Ore toſt, a ly ! a ly !
Þere þe kniʒttes of Achaye
Iuſted wiþ hem of Arabye ;
Þoo[3] of Rome, wiþ hem of Mede
Many londe wiþ oþere þede
Egipte iuſted wiþ hem of Tyre
Symple kniʒth wiþ riche ſyre ;
Þere nas foreʒifte ne for berynge ;
bituene vauaſoure[4] ne kynge,
Tofore, men miʒtten *and* byhynde
Cunteke[5] ſeke *and* cuntek fynde.
Wiþ Perciens fouʒtten þe gregeys ;[6]
Þere roos cry *and* grete honteys.
Hy kidden[7] þat hy neren merce
Hy braken ſperes alto ſlice :
Þere miʒth kniʒth fynde his pere,
Þere les many his deſtrere :
Þere was quyk in litel þrawe,[8]
Many gentil kniʒth yſlawe ;
Many Arme, many heued,[9]
Sone from þe body reued :
Many gentil lauedy[10]
Þere leſe quyke her amy :[11]
Þere was many maym ykede
Many fair penſel biblede.[12]
Þere was ſwerdes lik lakynge[13]
Þere was ſperes baþinge.[14]

---

[1] point.   [2] fellows.   [2] they.   [4] ſervant ; ſubjeĉt.   [5] ſtrife.
[6] Greeks.   [7] [ſhewed.]   [8] ſhort time.   [9] head.   [10] lady.
[11] paramour.   [12] " many a rich banner, or flag, ſprinkled with blood."
[13] claſhing. [This phraſe is one of frequent occurrence in Anglo-Saxon poetry,
and bears a very different import from that given by Mr. Weber : ſweord-lac, A.-S.
gladiorum ludus, from lacan, to play.—*Price*.]
[14] [Bathyng is the ſame as *Beating* ; but perhaps the true word is Bateing=
Fluttering.]

Boþe kynges þere, faunȝ doute
Beeþ in daſshet wiþ al her route ;
þe on to don men of hym ſpeke
þe oþere his harmes forto wreke.
Many londes neiȝ *and* ferre
Leſen her lorde in þat werre.
þe erþe quaked of her rydynge
þe weder [1] þicked of her crieynge
þe blood of hem þat weren yſlawe
Ran by flodes to þe lowe, &c.[2]

I have already mentioned Alexander's miraculous horn : [3]

He blew an horne quyke, faunȝ doute [4]
His folke com ſwiþe aboute :
And hem he ſeide wiþ voice clere,
Ich bidde, frendes, þat ȝe me here !
Aliſaunder is comen in þis londe
Wiþ ſtronge knniȝttes, wiþ miȝtty of honde.

Alexander's adventures in the deſerts among the Gymnoſophiſts, and in India, are not omitted. The authors, whom he quotes for his vouchers, ſhew the reading and ideas of the times : [5]

þoo Aliſaunder wente þorouȝ deſerte
Many wondres he ſeiȝ aperte [6]
Whiche he dude wel deſcryue
By gode clerkes in her lyue
By Ariſtotle his maiſter þat was
Better clerke ſiþen non nas.
He was wiþ hym *and* ſeiȝ *and* wroote
Alle þiſe wondres, (god it woote)
Salomon þat al þe werlde þorouȝ ȝede
In ſooþ witneſſe helde hym myde.
Yſidre [7] alſo, þat was ſo wys
In his bokes telleþ þis.
Maiſter euſtroge bereþ hym witneſſe
Of þe wondres more *and* leſſe.
Seint Jerome, ȝee ſhullen y-wyte
Hem haþ alſo in booke y-write ;
And Mageſtene, þe gode clerke
Haþ made þerof mychel werke.
Denys þat was of gode memorie
It ſheweþ al in his booke of ſtorie ;
And alſo Pompie [8] of Rome lorde,
Duke it writen euery worde.
Beheldeþ me þerof no fynder ; [9]
Her bokes ben my ſhewer
And þe lyf of Aliſaunder
Of whom fleȝ ſo riche ſklaunder.

---

[1] weather, ſky.   [2] (l. 3843, f. 45.)
[3] [It is moſt probable that Warton interpreted this paſſage of Alexander's horn : though the context plainly ſhews that it was Darius who blew it.—*Price*.]
[4] (l. 3848, f. 45.)   [5] line 4772.   [6] ſaw openly.
[7] *Iſidore.* He means, I ſuppoſe, Iſidorus Hiſpalenſis, a Latin writer of the ſeventh century.
[8] He means Juſtin's Trogus Pompeius the hiſtorian, whom he confounds with Pompey the Great.
[9] "don't look on me as the inventor."

Ʒif ʒee willeþ ʒiue liſtnynge
Now ʒee ſhullen here gode þinge
IN ſomers tyde þe day is longe ;
Foules ſyngeþ *and* makeþ ſonge
Kynge Aliſaunder y-wente is,
Wiþ dukes, Erles, *and* folke of pris,
Wiþ many kniʒth *and* douʒtty Men,
Toward the Cité of facen ;
After kynge Porus þat flowen[1] was
Into the Cité of Bandas :
He wolde wende þorouʒ deſerte
Þiſe wondres to ſeen aperte.
Gyoures he name[2] of þe londe
Fyue þouſande I vnderſtonde
Þat hem ſhulden lede riʒth,[3]
Þorouʒ deſerte by day *and* niʒth.
Þe Gyoures loueden þe kynge nouʒth
And wolden haue hym bicauʒth :
Hy ledden hym þerfore als I fynde
In þe ſtraungeſt peryl of ynde.
Ac, ſo ich fynde in the booke
Hy weren asſhreynte in her crooke.
Now rideþ Aliſaunder wiþ his Oſte,
Wiþ mychel pride *and* mychel booſte ;
Ac ar hy comen to Caſtel, oiþer toun
Hy ſhullen ſpeken anoþere leſſoun.
Lordynges, alſo I fynde
At Mede ſo bigynneþ ynde :
Forſoþe ich woote, it ſtretcheth ferreſte,
Of alle the londes in þe Eſte,
And oþ þe ſouþ half ſikerlyke
To þe cee takeþ of Affryke ;
And þe norþ half to a mountayne,
Þat is ycleped Caucaſayne.[4]
Forſoþe ʒee ſhullen vnderſtonde
Twyes is Somer in þe londe
And neuermore wynter ne chelen.[5]
Þat londe is ful of al wele ;
Twyes hy gaderen fruyte þere
And wyne *and* Corne in one ʒere.
In þe londe als I fynde, of ynde
Ben Citès fyue þouſynde ;
Wiþouten ydles *and* Caſtels,
And Boroughʒ tounes ſwiþe feles.[6]
In þe londe of ynde þou miʒth lere
Nyne þouſynde folk of ſelcouþ[7] manere
Þhat þer non is oþer yliche ;
Ne helde þou it nouʒth ferlich
Ac by þat þou vnderſtonde þe geſtes
Boþe of Men *and* eke of beeſtes, [&c.][8]

Edward II. is ſaid to have carried with him to the ſiege of Stirling Caſtle a poet named Robert Baſton.[9] He was a Carmelite friar of

---

[1] fled.   [2] took.   [3] ſtrait.   [4] Caucaſus.
[5] chill, cold.   [6] very many.   [7] uncommon.   [8] [l. 4831, f. 49 *b*.]
[9] [Winſtanley, in his *Account of the Engliſh Poets*, 1687, has introduced the name of BASTON, and has quoted the opening of his involuntary eulogium on Scotland and her king :

Scarborough; and the king intended that Baston, being an eye-witnefs of the expedition, fhould celebrate his conqueft of Scotland in verfe. Holinfhed, an hiftorian not often remarkable for penetration, mentions this circumftance as a fingular proof of Edward's prefumption and confidence in his undertaking againft Scotland: but a poet feems to have been a ftated officer in the royal retinue when the king went to war.[1] Baston, however, appears to have been chiefly a Latin poet, and therefore does not properly fall into our feries. At leaft his poem on the fiege of Stirling Caftle is written in monkifh Latin hexameters:[2] and our royal bard, being taken prifoner in the expedition, was compelled by the Scots, for his ranfom, to write a panegyric on Robert Brus, which is compofed in the fame ftyle and language.[3] Bale mentions his *Poemata et Rhythmi, Tragœdiæ et Comœdiæ vulgares.*[4] Some of thefe indeed appear to have been written in Englifh: but no Englifh pieces of this author now remain. In the meantime, the bare exiftence of dramatic compofitions in England at this period, even if written in the Latin tongue, deferve notice in inveftigating the progrefs of our poetry. I muft not pafs over a Latin [dialogue in verfe], written about the year [1367]. This [dialogue] is thus entitled in the Bodleian MS.: *De Babione et Croceo domino Babionis et Viola filiaftra Babionis quam Croceus duxit invito Babione, et Pecula uxore Babionis et Fodio fuo,* &c.[5] It is

---

"In dreery verfe my Rymes I make,
Bewailing whileft fuch Theme I take."

which appears to be Winftanley's own rendering of the opening lines.]

[1] Leland. *Script. Brit.* p. 338. Holinfh. *Hift.* ii. pp. 217, 220. Tanner mentions, as a poet of England, one Gulielmus Peregrinus, who accompanied Richard I. into the Holy Land, and fang his achievements there in a Latin poem, entitled *Odoeporicon Ricardi Regis,* lib. i. It is dedicated to Hurbert, archbifhop of Canterbury, and Stephen Turnham, a captain in the expedition. He flourifhed abou. A. D. 1200. *Bibl.* p. 591. See Vofs. *Hift. Lat.* p. 441. He is called "poeta per eam ætatem excellens." See Bale, iii. 45. Pits. 266. See Leland *Script. Brit.* p. 228. And a note in the editor's firft Index, under Gulielmus de Canno.

[2] It is extant in Fordun's *Scoti-Chron.* c. xxiii. l. 12.

[3] Leland. *ut fupr.* And MSS. Harl. 1819. Brit. Mus. See alfo Wood, *Hift. Ant. Univ. Oxon.* i. p. 101.

[4] Tanner, p. 79.

[5] Arch. B. 52. [In the Cotton MS. Titus A. xx. the feveral parts of the dialogue are diftinguifhed by initial capitals; and on the oppofite fide ftand marginal notices of the change of perfon. Thus: "Babio, Violæ; Viola, Babioni; Fodius, Babioni; Babio, Croceo." The *Geta* [by Vitalis Blefenfis], noticed below, and alfo occurring in the Cotton MS., is founded on the ancient fable of Jupiter's intrigue with Alcmena, [and is a mediæval verfion of the *Geta* of Plautus.] It is in the fame ftyle of dialogue with Babio, and has fimilar marginal directions; fuch as "Jupiter Alcmenæ; Alcmena Jovi," The line quoted by Warton occurs in what may be called the Prologue. The Cotton MS. affords no clue as to the date of thefe fingular productions, [but Mr. Wright has fhown the extreme probability that they belong to the middle of the thirteenth century.] It contains a farrago of rhythmical pieces from the time of Gualo (1160) to Bafton and perhaps later. But in France fuch pieces appear to have been current during the twelfth century. Du Boulay has noticed a tragedy *de Flaura et Marco,* and a comedy called *Alda,* written by [Matthæus Vindocinenfis].—*Price.* "Three manufcripts are known of this poem. One is in the Cotton MS. Titus, A. xx, which, amongft a vaft mafs of

written in long and fhort Latin verfes. The ftory is in Gower's *Confeffio Amantis.* Whether Gower had it from this performance I will not enquire. It appears at leaft that he took it from fome previous book.

> I find write of Babio,
> Which had a love at his menage,
> Ther was no fairer of her age,
> And highte Viola by name, &c.
> And had affaited to his honde
> His fervant, the which Spodius
> Was hote, &c.
> A frefshe a free a frendly man, &c.
> Which Croceus by name hight, &c.[1]

There is nothing dramatic in the ftructure of this nominal comedy ; and it has certainly no claim to that title, only as it contains a familiar and comic ftory carried on with much fcurrilous fatire intended to raife mirth. But it was not uncommon to call any fhort poem, not ferious or tragic, a comedy. In the Bodleian MS. which comprehends [the *Babio*] juft mentioned, there follows [the] *Geta :* this is in Latin long and fhort verfes,[2] and has no marks of dialogue.[3] In the library of Corpus Chrifti College at Cambridge is a piece entitled *Comedia ad monafterium de Hulme ordinis S. Benedicti Diocef. Norwic. directa ad Reformationem fequentem, cujus data eft primo die Septembris fub anno Chrifti* 1477, *et a morte Joannis Faftolfe militis eorum benefactoris*[4] *precipui* 17, *in cujus monafterii ecclefia humatur.*[5] This is nothing more than a fatirical ballad in Latin ; yet fome allegorical perfonages are introduced, which, however, are in no refpect accommodated to fcenical reprefentation. About the reign of Edward IV. one Edward Watfon, a fcholar in grammar at Oxford, is permitted to proceed to a degree in that faculty, on condition that within two years he would write one hundred verfes in praife of the univerfity, and alfo compofe a comedy.[6] The nature and fubject of Dante's *Commedia*, as it is ftyled, are well known.[7] The comedies

---

Anglo-Latin poetry of the twelfth, thirteenth, and fourteenth centuries, contains alfo a copy of the *Geta*. . . . The two other MSS. of the Babio are preferved in the Bodleian Library."—*Wright.*]

[1] [Gower's *C. F.* ed. Pauli, ii. 288-9.]

[2] Carmina compofuit, voluitque placere poeta. [The beft edition of the *Geta* of Vitalis *Blefenfis* is in Mr. Wright's volume of *Early Myfteries*, &c. 1838, 8vo. p. 79 *et feqq.*] [3] f. 121.

[4] In the epifcopal palace at Norwich is a curious piece of old wainfcot brought from the monaftery of Hulme at the time of its diffolution. Among other antique ornaments are the arms of Sir John Falftaff, their principal benefactor. This magnificent knight was alfo a benefactor to Magdalene College in Oxford. He bequeathed eftates to that fociety, part of which were appropriated to buy liveries for fome of the fenior fcholars. But this benefaction, in time, yielding no more than a penny a week to the fcholars who received the liveries, they were called, by way of contempt, *Falftaff's Buckram-men.*

[5] *Mifcell. M.* p. 274.

[6] *Hift. Antiq. Univ. Oxon.* ii. 4, col. 2.

[7] [In the dedication of his *Paradifo* to Can della Scala, Dante thus explains his own views of Tragedy and Comedy : " Eft comœdia genus quoddam poeticæ nar-

afcribed to Chaucer are probably his *Canterbury Tales.* We learn from Chaucer's own words, that tragic tales were called *Tragedies.* In the Prologue to the *Monkes Tale :*

> Tregedis is to fayn a certeyn ftorie,
> As olde bookes maken us memorie,
> Of hem that ftood in greet profperite,
> And is y-fallen out of heigh degre, &c.[1]

Some of thefe, the monk adds, were written in profe, others in metre. Afterwards follow many tragical narratives, of which he fays:

> *Tragidies* firft wol I tell
> Of which I have an hundred in my cell.

Lidgate further confirms what is here faid with regard to comedy as well as tragedy :

> My maifter Chaucer with frefh *comedies,*
> Is dead, alas! chief poet of Britaine :
> That whilom made ful piteous *tragedies.*[2]

The ftories in the *Mirror for Magiftrates* are called tragedies, fo late as the fixteenth century. Bale calls his play or Myftery of *God's Promifes,* which appeared about the year 1538, a tragedy.

I muft however obferve here that dramatic entertainments, reprefenting the lives of faints and the moft eminent fcriptural ftories, were known in England for more than [a century] before the reign of Edward II. Thefe fpeftacles they commonly ftyled miracles. I have already mentioned the play of Saint Catharine, afted at Dunftable about the year 1110.[3] [Two of the oldeft miracle-plays in the *Englifh* language are perhaps the *Harrowing of Hell*[4] and the *Incredulity of St. Thomas,* the latter of which was exhibited by the Scriveners' Guild at York.[5] The *Harrowing of Hell* exifts in a MS. which may

---

rationis ab omnibus aliis differens. Differt ergo in materia a tragœdia per hoc, quod tragœdia in principio eft admirabilis et quieta, in fine five exitu fœtida et horribilis. . . . . . Comœdia vero inchoat afperitatem alicujus rei, fed ejus materiam profpere terminatur. Similiter differunt *in modo loquendi.*" He has alfo expatiated upon the diftinftive ftyles peculiar to fuch compofitions in his treatife, *De vulgari Eloquentia;* though his precepts when oppofed to his practice have proved a fad ftumbling-block to the critics : " Per Tragœdiam fuperiorem ftylum induimus, per Comœdiam inferiorem. . . . . Si tragice canenda vicentur, tum adfumendum eft vulgare illuftre. Si vero comice, tum quandoque mediocre, quandoque humile vulgare fumatur." Lib. ii. c. iv.—*Price.*]

[1] v. 85. See alfo, *ibid.* v. 103, 786, 875.

[2] Prol. F. Pr. v. i. See alfo Chaucer's *Troil. and Cr.* v. 1785, 1787.

[3] Differtation ii. [The earlieft examples of fuch compofitions now known are three plays written in France by Hilarius, an Englifhman, and difciple of the famous Abelard, the fubjefts of which are the Raifing of Lazarus, a miracle of St. Nicholas, and the Hiftory of Daniel; they were written early in the twelfth century—*Wright.* There is an edition of them at Paris, 1838, 8vo.]

[Perhaps the plays of Rofwitha, a nun of Ganderfheim in Lower Saxony, who lived towards the clofe of the tenth century, afford the earlieft fpecimens of dramatic compofition, fince the decline of the Roman Empire. They were profeffedly written for the benefit of thofe Chriftians who, abjuring all other heathen writers, were irrefiftibly attracted by the graces of Terence, to the imminent danger of their

be nearly coeval with the performance itfelf; of the other piece we have apparently only a copy made at a much later date.] William Fitz-Stephen, a writer of the twelfth century, in his *Defcription of London*, relates that " London, for its theatrical exhibitions, has holy plays, or the reprefentation of miracles wrought by confeffors, and of the fufferings of martyrs."[6] Thefe pieces muft have been in high vogue at our prefent period; for Matthew Paris, who wrote about the year 1240, fays that they were fuch as " Miracula vulgariter

---

fpiritual welfare and the certain pollution of their moral feelings. Rofwitha appears to have been impreffed with a hope, that by contrafting the laudable chaftity of Chriftian virtue, as exhibited in her compofitions, with what fhe is pleafed to term the lewd voluptuoufnefs of the Grecian females, the Catholic world might be induced to forget the ancient claffic, and to receive with avidity an orthodox fubftitute, combining the double advantage of pleafure and inftruction. How far her expectations were gratified in this latter particular, it is impoffible to fay; but we can eafily conceive, that the almoft total oblivifcence of the Roman author during the fucceeding ages muft have furpaffed even her fanguine wifhes. It does not appear that thefe dramas were either intended for reprefentation, or exhibited at any fubfequent period. They have been publifhed twice: by Conrad Celtes in 1501, and Leonhard Schurzfleifch in 1707. They have alfo been analyfed by Gottfched in his Materials for a Hiftory of the German Stage. Leip. 1757.—Pez (in his *Thefaur. Novifs. Anecd.* vol. ii. p. iii. f. 185) has publifhed an ancient Latin Myftery, entitled *De Adventu et Interitu Antichrifti*, which he acknowledges to have copied from a manufcript of the twelfth century. It approaches nearer to the character of a pageant, than to the dramatic caft of the later myfteries. The dumb-fhow appears to have been confiderable, the dialogue but occafional; and ample fcope is given for the introduction of pomp and decoration. The paffages to be declaimed are written in Latin rhyme. Lebeuf alfo mentions a Latin Myftery written fo early as the time of Henry I. of France (1031—1061). In this Virgil is affociated with the prophets who come to offer their adorations to the new-born Meffiah; and at the conclufion he joins his voice with theirs in finging a long Benedicamus. A fragment of what may be a German tranflation of the fame myftery, copied from a manufcript of the thirteenth century, will be found in Dieterich's *Specimen Antiquitatum Biblicarum*, p. 122. But here Virgil appears as an acknowledged heathen; and he is only admitted with the other prophets from his fuppofed predictions of the coming Meffiah contained in his *Pollio*. In conformity with this opinion, Dante adopted him as his guide in the *Inferno.—Price.* Mr. Price's affertion as to the almoft total oblivifcence of Terence in the middle ages is not founded on fact. No claffic author is oftener quoted by monkifh writers, and in the Britifh Mufeum alone there are above thirty MSS. copies written between the tenth and fifteenth centuries.—*Madden.*]

⁴ [Edited from Harl. MS. 2253 by Mr. Halliwell, 1840, 8vo, and from the Auchinleck MS. by Mr. Laing (*Owain Miles and other Pieces of Ancient Englifh Poetry*, 1837, 8vo).]

⁵ [Printed in Croft's *Excerpta Antiqua*, 1797, and again by Collier, *Camden Mifcellany*, iv.]

⁶ " Lundonia pro fpectaculis theatralibus, pro ludis fcenicis, ludos habet fanctiores, reprefentationes miraculorum quæ fancti confeffores operati funt, feu reprefentationes paffionum quibus claruit conftantia martyrum." Stow's *Survey of London*, p. 480, edit. 1599. The reader will obferve, that I have conftrued *fanctiores* in a pofitive fenfe. [But here Warton merely follows Pegge in his tranflation of Fitz-Stephen: neither ftates a reafon. See Collier's *Hift. of E. D. P.* i. 2, *note*.] Fitz-Stephen mentions at the end of his tract, " Imperatricem Matildem, Henricum regem tertium, et beatum Thomam, &c." p. 483. [Fitz-Stephen is fpeaking of Henry the younger, fon of Henry II. and grandfon to the Emprefs Matilda, who was crowned king in the lifetime of his father, and is exprefsly ftyled Henricus Tertius by Matthew Paris, William of Newbury, and feveral other of our early hiftorians.—*Ritfon.*]

appellamus."[1]   And we learn from Chaucer, that in his time Plays of Miracles were the common resort of idle gossips in Lent :

> Therefore made I my visitations,
> To prechings eke and to pilgrimagis,
> To Plays of Miracles, and mariagis, &c.[2]

---

[1] *Vit. Abbat.* ad calc. *Hist.* p. 56, edit. 1639.

[William de Wadington (who possibly was a contemporary of Matthew Paris) has left a violent tirade against this general practice of acting miracles. As it contains some curious particulars relative to the manner in which they were conducted, and the places selected for exhibiting them, an extract from it may not be out of place here :

> " Une autre folie apert
> Unt les fols clers cuntrové ;
> Qe miracles sunt apelé.
> Lur faces unt la deguise,
> Par visers li forsene,
> Qe est defendu en decree ;
> Tant est plus grant lur peché.
> Fere poent representement,
> Mes qe ceo seit chastement.
> En office de seint eglise
> Quant hom fet la, Deu servise.
> *Cum Ihu Crist le fiz Dee,*
> *En sepulcre esteit posé;*
> *Et la resurrectiun :*
> Par plus aver devociun.
> Mes fere foles assemblez,
> En les rues des citez,
> Ou en cymiters apres mangers,
> Quant venent les fols volonters,
> Tut dient qe il le funt pur bien :
> Crere ne les devez pur rien,
> Qe fet seit pur le honur de Dee.
> E iuz del Deable pur verité.
> Seint Ysidre me ad testimonie,
> Qe fut si bon clerc lettré.
> Il dit qe cil qe funt spectacles,
> Cum lem fet en miracles,
> Ou iuჳ qe vus nomames einჳ,
> Burdiz ou turnemens,
> Lur baptesme unt refusez,
> E Deu de ciel reneiez, &c.
> Ke en lur iuz se delitera,
> Chevals ou harneis les aprestera,
> Vesture ou autre ournement,
> Sachez il fet folement.
> Si vestemens serent dediez,
> Plus grant dassez est le pechez.
> Si preste ou clerc le ust preste,
> Bien dust estre chaustie ;
> Car sacrilege est pur verité.
> E ki par vanite les verrunt,
> De lur fet partaverunt."
>   Harl. MS. 273, f. 141.—*Frice.*

This has been printed by Mr. Furnivall in his edition of Robert de Brunne's *Handlyng Synne*, Roxburghe Club, 1862.]

[2] *Prol. Wif. B.* v. 555.

This is the genial *Wife of Bath*, who amufes herfelf with thefe fafhionable diverfions, while her hufband is abfent in London, during the holy feafon of Lent. And in Pierce the Plowman's *Crede*, a friar Minorite mentions the miracles as not lefs frequented than markets or taverns :

> We haunten no tavernes, ne hobelen abouten,
> Att markets and Miracles we medeley us never.[1]

Among the plays ufually reprefented by the guild of Corpus Chrifti at Cambridge, on that feftival, *Ludus filiorum Ifraelis* was acted in the year 1355.[2] Our drama feems hitherto to have been almoft entirely confined to religious fubjects, and thefe plays were nothing more than an appendage to the fpecious and mechanical devotion of the times. I do not find exprefsly, that any play on a profane fubject, either tragic or comic, had as yet been exhibited in England. Our very early anceftors fcarce knew any other hiftory than that of their religion. Even on fuch an occafion as the triumphant entry of a king or queen into the city of London, or other places, the pageants were almoft entirely Scriptural.[3] I likewife find in the wardrobe-rolls of Edward III., 1348, an account of the dreffes, *ad faciendum Ludos domini regis ad ffeftum Natalis domini celebratos apud*

---

[1] Signat. A iii b, edit. 1561.

[2] Mafters' *Hift. C. C. C. C.* p. 5, vol. i. What was the antiquity of the *Guary-Miracle*, or *Miracle-Play* in Cornwall, has not been determined. In the Bodleian library are three Church interludes, written on parchment. [Bodley, 791.] In the fame library there is alfo another, written on paper in the year 1611. Arch. [N. 2·9.] Of this laft there is a tranflation in the Britifh Mufeum. MSS. Harl. 1867, 2. It is entitled the *Creation of the World,* [and bears traces of an obligation on the part of the compiler to the earlier production printed by Norris—the *Origo Mundi.*] It is called a Cornifh play or opera, and faid to be written by Mr. William Jordan. The tranflation into Englifh was made by John Keigwin of Moufhole in Cornwall, at the requeft of Trelawney, Bifhop of Exeter, 1691. Of this William Jordan I can give no account. [Mr. Davies Gilbert publifhed the *Creation of the World* in 1827, 8vo., and more recently, Mr. Edwin Norris has edited from the Bodleian MS. the three Cornifh Dramas, *Origo Mundi, Paffio Domini Noftri,* and *Refurrectio Domini Noftri,* 1859, 2 vols. 8vo. Mr. Gilbert alfo edited the poem of *Mount Calvary* in 1826, 8vo.; but his text is very bad both there and in the *Creation.* See Mr. Norris's remarks and explanations in his Appendix, ii. 439 *et feqq.* I fear that Mr. Norris's own text is not very truftworthy. In the library of Mr. C. Wynne, at Peniarth, Montgomeryfhire, is another Cornifh play, unknown to Gilbert and Norris.]

In the Britifh Mufeum there is an ancient Cornifh poem on the death and refurrection of Chrift. It is on vellum, and has fome rude pictures. The beginning and end are loft. The writing is fuppofed to be of the fifteenth century. MSS. Harl. 1782, 4to. [This is the poem on *Mount Calvary* already referred to, but three other copies are known.] See the learned Lwhyd's *Archæol. Brit.* p. 265. And Borlafe's *Cornwall, Nat. Hift.* p. 295, edit. 1758.

[3] When our Hen. VI. entered Paris in 1431, in the quality of King of France, he was met at the gate of Saint Denis by a Dumb Shew, reprefenting the birth of the Virgin Mary and her marriage, the adoration of the three kings, and the parable of the fower. This pageant indeed was given by the French : but the readers of Holinfhed will recollect many inftances immediately to our purpofe. See Monftrelet *apud* Fonten. *Hift. Theatr.* ut fupr. p. 37.

Guldeford, for furnishing the plays or sports of the king, held in the castle of Guildford at the feast of Christmas.[1] In these Ludi, says my record, were expended eighty tunics of buckram of various colours, forty-two visors of various similitudes, that is, fourteen of the faces of women, fourteen of the faces of men with beards, fourteen of heads of angels, made with silver; twenty-eight crests,[2] fourteen mantles embroidered with heads of dragons: fourteen white tunics wrought with heads and wings of peacocks, fourteen heads of swans with wings, fourteen tunics painted with eyes of peacocks, fourteen tunics of English linen painted, and as many tunics embroidered with stars of gold and silver.[3] In the *Wardrobe* rolls of Richard II. there is also an entry which seems to point out a sport of much the same nature [in 1389, 12 Rich. II.] " Pro xxi *coifs* de tela linea pro hominibus de lege contrafactis pro ludo regis tempore natalis domini anno xii."[4] That is, " for twenty-one linen coifs for counterfeiting men of the law in the king's play at Christmas." It will be sufficient to add here on the last record, that the serjeants at law at their creation anciently wore a cap of linen, lawn, or silk, tied under the chin: this was to distinguish them from the clergy who had the tonsure. Whether in both these instances we are to understand a dumb-shew, or a dramatic interlude with speeches, I leave to the examination of those who are professedly making enquiries into the history of our stage from its rudest origin. But that plays on general subjects were no uncommon mode of entertainment in the royal palaces of England, at least at the commencement of the fifteenth century, may be collected from an old memoir of shews and ceremonies exhibited at Christmas, in the reign of Henry VII. in the palace of Westminster. It is in the year 1489. "This cristmas I saw no disguysings, and but *right few* Plays. But ther

---

[1] Comp. J. Cooke, Provisoris Magnæ Garderob. *ab ann.* 21 Edw. [III.] *ad ann.* 23. Memb. ix.

[2] I do not perfectly understand the Latin original in the place, viz. " xiiij *Crestes* cum tibiis reversatis et calceatis, xiiij *Crestes* cum montibus et cuniculis." Among the stuffs are " viii pelles de Roan." In the same wardrobe rolls, a little above, I find this entry, which relates to the same festival. " Et ad faciendum vi pennecellos pro tubis et clarionibus contra Festum natalis domini, de syndone, vapulatos de armis regis quartellatis." Membr. ix.

[3] Some perhaps may think, that these were dresses for a Masque at court. If so, Holinshed is mistaken in saying, that in the year 1512, " on the daie of Epiphanie at night, the king with eleven others were disguised after the manner of Italie called a maske, *a thing not seen before in England.* They were apparalled in garments long and broad wrought all with gold, with visors and caps of gold," &c. *Hist.* vol. iii. p. 812, a, 40. Besides, these maskings most probably came to the English, if from Italy, through the medium of France. Holinshed also contradicts himself: for in another place he seems to allow their existence under our Henry IV., A.D. 1400. " The conspirators ment upon the sudden to have set upon the king in the castell of Windsor, under colour of a *maske* to *mummerie*," &c. *ibid.* p. 515, b. 50. Strype says there were Pageaunts exhibited in London when Queen Eleanor rode through the city to her coronation, in 1236. And for the victory over the Scots by Edward I. in 1298. *Anec. Brit. Topograph.* p. 725, edit. 1768.

[4] *Comp. Magn. Garderob.* an. 14 Ric. II. f. 198. b.

was an abbot of Misrule, that made much sport, and did right well his office." And again, " At nyght the kynge, the qweene, and my ladye the kynges moder, cam into the Whitehall, and ther hard a Play."[1]

As to the religious dramas, it was customary to perform this species of play on holy festivals in or about the churches. In the register of William of Wykeham, bishop of Winchester, under the year 1384, an episcopal injunction is recited, against the exhibition of *Spectacula* in the cemetery of his cathedral.[2] Whether or no these were dramatic *Spectacles*, I do not pretend to decide.[3] In several of our old scriptural plays, we see some of the scenes directed to be represented *cum cantu et organis*, a common rubric in the missal. That is, because they were performed in a church where the choir assisted. There is a curious passage in Lambarde's *Topographical Dictionary* written about 1570, much to our purpose, and which I am therefore tempted to transcribe :[4]—" In the Dayes of ceremonial religion, they used at *Wytney* (in Oxfordshire) to set foorthe yearly in maner of a Shew, or Enterlude, the Resurrection of our Lord, &c. For the which Purpose, and the more lyvely thearby to exhibite to the Eye the hole Action of the Resurrection, the Priestes garnished out certain smalle Puppets, representinge the Parsons of *Christe*, the Watchmen, *Marie*, and others ; amongest the which, one bare the Parte of a wakinge Watcheman, who (espiinge *Christ* to arise) made a continual Noyce, like to the Sound that is caused by the Metinge of two Styckes, and was therof comonly called *Jack Snacker of Wytney*. The like Toye I my selfe (beinge then a Childe,) once saw in *Poules* Churche at *London*, at a Feast of *Whitsuntyde ;* wheare the comynge downe of the *Holy Gost* was set forthe by a white Pigion, that was let to fly out of a Hole, that yet is to be sene in the mydst of the Roofe of the great Ile, and by a longe Cenfer, which descendinge out of the same Place almost to the verie Grounde, was swinged up and downe at suche a Lengthe, that it reached with thone Swepe almost to the West Gate of the Churche, and with the

---

[1] Leland, *Coll.* iii. *Append.* p. 256, edit, 1770.

[2] *Registr.* lib. iii. f. 88. " Canere Cantilenas, ludibriorum *spectacula* facere, saltationes et alios ludos inhonestos frequentare, choreas," &c. So in Statut. Eccles. Nannett. A. D. 1405. No "mimi vel joculatores, ad *monstra larvarum* in ecclesia et cemeterio," are permitted. Marten. *Thesaur. Anecd.* iv. p. 993. And again, " Joculatores, histriones, saltatrices, in ecclesia, cemeterio, vel porticu.—nec aliquæ choreæ." Statut. *Synod Eccles. Leod.* A.D. 1287, *apud* Marten. *ut supr.* 846. Fontenelle says, that anciently among the French, comedies were acted after divine service in the church-yard. " Au sortir du sermon ces bonnes gens alloient a la *Comedie*, c'est a dire, qu'ils changeoint de Sermon."—*Hist. Theatr.* ut supr. p. 24. But these were scriptural comedies, and they were constantly preceded by a Benedicite, by way of prologue. The French stage will occur again below.

[3] ["Had he (Warton) seen the passage in the *Manuel de Peché*, where *Miracles* are expressly called *Spectacles*, his doubt (as to the nature of these *Spectacula*) would have been removed. The author of the French original is very particular in stating to what performances he refers."—*Collier.*]

[4] 1730, 459. [Warton's transcript was full of errors in the orthography, although he must have copied from the ed. of 1730.]

other to the Quyre Staires of the fame; breathinge out over the whole Churche and Companie a moft p!eafant Perfume of fuch fwete Thinges as burned thearin; withe the like doome Shewes alfo, they ufed every whear to furnifhe fondrye Partes of their Churche Service, as by their Spectacles of the Nativitie, Paffion, and Afcenfion" &c.

This practice of acting plays in churches, had at laft grown to fuch an enormity, and was attended with fuch inconvenience confequences, that in the reign of Henry VIII., Bonner, bifhop of London, iffued a proclamation to the clergy of his diocefe, dated 1542, prohibiting " all maner of common plays, games, or interludes to be played, fet forth, or declared, within their churches, chapels," &c.[1] This fafhion feems to have remained even after the Reformation, and when perhaps profane ftories had taken place of religious.[2] Arch-bifhop Grindal, in the year 1563, remonftrated againft the danger of interludes : complaining that players " did, efpecially on holy days, fet up bills inviting to their play."[3] From this ecclefiaftical fource of the modern drama, plays continued to be acted on Sundays fo late as the reign of Elizabeth, and even till that of Charles I., by the chorifters or finging-boys of Saint Paul's Cathedral in London, and of the royal chapel.

It is certain that thefe *Miracle-plays* were the earlieft of our dra-matic exhibitions. But as thefe pieces frequently required the in-troduction of allegorical characters, fuch as Charity, Sin, Death, Hope, Faith, or the like, and as the common poetry of the times, efpecially among the French, began to deal much in allegory, at length plays were formed entirely confifting of fuch perfonifications. Thefe were called *Moralities.* The miracle-plays, or *Myfteries*, were totally deftitute of invention or plan : they tamely reprefented ftories according to the letter of fcripture, or the refpective legend. But the Moralities indicate dawnings of the dramatic art; they contain fome rudiments of a plot, and even attempt to delineate charac-ters, and to paint manners. Hence the gradual tranfition to real hiftorical perfonages was natural and obvious. It may be alfo ob-ferved, that many licentious pleafantries were fometimes introduced in thefe religious reprefentations. This might imperceptibly lead the way to fubjects entirely profane and to comedy, and perhaps earlier than is imagined. In a Myftery[4] of the *Maffacre of the Holy Innocents*, part of the fubject of a facred drama given by the Englifh fathers at the famous council of Conftance in the year 1417,[5] a

[1] Burnet, *Hift. Ref.* i. Coll. Rec. p. 225.

[2] From a puritanical pamphlet entitled *The [fecond and] third Blaft of Retrait from Plaies*, &c. 1580, p. 77 [*Englifh Drama & Stage*, 1869, p. 134.] Where the author fays, the players are " permitted to publifh their mamettree in euerie Temple of God, and that through England," &c. This abufe of acting plays in churches is mentioned in the canon of James I., which forbids alfo the profanation of churches by court-leets, &c. The canons were given in the year 1603.

[3] Strype's *Grindal*, p. 82.

[4] [Ancient Myfteries from the Digby MSS., 1835.]

[5] L'Enfant, ii. 440.

low buffoon of Herod's court is introduced, defiring of his lord to be dubbed a knight, that he might be properly qualified to *go on the adventure* of killing the mothers of the children of Bethlehem. This tragical bufinefs is treated with the moft ridiculous levity. The good women of Bethlehem attack our knight-errant with their fpinning-wheels, break his head with their diftaffs, abufe him as a coward and a difgrace to chivalry, and fend him home to Herod as a recreant champion with much ignominy. It is in an enlightened age only that fubjects of fcripture hiftory would be fupported with proper dignity. But then an enlightened age would not have chofen fuch fubjects for theatrical exhibition.[1] It is certain that our anceftors intended no fort of impiety by thefe monftrous and unnatural mixtures. Neither the writers nor the fpectators faw the impropriety, nor paid a feparate attention to the comic and ferious part of thefe motley fcenes; at leaft they were perfuaded that the folemnity of the fubject covered or excufed all incongruities. They had no juft idea of decorum, confequently but little fenfe of the ridiculous: what appears to us to be the higheft burlefque, on them would have made no fort of impreffion. We muft not wonder at this, in an age when courage, devotion, and ignorance compofed the character of European manners; when the knight, going to a tournament, firft invoked his God, then his miftrefs, and afterwards proceeded with a fafe confcience and great refolution to engage his antagonift. In thefe Myfteries I have fometimes feen grofs and open obfcenities. In a play of *the Old and New Teftament,*[2] Adam and

---

[1] [Even what may be called *the vices* of literature have their favourable fide; for, if in our early drama from the Myfteries downward, there had not been the uncouth vernacular diction, the grofs anachronifms, the ribaldry, and the totally un-artiftic conftruction, which we fee, thofe remains would never have poffeffed the intereft in our eyes, which under the circumftances they have, as ftorehoufes of information upon many points connected with ancient manners and opinions.]

[2] MSS. Harl. 2013, &c. Exhibited at Chefter in the year 1327, at the expenfe of the different trading companies of the city. *The Fall of Lucifer* by the Tanners. *The Creation* by the Drapers. *The Deluge* by the Dyers. *Abraham, Melchifedech,* and *Lot* by the Barbers. *Mofes, Balak,* and *Balaam* by the Cappers. *The Salutation* and *Nativity* by the Wrightes. *The Shepherds feeding their flocks by night* by the Painters and Glaziers. *The three Kings* by the Vintners. *The Oblation of the three Kings* by the Mercers. *The Killing of the Innocents* by the Goldfmiths. *The Purification* by the Blackfmiths. *The Temptation* by the Butchers. *The laft Supper* by the Bakers. *The Blindmen and Lazarus* by the Glovers. *Jefus and the Lepers* by the Corvefarys. *Chrift's Paffion* by the Bowyers, Fletchers, and Ironmongers. *Defcent into Hell* by the Cooks and Innkeepers. *The Refurrection* by the Skinners. *The Afcenfion* by the Taylors. *The election of S. Mathias, Sending of the holy ghoft, &c.* by the Fifhmongers. *Antechrift* by the Clothiers. *Day of Judgment* by the Webfters. The reader will perhaps fmile at fome of thefe combinations. This is the fubftance and order of the former part of the play :—God enters creating the world: he breathes life into Adam, leads him into Paradife, and opens his fide while fleeping. Adam and Eve appear naked and *not afhamed,* and the old ferpent enters lamenting his fall. He converfes with Eve. She eats of the forbidden fruit and gives part to Adam. They propofe, according to the ftage-direction, to make themfelves *fubligacula a foliis quibus tegamus Pudenda.* Cover their nakednefs with leaves, and converfe with God. God's curfe. The ferpent *exit* hiffing. They are driven from Paradife by four angels and the cherubim with a flaming fword. Adam appears digging the ground, and Eve fpinning.

Eve are both exhibited on the stage naked, and conversing about
their nakednefs : this very pertinently introduces the next scene, in
which they have coverings of fig-leaves. This extraordinary spec-
tacle was beheld [at Chester] by a numerous affembly of both sexes
with great composure : they had the authority of scripture for such
a representation, and they gave matters just as they found them in
the third chapter of Genesis. It would have been absolute herefy to
have departed from the facred text in perfonating the primitive appearance of our first parents, whom the spectators fo nearly resembled in
simplicity : and if this had not been the case, the dramatists were ignorant what to reject and what to retain.

[" The original date and the authorship of the Chester plays," says
Mr. Wright, " have been subjects of confiderable difcussion. My own
impression, from the phraseology and forms of words, which may frequently be discovered in the blunders of the modern scribes, is that
the original manuscript from which they copied was of the earlier part
of the fifteenth or of the end of the fourteenth century." The
transcript from which the edition superintended by Mr. Wright is
printed, appears to have been made late in the reign of Elizabeth.[1]
Besides the Coventry and Chester series, and the other miscel-
laneous productions of the same clafs in the Digby and other MSS.,
there were the York and Towneley or Widkirk Mysteries. The
former, in fact, have had a most unfortunate destiny in being secreted
by succeffive owners. It is to be regretted that they were not secured,
when they occurred for sale about twenty years ago, for the national
library, since only one of the York series, the Scriveners' Play, exifts in a duplicate copy. The Towneley plays, however, which are
alfo known only in one MS. (and that not entirely perfect), have been
published.][2]

In the meantime, profane dramas seem to have been known in
France at a much earlier period.[3] Du Cange gives the following

---

Their children Cain and Abel enter: The former kills his brother. Adam's
lamentation. Cain is banished, &c.

[The *Chester Mysteries* have been published entire by T. Wright, Efq., 2 vols.
8vo. 1843-7. Mr. Wright obferves : " The traditions adopted or imagined by
fome old Chefter antiquaries, which carried the compofition of thefe plays fo far
back as the mayoralty of John Arneway (1268 to 1270), and the suppofition of
Warton that they were the productions of Ralph Higden the chronicler, appear
to me too improbable to deferve our ferious confideration, unless they were founded
on more authentic statements, or on more substantial arguments."]

[1] [Mr. Whitley Stoke edited for the Philological Society (1860-1) *The Play of
the Sacrament*, which he terms a middle-Englifh " drama." A pageant called
The Salutation of Gabriel, was exhibited at Edinburgh in 1503, at the nuptials of
James IV. and the Princess Margaret.]

[2] [By the Surtees Society, 1836, 8vo.]

' At Conftantinople it feems that the stage flourished much under Juftinian and
Theodora, about the year 540. For in the Bafilical codes we have the oath of an
actrefs μη αναχωρειν της πορνειας. Tom. vii. p. 682, edit. Fabrot. Græco-Lat. The
ancient Greek fathers, particularly Saint Chryfoftom, are full of declamation againft
the drama, and complain that the people heard a comedian with much more
pleafure than a preacher of the Gofpel.

picture of the king of France dining in public before the year 1300. During this ceremony, a sort of farces or drolls seems to have been exhibited. All the great officers of the crown and the household, says he, were present. The company was entertained with instrumental music of the minstrels, who played on the kettle-drum, the flageolet,[1] the cornet, the Latin cittern, the Bohemian flute, the trumpet, the Moorish cittern, and the fiddle. Besides there were " des FARCEURS, des jougleurs, et des plaisantins, qui divertisseoient les compagnies par leur faceties et par leur COMEDIES, pour l'entretien." He adds, that many noble families in France were entirely ruined by the prodigious expenses lavished on those performers.[2] The annals of France very early mention buffoons among the minstrels at these solemnities; and more particularly that Louis le Debonnaire, who reigned about the year 830, never laughed aloud, not even when, at the most magnificent festivals, players, buffoons, minstrels, singers, and harpers, attended his table.[3] In some constitutions given to a cathedral church in France, in the year 1280, the following clause occurs: " Nullus SPECTACULIS aliquibus quæ aut in *Nuptiis* aut in *Scenis* exhibentur, intersit."[4] Where, by the way, the word *Scenis* seems to imply somewhat of a professed stage, although the establishment of the first French theatre is dated not before the year 1398.[5] The play of *Robin and Marian* is said to

---

[1] I believe, a sort of pipe. This is the French word, viz. Demy-canon. See Carpent. Du Cange, *Gl. Lat.* i. p. 760.

[2] *Dissertat. Joinv.* p. 161. [3] *Ibid.*

[4] Montfauc. *Cat. Manuscrip.* p. 1158. See also Marten. *Thesaur. Anecd.* tom. iv. p. 506. *Stat. Synod.* A. D. 1468. " Larvaria ad Nuptias," &c. Stow, in his *Survey of London*, mentions the practice of acting plays [masques] at weddings.

[5] [A modern French antiquary (M. Roquefort) has claimed a much higher antiquity for the establishment or rather origin of the French stage; though upon principles, it must be allowed, which have a decided tendency to confound all distinctions between the several kinds of poetic composition. The beautiful tale of Aucassin and Nicolette is the corner-stone upon which this theory reposes, and as the narrative is interspersed with song, seems to have induced a belief, that the recitations were made by a single Trouvere, and the poetry chaunted by a band of attendant minstrels. Admitting this to be the case—yet for it no authority is offered—the approximation to dramatic composition is as remote as when left in the hands of a solitary declaimer. Upon this ground every ballad or romantic tale, which is known to have been accompanied by music and the voice, might be styled " a monument of theatric art ; " and by analogy the rhapsodists of Greece, who sang the *Iliad* at the public games, might be said to have " enacted the plays" of Homer. Nor is the argument in favour of the *Jeux-partis* or such fabliaux as the *deux Bordeors ribauds*, in any degree more admissible. In all these pieces there is nothing more than a simple interchange of opinion, whether argumentative or vituperative, without pretension to incident, fable, or development of character. Indeed, if a multiplicity of interlocutors would alone constitute a drama, the claim of Wolfram von Eschenbach to be the founder of the German stage (as some of his countrymen have maintained) would be undeniable. In his *Krieg auf Wartburg*, a singular monument of early (1207) improvisatorial skill, the declaimers in the first part are six and in the second three Master or Minne-singers. But this poem, like the *Tensons* of the Troubadours, is a mere trial of poetical ingenuity, and bears a strong resemblance both in matter and manner to the *Torneyamens* of the same writers. That it was not considered a play in earlier

have been performed by the fchoolboys of Angiers, according to annual cuftom, in the year 1392.[1] A royal caroufal given by Charles V. of France to the emperor Charles IV. in the year 1378, was clofed with the theatrical reprefentation of the *Conqueft of Jerufalem by Godfrey of Bulloign,* which was exhibited in the hall of the royal palace.[2] This indeed was a fubjeét of a religious tendency; but not long afterwards, in the year 1395, perhaps before, the interefting ftory of *Patient Grifel* appears to have been aéted at Paris. This piece ftill remains, and is entitled *Le Myftere de Grifildis marquife de Saluce.*[3] For all dramatic pieces were indifcriminately called *Myfteries,* whether a martyr or a heathen god, whether Saint Catharine or Hercules was the fubjeét.

In France the religious *Myfteries,* often called *Piteaux,* or *Pitoux,* were certainly very fafhionable and of high antiquity : yet from any written evidence I do not find them more ancient than thofe of the Englifh. In the year 1384, the inhabitants of the village of Aunay, on the Sunday after the feaft of Saint John, played the *Miracle* of Theophilus, " ou quel Jeu avoit un perfonnage de un qui devoit getter d'un canon."[4] In the year 1398, fome citizens of Paris met

times, is clear from an illumination publifhed by Docen, where the aétors in this celebrated conteft are reprefented feated and finging together, and above them is this decifive infcription : " Hie krieget mit fange, Herr walther von der vogilweide," &c. *Here bataileth in fong,* &c. However, fhould this theory obtain, Solomon, bifhop of Conftance in the tenth century, will perhaps rank as the earlieft dramatift at prefent known : Metro primus et coram Regibus plerumque pro ludicro *cum aliis certator.* Ekkehardus *de Cafibus S. Galli,* p. 49.—*Price.*]

[1] The boys were *deguifiez,* fays the old French record : and they had among them *un Fillette defguifeè.* Carpent. *ubi fupr.* v. *Robinet Pentecofte.* Our old charaéter of *Mayd Marian* may be hence illuftrated. It feems to have been an early fafhion in France for fchoolboys to prefent thefe fhews or plays. In an ancient MS. under the year 1477, there is mentioned " Certaine MORALITE, ou FARÇE, que les efcolliers de Pontoife avoit fait, *ainfi qu'il eft de couftume."* Carpent. *ubi fupr.* v. *Moralitas.* The *Myftery of the old and new Teftament* is faid to have been reprefented in 1424 by the boys of Paris placed like ftatues againft a wall, without fpeech or motion, at the entry of the duke of Bedford, regent of France. See J. de Paris, p. 101. And Sauval, *Ant. de Paris,* ii. 101. [*Le Jeu de Robin et de Marion,* the piece alluded to in the text, has been analyfed by M. le Grand in the fecond volume of his *Fabliaux et Contes.* It is there called *Le Jeu du Berger et de la Bergere,* and by him attributed to Adan de la Hale, nicknamed le Boçu d'Arras. In this he is followed by M. Meon, the editor of Barbazan's *Fabliaux,* who alfo afcribes to the fame author a play called *Le Jeu du Mariage.* M. Roquefort catalogues *Robin et Marion* among the works of Jehan Bodel d'Arras, the author of three plays called *Le Jeu de Pelerin, Le Jeu d`Adam ou de la Feuillée, Le Jeu de St. Nicholas;* and a myftery called *Le Miracle de Theophile.* This latter may be the fame referred to below. Adan de la Hale appears to have lived in the early part of the thirteenth century (Roquefort, p. 103), and Jehan Bodel during the reign of Saint Louis (1226-70). Thefe perhaps are the earlieft fpecimens extant of anything refembling dramatic compofition in the French language.— *Price.*]

[2] Felib. tom. ii. p. 681. [The thirteenth century romance (on this fubjeét) was publifhed by M. Hippeau of Caen ; Paris, 1868, 8vo.—F.]

[3] [Printed at Paris about 1550, 4to, 20 leaves. See Brunet, *dern.* edit. iii. 1968-9.]

[4] Carpentier, Suppl. Du Cange, *Lat. Gl.* v. *Ludus.* [The ftory of a man who fold himfelf to the devil, and was redeemed by the virgin to whom he had recom-

at Saint Maur to play the *Paffion of Chrift*. The magiftrates of Paris, alarmed at this novelty, publifhed an ordonnance, prohibiting them to reprefent " aucuns jeux de perfonages foit de vie de faints ou autrement," without the royal licence, which was foon after-wards obtained.[1] In the year 1486, at Anjou, ten pounds were paid towards fupporting the charges of acting the *Paffion of Chrift*, which was reprefented by mafks, and, as I fuppofe, by perfons hired for the purpofe.[2] The chaplains of Abbeville, in the year 1455, gave four pounds and ten fhillings to the players of the Paffion ;[3] [and at Angiers, about the fame period, Jean Michel's very curious *miftere de la paffion iefu Crift* was performed; it was fubfequently exhibited at Paris in 1507 ; and the old editions of it are tolerably numerous]. But the French *Myfteries* were chiefly performed by the religious communities, and fome of their Fetes almoft entirely confifted of a dramatic or perfonated fhew. At the *Feaft of Affes*, inftituted in [com-memoration of the Flight into Egypt,] the clergy walked on Chrift-mas-day in proceffion, habited to reprefent the prophets and others. Mofes appeared in an alb and cope, with a long beard and rod. David had a green veftment. Balaam with an immenfe pair of fpurs, rode on a wooden afs, which inclofed a fpeaker. There were alfo fix Jews and fix Gentiles. Among other characters the poet Virgil was introduced as a gentile prophet and a tranflator of the Sibylline oracles. They thus moved in proceffion, chanting verficles, and converfing in character on the nativity and kingdom of Chrift, through the body of the church, till they came into the choir. Virgil fpeaks fome Latin hexameters during the ceremony, not out of his fourth eclogue, but wretched monkifh lines in rhyme. This feaft was, I believe, early fuppreffed. In the year 1445, Charles VII. of France ordered the mafters in theology at Paris to forbid the minifters of the collegiate[4] churches to celebrate at Chriftmas the

---

mended himfelf, occurs in a collection of miracles put in verfe by Guatier de Quenfi, a French poet of the thirteenth century, from whofe work and others of the fame kind an abridgment was printed at Paris in the beginning of the fix-teenth century. This was made by Jean le Comte, a friar minor. Quenfi's work is among the Harl. MSS. No. 4400.—*Douce*. It is alfo the legend of the *Knyght and his Wyfe* (*Rem. of the Early Pop. P. of Engl.* i. 16, *et feqq.* and Brunet, *ut fupr.* 1979).]

[1] Beauchamps, *ut fupr.* p. 90. This was the firft theatre of the French : the actors were incorporated by the king, under the title of the *Fraternity of the Paffion of our Saviour*. Beauch. *ibid.* See above, fect. ii. The *Jeu de perfonages* was a very common play of the young boys in the larger towns, &c. Carpentier, *ut fupr.* v. *Perfonagium*, and *Ludus Perfonag*. [But almoft all the old French miracle-plays purport to have been *jeux de perfonnages*.] At Cambray mention is made of the fhew of a boy *larvatus cum maza in collo* with drums, &c. Carpent. *ibid.* v. *Kalendæ Januar.*

[2] " Decem libr. ex parte nationis, ad onera fupportanda hujus Mifterii." Car-pent. *ut fupr.* v. *Perfonagium*.

[3] [Brunet, *ut fupr.* 1971.] Carpent. *ut fupr.* v. *Ludus*. He adds, from an ancient Computus, that three fhillings were paid by the minifters of a church, in the year 1537, for parchment for writing *Ludus Refurrectionis Domini*.

[4] Marten. *Anecd.* tom. i. col. 1804. See alfo Belet. *De Divin. Offic.* cap. 72. And Guffanvill. *poft. Not. ad Petr. Blefens.* Felibien confounds *La Fete de Fous et la*

Feaſt of Fools in their churches, where the clergy danced in maſques and antic dreſſes, and exhibited " pluſieurs mocqueries ſpectacles publics, de leur corps deguiſements, farces, rigmereis," with various enormities ſhocking to decency. In France as well as England it was cuſtomary to celebrate the feaſt of the boy-biſhop. In all the collegiate churches of both nations, about the feaſt of St. Nicholas,[1] or the Holy Innocents, one of the children of the choir, completely apparelled in the epiſcopal veſtments, with a mitre and croſier, bore the title and ſtate of biſhop, and exacted canonical obedience from his fellows, who were dreſſed like prieſts. They took poſſeſſion of the church, and performed all the ceremonies and offices,[2] the maſs excepted, which might have been celebrated by the biſhop and his prebendaries.[3] In the ſtatutes of the archiepiſcopal cathedral of Tulles, given in the year 1497, it is ſaid, that during the celebration of the feſtival of the boy-biſhop, " Moralities were preſented, and ſhews of Miracles, with farces and other ſports, but compatible with

---

Fete de Sotiſe. The latter was an entertainment of dancing called *Les Saultes,* and thence corrupted into *Soties* or *Sotiſe.* See *Mem. Acad. Inſcript.* xvii, 225, 226, and Probat. *Hiſt. Antiſſiodor.* p. 310. Again, the *Feaſt of Fools* ſeems to be pointed at in Statut. Senonens. A.D. 1445. Inſtr. tom. xii. *Gall. Chriſtian.* Coll. 96. " Tempore divini ſervitii larvatos et monſtruoſos vultus deferendo, cum veſtibus mulierum, aut lenonum, aut hiſtrionum, choreas in eccleſia et choro ejus ducendo," &c. With the moſt immodeſt ſpectacles. The nuns of ſome French convents are ſaid to have had *Ludibria* on Saint Mary Magdalene's and other feſtivals, when they wore the habits of ſeculars, and danced with them. Carpent. *ubi ſupr.* v. *Kalendæ.* There was the office of the *Rex Stultorum* in Beverley church, prohibited 1391. Dugd. *Mon.* iii. Append. 7. [In the Conſtitutions of Robert Groſſeteſte, biſhop of Lincoln, is the following prohibition : " Execrabilem etiam conſuetudinem quæ conſuevit in quibuſdam eccleſiis obſervari de faciendo Feſto Stultorum ſpeciali authoritate reſcripti Apoſtolici penitus inhibemus ; ne de domo orationis fiat domus ludibrii," &c. See Brown *Faſcicul. rerum expetendarum,* ii. 412. And in his 32nd Letter, printed in the ſame collection, ii. 331, after reciting that the houſe of God is not to be turned into a houſe of buffoonery, &c. he adds : " Quapropter vobis mandamus in virtute obedientiæ firmiter injungentes, quatenus Feſtum Stultorum, cum ſit vanitate plenum et voluptatibus ſpurcum, Deo odibile et dæmonibus amabile, de cætero in eccleſia Lincoln. die venerandæ ſolennitatis circumciſionis Domini nullatenus permittatis fieri."—*Douce.*]

[1] [This feaſt was probably celebrated on St. Nicholas's day, on account of his being the patron ſaint of children. See his legend, printed at Naples, 1645, 4to.— *Douce.* See alſo *Popular Antiquities of Great Britain,* by Hazlitt, i. 232-40.]

[2] In the ſtatutes of Eton College, given 1441, the *Epiſcopus Puerorum* is ordered to perform divine ſervice on Saint Nicholas's day. Rubr. xxxi. In the ſtatutes of Wincheſter College, given 1380, *Pueri,* that is, the boy-biſhop and his fellows, are permitted on Innocents'-day to execute all the ſacred offices in the chapel, according to the uſe of the church of Sarum. Rubr. xxix. This ſtrange piece of religious mockery flouriſhed greatly in Saliſbury cathedral. In the old ſtatutes of that church there is a chapter De Epiſcopo Choriſtarum : and their Proceſſionale gives a long and minute account of the whole ceremony, edit. 1555.

[3] This ceremony was aboliſhed by a proclamation, no later than 33 Hen. VIII. MSS. Cott. Tit. B 1, f. 208. In the inventory of the treaſury of York cathedral, taken in 1530, we have " Item una mitra parva cum petris pro epiſcopo puerorum," &c. Dugd. *Monaſt.* iii. 169, 170. See alſo 313, 314, 177, 279. See alſo Dugd. *Hiſt. S. Paul's,* pp. 205, 206, where he is called Epiſcopus Parvulorum, And Anſtis *Ord. Gart.* ii. 309, where, inſtead of Nihilenſis, read Nicolenſis, or Nicolatenſis.

decorum. After dinner they exhibited, without their maſks, but in proper dreſſes, ſuch farces as they were maſters of, in different parts of the city." [1] It is probable that the ſame entertainments attended the ſolemniſation of this ridiculous feſtival in England: [2] and from this ſuppoſition ſome critics may be inclined to deduce the practice of our plays being acted by the choir-boys of St. Paul's church and the chapel royal, which continued, as I before obſerved, till Cromwell's uſurpation. The Engliſh and French ſtages mutually throw light on each other's hiſtory. But perhaps it will be thought, that in ſome of theſe inſtances I have exemplified in nothing more than farcical and geſticulatory repreſentations. Yet even theſe traces ſhould be attended to. In the meantime we may obſerve upon the whole, that the modern drama had no foundation in our religion, and that it was raiſed and ſupported by the clergy. The truth is, the members of the eccleſiaſtical ſocieties were almoſt the only perſons who could read, and their numbers eaſily furniſhed performers: they abounded in leiſure, and their very relaxations were religious.

I did not mean to touch upon the Italian ſtage. But as ſo able a judge as Riccoboni ſeems to allow that Italy derived her theatre from thoſe of France and England, by way of an additional illuſtration of the antiquity of the two laſt, I will here produce one or two Miracle-Plays, acted much earlier in Italy than any piece mentioned by that ingenious writer or by Creſcimbeni. In the year 1298, on "the feaſt of Pentecoſt, and the two following holidays, the repreſentation of the *Play of Chriſt*, that is, of his paſſion, reſurrection, aſcenſion, judgment, and the miſſion of the holy ghoſt, was performed by the clergy of Civita Vecchia, 'in curia domini patriarchæ Auſtriæ civitatis honorifice et laudabiliter.'" [3] And again, "In 1304, the chapter of Civita Vecchia exhibited a play of the creation

---

[1] *Statut. Eccles. Tullens.* apud Carpent. *Suppl. Lat. Gl. Du Cang.* v. *Kalendæ.*

[2] It appears that in England the boy-biſhop with his companions went about to different parts of the town; at leaſt viſited the other religious houſes. As in *Rot. Comp. Coll. Winton.* A. D. 1461. "In Dat. epiſcopo Nicolatenſi." This I ſuppoſe was one of the children of the choir of the neighbouring cathedral. In the ſtatutes of the collegiate church of S. Mary Ottery, founded by Biſhop Grandiſon in 1337, there is this paſſage: "Item ſtatuimus, quod nullus canonicus, vicarius, vel ſecundarius, pueros choriſtas in feſto ſanctorum Innocentium extra Parochiam de Otery trahant, aut eis licentiam vagandi concedant."—cap. 50, *MS. Regiſtr. Priorat. S. Swithin. Winton.* quat. 9. In the wardrobe-rolls of Edward III. an. 12, we have this entry, which ſhews that our mock-biſhop and his chapter ſometimes exceeded their adopted clerical commiſſion, and exerciſed the arts of ſecular entertainment. "Epiſcopo puerorum eccleſiæ de Andeworp cantanti coram domino rege in camera ſua in feſto ſanctorum Innocentium, de dono ipſius dom. regis. xiii *s.* vi *d.*"

[3] *Chron. Forojul.* in Append. ad *Monum. Eccl. Aquilej.* p. 30, col. 1. [An earlier record of the exhibition of theſe miracle-plays in Italy will be found in the *Catalogo de' Podeſte di Padova:* "In queſt anno (1243) fu fatta la rappreſentazion della Paſſione e Reſurreccione di Chriſto nel Pra della Valle." Muratori, *Script. Rer. Ital* v. 8, p. 365.—The chief object of the Compagna del Confalone inſtituted at Rome in the year 1264, was to repreſent the Myſteries, "della Paſſione del Redentore." Tiraboſchi, vol. iv. p. 343.—*Price.*]

of our firft parents, the annunciation of the Virgin Mary, the birth of Chrift, and other paffages of facred fcripture."[1] In the mean time, thofe critics, who contend for the high antiquity of the Italian ftage, may adopt thefe inftances as new proofs in defence of that hypothefis.

This fhow of the BOY-BISHOP, not fo much for its fuperftition as its levity and abfurdity, had been formerly abrogated by King Henry VIII. fourteen years before, in the year 1542, as appears by a "Proclamation deuifed by the Kings Maiefty by the advys of his Highnefs Counfel the xxii day of Julie, 33 Hen. viij, commanding the Feafts of faint Luke, faint Mark, faint Marie Magdalene, In- uention of the Croffe, and faint Laurence, which had been abro- gated, fhould be nowe againe celebrated and kept holie days," of which the following is the concluding claufe. "And where as here- tofore dyuers and many fuperftitious and chyldyfh obferuances have be vfed, and yet to this day are obferued and kept, in many and fundry partes of this realm, as vpon faint Nicholas,[2] faint Catharine,[3] faint Clement,[4] the holie Innocents, and fuch like,[5] Children [boys]

---

[1] *Ibid.* p. 30, col. 1. It is extraordinary that the Miracle-plays, even in the churches, fhould not ceafe in Italy till the year 1660.

[2] In Barnaby Googe's *Popifh Kingdom*, 1570, a tranflation from Naogeorgus's *Regnum Antichrifti*, fol. 55:—

"Saint Nicholas monie vfde to give to maydens fecretlie,
Who that be ftill may vfe his wonted liberalitie:
The mother all their children on the Eeve do caufe to faft,
And when they euerie one at night in fenfeleffe fleepe are caft,
Both apples, nuts and payres they bring, and other thinges befide,
As cappes, and fhoes, and petticoates, wich fecretly they hide,
And in the morning found, they fay, that 'this Saint Nicholas brought,'" &c.

I have already given traces of this practice in the colleges of Winchefter and Eton. To which I have add another. *Regiftr. Coll. Wint. fub ann.* 1427. "Crux deaurata de cupro [copper] cum Baculo, pro Epifcopo puerorum." But it appears that the practice fubfifted in common grammar-fchools. "Hoc anno, 1464, in fefto fancti Nicolai non erat Epifcopus Puerorum in fchola grammaticali in civitate Cantuariæ ex defectu Magiftrorum, viz. J. Sidney et T. Hikfon," &c. *Lib. Jo- hannis Stone, Monachi Eccles. Cant.* fc. *De Obitibus et aliis Memorabilibus fui cœnobii ab anno* 1415, *ad annum* 1467. MS. C.C.C.C.Q. 8. The abufes of this cuftom in Wells Cathedral are mentioned fo early as Decemb. 1. 1298. *Regiftr. Eccl. Wellens.*

[3] The reader will recollect the old play of Saint Catharine, *Ludus Catharinæ,* exhibited at Saint Albans Abbey in 1160. Strype fays, in 1556, "On Saint Katharines day, at fix of the clock at night, S. Katharine went about the battle- ments of S. Paul's church accompanied with fine finging and great lights. This was faint Katharine's Proceffion." *Eccl. Mem.* iii. 309. ch. xxxix. Again, her proceffion in 1553 is celebrated with five hundred great lights, round Saint Paul's fteeple, &c. *Ibid.* p. 51. ch. v. And p. 57. ch. v.

[4] Among the church-proceffions revived by Queen Mary, that of S. Clement's church, in honour of this faint, was by far the moft fplendid of any in London. Their proceffion to Saint Paul's in 1557 "was made very pompous with fourfcore banners and ftreamers, and the waits of the city playing, and threefcore priefts and clarkes in copes. And divers of the Inns of Court were there, who went next the priefts," &c. Strype, *ubi fupr.* iii. 337, ch. xlix.

[5] In the Synodus Carnotenfis, under the year 1526, it is ordered, "In fefto fancti Nicolai, Catharinæ, Innocentium, aut alio quovis die, prætextu recreationis, ne Scholaftici, Clerici, Sacerdotefve, ftultum aliquod aut ridiculum faciant in

be ftrangelie decked and apparayled, to counterfeit Priefts, Bifshopes, and Women, and fo be ledde with Songes and Dances from houfe to houfe, bleffing the people, and gathering of money; and Boyes do finge maffe, and preache in the pulpitt, with fuch other vnfittinge and inconuenient vfages, rather to the deryfyon than anie true glorie of God, or honor of his fayntes: The Kynges maieftie therefore, myndinge nothing fo moche as to aduance the true glory of God without vain fuperftition, wylleth and commandeth, that from hence- forth all fvch fvperftitious obferuations be left and clerely extin- guifhed throwout all this his realme and dominions, for-as moche as the fame doth refemble rather the vnlawfull fuperftition of gentilitie, than the pvre and fincere religion of Chrifte." With refpect to the difguifings of thefe young fraternities, and their proceffions from houfe to houfe with finging and dancing, fpecified in this edict, in a very mutilated fragment of a Computus, or annual Accompt-roll, of Saint Swithin's Cathedral Priory at Winchefter, under the year 1441, a difburfement is made to the finging-boys of the monaftery, who, together with the chorifters of Saint Elizabeth's collegiate chapel near that city, were dreffed up like girls, and exhibited their fports before the abbefs and nuns of Saint Mary's Abbey at Winchefter, in the public refectory of that convent, on Innocents' day.[1] " Pro Pueris Eleemofynariæ una cum Pueris Capellæ fanctæ Elizabethæ, ornatis more puellarum, et faltantibus, cantantibus, et ludentibus, coram domina Abbatiffa et monialibus Abbathiæ beatæ Mariæ vir- ginis, in aula ibidem in die fanctorum Innocentium."[2] Again, in a fragment of an Accompt of the Cellarer of Hyde Abbey at Win-

---

ecclefia. Denique ab ecclefia ejiciantur veftes fatuorum perfonas fcenicas agen- tium." See Bochellus, *Decret. Eccles. Gall.* lib. iv. Tit. vii. C. 43. 44. 46. p. 586. Yet thefe fports feem to have remained in France fo late as 1585. For in the Synod of Aix, 1585, it is enjoined, " Ceffent in die Sanctorum Innocentium ludibria omnia et pueriles ac theatrales lufus." Bochell, *ibid.* C. 45. p. 586. A Synod of Tholoufe, an. 1590, removes plays, fpectacles, and *hiftrionum circulationes* from churches and their cemeteries. Bochell. *ibid.* lib. iv. tit. 1. c. 98, p. 560.

[1] In the Regifter of Wodeloke Bifhop of Winchefter, the following is an article among the injunctions given to the nuns of the convent of Rumfey in Hampfhire, in confequence of an epifcopal vifitation, under the year 1310. " Item prohi- bemus, ne cubent in dormitorio pueri mafculi cum monialibus, vel foemellæ, nec per moniales ducantur in Chorum, dum ibidem divinum officium celebratur." fol. 134. In the fame regifter thefe injunctions follow in a literal French tranflation, made for the convenience of the nuns.

[2] *MS. in Archiv. Wulves, apud Winton.* It appears to have been a practice for itinerant players to gain admittance into the nunneries, and to play Latin myfteries before the nuns. There is a curious canon of the council of Cologne, in 1549, which is to this effect. " We have been informed that certain Actors of Comedies, not content with the ftage and theatres, have even entertained the nunneries, in order to recreate the nuns, *ubi virginibus commoveant voluptatem,* with their pro- fane, amorous, and *fecular* gefticulations. Which fpectacles or plays, although they confifted of facred and pious fubjects, can yet notwithftanding leave little good, but on the contrary much harm, in the minds of the nuns, who behold and admire the outward geftures of the performers, and underftand not the words. Therefore we decree, that henceforward no plays, *Comediae,* fhall be admitted into the convents of nuns," &c. *Sur. Concil.* tom. iv. p. 852. Binius, tom. iv. p. 765.

chester, under the year 1490. "In larvis et aliis indumentis Puerorum visentium Dominum apud Wulsey, et Constabularium Castri Winton, in apparatu suo, necnon subintrantium omnia monasteria civitatis Winton, in Festo sancti Nicholai."[1]   That is, "In furnishing masks and dresses for the boys of the convent, when they visited the bishop at Wulvesey-palace, the constable of Winchester-castle, and all the monasteries of the city of Winchester, on the festival of saint Nicholas."   As to the divine service being performed by children on these feasts, it was not only celebrated by boys, but there is an injunction given to the Benedictine nunnery of Godstowe in Oxfordshire by Archbishop Peckham, in the year 1278, that on Innocents' day, the public prayers should not any more be said in the church of that monastery per parvulas, that is, by little girls.[2]

The ground-work of this religious mockery of the boy-bishop, which is evidently founded on modes of barbarous life, may perhaps be traced backward at least as far as the year 867.[3]   At the Constantinopolitan synod under that year, at which were present three hundred and seventy-three bishops, it was found to be a solemn custom in the courts of princes, on certain stated days, to dress some layman in the episcopal apparel, who should exactly personate a bishop both in his tonsure and ornaments: as also to create a burlesque patriarch, who might make sport for the company.[4]   This scandal to the clergy was anathematized.   But ecclesiastical synods and censures have often proved too weak to suppress popular spectacles, which take deep root in the public manners, and are only concealed for a while, to spring up afresh with new vigour.

After the form of a legitimate stage had appeared in England, mysteries and miracles were also revived by Queen Mary, as an appendage of the papistic worship:

> En, iterum crudelia retro
> Fata vocant![5]

In the year 1556 a goodly stage-play of the *Passion of Christ* was

---

[1] MS. *Ibid.* See *supr.*

[2] Harpsfield, *Hist. Eccl. Angl.* p. 441, edit. 1622.

[3] Or, 870. [See Mr. Strutt's *Sports and Pastimes of the People of England.*— Price.]

[A tract explaining the origin and ceremonial of the Boy-bishop was printed [by John Gregory] in 1649 with the following title: "*Episcopus puerorum in die Innocentium;* or a Discoverie of an ancient Custom in the church of Sarum, making an anniversarie Bishop among the Choristers." This tract was written in explanation of a stone monument still remaining in Salisbury Cathedral, representing a little boy habited in episcopal robes, with a mitre upon his head, a crosier in his hand, &c. and the explanation was derived from a chapter in the ancient statutes of that church entitled *De Episcopo Choristarum.* See a long account of the *Boy Bishop,* in Hawkins's *History of Music,* vol. ii.—*Park.* See *Handb. of E. E. Lit.* art. *Episcopus Puerorum.*]

[4] Surius, *Concil.* iii. 529. 539. Baron. *Annal.* Ann. 869. § 11. See *Concil.* Basil. num. xxxii.   The French have a miracle play, *Beau Miracle de S. Nicolas,* to be acted by twenty-four personages, printed at Paris, for Pierre Sergeant, in quarto, without date, Bl. lett. [Compare Brunet, iii. 1742-3.]

[5] Virgil, *Georg.* iv. 495.

preſented at the Grey-Friars in London, on Corpus-Chriſti day, before the lord mayor, the privy-council, and many great eſtates of the realm.[1] Strype alſo mentions, under the year 1557, a ſtage-play at the Grey-Friars, of the *Paſſion of Chriſt*, on the day that war was proclaimed in London againſt France, and in honour of that occaſion.[2] On Saint Olave's day in the ſame year, the holiday of the church in Silver-ſtreet which is dedicated to that ſaint, was kept with much ſolemnity. At eight of the clock at night began a ſtage-play of goodly matter, being the miraculous hiſtory of the life of that ſaint,[3] which continued four hours, and was concluded with many religious ſongs.[4]

Many curious circumſtances of the nature of theſe miracle-plays appear in a roll of the churchwardens of Baſſingborne in Cambridge-ſhire, which is an account of the expenſes and receptions for acting the play of *Saint George* at Baſſingborne, on the feaſt of Saint Margaret in the year 1511. They collected upwards of four pounds in twenty-ſeven neighbouring pariſhes for furniſhing the play. They diſburſed about two pounds in the repreſentation. Theſe diſburſements are to four minſtrels, or waits, of Cambridge for three days, v s. vj d. To the players, in bread and ale, iij s. ij d. To the garnement-man for garnements, and propyrts,[5] that is, for dreſſes, decorations, and implements, and for play-books, xx s. To John Hobard, brotherhoode preeſte, that is, a prieſt of the guild in the church, for the play-book, ij s. viij d. For the crofte, or field in which the play was exhibited, j s. For propyrte-making, or furniture, j s. iv d. "For fiſh and bread, and to ſetting up the ſtages, iv d." For painting three fanchoms and four tormentors, words which I do not underſtand, but perhaps phantoms and devils. . . . The reſt was expended for a feaſt on the occaſion, in which are recited, "Four chicken for the gentilmen, iv d." It appears from the *Coventry Plays* that a temporary ſcaffold only was erected for theſe performances; and Chaucer ſays of Abſolon, a pariſh-clerk,

---

[1] MSS. Cotr. Vitell. E. 5. Strype. See *Life of Sir Thomas Pope*, Pref. p. xii.

[2] Eccl. Mem. vol. iii. ch. xlix.

[3] Strype, *ibid.* p. 379. With the religious pageantries, other ancient ſports and ſpectacles alſo, which had fallen into diſuſe in the reign of Edward VI., began to be now revived. As thus, "On the 30th of May was a goodly May-game in Fenchurch-ſtreet, with drums, and guns, and pikes, with the Nine Worthies who rid. And each made his ſpeech. There was alſo the morice-dance, and an elephant and caſtle, and the lord and lady of the May appeared to make up this ſhow." Strype, *ibid.* 376, ch. xlix.

[4] Ludovicus Vives relates that it was cuſtomary in Brabant to preſent annual plays in honour of the reſpective ſaints to which the churches were dedicated : and he betrays his great credulity in adding a wonderful ſtory in conſequence of this cuſtom. *Not. in Auguſtin. De Civit. Dei*, lib. xii. cap. 25, C.

[5] The property-room is yet known at our theatres. ["Malone (Shakeſpeare by Boſwell, iii. 25), following Warton, has remarked upon the uſe of the word *properties* in the reign of Henry VIII., but we here (in the *Caſtle of Perſeverance*) find it employed, and in the ſame ſenſe of furniture, apparel, &c., a century earlier."— *Collier.*]

and an actor of King Herod's character in theſe dramas, in the *Miller's Tale:*

> And for to ſhew his lightneſſe and maiſtry
> He playith Herawdes on a ſcaffald hie.[1]

Scenical decorations and machinery[2] which employed the genius and invention of Inigo Jones, in the reigns of the firſt James and Charles, ſeem to have migrated from the maſques at court to the public theatre. In the inſtrument here cited, the prieſt who wrote the play, and received only two ſhillings and eight pence for his labour, ſeems to have been worſe paid in proportion than any of the other perſons concerned. The learned Oporinus, in 1547, pub-liſhed in two volumes a collection of religious interludes, which abounded in Germany. They are in Latin, and not taken from legends, but from the Bible.

The Puritans were highly offended at theſe religious plays now revived.[3] But they were hardly leſs averſe to the theatrical repre-

---

[1] *Mill. T.* v. 275. Mr. Steevens and Mr. Malone have ſhown that the accom-modations in our early regular theatres were but little better. That the old ſcenery was very ſimple, may partly be collected from an entry in a Computus of Wincheſter College, under the year 1579, viz. *Comp. Burs. Coll. Winton.* A. D. 1573. Eliz. xvº.—" Cuſtos Aulæ. Item, pro diverſis expenſis circa Scaffoldam erigendam et deponendam, et pro Domunculis de novo compoſitis cum carriagio et recarriagio *ly jovſtes*, et aliorum mutuatorum ad eandem Scaffoldam, cum vj *linckes* et jº [uno] duodeno candelarum, pro lumine expenſis, tribus noctibus in Ludis comediarum et tragediarum, xxv s. viij d." Again in the next quarter, " Pro vij *ly linckes* deli-beratis pueris per M. Informatorem [the ſchoolmaſter] pro Ludis, iij s." Again, in the laſt quarter, " Pro removendis Organis e templo in Aulam et præparandis eiſdem erga Ludos, v s." By Domunculis I underſtand little cells of board, raiſed on each ſide of the ſtage, for dreſſing-rooms, or retiring places. Strype, under the year 1559, ſays that after a grand feaſt at Guildhall, " the ſame day was a ſcaffold ſet up in the hall for a play." *Ann. Ref.* i. 197, edit. 1725.

[2] [Dr. Aſhby ſuggeſts that ſome diſtinction ſhould perhaps be made between ſcenery and machinery: and it may probably be ceded that ſcenic decoration was firſt introduced.—*Park.*]

[3] A very late ſcripture-play is *The Hiſtory of Jacob and Eſau*, 1568. But this play had appeared in Queen Mary's reign, " An enterlude vpon the hiſtory of Jacobe and Eſawe," &c. Licenſed to Henry Sutton in 1557. *Regiſtr. Station.* A. fol. 23, a. It is certain, however, that the faſhion of religious interludes was not entirely diſcontinued in the reign of Queen Elizabeth; for I find licenſed to T. Hackett, in 1561, " A newe enterlude of the ij ſynnes of Kynge Dauyde." *Ibid.* fol. 75, a. [For other pieces of the ſame nature, ſee *Handb. of E. E. Lit.* 1867, arts. *Plays, Wager,* &c. The " enterlude of the ſynnes of Kynge Dauyde" is not known, unleſs it was the *ballad* reprinted by Chappell (*Roxburghe Ballads,* vol. i. part ii.)] Ballads on Scripture ſubjects are now innumerable. Peele's *David and* [*Bethſabe*] is a remain of the faſhion of Scripture-plays. I have mentioned the play of *Holofernes* acted at Hatfield in 1556. *Life of Sir Thomas Pope,* p. 87. In 1556 was printed " A ballet intituled the hiſtorye of Judith and Holyfernes." *Regiſtr.* ut ſupr. fol. 154, b. And Regiſtr. B. fol. 227. In Hearne's *Manuſcript Collectanea* there is a licence, dated 1571, from the queen, directed to the officers of Middleſex, permitting one John Swinton Powlter, " to have and uſe ſome playes and games at or uppon nine ſeverall ſondaies," within the ſaid county. "And be-cauſe greate reſorte of people is lyke to come thereunto, he is required, for the preſervation of the peace and for the ſake of good order, to take with him four or five diſcreet and ſubſtantial men of thoſe places where the games ſhall be put in practice, to ſuperintend duringe the contynuance of the games or playes." Some of

fentation of the Chriftian than of the Gentile ftory : yet for different reafons. To hate a theatre was a part of their creed, and therefore plays were an improper vehicle of religion. The heathen fables they judged to be dangerous, as too nearly refembling the fuperftitions of popery.[1]

In this tranfient view of the origin and progrefs of our drama, which was incidentally fuggefted by the mention of Bafton's fuppofed comedies, I have trefpaffed upon future periods. But I have chiefly done this for the fake of connection, and to prepare the mind of the reader for other anecdotes of the hiftory of our ftage, which will occur in the courfe of our refearches, and are referved for their refpective places. I could have enlarged what is here loofely thrown together, with many other remarks and illuftrations : but I was unwilling to tranfcribe from the collections of thofe who have already treated this fubject with great comprehenfion and penetration, and efpecially from the author of the Supplement to the Tranflator's Preface of Jarvis's *Don Quixote*.[2] I claim no other merit from this digreffion, than that of having collected fome new anecdotes relating to the early ftate of the Englifh and French ftages, the original of both which is intimately connected, from books and manufcripts not eafily found, nor often examined. Thefe hints may perhaps prove of fome fervice to thofe who have leifure and inclination to examine the fubject with more precifion.

SECTION VII.

DWARD III. was an illuftrious example and patron of chivalry. His court was the theatre of romantic elegance. I have examined the annual rolls of his wardrobe, which record various articles of coftly ftuffs delivered occafionally for the celebration of his tournaments; fuch as ftandards, pennons, tunics, caparifons, with other fplendid furniture of the fame fort : and it appears that he commanded thefe folemnities to be kept, with a magnificence fuperior to that of former ages, at Lichfield, Bury, Guilford, Eltham, Canterbury, and twice at Windfor, in little more than the fpace of one year.[3] At his tri-

---

the exhibitions are then fpecified, fuch as "Shotinge with the brode arrowe, The lepping for men, The pitchynge of the barre," and the like. But then follows this very general claufe, "With all fuche other games, as haue at anye time heretofore or now be lycenfed, ufed, or played." *Coll. MSS. Hearne,* tom. lxi. p. 78. One wifhes to know whether any interludes, and whether religious or profane, were included in this inftrument.

[1] [Oppofite fects, as Romanifts and Proteftants, often adopt each other's arguments. See Bayle's *Dict.—Afhby*.]

[2] [This fubject is refumed in Sect. 34.]

[3] *Comp. J. Cooke, Proviforis Magn. Garderob.* ab ann. 21 Edw. III. ad ann. 23, *fupr. citat.* I will give, as a fpecimen, this officer's accompt for the tournament

umphant return from Scotland, he was met by two hundred and thirty knights at Dunftable, who received their victorious monarch with a grand exhibition of thefe martial exercifes. He eftablifhed in the caftle of Windfor a fraternity of twenty-four knights, for whom he erected a round table, with a round chamber ftill remaining, according to a fimilar inftitution of King Arthur.[1] Anftis treats the notion, that Edward in this eftablifhment had any retrofpect to King Arthur, as an idle and legendary tradition.[2] But the fame of Arthur was ftill kept alive, and continued to be an object of veneration long after-wards : and however idle and ridiculous the fables of the round table may appear at prefent, they were then not only univerfally known, but firmly believed. Nothing could be more natural to fuch a ro-mantic monarch, in fuch an age, than the renovation of this moft ancient and revered inftitution of chivalry. It was a prelude to the renowned order of the garter, which he foon afterwards founded at Windfor, during the ceremonies of a magnificent feaft, which had been proclaimed by his heralds in Germany, France, Scotland, Bur-gundy, Hainault, and Brabant, and lafted fifteen days.[3] We muft not try the modes and notions of other ages, even if they have arrived to fome degree of refinement, by thofe of our own. Nothing is more probable, than that this latter foundation of Edward III. took its rife from the exploded ftory of the garter of the Countefs of Salifbury.[4] Such an origin is interwoven with the manners and ideas of the times.

---

at Canterbury. " Et ad faciendum diverfos apparatus pro corpore regis et fuorum pro haftiludio Cantuarienfi, an. reg. xxii. ubi Rex dedit octo hernefia de fyndone ynde facta, et vapulata de armis dom. Stephani de Cofyngton militis, dominis prin-cipibus comiti Lancaftriæ, comiti Suffolciæ, Johanni de Gray, Joh. de Beauchamp, Roberto Maule, Joh. Chandos, et dom. Rogero de Beauchamp. Et ad faciendum unum harnefium de bokeram albo pro rege, extencellato cum argento, viz. tunicam et fcutum operata cum dictamine Regis,

> ' Hay Hay the wythe fwan
> By Godes foule I am thy man.'

Et croparium, pectorale, teftarium, et arcenarium extencellata cum argento. Et ad parandum i. tunicam Regis, et i. clocam et capuciam cum c. garteris paratis cum boucles, barris, et pendentibus de argento. Et ad faciendum unum dublettum pro Rege de tela linea habente, circa manicas et fimbriam, unam borduram de panno longo viridi operatam cum nebulis et vineis de auro, et cum dictamine Regis, *It is as it is.*" Membr. xi. [A.D. 1349.]

[1] Walfing. p. 117.   [2] *Ord. Gart.* ii. 92.
[3] Barnes, i. ch. 22, p. 292. Froiffart, c. 100. Anftis, *ut fupr.*
[4] Afhmole proves, that the orders of the Annunciada, and of the Toifon d'Or, had the like origin. *Ord. Gart.* pp. 180, 181. Even in the enfigns of the order of the Holy Ghoft, founded fo late as 1578, fome love-myfteries and emblems were con-cealed under ciphers introduced into the blafonry. See Le Laboureur, *Contin. des Mem. de Caftelnau*, p. 895. " Il y eut plus de myfteres d'amourettes que de reli-gion," &c. But I cannot in this place help obferving, that the fantaftic humour of unriddling emblematical myfteries, fuppofed to be concealed under all enfigns and arms, was at length carried to fuch an extravagance, at leaft in England, as to be checked by the legiflature. By a ftatute of Queen Elizabeth, a fevere penalty is laid, " on all fond phantaftical prophecies upon or by the occafion of any arms, fields, beaftes, badges, or the like things accuftomed in arms, cognifaunces, or fignetts," &c. *Statut.* c. Eliz. ch. 15, A.D. 1564.

Their attention to the fair ſex entered into every thing. It is by no means unreaſonable to ſuppoſe, that the fantaſtic Collar of SS., worn by the knights of this Order, was an alluſion to her name. Froiſſart, an eye-witneſs, and well acquainted with the intrigues of the court, relates at large the king's affection for the counteſs, and particularly deſcribes a grand carouſal which he gave in conſequence of that attachment.[1] The firſt feſtival of this order was not only adorned by the braveſt champions of Chriſtendom, but by the preſence of Queen Philippa, Edward's conſort, accompanied by three hundred ladies of noble families.[2] The tournaments of this ſtately reign were conſtantly crowded with ladies of the firſt diſtinction, who ſometimes attended them on horſeback, armed with daggers, and dreſſed in a ſuccinct ſoldier-like habit or uniform prepared for the purpoſe.[3] In a tournament exhibited at London, ſixty ladies on palfries appeared, each leading a knight with a gold chain. In this manner they paraded from the Tower to Smithfield.[4] Even Philippa, a queen of ſingular elegance of manners,[5] partook ſo much of the heroic ſpirit which was univerſally diſfuſed, that juſt before an engagement with the king of Scotland, ſhe rode round the ranks of the Engliſh army encouraging the ſoldiers, and was with ſome difficulty perſuaded or compelled to relinquiſh the field.[6] The Counteſs of Montfort is another eminent inſtance of female heroiſm in this age. When the ſtrong town of Hennebond, near Rennes, was beſieged by the French, this redoubted amazon rode in complete armour from ſtreet to ſtreet on a large courſer, animating the garriſon.[7] Finding from a high tower that the

---

[1] *Ubi ſupr.* [In *Notes and Queries,* from time to time, a good deal of information has been printed on this ſubject. See General Indices.]

[2] They ſoon afterwards regularly received robes, with the knights companions, for this ceremony, powdered with garters. Aſhmol. *Ord. Gart.* 217, 594. And Anſtis, ii. 123.

[3] Knyghton, *Dec. Script.* p. 2597.

[4] Froiſſart *apud.* Stow's *Surv. Lond.* p. 718, edit. 1616. At an earlier period, the growing gallantry of the times appears in a public inſtrument. It is in the reign of Edward I. Twelve jurymen depoſe upon oath the ſtate of the king's lordſhip at Woodſtock : and among other things it is ſolemnly recited, that Henry II. often reſided at Woodſtock, "pro amore cujuſdam mulieris nomine Roſamunda." Hearne's *Aveſbury,* Append. 331.

[5] And of diſtinguiſhed beauty. Hearne ſays, that the ſtatuaries of thoſe days uſed to make Queen Philippa a model for their images of the Virgin Mary. *Gloſs. Rob.* [*de*] *Brun.* p. 349. He adds, that the holy virgin, in a repreſentation of her aſſumption was conſtantly figured young and beautiful; and that the artiſts before the Reformation generally "had the moſt beautiful women of the greateſt quality in their view, when they made ſtatues and figures of her." *Ibid.* p. 550.

[6] Froiſſart, i. c. 138.

[7] Froiſſart ſays, that when the Engliſh proved victorious, the counteſs came out of the caſtle, and in the ſtreet kiſſed Sir Walter Manny the Engliſh general, and his captains, one after another, twice or thrice, *comme noble et valliant dame.* On another like occaſion, the ſame hiſtorian relates, that ſhe went out to meet the officers, whom ſhe kiſſed and ſumptuouſly entertained in her caſtle, i. c. 86. At many magnificent tournaments in France, the ladies determined the prize. See *Mem. anc. Cheval.* i. p. 175, *ſeq.* p. 223, *ſeq.* An Engliſh ſquire, on the ſide of the French, captain of the caſtle of Beaufort, called himſelf *le Pourſuivant d' amour,* in 1369. Froiſſart, l. i. c. 64. In the midſt of grand engagements between the French and Engliſh armies,

whole French army was engaged in the aſſault, ſhe iſſued, thus completely accoutred, through a convenient poſtern at the head of three hundred choſen ſoldiers, and ſet fire to the French camp.[1]   In the mean time riches and plenty, the effects of conqueſt, peace and proſperity, were ſpread on every ſide ; and new luxuries were imported in great abundance from the conquered countries. There were few families, even of a moderate condition, but had in their poſſeſſion precious articles of dreſs or furniture : ſuch as ſilks, fur, tapeſtry, embroidered beds, cups of gold, ſilver, porcelain and cryſtal, bracelets, chains, and necklaces, brought from Caen, Calais, and other opulent foreign cities.[2] The increaſe of rich furniture appears in a foregoing reign.   In an act of Parliament of Edward I.[3] are many regulations, directed to goldſmiths, not only in London, but in other towns, concerning the ſterling alloy of veſſels and jewels of gold and ſilver, &c.; and it is ſaid, " Gravers or cutters of ſtones and ſeals ſhall give every one their juſt weight of ſilver and gold." It ſhould be remembered, that about this period Europe had opened a new commercial intercourſe with the ports of India.[4] No fewer than eight ſumptuary laws, which had the uſual effect of not being obſerved, were enacted in one ſeſſion of parliament during this reign.[5] Amid theſe growing elegances and ſuperfluities, foreign manners, eſpecially of the French, were perpetually increaſing ; and the native ſimplicity of the Engliſh people was perceptibly corrupted and effaced. It is not quite uncertain that maſques had their beginning in this reign.   Theſe ſhews, in which the greateſt perſonages of the court often bore a part, and which arrived at their height in the reign of Henry VIII., encouraged the arts of addreſs and decorum, and are ſymptoms of the riſe of poliſhed manners.[6]

In a reign like this, we ſhall not be ſurpriſed to find ſuch a poet as Chaucer, with whom a new era in Engliſh poetry begins, and on whoſe account many of theſe circumſtances are mentioned, as they ſerve to prepare the reader for his character, on which they throw no inconſiderable light.

But before we enter on ſo ample a field, it will be perhaps leſs embarraſſing, at leaſt more conſiſtent with our preſcribed method,

---

when perhaps the intereſts of both nations are vitally concerned, Froiſſart gives many inſtances of officers entering into ſeparate and perſonal combat to diſpute the beauty of their reſpective miſtreſſes. *Hiſt.* l. ii. ch. 33, 43. On this occaſion an ingenious French writer obſerves, that Homer's heroes of ancient Greece are juſt as extravagant : who, in the heat of the fight, often ſtop on a ſudden, to give an account of the genealogy of themſelves or their horſes. *Mem. anc. Cheval.* ubi ſupr. Sir Walter Manny, in 1343, in attacking the caſtle of Guigard, exclaims, " Let me never be beloved of my miſtreſs, if I refuſe this attack," &c. Froiſſart, i. 81.

[1] Froiſſart, i. c. 80. Du Cheſne, p. 656. Mezeray, ii. 3, p. 19, *ſeq.*
[2] Walſing. *Ypodigm.* 121, *Hiſt.* 159.   [3] A.D. 1300, Edw. I. *an.* 28, cap. xx.
[4] Anderſon, *Hiſt. Comm.* i. p. 141.   [5] *Ann.* 37 Edw. III. cap. viii. *ſeq.*
[6] This ſpirit of ſplendour and gallantry was continued in the reign of his ſucceſſor. See the genius of that reign admirably characterized, and by the hand of a maſter, in Biſhop Lowth's *Life of Wykeham,* p. 222. See alſo Holinſh. *Chron.* ſub ann. 1399, p. 508, col. 1.

if we previoufly difplay the merits of two or three poets, who appeared in the former part of the reign of Edward III., with other incidental matters.

The firft of thefe is Richard [Rolle, of] Hampole, [near Don-cafter, commonly called Richard Hampole, who is faid to have been a hermit] of the Order of Saint Auguftine. He was a doctor of divinity, and lived a folitary life near the nuns of Hampole, four miles from Doncafter in Yorkfhire.[1] The neighbourhood of this female fociety could not withdraw our recluse from his devotions and his ftudies. He [died] in the year 1349.[2] His Latin theological tracts, both in profe and verfe, in which Leland juftly thinks he has difplayed more erudition than eloquence, are numerous. His prin-cipal pieces of Englifh rhyme are a *Paraphrafe of part of the Book of Job*, of the *Lord's Prayer*, and of the *feven penitential Pfalms*, and the *Pricke of Confcience*. But our hermit's poetry, which indeed from thefe titles promifes but little entertainment, has no tincture of fenti-ment, imagination, or elegance. The following verfes are extracted from the *Pricke of Confcience*, one of the moft common manufcripts in our libraries, and I prophefy that I am its laft tranfcriber.[3] But I muft obferve firft that this piece is divided into feven parts. I. Of man's nature. II. Of the world. III. Of death. IV. Of purgatory. V. Of the day of judgment. VI. Of the torments of hell. VII. Of the joys of heaven.[4]

---

[1] Wharton, App. ad Cave, p. 75. *Sæcul. Wickley.*

[2] [Of the Black Death of 1348, no doubt.—F. The fact of not finding MSS. older than the fourteenth century would feem to fhow that Hampole compiled the *Pricke of Confcience* but a few years before his death (A.D. 1349).—*Morris.*]

[3] [*The Pricke of Confcience*, notwithftanding Warton's prediction to the contrary, has been edited by Richard Morris, 1863, 8vo., his text being chiefly taken from Cotton. MS. Galba, E. ix.; an imperfect copy of the poem in Canterbury cathedral library exhibits, I am informed by Mr. Furnivall, dialectic changes, as *ho* for *wha*, *to* for *till*, *fchal* for *fal*, &c. The enfuing extracts are from edit. Morris, pp. 11-12. In the *Archæologia*, vol. xix. pp. 314-335, 4to. 1821, is a long analyfis of Hampole's poem, by Mr. J. B. Yates, illuftrated by extracts; in which the writer advocates with very doubtful fuccefs the poetical talent of the recluse againft the opinion of Warton. But it is fomewhat remarkable, that previous to the publication of Mr. Yates's paper, a pamphlet of limited circulation (only fifty copies having been printed), written by W. J. Walter, appeared, 8vo. London, 1816, pp. 17, under the title of *An Account of a MS. of ancient Englifh Poetry, entitled Clavis Scientiæ, or Bretayne's Skyll-kay of Knawing, by John de Dageby, monk of Fountains Abbey.* This MS. in reality, is only one of the numerous copies exifting of Hampole's *Pricke of Confcience*, fomewhat altered and abbreviated, with fome lines added at the conclu-fion by the fcribe John de Dageby, whofe name appears in the colophon. Mr. Walter gives a copious analyfis of the work; and, like his fucceffor Mr. Yates, is inclined to place the author much higher in the fcale of poets than Warton's critique would juftify.—*Madden.* The MS. was fubfequently fold to the Britifh Mufeum.]

[4] Stimulus Confcientiæ *thys boke ys namyd.* MS. Afhmol. fol. No. 41. There is much tranfpofition in this copy. In MS. Digb. Bodl. 87, it is called *The Key of knowing.* Princ.

    "The mift of the fader admiti
    The wifdom of the fone al witti."

[Mr. Corfer's MS. adds an eighth part of the ftate of the world after doomfday; it

Here bygynnes the firſt part
That es of mans wrechednes.
Firſt whan God made al thyng of noght,
Of the fouleſt matere man he wroght
That was of erthe ; for twa ſkyls to halde ;
The tane es forthy that God walde
Of foul matere, mak man in deſpite
Of Lucifer that fel als tyte
Til helle, als he had ſynned thurgh pryde,
And of alle that with him fel that tyde ;
For thai ſuld have than the mare ſhenſhepe,
And the mare ſorow when thai tuk kepe,
That men of ſwa foul matere ſuld duelle
In that place fra whilk thai felle.
The ather ſkille es this to ſe ;
For man ſuld here the meker be
Ay, when he ſeſe and thynkes in thoght,
Of how foul mater he is wroght ;
For God, thurgh his gudnes and his myght,
Wold, that then that place in heven bright
Was made voyde thurgh the ſyn of pryde,
It war filled ogayne on ilka ſyde
Thurgh the vertu of mekenes,
That euen contrary til pride es ;
Than may na man thider come
Bot he that meke es, and boghſome ;
That proves the goſpelle that ſays us,
How God ſayd till his diſciples thus :

Niſi efficiamini ſicut parvulus, non intrabitis in regnum celorum.

Bot yhe, he ſayde, be als a childe,
That es to ſay, bathe meke and mylde,
Yhe ſal noght entre, be na way
Hevenryke that ſal laſt ay, &c.

In the Bodleian library I find three copies of the *Pricke of Con
ſcience* very different from that which I have juſt cited. In theſe
this poem is given to Robert Groſſeteſte, biſhop of Lincoln, above
mentioned.[1] With what probability, [we need not] inquire ; but I
haſten to give a ſpecimen. I will premiſe, that the language and
handwriting are of conſiderable antiquity, and that the lines are
here much longer. The poet is deſcribing the future rewards and
puniſhments of mankind :[1]

The goode ſoule ſchal have in his herynge
Gret joye in hevene and grete lykynge :

---

is the end of the fifth in edit. Morris, with additions.—F.   But all theſe texts are
decidedly very inferior to the MS. in the Northern dialect ſelected by Dr. Morris.]
 [1] Compare Tanner, *Bibl.* p. 375, col. 1, and p. 374, col. 1, notes.   MSS. Aſh.
52, pergamen. 4to.   Laud. K. 65, pergamen.   And G. 21.   And MSS. Digb. 14
[and 87.   The former begins :]

" The miſt of the fader of hevene
The wit of his ſon with his giftes ſevene."

[Other copies are in Royal MS. Br. Mus. 18 A v ; Harl. MS. 2261 ; Add. MS.
11,305. See MS. Aſhmol. 60 (Catalogue, p. 306, col. 1), and MSS. 41 and 52.—F.]

For hi ſchulleth yhere the aungeles ſong,
And with hem hi ſchulleth[1] ſynge ever among,
With delitable voys and ſwythe clere,
And alſo with that hi ſchullen have [there]
All other maner of ech a melodye,
Off well lykyng noyſe and menſtralſye,
And of al maner tenes[2] of muſike,
The whuche to mannes herte[3] migte like,
Withoute eni maner of travayle,
The whuche ſchal never ceſſe ne fayle :
And ſo ſchil[4] ſchal that noyſe bi, and ſo ſwete,
And ſo delitable to ſmale and to grete,
That al the melodye of this worlde heer
That ever was yhuryd ferre or neer
Were therto bote[5] as ſorwe[6] and care
To the bliſſe that is in hevene well zare.[7]

Of the contrarie of that bliſſe.

Wel grete ſorwe ſchal the ſynfolke[8] bytyde,
For he ſchullen yhere in ech a ſyde[9]
Well gret noyſe that the feondes[10] willen make,
As thei al the worlde ſcholde alto ſchake ;
And alle the men lyvynge that migte hit yhure,
Scholde here wit[11] looſe, and no lengere alyve dure.[12]
Thanne hi[13] ſchulleth for ſorwe here hondes wringe,
And ever weilaway hi ſchullethe be cryinge, &c.
The gode men ſchullethe have worſchipes grete,
And eche of them ſchal be yſet in a riche ſete,
And ther as kynges be ycrownid fayre,
And digte with riche perrie[14] and ſo yſetun[15] in a chayre,
And with ſtones of vertu and precioſue of choyſe,
As David [thus ſayth[16]] to god with a mylde voyſe,
     Poſuiſti, domine, ſuper caput eorum, &c.
"Lorde," he ſeyth, " on his heved thou ſetteſt wel arigt
A coronne of a pretious ſton richeliche ydigt."
[Ac[17]] ſo fayre a coronne nas never non yſene,
In this worlde on kynges hevede,[18] ne on quene :
For this coronne is the coronne of bliſſe,
And the ſton is joye whereof hi ſchilleth never miſſe, &c.
The ſynfolke ſchulleth, as I have afore ytold,
Ffele outrageous hete, and afterwards to muche colde ;
For now he ſchullethe freoſe, and now brenne,[19]
And ſo be ypyned that non ſchal other kenne,[20]
And alſo be ybyte with dragonnes felle and kene,
The whuche ſchulleth hem deſtrye outrigte and clene,
And with other vermyn and beſtes felle,
The whiche beothe nougt but fendes of helle, &c.

We have then this deſcription of the New Jeruſalem :

[¹ Not Hampole's verſion ; I cannot find this in edit. Morris. See it, ſlightly altered, in Add. MS. 11,305, leaf 119, *verſo.*]

² tunes.	³ beorte. W.	⁴ ſhrill.	⁵ but.
⁶ ſorrow.	⁷ prepared.	⁸ ſinners.	⁹ either ſide.
¹⁰ devils.	¹¹ ſenſes.	¹² remain.	¹³ they.
¹⁴ precious ſtones.	¹⁵ ſeated.	¹⁶ thy ſaid. W.	¹⁷ and. W.
¹⁸ Head.	¹⁹ This is the Hell of the monks, which Milton has adopted.		
²⁰ know.			

This citie is yſet on an hei hille,
That no ſynful man may therto tille :[1]
Th° whuche ich likne to beril clene,
[Ac²] ſo fayr berel may non be yſene.
Thulke hyl is nougt elles to underſtondynge
Bote holi thugt, and deſyr brennynge,
The whuche holi men hadde heer to that place,
Whiles hi hadde on eorthe here lyves ſpace ;
And I likne, as ymay ymagene in my thougt,
The walles of hevene, to walles that wer° ywrougt
Of all maner preciouſe ſtones yſet yſere,°
And yſemented with gold brigt and clere ;
Bot ſo brigt gold, ne non ſo clene,
Was in this worlde never yſene, &c.
The wardes of the cite of hevene brigt
I likne to wardes that wel were ydygt,
And clenly ywrougt and ſotely enteyled,
And on ſilver and gold clenly anamayled,[4] &c.
The torettes[5] of hevene grete and ſmale
I likne to the torrettes of clene criſtale, &c.

I am not, in the mean time, quite convinced that any MS. of the *Pricke of Conſcience* in Engliſh belongs to Hampole. That this piece is a tranſlation from the Latin appears from theſe verſes :

Therefore this boke is in Englis drawe
Of fele[6] matters that bene unknawe
To lewed men that are unkonande,[7]
That con no latyn undirſtonde.[8]

" In perfit living which paſſeth poyſie
Richard hermite contemplative of ſentence
Drough in Engliſhe, the Pricke of Conſcience."—*Bochas,* f. 217, b.

And this opinion is confirmed by the expreſs acknowledgment of the King's MS.

" Now have I firſte as I undertoke
Fulfilled the ſevene materes of this boke,
And oute of Latyn I have hem idrawe,
The whiche to ſom man is unknawe,
And namely to lewed men of Yngelonde
That konneth no thinge but Engliſhe undirſtonde.
And therfor this tretys oute drawe I wolde
In Engliſhe that men undirſtonde hit ſholde,
And prikke of conſcience is this tretys yhote, &c.
For the love of our Lord Jeſu Chriſt now
Praieth ſpecially for hym that hit oute drow,
And alſo for hym that this boke hath iwrite here,
Whether he be in water, other in londe ferre or nere."

Indeed it would be difficult to account for the exiſtence of two Engliſh verſions, eſſentially differing in metre and language ; though generally agreeing in matter, unleſs we aſſume a common Latin original. Which of theſe is Hampole's tranſlation, can only be decided by inſpecting a copy once in the poſſeſſion of Dr. Monro; and which Hampole " left to the ſociety of Friers-minors at York, after his and his brother's death." No manuſcript, which has fallen under the Editor's notice,

The Latin original in profe, entitled *Stimulus Confcientiæ,*[1] was moft probably written by Hampole : and it is not very likely that he fhould tranflate his own work. The author and tranflator were eafily confounded. As to the copy of the Englifh poem given to Bifhop Grofetefte, he could not be the tranflator, to fay nothing more, if Hampole wrote the Latin original. On the whole, whoever was the author of the two tranflations, at leaft we may pronounce with fome certainty, that they belong to the reign of Edward III.

makes mention of Hampole in the text; nor has he been able to difcover any fhadow of authority for attributing to this fainted bard, the pieces numbered from 6 to 16 in Mr. Ritfon's *Bibliographia Poetica.*—Price.]

[1] In the Cambridge MS. of Hampole's *Paraphrafe on the Lord's Prayer*, above mentioned, containing a prolix defcription of human virtues and vices, at the end this remark appears. " Explicit quidam tractatus fuper Pater nofter *fecundum* Ric. Hampole qui obiit A.D. MCCCLXXXIV." [But the true date of his death is in another place, viz. 1349.] MSS. More, 215, Princ.

> " Almighty God in trinite
> In whom is only perfonnes thre."

The *Paraphrafe on the Book of Job,* mentioned alfo before, feems to have exifted firft in Latin profe under the title of *Parvum Job.* The Englifh begins thus :

> " Lieff lord my foul thou fpare."

In Bibl. Bodl. MSS. Laud. F 77. 5, &c. &c. It is a paraphrafe of fome Excerpta from the book of Job. The *feven penitential Pfalms* begin thus :

> " To goddis worfchippe that dere us bougt."

MSS. Bodl. Digb. 18. Hampole's *Expofitio in Pfalterium* is not uncommon in Englifh. [Copies are in Corpus Chrifti College, Cambridge, and at Eton College.—F.] It has a preface in Englifh rhymes in fome copies, in praife of the author and his work. Pr. " This bleffyd boke that hire." MSS. Laud. F 14, &c. Hampole was a very popular writer. Moft of his many theological pieces feem to have been tranflated into Englifh foon after they appeared : and thofe pieces abound among our MSS. Two of his tracts were tranflated by Richard Mifyn, prior of the Carmelites at Lincoln, about the year 1435. The *Incendium Amoris* at the requeft of Margaret Hellingdon a reclufe. Princ. " To the afkynge of thi defire." And *De Emendatione Vitæ.* " Tarry thou not to oure." They are in the tranf-lator's own handwriting in the library of C.C.C. Oxon. MSS. 237. I find other ancient tranflations of both thefe pieces. Particularly, *The Pricke of Love after Richard Hampol treting of the three degrees of love.* MSS. Bodl. Arch. B. 65, f. 109. As a proof of the confufions and uncertainties attending the works of our author, I muft add, that we have a tranflation of his tract *De Emendatione* under this title : *The form of perfyt living, which holy Richard the hermit wrote to a reclufe named Margarete.* MS. Vernon. But Margarete is evidently the reclufe, at whofe requeft Richard Mifyn, many years after Hampole's death, tranflated the *Incendium Amoris.* Thefe obfervations, to which others might be added, are fuf-ficient to confirm the fufpicions infinuated in the text. Many of Hampole's Latin theological tracts were printed very early at Paris and Cologne.

[In 1866, Mr. Perry edited fome of his Englifh Profe Treatifes for the Early Englifh Text Society. See Mr. Perry's Preface.]

SECTION VIII.[1]

N this section we shall proceed to give some account of the poem which is commonly called the *Vision of Piers the Plowman*, with several extracts from the best edition. The remarks of our earlier antiquaries upon the subject are frequently misleading; and in the following sketch the reader's attention will often be most invited to those points on which preceding writers have gone most widely astray.

The title of the poem has been constantly misunderstood. In the MSS. it is *Dialogus de Petro Plowman*, and is divided into two sections; the former being *Visio Willelmi de Petro Plowman*, and the latter *Visio ejusdem* [or *Vita*] *de Dowel, Dobet, et Dobest*; from which it follows that the author's name was *William*, and that " Piers Plowman" is the subject of the poem. Yet it is quite usual, in nearly all text books, to speak of *Piers Plowman's Vision* as though Piers Plowman were the author's name! But this mistake is made even by Spenser, in his epilogue to the *Shepheard's Calendar*, where he alludes to Chaucer under the name of Tityrus, and next speaks of " the Pilgrim that the Ploughman playde awhyle." Let it be noted that the term " Piers Plowman's Vision" is sheer nonsense, because the words " *of* Piers the Plowman" mean " *concerning* Piers the Plowman," *of* not being here the sign of a possessive case.

This blunder is frequently doubled by confusing the " VISION" with an imitation of it by another author, which will be considered in the next section.

The name of the author of the VISION is not certainly known, but all accounts agree in giving him the name of LANGLAND, whilst numerous allusions in the poem concur with the Latin title in assigning to him the Christian name of WILLIAM. There are two notices of him, in handwriting of the fifteenth century. The one, discovered on the flyleaf of a MS. of the poem in Trinity College, Dublin, by Sir F. Madden, is as follows, " Memorandum, quod Stacy de Rokayle, pater *Willielmi de Langlond*, qui Stacius fuit generosus, et morabatur in Schipton vnder Whicwode [about 4 miles from Burford, co. Oxford] tenens domini le Spenser in comitatu Oxon. qui predictus Willielmus fecit librum qui vocatur Perys Ploughman." The other is on the flyleaf of a MS. (numbered cxxx) now in the possession of Lord Ashburnham, which says—" Robert or william langland made pers ploughman ;" beneath which is added, in the handwriting of John Bale—" Robert Langlande, natus in comitatu Salopie in villa Mortimers Clybery in the Clayland and within viij miles of Malvern hills, scripsit piers ploughman," &c.

[1 Communicated by the Rev. W. W. Skeat, whose text and remarks have been for the most part substituted for those of Warton and his earlier editors.]

It has commonly been affumed that we know very little more about the author than this; but the internal evidence of his poem really reveals much more, quite enough, in fact, to give us a clear conception of him.   But it is neceffary firft to give fome account of the poem itfelf, and to correct the common notion which affigns to it the date 1362, as if it were moft of it written all at once.

The poem affumes at leaft five fhapes in the various MSS., of which more than forty are ftill extant.   Two of thefe are due to errors of copyifts, but it is clear that three of thefe forms are due to the author himfelf, and that he rewrote his poem, not once only, but twice, and that rather long intervals intervened between the firft and fecond, and between the fecond and third, verfions.

(A). The *firft* verfion, which is by much the fhorteft, and written with great rapidity and vigour, confifts of a prologue and twelve Paffus.   It may be called the A-text, or the " Vernon " text, as the beft copy of it exifts in the Vernon MS. in the Bodleian library, and it has been publifhed by the Early Englifh Text Society, with the title—" The Vifion of William concerning *Piers* [*the*] *Plowman*, together with *Vita de Dowel, Dobet, et Dobeft, fecundum Wit et Refoun*, by William Langland, A. D. 1362."[1]   None of thefe MSS. contains the twelfth Paffus, except the Univerfity Coll. MS., which preferves only eighteen lines of it ; but there is one *complete* copy in the Bodleian library, viz. MS. Rawl. Poet. 137, in which the twelfth Paffus begins at fol. 40.   The date 1362 was fuggefted by Tyrwhitt, who obferved with great fagacity and juftice, that the " Southweftern wind on a Saturday at even," which the author refers to as a recent event, was certainly the terrible ftorm of Saturday, Jan. 15, 1361-2, which is noticed by many writers, and in particular, is thus recorded by Thorn, apud Decem Scriptores : " A. D. MCCCLXII. 15 die Januarii, circa horam *vefperarum*, ventus vehemens notus auftralis Africus tantâ rabie erupit," &c.[2]   Mention is made in the fame paffage of the poem (p. 52) of " thefe peftilences," *i. e.* the peftilences of 1348-1349, and 1361-1362.   This verfion confifts of about 2567 lines.

(B). Not forefeeing the popularity which his poem was deftined to enjoy, the author reforted to the not uncommon device of killing himfelf off, in the concluding lines of the earlieft verfion, where he fays :

> " Wille[3] wifte thurgh inwit[4] · thou woft wel the fothe,
> That this fpeche was fpedelich · and fped him wel fafte,
> And wroughthe that here is wryten[5] · and other werkes bothe

---

[1] [Edited from the " Vernon " MS., collated with MS. R. 3. 14 in the library of Trinity College, Cambridge, MS. Harl. 875 and 6041, the MS. in Univerfity College, Oxford, MS. Douce, 323, &c. : by the Rev. W. W. Skeat ; London, 1867.]

[2] [Cf. Walfingham, ed. H. T. Riley, vol. i. p. 296, Fabyan's Chronicle, ed. Ellis, p. 475, Hardyng's Chronicle, ed. Ellis, p. 330.]

[3] [*i. e.* William, the author himfelf.]   [4] [confcience.]

[5] [*i. e.* the Vifion of Do-wel ; the " other werkes " refer to the Vifion of Piers the Plowman, properly fo called.]

Of *peres the plowman* · and mechel puple[1] alſo ;
And whan this werk was wrought · ere wille[2] myghte aſpie,
Deth delt him a dent[3] · and drof him to the erthe,
And [he] is cloſed vnder clom[4] · criſt haue his ſoule !"

And ſo the matter reſted for nearly fifteen years. But the grief of
the whole nation at the death of the Black Prince, the diſquieting
political events of 1377, the laſt year of Edward III., the diſſatisfac-
tion of the commons with the conduct of the Duke of Lancaſter,
rouſed our poet, as it rouſed other men. Then it was that, taking his
text from Eccleſiaſticus, x. 16, *Væ terræ ubi rex puer eſt*, he compoſed
his famous verſion of the well-known fable of the rats wiſhing to bell
the cat, a fable which has never been elſewhere told ſo well or ſo
effectively. Then it was that, taking advantage of his now more extenſive acquaintance with Scripture, and his familiarity with the
daily ſcenes of London life, he rewrote and added to his poem till he
had trebled the extent of it, and multiplied the number of his Latin
quotations by ſeven. The additions are, moſt of them, exceedingly
good, and diſtinguiſhed by great freedom and originality of thought ;
indeed, we may ſay that, upon the whole, the " B-text " is the beſt
of the three, and the beſt ſuited for giving us a fair idea of the
author's peculiar powers. The complete text compriſes the two
Viſions, viz. of Piers Plowman, and of Do-wel, Do-bet, and Dobeſt ; the former conſiſting of a Prologue and ſeven Paſſus, and the
latter of three Prologues and ten Paſſus, viz. a Prologue and ſix
Paſſus of Do-wel, a Prologue and three Paſſus of Do-bet, and a Prologue and 1 Paſſus of Do-beſt. But in many (perhaps all) of the
MSS. the diſtinctions between the component parts are not much
regarded, and in ſome there is no mention of Do-wel, Do-bet, and
Do-beſt whatever, but the whole is called *Liber* (or *Dialogus*) *de petro
plowman*, and made to conſiſt of a Prologue and *twenty* Paſſus. Not
to go into further details, it is neceſſary to add that there are two
perfect MSS. of it which are of ſpecial excellence, and which do not
greatly vary from each other ; from one of theſe, MS. Trin. Coll.
Camb. B. 15, 17, Mr. Wright printed his well-known and convenient edition of the whole poem, and the other, MS. Laud 581,
forms the baſis of the text publiſhed by the Early Engliſh Text Society in 1869. Other good MSS. of this verſion are Rawl. Poet. 38
(which contains ſome extra lines), MS. Dd. 1. 17, in the Cambridge
Univerſity library, MS. 79 in Oriel College, Oxford, &c.

The B-text was alſo printed by Robert Crowley, in 1550, from a
very good MS. Indeed, Crowley printed three impreſſions of it in
the ſame year, the firſt and ſcarceſt being the moſt correct, and the
third (called " ſecond " impreſſion on the title-page) being the worſt.
Crowley's edition was very incorrectly reprinted by Owen Rogers
in 1561.

The third verſion was probably not compoſed till 1380 or even
later, or, ſtill more probably, it contains additions and reviſions made

---

¹ [much people.]   ² [*i. e.* William, the author himſelf.]
³ [dint, blow.]   ⁴ [loam, clay.]

at various periods later than 1378. Throughout thefe the working of the fame mind is clearly difcernible, but there is a tendency to diffufenefs and to a love for theological fubtleties. It is of ftill greater length, containing a Prologue and nine Paffus of *Piers the Plowman*, a Prologue and fix Paffus of *Do-wel*, a Prologue and three Paffus of *Do-bet*, and a Prologue and one Paffus of *Do-beft*; or, according to the fhorter notation, a Prologue and twenty-two Paffus. It may be remarked that the fhort poem of *Do-beft* ftands almoft exactly the fame in both the B and C verfions.

An edition of this text was printed (very incorrectly) by Dr. Whitaker, in 1813, from a MS. now belonging to Sir Thomas Phillipps.[1]

We may fafely date the A-text about A.D. 1362, the B-text about A.D. 1377, and the C-text about A.D. 1380. To affume the date 1362 for all three is to introduce unneceffary confufion.

Befides this extraordinary work, with its three varying editions, I hold that we are indebted to the fame author for a remarkable poem on the *Depofition of Richard II.* of courfe written in 1399, and which has been twice printed by Mr. Wright, the more convenient edition being that publifhed for the Camden Society in 1838. This is not the place to difcufs a queftion of fome difficulty, and concerning which a careful reader may form an opinion for himfelf, and can come, I think, to no other conclufion. It is true that Mr. Wright has expreffed a different opinion, but he was mifled by a marginal note in his MS. to which he attached fome importance.[2]

Returning to the author, we may now piece together the following account of him, which is probably true, and, at any rate, refts chiefly upon his own ftatements. At the time of writing the B-text of *Do-wel*, he was forty-five years of age, and he was therefore born

---

[1] [For further information concerning the MSS. fee the prefaces to the Early Englifh Text Society's edition, and a pamphlet alfo publifhed by the fame fociety, with the title—"Parallel Extracts from twenty-nine MSS. of Piers Plowman," &c.: ed. Skeat, 1866.]

For general remarks upon the poem, fee the fame prefaces; Mr. Wright's preface to his edition of 1842, reprinted in 1856; Profeffor Morley's *Englifh Writers*, vol. i.: Marfh's *Lectures on the Origin and Hiftory of the Englifh Language*, 8vo., 1862, p. 296, &c.; and a fine paffage in Dean Milman's *Hiftory of Latin Chriftianity*, vol. vi. p. 536, ed. 1855. Refpecting Whitaker's edit. 1813, to extracts from which the former editors of Warton very ufelefsly, as the prefent writer thinks, devoted feveral pages, Mr. Wright has obferved: "Dr. Whittaker was not well qualified for this undertaking; he alfo laboured under many difadvantages; he had accefs to only three manufcripts, and thofe not very good ones; and he has not chofen the beft text even of thefe. Unlefs he had fome reafon to believe that the book was originally written in a particular dialect, he ought to have given a preference to that among the oldeft manufcripts, which prefents the pureft language."]

[2] [See his edition (Camd. Soc.) p. vi., where "liber hic" fhould have been printed "liber homo," an error which vitiates the whole argument. The unique copy of this poem is found in MS. Ll. 4. 14. in the Cambridge Univerfity library, where it follows a copy of *Piers the Plowman*, and is in the fame handwriting with it, though that of courfe proves but little. I argue from internal evidence, of which I can adduce a great deal.]

about A.D. 1332, probably at Cleobury Mortimer. His father and his friends put him to fchool (poffibly in the monaftery at Great Malvern), made a *clerk* or fcholar of him, and taught him what holy writ meant. In 1362, at the age of about thirty, he wrote the A-text of the poem, without any thought of continuing or enlarging it. In this he refers to Edward III. and his fon the Black Prince, to the murder of Edward II., to the great peftilences of 1348 and 1361, to the treaty of Bretigny in 1360, and Edward's wars in Normandy, and alfo moft particularly to the great ftorm of wind which took place on Saturday evening, Jan. 15th, 1361-2.[1] This verfion of the poem he defcribes as having been partly compofed in May, whilft wandering on Malvern Hills, which are thrice mentioned in the part rightly called *Piers the Plowman*. In the introduction or prologue to *Do-wel*, he defcribes himfelf as wandering about all the fummer till he met with two Minorite Friars, with whom he dif-courfed concerning *Do-wel*. It was probably not long after this that he went to refide in London, with which he already had fome acquaintance; there he lived in Cornhill, with his wife Kitte and his daughter Calote, for many long years.[2] In 1377, he began to expand his poem into the B-text, wherein he alludes to the acceffion of Richard II. in the words—"ʒif I regne any while,"[3] and alfo explicitly to the dearth in the dry month of April, 1370, when Chichefter was mayor; a dearth due to the exceffive rains in the autumn of 1369. Chichefter was elected in 1369 (probably in October) and was ftill mayor in 1370. In Riley's *Memorials of London*, p. 344, he is mentioned as being mayor in that very month of April in that very year in the words—"Afterwards, on the 25th day of April in the year above-mentioned, it was agreed by John de Chicheftre, Mayor," &c. It is important to infift upon this, becaufe the MS. followed by Mr. Wright, in company with many inferior ones, has a corrupt reading which turns the words—"A þoufand and thre hondreth · tweis *thretty* and ten" into "twice *twenty* and ten," occafioning a great difficulty, and mifleading many modern writers and readers, fince the fame miftake occurs in Crowley's edition. Fortunately, the Laud MS. 581 and MS. Rawl. Poet. 38 fet us right here, and all difficulty now vanifhes; for it is eafily afcertained that Chichefter was mayor in 1369-70, and at no other time, having never been re-elected. Stow and other old writers have the right date. In the C-text, written at fome time after 1378, the poet reprefents himfelf as ftill in London, and in the commencement of Paffus v. (alfo called Paffus vi, as in Whitaker) gives us feveral particulars concerning himfelf, wherein he alludes to his own tall-nefs, faying that he is too "long" to ftoop low, and he has alfo fome remarks concerning the fons of freemen which imply that he

---

[1] [That is, the year 1362, which was formerly called 1361, when the year was fuppofed not to begin till March. See, for thefe allufions, B-text, Paff. iii. 186, 188; iv. 45; and v. 14.]

[2] [C-Text, Paff. v.] [3] [B. iv. 177.]

was himſelf the ſon of a franklin or freeman, and born in lawful
wedlock. He wore the clerical tonſure, probably as having taken
minor orders, and earned a precarious living by ſinging the *placebo*,
dirige, and "ſeven pſalms" for the good of men's ſouls; for, ever
ſince his friends died who had firſt put him to ſchool, he had found
no kind of life that pleaſed him except to be in "theſe long clothes,"
and by help of ſuch (clerical) labour as he had been bred up to he
contrived not only to live "*in* London, but *upon* London" alſo.
The ſuppoſition that he was married (as he ſays he was) may, perhaps explain why he never roſe in the church. He has many alluſions to his extreme poverty. Laſtly, in the depoſition of Richard
II. he deſcribes himſelf as being in Briſtol in the year 1399, when
he wrote his laſt poem. This poem is but ſhort, and in the only
MS. wherein it exiſts, terminates abruptly in the middle of a page,
and it is quite poſſible that it was never finiſhed. This is the laſt
trace of him, and he was then probably about ſixty-ſeven years of
age, ſo that he may not have long ſurvived the acceſſion of Henry
IV. In perſonal appearance, he was ſo tall that he obtained the
nickname of "Longe Wille," as he tells us in the line :

"I have lyued in londe," quod I · "my name is Longe wille."[1]

This nickname may be paralleled from Mr. Riley's *Memorials of
London*, p. 457, where we read of John Edward, "otherwiſe called
Longe Jack," under the date 1382. In Paſſus xv (B-text) he ſays
that he was loath to reverence lords or ladies, or perſons dreſſed in
fur, or wearing ſilver ornaments; he never would ſay "God ſave
you" to ſerjeants whom he met, for all of which proud behaviour,
then very uncommon, people looked upon him as a fool. It requires
no great ſtretch of imagination to picture to ourſelves the tall gaunt
figure of Long Will in his long robes and with his ſhaven head,
ſtriding along Cornhill, ſaluting no man by the way, minutely obſer-
vant of the gay dreſſes to which he paid no outward reverence. It
ought alſo to be obſerved how very frequent are his alluſions to
lawyers, to the law-courts at Weſtminſter, and to legal proceſſes.
He has a mock-charter, beginning with the ordinary formula *Sciant
præſentes et futuri*, a form of making a will, and in one paſſage (B-
text, Paſs. xi.) he ſpeaks with ſuch ſcorn of a man who draws up a
charter badly, who interlines it, or leaves out ſentences, or puts falſe
Latin in it, that I think we may fairly ſuppoſe him to have been
converſant with the writing out of legal documents, and to have
eked out his ſubſiſtence by the ſmall ſums received for doing ſo.
The various texts are ſo conſiſtent, that we may well ſuppoſe him
to have been his own ſcribe in the firſt inſtance. Indeed, there are
ſome reaſons for ſuppoſing the MS. *Laud Miſc.* 581 to be an
autograph copy.

Wood confuſes Langland with John Maluerne, a continuation of

---

[1] [See Wright's edition, p. 304, where "quod *I*" is printed "quod *he*," an error
which a collation of many MSS. has removed. It is very curious that the words
londe, *longe*, and *wille* in this line form *Wille Longelonde* when read backwards.]

the *Polychronicon,* who is faid to have been a fellow of Oriel, and was certainly a prior of the Benedictine monaftery at Worcefter.

The poem itfelf contains a feries of diftinct vifions, which the author imagines himfelf to have feen, while he was fleeping, after a long ramble on Malverne-hills in Worcefterfhire. It is a fatire on the vices of almoft every profeffion; but particularly on the corruptions of the clergy, and the abfurdities of fuperftition. Thefe are ridiculed with much humour and fpirit, couched under a ftrong vein of allegorical invention.

But it is untrue that Langland adopts the ftyle of the Anglo-Saxon poets, as has been well fhown by Mr. Marfh who, in the paffage already referred to, thus refutes this notion:

" The Vifion of the Ploughman furnifhes abundant evidence of the familiarity of its author with the Latin Scriptures, the writings of the fathers, and the commentaries of Romifh expofitors, but exhibits very few traces of a knowledge of romance literature. Still the proportion of Norman-French words, or at leaft of words which, though of Latin origin, are French in form, is quite as great as in the works of Chaucer.[1] The familiar ufe of this mixed vocabulary, in a poem evidently intended for the popular ear, and compofed by a writer who gives no other evidence of an acquaintance with the literature of France, would, were other proof wanting, tend ftrongly to confirm the opinion I have before advanced, that a large infufion of French words had been not merely introduced into the literature, but incorporated into the common language of England; and that only a very fmall proportion of thofe employed by the poets were firft introduced by them.

" The poem, if not altogether original in conception, is abundantly fo in treatment. The fpirit it breathes, its imagery, the turn of thought, the ftyle of illuftration and argument it employs, are *as remote as poffible from the tone of Anglo-Saxon poetry,* but exhibit the characteriftic moral and mental traits of the Englifhman as clearly and unequivocally as the moft national portions of the works of Chaucer or of any other native writer."

The whole poem is in alliterative verfe, not becaufe Langland wifhed here again to " imitate the Anglo-Saxon ftyle," but becaufe that rhythm was more thoroughly Englifh than any other kind, and familiar to moft Englifhmen, efpecially in the northern and weftern parts. Neither did the neceffity of finding fimilar initial letters cramp his expreffion, as Warton intimated; for it is clear that Langland was often carelefs about his alliteration, and wrote with great eafe, facrificing found to fenfe in every cafe of perplexity. It ought further to be noticed that the poem is fomething more than a fatire; the author, dreaming like another Bunyan, fees his ideal type of excellence in the fhape of Piers the Ploughman, and his chief

---

[1] [The Prologue to Piers the Plowman and the firft 420 lines of Chaucer's Prologue alike contain 88 per cent. of Anglo-Saxon words. See Marfh, *Lectures on English;* 1st Series, p. 124.]

aim is to develcp the whole hiftory of the religious life of man, fo that Piers anfwers in fome fenfe to Bunyan's "Chriftian," though he is ftill more like "Greatheart." In fact, Piers is fpoken of under feveral afpects. At one time he is the honeft and utterly truthful labourer, whofe ftrong common fenfe can give good advice to his betters; at another, he is identified with the human nature of Chrift; and again, he reprefents the whole Chriftian church in its primitive and beft condition. At all times he is the imperfonation of the fpiritual part of human nature which ever wars againft evil, but which can never wholly triumph in this world. Unlefs this be kept in view, the poem indeed feems wanting in unity.

The fatire is conducted by the agency of feveral allegorical perfonages, fuch as Avarice, Bribery, Simony, Theology, Confcience, &c. There is much imagination in the following picture, which is intended to reprefent human life and its various occupations :

> Thanne gan I to meten · a merueiloufe fweuene,[1]
> That I was in a wildernefle · wift I neuer where;
> As I bihelde in-to þe eft · an hiegh to þe fonne,
> I feigh a toure on a toft · trielich ymaked;
> A depe dale binethe · a dongeon þere-Inne,
> With depe dyches & derke · and dredful of fight.
> A faire felde ful of folke · fonde I there bytwene,
> Of alle maner of men · þe mene and þe riche,
> Worchyng and wandryng · as þe worlde afketh.
> Some putten hem to þe plow · pleyed ful felde,
> In fettyng and in fowyng · fwonken ful harde,
> And wonnen that waftours · with glotonye deftruyeth.
> And fome putten hem to pruyde, &c.

The following extracts from Paffus viii-x. (Text B.) are not only ftriking fpecimens of our author's allegorical fatire, but contain much fenfe and obfervation of life, with fome ftrokes of poetry :

> Thus yrobed in ruffet · I romed aboute
> Al a fomer fefou*n* · for to feke dowel,[2]
> And frayned[3] ful oft · of folke þat I mette,
> If ani wiȝte wifte · where dowel was at Inne,[4]
> And what man he miȝte be · of many man I axed.
> ¶ Was neuere wiȝte, as I went · þat me wifle couthe[5]
> Where þis lede lenged[6] · laffe ne more;
> ¶ Tyl it bifel on a fryday · two freres I mette,
> Maiftres of þe Menoures[7] · men of grete witte.
> I hailfed hem hendely[8] · as I hadde lerned,
> And preyed hem *par* charitee · ar þei paffed forther,
> If þei knewe any contre · or coftes, as þei went,
> Where þat dowel dwelleth · doth me to wytene.[9]
> ¶ For þei ben men on þis molde · þat mofte wyde walken,
> And knowen contrees, and courtes · and many kynnes places,[10]
> Bothe prynces paleyfes · and pore mennes cotes,
> And do-wel and do-yuel · where þei dwelle bothe.
> ¶ "Amonges vs," quod þe Menours · "þat man is dwellyng*e*,
> And euere hath, as I hope · and euere fhal here-after."

---

[1] B-text; Prol. ll. 11-22 (ed. Skeat).
[2] [Do-well.]   [3] [inquired.]   [4] [lived.]   [5] [could inform me.]
[6] [lingered, dwelt.]   [7] [Friars Minors.]   [8] [faluted them civilly.]
[9] [know.]   [10] [Places of many a kind; *i. e.* many forts of places.]

¶ " Contra," quod I as a clerke · and comſed to diſputen,
And ſeide hem ſothli, "*ſepcies · in die cadit iuſtus;*
Seuene ſythes,[1] ſeith þe boke · ſynneth þe riȝtful.
And who-ſo ſynneth," I ſeyde · " doth yuel, as me þinketh,
And dowel and do-yuel · mow nouȝt dwelle togideres.
Erȝo, he nys nauȝt alway · amonge ȝow freres;
He is otherwhile ellis where · to wiſſe þe peple."
¶ " I ſhal ſey þe, my ſone " · ſeide þe frere þanne,
" How ſeuene ſithes þe ſad man[2] · on þe day ſynneth;
By a forbiſene,"[3] quod þe frere · " I ſhal þe faire ſhewe.
¶ Lat Brynge a man in a bote · amydde a brode water,
þe wynde and þe water · and the bote waggynge
Maketh þe man many a tyme · to falle and to ſtonde;
For ſtonde he neuere ſo ſtyf · he ſtombleth ȝif he moeue;
Ac ȝit is he ſauf and ſounde · and ſo hym bihoueth,
For ȝif he ne ariſe þe rather · and rauȝte to þe ſtiere;
þe wynde wolde, wyth þe water · þe bote ouerthrowe;
And þanne were his lyf loſte · þourgh laccheſſe[4] of hym-ſelf.
¶ And þus it falleth," quod þe frere · " bi folke here on erthe;
þe water is likned to þe worlde · þat wanyeth and wexeth,
þe godis of þis grounde aren like · to þe grete wawes,
þat as wyndes and wederes · walweth aboute.
þe bote is likned to owre body · þat brutel is of kynde,
þat þorugh þe fende and þe fleſhe · and þe frele worlde
Synneth þe ſadman · a day, ſeuene ſythes.
¶ Ac dedly ſynne doth he nouȝt · for dowel hym kepith,
And þat is charite þe champioun · chief help aȝein ſynne;
For he ſtrengtheth man to ſtonde · and ſtereth mannes ſoule,
And þowgh þi body bow · as bote doth in þe water,
Ay is þi ſoule ſauf · but if þi-ſelf wole
Do a dedly ſynne · and drenche ſo þi ſoule;
God wole ſuffre wel þi ſleuthe · ȝif þi-ſelf lyketh.
For he ȝaf þe to ȝeresȝyue · to ȝeme wel þi-ſelue,
And þat is witte and fre wille · to euery wyȝte a porcioun,
To fleghyng foules · to fiſſches & to beſtes.
Ac man hath moſte þerof · and moſte is to blame,
But if he worche wel þer-with · as dowel hym techeth."
¶ " I haue no kyn᷈ᷤe knowyng," quod I · " to conceyue alle ȝowre wordes,
Ac if I may lyue and loke · I ſhal go lerne bettere."
" I bikenne þe cryſt, quod he · þat on þe croſſe deyde."
And I ſeyde, " þe ſame · ſaue ȝow fro myſchaunce,
And ȝiue ȝow grace on þis grounde · good men to worthe."
¶ And þus I went wide-where · walkyng myne one,
By a wilde wilderneſſe · and bi a wode-ſyde.
Bliſſe of þo briddes · abyde me made,
And vnder a lynde[5] vppon a launde · lened I a ſtounde,[6]
To lythe[7] þe layes · þe louely foules made.
Murthe of her mouthes · made me þere to ſlepe;
þe merueilloufeſt meteles · mette me[8] þanne
þat euer dremed wyȝte · in worlde, as I wene.
¶ A moche man, as me þouȝte · and lyke to my-ſelue
Come and called me · by my kynde[9] name.
" What artow," quod I þo · " þat þou my name knoweſt?"
" þat þou woſt wel," quod he · " and no wyȝte bettere."

---

[1] [times.]　　　[2] [ſober, good man.]　　　[3] [ſimilitude, example.]
[4] [lazineſs.]　　　[5] [lime-tree.]　　　[6] [a while.]
[7] [liſten to.]　　　[8] [I dreamed.]
[9] [own; *i. e.* Chriſtian name of " Will."]

¶ " Wote I what þow art ?" · " þought," ſeyde he þanne,
" I haue ſuwed¹ þe þis ſeuene ȝere · ſey þow me no rather ? "
¶ " Art þow thought ?" quod I þo · " þow coutheſt me wiſſe
Where þat dowel dwelleth · and do me þat to knowe ?"
¶ " Dowel and dobet · and dobeſt þe thridde," quod he,
" Aren three faire vertues · and beth nauȝte fer to fynde.
Who-ſo is trewe of his tonge · and of his two handes,
And þorugh his laboure or þorugh his londe · his lyflode wynneth,²
And is truſti of his tailende³ · taketh but his owne,
And is nouȝt dronkenlew⁴ ne dedeignous · dowel hym folweth.
Dobet doth ryȝt þus · ac he doth moche more ;
He is as low as a lombe · and loueliche of ſpeche,
And helpeth alle men · after þat hem nedeth ;
þe bagges and þe bigurdeles · he hath to-broken⁵ hem alle,
þhat þe Erl auarous · helde, and his heires ;
And þus with Mammonaes moneie · he hath made hym frendes,
And is ronne in-to Religioun · and hath rendred⁶ þe bible,
And precheth to the poeple · ſeynt Poules wordes,
      Libenter ſuffertis inſipientes, cum ſitis ipſi ſapientes,
' And ſuffreth þe vnwiſe · with ȝow for to libbe,
And with gladde wille doth hem gode · for ſo god ȝow hoteth.'
¶ Dobeſt is aboue bothe · and bereth a biſſchopes croſſe,
Is hoked on þat one ende · to halie⁷ men fro helle.
A pyke is on þat potente⁸ · to pulte adown þe wikked,
þat wayten any wikkedneſſe · dowel to tene.
And dowel and dobet · amonges hem ordeigned
To croune one to be kynge · to reule hem bothe ;
þat ȝif dowel or dobet · did aȝein dobeſt,
þanne ſhal þe kynge come · and caſten hem in yrens,
And but if dobeſt bede for hem · þei to be þere for euere.
¶ Thus dowel and dobet · and dobeſt þe thridde,
Crouned one to be kynge · to kepen hem alle,
And to reule þe Reume · bi her⁹ thre wittes,
And none other-wiſe · but as þei thre aſſented."
¶ I thonked thouȝt þo · þat he me þus tauȝte ;
" Ac ȝete ſauoureth me nouȝt þi ſeggyng · I coueite to lerne
How dowel, dobet, and dobeſt · don amonges þe peple."
¶ " But witte conne wiſſe þe," quod þouȝt · where þo¹⁰ thre dwelle ;
Ellis wote I none þat can · þat now is alyue."
¶ þouȝte and I thus · thre days we ȝeden,¹¹
Diſputyng vppon dowel · day after other,
And ar we were ywar · with witte gan we mete.
He was longe and lene · liche to none other,
Was no pruyde on his apparaille · ne pouerte noyther,
Sadde of his ſemblaunt · and of ſoft chiere.
I dorſte meue no matere · to make hym to iangle,
But as I bad þouȝt þo · be mene bitwene,
And put forth ſomme purpos · to prouen his wittes,
What was dowel fro dobet · and dobeſt fram hem bothe.
¶ þanne þouȝt in þat tyme · ſeide þiſe wordes,
" Where dowel, dobet · and dobeſt ben in londe,
Here is wille wolde ywyte · ȝif witte couthe teche hym,
And whether he be man or [no] man · þis man fayne wolde aſpye,
And worchen as þei thre wolde · þis is his entente."

---

¹ [followed.]   ² [earns.]
³ [The Oriel MS. has *tayling*, i.e. dealing, reckoning.]   ⁴ [drunken.]
⁵ [broken in pieces.]   ⁶ [tranſlated.]   ⁷ [hale, draw.]
⁸ [ſtaff.]   ⁹ [their.]   ¹⁰ [thoſe.]
¹¹ [went, travelled.]

PASSUS IX. (B-TEXT).

" Sire dowel dwelleth," q*uod* witte · " nou3t a day hennes,
In a caftel þat kynde[1] made · of foure kynnes þinges;
Of erthe and eyre is it made · medled togideres,
With wynde and with water · witterly[2] enioyned.
Kynde hath clofed þere-Inne · craftily with-alle,
A lemman[3] þat he loueth · like to hym-felue,
Anima fhe hatte · ac enuye hir hateth,
A proude pryker of Fraunce · *prynceps huius mundi*,
And wolde winne hir awey · with wyles, and he my3te.
¶ Ac kynde knoweth þis wel · and kepeth hir þe bettere,
And hath do hir with fire dowel · is duke of þis marches.
Dobet is hir damoifele · fire doweles dou3ter,
To ferue this lady lelly[4] · bothe late and rathe.[5]
Dobeft is aboue bothe · a biflchopes pere;
Þat he bit, mote be do[6] · he reuleth hem alle;
Anima þat lady · is ladde bi his lerynge.
¶ Ac þe conftable of þat caftel · þat kepeth al þe wacche,
Is a wys kni3te with-al · fire Inwitte he hatte,
And hath fyue feyre fones · bi his firft wyf;
Sire fewel and faywel · and herewel þe hende,
Sire worche-wel-wyth-þine-hande · a wi3te man of ftrengthe,
And fire godfrey gowel · gret lordes for fothe.
Þife fyue ben fette · to faue þis lady *anima*,
Tyl kynde come or fende · to faue hir for euere."
¶ " What kynnes thyng is kynde," q*uod* I · " canftow me telle?"
¶ " Kynde," q*uod* witte, " is a creatour · of alle kynnes þinges;
Fader and fourmo*ur* · of al þat euere was maked;
And þat is þe gret god · þat gynnynge had neuere,
Lorde of lyf and of ly3te · of lyffe and of peyne.
Angeles and al þing · aren at his wille.
Ac man is hym mofte lyke · of marke[7] and of fchafte;
For þorugh þe worde þat he fpake · wexen forth beftes,
       Dixit, & faƐa funt;
¶ And made man likkeft · to hym-felf one,
And Eue of his ribbe-bon · with-outen eny mene.
For he was fynguler hym-felf · and feye *faciamus,*
As who feith, ' more mote here-to · þan my worde one;
My my3te mote helpe · now with my fpeche.'
Ri3te as a lorde fholde make *lettres* · and hym lakked p*ar*chemyn,
Þough he couth write neuere fo wel · 3if he had no penne,
Þe *lettre*[s] for al þe lordfhip · I leue were neuere ymaked.
¶ And fo it femeth bi hym · as þe bible telleth,
       Þere he feyde, *dixit, & faƐa funt;*
He mofte worche with his worde · and his witte fhewe.
And in þis manere was man made · þorugh my3te of god almi3ti,
With his worde and werkemanfchip · and with lyf to lafte.
And þus god gaf hym a gooft[8] · of þe godhed of heuene,
And of his grete grace · graunted hym bliffe,
And þat is lyf þat ay fhal laft · to al his lynage after.
And þat is þe caftel þat kynde made · *caro* it hatte,
And is as moche to mene · as man with a foule;
And þat he wrou3t with werke · and with worde bothe,
Þorugh my3te of þe maiefte · man was ymaked.

---

[1] [nature.]   [2] [verily, truly.]   [3] [lover.]
[4] [loyally.]   [5] [early.]   [6] [What he bids, muft be done.]
[7] [form, fafhion.]   [8] [fpirit.]

¶ Inwit and alle wittes · clofed ben þer-inne,
For loue of þe lady *anima* · þat lyf is ynempned ;[1]
Ouer al in mannes body · he walketh and wandreth,
Ac in þe herte is hir home · and hir mofte[2] refte.
Ac Inwitte is in þe hed · and to the herte he loketh,
What *anima* is lief or loth[3] · he lat[4] hir at his wille ;
For after þe grace of god · þe grettest is Inwitte.

*   *   *   *   *   *   *

PASSUS X. (B-TEXT.)

Thanne hadde witte a wyf · was hote dame ftudye,
Þat lene was of lere · and of liche bothe.
She was wonderly wroth · þat witte me þus tauȝte,
And al ftarynge dame ftudye · fternelich feyde,
" Wel artow wyfe," quod fhe to witte · " any wyfdomes to telle
To flatereres or to folis · þat frantyk ben of wittes!"
And blamed hym and banned hym · and badde hym be ftylle,
With fuche wife wordes · to wiffen any fottes ;
And feyde, " *noli mittere*, man · margerye perlis
Amanges hogges, þat han · hawes at wille.
þei don but dryuele þer-on · draffe[5] were hem leuere[6]
þan al þe *precious* perre · þat in paradys wexeth.[7]
I fey it bi fuche," quod fhe · " þat fheweth bi her werkes,
Þat hem were leuer[6] londe · and lordfhip on erthe,
Or ricchefle or rentis · and refte at her wille,
Þan alle þe fothe fawes · þat falamon feyde euere.
¶ Wifdome and witte now · is nouȝt worth a carfe,[8]
But if it be carded with coueytife[9] · as clotheres kemben here wolle.
Who-fo can contreue deceytes · an confpire wronges,
And lede forth a loue-day[10] · to latte with treuthe ;
He þat fuche craftes can · to confeille is clepid ;
þei lede lordes with lefynges · and bilyeth treuthe.
¶ Iob þe gentel · in his geftes witneffeth,
Þat wikked men, þei welden · þe welthe of þis worlde,
And þat þei ben lordes of eche a londe · þat oute of lawe libbeth ;
    Quare impij viuunt ? bene eft omnibus, qui preuaricantur & inique
        agunt ?
¶ Þe fauter feyth þe fame · bi fuche þat don ille,
    Ecce ipfi peccatores habundantes ; in feculo optinuerunt diuicias.
' Lo !' feith holy letterrure · ' whiche lordes beth þis fhrewes !'
þilke þat god mofte gyueth · lefte good þei deleth,
And mofte vnkynde to þe comune · þat mofte catel weldeth ;[11]
    Que perfecifti, deftruxerunt ; iuftus autem quid fecit !
Harlotes for her harlotrye · may haue of her godis,
And iaperes and iogeloures[12] · and iangelers of geftes.
¶ Ac he þat hath holy writte · ay in his mouth,
And can telle of Tobye · and of þe twelue apoftles,
Or *prechen* of þe penaunce þat pilat wrouȝt
To Ihefu þe gentil · þat Iewes to-drowe :—
Litel is he loued · þat fuche a leffoun fcheweth,
Or daunted or drawe forth · I do it on god hym-felf !

---

[1] [named.]   [2] [greateft, chief.]   [3] [unwilling.]   [4] [leadeth.]
[5] [dregs, refufe ; ufed by Chaucer.]
[6] [dearer to them ; *i. e.* they would rather have.]   [7] [grows.]
[8] [Some MSS. have *kerfe*, i. e. a water-crefs.]   [9] [covetoufnefs.]
[10] [A day for the amicable fettlement of differences was called a *love-day*.]
[11] [wields ; *i. e.* poffeffes.]   [12] [jugglers.]

¶ But þo[1] þat feynen hem folis · and with faityng[2] libbeth,
Aȝein þe lawe of owre lorde · and lyen on hem-selue,
Spitten and spewen · and speke foule wordes,
Drynken and dryuelen · and do men for to gape,
Lickne men and lye on hem · þat leneth hem no ȝiftes,
þei conne[3] namore mynſtralcye · ne muſyke, men to glade,
Than Munde þe mylnere · of *multa fecit deus!*
Ne were here vyle harlotrye · haue god my treuthe,
Shulde neuere Kyng ne kniȝt · ne chanoun of ſeynt Poules
Ȝyue hem to her ȝereſȝiue · þe ȝifte of a grote !
¶ Ac murthe and mynſtralcye · amonges men is nouthe
Leccherye, loſengerye,[4] · and loſeles tales ;
Glotonye and grete othes · þis murthe þei louieth.
¶ Ac if þei carpen[5] of cryſt · þis clerkis and þis lewed,
Atte mete in her murthes · whan mynſtralles ben ſtille,
þanne telleth þei of þe trinite · a tale other tweyne,
And bringen forth a balled reſoun · and taken Bernard[6] to witneſſe,
And putten forth a preſumpſioun · to preue þe ſothe.
þus þei dryuele at her deyſe[7] · þe deite to knowe,
And gnawen god with þe gorge[8] · whan her gutte is fulle.
¶ Ac þe careful[9] may crye · and carpen atte ȝate,
Bothe afyngred[10] and a-thurſt · and for chele[11] quake ;
Is none to nymen hym nere · his noye[12] to amende,
But hoen on hym as an hounde · and hoten hym go þennes.
Litel loueth he þat lorde · þat lent hym al þat bliſſe,
þat þus parteth with þe pore · a parcel whan hym nedeth.
Ne were mercy in mene men · more þan in riche,
Mendinantȝ meteles[13] · miȝte go to bedde.
God is moche in þe gorge · of þiſe grete mayſtres,
Ac amonges mene men · his mercy and his werkis ;
And ſo ſeith þe ſauter · I haue yſeye it ofte,

    Ecce audiuimus eam in effrata, inuenimus eam in campis
    ſilue.

Clerkes and other kynnes men · carpen of god faſte,
And haue hym moche in þe mouthe · ac mene men in herte.
¶ Freres and faitoures · han founde ſuche queſtiouns
To pleſe with proude men · ſithen þe peſtilence tyme,
And prechen at ſeint poules · for pure enuye of clerkis,
þat folke is nouȝte fermed in þe feith · ne fre of her goodes,
Ne ſori for her ſynnes · ſo is pryde waxen
In religioun in alle þe rewme · amonges riche & pore,
þat prayeres haue no power · þe peſtilence to lette.
And ȝette þe wrecches of þis worlde · is none ywar bi other,
Ne for drede of þe deth · withdrawe nouȝt her pryde,
Ne beth plentyuous to þe pore · as pure charite wolde,
But in gayneſſe and in glotonye · for-glotton her goode hem-ſelue,
And breken nouȝte to þe beggar · as þe boke techeth,

    Frange eſurienti panem tuum, &c.

And þe more he wynneth and welt · welthes & riccheſſe,
And lordeth in londes · he laſſe good he deleth.
¶ Thobye telleth ȝow nouȝt ſo · take hede, ȝe riche,
How þe boke bible · of hym bereth witneſſe :

    Si tibi ſit copia, habundanter tribue ; ſi autem exiguum,
    illud impertiri ſtude libenter :—

Who-ſo hath moche, ſpene manliche · ſo meneth Thobie,

---

[1] [thoſe.] [2] [deceit.] [3] [know.] [4] [flattery.]
[5] [ſpeak.] [6] [St. Bernard.] [7] daïs, high table. [8] [throat.]
[9] [poor.] [10] [very hungry.] [11] [cold.] [12] [trouble.]
[13] [Beggars ſupperleſs.]

And who-ſo litel weldeth · reule him þer-after ;
For we haue no *lettre* of owre lyf · now longe it ſhal dure.
Suche leſſounes lordes ſhulde · louie to here,
And how he myȝte moſt meyne · manliche fynde.
¶ Nouȝt to fare as a fitheler or a frere · for to ſeke feſtes,
Homelich at other mennes houſes · and hatyen her owne.
Elyng[1] is þe halle · vche daye in þe wyke,
þere þe lorde ne þe lady · liketh nouȝte to ſytte.
Now hath vche riche a reule[2] · to eten bi hym-ſelue
In a pryue parloure · for pore mennes ſake,
Or in a chambre with a chymneye · and leue þe chief halle,
þat was made for meles · men to eten Inne;
And al to ſpare to ſpille · þat ſpende ſhal an other.
¶ And whan þat witte was ywar · what dame ſtudye tolde,
He bicome ſo confus · he couth nouȝte loke,
And as doumbe as deth · and drowe hym arrere[3] ;
¶ And for no carpyng I couth after · ne knelyng to þe grounde,
I myȝte gete no greyne · of his grete wittis,
But al laughyng he louted · and loked vppon ſtudye,
In ſigne þat I ſhulde · biſeche hir of grace.
¶ And whan I was war of his wille · to his wyf gan I loute,
And ſeyde, "mercy, madame · ȝowre man ſhal I worthe,
As longe as I liue · bothe late & rathe,
Forto worche ȝowre wille · þe while my lyf dureth,
With þat ȝe kenne me kyndely · to knowe what is dowel."
¶ "For þi mekeneſſe, man," quod ſhe · "and for þi mylde ſpeche,
I ſhal kenne þe to my coſyn · þat clergye is hoten.[4]
He hath wedded a wyf · with-Inne þis ſyx monethes,
Is ſybbe[5] to þe ſeuene artz · ſcripture is hir name.
þei two, as I hope · after my techyng,
Shullen wiſſen þe to dowel · I dar it vndertake."
¶ þanne was I alſo fayne[6] · as foule[7] of faire morwe,
And gladder þan þe gleman[8] · þat golde hath to ȝifte,
And axed hir þe heighe weye · where þat clergye[9] dwelte,
"And telle me ſome token," quod I · "for tyme is þat I wende."
¶ "Axe þe heighe waye," quod ſhe · "hennes to ſuffre-
Bothe-wel-&-wo · ȝif þat þow wolt lerne,
And ryde forth by riccheſſe · ac reſt þow nauȝt þerinne,
For if þow coupleſt þe þer-with · to clergye comeſtow neuere.
¶ And alſo þe likerouſe launde · þat leccherye hatte,
Leue hym on þi left halue · a large myle or more,
Tyl þow come to a courte · kepe-wel-þi-tonge-
Fro-leſynges-and-lither[10]-ſpeche- and-likerouſe-drynkes.
þanne ſhaltow ſe ſobrete · and ſymplete-of-ſpeche,
þat eche wiȝte be in wille · his witte þe to ſhewe,
And þus ſhaltow come to clergye · þat can many þinges.
¶ Saye hym þis ſigne · I ſette hym to ſcole,
And þat I grete wel his wyf · for I wrote hir many bokes,
And ſette hir to ſapience · and to þe ſauter gloſe.
Logyke I lerned hir · and many other lawes,
And alle þe muſouns in muſike · I made hir to knowe.
¶ Plato þe poete · I put hym fyrſte to boke,
Ariſtotle and other moo · to argue I tauȝte.
Grammer for gerles · I garte firſt wryte,
And bette hem with a baleis · but if þei wolde lerne.

---

[1] [ſtrange, deſerted. Henry VIII. in a letter to Anne Bullen ſpeaks of his *El-lengneſs* ſince her departure. Hearne's *Aveſbury*, p. 360.]   [2] [cuſtom.]
[3] back.   [4] named.   [5] akin.   [6] glad.
[7] bird.   [8] harper.   [9] learning.   [10] wanton, bad.

Of alkinnes craftes · I contreued toles,
Of carpentrie, of kerueres · and compaſſed maſouns,
And lerned hem leuel and lyne · þough I loke dymme.
¶ Ac theologie hath tened me · ten ſcore tymes,
The more I muſe þere-Inne · þe miſtier it ſemeth,
And þe depper I deuyne · þe derker me it þinketh;
It is no ſcience for ſothe · forto ſotyle Inne;
A ful lethy þinge it were · ȝif þat loue nere.
Ac for it let beſt by loue · I loue it þe bettre;
For þere þat loue is leder · ne lacked neuere grace, &c.]

The artifices and perſuaſions of the monks to procure donations
to their convents are thus humorouſly ridiculed, in a ſtrain which
ſeems to have given riſe to Chaucer's *Sompnour's Tale :*—

Thanne he aſſoilled hir ſone · and ſithen he ſeyde,
" We han a wyndowe a wirchyng · wil ſitten vs ful heigh;
Woldeſtow glaſe þat gable · and graue þere-innc þi name,
Siker ſholde þi ſoule be · heuene to haue." [B. iii. 47.][1]

Covetiſe or Covetouſneſs is thus drawn in the true colours of
ſatirical painting.

And þanne cam coueytiſe · can I hym nouȝte deſcryue,
So hungriliche and holwe · ſire Heruy hym loked.
He was bitelbrowed · and baberlipped alſo,
With two blered eyghen · as a blynde hagge;
And as a letheren purs · lolled his chekes,
Wel ſydder þan his chyn · þei chiueled for elde;
And as a bondman of his bacoun · his berde was bidraueled.
With an hode on his hed · a louſi hatte aboue,
And in a tauny tabarde[2] · of twelue wynter age,
Al totorne and baudy · and ful of lys crepynge;
But if þat a lous couthe · haue lopen þe bettre,
She ſholde nouȝte haue walked on þat welche · ſo was it thredebare.
" I haue ben coueytouſe," quod þis caityue · " I biknowe it here;
For ſome tyme I ſerued · Symme atte Stile,

---

[1] Theſe, and the following lines, are plainly copied by Chaucer, viz. :—
" And I ſhall cover your kyrke, and your cloiſture do maken."
Chaucer, *Sompn. T.* v. 399, Morris edit. But with new ſtrokes of humour.
" ' Yif me than of thy good to make our cloyſter,'
Quod he, ' for many a muſcle and many an oyſter
Hath ben oure foode, our cloyſter to arreyſe,
Whan other men han ben ful wel at eyſe;
And yit, God wot, unnethe the foundement
Parformed is, ne of oure pavyment
Is nought a tyle yit withinne our wones;
Bi God, we owe yit fourty pound for ſtones.' "
So alſo in the *Ploughman's Crede,* hereafter mentioned, l. 396, a friar ſays—
" So that thou mowe amenden our hous · with money other elles,
With ſom katell, other corne · or cuppes of ſiluer."
And again, l. 123—
" And mighteſtou amenden vs · with money of thyn owne,
Thou ſholdeſt cnely bifore Criſt · in compas of gold,
In the wide windowe · weſtwarde · wel nighe in the myddell."
That is, " your figure ſhall be painted in glaſs, in the middle of the weſt window,"
&c. But of this paſſage hereafter.
[2] tabard. A coat.

And was his prentis ypli3te • his profit to wayte.
Firft I lerned to lye • a leef other tweyne,
Wikkedlich to weye • was my furft leſſou*n*.
To Wy¹ and to Wyncheſtre² I went to þe faire,

---

¹ Wy is probably Weyhill in Hampſhire, where a famous fair ſtill ſubſiſts.

² Anciently, before many flouriſhing towns were eſtabliſhed, and the neceſſaries or ornaments of life, from the convenience of communication and the increaſe of provincial civility, could be procured in various places, goods and commodities of every kind were chiefly ſold at fairs, to which, as to one univerſal mart, the people reſorted periodically, and ſupplied moſt of their wants for the enſuing year. The diſplay of merchandiſe, and the conflux of cuſtomers at theſe principal and almoſt only emporia of domeſtic commerce, was prodigious; and they were often held on open and extenſive plains. One of the chief of them ſeems to have been that of St. Giles's hill or down near Wincheſter, to which our poet here refers. It was inſtituted and given as a kind of revenue to the biſhop of Wincheſter by William the Conqueror, who by his charter permitted it to continue for three days. But in conſequence of new royal grants, Henry III. prolonged its continuance to ſixteen days. Its juriſdiction extended ſeven miles round, and comprehended even Southampton, then a capital trading town: and all merchants who ſold wares within that circuit forfeited them to the biſhop. Officers were placed at a conſiderable diſtance, at bridges and other avenues of acceſs to the fair, to exact toll of all merchandiſe paſſing that way. In the meantime all ſhops in the city of Wincheſter were ſhut. In the fair was a court called the pavilion, at which the biſhop's juſticiaries and other officers aſſiſted, with power to try cauſes of various ſorts for ſeven miles round: nor among other ſingular claims could any lord of a manor hold a court-baron within the ſaid circuit without licence from the pavilion. During this time the biſhop was empowered to take toll of every load or parcel of goods paſſing through the gates of the city. On Saint Giles's eve the mayor, bailiffs, and citizens of the city of Wincheſter delivered the keys of the four city gates to the biſhop's officers who, during the ſaid ſixteen days, appointed a mayor and bailiff of their own to govern the city, and alſo a coroner to act within the ſaid city. Tenants of the biſhop, who held lands by doing ſervice at the pavilion, attended the ſame with horſes and armour, not only to do ſuit at the court there, but to be ready to aſſiſt the biſhop's officers in the execution of writs and other ſervices. But I cannot here enumerate the many extraordinary privileges granted to the biſhop on this occaſion, all tending to obſtruct trade and to oppreſs the people. Numerous foreign merchants frequented this fair; and it appears that the juſticiaries of the pavilion, and the treaſurer of the biſhop's palace of Wolveſey, received annually for a fee, according to ancient cuſtom, four baſins and ewers of thoſe foreign merchants who ſold brazen veſſels in the fair, and were called *mercatores diaunteres.* In the fair ſeveral ſtreets were formed, aſſigned to the ſale of different commodities, and called the Drapery, the Pottery, the Spicery, &c. Many monaſteries in and about Wincheſter had ſhops or houſes in theſe ſtreets, uſed only at the fair, which they held under the biſhop, and often let by leaſe for a term of years. One place in the fair was called *Speciarium Sancti Swythini*, or the Spicery of Saint Swithin's monaſtery. In the revenue rolls of the ancient biſhops of Wincheſter, this fair makes a grand and ſeparate article of reception, under this title: *Feria. Computus Feriæ ſancti Egidii.* But in the revenue roll of biſhop Will. of Waynflete [an. 1471], it appears to have greatly decayed: in which, among other proofs, I find mention made of a diſtrict in the fair being un-occupied, "*Ubi homines Cornubiæ ſtare ſolebant.*" From whence it likewiſe appears that different counties had their different ſtations. The whole reception to the biſhop this year from the fair amounted only to 45*l*. 18*s*. 5*d*. Yet this ſum, ſmall as it may ſeem, was worth upwards of 400*l*. Edward I. ſent a precept to the ſheriff of Hampſhire to reſtore to the biſhop this fair, which his eſcheator Malcolm de Harlegh had ſeized into the king's hands, without command of the treaſurer and barons of the exchequer, in the year 1292. *Regiſtr. Joh. de Pontiſſara, Epiſc. Wint.* fol. 195. After the charter of Henry III. many kings by charter confirmed this

With many maner*e* marchandife · as my Maiftre me hi3te ;
Ne had þe gr*ace* of gyle · ygo amonge my ware,
It had be vnfolde þis feuene 3ere · fo me god helpe !
   Thanne drowe I me amonges draperes · my donet[1] to lerne,
To drawe þe lyfer alonge · þe lenger it femed ;
Amonge þe riche rayes · I rendred a leffou*n*, &c. [B. v. 188.]

---

fair with all its privileges to the bifhops of Winchefter. The laft charter was of Henry VIII. to Bifhop Richard Fox and his fucceffors, in the year 1511. But it was followed by the ufual confirmation-charter of Charles II. In the year 1144, when Brian Fitz-count, lord of Wallingford in Berkfhire, maintained Wallingford Caftle, one of the ftrongeft garrifons belonging to Maud the emprefs, and confequently fent out numerous parties for contributions and provifions, Henry de Blois, bifhop of Winchefter, enjoined him not to moleft any paffengers that were coming to his fair at Winchefter, under pain of excommunication. *Omnibus ad feriam meam venientibus,* &c. *MSS. Dodfworth,* vol. 89, fol. 76, Bibl. Bodl. This was in King Stephen's reign. In that of Richard I., in the year 1194, the king grants to Portfmouth a fair lafting for fifteen days, with all the privileges of Saint Giles's fair at Winchefter. Anders. *Hift. Com.* i. 197. In the year 1234, the eighteenth of Henry III., the fermier of the city of Winchefter paid twenty pounds to Ailward chamberlain of Winchefter Caftle, to buy a robe at this fair for the king's fon, and divers filver implements for a chapel in the caftle. Madox, *Exch.* p. 251. It appears from [the *Northumb. Houfh. Book*], that the ftores of his lordfhip's houfe at Wrefille, for the whole year, were laid in from fairs. "He that ftandes charged with my lordes houfe for the houll yeir, if he may poffible, fhall be at all Faires where the groice emptions fhall be boughte for the houfe for the houlle yeire, as wine, wax, beiffes, multons, wheite, and maltie," p. 407. This laft quotation is a proof that fairs ftill continued to be the principal marts for purchafing neceffaries in large quantities, which now are fupplied by frequent trading towns: and the mention of "beiffes" and "multons," which were falted oxen and fheep, fhews that at fo late a period they knew but little of breeding cattle. Their ignorance of fo important an article of hufbandry is alfo an evidence that in the reign of Henry VIII. the ftate of population was much lower among us than we may imagine.

In the ftatutes of Saint Mary Ottery's college in Devonfhire, given by Bifhop Grandifon the founder, the ftewards and facrift are ordered to purchafe annual'y two hundred pounds of wax for the choir of the college, at this fair. "Cap. lxvii.— Pro luminaribus vero omnibus fupradictis inveniendis, etiam ftatuimus, quod fenefcalli fcaccarii per vifum et auxilium facrifte, omni anno, in nundinis Wynton, vel alibi apud Toryngton et in partibus Barnftepol, ceram fufficientem, quam ad ducentas libras æftimamus pro uno anno ad minus faciant provideri." Thefe ftatutes were granted in the year 1338. MS. apud Regiftr. Priorat. S. Swithin. Winton. In Archiv. Wolves. In the accompts of the Priories of Maxtoke in Warwickfhire, and of Bicefter in Oxfordfhire, under the reign of Henry VI., the monks appear to have laid in yearly ftores of various yet common neceffaries, at the fair of Sturbridge in Cambridgefhire, at leaft one hundred miles diftant from either monaftery. It may feem furprifing, that their own neighbourhood, including the cities of Oxford and Coventry, could not fupply them with commodities neither rare nor coftly, which they thus fetched at a confiderable expence of carriage. It is a rubric in fome of the monaftic rules *De Euntibus ad Nundinas.* See Dugd. Mon. Angl. ii. p. 746. It is hoped the reader will excufe this tedious note, which at leaft developes ancient manners and cuftoms.

[1] Leffon. Properly a *Grammar,* from *Ælius Donatus* the grammarian. *Teftam. L.* p. 504, b. edit. Urr. "No paffef to vertues of this Margarite, but therin al my *donet* can I·lerne." In the ftatutes of Winchefter-college, [written about 1386,] grammar is called "Antiquus donatus," *i. e.* the *old d.nat,* or the name of a fyftem of grammar at that time in vogue, and long before. The French have a book entitled "*Le Donnet, traité de grammaire, baillé a feu roi Charles* viii." Among Rawlinfon's MSS. at Oxford, I have feen *Donatus optimus noviter compi-*

Our author, who probably could not get preferment, thus inveighs against the luxury and diversions of the prelates of his age :

> Ac now is religioun a ryder [1] a rowmer bi ftretes,
> A leder of louedayes [2] · and a londe-bugger,
> A priker on a palfray · fro maner*e* to maner*e*,
> An heep of houndes at his ers · as he a lorde were.[1]
> And but if his knaue knele · þat fhal his cuppe brynge,
> He loureth on hym and axeth hym · who tau3te hym curteifye ?[3]

There is great picturefque humour in the following lines :

---

latus, a manufcript on vellum, given to Saint Alban's, by John Stoke, abbot, in 1450. In the introduction, or *lytell Proheme*, to Dean Colet's *Grammatices Rudimenta*, we find mention made of "certayne introducyons into latyn fpeche called *Donates*," &c. Among the books written by Bifhop Pecock, there is the *Donat into chriftian religion*, and the *Folower to the Donat*. Lewis's *Pecock*, p. 317. I think I have before obferved, that John of Bafing, who flourifhed in the year 1240, calls his Greek Grammar *Donatus Græcorum*. Pegge's *Wefeham*, p. 51. Wynkyn de Worde printed *Donatus ad Anglicanarum fcholarum ufum*. [But fee *Handb. of E. E. Lit.* art. *Children.*] Cotgrave (in v.) quotes an old French proverb, "Les diables eftoient encores *a leur Donat*, *The devils were but yet in their grammar*."

[1] Walter de Suffield, bifhop of Norwich, bequeaths by will his pack of hounds to the king in 1256. Blomefield's *Norf.* ii. 347. See Chaucer's *Monkes Prol.* v. 165. This was a common topic of fatire. It occurs again, fol. xxvii. a. See [the] *Teftament of Love*, p. 492, col. ii. Urr. The archdeacon of Richmond, on his vifitation, comes to the priory of Bridlington in Yorkfhire, in 1216, with ninety-feven horfes, twenty-one dogs, and three hawks, Dugd. *Mon.* ii. 65.

[2] [love-days.]

[3] B. x. 306. The following prediction, although a probable conclufion, concerning a king, who after a time would fupprefs the religious houfes, is remarkable. I imagined it was foifted into the copies, in the reign of Henry VIII. But it is in [all the] MSS. of this poem [which exhibit the *fecond* verfion, many of which are] older than the year 1400.

> " ¶ Ac þere fhal come a kyng · and confeffe 3ow religioufes,
> And bete 3ow as þe bible telleth · for brekynge of 3owre reule,
> And amende monyales · monkes and chanouns—
> ¶ And þanne Freres in here freitoure · fhal fynden a keye
> Of coftantynes coffres · in which is þe catel
> Þat Gregories god-children · han yuel difpended.
> ¶ And þanne fhal þe abbot of Abyndoun · and alle [his] iffu for euere
> *Haue a knokke of a kynge · and incurable þe wounde.*"   [B. x. 317.]

Again, where he alludes to the knights-templers, lately fuppreffed :

> " Men of holy kirke
> Shul tourne as templeres did, *the tyme approcheth fafte.*"
>   [B. xv. 507.]

This, I fuppofe, was a favourite doctrine in Wickliffe's difcourfes. I cannot help taking notice of a paffage in *Piers Plowman*, which fhews how the reigning paffion for chivalry infected the ideas and expreffions of the writers of this period. The poet is defcribing the crucifixion, and fpeaking of the perfon who pierced our Saviour's fide with a fpear. This perfon our author calls a knight, and fays that he came forth "with his fpere in hand, and jufted with Jefus." Afterwards for doing fo bafe an act as that of wounding a dead body, he is pronounced a difgrace to knighthood : and [this "champioun chiualer, chief knyght of yow alle" is declared to have yielded himfelf recreant. B. xviii. 99.] This knight's name is Longis, and he is blind ; but receives his fight from the blood which fprings from our Saviour's fide. This miracle is recorded in the *Golden Legend*. He is called Longias, "A blinde knight men ycallid Longias," in Chaucer, *Lam. Mar. Magd.* v. 177.

> Hunger in haſte þo · hent waſtour bi þe mawe,
> And wronge hym ſo bi þe wombe · þat bothe his eyen wattered ;
> He buffeted þe Britoner · aboute þe chekes,
> Þat he loked like a lanterne · al his lyf after.[1]

And in the following, where the Vices are repreſented as converted and coming to confeſſion, among which is the figure of Envy :

> Of a freres frokke · were þe forſleues.
> And as a leke hadde yleye · longe in þe ſonne,
> So loked he with lene chekes · lourynge foule.   [B. v. 81.]

It would be tedious to tranſcribe other ſtrokes of humour, with which this poem abounds.   Before one of the Viſions the poet falls aſleep, while he is bidding his beads.   In another he deſcribes Antichriſt, whoſe banner is borne by Pride, as welcomed into a monaſtery with ringing of bells, and a ſolemn congratulatory proceſſion of all the monks as marching out to meet and receive him.[2]

Theſe images of mercy and truth are in a different ſtrain :

> Out of þe weſt coſte · a wenche, as me thouȝte,
> Cam walkynge in þe wey · to-helle-ward ſhe loked.
> Mercy hiȝt þat mayde · a meke þynge with-alle,
> A ful benygne buirde · and boxome of ſpeche.
> Her ſuſter, as it ſemed · cam ſoftly walkynge,
> Euene out of þe eſt · and weſtward ſhe loked.
> A ful comely creature · treuth ſhe hiȝte,
> For þe vertue þat hir folwed · aferd was ſhe neuere.
> Whan þis maydenes mette · mercy and treuth,
> Eyther axed other · of þis grete wonder,
> Of þe dyne & of þe derkneſſe, &c.[3]

The imagery of Nature, or Kinde, ſending forth his diſeaſes from the planets, at the command of Conſcience, and of his attendants Age and Death, is conceived with ſublimity :

> Kynd Conſcience tho herde · and cam out of the planets,
> And ſent forth his foreioures · feures & fluxes,
> Coughes, and cardiacles · crampes, and tothaches,
> Rewmes, & radegoundes · and roynouſe ſcalles,
> Byles, and bocches · and brennyng agues ;
> Freneſyes, & foule yueles · forageres of kynde,
> Hadde yprykked and prayed · polles of peple,
> Þat largelich a legioun · leſe her lyf ſone.
> ¶ There was—" harrow and help ! · here cometh kynde,
> With deth þat is dredful · to vndone vs alle ! "
> ¶ The lorde that lyued after luſt · tho alowde cryde
> After conforte, a knyghte · to come and bere his banere
> ¶ Elde þe hore · he was in þe vauntwarde,
> And bare þe banere bifor deth · by riȝte he it claymed.
> Kynde come after · with many kene ſores,
> As pokkes and peſtilences · and moche poeple ſhente ;
> So kynde þorw corupciouns · kulled ful manye.
> ¶ Deth cam dryuende after · and al to douſt paſſhed
> Knyges & knyȝtes · kayſeres and popes ;
> Many a louely lady · and lemmanes of knyghtes
> Swouned and ſwelted · for ſorwe of dethes dyntes.
> ¶ Conſcience of his curteiſye · to kynde he biſouȝte,
> To ceſſe & ſuffre · and ſee where þei wolde

---

[1] [B. text ; vi. 176.]   [2] [B. xx. 57.]   [3] [B. xviii. 113.]

Leue pryde pryuely · and be parfite criſtene.
¶ And kynde ceſſed tho · to ſe þe peple amende.[1]

Theſe lines at leaſt put us in mind of Milton's *Lazarhouſe* :[2]

. . . . . Immediately a place
Before his eyes appeared, ſad, noiſome, dark :
A lazar-houſe it ſeem'd, wherein were laid
Numbers of all diſeas'd : all maladies
Of gaſtly ſpaſm, or racking torture, qualms
Of heart-ſick agony, all feverous kinds,
Convulſions, epilepſies, fierce catarrhs,
Inteſtine ſtone, and ulcer, cholic pangs,
Demoniac phrenzy, moping melancholy,
And moon-ſtruck madneſs, pining atrophy,
Maraſmus, and wide-waſting Peſtilence :
Dropſies and aſthma, and joint-racking rheum.
Dire was the toſſing ! Deep the groans ! Deſpair
Tended the ſick, buſy from couch to couch ;
And over them triumphant Death his dart
Shook, but delay'd to ſtrike, &c.

At length Fortune or Pride ſends forth a numerous army led by
Luſt, to attack Conſcience.

And gadered a gret hoſte · al agayne CONSCIENCE :
This LECHERYE leyde on · with a laughyng chiere,
And with pryue ſpeche · and peynted wordes,
And armed hym in ydelneſſe · and in hiegh berynge.
He bare a bowe in his hande · and manye blody arwes,
Weren fethered with faire biheſte · and many a falſe truthe.[3]

Afterwards Conſcience is beſieged by Antichriſt and ſeven great
giants, who are the ſeven capital or deadly ſins : and the aſſault is
made by Sloth, who conducts an army of more than a thouſand
prelates.

It is not improbable, that Langland here had his eye on the old
French *Roman d' Antechriſt*, a poem written by Huon de Meri, about
the year 1228. The author of this piece ſuppoſes that Antichriſt is
on earth, that he viſits every profeſſion and order of life, and finds
numerous partiſans. The Vices arrange themſelves under the
banner of Antichriſt, and the Virtues under that of Chriſt. Theſe
two armies at length come to an engagement, and the battle ends to
the honour of the Virtues, and the total defeat of the Vices. The
banner of Antichriſt has before occurred in our quotations from
Longland. The title of Huon de Meri's poem deſerves notice. It
is [*Le*] *Turnoyement de l' Antechriſt*. Theſe are the concluding lines :

Par ſon droit nom a peau cet livre
Qui treſbien s'avorde a l' eſcrit
Le *Tournoiement de l' Antechriſt*.

The author appears to have been a monk of St. Germain des Pres,
near Paris.[4] This allegory is much like that which we find in the old
dramatic Moralities. The theology of the middle ages abounded
with conjectures and controverſies concerning Antichriſt, who at a
very early period was commonly believed to be the Roman pontiff.[5]

---

[1] [B. xx. p. 372, edit. Skeat.]   [2] *Par. L.* ii. 475.   [3] [B. xx. 112.]
[4] [See ſome account of this poem in Mr. Wright's *St. Patrick's Purgatory.*]
[5] See this topic diſcuſſed with ſingular penetration and perſpicuity, by Dr. Hurd.
in *Twelve Sermons Introductory to the Study of the Prophecies*, 1772, p. 206, *ſeq.*

SECTION IX.

TO the *Vision of* [*William concerning*] *Pierce Plowman* has been commonly annexed a poem called *Pierce the Plowman's Crede.*[1]

The author, in the character of a plain uninformed person, pretends to be ignorant of his creed, to be instructed in the articles of which, he applies by turns to the four orders of Mendicant friars. This circumstance affords an obvious occasion of exposing in lively colours the tricks of those societies. After so unexpected a disappointment, he meets one Pierce or Peter, a ploughman, who resolves his doubts, and teaches him the principles of true religion. In a copy of the [edition of the] *Crede,* [printed in 1561], presented to me by the Bishop of Gloucester, and once belonging to Mr. Pope, the latter in his own hand has inserted the following abstract of its plan. "An ignorant plain man having learned his Pater-noster and Ave-Mary, wants to learn his creed. He asks several religious men of the several orders to teach it him. First a friar Minor, who bids him beware of the Carmelites, and assures him they can teach him nothing, describing their faults, &c. but that the friars Minors shall save him, whether he learns his creed or not. He goes next to the friars Preachers, whose magnificent monastery he describes: there he meets a fat friar, who declaims against the Augustines. He is shocked at his pride, and goes to the Augustines. They rail at the Minorites. He goes to the Carmelites: they abuse the Dominicans, but promise him salvation, without the creed, for money. He leaves them with indignation, and finds an honest poor Ploughman in the field, and tells him how he was disappointed by the four orders. The ploughman answers with a long invective against them."

The language of the *Crede* is less embarrassed and obscure than that of the *Vision.* But before I proceed to a specimen, it may not

[1] The first edition [was printed by Reynold Wolfe in 1553.] It was reprinted, and added to Rogers's, or the fourth, edition of the *Vision,* 1561. It was evidently written after the year 1384. Wickliffe died in that year, and he is mentioned as no longer living, in signat.—C ii. edit. 1561 [l. 528]. Walter Britte or Brithe, a follower of Wickliffe, is also mentioned [l. 657] signat. C iii. [The *Crede* is in no sense an appendage to the *Vision,* but upon a totally different plan. The proper sequel to the *Vision* is the piece called the *Deposition of Richard II.,* probably also by Langland. But *Pierce the Plowman's Crede* is by another author, a professed follower of Wickliffe, written about A.D. 1394, in order to discredit the four orders of Mendicant Friars. The only points of connection with the *Vision* are the title, which was imitated from it; the rhythm, and the fact that some have thought fit to print both poems in one volume, to the intense confusion of hasty students, who mix the two together in a most unscholarly fashion.—*Skeat.*] Britte is placed by Bale in 1390. Cent. vi. 94. See also Fuller's *Worth.* p. 8, *Wales,* [and Pref. to edit. Skeat.] The reader will pardon this small anticipation for the sake of connection.

be perhaps improper to prepare the reader, by giving an outline of
the conftitution and character of the four orders of Mendicant friars,
the object of our poet's fatire: an enquiry in many refpects connected with the general purport of this hiftory, and which, in this
place at leaft, cannot be deemed a digreffion, as it will illuftrate the
main fubject, and explain many particular paffages, of the *Plowman's
Crede*.[1]

Long before the thirteenth century, the monaftic orders, as we
have partly feen in the preceding poem, in confequence of their
ample revenues, had degenerated from their primitive aufterity, and
were totally given up to luxury and indolence. Hence they became
both unwilling and unable to execute the purpofes of their eftablifhment: to inftruct the people, to check the growth of herefies, or to
promote in any refpect the true interefts of the church. They
forfook all their religious obligations, defpifed the authority of their
fuperiors, and were abandoned without fhame or remorfe to every
fpecies of diffipation and licentioufnefs. About the beginning therefore of the thirteenth century, the condition and circumftances of
the church rendered it abfolutely neceffary to remedy thefe evils, by
introducing a new order of religious, who being deftitute of fixed
poffeffions, by the feverity of their manners, a profeffed contempt of
riches, and an unwearied perfeverance in the duties of preaching
and prayer, might reftore refpect to the monaftic inftitution, and
recover the honours of the church. Thefe were the four orders of
mendicant or begging friars, commonly denominated the Francifcans,
the Dominicans, the Carmelites, and the Auguftines.[2]

Thefe focieties foon furpaffed all the reft, not only in the purity of
their lives, but in the number of their privileges and the multitude of
their members. Not to mention the fuccefs which attends all novelties, their reputation arofe quickly to an amazing height. The popes,
among other uncommon immunities, allowed them the liberty of
travelling wherever they pleafed, of converfing with perfons of all
ranks, of inftructing the youth and the people in general, and of
hearing confeffions, without referve or reftriction: and as on thefe
occafions, which gave them opportunities of appearing in public and
confpicuous fituations, they exhibited more ftriking marks of gravity
and fanctity than were obfervable in the deportment and conduct of
the members of other monafteries, they were regarded with the

---

[1] And of fome perhaps quoted above from the *Vifion*. ["Of the creed there
does not appear to exift any manufcript older than the firft printed edition."—
Wright. But fee Mr. Skeat's notice of a MS. in Trin. Coll. Camb. which, though
a late tranfcript, is obvioufly exactly copied from a MS. of the firft half of the
fifteenth century.]

[2] The Francifcans were often ftyled friars-minors, or minorites, and greyfriars:
the Dominicans, friars-preachers, and fometimes black-friars; the Carmelites, white-
friars; and the Auftins, grey-friars. The firft eftablifhment of the Dominicans in
England was at Oxford in 1221; of the Francifcans, at Canterbury. Thefe two
were the moft eminent of the four orders. The Dominican friary at Oxford ftood
in an ifland on the fouth of the city, fouth-weft of the Francifcan friary, the fite of
which is hereafter defcribed.

higheſt eſteem and veneration throughout all the countries of Europe.

In the mean time they gained ſtill greater reſpeсt, by cultivating the literature then in vogue with the greateſt aſſiduity and ſucceſs. Giannone ſays, that moſt of the theological profeſſors in the univerſity of Naples, newly founded in the year 1220, were choſen from the Mendicants.[1] They were the principal teachers of theology at Paris, the ſchool where this ſcience had received its origin.[2] At Oxford and Cambridge reſpeсtively, all the four orders had flouriſhing monaſteries. The moſt learned ſcholars in the univerſity of Oxford, at the cloſe of the thirteenth century, were Franciſcan friars: and long after this period, the Franciſcans appear to have been the ſole ſupport and ornament of that univerſity.[3] Hence it was that Biſhop Hugh de Balſham, founder of Peter-houſe at Cambridge, orders in his ſtatutes given about the year 1280, that ſome of his ſcholars ſhould annually repair to Oxford for improvement in the ſciences.[4] That is, to ſtudy under the Franciſcan readers. Such was the eminence of the Franciſcan friary at Oxford, that the learned Biſhop Groſeteſte, in the year 1253, bequeathed all his books to that celebrated ſeminary.[5] This was the houſe in which the renowned Roger Bacon was educated; who revived in the midſt of barbariſm, and brought to a conſiderable degree of perfeсtion, the knowledge of mathematics in England, and greatly facilitated many modern diſcoveries in experimental philoſophy.[6] The ſame fraternity is likewiſe ſaid to have ſtored their

---

[1] *Hiſt. Nap.* xvi. 3.

[2] See Boul. *Hiſt. Academ. Paris*, iii. pp. 138, 240, 244, 248, &c.

[3] This circumſtance in ſome degree rouſed the monks from their indolence, and induced the greater monaſteries to procure the foundation of ſmall colleges in the univerſities for the education of their novices. At Oxford the monks had alſo ſchools which bore the name of their reſpeсtive orders: and there were ſchools in that univerſity which were appropriated to particular monaſteries. Kennet's *Paroch. Ant.* p. 214. Wood, *Hiſt. Ant. Univ. Oxon.* i. 119. Leland ſays, that even in his time at Stamford, a temporary univerſity, the names of halls inhabited by the novices of Peterborough, Sempringham, and Vauldrey abbeys, were remaining. *Itin.* vi. p. 21. And it appears, that the greater part of the proceeders in theology at Oxford and Cambridge, juſt before the Reformation, were monks. But we do not find that, in conſequence of all theſe efforts, the monks made a much greater figure in literature. In this rivalry which ſubſiſted between the mendicants and the monks, the latter ſometimes availed themſelves of their riches: and with a view to attraсt popularity, and to eclipſe the growing luſtre of the former, proceeded to their degrees in the univerſities with prodigious parade. In the year 1298, William de Brooke, a Benediсtine of St. Peter's abbey at Glouceſter, took the degree of doсtor in divinity at Oxford. He was attended on this important occaſion by the abbot and whole convent of Glouceſter, the abbots of Weſtminſter, Reading, Abingdon, Eveſham, and Malmeſbury, with one hundred noblemen and eſquires, on horſes richly capariſoned. Theſe were entertained at a ſumptuous feaſt in the refeсtory of Glouceſter college. But it ſhould be obſerved, that he was the firſt of the Benediсtine order that attained this dignity. Wood, *Hiſt. Ant. Univ. Oxon.* i. 25, col. 1. See alſo Dugdale, *Mon.* [edit. Stevens,] i. 70.

[4] " De ſcholaribus emittendis ad univerſitatem Oxonie pro doсtrina." Cap. xviii.

[5] Leland. *Script. Brit.* p. 283. This houſe ſtood juſt without the city walls, near Little-gate. The garden called Paradiſe was their grove or orchard.

[6] It is probable that the treatiſes of many of Bacon's ſcholars and followers, col-

valuable library with a multitude of Hebrew manuscripts, which they purchased of the Jews on their banishment from England.[1] Richard de Bury, Bishop of Durham, author of *Philobiblon*, and the founder of a library at Oxford, is prolix in his praises of the Mendicants for their extraordinary diligence in collecting books.[2] Indeed it became difficult in the beginning of the fourteenth century to find any treatise in the arts, theology, or canon law, commonly exposed to sale: they were all universally bought up by the friars.[3] This is mentioned by Richard Fitzralph, archbishop of Armagh, in his discourse before the Pope at Avignon in 1357 ; he was their bitter and professed antagonist, and adds, without any intention of paying them a compliment, that all the Mendicant convents were furnished with a "grandis et nobilis libraria."[4] Sir Richard Whittington built the library of the Grey Friars in London, which was one hundred and twenty-nine feet long, and twelve broad, with twenty-eight desks.[5] About the year 1430, one hundred marks were paid for transcribing the profound Nicholas de Lyra, in two volumes, to be chained in this library.[6] Leland relates that Thomas Wallden, a learned Carmelite, bequeathed to the same library as many MSS. of approved authors, written in capital Roman characters, as were then estimated at more than two thousand pieces of gold.[7] He adds that this library even in his time exceeded all others in London for multitude of books and antiquity of copies.[8] Among many other instances which might be given of the learning of the Mendicants, there is one which greatly contributed to establish their literary character. In the eleventh century, Aristotle's philosophy had been condemned in the university of Paris as heretical. About a hundred years afterwards, these prejudices began to subside ; and new translations of Aristotle's writings were published in Latin by our countryman Michael Scotus, and others, with more attention to the original Greek, at least without the pompous and perplexed

lected by Thomas Allen in the reign of James I. still remain among the MSS. of Sir Kenelm Digby in the Bodleian library.

[1] Wood, *ubi supr.* 1, 77, col. 2.
[2] *Philobibl.* cap. v. This book was written in 1344.
[3] Yet I find a decree made at Oxford, where these orders of friars flourished so greatly, in the year 1373, to check the excessive multitude of persons selling books in the university without licence. *Vet. Stat. Univ. Oxon.* D. fol. 75. Archiv. Bodl.
[4] MSS. Bibl. Bodl. Propositio coram papa, &c. And MSS. C.C.C. Oxon. 182. Propositio coram, &c. See a translation of this Sermon by Trevisa, MSS. Harl. 1900, 2. See f. 11. See also Browne's *append. Fascic. Rer. expetend. fugiend.* ii. p. 466. I believe this discourse has been printed twice or thrice at Paris. In which, says the archbishop, there were thirty thousand scholars at Oxford in my youth, but now (1357) scarce six thousand. At Bennet in Cambridge, there is a curious MS. of one of Fitzrauf's Sermons, in the first leaf of which there is a drawing of four devils, hugging four mendicant friars, one of each of the four orders, with great familiarity and affection. MSS. L. 16. This book belonged to Adam Eston, a very learned Benedictine of Norwich, and a witness against Wickliffe at Rome, where he lived the greatest part of his life, in 1370.
[5] Stow's *Surv. Lond.* p. 255, edit. 1599.
[6] Stow, *ibid.* p. 256, Dugd. *Monast.* [ed. Stevens] i. 112.　　[7] Aurei.
[8] *Script. Brit.* p. 441, and *Collectan.* iii. p. 52.

circumlocutions which appeared in the Arabic verſions hitherto uſed. In the mean time ſprang up the Mendicant orders who, happily availing themſelves of theſe new tranſlations, and making them the conſtant ſubjeƈt of their ſcholaſtic leƈtures, were the firſt who revived the doƈtrines of this philoſopher, and acquired the merit of having opened a new ſyſtem of ſcience.[1] The Dominicans of Spain were accompliſhed adepts in the learning and language of the Arabians; and were employed by the kings of Spain in the inſtruƈtion and converſion of the numerous Jews and Saracens who reſided in their dominions.[2]

The buildings of the Mendicant monaſteries, eſpecially in England, were remarkably magnificent, and commonly much exceeded thoſe of the endowed convents of the ſecond magnitude. As theſe fraternities were profeſſedly poor, and could not from their original inſtitution receive eſtates, the munificence of their benefaƈtors was employed in adorning their houſes with ſtately refeƈtories and churches: and for theſe and other purpoſes they did not want addreſs to procure abundance of patronage, which was facilitated by the notion of their ſuperior ſanƈtity. It was faſhionable for perſons of the higheſt rank to bequeath their bodies to be buried in the friary churches, which were conſequently filled with ſumptuous ſhrines and ſuperb monuments.[3] In the noble church of the Grey friars in London, finiſhed in the year 1325, but long ſince deſtroyed, four queens, beſides upwards of ſix hundred perſons of quality, were buried, whoſe beautiful tombs remained till the diſſolution.[4] Theſe interments imported conſiderable ſums of money into the mendicant

---

[1] See Joann. Laun. *de varia Ariſtotel. Fortun. in Acad. Paris,* p. 78, edit. 1662.

[2] R. Simon's *Lett. Chois.* tom. iii. p. 112. They ſtudied the arts of popular entertainment. The Mendicants, I believe, were the only religious in England who aƈted plays. The *Creation of the World,* annually performed by the Grey friars at Coventry, is ſtill extant. And they ſeem to have been famous abroad for theſe exhibitions. De la Flamma, who flouriſhed about the year 1340, has the following curious paſſage in his chronicle of the Viſconti of Milan, publiſhed by Muratori. In the year 1336, ſays he, on the feaſt of Epiphany, the firſt feaſt of the three kings was celebrated at Milan by the convent of the friars Preachers. The three kings appeared crowned on three great horſes, richly habited, ſurrounded by pages, bodyguards, and an innumerable retinue. A golden ſtar was exhibited in the ſky, going before them. They proceeded to the pillars of S. Lawrence, where King Herod was repreſented with his ſcribes and wiſe men. The three kings aſk Herod where Chriſt ſhould be born: and his wiſe men having conſulted their books, anſwer him at Bethlehem. On which, the three kings with their golden crowns, having in their hands golden cups filled with frankincenſe, myrrh, and gold, the ſtar ſtill going before, marched to the church of S. Euſtorgius with all their attendants, preceded by trumpets and horns, apes, baboons, and a great variety of animals. In the church, on one ſide of the high altar, there was a manger with an ox and an aſs, and in it the infant Chriſt in the arms of his mother. Here the three kings offer their gifts, &c. The concourſe of the people, of knights, ladies, and eccleſiaſtics, was ſuch as never before was beheld, &c. *Rer. Italic. Scriptor.* tom. xii. col. 1017. D. This feaſt in the ritual is called The feaſt of the Star. Joann. Epiſcop. Abrinc. *de Offic. Eccl.* p. 30.

[3] Their churches were eſteemed more ſacred than others.

[4] Weev. *Fun. Mon.* p. 388.

focieties. It is probable that they derived more benefit from cafual
charity, than they would have gained from a regular endowment.
The Francifcans indeed enjoyed from the popes the privilege of
diftributing indulgences, a valuable indemnification for their voluntary poverty.[1]

On the whole, two of thefe Mendicant inftitutions, the Dominicans
and the Francifcans, for thc fpace of nearly three centuries appear
to have governed the European church and ftate with an abfolute
and univerfal fway; they filled, during that period, the moft eminent
ecclefiaftical and civil ftations, taught in the univerfities with an
authority which filenced all oppofition, and maintained the difputed
prerogative of the Roman pontiff againft the united influence of
prelates and kings, with a vigour only to be paralleled by its fuccefs.
The Dominicans and Francifcans were, before the Reformation,
exactly what the Jefuits have been fince. They difregarded their
monaftic character and profeffion, and were employed not only in
fpiritual matters, but in temporal affairs of the greateft confequence ;
in compofing the differences of princes, concluding treaties of peace,
and concerting alliances ; they prefided in cabinet councils, levied
national fubfidies, influenced courts, and managed the machinery of
every important operation and event, both in the religious and political world.

From what has been here faid, it is natural to fuppofe that the
Mendicants at length became univerfally odious. The high efteem
in which they were held, and the tranfcendent degree of authority
which they had affumed, only ferved to render them obnoxious to
the clergy of every rank, to the monafteries of other orders, and to
the univerfities. It was not from ignorance, but from a knowledge
of mankind, that they were active in propagating fuperftitious notions,
which they knew were calculated to captivate the multitude, and to
ftrengthen the papal intereft ; yet at the fame time, from the vanity
of difplaying an uncommon fagacity of thought and a fuperior fkill
in theology, they affected novelties in doctrine, which introduced
dangerous errors, and tended to fhake the pillars of orthodoxy.
Their ambition was unbounded, and their arrogance intolerable.
Their increafing numbers became, in many ftates, an enormous and
unwieldy burthen to the commonwealth. They had abufed the
powers and privileges which had been intrufted to them ; and the
common fenfe of mankind could not long be blinded or deluded by
the palpable frauds and artifices, which thefe rapacious zealots fo
notorioufly practifed for enriching their convents. In England, the
univerfity of Oxford refolutely refifted the perpetual encroachments of
the Dominicans ;[2] and many of our theologifts attacked all the four
orders with great vehemence and feverity. Exclufively of the jealoufies
and animofities which naturally fubfifted between four rival inftitutions, their vifionary refinements and love of difputation introduced

---

[1] See Baluz. *Mifcellan.* tom. iv. 490, vii. 392.
[2] Wood, *ut fupr.* i. 150, 154, 196.

among them the moſt violent diſſenſions. The Dominicans aimed
at popularity by an obſtinate denial of the immaculate conception.
Their pretended ſanctity became at length a term of reproach, and
their learning fell into diſcredit. As polite letters and general knowledge increaſed, their ſpeculative and pedantic divinity gave way to a
more liberal turn of thinking and a more perſpicuous mode of writing.
Bale, who was himſelf a Carmelite friar, ſays that his order, which
was eminently diſtinguiſhed for ſcholaſtic erudition, began to loſe
their eſtimation about the year 1460. Some of them were impru-
dent enough to engage openly in political controverſy ; and the Au-
guſtines deſtroyed all their repute and authority in England by ſedi-
tious ſermons, in which they laboured to ſupplant the progeny of
Edward IV., and to eſtabliſh the title of the uſurper Richard.[1] About
the year 1530, Leland viſited the Franciſcan friary at Oxford, big
with the hopes of finding in their celebrated library, if not many
valuable books, at leaſt thoſe which had been bequeathed by the
learned biſhop Groſeteſte. The delays and difficulties, with which
he procured admittance into this venerable repoſitory, heightened
his curioſity and expectations. At length, after much ceremony,
being permitted to enter, inſtead of an ineſtimable treaſure, he
ſaw little more than empty ſhelves covered with cobwebs and
duſt.[2]

After ſo prolix an introduction, I cannot but give a large quotation from our *Crede*, the humour and tendency of which will now be
eaſily underſtood ; eſpecially as this poem is ſo curious and lively a
picture of an order of men who once made ſo conſpicuous a figure
in the world :[3]

> For firſt y fraynede þe freres · and þey me fulle tolden,
> Þat all þe frute of þe fayþ · was in here foure ordres,
> And þe cofres of criſtendam · & þe keye boþen,
> And þe lok [of beleve · lyeth] loken in her hondes.

---

[1] Newcourt, *Repert.* i. 289.

[2] Leland deſcribes this adventure with ſome humour. " Contigit ut copiam
peterem videndi bibliothecam Franciſcanorum, ad quod obſtreperunt aſini aliquot,
rudentes nulli prorſus mortalium tam ſanctos aditus et receſſus adire, niſi Gardiano
et ſacris ſui collegii baccalariis. Sed ego urgebam, et principis diplomate munitus,
tantum non coegi, ut ſacraria illa aperirent. Tum unus e majoribus aſinis multa
ſubrudens tandem fores ægre reſeravit. Summe Jupiter ! quid ego illic inveni ?
Pulverem autem inveni, telas aranearum, tineas, blattas, ſitum denique et ſqual-
lorem. Inveni etiam et libros, ſed quos tribus obolis non emerem."—*Script. Brit.*
p. 286.

[3] [The Britiſh Muſeum contains but one MS. (King's MSS. 18. B. xvi.) of the
Crede, and that of no early date. It agrees cloſely in orthography and matter with
the printed copy, and is perhaps not much older.—*Price.* There is another MS. in
the library of Trinity College, Cambridge. Both MSS., as well as the old printed
edition, are evidently derived from one and the ſame older MS., now loſt, of the
early part of the fifteenth century. The Trinity MS. is a very faithful tranſcript,
and far more correct than the Muſeum copy ; both the MSS. copies are more
correct than the printed edition. The *Crede*, as printed by Warton and his
editors, has now been adjuſted to the *Early Engliſh Text Society's* edition, 1867, ed.
by Rev. W. W. Skeat.]

Þanne [wende] y to wyten · & wiþ a whiȝt y mette,
A Menoure in a morrow-tide · & to þis man I faide,
"Sire, for grete god[e]s loue · þe graiþ þou me telle,
Of what myddelerde man · miȝte y beft lerne
My Crede? For I can it nouȝt · my kare is þe more;
& þerfore, for Criftes loue · þi councell y praie.
A Carm me haþ y-couenaunt · þe Crede me to teche;
But for þou knoweft Carmes well · þi counfaile y afke."
Þis Menour loked on me · and lawȝyng he feyde,
"Leue Criften man · y leue þat þou madde!
Whouȝ fchulde þei techen þe God · þat con not hemfelue?
Þei ben but jugulers · and iapers, of kynde,
Lorels and Lechures · & lemmans holden;
Neyþer in order ne out · but vn-neþe lybbeþ,
And byiapeþ þe folke · wiþ geftes of Rome!
It is but a faynt folk · i-founded vp-on iapes,
Þei makeþ hem Maries men¹ · (fo þei men tellen),
And lieþ on our Ladie · many a longe tale.
And þat wicked folke · wymmen bi-traieþ,
And bigileþ hem of her good · wiþ glauerynge wordes,
And þerwiþ holden her hous · in harlotes werkes.
And, fo faue me God! · I hold it gret fynne
To ȝyuen hem any good · fwiche glotones to fynde,
To maynteyne fwiche maner men · þat mychel good deftruyeþ.
Ȝet feyn in here futilte · to fottes in townes,
Þei comen out of Carmeli² · Crift for to followen,
& feyneþ hem with holynes · þat yuele hem bifemeþ.
Þei lyuen more in lecherie · and lieth in her tales
Þan fuen any god liife; · but [lurken] in her felles,
[And] wynnen werldliche god · & waften it in fynne.
And ȝif þei couþen her crede · oþer on Crift leueden,
Þei weren nouȝt fo hardie · fwich harlotri vfen.
Sikerli y can nouȝt fynden · who hem firft founded,
But þe foles foundeden hem-felf · freres of the Pye,
And maken hem mendynauns · & marre þe puple.
But what glut of þo gomes · may any good kachen,
He will kepen it hym-felf · & cofren it fafte,
And þeiȝ his felawes fayle good · for him he may fteruen.
Her money may bi-queft · & teftament maken,
And no obedience bere · but don as [hem] lufte.
[And] ryȝt as Robertes men³ · raken aboute,
At feires & at ful ales · & fyllen þe cuppe,
And precheþ all of pardon · to plefen the puple.

---

¹ The Carmelites, fometimes called the brethren of the Bleffed Virgin, were fond of boafting their familiar intercourfe with the Virgin Mary. Among other things, they pretended that the Virgin affumed the Carmelite habit and profeffion: and that fhe appeared to Simon Sturckius, general of their order, in the thirteenth century, and gave him a folemn promife, that the fouls of thofe Chriftians who died with the Carmelite fcapulary upon their fhoulders fhould infallibly efcape damnation.

² The Carmelites pretended that their order was originally founded on Mount Carmel where Elias lived: and that their firft convent was placed there, within an ancient church dedicated to the Virgin Mary in 1121.

³ Robartes men, or Roberdfmen, were a fet of lawlefs vagabonds, notorious for their outrages when *Pierce Plowman* was written, that is, about the year [1362]. The ftatute Edw. III. (*an. reg.* 5. c. xiv.) fpecifies "divers manflaughters, felonies, and robberies, done by people that be called *Roberdefmen*, Waftours, and drawlatches." And the ftatute (*an. reg.* 7. c. v.) ordains, that the ftatute of King Edward concerning *Roberdfmen* and *Drawlacches* fhall be rigoroufly obferved.

Her pacience is all paſed · & put out to ferme,
And pride is in her pouerte · þat litell is to preiſen.
And at þe lulling of oure Ladye · þe wymmen to lyken,
And miracles of mydwyves · & maken wymmen to wenen
þat þe lace of oure ladie ſmok · liȝteþ hem of children.
þei ne prechen nouȝt of Powel · ne penaunce for ſynne,
But all of mercy & menſk · þat Marie maie helpen.
Wiþ ſterne ſtaues and ſtronge · þey ouer lond ſtrakeþ
þider as her lemmans liggeþ · and lurkeþ in townes,
(Grey grete-hedede quenes · wiþ gold by þe eiȝen),
And ſeyn, þat here ſuſtren þei ben · þat ſoiourneþ aboute ;
And þus about þey gon · & godes folke by-traieþ.
It is þe puple þat Powel · preched of in his tyme ;
He ſeyde of ſwich folk · þat ſo aboute wente,
' Wepyng, y warne ȝow · of walkers aboute ;
It beþ enemyes of þe cros · þat criſt opon þolede.
Swiche ſlomerers in ſlepe · ſlauþe is her ende,
And glotony is her God · wiþ g[l]oppyng of drynk,[1]
And gladnes in glees · & gret ioye y-maked ;
In þe ſchendyng of ſwiche · ſcha[l]l mychel folk lawȝe.'
þerfore, frend, for þi feyþ · fond to don betere,
Leue nouȝt on þo loſels · but let hem forþ paſen,
For þei ben fals in her feiþ · & fele mo oþere."
" Alas! frere," quaþ I þo · " my purpos is i-failed,
Now is my counfort a-caſt ! · canſtou no bote,
Where y myȝte meten wiþ a man · þat myȝte me [wiſſen]
For to conne my Crede · Criſt for to folwen ?"
" CERTEYNE, felawe," quaþ þe frere · " wiþ-outen any faile.
Of all men opon mold · we Menures moſt ſcheweþ
þe pure Apoſtell[e]s life · wiþ penance on erþe,
And ſuen hem in ſaunctite · & ſuffren well harde.
We haunten none tauernes · ne hobelen abouten ;
At marketts & myracles · we medleþ vs nevere ;
We hondlen no money · but menelich faren,
And haven hunger at [the] meate · at ich a mel ones.
We hauen forſaken the worlde · & in wo lybbeþ.
In penaunce & pouerte · & precheþ þe puple,
By enſample of oure life · ſoules to helpen ;
And in pouertie praien · for all oure parteners
þat ȝyueþ vs any good · god to honouren,
Oþer bell oþer booke · or breed to our fode,
Oþer catell oþer cloþ · to coveren wiþ our bones,
Money or money-worthe ; · here mede is in heven.
For we buldeþ a burwȝ · a brod and a large,
A Chirche and A Chapaile · with chambers a-lofte,
Wiþ wide windowes y-wrouȝt · & walles well heye,
þat mote bene portreid and paynt · & pulched ful clene [2]
Wiþ gaie glittering glas · glowing as þe ſonne.
And myȝteſtou amenden vs · wiþ money[3] of þyn owne,
þou chuldeſt cnely bifore Criſt · in compas of gold
In þe wide windowe weſtwarde · wel niȝe in the myddell,[4]
And ſeynt Fraunces him-ſelf · ſchall folden the in his cope,

---

[1] In the *Liber Pœnitentialis* there is this injunction, " Si monachus per ebrietatem *vomitum fecerit*, triginta dies *pæniteat*." MSS. James V. 237, Bibl. Bodl.

[2] Muſt be painted and beautifully adorned. *Mote* is often uſed in Chaucer for muſt.

[3] If you would help us with your money.

[4] Your figure kneeling to Chriſt ſhall be painted in the great weſt window. This was the way of repreſenting benefactors in painted glaſs. See *ſupr.*

And preſente the to the trynitie · and praie for thy ſynnes;
Þi name ſchall noblich ben wryten · & wrouȝt for the nones,
And, in remembrance of þe · y-rade þer for euer.[1]
And, broþer, be þou nouȝt aferd; · [bythenk in] thyn herte,
Þouȝ þou conne nouȝt þi Crede · kare þou no more.
I ſchal aſoilen þe, ſyre · & ſetten it on my ſoule,
And þou maie maken þis good · þenk þou non oþer."
"SIRE," y ſaide, "in certaine · y ſchal gon & aſaye;"--
And he ſette on me his honde · & aſoilede me clene,
And þeir y parted him fro · wiþ-outen any peine,
In couenant þat y come aȝen · Criſt he me be-tauȝte.
Þanne ſaide y to my-ſelf · "here ſemeþ litel trewþe!
Firſt to blamen his broþer · and bacbyten him foule,
Þeire-as curteis Criſt · clereliche ſaide,
' Whow myȝt-tou in thine broþer eiȝe · a bare mote loken,
And in þyn owen eiȝe · nouȝt a bem toten ?
See fyrſt on þi-ſelf · and ſiþen on anoþer,
And clenſe clene þi ſyȝt · and kepe well þyn eiȝe,
And for anoþer mannes eiȝe · ordeyne after.'
And alſo y ſey coueitiſe · catel to fongen,
Þat Criſt haþ clerliche forboden · & clenliche deſtruede,
And ſaide to his ſueres · forſoþe on þis wiſe,
' Nouȝt þi neiȝbours good · couet yn no tyme.'
But charite & chaſtete · ben chaſed out clene,
But Criſt ſeide, ' by her fruyt · men ſhall hem ful knowen.' "
Þanne ſaide y, "certeyn, ſire · þou demeſt full trewe !"
Þanne þouȝt y to frayne þe firſt · of þis foure ordirs,
And preſede to þe prechoures · to proven here wille.
[Ich] hiȝede to her houſe · to herken of more;
And whan y cam to þat court · y gaped aboute.
Swich a bild bold, y-buld · opon erþe heiȝte
Say i nouȝth in certeine · ſiþþe a longe tyme.
Y ȝemede vpon þat houſe · & ȝerne þeron loked,
Whouȝ þe pileres weren y-peynt · and pulched ful clene,
And queynteli i-coruen · wiþ curiouſe knottes,
Wiþ wyndowes well y-wrouȝt · wide vp o-lofte.
And þanne y entrid in · and even-forþ went,
And all was walled þat wone · þouȝ it wid were,
Wiþ poſternes in pryuytie · to paſen when hem liſte;
Orcheȝardes and erberes · eueſed well clene,
And a curious cros · craftly entayled,
Wiþ tabernacles y-tiȝt · to toten all abouten.
Þe pris of a plouȝ-lond · of penyes ſo rounde
To aparaile þat pyler · were pure lytel.
Þanne y mynſtre me forþ · þe mynſtre to knowen,
And a-waytede a woon · wonderlie well y-beld,
Wiþ arches on eueriche half · & belliche y-corven,
Wiþ crochetes on corners · wiþ knottes of golde,
Wyde wyndowes y-wrouȝt · y-written full þikke,
Schynen wiþ ſchapen ſcheldes[2] · to ſchewen aboute,

---

[1] Your name ſhall be written in our table of benefactors for whoſe ſouls we pray. This was uſually hung up in the church. Or elſe he means, Written in the windows, in which manner benefactors were frequently recorded.

Moſt of the [later] printed copies read *praid.* Hearne, in a quotation of this paſſage, reads *yrad. Gul. Newbrig.* p. 770. He quotes [the] edition of 1553. " Your name ſhall be richly written in the windows of the church of the monaſtery which men will read there for ever." This ſeems to be the true reading [unqueſtionably.]

[2] That is, coats of arms of benefactors painted in the glaſs. So in an ancient

Wiþ merkes of marchauntes[1] · y-medled bytwene,
Mo þan twenty and two · twyes y-noumbred.
Þer is none heraud þat haþ · half fwich a rolle,
Riȝt as a rageman · haþ reckned hem newe.
Tombes opon tabernacles · tyld opon lofte,
Houfed[2] in hirnes · harde fet abouten,
Of armede alabauftre · clad for þe nones,
[Made vpon marbel · in many maner wyfe,
Knyght*es* in her conifant*es*[3] · clad for þe nones,]

---

roll in verfe, exhibiting the defcent of the family of the lords of Clare in Suffolk, preferved in the Auftin friary at Clare, and written in the year 1356.

> " Dame Mault, a lady full honorable
> Borne of the Ulfters, as fheweth ryfe
> Hir armes of glaffe in the eaftern gable.
> —— So conjoyned be
> Ulftris armes and Gloceftris thurgh and thurgh,
> As fhewith our Wyndowes in houfes thre,
> Dortur, chapiter-houfe, and fraitour, which fhe
> Made out the grounde both plancher and wall."

Dugdale cites this roll, *Mon. Angl.* i. p. 535. As does Weever, who dates it in 1460. *Fun. Mon.* p. 734. But I could prove this fafhion to have been of much higher antiquity.

[1] By merkes of merchauntes we are to underftand their fymbols, ciphers, or badges, drawn or painted in the windows. [A great variety of them may be feen in *Current Notes*.] Of this paffage I have received the following curious explication from Mr. Cole, reƈtor of Blechley in Bucks, a learned antiquary in the heraldic art. " Mixed with the arms of their founders and benefaƈtors ftand alfo the marks of tradefmen and merchants, who had no Arms, but ufed their Marks in a Shield like Arms. Inftances of this fort are very common. In many places in Great Saint Mary's church in Cambridge fuch a Shield of Mark occurs : the fame that is to be feen in the windows of the great fhop oppofite the Conduit on the Market-hill, and the corner houfe of the Petty Curry. No doubt, in the reign of Henry VII., the owner of thefe houfes was a benefaƈtor to the building, or glazing Saint Mary's church. I have feen like inftances in Briftol cathedral ; and the churches at Lynn are full of them."—In an ancient fyftem of heraldry in the Britifh Mufeum, I find the following illuftration, under a fhield of this fort. " Theys be none armys, bvt a Marke as Marchaunts vfe, for every mane may take hyme a Marke, but not armys, without an herawde or purcyvaunte." MSS. Harl. 2259, 9, fol. 110.

[2] Hurnes, interpreted, in the fhort Gloffary to the *Crede*, Caves, that is, in the prefent application, niches, arches. See *Glofs. Rob. Glouc.* p. 660, col. i. Hurn, is angle, corner. From the Saxon Þyꞃn, Angulus. Chaucer, *Frankel.* T. v. 393.

> " Seeken in every halke [nook], and every herne."

And again, *Chan. Yem. Prol.* ver. 105.

> " Lurking in hernes and in lanes blynde."

Read the line, thus pointed.

> " Houfed in hurnes hard fet abouten."

The fenfe is therefore : " The tombs were within lofty-pinnacled tabernacles, and enclofed in a multiplicity of thick-fet arches." Hard is clofe, or thick. This conveys no bad idea of a Gothic fepulchral fhrine.

[3] In their proper habiliments. In their cognifances, or furcoats of arms. So again, fignat. C ii b.

> " For though a man in her minftre a maffe wolde heren,
> His fight fhall alfo byfet on fondrye workes,
> The pennons, and the poinells, and pointes of fheldes
> Withdrawen his devotion and dufken his harte."

That is, the banners, atchievements, and other armorial ornaments, hanging over the tombs.

All it femed feyntes · y-facred open erþe;
And louely ladies y-wrouȝt · leyen by her fydes
In many gay garmentes · þat weren gold-beten.
Þouȝ þe tax of ten ȝer · were trewly y-gadered,
Nolde it nouȝt maken þat hous · half, as y trowe.
Þanne kam I to þat cloifter · & gaped abouten
Whouȝ it was pilered and peynt · & portred well clene,
All y-hyled wiþ leed · lowe to þe ftones,
And y-paued wiþ peynt til · iche poynte after oþer;
Wiþ kundites of clene tyn · clofed all aboute,
Wiþ lauoures of latun · louelyche y-greithed.
I trowe þe gaynage of þe ground · in a gret fchire
Nolde aparaile þat place · oo poynt til other ende.
Þanne was þe chaptire-hous wrouȝt · as a greet chirche,
Coruen and couered · and queyntliche entayled;
Wiþ femlich felure · y-fet on lofte;
As a Parlement-hous · y-peynted aboute.[1]

---

[1] That they painted the walls of rooms, before tapeftry became fafhionable, I have before given inftances, *Obfervat. Spens.* vol. ii. § p. 232. I will here add other proofs. In an old French romance on the *Miracles of the Virgin*, liv. i. Carpent. *Suppl. Lat. Gl. Du Cang.* v. *Lambroiffare.*

> " Lors mouftiers tiennent ors et fales,
> Et lor cambres, et lor grans fales,
> Font lambroiffier, paindre et pourtraire."

Gervafius Dorobernenfis, in his account of the burning of Canterbury Cathedral in the year 1174, fays, that not only the beam-work was deftroyed, but the ceiling underneath it, or concameration called cœlum, being of wood beautifully painted, was alfo confumed. " Cœlum inferius egregie depictum," &c. p. 1289. *Dec. Script.* 1652. And Stubbes, *Actus Pontif. Eboracenfium*, fays that Archbifhop Aldred, about 1060, built the whole church of York from the prefbytery to the tower, and " fuperius opere pictorio quod Cœlum vocant auro multiformiter intermixto, mirabili arte conftruxit." p. 1704. *Dec. Script.* ut fupr. There are many inftances in the pipe-rolls. The roof of the church of Caffino in Italy is ordered to be painted in 1349, like that of St. John Lateran at Rome. *Hift. Caffin.* tom. ii. p. 545, col. i. Dugdale has printed an ancient French record, by which it appears that there was a hall in the caftle of Dover called Arthur's hall, and a chamber called Geneura's chamber. *Monaft.* ii. 2. I fuppofe, becaufe the walls of thefe apartments were refpectively adorned with paintings of each. Geneura is Arthur's queen. In the pipe-rolls, Hen. III., we have this notice, A.D. 1259. " Infra portam caftri et birbecanam, etc. ab exitu Cameræ Rofamundæ ufque capellam fancti Thomæ in Caftro Wynton." *Rot. Pip. Hen. III.* an. 43.—This I once fuppofed to be a chamber in Winchefter caftle, fo called becaufe it was painted with the figure or fome hiftory of fair Rofamond. But a Rofamond-chamber was a common apartment in the royal caftles, perhaps in imitation of her bower at Woodftock, literally nothing more than a chamber, which yet was curioufly conftructed and decorated, at leaft in memory of it. The old profe paraphraft of the Chronicle of Robert of Gloucefter fays, " Boures hadde the Rofamonde a bout in Engelonde, which this kynge [Hen. II.] for hir fake made: atte Waltham bifhopes, in the caftelle of Wynchefter, atte park of Fremantel, atte Marteleston, atte Woodeftoke, and other fele [many] places." *Chron.* edit. Hearne, 479. This paffage indeed feems to imply, that Henry II. himfelf provided for his fair concubine a bower, or chamber of peculiar conftruction, not only at Woodftock, but in all the royal palaces: which, as may be concluded from the pipe-roll juft cited, was called by her name. Leland fays, that in the ftately caftle of Pickering in Yorkfhire, " in the firft court be a foure Toures, of the which one is caullid Rofamundes Toure." *Itin.* fol. 71. Probably becaufe it contained one of thefe bowers or chambers. Or, perhaps we fhould read Rofamundes Boure. Compare Walpole's *Anecd. Paint.* i. pp. 10, 11.

Þanne ferd y into fraytour · and fond þere an oþer,
An halle for an heyȝ kinge · an housholde to holden,
Wiþ brode bordes aboute · y-benched wel clene,
Wiþ windowes of glas · wrouȝt as a Chirche.
Þanne walkede y ferrer · & went all abouten,
And seiȝ halles full hyȝe · & houses full noble,
Chambers wiþ chimneyes · & Chapells gaie ;
And kychens for an hyȝe kinge · in castells to holden,
And her dortour y-diȝte · wiþ dores ful stronge ;
Fermery and fraitur · with fele mo houses,
And all strong ston wall · sterne opon heiþe,
Wiþ gaie garites & grete · & iche hole y-glased ;
[And oþere] houses y-nowe · to herberwe þe queene.
And ȝet þise bilderes wilne beggen · a bagg-ful of wheate
Of a pure pore man · þat maie oneþe paie
Half his rente in a ȝer · and half ben behynde !
Þanne turned y aȝen · whan y hadde all y-toted,
And fond in a freitour · a frere on a benche,
A ꞏ ꞏꞏ ꞏ ꞏ & a grym · growen as a tonne,
Wiȝ ꞏꞏꞏ ꞏꞏ fat · as a full bledder,
Blowen bretfull of breþ · & as a bagge honged
On boþen his chekes, & his chyn · wiþ a chol lollede,
As greet as a gos eye · growen all of grece ;
Þat all wagged his fleche · as a quyk myre.
His cope þat biclypped him · wel clene was it folden,
Of double worstede y-dyȝt · doun to þe hele ;
His kyrtel of clene whijt · clenlyche y-sewed ;
Hyt was good y-now of ground · greyn for to beren.
I haylsede þat herdeman · & hendliche y saide,
" Gode syre, for Godes loue · canstou me graiþ tellen
To any worþely wijȝt · þat [wissen] me couþe
Whou y schulde conne my Crede · Crist for to folowe,
Þat leuede lelliche him-self · & lyuede þerafter,
Þat feynede non falshede · but fully Crist suwede ?
For sich a certeyn man · syker wold y trosten,
Þat he wolde telle me þe trewþe · and turne to none oþer.
And an Austyn þis ender daie · egged me faste ;
Þat he wolde techen me wel · he plyȝt me his treuþe,
And seyde me, ' serteyne · syþen Crist died
Oure ordir was [euelles] · & erst y-founde.' "
" Fyrst, felawe !" quaþ he · " fy on his pilche !
He is but abortijf · eked wiþ cloutes !
He holdeþ his ordynaunce · wiþe hores and þeues,
And purchaseþ hem pryuileges · wiþ penyes so rounde ;
It is a pur pardoners craft · proue & asaye !
For haue þei þi money · a moneþ þerafter,
Certes, þeiȝ þou come aȝen · he nyl þe nouȝt knowen.
But, felawe, *our* foundement · was first of þe opere,
And we ben founded fulliche · wiþ-outen fayntise ;
And we ben clerkes y-cnowen · cunnynge in scole,
Proued in procession · by procesʃe of lawe.
Of oure ordre þer beþ · bichopes wel manye,
Seyntes on sundry stedes · þat suffreden harde ;
And we ben proued þe prijs · of popes at Rome,
And of greteʃt degre · as godspelles telleþ."

I muʃt not quit our Ploughman without obʃerving, that ʃome other
ʃatirical pieces anterior to the Reformation bear the adopted name
of *Piers the Plowman.* Under the character of a ploughman the religious are likewiʃe laʃhed in a poem written in apparent imitation of

Langland's *Vision*, and [falsely] attributed to Chaucer. I mean the *Plowman's Tale.*[1] The meafure is different, and it is in rhyme. But it has Langland's alliteration of initials; as if his example had, as it were, appropriated that mode of verfification to the fubject, and the fuppofed character which fupports the fatire.[2] All thefe poems [or rather, the *Crede* and the *Tale*] were, for the moft part, founded on the doctrines newly broached by Wickliffe :[3] who maintained, among other things, that the clergy fhould not poffefs eftates, that the eccle-fiaftical ceremonies obftructed true devotion, and that Mendicant friars, the particular object of our *Plowman's Crede*, were a public and infupportable grievance. But Wickliffe, whom Mr. Hume pro-nounces to have been an enthufiaft, like many other reformers, carried his ideas of purity too far, and, as at leaft it appears from the two firft

---

[1] [In the] *Plowman's Tale* this Crede is alluded to, v. 3005 :

> " And of *Freris* I have *before*
> Told in a making of a *Crede ;*
> And yet I could tell worfe and more."

This paffage at leaft brings the *Plowman's Tale* below the *Crede* in time. But fome have thought, very improbably, that this Crede is *Jack Upland.* [Internal evidence clearly fhows that the author of the *Plowman's Tale* was alfo author of the *Crede*, as he claims to have been. In imitation of Langland, he named one of his poems the *Plowman's Crede*, and the other the *Plowman's Tale.* The probable date of the former is A. D. 1394, and of the latter A. D. 1395.]

[2] It is extraordinary that we fhould find in this poem one of the abfurd argu-ments of the puritans againft ecclefiaftical eftablifhments, v. 2253 :

> " For Chrift made no cathedralls,
> Ne with him was no Cardinalls."

But fee what follows, concerning Wickliffe.

[3] It is remarkable, that they touch on the very topics which Wickliffe had juft publifhed in his *Objections of Freres*, charging them with fifty herefies. As in the following : " Alfo Freres buildin many great churches, and cofty waft houfes and cloifteres, as it wern cafteles, and that withouten nede," &c. Lewis's *Wickliff*, p. 22. I will here add a paffage from Wickliffe's tract entitled *Why poor Priefts have no Benefices.* Lewis, App. Num. xix. p. 289. " And yet they [lords] wolen not prefent a clerk able of kunning of god's law, but a kitchen clerk, or a penny clerk, or wife in building caftles, or worldly doing, though he kunne not reade well his fauter," &c. Here is a manifeft piece of fatire on Wykeham, bifhop of Winchefter, Wickliffe's cotemporary ; who is fuppofed to have recommended him-felf to Edward III. by rebuilding the caftle of Windfor. This was a recent and notorious inftance. But in this appointment the king probably paid a compliment to that prelate's fingular talents for bufinefs, his activity, circumfpection, and management, rather than to any fcientific and profeffed fkill in architecture which he might have poffeffed. It feems to me that he was only a fupervifor or comp-troller on this occafion. It was common to depute churchmen to this department, from an idea of their fuperior prudence and probity. Thus John, the prior of St. Swithin's at Winchefter in 1280, is commiffioned by brief from the king to fuper-vife large repairs done by the fheriff in the caftle of Winchefter and the royal manor of Wolmer. *MS. Regiftr. Priorat.* Quat. 19, fol. 3. The bifhop of S. David's was mafter of the works at building King's College. Hearne's *Elmh.* p. 353. Alcock, bifhop of Ely, was comptroller of the royal buildings under Henry VII. Parker's *Hift. Cambr.* p. 119. He, like Wykeham, was a great builder, but not therefore an architect. Richard Williams, dean of Lichfield, and chaplain to Henry VIII. bore the fame office. MSS. Wood, Lichfield, D. 7. Afhmol. Nicholas Townley, clerk, was mafter of the works at Cardinal College. MS. Twyne, 8, f. 351. See alfo Walpole, *Anecd. Paint.* i. p. 40.

of thefe opinions, under the defign of deftroying fuperftition, his un-diftinguifhing zeal attacked even the neceffary aids of religion. It was certainly a lucky circumftance that Wickliffe quarrelled with the Pope. His attacks on fuperftition at firft probably proceeded from refentment. Wickliffe, who was profeffor of divinity at Ox-ford, finding on many occafions not only his own province invaded, but even the privileges of the univerfity frequently violated by the pretenfions of the Mendicants, gratified his warmth of temper by throwing out fome flight cenfures againft all the four orders, and the popes their principal patrons and abettors. Soon afterwards he was deprived of the wardenfhip of Canterbury hall by the Archbifhop of Canterbury, who fubftituted a monk in his place. Upon this he appealed to the Pope, who confirmed the archiepifcopal fentence, by way of rebuke for the freedom with which he had treated the mo-naftic profeffion. Wickliffe, highly exafperated at this ufage, imme-diately gave a loofe to his indignation, and without reftraint or dif-tinction attacked in numerous fermons and treatifes not only the fcandalous enormities of the whole body of monks, but even the ufurpations of the pontifical power itfelf, with other ecclefiaftical corruptions. Having expofed thefe palpable abufes with a juft ab-horrence, he ventured ftill farther, and proceeded to examine and refute with great learning and penetration the abfurd doctrines which prevailed in the religious fyftem of his age: he not only ex-horted the laity to ftudy the Scriptures, but tranflated the Bible into Englifh for general ufe and popular infpection. Whatever were his motives, it is certain that thefe efforts enlarged the notions of mankind, and fowed thofe feeds of a revolution in religion, which were quick-ened at length and brought to maturity by a favourable coincidence of circumftances, in an age when the increafing growth of literature and curiofity naturally led the way to innovation and improvement. But a vifible diminution of the authority of the ecclefiaftics, in Eng-land at leaft, had been long growing from other caufes. The difguft which the laity had contracted from the numerous and arbitrary en-croachments both of the court of Rome and of their own clergy, had greatly weaned the kingdom from fuperftition; and confpicuous fymptoms had appeared, on various occafions, of a general defire to fhake off the intolerable bondage of papal oppreffion.

SECTION X.

ANGLAND'S peculiarity of ftyle and verfification feems to have had many imitators. One of thefe is a namelefs author on the fafhionable hiftory of Alexander the Great : and his poem on this fubject is inferted at the end of the beautiful Bodleian copy of the French *Roman d'Alexandre*, before mentioned, with this reference :[1] *Here fayleth a proffeffe of this romaunce of Alixaunder the whiche proffeffe that fayleth ye fchulle fynde at the ende of thys boke ywrete in Engeliche ryme.* It is imperfect, and begins and proceeds thus :[2]

How Alexander partyd thennys.[3]
When this weith at his wil weduring hadde,
Ful rathe rommede he rydinge thederre ;
To Oridrace with his oft Alixandre wendus :
There wilde contre was wift, and wondurful peple,
That weren proved ful proude, and prys of hem helde ;
Of bodi went thei bare withoute any wede,
And had grave on the ground many grete cavys ;
There here wonnynge was wynturus and fomerus.
No fyte nor no fur ftede fothli thei ne hadde,
But holus holwe in the grounde to hide hem inne ;
The proude Genofophiftiens[4] were the gomus called,

---

[1] It is in a different hand, yet with Saxon characters. See ad calc. cod. f. 209. It has miniatures in water colours. [See Mr. Skeat's *Effay on Alliterative Poetry* in the third volume of the lately-edited Percy folio MS. (1868).—F.]

[2] There is a poem in the [Bodleian library,] complete in the former part, which is [certainly] the fame. [Sir F. Madden affigns the former to the reign of Henry VI. That gentleman alfo informs us that in the Bodleian is a fragment of anothers and quite different alliterative romance of Alexander, compofed, he believe, by the perfon who wrote the Englifh alliterative romance of *William and the Werwolf*, ed. 1832.] MSS. Afhm. 44. It has twenty-feven paffus, and begins thus :

" Whener folker faftid and fed, fayne wolde thei her
Some farand thing," &c.

[3] [Printed in Weber's collection, 1810.] At the end are thefe rubrics, with void fpaces, intended to be filled :

" How Alexandre remewid to a flood that is called Phifon."
" How king Duidimus fente lettres to king Alexandre."
" How Duidimus enditid to Alexaundre of here levyng."
" How he fpareth not Alexandre to telle hym of hys governance."
" How he telleth Alexandre of his maumetrie."
" How Alexandre fente aunfwere to Duidimus by lettres."
" How Duidimus fendyd an anfwere to Alexandre by lettre."
" How Alexandre fente Duidimus another lettre."
" How Alexandre pight a pelyr of marbyl ther."

[The laft of thefe rubrics only is followed by a void fpace in the Bodleian copy ; the former being filled up with fuch verfification as is given in Mr. Warton's text, which led Ritfon to confider it a much earlier compofition than Piers Plowman.— *Park.*]

[4] Gymnofophifts.

Now is that name to mene the nakid wife.
Wan the kiddefte of the cavus, that was kinge holde,
Hurde tydinge telle and toknynge wifte,
That Alixaundre with his oft atlede thidirre,
To beholden of hom hure hieʒeft prynce,
Than waies of worfhipe wittie and quainte
With his lettres he let to the lud fende.
Thanne fouthte thei fone the forefaide prynce,
And to the fchamlefe fchalk fchewen hur lettres.
Than rathe let the rink reden the fonde,
That newe tythingeit tolde in this wife :
The gentil Geneofophiftians, that gode were of witte,
To the emperour Alixandre here aunfweris wreten.
That is worfchip of word worthi to have,
And is conquerer kid in contres manie.
Us is fertefyed, feg, as we foth heren
That thou haft ment with thi man amongis us ferre
But yf thou kyng to us come with caere to fiʒte
Of us getift thou no good, gome, we the warne.
For what richeffe, rink, us might you us bi-reve,
Whan no wordliche wele is with us founde ?
We ben fengle of us filfe, and femen ful bare,
Nouht welde we nowe, but naked we wende,
And that we happili her haven of kynde
May no man but God maken us tine.
Thei thou fonde with thi folke to fighte with us alle,
We fchulle us kepe on cauʒt our cavus withinne.
Nevere werred we with wiʒth upon erthe ;
For we ben hid in oure holis or we harme laache.
Thus faide fothli the fonde that thei fente hadde,
And al fo cof as the king kende the fawe,
New lettres he let the ludus bitake,
And with his fawes of foth he fikerede hem alle,
That he wolde faire with his folke in a faire wife,
To b'holden here home, and non harme wurke.
So hath the king to hem fente, and fithen with his p'eple,
Kaires cofli til hem, to kenne of hure fare.
But whan thai fieu the feg with fo manye ryde,
Thei war agrifen of hys grym, and wende gref tholie ;
Faft heiede thei to holis, and hidden there,[1]
And in the cavus hem kept from the king fterne, &c.

Another piece, written in Langland's manner, is entitled, [*The
Deftruction of Jerufalem*]. This was a favourite fubject, as I have
before obferved, drawn from the Latin hiftorical romance, which
paffes under the name of *Hegefippus de Excidio Hierufalem* :

In Tyberyus tyme the trewe emperour[2]

---

[1] [In the Bodleian Library, MS. Greaves 60, is a fragment of another alliterative romance on the fubject of Alexander, totally different from the former one,
and which I have good grounds to believe was compofed by the fame poet who
wrote the Englifh alliterative romance of *William and the Werwolf*, edited by me
for the Roxburghe Club, in 1832.—M.]

[2] [The prefent text has been collated with the Cott. MS. Calig. A. ii. The
orthographical differences between this and the Laud MS. are numerous though
not important. All its readings improving the fenfe have been adopted ; though
this perhaps would have been wholly fuperfluous, had the original tranfcript been
correctly made.—*Price.*]

Syr Seſar hym [ſelf ſeſed [1]] in Rome
Whyl Pylot was provoſt under that prynce ryche
And [jewes [2]] juſtice alſo in Judens londis
Herode under his empire as heritage wolde
King of Galile was ycallid, whan that Criſt deyad
They [3] Seſar ſakles wer, that oft ſyn hatide
Throw Pilet pyned he was and put on the rode
A pyler was down pyʒt [4] upon the playne erthe
His body [bowndone [5]] therto beten with ſcourgis,
Whippes of [wherebole [6]] bywent his white ſides
Til he al on rede blode ran as rayn on the ſtrete;
[Sith [7]] ſtockyd hym an a ſtole with ſtyf menes hondis,
Blyndfelled hym as a be and boffetis hym raʒte
ʒif you be a prophete of pris, prophecie, they ſayde
Which man her aboute [bolled [8]] the laſte,
A ſtrange thorn crown was thraſte on his hed
[They [9]] caſten [up a grete] cry [that hym on] cros ſlowen,
For al the harme that he had, haſted he noʒt
On hym the vyleny to venge that hys venys broſten,
Bot ay taried on the tyme, ʒif they [turne [10]] wolde
Gaf [hem [11]] ſpace that him ſpilede they [hit ſpedde [12]] lyte
[Fourty wynter [13]] as y fynde, and no fewer, &c. [14]

Notwithſtanding what has been ſuppoſed above, it is not quite cer-

---

[1] ſuls ſayſed.   [2] ſewen.
[3] This is the orthography obſerved for both *though* and *they*. It occurs again below : "they it," though it.
[4] pygt was don.   [5] bouden.
[6] quyrbole;—which might have ſtood, ſince it only deſtroys the alliteration to the eye.
[7] Warton read "Such;" the Cotton MS. "And ſythen ſette on a ſete;" whence the genuine reading of the Laud MS. was obvious.
[8] bobette, Cot. MS.
[9] . . . caſten hym with a cry and on a croſs ſlowen.
[10] tone, which if intended for atone (like duie for endure, ſperſt for diſperſed, &c.) might be allowed to ſtand. The probability is that it is an erroneous tranſcript for torne.
[11] he.   [12] he ſpedde.
[13] Yf aynt was. Perhaps: xl. wynterit was, &c.
[14] Laud. . . 22, MSS. Bibl. Bodl. Ad calc. "Hic tractatur bellum Judaicum apud Jeruſalem," f. 19, b. It is alſo in Brit. Mus. Cot. MSS. *Calig.* A. ii. fol. 109-123. Gyraldus Cambrenſis ſays, that the Welſh and Engliſh uſe alliteration "in omni ſermone exquiſito." *Deſcript. Cambr.* cap. xi. p. 889. O'Flaherty alſo ſays of the Iriſh, "Non parva eſt apud nos in oratione elegantiæ ſchema, quod Paromæon, *i. e. Aſſimile*, dicitur: quoties multæ dictiones, ab eadem litera incipientes, ex ordine collocantur." *Ogyg.* part iii. 30, p. 242. [An objection has been taken to the antiquity of the Welſh poetry, from its ſuppoſed want of alliteration. But this is not the caſe. For the alliteration has not been perceived by thoſe ignorant of its conſtruction, which is to make it in the middle of words, and not at the beginning, as in this inſtance :

Yn   ias   ir   ei   naws   eirian.

This information was imparted to Mr. Douce by the ingenious Edward Williams, the Welſh bard.—*Park.* See alſo, ſays Sir F. Madden, Conybeare's *Illuſtr. of Anglo-Saxon Poetry*, (1826) Introduction.]

tain that Langland was the first who led the way in this singular species of versification. His *Vision* was written on a popular subject, and [was formerly] the only poem, composed in this capricious sort of metre, which [existed in print]. It is easy to conceive how these circumstances contributed to give him the merit of an inventor on this occasion.

Percy has exhibited specimens of two or three other poems belonging to this class.[1] One of these is entitled *Death and Life:* it consists of two hundred and twenty-nine lines, and is divided into two parts or *Fitts.* It begins thus :

> Christ, christen king, that on the crosse tholed,
> Hadd paines & passyons to deffend our soules ;
> Give us grace on the ground the greatlye to serve
> For that royall red blood that rann from thy side.

The subject of this piece is a *Vision,* containing a contest for superiority between *Our lady Dame Life,* and the *ugly fiend Dame Death :* who with the several attributes and concomitants are personified in a beautiful vein of allegorical painting. Dame Life is thus forcibly described :

> Shee was brighter of her blee then was the bright sonn :
> Her rudd redder then the rose that on the rise hangeth :
> Meekely smiling with her mouth, & merry in her lookes ;
> Ever laughing for love, as shee like wold :
> & as she came by the bankes, the boughes eche one
> They lowted to that Ladye & layd forth their branches ;
> Blossomes and burgens breathed full sweete,
> Flowers flourished in the frith where shee forth stepedd,
> And the grasse that was gray greened belive.

The figure of Death follows, which is equally bold and expressive. Another piece of this kind, also quoted by Dr. Percy, is entitled *Chevelere Assigne,* or *De Cigne,* that is, *Knight of the Swan.*[2] Among the Royal MSS. in the British Museum, there is a French metrical romance on this subject, entitled *L'Ystoire du Chevalier au Signe,*[3] [of which *Le Chevelere Assigne* is an abridgment]. Our English poem begins thus :[4]

---

[1] *Essay on the Metr. of P. P. Vis.* p. 8, *seq.* [The poem is printed in Bishop Percy's folio MS. 1868, vol. iii.—F.]

[2] MS. Cotton. Caligula, A. 2. Printed by Mr. E. V. Utterson, for the Roxburghe Club, 1820, and again by Mr. H. H. Gibbs for the Early English Text Society, 1868, with a series of photographs from a very curious ivory-casket in the editor's family, containing various illustrations of the story.]

[3] 15 E. vi. 9. fol. And in the Royal library at Paris, MS. 7192. *Le Roman du Chevalier au Cigne en vers.* Montf. Cat. MSS. ii. p. 789. [There are six romance sin the cycle. M. Paullin Paris has edited *Le Chanson d'Antioche.* See *Histoire Litteraire de la France,* tome 22.—F.]

[4] See MSS. Cott. Calig. A. ii. f. 109. 123.

[The celebrated Godfrey of Bullogne was said to have been lineally descended from the Chevalier au Cigne. *Melanges d'une Gr. Biblioth.* vol. v. c. iii. p. 148. The tradition is still current in the Duchy of Cleves, and forms one of the most interesting pieces in Otmar's Volkssagen. It must have obtained an early and general circulation in Flanders ; for Nicolaes de Klerc, who wrote at the com-

Alle-weldynge god whenne it is his wylle,
Wele he wereth his werke with his owne honde :
For ofte harmes were hente · that helpe we ne myȝte ;
Nere the hyȝnes of hym that lengeth in heuene
For this, &c.

This alliterative meaſure, unaccompanied with rhyme, and including many peculiar Saxon idioms appropriated to poetry, remained
in uſe ſo low as the ſixteenth century. In [the newly-edited Percy
MS.] there is one of this claſs called *Scottiſh Feilde*, containing a
very circumſtantial narrative of the battle of Flodden fought in 1513.

[There is alſo an Engliſh romance in proſe, entitled *The Knight
of the Swanne*, of which there ſeems to have been an edition by W.
de Worde in 1512. It is a tranſlation by Robert Copland, the in-
duſtrious typographer, of chapters 1-38 of a French romance entitled
"La Genealogie avecques les Geſtes & Nobles Faitz darmes du
tres preux & renomme prince Godeffroy de Boulion & de ſes cheua-
lereux freres Baudouin et Euſtace : yſſus & deſcendus de la très
noble & illuſtre lignée du vertueux Chevalier au Cyne." *The Knight
of the Swanne* was reprinted by William Copland about 1560, and it
is included in a modern collection.] [1]

In ſome of the earlieſt of our ſpecimens of old Engliſh poetry, [2]
we have long ago ſeen that alliteration was eſteemed a faſhionable
and favourite ornament of verſe. For the ſake of throwing the ſubject into one view, and further illuſtrating what has been here ſaid
concerning it, I chooſe to cite in this place a very ancient hymn to
the Virgin Mary, where this affectation profeſſedly predominates. [3]

I.
Hail beo yow [4] Marie, moodur and may,
Mylde, and meke, and merciable ;

---

mencement of the 14th century (1318), thus refers to it in his *Brabandſche
Yeeſten :*

"Om dat van Brabant die Hertoghen
Voormaels dicke ſyn beloghen
Alſe dat ſy quamen metten Swane
Daar by hebbics my genomen ane
Dat ic die waerheit wil out decken
Ende in Duitſche Rime vertrecken,

i. e. becauſe *formerly* the dukes of Brabant have been much belied, to wit, *that they
came with a Swan,* I have undertaken to diſcloſe the truth, and to propound it in
Dutch Rhyme. See Van Wynut *ſupra,* p. 270. The French romance upon this
ſubject, conſiſting of about 30,000 verſes, was begun by one Renax or Renaux,
and finiſhed by Gandor de Douay.—*Price.*]

  [1] [Thoms' *Early Proſe Romances,* 1828, iii.]
  [2] See ſect. i.
  [3] Among the Cotton MSS. there is an [Early Engliſh] alliterative hymn to the
Virgin Mary. *Ner.* A. xiv. f. 240, cod. membran. 8vo. "On ȝou ureiſun to ure
lefdi." That is, *A good prayer to our lady.*

"Criſteſ milſe moſer ʀeynꞇe Marie
Miner hueʀ leonie, mi leoue leꝼꞇi."

  [4] See ſome pageant-poetry, full of alliteration, written in the reign of Henry
VII., Leland, *Coll.* iii. App. 180, edit. 1770.

Heyl folliche fruit of fothfaſt fay,
Agayn vche ſtryf ſtudefaſt and ſtable !
Heil ſothfaſt ſoul in vche a ſay,
Undur the ſon is non ſo able.
Heil logge that vr lord in lay,
The formaſt that never was founden in fable,
Heil trewe, trouthfull, and tretable,
Heil cheef j choſen of chaſtite,
Heil homely, hende, and amyable
To preye for us to thi ſone ſo fre ! AVE.

II.

Heil ſtern, that never ſtinteth liht ;
Heil buſh, brennyng that never was brent ;
Heil rihtful rulere of everi riht,
Schadewe to ſchilde that ſcholde be ſchent.
Heil, bleſſed be yowe bloſme briht,
To trouthe and truſt was thine entent ;
Heil mayden and modur, moſt of miht,
Of all miſcheves and amendement ;
Heil ſpice ſprong that never was ſpent,
Heil trone of the trinitie ;
Heil ſoiene¹ that god us ſone to ſent
Yowe preye for us thi ſone fre ! AVE.

III.

Heyl hertely in holineſſe.
Heyl hope of help to heighe and lowe,
Heyl ſtrength and ſtel of ſtabylneſſe,
Heyl wyndowe of hevene wowe,
Heyl reſon of rihtwyſneſſe,
To vche a caityf comfort to knowe,
Heyl innocent of angerneſſe,
Vr takel, vr tol, that we on trowe,
Heyl frend to all that beoth fortth flowe
Heyl liht of love, and of bewte,
Heyl brihter then the blod on ſnowe,
Yow preye for us thi ſone ſo fre ! AVE.

IV.

Heyl mayden, heyl modur, heyl martir trowe,
Heyl kyndly i knowe confeſſour,
Heyl evenere of old lawe and newe,
Heyl buildor bold of criſtes bour,
Heyl roſe higeſt of hyde and hewe,
Of all ffruytes feireſt fflour,
Heyl turtell truſtieſt and trewe,
Of all trouthe thou art treſour,
Heyl puyred princeſſe of paramour,
Heyl bloſme of brere brihteſt of ble,
Heyl owner of eorthly honour,
Yowe preye for us thi ſone ſo fre ! AVE, &c.

V.

Heyl hende, heyl holy empereſſe,
Heyle queene corteois, comely, and kynde,
Heyl diſtruyere of everi ſtriſſe,
Heyl mender of everi monnes mynde,
Heil bodi that we ouht to bleſſe,
So feythful frend may never mon fynde,

---

¹ F. Seyen. *Scyon.*

Heil levere and lovere of largenesse
Swete and sweteft that never may swynde,
Heil botenere of everie bodi blynde,
Heil borgun brihtes of all bounte,
Heyl trewore then the wode bynde,
Yow preye for us thi sone so fre! AVE.

VI.

Heyl modur, heyl mayden, heyl hevene quene,
Heyl gatus of paradys,
Heyl sterre of the se that ever is sene,
Heyl riche, royall, and ryhtwys,
Heyl burde i blessed mote yowe bene,
Heyl perle of al perey the pris,
Heyl schadewe in vche a schour schene,
Heyl fairer thae that flour de lys,
Heyl cher chosen that never nas chis
Heyl chef chamber of charite
Heyl in wo that ever was wis
Yowe preye for us thi sone so fre! Ave, &c. &c.[1]

These rude stanzas remind us of the Greek hymns ascribed to Orpheus, which entirely consist of a cluster of the appellations appropriated to each divinity.

SECTION XI.

ALTHOUGH this work is professedly confined to England, yet I cannot pass over [a Scotish poet] of this period who ha[s] adorned the English language by a strain of versification, expression, and poetical imagery, far superior to [his] age; and who consequently deserve[s] to be mentioned in a general review of the progress of our national poetry. [His name] is John Barbour, archdeacon of Aberdeen. He was educated at Oxford; and Rymer has printed an instrument for his safe passage into England, in order to prosecute his studies in that university, in the years 1357 and 1365.[2] David Bruce, king of Scotland, gave him a pension for life, as a reward for his poem called the [*Brus*]. It was printed at [Edinburgh about 1570,[3] and often afterwards].[4]

---

[1] MS. Vernon. f. 122. In this manuscript are several other pieces of this sort. The Holy Virgin appears to a priest who often sang to her, and calls him her *joculator.* MSS. James, xxvi. p. 32.

[2] *Fœd.* vi. 31, 478.

[3] Tanner, *Bibl.* p. 73. [See our *List of Early English Poems,* supra. Mr. Henry Bradshaw assigns to Barbour two works hitherto unknown to have been by him: 1. Fragments of a *Troy-Book,* mixed up with some copies of Lydgate's *Troy-book;* 2. Nearly 40,000 lines of *Lives of Saints* (MSS. Camb. Univ. and Queen's Coll. Oxford).—F.]

[4] [Mr. D. Laing has a copy, wanting the title, of a 4to edit., which he assigns to this date. Extracts have now been taken from Mr. Skeat's new edition for the Early English Text Society, of which only Part I. (ten books) has yet appeared, 1870.

[The following is the account of the battle of Methven, near Perth, and the firſt diſcomfiture of King Robert :] [1].

On at*h*ir ſyd *th*us war *th*ai yhar,[2]
And till aſſemble[3] all redy war.
*Th*ai ſtraucht *th*ar ſperi*s*, on a*th*ir ſyd,
And ſwa ruydly gan Samyn[4] ryd,
*Th*at ſperi*s* [all] to-fruſchyt[5] war,
And feyle men dede, and woundyt far ;
*Th*e blud owt at *th*ar byrnys[6] breſt.
For *th*e beſt, and *th*e worthieſt,
*Th*at wilfull war to wyn honour,
Plungyt in *th*e ſtalwart ſtour,
And rowt*is* ruyd about *th*aim dang.[7]
Men my*ch*t haiff ſeyn in-to *th*at thrang
Kny*ch*ti*s* *th*at wy*ch*t and hardy war,
Wndyr horſs feyt defoulyt *th*ar ;
Sum woundyt, and ſum all ded :
*Th*e greſs woux[8] off *th*e blud all rede,
And *th*ai, *th*at held on horſs, in hȳ[9]
Swappyt owt ſwerdi*s* ſturdyly ;
And ſwa fell ſtrakys gave and tuk,
*Th*at all the renk[10] about *th*aim quouk.
*Th*e bruyſſis folk full hardely
Schawyt *th*ar gret chewalry :
And he him-ſelff, atour *th*e lave,[11]
Sa hard and hewy dynti*s* gave,
*Th*at quhar he come *th*ai maid hi*m* way.
His folk *th*aim put in hard aſſay,
To ſtynt[12] *th*ar fais mekill my*ch*t,
*Th*at then ſo fayr had off *th*e fy*ch*t,
*Th*at *th*ai wan feild ay mar & mar :
*Th*e king*is* ſmall folk ner wencuſyt ar.
And quhen *th*e king his folk has ſene
Begyn to faile, for propyr tene,[13]
Hys aſſenȝhe[14] gan he cry ;
And in *th*e ſtour ſa hardyly
He ruſchyt, *th*at all *th*e ſemble[15] ſchuk :
He all till-hewyt[16] *th*at he our-tuk ;
And dang on *th*aim quhill he my*ch*t drey.[17]
And till his folk he cri*y*t hey ;
" On *th*aim ! On *th*aim ! *th*ai feble faſt !
*Th*is bargane neu*ir* may lang*ar* laſt ! "
And with *th*at word ſa wilfully
He dang on, and ſa hardely,
*Th*at quha had ſene him in *th*at fy*ch*t
Suld hald him for A douchty kny*ch*t.
Bot tho*ch*t[18] he wes ſtout and hardy,

In all the preceding editions of Warton, the account of Blind Harry's *Wallace* has been improperly inſerted in the preſent ſection ; it has now been transferred to its correct place.]

[1] [Skeat's ed. pp. 38-42. " On the 19th June, 1306, the new king was completely defeated near Methven by the Engliſh Earl of Pembroke (Sir Aymer de Valence.)"—Scott's *Tales of a Grandfather.*]

[2] [ready.] [3] [to encounter.] [4] [together.]
[5] [all broken in pieces ; the word *all* is ſupplied from Hart's edition, 1616.]
[6] [breaſt-plates.] [7] [dealt ſtern ſtrokes about them.]
[8] [graſs became.] [9] [haſte.] [10] [ring ; Hart prints *rinke*.]
[11] [above the reſt.] [12] [ſtop.] [13] [very grief.] [14] [battle-cry.]
[15] [aſſembly.] [16] [hewed in pieces.] [17] [hold out.] [18] [though.]

And othir als off his cumpany,
Thar mycht na worschip thar awailȝe ; [1]
For thar sm   all folk begouth to failȝe,
Aud fled all skalyt[2] her and thar.
Bot the gude, at enchaufyt[3] war
Off Ire, abade and held the stour
To conquyr thaim endles honour.
And quhen schir Amer[4] has sene
The sm003Ball folk fle all bedene,[5]
And sa few abid to fycht,
He releyt[6] to him mony A knycht ;
And in the stour sa hardyly
He ruschyt with hys chewalry,
That he ruschyt[7] his fayis Ilkane.
Schir Thomas Randell[8] thar wes tane,
That then wes A ȝoung bacheler ;
And schir Alexander fraseyr ;
And schir dauid the breklay,
Inchmertyne, and hew de le hay,
And somerweil,[9] and othir ma ;
And the king him-selff alsua
Wes set in-till full hard assay,
Throw schir philip the mowbray,[10]
That raid till him full hardyly,
And hynt hys rengȝe,[11] and syne gan cry
"Help ! help ! I have the new-maid king ! "
With that come gyrdand, in A lyng,[12]
Cryſtall off Seytoun,[13] quhen he swa
Saw the king sesyt with his fa ;
And to philip sic rout he raucht,[14]
That thocht he wes of mekill maucht,
He gert him galay[15] disyly ;
And haid till erd gane fullyly,
Ne war he hynt him by his sted ;
Then off his hand the brydill yhed ;[16]
And the king his enssenȝe[17] gan cry,
Releyt[18] his men that war him by,
That war sa few that thai na mycht
Endur the forss mar off the fycht.
Thai prikyt then out off the press ;
And the king, that angry wes,
For he his men saw fle him fra,
Said then : "lordingis, sen It is swa
That vre[19] rynnys agane ws her,
Gud Is we pass off thar daunger,[20]
Till god ws send eftsonys grace :
And ȝeyt may fall, giff thai will chace,
Quyt thaim torn[21] but sum-dele we sall."
To this word thai assentyt all,
And fra thaim walopyt[22] owyr mar.

---

[1] [avail.] [2] [disperſed.] [3] [good ones, that enraged.]
[4] [Sir Aymer de Valence.] [5] [quickly.] [6] [rallied.]
[7] [overthrew.] [8] [Randolph.]
[9] [Sir David Barclay, Inchmartin, Hugh de la Haye, and Somerville.]
[10] [Philip de Mowbray.] [11] [caught his rein.]
[12] [charging in a direct line.] [13] [Sir Chriſtopher Seton.] [14] [blow he gave.]
[15] [made him ſtagger.] [16] [went.] [17] [war-cry.] [18] [rallied.] [19] [fortune.]
[20] [out of their power to harm.] [21] [requite them a turn.] [22] [galloped.]

*Th*ar fayis al*s*ua wery war,
*Th*at off *th*aim all *thar* cha*ff*yt nane :
Bot wi*th* pri*f*oneri*s, that th*ai had tane,
Rycht to *th*e toune¹ *th*ai held *thar* way,
Ry*ch*t glaid and Ioyfull off *thar* pray.

[As a further *f*pecimen of the poem, the opening of the de*f*crip-
tion·in the fifth book of Bruce's " han*f*aling in Carrik, at his fir*f*t
arriuing" may be *f*ufficient :]²

This wes in were,³ quhen vynt*ir*-tyde
Vith his bla*f*tis, hydwi*f*s to byde,
Wes ourdriffin :⁴ and byrdis *f*male,
As thri*f*till and *th*e nychtingale,
Begouth⁵ rycht mealy to *f*yng,
And for to mak in *th*air *f*ynging
Syndry notis, and *f*ound*is f*ere,⁶
And melody plea*f*ande to her*e*.
And *th*e treis begouth to ma
Burgeonys⁷ and bry*ch*t blwmys al*f*ua,
To vyn *th*e heling of *th*ar hevede,⁸
*Th*at vikkit vynt*ir* had *th*ame revede ;
And al grewis⁹ begouth to *f*pryng.

[To the latter half of the fifteenth century we mu*f*t refer another
Scoti*f*h writer, Andrew of Wyntown, who compo*f*ed the *Original
Chronicle of Scotland.* Wyntown was born in all probability at the
clo*f*e of the fourteenth, or beginning of the fifteenth century ; but
the exa*ct* date is wanting. It is difficult to allow that he *f*aw the
light during the reign of David II. (1329-71), *f*ince Dunbar, in his
Lament for the Makaris, compo*f*ed mo*f*t probably not earlier than
the year 1500, *f*eems to refer to this author as one whom he had
known, and who at that time had not been very long decea*f*ed.¹⁰ A
tolerably copious account of Wyntoun and his writings is readily
acce*ff*ible el*f*ewhere ;¹¹ and his *Original Chronicle of Scotland* has been
printed entire by Macpher*f*on.]¹²

About the pre*f*ent period, hi*f*torical romances of recent events
*f*eem to have commenced. Many of the*f*e appear to have been
written by heralds.¹³ In the library of Worce*f*ter college at Oxford,
there is a poem in French, reciting the achievements of Edward the
Black Prince, who died in the year 1376. It is in the *f*hort ver*f*e
of romance, and was written by the prince's herald, who attended
clo*f*e by his per*f*on in all his battles, according to the e*f*tabli*f*hed mode
of tho*f*e times. This was Chandos Herald, frequently mentioned in
Froi*ff*art. In this piece, which is of con*f*iderable length, the names

---

¹ [Perth.]   ² [Skeat's edit. p. 105.]   ³ [*f*pring.]   ⁴ [overpa*f*t.]
⁵ [began.]   ⁶ [various.]   ⁷ [buds.]
⁸ [to get the covering of their head. *Hevede* is clearly the reading, though *f*pelt
hede in the Cambridge, and *hewid* in the Edinburgh MS.]
⁹ [growing things ; the Edinb. MS. has *greffys,* gra*ff*es.]
¹⁰ [Works by Laing, 1834, i. 213.]
¹¹ [Irving's *Hiftory of Scotifh Poetry,* edit. 1861, chap. v.]
¹² [1795, 2 vols. large 8vo. A new edition by Dr. Laing has been promi*f*ed.]
¹³ See Le Pere Mene*f*trier, *Cheval. Ancien.* c. v. p. 225.

of the Englifhmen are properly fpelled, the chronology exact, and the
epitaph,[1] forming a fort of peroration to the narrative, the fame as
was ordered by the prince in his will.[2] This poem, indeed, may
feem to claim no place here, becaufe it happens to be written in the
French language : yet, exclufive of its fubject, a circumftance I have
mentioned, that it was compofed by a herald, deferves particular attention, and throws no fmall illuftration on the poetry of this era.
There are feveral proofs which indicate that many romances of the
fourteenth century, if not in verfe, at leaft thofe written in profe,
were the work of heralds. As it was their duty to attend their
mafters in battle, they were enabled to record the moft important
tranfactions of the field with fidelity. It was cuftomary to appoint
none to this office but perfons of difcernment, addrefs, experience,
and fome degree of education.[3] At folemn tournaments they made

---

[1] It is a fair and beautiful MS. on vellum. It is an oblong octavo, and formerly
belonged to Sir William Le Neve Clarencieux herald. [It has been edited by the
Rev. H. O. Coxe, M.A. the prefent keeper of Bodley, for the Roxburghe Club,
1842.]
[2] The hero's epitaph is frequent in romances. In the French romance of [*Le
Petit Jean de*] *Saintre*, written about this time, his epitaph is introduced.
[3] Le Pere Meneftrier, *Cheval Ancien.* ut fupr. p. 225, ch. v. "Que l'on croyoit
avoir *l'Efprit*," &c. Feron fays that they gave this attendance in order to make a
true report. *L'Inftit. des Roys et Herauds*, p. 44, a. See alfo Favin. p. 57. See
a curious defcription, in Froiffart, of an interview between the Chandois-herald,
mentioned above, and a marfhal of France, where they enter into a warm and very
ferious difpute concerning the *devices d'amour* borne by each army. Liv. i. ch. 161.
[A curious collection of German poems, evidently compiled from thefe heraldic
regifters, was formerly difcovered in the library of Prince Sinzendorf. The reader
will find an account of them and their author Peter Suchenwirt (who lived at the
clofe of the fourteenth century) in the 14th volume of the *Vienna Annals of Literature (Jahrbücher der Literatur*, Wien. 1821). They are noticed here for their
occafional mention of Englifh affairs. The life of Burkhard v. Ellerbach recounts
the victory gained by the Englifh at the battle of Creffy; in which this terror of
Pruffian and Saracen infidels was left for dead on the field, " the blood and the grafs,
the green and the red, being fo completely mingled in one general mafs," that no
one perceived him. Friedrich v. Chreuzpeckh ferved in Scotland, England, and
Ireland. In the latter country he joined an army of 60,000 (!) men, about to form
the fiege of a town called Trachtal (?) ; but the army broke up without an engagement. On his return thence to England, the fleet in which he failed fell in
with a Spanifh fquadron, and deftroyed or captured fix-and-twenty of the enemy.
Thefe events occurred between the years 1332-36. Albrecht v. Nürnberg followed
Edward III. into Scotland, and appears to have been engaged in the battle of
Halidown-hill. But the " errant knight" moft intimately connected with England
was Hans v. Traun. He joined the banner of Edward III. at the fiege of Calais,
during which he was engaged in cutting off fome fupplies fent by fea for the relief
of the befieged. He does ample juftice to the valour and heroic refiftance of the
garrifon, who did not furrender till their ftock of leather,[1] rope and fimilar materials,—which had long been their only food,—was exhaufted. Rats were fold at a
crown each. In the year 1356 he attended the Black Prince in the campaign which
preceded the battle of Poictiers ; and on the morning of that eventful fight, Prince
Edward honoured him with the important charge of bearing the Englifh ftandard.
The battle is defcribed with confiderable animation. The hoftile armies advanced

---

[1] [The original reads " fchuch, fil, chvnt und hewt ;" the two laft I interpret
" kind und haut."]

an effential part of the ceremony. Here they had an opportunity of obferving accoutrements, armorial diftinctions, the number and appearance of the fpectators, together with the various events of the turney, to the beft advantage : and they were afterwards obliged to compile an ample regifter of this ftrange mixture of foppery and ferocity.[1] They were neceffarily connected with the minftrels at public feftivals, and thence acquired a facility of reciting adventures. A learned French antiquary is of opinion, that anciently the French heralds, called Hiraux, were the fame as the minftrels, and that they fung metrical tales at feftivals.[2] They frequently received fees or largefs in common with the minftrels.[3] They travelled into different countries, and faw the fafhions of foreign courts, and foreign tournaments. They not only committed to writing the procefs of the lifts, but it was alfo their bufinefs, at magnificent feafts, to defcribe the number and parade of the difhes, the quality of the guefts, the brilliant dreffes of the ladies, the courtefy of the knights, the revels, difguifings, banquets, and every other occurrence moft obfervable in the courfe of the folemnity. Spenfer alludes exprefsly to thefe heraldic details, where he mentions the fplendour of Florimel's wedding :

---

on foot, the archers forming the vanguard. "This was not a time," fays the poet, "for the interchange of chivalric civilities, for friendly greetings and cordial love : no man afked his fellow for a violet or a rofe ;[*] and many a hero, like the oftrich, was obliged to digeft both iron and fteel, or to overcome in death the fenfations inflicted by the fpear and the javelin. The field refounded with the clafh of fwords, clubs, and battle-axes ; and with fhouts of Nater Dam and Sand Jors." But Von Traun, mindful of the truft repofed in him, rufhed forward to encounter the ftandard-bearer of France : "He drove his fpear through the vizer of his adverfary—the enemy's banner fank to the earth never to rife again—Von Traun planted his foot upon its ftaff ; when the king of France was made captive, and the battle was won." For his gallantry difplayed on this day Edward granted him a penfion of a hundred marks. He is afterwards mentioned as being intrufted by Edward III. with the defence of Calais during a ten weeks' fiege ; and at a fubfequent period as croffing the channel, and capturing a (French ?) fhip, which he brought into an Englifh port and prefented to Edward.— *Price.* The Poems were publifhed at Vienna in 1827 by Primiffer under the title : Peter Suchenwirt *Werke aus dem vierzehuten Jahr-hunderte.* With an introduction, notes, and a gloffary. See alfo Hormayr's *Tafchenbuch für die vaterlandifche Gefchichte.* Vienna, 1828.—*Rye.*]

[1] "L'un des principaux fonctions des Herauts d'armes etoit fe trouver au joufts, &c. ou ils gardoient les ecus pendans, recevoient les noms et les blafons des chevaliers, en tenoient regiftre, et en compofoient recueils," &c. Meneftr. *Orig. des Armoir.* p. 180. See alfo p. 119. Thefe regifters are mentioned in Perceforeft, xi. 68, 77.

[2] Carpentier, *Suppl. Du-Cang. Glofs. Lat.* p. 750, tom. ii.

[3] Thus at St. George's feaft at Windfor we have, "Diverfis heraldis et miniftrallis," &c. Ann. 21 Ric. ii. 9 Hen. vi. apud Anftis, *Ord. Gart.* i. 56, 108. And again, *Exit. Pell.* M. *ann.* 22 *Edw.* iii. "Magiftro Andreæ Roy Norreys, [a herald,] Lybekin le Piper, et Hanakino filio fuo, et fex aliis meneftrallis regis in denariis eis liberatis de dono regis, in fubfidium expenfarum fuarum, lv. *s.* iv. *d.*"—*Exit. Pell. P. ann.* 33 *Edw.* ii. "Willielmo Volaunt regi heraldorum et miniftrallis exiftentibus apud Smithfield in ultimo haftiludio de dono regis, x *l.*" I could give many other proofs.

---

[*] [So I interpret "umb veyal (veilchen) noch umb rofen."]

> To tell the glorie of the feaſt that day,
> The goodly ſervyſe, the devicefull ſighᵗs,
> The bridegromes ſtate, the brides moſt rich aray,
> The pride of Ladies, and the worth of knights,
> The royall banquet, and the rare delights,
> Were worke fit for an herauld, not for me : [1]—

I ſuſpeɕt that Chaucer, not perhaps without ridicule, glances at ſome of theſe deſcriptions, with which his age abounded ; and which he probably regarded with leſs reverence, and read with leſs edification, than did the generality of his cotemporary readers :

> What ſchuld I telle of the realté [2]
> Of this mariage, or which cours goth biforn,
> Who bloweth in a trompe or in an horn ?

Again, in deſcribing Cambuſcan's feaſt :

> Of which if I ſchal tellen al tharray, [3]
> Than wold it occupie a ſomeres day ;
> And eek it needith nought for to devyſe
> At every cours the ordre and the ſervyſe.
> I wol nat tellen of her ſtraunge ſewes,
> Ne of her ſwannes, ne here heroun-ſewes.

And at the feaſt of Theſeus, in the *Knight's Tale* :

> The mynſtralcye, the ſervyce at the feſte, [4]
> The grete yiftes to the moſt and leſte,
> The riche aray of Theſeus paleys,
> Ne who ſat firſt ne laſt upon the deys,
> What ladieſ fayreſt ben or beſt daunſyngₑ,
> Or which of hem can daunce beſt or ſyngₑ,
> Ne who moſt felyngly ſpeketh of love ;
> What haukes ſitten on the perche above,
> What houndes lyen in the floor adoun :
> Of al this make I now no mencioun.

In the *Flower and the Leaf*, the [author] has deſcribed in eleven long ſtanzas the proceſſion to a ſplendid tournament, with all the prolixity and exaɕtneſs of a herald. [5] The ſame affeɕtation, derived from the ſame ſources, occurs often in Arioſto.

It were eaſy to illuſtrate this doɕtrine by various examples. The famous French romance of [Le Petit Jean de] *Saintre* was evidently the performance of a herald. [Jean de] Saintre, the knight of the piece, was a real perſon, and, according to Froiſſart, was taken priſoner at the battle of Poitiers in 1356. [6] But the compiler confounds chronology, and aſcribes to his hero many pieces of true hiſtory belonging to others. This was a common praɕtice in theſe books. Some authors have ſuppoſed that this romance appeared before the year 1380. [7] But there are reaſons to prove, that it was written by Antony de la Sale, a Burgundian, author of a book of Ceremonies, from his name very quaintly entitled *La Sallade*, and

---

[1] *F. Q.* v. iii. 3 [edit. Morris, 1869, p. 306.]
[2] [Morris's *Chaucer*, ii. 191, ver. 605.]
[3] [*Ibid.* ii. 356, ver. 55.]   [4] [*Ibid.* ii. 68, ver. 1339.]
[5] From ver. 204 to ver. 287.   [6] Froiſſart, *Hiſt.* i. p. 178.
[7] Byſshe, *Not. in Upton. Milit. Offic.* p. 56. Meneſtrier, *Orig. Arm.* p. 23.

frequently cited by our learned antiquary Selden.[1] This Antony
came into England to fee the folemnity of the queen's coronation in
the year 1445.[2] I have not feen any French romance which has
preferved the practices of chivalry more copioufly than this of *Saintre*.
It muft have been an abfolute mafter-piece for the rules of tilting,
martial cuftoms, and public ceremonies prevailing in its author's age.
In the library of the [College] of Arms, there remains a very accurate
defcription of a feaft of Saint George, celebrated at Windfor in 1471.[3]
It appears to have been written by the herald Blue-Mantle Pur-
fuivant. Meneftrier fays, that Guillaume Rucher, herald of Henault,
has left a large treatife, defcribing the tournaments annually celebrated at Lifle in Flanders.[4] In the reign of Edward IV., John
Smarte, a Norman, garter king at arms, defcribed in French the
tournament held at Bruges, for nine days, in honour of the marriage
of the duke of Burgundy with Margaret the king's daughter.[5] There
is a French poem [on the fiege of the Caftle of Karlaverock in the
year] 1300.[6] This was [probably, however, the production of Walter
of Exeter, whom Carew fuppofes to have written the original Latin
profe romance of *Guy of Warwick*.] The author thus defcribes the
banner of John of Brittany, [nephew of the duke]:

> Baniere avoit cointe et paree
> De or et de açur efchequeree
> Au rouge ourle o iaunes lupars
> Dermine eftoit la quarte pars.[7]

The pompous circumftances of which thefe heraldic narratives

---

[1] *Tit. Hon.* p. 413, &c.　　　　　　　[2] Anft. *Ord. Gart.* ii. 321.

[3] MSS. Offic. Arm. M. 15, fol. 12, 13.

[4] "Guillaume Rucher, heraut d'armes du titre de Heynaut, a fait un gros
volume des rois de l'Epinette a Lifle en Flanders; c'eft une ceremonie, ou un fefte,
dont il a decrit les jouftes, tournois, noms, armoiries, livrees, et equipages de divers
feigneurs, qui fe rendoient a divers endroits, avec le catalogues de rois de cette
fefte." Meneftr. *Orig. des Armoir*, p. 64.

[5] See many other inftances in MS. Harl. 69, entit. *The Booke of certaine Triumphes*.
See alfo Appendix to the [laft] edition of Leland's *Collectanea*.

[6] MSS. Cott. [Caligula, A xviii. *The Siege of Carlaverock*, in the xxviii
Edward I. A.D. MCCC: &c., from a MS. in the handwriting of Robert Glover the
herald. Edited by H. N. Nicolas, Lond. 1828, 4to. In fome copies the plates of arms
are coloured. A reprint of the poem, with the roll of arms emblazoned, appeared in
1860, from which text the prefent extract has been taken, that of Warton being incorrect. The piece itfelf is alfo inferted from a collation of the two known copies
in the *Antiquarian Repertory*, edit. 1807, iv. 469. See Black's *Illuftrations of
Ancient State and Chivalry*, 1840, and *A Booke of Precedence*, &c. edit. Furnivall,
1869. The Britifh Mufeum has quite lately (Dec. 1870) acquired a curious volume
of French and Latin pieces on this fubject.]

[7] The bifhop of Gloucefter [fays Warton] has moft obligingly condefcended to
point out to me another fource, to which many of the romances of the fourteenth
century owed their exiftence. Montfaucon, in his *Monumens de la Monarchie
Françoife*, has printed the "Statuts de l'Ordre du Saint Efprit au droit defir ou du
Noeud etabli par Louis d'Anjou roi de Jerufalem et Sicile en 1352-3-4," tom. ii. p.
329. This was an annual celebration "au Chaftel de l'Euf enchanti du merveilleux
peril." The caftle, as appears by the monuments which accompany thefe ftatutes,
was built at the foot of the obfcure grot of the enchantments of Virgil. The
ftatutes are as extraordinary as if they had been drawn up by Don Quixote himfelf,
or his affeffors, the curate and the barber. From the feventh chapter we learn that

confifted, and the minute prolixity with which they were difplayed, feemed to have infected the profeffed hiftorians of this age. Of this there are various inftances in Froiffart, who had no other defign than to compile a chronicle of real facts. I will give one example out of many. At a treaty of marriage between our Richard II. and Ifabel daughter of Charles V. king of France, the two monarchs, attended with a noble retinue, met and formed feveral encampments in a fpacious plain, near the caftle of Guynes. Froiffart expends many pages in relating at large the coftly furniture of the pavilions, the riches of the fide-boards, the profufion and variety of fumptuous liquors, fpices, and difhes, with their order of fervice, the number of the attendants, with their addrefs and exact difcharge of duty in their refpective offices, the prefents of gold and precious ftones made on both fides, and a thoufand other particulars of equal importance, relating to the parade of this royal review.[1] On this account, Caxton, in his exhortation to the knights of his age, ranks Froiffart's hiftory, as a book of chivalry, with the romances of Lancelot and Percival, and recommends it to their attention, as a manual equally calculated to inculcate the knightly virtues of courage and courtefy.[2] This indeed was in an age when not only the courts of princes, but the caftles of barons, vied with one another in the luftre of their fhews; when tournaments, coronations, royal interviews, and folemn feftivals, were the grand objects of mankind. Froiffart was an eye-witnefs of many of the ceremonies which he defcribes. His paffion feems to have been that of feeing magnificent fpectacles, and of hearing reports concerning them.[3] Although a canon of two churches, he paffed his life in travelling from court to court, and from caftle to caftle.[4] He thus, either from his own obfervation or the credible information of others, eafily procured fuitable materials for a hiftory, which profeffed only to deal in fenfible objects, and thofe of the moft fplendid and confpicuous kind. He was familiarly known to two kings of England and one of Scotland.[5] But the court which he

---

the knights who came to this yearly feftival at the *chatel de l'euf*, were obliged to deliver in writing to the clerks of the chapel of the caftle their yearly adventures. Such of thefe hiftories as were thought worthy to be recorded, the clerks are ordered to tranfcribe in a book, which was called "Le livre des avenements aux chevaliers, &c. Et demeura le dit livre toujours en la dicte chapelle." This facred regifter certainly furnifhed from time to time ample materials to the romance-writers. And this circumftance gives a new explanation to a reference which we fo frequently find in romances: I mean, that appeal which they fo conftantly make to fome authentic record. [Warton's epifcopal informant was, of courfe, his friend Warburton.]

[1] See Froiffart's *Cronycle*, tranflated by Lord Berners, 1523, vol. ii. f. 242.

[2] [*Book of the ordre of chyualry or knyghthode* (circà 1484).]

[3] His father was a painter of armories. This might give him an early turn for fhews. See Sainte-Palaye, *Mem. Lit.* tom. x. p. 664, edit. 4to.

[4] He was originally a clerk of the chamber to Philippa, queen of Edward III. He was afterwards canon and treafurer of Chimay in Henault, and of Lifle in Flanders; and chaplain to Guy earl of Caftellon. Labor. *Introd. a l'Hift. de Charles VI.* p. 69. Compare alfo Froiffart's *Chron.* ii. f. 29, 305, 319. And Bullart, *Academ. des Arts et des Scienc.* i. p. 125, 126.

[5] *Cron.* ii. f. 158, 161.

moſt admired was that of Gaſton, Comte de Foix, at Orlaix in Bearn; for, as he himſelf acquaints us, it was not only the moſt brilliant in Europe, but the grand centre for tidings of martial adventures.[1] It was crowded with knights of England and Arragon. In the meantime it muſt not be forgotten that Froiffart, who from his childhood was ſtrongly attached to carouſals, the muſic of minſtrels, and the ſports of hawking and hunting,[2] cultivated the poetry of the troubadours, and was a writer of romances.[3] This turn, it muſt be confeſſed, might have ſome ſhare in communicating that romantic caſt to his hiſtory which I have mentioned. During his abode at the court of the Comte de Foix, where he was entertained for twelve weeks, he preſented to the earl his collection of the poems of the duke of Luxemburg, conſiſting of ſonnets, balades, and virelays. Among theſe was included a romance, compoſed by himſelf, called *Meliade*[s] *or The Knight of the Sun of Gold.* Gaſton's chief amuſement was to hear Froiffart read this romance[4] every evening after ſupper.[5] At his introduction to Richard II. he preſented that brilliant monarch with a book beautifully illuminated, engroſſed with his own hand, bound in crimſon velvet, and embelliſhed with ſilver boſſes, claſps, and golden roſes, comprehending all the matters of Amours and Moralities, which in the courſe of twentyfour years he had compoſed.[6] This was in 1396. When he left

---

[1] *Cron.* ii. f. 30. This was in 1381.

[2] See *Mem. Lit.* ut ſupr. p. 665.

[3] Speaking of the death of King Richard, Froiffart quotes a prediction from the old French proſe romance of Brut, which he ſays was fulfilled in that cataſtrophe, liv. iv. c. 119. Froiffart will be mentioned again as a poet.

[4] I take this opportunity of remarking, that romantic tales or hiſtories appear at a very early period to have been read as well as ſung at feaſts. So Wace in the *Roman du Rou,* in the Britiſh Muſeum, above mentioned :

"Doit l'en les vers et les regeſtes
Et les eſtoires *lire* as feſtes.''

[5] Froiffart brought with him for a preſent to Gaſton Comte de Foix four greyhounds, which were called by the romantic names of Triſtram, Hector, Brut, and Roland. Gaſton was ſo fond of hunting, that he kept upwards of ſix hundred dogs in his caſtle. Sainte-Palaye, *ut ſupr.* pp. 676, 678. He wrote a treatiſe on hunting, printed [about 1507. See Brunet, *dern.* edit. art. *Phebus.*] In illuſtration of the former part of this note, Creſcimbeni ſays, "Che in molte nobiliſſime famiglie Italiane, ha 400 e più anni, paſſarono` i nomi de' *Lancillotti,* de' *Triſtani,* de *Galvani,* di *Galeotti,* delle [Iſoulde], delle *Genevre,* e d'altri cavalieri, à dame in eſſe Tavola Roitonda operanti,'' &c. *Iſtor. Volg. Poes.* vol. i. lib. v. p. 327.

[6] I ſhould think that this was his romance of *Meliadus.* Froiffart ſays, that the king at receiving it aſked him what the book treated of. He anſwered *d'Amour.* The king, adds our hiſtorian, ſeemed much pleaſed at this, and examined the book in many places, for he was fond of reading as well as ſpeaking French. He then ordered Richard Crendon, the chevalier in waiting, to carry it into his privy chamber, *dont il me fit bonne chere.* He gave copies of the ſeveral parts of his chronicle, as they were finiſhed, to his different patrons. Le Laboureur ſays, that Froiffart ſent fifty-ſix quires of his *Roman au Croniques* to Guillaume de Bailiy, an illuminator; which, when illuminated, were intended as a preſent to the king of England. *Hiſt.* ch. vi. En *la vie de Louis duc d'Anjou,* p. 67, *ſeq.* See alſo *Cron.* i. iv. c. i.—iii. 26. There are two or three fine illuminated copies of Froiffart

England the fame year,[1] the king fent him a maffive goblet of filver, filled with one hundred nobles.[2]

As we are approaching to Chaucer, let us here ftand ftill, and take a retrofpect of the general manners. The tournaments and caroufals of our ancient princes, by forming fplendid affemblies of both fexes, while they inculcated the moft liberal fentiments of honour and heroifm, undoubtedly contributed to introduce ideas of courtefy, and to encourage decorum. Yet the national manners ftill retained a great degree of ferocity, and the ceremonies of the moft refined courts in Europe had often a mixture of barbarifm which rendered them ridiculous. This abfurdity will always appear at periods when men are fo far civilized as to have loft their native fimplicity, and yet have not attained juft ideas of politenefs and propriety. Their luxury was inelegant, their pleafures indelicate, their pomp cumberfome and unwieldy. In the meantime it may feem furprifing that the many fchools of philofophy which flourifhed in the middle ages fhould not have corrected and polifhed the times. But as their religion was corrupted by fuperftition, fo their philofophy degenerated into fophiftry. Nor is it fcience alone, even if founded on truth, that will polifh nations. For this purpofe, the powers of imagination muft be awakened and exerted, to teach elegant feelings, and to heighten our natural fenfibilities. It is not the head only that muft be informed, but the heart muft alfo be moved. Many claffic authors were known in the thirteenth century, but the fcholars of that period wanted tafte to read and admire them. The pathetic or fublime ftrokes of Virgil would be but little relifhed by theologifts and metaphyficians.

---

among the Royal MSS. in the Britifh Mufeum. Among the ftores of Henry VIII. at his manor of Beddington in Surrey, I find the fafhionable reading of the times exemplified in the following books, *viz.* " *Item*, a great book of parchmente written and lymned with gold of graver's work *De confeffione Amantis*, with xviii. other bookes, Le premier volume de Lancelot, Froiffart, Le grant voiage de Jerufalem, Enguerain de Monftrellet," &c. MSS. Harl. 1419, f. 382. Froiffart was here properly claffed.

[1] Froiffart fays, that he accompanied the king to various palaces, " A Elten, a Ledos, a Kinkeftove, a Cenes, a Certefée et a Windfor." This is, Eltham, Leeds, Kingfton, Chertfey, &c. *Cron.* liv. iv. c. 119, p. 348. The French are not much improved at this day in fpelling Englifh places and names.

Perhaps by *Cenes*, Froiffart means Shene, the royal palace at Richmond.

[2] *Cron.* f. 251, 252, 255, 319, 348. Bayle, who has an article on Froiffart, had no idea of fearching for anecdotes of Froiffart's life in his *Chronicle*. Inftead of which, he fwells his notes on this article with the contradictory accounts of Moreri, Voffius, and others, whofe difputes might have been all eafily fettled by recurring to Froiffart himfelf, who has interfperfed in his hiftory many curious particulars relating to his own life and works.

SECTION XII.

THE moſt illuſtrious ornament of the reign of Edward III. and of his ſucceſſor Richard II. was Geoffrey Chaucer, a poet with whom the hiſtory of our poetry is by many ſuppoſed to have commenced, and who has been pronounced, by a critic of unqueſtionable taſte and diſcernment, to be the firſt Engliſh verſifier who wrote poetically.[1] He was born [about] the year [1340, and was probably in his youth a page of Elizabeth, wife of Prince Lionel, third ſon of Edward III.]:[2] but the livelineſs of his parts, and the native gaiety of his diſpoſition, ſoon recommended him to the patronage of a magnificent monarch, and rendered him a very popular and acceptable character in the brilliant court which I have above deſcribed. In the meantime he added to his accompliſhments by frequent tours into France and Italy, which he ſometimes viſited under the advantages of a public character. Hitherto our poets had been perſons of a private and circumſcribed education, and the art of verſifying, like every other kind of compoſition, had been confined to recluſe ſcholars. But Chaucer was a man of the world; and from this circumſtance we are to account, in great meaſure, for the many new embelliſhments which he conferred on our language and our poetry. The deſcriptions of ſplendid proceſſions and gallant carouſals with which his works abound are a proof that he was converſant with the practices and diverſions of polite life. Familiarity with a variety of things and objects, opportunities of acquiring the faſhionable and courtly modes of ſpeech, connections with the great at home, and a perſonal acquaintance with the vernacular poets of foreign countries, opened his mind, and furniſhed him with new lights.[3] In Italy he [is ſaid to have met] Petrarch, at the wedding of Violante, daughter of Galeazzo, duke of Milan, with the duke of Clarence; and it is [even alleged] that Boccaccio was of the party.[4] Although Chaucer had undoubtedly ſtudied the works of theſe celebrated writers, and particularly of Dante, before this, yet it ſeems likely that theſe excurſions gave him a new reliſh for their compoſitions, and enlarged his knowledge of the Italian fables. His travels likewiſe enabled him to cultivate the Italian and [French] languages with

---

[1] Johnſon's *Diction.* Pref. p. 1.

[2] [*New Facts in the Life of Geoffrey Chaucer*, by E. A. Bond, *Fortnightly Rev.*, Aug. 15, 1866.]

[3] The earl of Saliſbury, beheaded by Henry IV., could not but patronize Chaucer. I do not mean for political reaſons. The earl was a writer of verſes, and very fond of poetry. On this account his acquaintance was much cultivated by the famous Chriſtina of Piſa, whoſe works, both in proſe and verſe, compoſe ſo conſiderable a part of the old French literature. She uſed to call him, " Gracieux chevalier, aimant dictiez, et lui-meme gracieux dicteur." See M. Boivin, *Mem. Lit.* tom. ii. p. 767, *ſeq.* 4to.

[4] Froiſſart was alſo preſent. *Vie de Petrarque*, 1766, iii. 772. I believe Paulus Jovius is the firſt who mentions this anecdote. *Vit. Galeaz.* ii. p. 153.

the greatest fuccefs, and induced him to polifh the afperity, and enrich the fterility of his native verfification with fofter cadences, and a more copious and variegated phrafeology. [This attempt was] authorized by the recent and popular examples of Petrarch in Italy and [Jean de Meun and others] in France.[1] The revival of learning in moft countries appears to have firft owed its rife to tranflation. At rude periods the modes of original thinking are unknown, and the arts of original compofition have not yet been ftudied. The writers, therefore, of fuch periods are chiefly and very ufefully employed in importing the ideas of other languages into their own. They do not venture to think for themfelves, nor aim at the merit of inventors, but they are laying the foundations of literature; and while they are naturalizing the knowledge of more learned ages and countries by tranflation, they are imperceptibly improving the national language. This has been remarkably the cafe, not only in England, but in France and Italy. [To mention only a few inftances: Laʒamon tranflated and enlarged Wace; Robert of Brunne tranflated William of Waddington, Wace, and Langtoft; and] in the year 1387, John Trevifa, canon of Weftbury in Gloucefterfhire and a great traveller, not only finifhed a tranflation of the Old and New Teftaments at the command of his munificent patron, Thomas Lord Berkley,[2] but alfo tranflated Higden's *Polychronicon* and other Latin pieces.[3] But thefe tranflations would have been alone infufficient to have produced or fuftained any confiderable revolution in our language: the great work was referved for Gower and Chaucer. Wickliffe had alfo tranflated the Bible;[4] and in other refpeéts his attempts to bring about a reformation in religion at this time proved beneficial to Englifh literature. The orthodox divines of this period generally wrote in Latin: but Wickliffe, that his arguments might

---

[1] [Not Alain Chartier, as Warton fays; for Alain Chartier was born at Bayeux not later than 1395, and did not compofe his firft work till after the battle of Agincourt (25 Oét. 1415); it was *Le Livre des Quatre Dames.* He was fent to Scotland on an embaffy in June or July, 1428. See *Memoires de la Société des Antiquaires de Normandie*, tome xxviii. and *Revue Critique*, Aug. 28, 1869.—F. The example of Chartier could not have been, confequently, of much fervice to our Chaucer!]

[2] See Wharton, *Append. Cav.* p. 49.

[3] Such as Bartholomew Glanville *De Proprietatibus Rerum*, lib. xix. and Vegetius *De Arte Militari.* MSS. Digb. 233. Bibl. Bodl. In the fame manufcript is Ægidius Romanus *De Regimine Principum*, a tranflation by [Occleve. It was edited for the Roxburghe Club, by Mr. T. Wright, 1860.] He alfo tranflated fome pieces of Richard Fitzralph, archbifhop of Armagh. See *fupr.* He wrote a traét, prefixed to his verfion of the *Polychronicon*, on the utility of tranflations: *De Utilitate Tranflationum, Dialogus inter Clericum et Patronum.* See more of his tranflations in MSS. Harl. 1900. I do not find his *Englifh Bible* in any of our libraries, nor do I believe that any copy of it now remains. Caxton mentions it in the preface to his edition of the Englifh *Polychronicon.* See Lewis's *Wickliffe*, p. 66, 329, and Lewis's *Hiftory of the Tranflations of the Bible*, p. 66.

[4] It is obfervable that he made his tranflation from the vulgate Latin verfion of Jerom. See MS. Cod. Bibl. Coll. Eman. Cant. 102. [There is nothing in the MS. to warrant the ftatement in the former editions as to the work having been finifhed in 1383, which date is fimply added in a note written in a fecond hand.— *Madden.*]

be familiarized to common readers and the bulk of the people, was obliged to compofe in Englifh his numerous theological treatifes againft the papal corruptions. Edward III. while he perhaps intended only to banifh a badge of conqueft, greatly contributed to eftablifh the national dialect, by abolifhing the ufe of the Norman tongue in the public acts and judicial proceedings, as we have before obferved, and by fubftituting the natural language of the country. But Chaucer manifeftly firft taught his countrymen to write Englifh, and formed a ftyle by naturalizing words from the [Langue d'Oye],[1] at that time the [richeft] dialect of any in Europe, and the beft adapted to the purpofes of poetical expreffion.

It is certain that Chaucer abounds in claffical allufions; but his poetry is not formed on the ancient models. He appears to have been an univerfal reader, and his learning is fometimes miftaken for genius; but his chief fources were the French and Italian poets. From thefe originals two of his capital poems, the *Knight's Tale*,[2] and the *Romaunt of the Rofe* [if his] are imitations or tranflations. The firft of thefe is taken from Boccaccio. [Chaucer, out of the 2250 lines of his *Knight's Tale*, has tranflated 270 (lefs than one-eighth) from the 9054 of Boccaccio's original: 374 more lines

---

[1] The ingenious editor of the *Canterbury Tales* treats the notion, that Chaucer imitated the Provençal poets, as totally void of foundation. He fays, " I have not obferved in any of his writings a fingle phrafe or word, which has the leaft appearance of having been fetched from the South of the Loire. With refpect to the manner and matter of his compofitions, till fome clear inftance of imitation be produced, I fhall be flow to believe, that in either he ever copied the poets of Provence; with whofe works, I apprehend, he had very little, if any acquaintance," vol. i. *Append. Pref.* p. xxxvi. I have advanced the contrary doctrine, at leaft by implication : and I here beg leave to explain myfelf on a fubject materially affecting the fyftem of criticifm that has been formed on Chaucer's works. I have never affirmed that Chaucer imitated the Provençal bards; although it is by no means improbable that he might have known their tales. But as the peculiar nature of the Provençal poetry entered deeply into the fubftance, caft, and character, of fome of thofe French and Italian poets, which he is allowed to have followed, he certainly may be faid to have copied, although not immediately, the *matter* and *manner* of thefe writers. I have called his *Houfe of Fame* originally a Provençal compofition. I did not mean that it was written by a Provençal troubadour : but that Chaucer's original was compounded of the capricious mode of fabling, and that extravagant ftyle of fiction, which conftitute the effence of the Provençal poetry. As to the *Flower and the Leaf*, which Dryden pronounces to have been compofed *after their manner*, it is framed on the old allegorifing fpirit of the Provençal writers, refined and disfigured by the fopperies of the French poets in the fourteenth century. The ideas of thefe fablers had been fo ftrongly imbibed, that they continued to operate long after Petrarch had introduced a more rational method of compofition.

[2] Chaucer alludes to fome book whence this tale was taken, more than once, viz. v. 1. " Whilom, as *olde ftories* tellin us." v. 1465. " As *olde bookes* to us faine, that *all this ftorie telleth more plain*." v. 2814. " Of foulis fynd I nought in this *regiftre.*" That is, this hiftory, or narrative. See alfo v. 2297. In the *Legend of good women*, where Chaucer's works are mentioned, is this paffage, v. 420.

"And al the love of Palamon and Arcite Of Thebis, *though the ftoreis known lite.*"

[The laft words feem to imply that it had not made itfelf very popular.—*Tyrwhitt.*]

bear a general likenefs to the Italian poets, and 132 more, a flight likenefs.[1]]

Boccaccio was the difciple of Petrarch : and although principally known and defervedly celebrated as a writer or inventor of tales, he was by his cotemporaries ufually placed in the third rank after Dante and Petrarch. But Boccaccio having feen the Platonic fonnets of his mafter Petrarch, in a fit of defpair committed [a portion of his own] to the flames,[2] except [only certain pieces, of which perhaps] his good tafte had taught him to entertain a more favourable opinion, [one] thus happily refcued from deftruction [was formerly] fo little known even in Italy, as to have left its author but a flender proportion of that eminent degree of poetical reputation which he might have juftly claimed from fo extraordinary a performance. It is an heroic poem, in twelve books, entitled La Tefeide, and written in the octave ftanza, called by the Italians *ottava rima*, which Boccaccio adopted from the old French chanfons, and here firft introduced among his countrymen.[3] It was printed at Ferrara, but with fome deviations from the original, and even mifreprefentations of the ftory, in 1475.[4] [It was reprinted without date in 4to, and again in 1528. The poem has alfo been tranflated into Italian and French profe.]

Whether Boccaccio was the inventor of the ftory of this poem [feems rather doubtful]. It is certain that Thefeus was an early hero of romance.[5] He was taken from that grand repofitory of the Grecian heroes, the *Hiftory of Troy*, [compofed from various materials] by Guido de Colonna. In the royal library at Paris there is a MS. entitled, *Roman de Thefeus et de Gadifer*.[6] Probably, this is the French romance, [printed at Paris in two folio volumes in 1534.[7]] Gadifer, with whom Thefeus is joined in this ancient tale, written probably by a troubadour of Picardy, is a champion in the oldeft French romances.[8] He is mentioned frequently in the *Roman d'Alexandre*. In the romance of *Perceforreft*, he is called king of Scotland, and faid to be crowned by Alexander the Great.[9] [But this Thefeus, as Mr. Douce has pointed out, is a different perfon altogether from the claffical hero, being the fon of Floridas, king of

---

[1] [*Temporary Preface*, by F. J. F., pp. 104-5.]

[2] Goujet, *Bibl. Fr.* tom. vii. p. 328.

[3] See Crefcimbeni *Iftor. Volgar. Poes.* vol. i. l. i. p. 65.

[4] [See the correct title in Brunet, laft edit. i. 1016-17. A purer text of the poem appeared in 1819, 8vo, in which it was taken from a MS. The *Thefeid* forms vol. 9 of the collected edit. of Boccaccio, publifhed at Florence, 1827-31, 13 vols. 8vo.]

[5] In Lydgate's *Temple of Glas*, among the lovers painted on the wall is Thefeus killing the Minotaur. I fuppofe from Ovid, or from Chaucer's *Legend of Good Women*. Bibl. Bodl. MSS. Fairfax, 16.

[6] MSS. Bibl. Reg. Paris. tom. ii. 974. E.

[7] [See the full and correct title in the laft edition of Brunet, v. 808. There was a later edition about 1550.]

[8] The chevaliers of the courts of Charles V. and VI. adopted names from the old romances, fuch as Lancelot, Gadifer, Carados, &c. *Mem. Anc. Cheval.* i. p. 340.

[9] [See Brunet, *dern.* edit. in v. *Perceforeft*. This tedious ftory was printed at Paris in 1528, in fix folio volumes, ufually bound in three.]

Cologne, in the year 682.] There is in the fame library a MS.
called by Montfaucon *Historia Thesei in lingua vulgari*, in ten books.[1]
The Abbé Goujet obferves, that there is in fome libraries of France
an old French tranflation of Boccaccio's *Thefeid*, from which Anna
de Graville formed the French poem of *Palamon and Arcite*, at the
command of Queen Claude, wife of Francis I., about the year 1487.
Either the tranflation ufed by Anna de Graville, or her poem, is
perhaps the fecond of the MSS. mentioned by Montfaucon. Boccaccio's *Thefeid* has alfo been tranflated into Italian profe by
Nicolas Granuci, and printed at Lucca in 157[9].[2] In the *Dedication* to this work, which was printed about one hundred years after
the Ferrara edition of the *Thefeide* appeared, Granucci [wrongly
and even ignorantly, as we are much inclined to think], mentions
Boccaccio's work as a tranflation from the barbarous Greek poem
cited below.[3] Boccaccio himfelf mentions the ftory of Palamon
and Arcite. This may feem to imply that the ftory exifted before
his time : unlefs he artfully intended to recommend his own poem
on the fubject by ſuch an allufion. It is where he introduces two
lovers finging a portion of this tale :—" Dioneo e Fiametta gran
pezza canterono infieme d'Arcite e di Palamone."[4] By Dioneo
Boccaccio reprefents himfelf ; and by Fiametta, his miftrefs, Mary
of Arragon, a natural daughter of Robert, king of Naples.

I confefs I am of opinion, that Boccaccio's *Thefeid* is [to a great
extent] an original compofition [though bafed on, and improved
from, the *Thebais* of Statius]. But there is a Græco-barbarous
poem extant on this fubject, which, if it could be proved to be antecedent in point of time to the Italian poem, would degrade Boccaccio
to a mere tranflator on this occafion. It is a matter that deferves
to be examined at large, and to be traced with accuracy.

This Greek poem is [by no means fo well] known as Boccaccio's.
It is entitled Θησευς και Γαμοι της Εμιλιας. It was printed at Venice
in 1529.[5] It is often cited by Du Cange in his Greek gloffary under
the title, *De Nuptiis Thefei et Æmiliæ*. The heads of the chapters
are adorned with rude wooden cuts of the ftory. I once fufpected
that Boccaccio, having received this poem from fome of his learned
friends among the Grecian exiles, who being driven from Conftantinople took refuge in Italy about the fourteenth century, tranflated it
into Italian. Under this fuppofition, I was indeed furprifed to find

---

[1] Bibl. MSS. *ut fupr.*
[2] [But fee Brunet, i. 1017.] The *Thefeid* has alfo been tranflated into French
pro , 1597, 12mo.—[Ibid.] Jeanne de la Fontaine tranflated into French verfe
it is poem. She died 1536. Her tranflation was never printed. It is applauded
by Joannes Secundus, *Eleg.* xv.
[3] *Dedicaz.* fol. 5. " Volendo far cofa, que non fio ftata fatta da loro, pero
mutato parere mi dicoli a ridurre in profa quefto Innamoramento, Opera di M.
Giovanni Boccaccio, quale egli transforto dal Greco in octava rima per compiacere
alla fua Fiametta," &c. See Sloane MS. 1614. Brit. Muſ.
[4] Giorn. vii. Nov. 10, p. 348, edit. 1548. Chaucer himfelf alludes to this ftory,
Bl. Kn. v. 369. Perhaps on the fame principle.
[5] A MS. of it is in the Royal Library at Paris, Cod. 2569. Du Cange, *Ind.
Auct. Glofs. Gr. Barb.* ii. p. 65, col. 1.

the ideas of chivalry and the ceremonies of a tournament minutely defcribed, in a poem which appeared to have been written at Conftantinople. But this difficulty was foon removed, when I recollected that the [Latins, in which name we include the French, Flemings, Italians, and] Venetians, had been in poffeffion of that city for more than one hundred years, Baldwin, earl of Flanders, having been elected emperor of Conftantinople in 1204.[1] Add to this, that the word, τερνεμεντον, a tournament, occurs in the Byzantine hiftorians.[2] From the fame communication likewife, I mean the Greek exiles, I fancied Boccaccio might have procured the ftories of feveral of his tales in the *Decameron:* as, for inftance, that of *Cymon and Iphigenia,* where the names are entirely Grecian, and the fcene laid in Rhodes,

---

[1] About which period it is probable that the anonymous Greek poem, called the *Loves of Lybifter and Rhodamna,* was written. This appears by the German name Frederic, which often occurs in it, and is grecifed, with many other German words. In a MS. of this poem which Crufius faw, were many paintings and illuminations; where, in the reprefentation of a battle, he obferved no guns, but javelins and bows and arrows. He adds, " et muficæ teftudines." It is written in the iambic meafure mentioned below. It is a feries of wandering adventures with little art or invention. Lybifter, the fon of a Latin king, and a Chriftian, fets forward accompanied with an hundred attendants in fearch of Rhodamna, whom he had loft by the ftratagems of a certain old woman fkilled in magic. He meets Clitophon fon of a king of Armenia. They undergo various dangers in different countries. Lybifter relates his dream concerning a partridge and an eagle; and how from that dream he fell in love with Rhodamna daughter of Chyfes a pagan king, and communicated his paffion by fending an arrow, to which his name was affixed, into a tower, or caftle, called Argyrocaftre, &c. See Crufius, *Turko-Græcia,* p. 974. But we find a certain fpecies of erotic romances, fome in verfe and fome in profe, exifting in the Greek empire, the remains and the dregs of Heliodorus, Achilles Tatius, Xenophon the Ephefian, Charito, Euftathius or Eumathius, and others, about or rather before the year 1200. Such are the *Loves of Rhodante and Dofilcs,* by Theodorus Prodromus, who wrote about the year 1130. This piece was imitated by Nicetas Eugenianus in the *Loves of Charicell and Drofilla.* See Labb. *Bibl. Nov. Manufcript.* p. 220. *The Loves of Callimachus and Chryforrhoe, The Erotic hiftory of Hemperius, The hiftory of the Loves of Florius and Platzaftora,* with fome others, all by anonymous authors, and in Græco-barbarous iambics, were written at Conftantinople, [and were probably tranflations from another language.] See Neffel. i. p. 342-343. Meurs. *Glofs. Gr. Barb.* v. Βανενι. And Lambecc. v. p. 262, 264.

[2] As alfo Τορνε, *Haftiludium.* Fr. *Tournoi.* And Τουρνεσειν, *haftiludio contendere.* Johannes Cantacuzenus relates, that when Anne of Savoy, daughter of Amadeus, the fourth earl of Savoy, was married to the Emperor Andronicus, junior, the Frankifh and Savoyard nobles, who accompanied the princefs, held tilts and tournaments before the court at Conftantinople; which, he adds, the Greeks learned of the Franks. This was in 1326. *Hift. Byzant.* l. i. cap. 42. But Nicetas fays, that when the Emperor Manuel [Comnenus] made fome ftay at Antioch, the Greeks held a folemn tournament againft the Franks. This was about 1160. *Hift. Byzant.* l. iii. cap. 3. Cinnamus obferves, that the fame Emperor Manuel altered the fhape of the fhields and lances of the Greeks to thofe of the Franks. *Hift.* lib. iii. Nicephorus Gregoras, who wrote about the year 1340, affirms that the Greeks learned this practice from the Franks. *Hift. Byzant.* l. x. p. 339, edit. fol. Genev. 1615. The word Καβαλλαριοι, knights, chevaliers, occurs often in the Byzantine hiftorians, even as early as Anna Comnena, who wrote about 1140. *Alexiad,* lib. xiii. p. 411. And we have in J. Cantacuzenus, " την Καβαλαριων παρειχε τιμην:"--He conferred the honour of Knighthood. This indeed is faid of the Franks. *Hift.* ut fupr. l. iii. cap. 25. And in the Greek poem now under confideration, one of the titles is, " Πως εποικεν ὁ Θεσευς της δυο Θηβαιης Καβαλαρινς:"--How Thefeus dubbed the two Thebans knights. Lib. vii. fignatur ν*ιιι* fol. vers.

Cyprus, Crete, and other parts of Greece belonging to the imperial territory.[1] But, to ſay no more of this, I have at preſent no ſort of doubt of what I before aſſerted, that Boccaccio is the writer and inventor of this piece. Our Greek poem is in faƈt a literal tranſlation from the Italian *Theſeid*. The writer has tranſlated the prefatory epiſtle addreſſed by Boccaccio to the *Fiametta*. It conſiſts of twelve books, and is written in Boccaccio's oƈtave ſtanza, the two laſt lines of every ſtanza rhyming together. The verſes are of the iambic kind, and ſomething like the *Verſus Politici*, which were common among the Greek ſcholars a little before, and long after, Conſtantinople was taken by the Turks in 1453. It will readily be allowed, that the circumſtance of the ſtanzas and rhymes is very ſingular in a poem compoſed in the Greek language, and is alone ſufficient to prove this piece to be a tranſlation from Boccaccio. I muſt not forget to obſerve, that the Greek is extremely barbarous, and of the loweſt period of that language.

It was a common praƈtice of the learned and indigent Greeks, who frequented Italy and the neighbouring ſtates about the fifteenth and ſixteenth centuries, to tranſlate the popular pieces of Italian poetry, and the romances or tales moſt in vogue, into theſe Græco-barbarous iambics.[2] *Paſtor Fido* was thus tranſlated. The romance of *Alexander the Great* was alſo tranſlated in the ſame manner by Demetrius Zenus, who flouriſhed in 1530, under the title of Αλεξανδρευς ὁ Μακεδων, and printed at Venice in 1529.[3]

In the very year, and at the ſame place, when and where our Greek poem on Theſeus, or Palamon and Arcite, was printed, *Apollonius of Tyre*, another famous romance of the middle ages, was tranſlated in the ſame manner, and entitled Διηγησις ὡραιωτατη Απολλωνιου του εν Τυρω[4] ρημαδα.[5] The ſtory of King Arthur they alſo reduced into the ſame language. The French hiſtory or [rather] romance

---

[1] Giorn. v. Nov. 1.

[2] That is *verſus politici* above mentioned, a ſort of looſe iambic. See Langius, *Philologia Græco-barbara*. Tzetzes's Chiliads are written in this verſification. See Du Cange, *Gl. Gr.* ii. col. 1196.

[3] Crus. *ut ſupr.* pp. 373, 399.

[4] That is, Rythmically, poetically, *Gr. Barb.*

[5] Du Cange mentions, " Μεταγλωττισμα απο Λατινικης εις Ραμαικην διηγησις πολληπαθους Απολλωνιου του Τυρου." *Ind. Auƈt. Gloſſ. Gr. Barb.* ii. p. 36, col. b. Compare Fabricius, *Bibl. Gr.* vi. 821. Firſt printed at Venice [in 1534. See Brunet, i. 350-1, where other editions are quoted.] In the works of Velſerus there is *Narratio Eorum quæ Apollonio regi acciderunt*, &c. He ſays it was firſt written by ſome Greek author. Velſeri Op. p. 697, edit. 1682. The Latin is in Bibl. Bodl. MSS. Laud, 39.—Bodl. F. 7, and F. 11.45. In the preface, Velſerus, who died 1614, ſays that he believes the original in Greek ſtill remains at Conſtantinople, in the library of Manuel Eugenicus. Montfaucon mentions a noble copy of this romance, written in the xiii[th]. century, in the royal library at Paris. Bibl. MSS. p. 753. Compare MSS. Langb. Bibl. Bodl. vi. p. 15. *Geſta Apollonii*, &c. There is a [verſion] in [Anglo-]Saxon of the romance. Wanley's Catal. *apud* Hickes, ii. 146, [printed by Thorpe, 1834, 8vo.] See Martin. Cruſii *Turco Græc.* p. 209, edit. 1594. Gower recites many ſtories of this romance in his *Confeſſio Amantis*. He calls Apollonius " a yonge, a freſhe, a luſtie knight." See lib. viii. fol. 175, b.—185, a. But he refers to Godfrey of Viterbo's *Pantheon*, or univerſal Chronicle, called alſo *Me-*

of *Bertrand du Guefcelin,* printed at Abbeville in 1487,[1] and that of *Belifaire* or *Belifarius,* they rendered in the fame language and metre, with the titles Διηγησις εξαιρετος Βελθανδρου του Ρωμαιου,[2] and Ἱστορικη εξηγησις περι Βελλισαριου, &c.[3]   Boccaccio himfelf, in the *Decameron,*[4]

---

moriæ Sæculorum, partly in profe, partly verfe, from the creation of the world to the year 1186. The author died in 1190.
> " —A Cronike in daies gone
> The which is cleped Panteone," &c.

fol. 175, a. [There is a fragment of 140 lines of a fifteenth-century Englifh verfe tranflation of this romance in MS. Douce 216.—F. Another is in the poffeffion of Sir Thomas Philipps. Neither has any connection with the Englifh (profe) verfion of *Apollonius of Tyre,* executed by Robert Copland, and printed in 1510. The Duke of Devonfhire's copy of the latter, purchafed at the Roxburghe fale in 1812, feems to be unique. It has been lately (1870) reprinted in facfimile by Afh-bee. Refpecting *Apollonius of Tyre,* fee the prefent work *infra,* Collier's *Shakefpeare's Library,* 1843, and Halliwell's *New Boke about Shakefpeare and Stratford-on-Avon,* 1850, where the Philipps fragment is printed for the firft time. It formerly belonged to Dr. Farmer.] The play called *Pericles Prince of Tyre,* attributed to Shakefpeare, is taken from this ftory of Apollonius as told by Gower, who fpeaks the prologue. It exifted in Latin before the year 900. See Barth. *Adverfar.* lviii. cap. i. Chaucer calls him " of Tyre Apolloneus " (*Prol. Man. L. Tale,* ver. 82), and quotes from this romance :
> " How that the curfed kyng Anteochus
> Byreft his doughter of hir maydenhede,
> That is fo horrible a tale as man may reede,
> Whan he hir threw upon the pament."

[But Shakefpeare is alfo fuppofed to have been indebted to Lawrence Twyne's compilation : " The Patterne of painefull Aduentures," firft publifhed probably in 1576, and reprinted from a later ed. in the firft vol. of *Shakefpeare's Library,* 1843.] In the Britifh Mufeum there is *Hiftoire d'Apollin roy de Thir.* MSS. Reg. 20 C. ii. 2. With regard to the French editions of this romance, [the oldeft is probably that of Geneva, *fine ulla nota,* folio. See Brunet, i. 351. Thofe of 1530 and *fans date* (Paris, Jehan Boufont) are later, curtailed, and of courfe lefs valuable.] At length the ftory appeared in a modern drefs by M. le Brun, under the title of *Avantures d'Apollonius de Thyr,* printed in 1710, and again the following year. In the edition of the *Gefta Romanorum,* printed at Rouen in 1521, and containing 181 chapters, [as well as in that of 1488 and others,] the hiftory of Apollonius of Tyre occurs, ch. 153. This is the firft of the additional chapters.

[1] At the end of *Le Triumphe des neuf Preux:* that is, *The Nine Worthies.* [Compare Brunet, i. 44, with *ibid.* ii. 809.]

[2] See Du Cange, *Gl. Gr. Barb.* ii. *Ind. Auctor.* p. 36, col. b. This hiftory contains Beltrand's or Bertrand's amours with Χρυσατζα, Chryfatfa, the king of Antioch's daughter.

[3] See Lambecc. *Bibl. Cæfar.* lib. v. p. 264. It is remarkable that the ftory of *Date obolum Belifario* is not in Procopius, but in this romance. Probably Vandyck got this ftory from a modernized edition of it, called *Bellifaire ou le Conquerant,* Paris, 1643. It, however, is faid in the title-page to be taken from Procopius. It was written by [François de Grenaille, fieur de Chateaunieres.]

[4] They fometimes applied their Greek iambics to the works of the ancient Greek poets. Demetrius Zenus, above mentioned, tranflated Homer's Βατραχομυομαχια ; and Nicolaus Lucanus the *Iliad.* The firft was printed at Venice, and afterwards reprinted by Crufius, *Turco-Græc.* p. 373; the latter was alfo printed at Venice, 1526. This Zenus is faid to be the author of Γαλεωμυομαχια, or *Battle of the Cats and Mice.* See Crus. *ubi fupr.* 396, and Fabric. *Bibl. Gr.* i. 264, 223. [But the true writer was Theodorus Prodronus.— *Rye.*] On account of the Græco-barbarous books, which began to grow common, chiefly in Italy about the year 1520, Sabius above-mentioned, the printer of many of them, publifhed a Græco-barbarous lexicon at Venice, 1527: [*Introduttorio nuovo intitolato Corona preciofa,* &c. See Brunet, *dern. edit.* v. 7, and *ibid.* ii. 293.] It is a mixture of

mentions the ftory of Troilus and Creffida in Greek verfe, which I
fuppofe had been tranflated by fome of the fugitive Greeks with
whom he was connected, from a romance on that fubject, many
ancient copies of which now remain in the libraries of France.[1]
The ftory of *Florius and Platzflora*, a romance which Ludovicus
Vives with great gravity condemns under the name of *Florian and
Blanca-Flor*, as one of the pernicious and unclaffical popular hiftories
current in Flanders about the year 1523,[2] of which there are old
editions in French, Spanifh,[3] and perhaps Italian, is likewife extant
very early in Greek iambics, moft probably as a tranflation into that
language.[4]   I could give many others, but I haften to lay before my
readers fome fpecimens both of the Italian and the Greek *Palamon
and Arcite*:[5] only premifing that both have about a thoufand verfes

---

modern and ancient Greek words, Latin and Italian.   It was reprinted at Venice
[in 1543, of which there was a re-iffue in] 1546.

[1] See *Le Roman de Troylus*, [a profe French copy of the *Filoftrato*, in *Nouvelles
Françoifes du XIVme Siècle*, 1858,] and Montfaucon, *Bibl. MSS.* p. 792, 793, &c.
&c.   There is, "L'Amore di Troleo et Grifeida, ove fi tratta in buone parte la
Guerra di Troja," d'Angelo Leonico, Ven. 1553, in octave rhyme.

[2] Lud. Viv. *de Chriftiana Femina*, lib. i. cap. *cui tit.   Qui non legendi Scriptores*,
&c.   He lived at Bruges.   He mentions other romances common in Flanders,
Leonela and Canamor, Curias and Florela, and *Pyramus and Thifbe*.

[3] *Flores y Blancaflor*.   En Alcala, 1512, 4to.   See Brunet's remarks, ii. 1300.
This Spanifh verfion was tranflated into French, under the title:] *Hiftoire Amoreufe
de Flores et de Blanchefleur*, traduite de l'Efpagnol par Jacques Vincent.   Paris,
1554, 8vo.   *Florimont et Pafferoze*, traduite de l'Efpagnol en profe Françoife, Lyon,
15—, 8vo.   There is a French edition at Lyons, 1571; it was, perhaps, originally
Spanifh.   [Compare Brunet, ii. 1307.]
The tranflation of *Flores and Blanca[f]lore* in Greek iambics might alfo be
made in compliment to Boccaccio.   Their adventures make the principal fubject
of his *Philocopo:* but the ftory exifted long before, as Boccaccio himfelf informs us,
lib. i., edit. [1827-31.]   Flores and Blancaflore are mentioned as illuftrious lovers
by Matfres Eymengau de Bezers, a poet of Languedoc, in his *Breviari d'Amor*,
dated 1288.   MSS. Reg. 19 C. i. fol. 199.   This tale was probably enlarged in
paffing through the hands of Boccaccio.   [The two different verfions of the
French thirteenth century romance of *Florice and Blancheflore* (Bibl. Imperiale,
No. 6987; Paulin-Paris, vol. 3, pp. 215-16) have been printed at Berlin in 1844,
and at Paris in 1856.   Read in the latter M. du Méril's excellent introduction.
Several MSS. of the Englifh verfion are extant.   There is a copy in the
Auchinleck MS. printed in *Antient Englifh Poetry*, 1857; in Cotton. MS. Vitellius,
D, 111, printed by Early Engl. Text Society (with *King Horn*), 1866; and at
Cambridge, printed (probably very badly) in Hartfhorne's *Ancient Metrical Tales*,
1829.   The Cotton. MS. is fadly mutilated.—F.]
[A German romance on this fubject was tranflated by Konrad Flecke from the
French of Robert d'Orleans, in the early part of the thirteenth century.   The
fubject is referred to at an earlier period by feveral Provençal poets, and this,
coupled with the theatre of its events, makes Warton's conjecture extremely probable that it is of Spanifh origin.—*Price.*   For the fulleft account of the biblio-
graphy of this popular romance fee Hoffmann's *Horæ Belgicæ*, 1830, part 3.   See
alfo art. *Affenede* in the *Dict. Soc. Ufeful Knowledge.—Rye.*]

[4] [Dr. Wagner is editing a Middle-Greek *Floris* for the Philological Society.—F.]

[5] [Warton was indebted, he tells us, to Mr. Stanley for the ufe of the Greek
Thefeus, printed at Venice in 1529, with woodcuts.   Another copy was at that
time in the hands of Ramfay the painter.   The firft edition of the original Italian,
Ferrara, 1475, folio, was in Dr. Afkew's collection.   Conful Smith's copy was
bought for King George III.   Another copy is at Althorp, and a fourth fold at

in each of the twelve books, and that the two first books are introductory; the first containing the war of Theseus with the Amazons,
and the second that of Thebes, in which Palamon and Arcite are
taken prisoners.   Boccaccio thus describes the Temple of Mars:

Ne' campi tracii sotto i cieli iberni
Da tempesta continova agitati
Dove schieré di nembi sempiterni
Da venti or qua ed or la trasmutati
In varii luoghi ne guazzori verni
E d' acqua globi per freddo aggroppati
Gittati sono, e neve tuttavia,
Che 'n ghiaccio a mano a man' s' indura e cria:

E 'n una selva steril di robusti
Cerri, dov' eran folti ed alti molte,
Nodosi ed aspri, rigidi e vetusti,
Che d' ombra eterna ricuoprono il volto
Del tristo suolo, e in fra gli antichi fusti,
Da ben mille furor sempre ravvolto
Vi si sentia grandissimo romore,
Ne v' era bestia encora nè pastore

In questa vide la ca' dello iddio
Armipotente, e questa è edificata
Tutta d' acciaio splendido e pulio,
Dal quale era dal sol riverberata
La luce, che aborriva il luogho rio:
Tutta di ferro era la stretta entrata
E le porte eran d' eterno diamante
Ferrate d' ogni parte tutte quante,

E le colonne di ferro custei
Vide, che l' edificio sostenieno
Li gl' Impeti dementi parve a lei
Veder, che fier fuor della uscieno,
Ed il cieco Peccare, ed ogni Omei
Similemente quivi si vedieno;
Videvi l' Ire rosse come fuoco,
E la Paura pallida in quel loco.

E con gli occulti ferri i Tradimenti
Vide, e le Insidie con giusta apparenza:
Li Discordia sedeva, e sanguinenti
Ferri avie in mano, e d' ogni differenza;
E tutti i luoghi pareano strepenti
D' aspre minacce e di crudele intenza:
E 'n mezzo il loco la Virtù tristissima
Sedie di degne lode poverissima.

Videvi ancora l' allegro Furore,
E oltre a ciò con volto sanguinoso
La Morte armata vide e lo Stupore;
Ed ogni altare quivi era copioso
Di sangue sol nelle battaglie fuore
De' corpi uman cacciato, e luminoso
Era ciascun di fuoco tolto a terre
Arse e disfatte per le triste guerre.

Ed era il tempio tutto istoriato[1]

Hibbert's sale in 1829 for £160.   See Dibdin's *Biblioth. Spencer.* iv. 84, and
Brunet, i. 1015-16.]

[1] Thus, Στορισματα means paintings, properly history-paintings, and ιςορειν, and

Da fottil mano e di fopra e d' intorno
E ciò che pria vi vide difegnato
Eran prede di notte e di giorno
Tolti alle terre, e qualunque isforzato
Fu era quivi in abito muforno :
Vedevanfi le genti incatenate,
Porti di ferro e fortezze fpezzate

Videvi ancor le navi bellatrici,
I vòti carri, e li volti guaftati,
E li miferi pianti ed infelici,
Ed ogni forza cogli afpetti elati,
Ogni fedita ancor fi vedea lici :
E fangui colle terre mefcolati :
E 'n ogni loco nell' afpetto fiero
Si vedea Marte torbido ed altiero, &c.[1]

The Temple of Venus has thefe imageries :

Poi vide preffo a fè paffar Bellezza
Senz' ornamento alcun fè riguardando,
E vide gir con lei Piacevolezza,
E l' una e l' altra feco commendano;
Poi con lor vide ftarfi Giovinezza
Deftra ed adorna molto fefteggiando :
E d' altra parte vide il folle Ardire
Lufinghe e Ruffianie infieme gire.

E 'n mezzo il loco in fu alte colonne
Di rame vide un tempio, al qual d' intorno
Danzando giovinetti vide e donne,
Qual da fè belle : e qual d' abito adorno,
Difcinte e fcalze, in capelli e gonne,
Che in quefto folo difpendeano il giorno :
Poi fopra il tempio vide volitare
Paffere molte e columbe rucchiare.

Ed all' entrata del tempio vicina
Vide che fi fedeva pianamente
Madonna Pace, e in mano una cortina
'Nanzi alla porta tenea lievemente :
Appreffo a lei in vifta affai tapina
Pacienza fedea difcretamente,

ανιϛορειν, is to *paint*, in barbarous Greek. There are various examples in the Byzantine writers. In middle Latinity *Hiftoriographus* fignifies literally a painter. Perhaps our hiftoriographer royal was originally the king's illuminator. 'Iϛοριο-γραφος μουϛιατωρ occurs in an infcription publifhed by Du Cange, *Differtat. Joinv.* xxvii. p. 319. Where μουϛιατωρ implies an artift who painted in mofaic work called μουϛαιον, or μουϛιον, *mufivum.* In the Greek poem before us 'Iϛοριτας is ufed for a painter, lib. ii. :

Εκ την παρουσαν την ζωην ὁλεποικειν ὁ 'Iϛοριτας.

In the middle Latin writers we have *depingere hiftorialiter*, to paint with hiftories or figures, viz. "Forinfecus dealbavit illud [delubrum,] intrinfecus autem *depinxit hiftorialiter.*" Dudo, *De Act. Norman.* l. iii. p. 153. Dante ufes the Italian word before us in the fame fenfe. Dante, *Purgat.* Cant. x. :

" Quivi era hiftoriata l'alta gloria
Del Roman Principe."

'Iϛορια frequently occurs, fimply for picture or reprefentation in colours. Nilus Monach. lib. iv. *Epift.* 61. Και ιϛοριας πτηνων και ἑρπετων και βλαϛημματων. " Pictures of birds, ferpents, and plants." And in a thoufand other inftances.

[1] L. vii. [Ed. 1827-31, ix. 221-3. In all the former editions, the extract, as well as that which fucceeds, was fo disfigured by errors, as to be abfoluteiy unintelligible.]

Pallida nell' afpecto : e d' ogni parte
D' intorno a lei vide Promeffe ad arte.
Poi dentro al tempio entrata, di fofpiri
Vi fenti un tumulto, che girava
Focofo tutto di caldi difiri:
Quefto gli altari tutti aluminaua
Di nuove fiamme nate di martiri,
De' qua' ciafcun di lagrime grondava,
Moffe da una dona cruda e ria,
Che vide li, chiamata Gelofia. &c.[1]

It is highly probable that Boccaccio learned many anecdotes of Grecian hiftory and Grecian fable, not to be found in any Greek writer now extant, from his preceptors Barlaam, Leontius, and others, who had lived at Conftantinople, while the Greek literature was yet flourifhing. Some of thefe are perhaps fcattered up and down in the compofition before us, which contains a confiderable part of the Grecian ftory ; and efpecially in his Treatife of the Genealogies of the Gods.[2] Boccaccio himfelf calls his mafter Leontius an inexhauftible archive of Grecian tales and fables, although not equally converfant with thofe of the Latins.[3] He confeffes that he took many things in his book of the genealogies of the gods from a vaft work entitled *Collectivum*, now loft, written by his cotemporary Paulus Perufinus, the materials of which had in great meafure been furnifhed by Barlaam.[4] We are informed alfo, that Perufinus made

---

[1] [*Ibid.* pp. 230-1.] Some of thefe ftanzas are thus expreffed in the Græco-barbarous tranflation :

Εἰς τοῦτον εἶδε τοῦ θεοῦ, τὸν οἶκον τὸν μεγάλον,
ἀπαρματα πολλὰ σκληρὰ, κτισμένος ἥτον ὅλος.
Ὁ λόλαμπρος γὰρ ἥτοναι, ἔλαμπεν ὡς τὸν ἥλιον,
ὅταν ὁ ἥλιος ἔκρουε, ἀστραπτεν ὡς τὸν φέγγος.
Ὁ τόπος ὅλος ἔλαμπεν, ἐκτὴν λαμπρότητάντου,
τὸ ἔμπατου ὁλοσίδηρον, καὶ τὰ στενώματάτου.
Ἀπὸ διαμάντη πόρτεστου, ἦσαν καὶ τὰ καρφία,
σιδερομέναις δυνατὰ, ἀπάπασαν μερία.

Κολόναις ἦσαν σιδηρὲς, πολλὰ χοντρὲς μεγάλαις,
ἀπάνωτους ἐβάστεναν, ὅλον τὸν οἶκον κεῖνον.
Ἐκεῖδε τὴν βουρκότητταν, τὸν λογισμὸν ἐκείνων,
ὁποκτὴν πόρταν βγένασι, ἄγροι καὶ θυμωμένοι.
Καὶ τὴν τυφλὴ τὴν ἁμαρτίαν καὶ τὸ οὐαὶ καὶ ὄχου
ἐκεῖσε ἐφαινόντησαν, ὅμοιον σὰν καὶ τ'ἄλλα.
Καὶ ταῖς ὀργαῖς ἐσκεύθηκεν, κόκιναις ὡς φωτία,
τὸν φόβον εἶδε λόχλομον, ἐκεῖσε σμίαν μερία.

Μετὰ κοιφὰ τὰ σίδερα, εἶδε δημηηγερσίαις,
καὶ ταῖς φαλσίαις πουγίνονται, καὶ μοίαζουν δικαιοσούνες.
Ἐκεῖτον ἀσυνηβασία, μεταῖς διαφωνίαις,
ἐβάσα εἰς τὸ χέρητης, σίδερα ματομένα.
Ὅλος ὁ τόπος ἔδειχνε, ἄγριος καὶ χολιασμένος,
ἀγρίους γὰρ φοβερισμοὺς, κιωμόταπην μαλεαν.
Μέσα τον τόπον τούτονε, ἡ χάρπα τυχεμένη,
ἐκάθετον ὁ πόπρεπε, νὰ ἔναι παινεμένη.

[2] In fifteen books. Firft printed in 1481, fol. And in Italian by Betuffi, Venet. 1553. In French at Paris, 1531, fol. In the interpretation of the fables he is very prolix and jejune.

[3] *Geneal. Deor.* lib. xv. cap. vi.

[4] " Quicquid apud Græcos inveniri poteft, adjutorio Barlaæ arbitror collegiffe." —*Ibid.*

ufe of fome of thefe fugitive Greek fcholars, efpecially Barlaam, for
colleﬁing rare books in that language. Perufinus was librarian,
about the year 1340, to Robert, king of Jerufalem and Sicily, and
was the moſt curious and inquiſitive man of his age for fearching
after unknown or uncommon manufcripts, efpecially hiſtories and
poetical compoſitions, and particularly fuch as were written in
Greek. I will beg leave to cite the words of Boccaccio, who
records this anecdote.[1] By the *Hiſtoriæ* and *Poetica Opera*, [men-
tioned below as] brought from Conſtantinople by Barlaam, undoubtedly works of entertainment, and perhaps chiefly of the
romantic and fiﬁitious fpecies, I do not underſtand the claffics. It
is natural to fuppofe that Boccaccio, both from his conneﬁions and
his curioſity, was no ſtranger to thefe treafures: and that many of
thefe pieces, thus imported into Italy by the difperfion of the
Conſtantinopolitan exiles, are only known at prefent through the
medium of his writings. It is certain that many oriental fiﬁions
found their way into Europe by means of this communication.

Boccaccio borrowed the ſtory of Titus and Geſippus from the
Geſta Romanorum, or from the fecond fable of Alphonfus. There is
another Latin hiſtory of thefe two friends, a tranflation from [the
eighth novel of the tenth day of the *Decameron,*] by Bandello, and
printed at Milan in 1509. An exceedingly fcarce book.[2]

I take this opportunity of pointing out another fource of Boccaccio's *Tales.* Friar Philip's ſtory of the *Goofe,* or of the young
man who had never feen a woman, in the prologue to the fourth day
of the *Decameron,* is taken from a fpiritual romance, called the
Hiſtory of Barlaam and Jofaphat. This fabulous narrative, in which
Barlaam is a hermit and Jofaphat a king of India, is fuppofed to have
been originally written in Greek by Johannes Damafcenus. The
Greek is no uncommon manufcript.[3] It was from the old Latin
tranflation, which is mentioned by Vincent of Beauvais, that it became a favourite in the dark ages. The Latin, which is alfo a
common manufcript, was printed fo early as the year 1470. It has
often appeared in French. A modern Latin verfion was publiſhed at
Paris in 1577. The legendary hiſtorians, who believed everything,
and even Baronius, have placed Barlaam and Jofaphat in their catalogues of confeffors. Saint Barlaam and Saint Jofaphat occur in
the *Metrical Lives of the Saints.*[4] This hiſtory feems to have been
compofed by an oriental Chriſtian: and, in fome manufcripts, is faid
to have been brought by a monk of Saint Saba into the holy city from
Ethiopia. Among the Baroccian MSS. Cod. xxi. there was an office
in Greek for thefe two fuppofed faints.

In paffing through Chaucer's hands, this poem has received many
new beauties. Not only thofe capital fiﬁions and defcriptions, the

---

[1] " Et, fi ufquam curiofiffimus fuit homo in perquirendis, juffu etiam principis,
peregrinis undecunque libris, *Hiſtoriis et Poeticis* operibus, iſte fuit. Et ob id, fin-
gulari amicitiæ Barlaæ conjunﬁus, quæ a Latinis habere non poterat eo medio
innumera exhauſit a Græcis."—*Geneal. Deor.* lib. xv. cap. vi.

[2] [See, for the correﬁ title, *Brunet,* i. 636.]   [3] See MSS. Laud. C. 72.

[4] MSS. Bodl. 72, fol. 288, b, [Vernon MS., &c.]

temples of Mars, Venus, and Diana, with their allegorical paintings, [but alſo] the figures of Lycurgus and Emetrius with their retinue, are ſo much heightened by the bold and ſpirited manner of the Britiſh bard, as to ſtrike us with an air of originality. Boccaccio's ſituations and incidents reſpecting the lovers are often inartificial and unaffecting. In the Italian poet, Emilia walking in the garden and ſinging is ſeen and heard firſt by Arcite, who immediately calls Palamon. They are both equally, and at the ſame point of time, captivated with her beauty ; yet without any expreſſions of jealouſy, or appearance of rivalry. But in Chaucer's management of the commencement of this amour, Palamon by ſeeing Emilia firſt acquires an advantage over Arcite, which ultimately renders the cataſtrophe more agreeable to poetical juſtice. It is an unnatural and unanimated picture which Boccaccio preſents, of the two young princes violently enamoured of the ſame object, and ſtill remaining in a ſtate of amity. In Chaucer, the quarrel between the two friends, the foundation of all the future beautiful diſtreſs of the piece, commences at this moment, and cauſes a converſation full of mutual rage and reſentment. This rapid tranſition, from a friendſhip cemented by every tie to the moſt implacable hoſtility, is on this occaſion not only highly natural, but produces a ſudden and unex-pected change of circumſtances, which enlivens the detail and is always intereſting. Even afterwards, when Arcite is releaſed from the priſon by Pirithous, he embraces Palamon at parting ; and in the fifth book of *La Teſeide,* when Palamon goes armed to the grove in ſearch of Arcite, whom he finds ſleeping, they meet on terms of much civility and friendſhip, and in all the mechanical formality of the manners of romance. In Chaucer, this dialogue has a very dif-ferent caſt. Palamon, at ſeeing Arcite, feels a " colde ſwerde " glide throughout his heart : he ſtarts from his ambuſcade, and inſtantly ſalutes Arcite with the appellation of " falſe traitour ; " and although Boccaccio has merit in diſcriminating the characters of the two princes, by giving Palamon the impetuoſity of Achilles, and Arcite the mildneſs of Hector, yet Arcite by Boccaccio is here injudiciouſly repreſented as too moderate and pacific. In Chaucer he returns the ſalute with the ſame degree of indignation, draws his ſword, and defies Palamon to ſingle combat. So languid is Boccaccio's plan of this amour, that Palamon does not begin to be jealous of Arcite till he is informed in the priſon that Arcite lived as a favourite ſervant with Theſeus in diſguiſe, yet known to Emilia. When the lovers ſee Emilia from the window of their tower, ſhe is ſuppoſed by Boc-caccio to obſerve them, and not to be diſpleaſed at their ſigns of ad-miration. This circumſtance is juſtly omitted by Chaucer, as quite unneceſſary, and not tending either to promote the preſent buſineſs or to operate in any diſtant conſequences. On the whole, Chaucer has eminently ſhewn his good ſenſe and judgment in rejecting the ſuperfluities and improving the general arrangement of the ſtory. He frequently corrects or ſoftens Boccaccio's falſe manners ; and it is with ſingular addreſs he has often abridged the Italian poet's oſtentatious and pedantic parade of ancient hiſtory and mythology.

Therefore it is to be remarked, that as Chaucer in fome places
has thrown in ftrokes of his own, fo in others he has contracted
the uninterefting and tedious prolixity of narrative, which he
found in the Italian poet; and that he might avoid a fervile
imitation, and indulge himfelf as he pleafed in an arbitrary departure
from the original, it appears that he neglected the embarraffment of
Boccaccio's ftanza, and preferred the Englifh heroic couplet, of
which this poem affords the firft confpicuous example extant in our
language.

The fituation and ftructure of the temple of Mars are thus
defcribed :

> A forefte,[1]
> In which ther dwellede neyther man ne befte,
> With knotty knarry bareyn trees olde
> Of ftubbes fcharpe and hidous to byholde ;
> In which ther ran a fwymbul in a fwough,
> As it were a ftorme fchulde berft every bough :
> And downward on an hil under a bent,[2]
> Ther ftood the tempul of Marz armypotent,
> Wrought al of burned[3] fteel, of which thentre
> Was long and ftreyt, and gaftly for to fee.
> And therout came a rage of fuche a prife,
> That it maad al the gates for to rife.
> The northen light in at the dore fchon,
> For wyndow on the walle *ne* was ther noon,
> Thorugh the which men might no light difcerne.
> The dores wer alle ademaunte eterne,
> I-clenched overthward and endelong
> With iren tough ; and, for to make it ftrong,
> Every piler the tempul to fufteene
> Was tonne greet of iren bright and fchene.

The gloomy fanctuary of this tremendous fane, was adorned with
thefe characteriftical imageries.

> Ther faugh I furft the derk ymaginyng[4]
> Of felony, and al the compaffyng ;
> The cruel ire, as reed as eny gleede ;
> The pikepurs, and eek the pale drede;
> The fmyler with the knyf under his cloke ;
> The fchipne brennyng with the blake fmoke ;
> The trefoun of the murtheryng in the bed ;
> The open werres, with woundes al bi-bled ;
> *Contek* with bloody knyf,[5] and fcharp manace.
> Al ful of chirkyng[6] was that fory place.
> The fleer of himfelf yet faugh I there,
> *His* herte-blood hath bathed al his here ;
> The nayl y-dryve in the fchode a-nyght ;

---

[1] [Morris's *Chaucer*, ii. 61, ver. 1117.]
[2] [declivity].   [3] burnifhed.   [4] [Morris's *Chaucer*, ii. 62, ver. 1137.]
[5] This image is likewife entirely mifreprefented by Dryden, and turned to a
fatire on the Church :

> " Conteft with fharpen'd knives in *cloyfters* drawn,
>   And all with blood befpread the *holy lawn.*"

[6] Any difagreeable noife, or hollow murmur. Properly, the jarring of a door
upon the hinges. See alfo Chaucer's *Boeth.* p. [25, edit. Morris:] "Whan the
felde *chirkynge* agrifethe of colde by the fellneffe of the wynde that hyʒt aquilon."
The original is, " Vento Campus inhorruit."

The colde deth, with mouth gapyng upright.[1]
Amyddes of the tempul fet mefchaunce,
With fory comfort and evel contynaunce.
Yet I faugh woodnes laughyng in his rage ;
The hunte ftrangled with wilde bores corage.
The caraigne in the bufche, with throte i-korve :
A thoufand flayne, and not of qualme i-ftorve ;[2]
The tiraunt, with the pray bi force i-rafte ;
The toune deftroied, there was no thing lafte.
Yet faugh I brent the fchippis hoppefteres ;[3]
The hunte[4] *ftrangled with the wilde beeres.*
The fowe freten the child right in the cradel ;
The cook i-fkalded, for al his longe ladel.
Nought beth forgeten the infortune of Mart ;
The carter over-ryden with his cart,
Under the whel ful lowe he lay adoun.
Ther wer alfo of Martz divifioun,
The barbour, and the bowcher, and the fmyth,
That forgeth fcharpe fwerdes on his ftith.
And al above depeynted in a tour
Saw I conqueft fittyng in gret honour,
With the fcharpe fwerd over his heed
Hangynge by a fotil twyne threed.

This group is the effort of a ftrong imagination, unacquainted with felection and arrangement of images. It is rudely thrown on the canvas without order or art. In the Italian poets, who defcribe every thing, and who cannot, even in the moft ferious reprefentations, eafily fupprefs their natural predilection for burlefque and familiar imagery, nothing is more common than this mixture of fublime and comic ideas.[5] The form of Mars follows, touched with the impetuous dafhes of a favage and fpirited pencil :

The ftatue[6] of Mars upon a carte ftood,
Armed, and lokede grym as he were wood ;

*   *   *   *   *

---

[1] This couplet refers to the fuicide in the preceding one, who is fuppofed to kill himfelf by driving a nail into his head [in the night], and to be found dead and cold in his bed, with his "mouth gapyng upryght." This is properly the meaning of his "hair being bathed in blood." *Shode,* in the text, is literally *a bufh of hair.* Dryden has finely paraphrafed this paffage.

[2] "flain—not deftroyed by ficknefs or dying a natural death."

[3] A writer in *Notes and Queries* (1ft S. ii. 31,) conjectures, that Chaucer may have mifread the *bellatrici* of Statius *ballatrici.* Another writer in the fame mifcellany (2nd S. iv. 407) thinks that it fhould be *hoppofteres* quafi upholfteries= dock-yards. Now, a *hopyr* is the old word for the *trough,* in which the grain is placed to be ground, and there may have been a term, now loft, but known to Chaucer, founded upon *hopyr,* and having the fenfe of fhip's ftocks. This appears to be on the whole the moft probable folution :

"By God ! right by the *hoper* wol I ftande,
Quod Johan, ' And fe how that the corn gus inne.' "
Reeves Tale, l. 4034, ed. Wright.]

[4] [The huntfman ; from the Saxon *hunta.*—Tyrwhitt.]

[5] There are many other inftances of this mixture. v. 319. "We ftrive as did the houndis for the bone." v. 403. "We fare he that dronk is as a moufe, &c." "Farewel phyfick ! Go bere the corfe to church ;" "Some faid he lokid grim and he wolde fight," &c. *infra.*

[6] [Morris's *Chaucer,* ii. 63, ver. 1183.] Statuary is not implied here. Thus he mentions the *ftatue* of Mars on a banner, *fupr.* v. 117. I cannot forbear adding in

A wolf ther ftood byforn him at his feet
With eyen reed, and of a man he eet;
With fotyl pencel depeynted was this ftorie,
In redoutyng¹ of Mars and of his glorie.

But the groundwork of this whole defcription is in the *Thebais* of Statius. I will make no apology for tranfcribing the paffage at large, that the reader may judge of the refemblance. Mercury vifits the temple of Mars fituated in the frozen and tempeftuous regions of Thrace:—²

Hic fteriles delubra notat Mavortia filvas,
Horrefcitque tuens: ubi mille furoribus illi
Cingitur adverfo domus immanfueta fub Hæmo.
Ferrea compago laterum, ferro arcta teruntur
Limina, ferratis incumbunt tecta columnis.
Læditur adverfum Phœbi jubar, ipfaque fedem
Lux timet, et dirus contriftat fidera fulgor.
    Digna loco ftatio? primis falit Impetus amens
E foribus, cæcumque Nefas, Iræque rubentes,
Exfanguefque Metus; occultifque enfibus adftant
Infidiæ, geminumque tenens Difcordia ferrum.
Innumeris ftrepit aula Minis: triftiffima Virtus
Stat medio, lætufque Furor, vultuque cruento
Mors armata fedet: bellorum folus in aris
Sanguis, et incenfis qui raptus ab urbibus ignis.
Terrarum exuviæ circum, et faftigia templi
Captæ infignibant gentes, cœlataque ferro
Fragmina portarum, bellatricefque carinæ,
Et vacui currus, protritaque curribus ora.³

---

this place thefe fine verfes of Mars arming himfelf in hafte, from our author's *Complaint of Mars and Venus*, v. 99:

"He throwe*th* on him his helme of huge wyghte,
And girt him with his fwerde; and in his honde
His myghty fpere, as he was wont to fygh*te*,
He fhaketh fo, that almoft it to-wonde;"

Here we fee the force of defcription without a profufion of idle epithets. Thefe verfes are all finew: they have nothing but verbs and fubftantives.

¹ recording, [reverence, *T*.]

² Chaucer points out this very temple in the introductory lines, v. 1113:

"Like to the eftres of the grifly place,
That hight the gret tempul of Mars in Trace,
In that colde and frofty regioun,
Ther as Mars hath his fovereyn mancioun."

³ Stat. *Theb.* vii. 40 [Edit. Paris, 1827, iii. 9-10]. And below we have Chaucer's *Doors of adamant eterne*, viz. v. 68.

"Claufæque adamante perenni
Diffiluere fores."

Statius alfo calls Mars, *Armipotens*, v. 78. A facrifice is copied from Statius, where, fays Chaucer (v. 1435):

"And did hir thinges, as men may biholde
In Stace of Thebes."

I think Statius is copied in a fimile, v. 1640. The introduction of this poem is alfo taken from the *Thebaid*, xii. 545, 481, 797. Compare Chaucer's lines, v. 870, *feq.* v. 917, *feq.* v. 996, *feq.* The funeral pyre of Arcite is alfo tranflated from *Theb.* vi. 195, *feq.* See Ch. v. 2940, *feq.* I likewife take this opportunity of

Statius was a favourite writer with the poets of the middle ages.
His bloated magnificence of defcription, gigantic images, and pompous diction, fuited their tafte, and were fomewhat of a piece with
the romances they fo much admired. They neglected the gentler
and genuine graces of Virgil, which they could not relifh. His
pictures were too correctly and chaftely drawn to take their fancies :
and truth of defign, elegance of expreffion, and the arts of compofition were not their objects.[1] In the meantime we muft obferve,
that in Chaucer's *Temple of Mars* many perfonages are added : and
that thofe which exifted before in Statius have been retouched,
enlarged, and rendered more diftinct and picturefque by Boccaccio

---

obferving, that Lucretius and Plato are imitated in this poem, together with many
paffages from Ovid and Virgil.

[1] In *Troilus and Creffide* he has tranflated the arguments of the twelve books of
the *Thebais* of Statius. See B. v. p. 1479, *feq.*

But to be more particular as to thefe imitations, ii. 28, v. 40 :—

> " A companye of ladies, tweye and tweye," &c.

Thus Thefeus, at his return in triumph from conquering Scythia, is accofted by
the dames of Thebes, Stat. *Theb.* xii. 519 :—

> " Jamque domos patrias, Scythicæ poft afpera gentis
> Prælia, laurigero fubeuntem Thefea curru
> Lætifici plaufus, &c. &c.
> Paulum et ab inseffis mœftæ Pelopeides aris
> Promovere gradum, feriemque et dona triumphi
> Mirantur, victique animo rediere mariti.
> Atque ubi tardavit currus, et ab axe fuperbo
> Explorat caufas victor, pofcitque benigna
> Aure preces; orfa ante alias Capaneia conjux,
> Belliger Ægide," &c.

Chaucer here copies Statius (*Theb.* v. 861-966). *Kn. T.* from [v. 70 to v. 151,]
See alfo *ibid.* v. 70, *feq.* v. 930 :

> " Here in the Temple of the goddefs Clemence," &c.

Statius mentions the temple of Clemency as the afylum where thefe ladies were
affembled, *Theb.* xii. 481 :

> " Urbe fuit media, nulli conceffa potentum
> Ara deum, mitis pofuit Clementia fedem," &c.

Ver. 2087.
> " Ne what jewels men in the fyr cafte," &c.

Literally from Statius, *Theb.* vi. 206 :

> " Ditantur flammæ, non unquam opulentior illa
> Ante cinis; crepitant gemmæ," &c.

But the whole of Arcite's funeral is minutely copied from Statius. More than a
hundred parallel lines on this fubject might be produced from each poet. In
Statius the account of the trees felled for the pyre, with the confternation of
the Nymphs, takes up more than twenty-four lines, v. 84-116. In Chaucer
about thirteen, v. 2060-2072. In Boccaccio, fix ftanzas, B. xi. Of the three
poets, Statius is moft reprehenfible, the firft author of this ill-placed and unneceffary
defcription, and who did not live in a Gothic age. The ftatues of Mars and
Venus I imagined had been copied from Fulgentius, Boccaccio's favourite mytho-
grapher. But Fulgentius fays nothing of Mars : and of Venus, that fhe only ftood
in the fea on a couch, attended by the Graces. It is from Statius that Thefeus
became a hero of romance.

and Chaucer. Arcite's addrefs to Mars, at entering the temple, has great dignity, and is not copied from Statius :

> O ftronge god, that in the reynes colde[1]
> Of Trace honoured and lord art thou y-holde,
> And haft in every regne and every land
> Of armes al the bridel in thy hand,
> And hem fortuneft as the lufte devyfe,
> Accept of me my pitous facrififse.

The following portrait of Lycurgus, an imaginary king of Thrace, is highly charged, and very great in the Gothic ftyle of painting :

> Ther maiftow fe comyng with Palomoun[2]
> Ligurge himfelf, the grete kyng of Trace ;
> Blak was his berd, and manly was his face.
> The cercles of his eyen in his heed
> They gloweden bytwixe yolw and reed,
> And lik a griffoun loked he aboute,
> With kempe heres on his browes ftowte ;
> His lymes greet, his brawnes hard and ftronge,
> His fchuldres brood, his armes rounde and longe.
> And as the gyfe was in his contré,
> Ful heye upon a chare of gold ftood he,
> With foure white boles in a trays.
> In ftede of cote armour in his harnays,
> With nales yolwe, and bright as eny gold,
> He had a bere[3] fkyn, cole-blak for old.
> His lange heer y-kempt byhynd his bak,
> As eny raven fether it fchon for blak.
> A wrethe of gold arm-gret, and huge of wighte,
> Upon his heed, fet ful of ftoones brighte,
> Of fyne rubeus and of fyn dyamauntz.
> Aboute his chare wente white alauntz,[4]
> Twenty and mo, as grete as eny ftere,
> To hunt at the lyoun or at the bere,
> And folwed him, with mofel faft i-bounde,
> Colerd with golde, and torettz[5] fyled[*] rounde.

---

[1] [Morris's *Chaucer*, ii. 73, ver. 1515.]   [2] [*Ibid.* ii. 66, ver. 1270.]   [3] A bear's.

[4] Greyhounds. A favourite fpecies of dogs in the middle ages. In the ancient pipe-rolls, payments are frequently made in greyhounds. *Rot. Pip. an.* 4, *Reg. Johann.* [A.D. 1203.] " Rog. Conftabul. Ceftrie debet D. Marcas, et x. palfridos et x. *laiffas Leporariorum* pro habenda terra Vidonis de Loverell de quibus debet reddere per ann. C. M." Ten leafhes of greyhounds, *Rot. Pip. an.* 9 *Reg. Johann.* [A.D. 1208.] " Suthant. Johan. Teingre debet C. M. et *x. leporarios magnos, pulchros, et bonos*, de redemtione fua." &c. *Rot. Pip. an.* 11, *Reg. Johan.* [A.D. 1210.] " Everveycfire. Rog. de Mallvell redd. comp. de I. palefrido velociter currente, et ii. *Laifiis leporariorum* pro habendis literis deprecatoriis ad Matildam de M." I could give a thoufand other inftances of the fort. [" Speght interprets *alaunz*, greyhounds ; Tyrrwhitt, maftiffs. The latter was apparently mifled by the fact that the wolf-dog, generally known by the name of the *Irifh greyhound*, becaufe ufed moft recently in that country, is called by Buffon *le matin*."—*Bell*.]
In Hawes's *Paftime of Pleafure*, Fame is attended with two greyhounds, on whofe golden collars Grace and Governaunce are infcribed in diamond letters. See next note.

[5] Rings ; the faftening of dogs' collars. They are often mentioned in the inventory of furniture, in the royal palaces of Henry VIII. above cited. MSS. Harl. 1419. In the *Caftle of Windfor*, article Collars, f. 409. " Two grey-

---

[*] Filed ; highly polifhed.

> An hundred lordes had he in his route
> Armed ful wel, with hertes ftern and ftoute.

The figure of Emetrius, king of India, who comes to the aid of
Arcite, is not inferior in the fame ftyle, with a mixture of grace:

> With Arcita, in ftories as men fynde,[1]
> The gret Emetreus, the kyng of Ynde,
> Uppon a fteede bay, trapped in fteel,
> Covered with cloth of gold dyapred wel,
> Cam rydyng lyk the god of armes Mars.
> His coote armour was of a cloth of Tars,[2]
> Cowched of perlys whyte, round and grete.
> His fadil was of brend gold newe *i*-bete;
> A mantelet upon his fchuldre hangyng
> Bret-ful of rubies reed, as fir fparclyng.
> His crifpe her lik rynges was i-ronne,
> And that was yalwe, and gliteryng as the fonne.
> His nofe was heigh, his eyen *bright* cytryne,
> His lippes rounde, his colour was fangwyn,
> A fewe freknes in his face y-fpreynd,
> Betwixe yolwe and fomdel blak y-meynd,
> And as a lyoun he his lokyng cafte.
> Of fyve and twenty yeer his age I cafte.
> His berd was wel bygonne for to fprynge;
> His voys was as a trumpe thunderynge.
> Upon his heed he wered *of* laurer grene
> A garlond freifch and lufty for to fene.
> Upon his hond he bar for his delyt
> An egle tame, as eny lylie whyt.
> An hundred lordes had he with him ther,
> Al armed fauf here hedes in here ger,
>
> *   *   *   *   *
>
> Aboute the kyng ther ran on every part
> Ful many a tame lyoun and lepart.

The banner of Mars difplayed by Thefeus, is fublimely conceived:

> The reede ftatue of Mars with fpere and targe[3]
> So fchyneth in his white baner large,
> That alle the feeldes gliteren up and doun.

This poem has many ftrokes of pathetic defcription, of which
thefe fpecimens may be felected:

---

houndes collars of crimfun velvett and cloth of gold, lacking *torrettes*."--" Two
other collars with the kinges armes, and at the ende portcullis and rofe."—"Item,
a collar embrawdered with pomegranates and rofes with *turrets* of filver and gilt."
—"A collar garnifhed with ftole-worke with one fhallop fhelle of filver and gilte,
with *torrettes* and pendauntes of filver and guilte."—"A collar of white velvette,
embrawdered with perles, the fwivels of filver."

[1] [Morris's *Chaucer*, ii. 67, ver. 1297.]
[2] Not of Tarfus in Cilicia. It is rather an abbreviation for Tartarin, or Tar-
tarium. See [the] *Flower and Leaf*, [*ibid.* iv. 94, ver. 211:]

> "On every trumpe hanging a broad banere
> Of fine tartarium ful richely bete."

That it was a coftly ftuff appears from hence. " Et ad faciendum unum Jupoun
de *Tartaryn* blu pouderat. cum garteriis blu paratis cum boucles et pendants de
argento deaurato."—*Comp. J. Coke Proviforis Magn. Garderob. temp. Edw. III.*
ut fupr. It often occurs in the wardrobe-accounts for furnifhing tournaments.
Du Cange fays, that this was a fine cloth manufactured in Tartary.— *Glofs.* v. Tar-
arium. But Skinner in v. derives it from Tortona in the Milanefe. He cites
tat. 4, Hen. VIII. c. vi.   [3] [Morris's *Chaucer*, ii. 31, ver. 117.]

> Uppon that other fyde Palomon,[1]
> Whan he wifte that Arcite was agoon,
> Such forwe maketh, that the grete tour
> Refowneth of his yollyng and clamour.
> The pure feteres of his fchynes grete
> Weren of his bitter falte teres wete.

Arcite is thus defcribed, after his return to Thebes, where he defpairs of feeing Emilia again :

> His fleep, his mete, his drynk is him byraft,[2]
> That lene he wexe, and drye as eny fchaft.
> His eyen holwe, grifly to biholde ;
> His hewe falwe, and pale as affchen colde,
> And folitary he was, and ever alone,
> And dwellyng al the night, making his moone.
> And if he herde fong or inftrument,
> Then wolde he wepe, he mighte nought be ftent ;
> So feble were his fpirites, and fo lowe.
> And chaunged fo, that no man couthe knowe
> His fpeche nother his vois, though men it herde.

Palamon is thus introduced in the proceffion of his rival Arcite's funeral :

> Tho cam this woful Theban Palomoun,[3]
> With flotery [4] berd, and ruggy afshy heeres,
> In clothis blak, y-dropped al with teeres,
> And, paffyng other, of wepyng Emelye,
> The rewfulleft of al the companye.

To which may be added the furprife of Palamon, concealed in the foreft, at hearing the difguifed Arcite, whom he fuppofes to be the fquire of Thefeus, difcover himfelf at the mention of the name of Emilia :

> Thurgh his herte [5]
> He felt a cold fwerd fodeynliche glyde :
> For ire he quook, he nolde no lenger abyde.
> And whan that he hath herd Arcites tale,
> As he were wood, with face deed and pale,
> He fterte him up out of the buffches thikke, &c.

A defcription of the morning muft not be omitted ; which vies both in fentiment and expreffion with the moft finifhed modern poetical landfcape, and finely difplays our author's talent at delineating the beauties of nature :

> The bufy larke, meffager of *day*,[6]
> Salueth in hire fong the morwe gray ;
> And fyry Phebus ryfeth up fo bright,
> That al the orient [7] laugheth of the light,[8]
> And with his ftremes dryeth in the greves
> The filver dropes, hongyng *on* the leeves.

---

[1] [Morris's *Chaucer*, ii. 40, ver. 417.]   [2] [*Ibid.* ii. 42, ver. 503.]

[3] [*Ibid.* ii. 89, ver. 2024.]

[4] fqualid. [*Flotery* feems literally to mean floating ; as hair difhevelled (*rabuffata*) may be faid to float upon the air.—*Tyrwhitt.*]

[5] [Morris's *Chaucer*, ii. 49, ver. 716.]   [6] [*Ibid.* ii. 46, ver. 633.]

[7] For *Orient*, perhaps *Orifount*, or the *horifon*, is the true reading. So the edition of Chaucer in 1561. So alfo the barbarous Greek poem on this ftory, Ὁ Οὐρανος ὁλος γελα. Dryden feems to have read, or to have made out of this miffpelling of Horifon, Orient.—The ear inftructs us to reject this emendation.

[8] See Dante, *Purgat.* c. 1. p. 234.

Nor muſt the figure of the blooming Emilia, the moſt beautiful objeckt of this vernal pickture, paſs unnoticed :

> Emelie, that fairer was to ſeene[1]
> Than is the lilie on hire ſtalkes grene.
> And freſcher than the May with floures newe—
> For with the roſe colour ſtrof hire hewe.

In other parts of his works he has painted morning ſcenes *con amore :* and his imagination ſeems to have been peculiarly ſtruck with the charms of a rural proſpeckt at ſun-riſing.

We are ſurpriſed to find, in a poet of ſuch antiquity, numbers ſo nervous and flowing : a circumſtance which greatly contributed to render Dryden's paraphraſe of this poem the moſt animated and harmonious piece of verſification in the Engliſh language. I cannot leave the *Knight's Tale* without remarking, that the inventor of this poem appears to have poſſeſſed conſiderable talents for the artificial conſtrucktion of a ſtory. It exhibits unexpeckted and ſtriking turns of fortune, and abounds in thoſe incidents which are calculated to ſtrike the fancy by opening reſources to ſublime deſcription, or to intereſt the heart by pathetic ſituations. On this account, even without conſidering the poetical and exterior ornaments of the piece, we are hardly diſguſted with the mixture of manners, the confuſion of times, and the like violations of propriety, which this poem, in common with all others of its age, preſents in almoſt every page. The acktion is ſuppoſed to have happened ſoon after the marriage of Theſeus with Hippolita, and the death of Creon in tl . ſiege of Thebes : but we are ſoon tranſported into more recent periods. Sunday, the celebration of matins, judicial aſtrology, heraldry, tilts and tournaments, knights of England and targets of Pruſſia,[2] occur in the city of Athens under the reign of Theſeus.

SECTION XIII.

HAUCER'S *Romaunt of the Roſe*[3] is tranſlated from a French poem entitled *Le Roman de la Roſe.* It was begun by William of Lorris, a ſtudent in juriſprudence, who died about the year 1260. Being left unfiniſhed, it was completed by John of Meun, a native of a little town of that name, ſituated on the River Loire near Orleans, who

---

[1] [Morris's *Chaucer*, ii. 33, ver. 177.]

[2] The knights of the Teutonic order were ſettled in Pruſſia, before 1300. See alſo Ch. Prol. v. 53 ; where tournaments in Pruſſia are mentioned. Arcite quotes a fable from Æſop (v. 1179).

[3] [The one fifteenth century MS. of this poem that we poſſeſs (in the Hunterian Muſeum, at Glaſgow) is a very faulty one. Mr. Bradſhaw contends that it is not Chaucer's tranſlation at all, but that of a fifteenth century poet, mainly becauſe it contains ſo many falſe rhymes of the final *e*—falſe according to Chaucer's uniform

feems to have flourifhed about the year 1310.[1] This poem is
efteemed by the French the moft valuable piece of their old poetry.
It is far beyond the rude efforts of all their preceding romancers:
and they have nothing equal to it before the reign of Francis I., who
died in the year 1547. But there is a confiderable difference in
the merit of the two authors. William of Lorris, who wrote not
one quarter of the poem, is remarkable for his elegance and luxuri-
ance of defcription, and is a beautiful painter of allegorical perfonages.
John of Meun is a writer of another caft. He poffeffes but little of
his predeceffor's inventive and poetical vein; and in that refpect
was not properly qualified to finifh a poem begun by William of
Lorris. But he has ftrong fatire and great livelinefs.[2] He was
one of the wits of the court of Charles le Bel.

The difficulties and dangers of a lover, in purfuing and obtaining
the object of his defires, are the literal argument of this poem. This
defign is couched under the allegory of a Rofe, which our lover after
frequent obftacles gathers in a delicious garden. He traverfes vaft
ditches, fcales lofty walls, and forces the gates of adamantine and
almoft impregnable caftles. Thefe enchanted fortreffes are all inhabited by various divinities, fome of which affift, and fome oppofe,
the lover's progrefs.[3]

Chaucer has luckily tranflated all that was written by William of
Lorris:[4] he gives only part of the continuation of John of Meun.[5]

---

practice in his genuine poems. For inftance, the Romaunt rhymes the infinitives
ly-e, *li-e*, with the adverbs *erly*, *tendirly*, l. 264, p. 2738; *maladie*, *jeloufie*, with I,
l. 1850, 3910, 4146, &c. &c. See *Temporary Preface to Six-Text Chaucer*, pp. 107-
11. Prof. Child of Harvard alfo holds the *Romaunt* not to be Chaucer's.—F.]

[1] Fauchet, pp. 198-200. He alfo tranflated Boethius *De Confolatione*, [recently
edited by Dr. Morris (1868, 8°) from Addit. MS. Br. Mus. 10,340, collated
with MS. Univ. Lib. Cam. I. 3, 21,] and *Abelard's Letters*, and wrote *Anfwers of
the Sibyls*, &c.

[2] The poem confifts of 22734 verfes. William of Lorris's part ends with v.
4149, viz:
" A peu que je ne m'en defefpoir."

[3] In the preface of the edition printed in the year 1538, all this allegory is turned
to religion. The Rofe is proved to be a ftate of grace, or divine wifdom, or eternal
beatitude, or the Holy Virgin to which heretics cannot gain accefs. It is the white
Rofe of Jericho, *Quafi plantatio Rofæ in Jericho*, &c. &c. The chemifts, in the
mean time, made it a fearch for the philofopher's ftone: and other profeffions, with
laboured commentaries, explained it into their own refpective fciences.

[4] See Occleve (*Letter of Cupide*, written 1402. Urry's *Chaucer*, p. 536, v. 283),
who calls John of Meun the author of the *Romaunt of the Rofe*. ·

[5] Chaucer's poem confifts of 7699 verfes: and ends with this verfe of the original,
viz. ver. 13105.
" Vous aurez abfolution."
But Chaucer has made feveral omiffions in John of Meun's part, before he comes to
this period. He has tranflated all William of Lorris's part, as I have obferved;
and his tranflation of that part ends with ver. 4432, viz.
" Than fhuldin I fallin in wanhope."
Chaucer's cotemporaries called his *Romaunt of the Rofe* a tranflation. Lydgate fays
that Chaucer
" Notably did his bufineffe

How far he has improved on the French original, the reader shall judge. I will exhibit passages selected from both poems : respectively placing the French beside the English, for the convenience of comparison. The renovation of nature in the month of May is thus described.

That it was May, thus dremede me,[1]	Qu'on joli moys de May songeoye,
In tyme of love and jolité,	Ou temps amoreux plein de joye,
That al thing gynneth waxen gay,	Que toute chose si s'esgaye,
For ther is neither busk nor hay	Si qu'il n'y a buissons ne haye
In May, that it nyl shrouded bene,	Qui en May parer ne se vueille,
And it with newe leves wrene.	Et couvrir de nouvelle fueille :
These wodes eek recoveren grene,	Les boys recouvrent leur verdure,
That drie in wynter ben to sene ;	Qui sont secs tant qui l'hiver dure ;
And the erth wexith proude withalle,	La terre mesmes s'en orgouille
For swote dewes that on it falle ;	Pour la rousée qui la mouille,
And the pore estat forgette,	En oublian la povretè
In which that wynter had it sette.	Où elle a tout l'hiver estè ;
And than bycometh the ground so proude,	Lors devient la terre si gobe,
That it wole have a newe shroude,	Qu'elle veult avoir neusve robe ;
And makith so queynt his robe and faire,	Si scet si cointe robe faire,
That it had hewes an hundred payre,	Que de couleurs y a cent paire,
Of gras and flouris, ynde and pers,	D'herbes, de fleures Indes et Perses :
And many hewes ful dyvers :	Et de maintes couleurs diverses,

> By grete avyse his wittes to dispose,
> To translate the *Romans of the Rose.*"

Prol. Boch. st. vi. It is manifest that Chaucer took no pains to disguise his translation. He literally follows the French, in saying, that a river was " lesse than Saine." *i. e.* the Seine at Paris, ver. 118. " No wight in all Paris," ver. 7157. A grove has more birds " than ben in all the relme of Fraunce," ver. 495. He calls a pine, " A tree in France men call a pine," ver. 1457. He says of roses, " so faire werin never in Rone," ver. 1674. " That for Paris ne for Pavie," ver. 1654. He has sometimes reference to French ideas, or words, not in the original. As " Men clepin hem Sereins in France," ver. 684. " From Jerusalem to Burgoine," ver. 554. " Grein de Paris," ver. 1369. In mentioning minstrells and jugglers, he says, that some of them " Songin songes of Loraine," ver. 776. He adds,

> " For in Loraine there notis be
> Full swetir than in this contre."

There is not a syllable of these songs and singers of Lorraine, in the French. By the way, I suspect that Chaucer translated this poem while he was at Paris. There are also many allusions to English affairs, which I suspected to be Chaucer's ; but they are all in the French original. Such as, " Hornpipis of Cornevaile," v. 4250. These are called in the original, " Chalemeaux de Cornouaille," ver. 3991. [Cornouaille here mentioned was a part of the province of Bretagne in France. Mr. Warton must have consulted some French MS. respecting the singers of Lorraine, for the passage certainly occurs in some of the printed editions, and in several MSS. —*Douce.*] A knight is introduced, allied to king " Arthour of Bretaigne," ver. 1199. Who is called, " Bon roy Artus de Bretaigne," Orig. ver. 1187. Sir Gawin and Sir Kay, two of Arthur's knights, are characterised, ver. 2206, *seq.* See Orig. ver. 2124. Where the word Keulx is corrupt for Keie. But there is one passage, in which he mentions a Bachelere as fair as " The Lordis sonne of Windisore," ver. 1250. This is added by Chaucer, and intended as a compliment to some of his patrons. In the *Legend of Good Women*, Cupid says to Chaucer, ver. 329 :

> " For in pleyne text, withouten nede of glose,
> Thou hast *translated* the *Romaunce of the Rose.*"

[1] [Morris's *Chaucer*, vi. 2, ver. 51.]

That is the robe I mene, iwis,   Eſt la robe que je deviſe
Through which the ground to preiſen is.   Parquoy la terre mieulx ſe priſe.

  *The briddes, that hav*en lefte her ſong,   Les oiſeaulx qui tant ſe ſont teuz
While thei *han ſuff*ride cold ſo ſtrong   Pour l'hiver qu'ils ont tous ſentuz,
In wedres gryl and derk to ſight*e*,   Et pour le froit et divers temps,
Ben in May for the ſonne bright*e*,   Sont en May, et par la printemps,
So glade, &c.   Si liez, &c.

In the deſcription of a grove, within the garden of Mirth, are many natural and picturesque circumſtances, which are not yet got into the ſtorehouſe of modern poetry :[1]

  Theſe trees were ſette, that I devyſe,   Mais ſachiès que les arbres furent
One from another in aſſyſe   Si loing a loing comme eſtre durent
Five fadome or ſyxe, I trowe ſo,   L'ung ſut de l'autre loing aſſis
But they were hye and great alſo :   De cinque toiſes voyre de ſix,
And for to kepe oute well the ſonne,   Mais moult furent fueilluz et haulx
The croppes were ſo thycke yronne,[2]   Pour gardir de l'eſte le chaulx
And every braunche in other knytte,   Et ſi eſpìs par deſſus furent
And full of grene leves ſytte,   Que chaleurs percer ne lis peurent
That ſonne myght*e* there noon dyſcende,   Ne ne povoient bas deſcendre
Leſt the tender graſſes ſhende.   Ne faire mal a l'erbe tendre.
There myght*e* men does and roes yſe,   Au vergier eut dains & chevreleux,
And of ſquyrels ful gret plenté,   Et auſſi beaucoup d'eſcureux,
From bowe to bowe alwaye lepynge.   Qui par deſſus arbres ſailloyent ;
Connies there were alſo playenge,[3]   Connins y avoit qui yſſoient
That comyn out of her clapers   Bien ſouvent hors de leurs tanieres,
Of ſondry colours and maners,   En moult de diverſes manieres,[4]
And maden many a tourneynge   [Aloient entr'eus tornoiant
Upon the freſhe graſſe ſpryngynge.   Sor l'erbe freſche verdoiant.[5]]

Near this grove were ſhaded fountains without frogs, running into murmuring rivulets, bordered with the ſofteſt graſs enamelled with various flowers.[6]

  In places ſawe I welles there,   Par lieux y eut cleres fontaines,
In whych there no frogges were,   Sans barbelotes & ſans raines,
And fayre in ſhadowe was every well*e* ;[7]   Qui des arbres eſtoient umbrez,
But I ne can the nombre tell*e*   Par moy ne vous ſeront nombrez,
Of ſtremys ſmal*e*, that by devyſe   Et petit ruiſſeaulx, que Deduit
Myrthe had*de* done come through con-   Avoit la trouvés par conduit ;
    dyſe,[8]   L'eaue alloit aval faiſant
Of whych the water in rennynge   Son melodieux et plaiſant.
Gan make a noyſe full lykynge.   Aux bortz des ruiſſeaulx et des rives
  Aboute the brynkes of theſe welles,   Des fontaines cleres et vives
And by the ſtremes over al elles   Poignoit l'erbe dru et plaiſant
Sprange up the graſſe, as thycke yſet   Grant ſoulas et plaiſir faiſant.
And ſofte as any velvet,   Amy povoit avec ſa mye
On whych men myght hys lemman ley*e*,   Soy deporter ne'en doubtez mye.—
As on a fetherbed to pley*e*,

    *   *   *   *   *   *   *

  There ſprange the vyolet al newe,   Violette y fut moult belle
And freſhe pervynke[9] ryche of hewe,   Et auſſi parvenche nouvelle ;

---

[1] [Morris's *Chaucer*, vi. 43, ver. 1391.]
[2] " the tops, or boughs, were ſo thickly twiſted together."
[3] Chaucer imitates this paſſage in the *Aſſemble of Foules*, v. 190, *ſeq.* Other paſſages of that poem are imitated from the *Roman de la Roſe*.
[4] ver. 1348.   [5] ed. Michel, p. 46.   [6] [Morris's *Chaucer*, vi. 43, ver. 1409.]
[7] A ſpecies of inſect often found in ſtagnant water.   [8] conduits.   [9] periwinkle.

And floures yelow*e*, white, and rede ;	Fleurs y eut blanches et vermeilles,
Suche plenté grewe there never in mede.	Ou ne pourroit trouver pareilles,
Ful gaye was al the grounde, and queynt,	De toutes diverſes couleurs,
And poudred, as men had it peynt,	De haulx pris et de grans valeurs,
With many a freſhe and ſondrye floure,	Si eſtoit ſoef flairans
That caſten up ful good ſavoure.	Et reflagrans et odorans.[1]

But I haſten to diſplay the peculiar powers of William de Lorris in delineating allegorical perſonages ; none of which has ſuffered in Chaucer's tranſlation. The poet ſuppoſes that the garden of Mirth, or rather Love, in which grew the Roſe, the object of the lover's wiſhes and labours, was encloſed with embattled walls, richly painted with various figures, ſuch as Hatred, Avarice, Envy, Sorrow, Old Age, and Hypocriſy. Sorrow is thus repreſented :

Sorowe was peynted next Envie[2]	De les Envie etoit Triſteſſe
Upon that walle of maſonrye.	Painte auſſi et garnye d'angoiſſe.
But wel ſhe was ſeyn in hir colour	Et bien paroit à ſa couleur
That ſhe hadde lyved in langour ;	Qu'elle avoit a cueur grant douleur :
Hir ſemede to have the jaunyce.	Et ſembloit avoir la jaunice,
Nought half ſo pale was Avarice,	La n'y faiſoit riens Avarice,
Nor no thyng lyk of leneſſe ;	Ne de paleur ne de maigreſſe ;
For ſorowe, thought, and gret diſtreſſe.	Car le travaile et la deſtreſſe, &c.
* * * * *	* * * * *
A ſorowful thyng wel ſemed*e* ſhe.	Moult ſembloit bien que fuſt dolente ;
Nor ſhe hadde no thyng ſlowe be	Car el n'avoit pas eſte lente
For to forcracchen al hir face,	D'eſgratignier toute ſa chiere ;
And for to rent in many place	Sa robe ne luy eſtoit chiere
Hir clothis, and for-to tere hir ſwire,	En mains lieux l'avoit deſſirée,
As ſhe that was fulfilled of ire ;	Comme celle qui moult fut yrée.
And al-to-torn lay eek hir here	Ses cheveulx dérompus eſtoient,
Aboute hir ſhuldris, here and there,	Qu'autour de ſon col pendoient,
As ſhe that hadde it al to-rent	Preſque les avoit tous deſroux
For angre and for maltalent.	De maltalent et de corroux.[3]

Nor are the images of Hatred and Avarice inferior :

Amyd ſaugh I a Hate ſtonde,[4]	Au milieu de mur je vy Hayne.
* * * * *	
And ſhe was no thyng wel arraied,	Si n'eſtoit pas bien atournée,
But lyk a wode womman afraied,	Ains ſembloit eſtre forcenée,
Frounced foule was hir viſage,	Rechignée eſtoit et froncé,
And grennyng for diſpitous rage,	
Hir noſe ſnorted up for tene.	Le vis et le nez rebourſé.
Ful hidous was ſhe for to ſene,	Moult hydeuſe eſtoit et ſouilleè,
Ful foule and ruſty was ſhe this.	
Hir heed ywrithen was, y-wis,	Et fut ſa teſte entortilleè
Ful grymly with a greet towayle.	Tres ordement d'un touaille.[5]

The deſign of this work will not permit me to give the portrait of Idleneſs, the portreſs of the garden of Mirth, and of others, which form the group of dancers in the garden : but I cannot reſiſt the pleaſure of tranſcribing thoſe of Beauty, Franchiſe, and Richeſſe, three capital figures in this genial aſſembly :

---

[1] v. 1348. [Warton quotes a very late and poor French text, much modernized. —F.]

[2] [Morris's *Chaucer*, vi. 10, ver. 301.]

[3] ver. 300.

[4] [*Ibid.* vi. 5, ver. 147.]

[5] ver. 143.

The God of Love, jolyf and lyght,[1]	Le Dieu d'amours ſi s'eſtoit pris
Ladde on his honde a lady bright,	A une dame de hault pris,
Of high prys, and of grete degré.	Pres ſe tenoit de ſon coſté,
This lady called was Beauté,	Celle dame eut nom Beaulte.
And an arowe, of which I tolde.	Ainſi comme une des cinque fleſches
Ful wel thewed[2] was ſhe holde,	En elle aut toutes bonnes taiches :
Ne ſhe was derk ne broun, but bright,	Point ne fut obſcur, ne brun,
And clere as the mone-lyght.	Mais fut clere comme la lune.—

* * * * * 　　　　　 * * * * *

Hir fleſh was tendre as dewe of flour,	Tendre eut la chair comme rouſée,
Hir chere was ſymple as byrde in bour ;	Simple fut comme une eſpouſée.
As whyte as lylye or roſe in rys,[3]	Et blanche comme fleur de lis,
Hir face gentyl and tretys.	Viſage eut bel doulx et alis,
Fetys[4] ſhe was, and ſmale to ſe,	Elle eſtoit greſle et alignée
No wyntred[5] browis hadde ſhe,	N'eſtoit fardie ne pignée,
Ne popped hir, for it nedede nought	Car elle n'avoit pas meſtier
To wyndre hir, or to peynte hir ought.	De ſoy farder et affaictier.
Hir treſſes yelowe, and longe ſtraughten,	Les cheveulx eut blons et ſi longs
Unto hir helys doun they raughten.	Qu'ils batoient aux talons.[6]

Nothing can be more ſumptuous and ſuperb than the robe and other ornaments of Richeſſe, or Wealth. They are imagined with great ſtrength of fancy. But it ſhould be remembered, that this was the age of magnificence and ſhow ; when a profuſion of the moſt ſplendid and coſtly materials was laviſhed on dreſs, generally with little taſte and propriety, but often with much art and invention :

Richeſſe a robe of purpur on hadde,[7]	De pourpre fut le veſtement
Ne trowe not that I lye or madde ;	A Richeſſe, ſi noblement,
For in this world is noon hir lyche,	Qu'en tout le monde n'euſt plus bel,
Ne by a thouſand deelle ſo riche,	Mieulx fait, ne auſſi plus nouvel :
Ne noon ſo faire ; for it ful welle	Pourtraictes y furent d'orfroys,
With orfrays leyd was everydeelle,	Hyſtoryes d'empereurs et roys.
And portraied in the ribanynges	Et encores y avoit-il
Of dukes ſtoryes, and of kynges.	Un ouvrage noble et ſobtil ;
And with a bend of gold taſſeled,	A noyaulx d'or au col fermoit,
And knoppis fyne of gold enameled.[8]	Et a bendes d'azur tenoit ;

---

[1] [Morris's *Chaucer*, vi. 31, ver. 1003.]

[2] Having good qualities. See *ſupr.* ver. 939, *ſeq.*

[3] [On the branch. Sax. hɲıs, virgulta.] 　　[4] [well-made, neat.—*T.*]

[5] contracted. 　　[6] ver. 1004. 　　[7] [Morris's *Chaucer*, vi. 33, ver. 1071.]

[8] Enameling, and perhaps pictures in enamel, were common in the Middle Ages. From the Teſtament of Joh. de Foxle, knight, Dat. apud Bramſhill co. Southampt. Nov. 5, 1378. "Item lego domino abbati de Waltham unum annulum auri groſſi, cum uno ſaphiro infixa, et nominibus trium regum [of Cologne] ſculptis in eodem annulo. Item lego Margarite ſorori mee unam tabulam argenti deaurati et amelitam, minorem de duabus quas habeo, cum diverſis ymaginibus ſculptis in eadem.—Item lego Margerite uxori Johannis de Wilton unum monile auri, cum S. litera ſculpta et amelita in eodem." *Regiſtr. Wykeham Epiſc. Winton.* p. ii. fol. 24. See alſo Dugd. *Bar.* i. 234, a.

Enameled is from the French *email*, or enamel. This art flouriſhed moſt at Limoges in France. So early as the year 1197, we have "Duas tabulas æneas ſuperauratas de labore Limogiæ." Chart. ann. 1197, apud Ughelin.—*Ital. Sacr.* vii. 1274. It is called *Opus Lemnoviticum*, in Dugdale's *Mon.* iii. 310, 313, 331. In Wilkins's *Concil.* i. 666, two cabinets for the hoſt are ordered, one of ſilver or of ivory, and the other *de opere Lemovicino. Synod. Wigorn.* A.D. 1240. And in many other places. I find it called *Limaiſe* in a metrical romance the name of which I have forgotten, where a tomb is deſcribed,

Aboute hir nekke of gentyl entayle
Was fhete the riche chevefaile,
In which ther was fulle gret plenté
Of ftones clere and bright to fee.
Rycheffe a girdelle hadde upon,
The bokele of it was of a ftoon,
Of vertu gret, and mochel of myght
For who fo bare the ftoon fo bright,
Of venym durft hym no thing doute,
While he the ftoon hadde hym aboute.

*　　*　　*　　*　　*

The mourdaunt, wrought in noble wife,
Was of a ftoon fulle precious,
That was fo fyne and vertuous,
That hole a man it koude make
Of palafie, and tothe ake.
And yit the ftoon hadde fuch a grace,
That he was fiker in every place
Alle thilke day not blynde to bene,
That faftyng myghte that ftoon feene.
The barres were of gold ful fyne,
Upon a tyffu of fatyne,
Fulle hevy, gret, and no thyng lyght,
In everiche was a befaunt wight.
Upon the treffes of Richeffe
Was fette a cercle for nobleffe
Of brend gold, that fulle lyghte fhoon ;
So faire trowe I was never noon.
But fhe were kunnyng for the nonys,
That koude devyfe alle the ftonys
That in that cercle fhewen clere ;
It is a wondir thing to here.
For no man koude preyfe or geffe
Of hem that valewe or richeffe.

Noblement eut le chief parè,
De riches pierres decorè,
Qui gettoient moult grant clartè ;
Tout y eftoit bien affortè.
Puis eut une riche fainture,
Sainte par deffus fa vefture :
Le boucle d'une pierre fu,
Groffe, et de moult grant vertu :
Celluy qui fur foy la portoit,
De tous venins garde eftoit.—

*　　*　　*　　*　　*

D'une pierre fut le mordans

Qui gueriffoit du mal des dens.

Ceft pierre portoit bon eur,
Qui l'avoit pouvoit eftre affeur
De fa fantè et de fa vei,
Quant à jeun il l'avoit vei :
Les cloux furent d'or epurè,
Par deffus le tiffu dorè,
Qui eftoient grans et pefans ;
En chafcun avoit deux befans.
Si eut avecques à Richeffe
Uns cadre d'or mis fur la treffe,
Si riche, fi plaifant, et fi bel,
Qu'onques on ne veit le pareil :
De pierres eftoit fort garny,
Precieufes et aplany,
Qui bien en vouldroit devifer,

On ne les pouvroit pas prifer :

" And yt was, the Romans fayes,
All with golde and limaife."

[Du Cange v. Limogia], obferves, that it was anciently a common ornament of
fumptuous tombs. He cites a Teftament of the year 1327, " Je lais huit cent livres
pour faire deux tombes hautes et levées de l'Euvre de Limoges." The original
tomb of Walter de Merton, Bifhop of Rochefter, erected in his cathedral about the
year 1276 [?], was made at Limoges. This appears from the accompts of his
executors, viz. " Et computant xl l. v s. vi d. liberat. Magiftro Johanni Linnom-
cenfi, pro tumba dicti Epifcopi Roffenfis, fcil. pro Conftructione et carriagio de
Lymoges ad Roffam. Et xl s. viii d. cuidam Executori apud Lymoges ad ordi-
nandam et providendam Conftructionem dictæ Tumbæ. Et x s. viii d. cuidam
garcioni eunti apud Lymoges quærenti dictam tumbam conftructam, et ducenti eam
cum dicto Mag. Johanne ufque Roffam. Et xxii l. in maceoneria circa dictam
tumbam defuncti. Et vii marcas, in ferramento ejufdem, et carriagio a Londin.
ufque ad Roff. et aliis parandis ad dictam tumbam. Et xi s. cuidam vitriario pro
vitris feneftrarum emptarum juxta tumbam dicti Epifcopi apud Roffam." Ant.
Wood's *MS. Merton Papers*, Bibl. Bodl. Cod. Ballard, 46.

[1] I cannot give the precife meaning of *Barris*, nor of *Cloux* in the French. It
feems to be part of a buckle. In the wardrobe-roll, quoted above, are mentioned,
" One hundred garters *cum boucles*, barris, *et pendentibus de argento*." For which
were delivered, " ccc barrs argenti." An. 21, Edw. III.—[*Clavus* in Latin,
whence the Fr. *cloux* is derived, feems to have fignified not only an outward border,
but alfo what we call a ftripe. Montfaucon, t. iii. P. i. ch. vi. A bar in heraldry
is a narrow ftripe or fafcia.—*Tyrwhitt.*]

Rubyes there were, faphires, jagounces,[1]	Rubis y eut, faphirs, jagonces,
And emeraudes, more than two ounces.	Efmeraudes plus de cent onces :
But alle byfore ful fotilly	Mais devant eut, par grant maiftrife,
A fyn charboncle fette faugh I.	Un efcarboucle bien affife,
The ftoon fo clere was and fo bright,	Et le pierre fi clere eftoit,
That, a. o foone as it was nyght,	Que cil qui devant la mettoit,
Men myghte feen to go for nede	Si en povoit veoir au befoing
A myle or two, in lengthe and brede.	A foy conduire une lieue loing.
Sich lyght *tho* fprang oute of the ftone,	Telle clartè fi en yffoit
That Richeffe wondir brighte fhone	Que Richeffe en refplendiffoit
Bothe hir heed, and alle hir face,	Par tout le corps et par fa face,
And eke aboute hir al the place.	Auffi d'autour d'elle la place.[2]

The attributes of the portrait of Mirth are very expreffive :

Of berde unnethe hadde he no thyng,[3]	Et fi n'avoit barbe a menton,
For it was in the firfte fpryng.	Si non petit poil follaton ;
Ful yonge he was, and mery of thought,	Il etoit jeune damoyfaulx ;
And in famette,[4] with briddis wrought,	Son bauldrier fut portrait d'oifeaulx

---

[1] The gem called a jacinth. The knowledge of precious ftones was a grand article in the natural philofophy of this age ; and the medical virtue of gems, alluded to above, was a doctrine much inculcated by the Arabian naturalifts. Chaucer refers to a treatife on gems, called the *Lapidary*, famous in that time. *Houfe of Fame*, L. iii. ver. 260 [edit. Morris]:

> " And they were fet as thik of nouchis
> Fyne, of the fyneft ftones faire
> That men reden in the Lapidaire."

Montfaucon, in the royal library at Paris, recites, " Le Lapidaire, de la vertu des pierres."—*Catal. MSS.* p. 794. This I take to be the book here referred to by Chaucer. Henry of Huntingdon [has, among his minor productions (of which there is a copy in Royal MS. 13, c. 11), fome verfes on precious ftones. See Wright's *Biog. Brit. Literaria*, Anglo-Norman period, p. 169. This writer was living in 1154]. See Du Cange, *Gloff. Gr. Barb.* ii. *Ind. Auctor.* p. 37, col. 1. In the Cotton library is a Saxon Treatife on precious ftones. *Tiber.* A. 3, liii. fol. 98. The writing is [very] ancient. [The treatife referred to contains a meagre explanation of the twelve precious ftones mentioned in the Apocalypfe.] Pelloutier mentions a Latin poem of the eleventh century on precious ftones, written by Marbode, bifhop of Rennes [who died in the year 1123], and foon afterwards tranflated into French verfe. *Mem. Lang. Celt.* part i. vol. i. ch. xiii. p. 26. The tranflation begins :

> " Evax fut un mult riche reis
> Lu reigne tint d'Arabeis."

It was printed in [the folio edit. (1708) of the works of St. Hildebert,] col. 1638. This may be reckoned one of the oldeft pieces of French verfification. A MS. *De Speciebus Lapidum*, occurs twice in the Bodleian library, falfely attributed to one Adam Nidzarde, Cod. Digb. 28, f. 169. and Cod. Laud. C. 3, *Princ.* " Evax rex Arabum legitur fcripfiffe." But it is, I think, Marbode's book above mentioned. Evax is a fabulous Arabian king, faid to have written on this fubject. Of this Marbode or Marbodæus, fee Ol. Borrich. Diff. Acad. de Poet. p. 87, fect. 78, edit. Francof. 1683, 4to. His poem was publifhed, with notes, by Lampridius Alardus. The eaftern writers pretend that King Solomon, among a variety of phyfiological pieces, wrote a book on gems : one chapter of which treated of thofe precious ftones which refift or repel evil Genii. They fuppofe that Ariftotle ftole all his philofophy from Solomon's books. See Fabric. *Bibl. Gr.* xiii. 387, *feq.* and i. p. 71. Compare Herbelot, *Bibl. Oriental*, p. 962, b. Artic. *Ketab alahgiar feq.*

[2] ver. 1066.   [3] [Morris's *Chaucer*, vi. 26, ver. 833.]   [4] *famite;* fattin.

And with gold beten ful fetyſly,	Qui tout etoit è or batu,
His body was clad ful richely.	Tres richement eſtoit veſtu
Wrought was his robe in ſtraunge giſe,	D'un' robe moult deſgyſée,
And al to-flytered for queyntiſe	Qui fut en maint lieu inciſée,
In many a place, lowe and hie.	Et decouppeè par quointiſe.
And ſhode he was with grete maiſtrie,	Et fut chauſſé par mignotiſe
With ſhoon decoped,[1] and with laas,	D'un ſouliers decouppés à las,
By druery,[2] and by ſolas.	Par joyeuſete et ſoulas,
His leef a roſyn chapelet	Et ſa neye luy fiſt chapeau
Hadde made, and on his heed it ſet.	De roſes gracieux et beau.[3]

Franchiſe is a no leſs attractive portrait, and ſketched with equal grace and delicacy :

And next hym dauncede dame Fraun-chiſe,[4]	Apres tous ceulx eſtoit Franchiſe,
Arayed in fulle noble gyſe.	
She was not broune ne dunne of hewe,	Qui ne fut ne brune ne biſe ;
But white as ſnowe falle newe.	Ains fut comme la neige blanche
Hir noſe was wrought at poynt devys,	Courtoiſe eſtoit, joyeuſe et franche,
For it was gentyl and tretys ;	Le nez avoit long et tretis
With eyen gladde, and browes bente ;	Yeulx vers rins, ſoureils ſaitis,
Hir here doun to hir helis wente [5]	Les cheveulx eut tres-blons et longs,
And ſhe was ſymple as dowve of tree,	Simple feut comme les coulons.
Ful debonaire of herte was ſhe.	Le cueur eut doulx et debonnaire.[6]

The perſonage of Danger is of a bolder caſt, and may ſerve as a contraſt to ſome of the preceding. He is ſuppoſed ſuddenly to ſtart from an ambuſcade, and to prevent Bialcoil, or *Kind Reception*, from permitting the lover to gather the roſe of beauty :

With that ſterte oute anoon Daungere,[7]	A tant ſaillit villain Dangere,
Out of the place where he was hidde.	De là ou il eſtoit mucè ;
His malice in his chere was kidde ;[8]	
Fulle grete he was and blak of hewe,	Grant fut, noir, et tout hericè,
Sturdy, and hidous, who-ſo hym knewe,	
Like ſharp urchouns[9] his here was growe,	
His eyes rede ſparkling as the fire glowe,	S'ot les yeulx rouges comme feux,
His noſe frounced fulle kirked ſtoode,	Le vis froncè, le nez hydeux
He come criande as he were woode.	Et s'eſcrie tout forcenez.[10]

Chaucer has enriched this figure. The circumſtance of Danger's hair ſtanding erect like the prickles on the urchin or hedge-hog is his own, and finely imagined.

Hitherto ſpecimens have been given from that part of this poem

---

[1] cut or marked with figures. From *decouper*, Fr. to *cut*. I ſuppoſe *Poulis windows* was a cant phraſe for a fine device or ornament. [Compare *infrâ*, p. 358, and Note 12.]

[2] [courtſhip, gallantry, T.]   [3] v. 832.

[4] [Morris's *Chaucer*, vi. 37, ver. 1211.]

[5] All the females of this poem have grey eyes and yellow hair. One of them is ſaid to have " Hir yen grey as is a faucoun," v. 546. Where the original word, tranſlated *grey*, is *vers*. v. 546. We have this colour again, Orig. v. 822. " Les yeulx eut *vers*." This too Chaucer tranſlates, " Hir yen greye," v. 862. The ſame word occurs in the French text before us, v. 1195. This compariſon was natural and beautiful, as drawn from a very familiar and favourite-object in the age of the poet. Perhaps Chaucer means " grey as a falcon's *eyes*."

[6] v. 1190.   [7] [Morris's *Chaucer*, vi. 96, 3130.]

[8] " was diſcovered by his behaviour, or countenance."

[9] *urchins*, hedge-hogs.   [10] v. 2959.

which was written by William de Lorris, its firſt inventor. Here Chaucer was in his own walk. One of the moſt ſtriking pictures in the ſtyle of allegorical perſonification, which occurs in Chaucer's tranſlation of the additional part, is much heightened by Chaucer, and indeed owes all its merit to the tranſlator ; whoſe genius was much better adapted to this ſpecies of painting than that of John of Meun, the continuator of the poem :

With hir Labour and Travaile[1]	Travaile et Douleur la herbergent,
Logged ben with Sorwe and Woo,	Mais il la lient et la chargent,
That never out of hir court goo.	
Peyne and Diſtreſſe, Sykneſſe, and Ire,	
And Malencoly, that angry ſire,	
Ben of hir paleys[2] ſenatours.	
Gronyng and Grucchyng, hir herbe-jours,[3]	
The day and nyght, hir to turmente,	Et tant la batent et tormentent,
With cruelle Deth they hir preſente.	Que mort prochaine luy preſentent,
And tellen hir, erliche[4] and late,	Et talent de ſe repentir ;
That Deth ſtondith armed at hir gate.	Tant luy ſont de fleaux ſentir.
Thanne brynge they to her remem-braunce	Adonc luy vient en remembraunce, En ceſt tardifve peſance,
The foly dedis of hir infaunce,	Quant el ſe voit foible et chenue,[5]
Whiche cauſen hir to mourne in woo	Que malement l'a décéue
That Youthe hath hir bigiled ſo.	Joueſce . . .

The fiction that Sickneſs, Melancholy, and other beings of the like ſort were counſellors in the palace of Old Age, and employed in telling her day and night, that " Death ſtood armed at her gate," was far beyond the ſentimental and ſatirical vein of John of Meun, and is conceived with great vigour of imagination.

Chaucer appears to have been early ſtruck with this French poem.[6] [So were many other Engliſh poets. The author of the *Yle of Ladyes*, called generally *Chaucer's Dreme*,[7] ſuppoſes that the chamber in which he ſlept was richly painted with the ſtory of the *Romaunt of the Roſe*.[8] It is natural to imagine that ſuch a poem muſt have been a favourite with Chaucer. No poet, before William of Lorris, either Italian or French, had delineated allegorical per-ſonages in ſo diſtinct and enlarged a ſtyle, and with ſuch a fulneſs of characteriſtical attributes : nor had deſcriptive poetry ſelected ſuch a variety of circumſtances, and diſcloſed ſuch an exuberance of embelliſhment, in forming agreeable repreſentations of nature. On this account, we are ſurpriſed that Boileau ſhould mention Villon as the firſt poet of France who drew form and order from the chaos of the old French romancers :

---

[1] [Morris's *Chaucer*, vi. 152, 4997.]   [2] palace.

[3] [providers of lodgings, harbingers.—T.]   [4] early.   [5] v. 4733.

[6] [See M. Sandras's *Etude ſur Chaucer conſidéré comme Imitateur des Trouvères*, Paris, 1859, arguing that Chaucer owed nearly everything to Jean de Meun's and other French influence on him. See on the other ſide as to the greater influence of Italian on him.—Ebert's review of Sandras in the Chaucer Society's Eſſays, p. 5, and Prof. Ten Brink's *Studien.*—F.]

[7] [Mr. Bradſhaw and Prof. Ten Brink contend that the poem called Chaucer's *Dreme* is decidedly not his.—F.]

[8] v. 322. Chaucer alludes to this poem in *The Marchaunt's Tale*, v. 1548.

Villon ſçeut le Premier, dans ces ſiecles groſſiers,
Debroüiller l'art confus de nos vieux romanciers.[1]

But the poetry of William of Lorris was not the poetry of Boileau. That this poem ſhould not pleaſe Boileau, I can eaſily conceive. It is more ſurpriſing that it ſhould have been cenſured as a contemptible performance by Petrarch, who lived in the age of fancy. Petrarch having deſired his friend Guido di Gonzaga to ſend him ſome new piece, he ſent him the *Roman de la Roſe.* With the poem, inſtead of an encomium, he returned a ſevere criticiſm; in which he treats it as a cold, inartificial, and extravagant compoſition: as a proof how much France, who valued this poem as her chief work, was ſurpaſſed by Italy in eloquence and the arts of writing.[2] In this opinion we muſt attribute ſomething to jealouſy. But the truth is, Petrarch's genius was too cultivated to reliſh theſe wild excurſions of imagination: his favourite claſſics, whom he revived, and ſtudied with ſo much attention, ran in his head. Eſpecially Ovid's *Art of Love,* a poem of another ſpecies, and evidently formed on another plan; but which Petrarch had been taught to venerate, as the model and criterion of a didactic poem on the paſſion of love reduced to a ſyſtem. We may add that, although the poem before us was founded on the viſionary doctrines and refinements concerning love invented by the Provençal poets, and conſequently leſs unlikely to be favourably received by Petrarch, yet his ideas on that delicate ſubject were much more Platonic and metaphyſical.

SECTION XIV.

 HAUCER'S poem of *Troilus and Creſſeide* is ſaid to be formed on an old hiſtory, written by Lollius, a native of Urbino in Italy.[3] Lydgate ſays that Chaucer in this poem

made a tranſlacion
Of a boke which called is Trophe
In Lumbarde tongue, &c.[4]

---

[1] *Art. Poet.* ch. i.   He died about the year 1456.

[2] See Petrarch, *Carm.* i. i. ep. 30.

[3] Petrus Lambeccius enumerates Lollius Urbicus among the *Hiſtorici Latini profani* of the third century. Prodrom. p. 246. Hamb. 1659.   See alſo Voſs. *Hiſtoric. Latin.* ii. 2, p. 163, edit. Lugd. Bat.   But this could not be Chaucer's Lollius. Chaucer places Lollius among the hiſtorians of Troy, in his *Houſe of Fame,* iii. 380.   It is extraordinary, that Du [Cange] in the *Index Auctorum,* uſed by him for his Latin gloſſary, ſhould mention this Lollius Urbicus of the third century. Tom. vii. p. 407, edit. [1850.]   As I apprehend, none of his works remain. A proof that Chaucer tranſlated from ſome Italian original is, that in a manuſcript which I have ſeen of this poem, I find, *Moneſteo* for *Meneſtes, Rupheo* for *Ruphes, Phebuſeo* for *Phebuſes,* lib. iv. 50, *ſeq.*   Where, by the way, Xantippe, a Trojan chief, was perhaps corruptly written for Xantippo, *i. e.* Xantippus. As Joſeph. Iſcan iv. 10. In Lydgate's *Troy, Zantiphus,* iii. 26.   All corrupted from Antiphus, (Dict. Cret. p. 105).   In the printed copies we have *Aſcalapho* for Aſcalaphus, lib. v. 319.

[4] Prol. *Boch.* ſt. iii.

It is certain that Chaucer frequently refers to " *Myne auctor Lollius.*"[1] But he hints, at the same time, that Lollius wrote in Latin.[2] I have never seen this history either in the Italian or Latin language. I have before observed, that it is mentioned in Boccaccio's *Decameron,* and that a translation of it was made into Greek verse by some of the Greek fugitives in the fourteenth century. Du Fresnoy mentions it in Italian.[3] In the Royal Library at Paris it occurs often as an ancient French romance.[4] Much fabulous history concerning Troilus is related in Guido de Columna's *Destruction of Troy.*[5] Whatever were Chaucer's materials, he has on this subject constructed a poem of considerable merit, in which the vicissitudes of love are depicted in a strain of true poetry, with much pathos and simplicity of sentiment.[6] He calls it, " a litill tragedie."* Troilus is supposed to have seen Cresside in a temple,

---

[1] See lib. i. v. 395.　　　　　　　　[2] Lib. ii. v. 10.

[3] [*L'Amore di Troilo e Griseida,* di Angelo Leonico, Ven. 1553, 8vo. Du Fresnoy, *Bibl. des Romans,* i. 217.—*Douce.*]

[4] " Cod. 7546. *Roman de Troilus.*"—" Cod. 7564. *Roman de Troilus et de Briseida ou Criseida.*"—Again, as an original work of Boccaccio. " Cod. 7757. *Philostrato dell' amorose fatiche de Troilo per Giovanni Boccaccio.*" † " Les suivans (adds Montfaucon ‡) contiennent les autres œuvres de Boccace."

[5] [See M. Joly's *Benoit de Ste.-More et le Roman de Troie,* 1870, and the very valuable Introduction by MM. Moland and D'Hericault, in *Nouvelles Françoises en prose du xiv⁰ siecle,* 1858, where they have printed the prose French version of the *Filostrato,* entitled *Le Roman de Troilus.*]

[6] Chaucer however claims no merit of invention in this poem. He invokes Clio to favour him with rhymes only ; and adds:

> " To every lover I me excuse,
> That of no sentement I this endyte,
> But out of Latyn in my tonge it write."

L. ii. ver. 12. *seq.* But Sir Francis Kinaston who translated *Troilus and Cresseide* into

---

* L. ult. v. 1785.

† Boccaccio *Filostrato* was printed [at Venice before 1483 (see Brunet, i. 1013), and was reprinted at Bologna in 1498, and at Milan in 1499.] It is in the octave stanza. The editor of the *Canterbury Tales* [Tyrwhitt] informs me, that Boccaccio himself, in his *Decameron,* has made the same honourable mention of this poem as of the *Teseide :* although without acknowledging either for his own. In the Introduction to the Sixth Day, he says that " Dioneo insieme con Lauretta de *Troile et di Criseida* cominciarono cantare." Just as, afterwards, in the conclusion of the Seventh Day, he says that the same " Dioneo et Fiametta gran pezzi cantarono insieme d'Arcita et di Palamone." See *Canterb. T.* vol. iv. p. 85; iii. p. 311 [edit. Tyrwhitt.] Chaucer appears to have been as much indebted to Boccaccio in his *Troilus and Cresseide,* as in his *Knightes Tale.* At the same time we must observe, that there are several long passages, and even episodes, in *Troilus,* of which no traces appear in the *Filostrato.* Chaucer speaks of himself as a translator *out of Latin,* B. ii. 14. And he calls his author *Lollius,* B. i. 394-421, and B. v. 1652. The latter of these two passages is in the *Filostrato :* but the former, containing Petrarch's sonnet, is not. And when Chaucer says, he *translates from Latin,* we must remember that the *Italian* language was called *Latino volgare.* Shall we suppose, that Chaucer followed a more complete copy of the *Filostrato* than that we have at present, or one enlarged by some officious interpolater ? The Parisian manuscript might perhaps clear these difficulties. In Bennet Library at Cambridge, there is a MS. of Chaucer's *Troilus,* elegantly written, with a frontispiece beautifully illuminated, LXI.

‡ Bibl. p. 793, col. 2. Compare Lengl. *Bibl. Rom.* ii. p. 253.

and, retiring to his chamber, is thus naturally deſcribed in the critical ſituation of a lover examining his own mind after the firſt impreſſion of love.

> And when that he in chaumber was allon,[1]
> He down upon his beddes feet him ſette,
> And firſt he gan to ſyke, and eft to grone,
> And thoughte ay on hire ſo, withouten lette,
> That as he ſatt and woke, his ſpirit mette
> That he hire ſaugh, and temple, and al the wyſe
> Right of hire loke, and gan it new aviſe.

There is not ſo much nature in the ſonnet to Love, which follows. It is tranſlated from Petrarch ; and had Chaucer followed his own genius, he would not have diſguſted us with the affected gallantry and exaggerated compliments which it extends through five tedious ſtanzas.   The doubts and delicacies of a young girl diſcloſing her heart to her lover are exquiſitely touched in this compariſon :

> And as the new abayſed nyghtyngale,[2]
> That ſtynteth firſt, when *ſhe* bygynneth ſynge,
> When that ſhe hereth any *herdes* tale,
> Or in the hegges any wight ſterynge ;
> And, after, ſyker doth hire vois oute rynge ;
> Right ſo Criſeyde, when hire drede ſtente,
> Opned hire herte, and told hym hire entente.

The following pathetic ſcene may be ſelected from many others. Troilus, ſeeing Creſſide in a ſwoon, imagines her to be dead. He unſheaths his ſword with an intent to kill himſelf, and utters theſe exclamations :

> " And thow cité, in *which* I lyve in wo![3]
> And thow Priam, and bretheren alle iſere !
> And thow *my* moder, farwel, for I go !
> And, Attropes, mak redy thow my beere !
> And thow Criſeyde, O ſwete herte deere,
> Receyve now my ſpirit !" wolde he ſeye,
> With ſwerd at herte, al redy for to dye.
>
> But, as God wold, of ſwough ſhe therwith brayde,
> And gan to ſike, and " Troilus," ſhe cryede ;
> And he anſwerde, " Lady myn Criſeyde,
> Lyve ye yit ?" and lete his ſwerde down glide :
> " Ye, herte myn, that thanked be Cupide !"
> Quod ſhe, and therwithal *ſhe ſore* ſighte,
> And he bigan to glad hire as he myghte.

Latin rhymes, ſays that Chaucer in this poem " has taken the liberty of his own inventions." [The two firſt books of Kinaſton's tranſlation were printed in 1635 ; but a MS. of the whole work is in the poſſeſſion of Mr. James Croſſley, of Mancheſter.]   In the mean time, Chaucer, by his own references, ſeems to have been ſtudious of ſeldom departing from Lollius.   In one place, he pays him a compliment, as an author whoſe excellences he could not reach. L. iii. v. 1330.

> " But ſothe is, though I can not telln all,
>   As can mine author *of his excellence.*"

See alſo l. iii. 576, 1823.
 [1] [Morris's *Chaucer*, iv. 122, lib. i. ver. 358.]
 [2] [*Ibid.* iv. 275, lib. iii. ver. 1184.]   [3] [*Ibid.* iv. 349, lib. iv. ver. 1177.]

> Took hire in armes two, and kyſte hire ofte,
> And hire to glade, he dide al his entente,
> For which hire gooſte, that fliked ay o lofte,
> Into hire woful herte ayein it wente :
> But, at the laſte, as that hire eye glente
> Aſyde, anon ſhe gan his ſwerde aſpye,
> As it lay bare, and gan for feere crie,
>
> And aſked hym whi he it hadde out drawe ;
> And Troilus anon the cauſe hire tolde,
> And how hymſelf therwith he wolde han ſlawe ;
> For which Criſeyde upon hym gan byholde,
> And gan hym in *hire* armes faſte folde,
> And ſeyde, " O mercy God, lo, which a dede !
> Allas! how neigh we weren bothe dede !''

Pathetic deſcription is one of Chaucer's peculiar excellences.

In this poem are various imitations from Ovid, which are of too particular and minute a nature to be pointed out here, and belong to the province of a profeſſed and formal commentator on the piece. The Platonic notion in the third book about univerſal love, and the doctrine that this principle acts with equal and uniform influence both in the natural and moral world, are a tranſlation from Boethius.[1] In the *Knight's Tale* he mentions from the ſame favourite ſyſtem of philoſophy, the *Fair Chain of Love.* It is worth obſerving, that the reader is referred to Dares Phrygius, inſtead of Homer, for a diſplay of the achievements of Troilus :

> His worthy dedes, who-ſo leſt hem here,[2]
> Rede Dares ; he kan telle hem alle iſeere.

Our author, from his [ſomewhat unguarded imitation of Boccaccio] has been guilty of a very diverting and what may be called a double anachroniſm. He repreſents Creſſide, with two of her female companions, ſitting in a " pavid parlour," and reading the *Thebais* of Statius, which is called *The Geſt of the Siege of Thebes,* and *The Romance of Thebes.*[3] In another place, Caſſandra tranſlates the Arguments of the twelve books of the *Thebais.*[4] In the fourth book of this poem, Pandarus endeavours to comfort Troilus with arguments concerning the doctrine of predeſtination, taken from [Boethius

---

[1] *Conſolat. Philoſoph.* l. ii. Met. *ult.* iii. Met. 2. Spenſer is full of the ſame doctrine. See *Fairy Queen,* i. ix. 1, iv. x. 34, 35, &c. &c. I could point out many other imitations from Boethius in this poem.

[2] [Morris's *Chaucer,* v. 73, ver. 1784.]

[3] L. ii v. 100. *Biſhop Amphiorax* is mentioned, ib. v. 104. Pandarus ſays, v. 106 :

> " All this I know my ſelve,
> And all the aſſiege of Thebes, and all the care ;
> For herof ben ther makid *bokis twelve.*''

In his *Boke of the Ducheſſe* (Works, v. 156, l. 47-51), Chaucer, to paſs the night away, rather than play at cheſs, calls for a *Romaunce* ; in which " were writtin fables of quenis livis and of kings, and many othir thingis ſmale." This proves to be Ovid, v. 52, *ſeq.* See *Man of L. T.* v. 54.

[4] L. v. v. 1490. I will add here, that Creſſide propoſes the trial of the Ordeal to Troilus, l. iii. v. 1048. Troilus, during the times of truce, amuſes himſelf with hawking, l. iii. v. 1785.

De Confolatione Philofophiæ—a book which Chaucer himfelf tranflated.[1]]

This poem, although almoft as long as the Eneid, was intended
to be fung to the harp, as well as read.

> And red wher fo thow be, or elles fonge.[2]

It is dedicated to the " morall " Gower, and to the " philofophical "
Strode. Gower will occur as a poet hereafter. Strode was eminent
for his fcholaftic knowledge, and tutor to Chaucer's fon Lewis at
Merton college in Oxford.

Whether the *Houfe of Fame* is Chaucer's invention, or fuggefted
by any French or Italian poet, I cannot determine. But I am apt
to think it was originally a Provençal compofition,—among other
proofs, from this paffage:

> And theroute come fo grete a noyfe,[3]
> That had hyt ftonde upon Oyfe,
> Men myght hyt han herd efely
> To Rome, Y trowe fikerly.

The Oyfe is a river in Picardy, which falls into the River Seine, not
many leagues from Paris. An Englifhman would not have expreffed
diftance by fuch an unfamiliar illuftration. Unlefs we reconcile the
matter by fuppofing that Chaucer wrote this poem during his travels.
There is another paffage where the ideas are thofe of a foreign romance. To the trumpeters of renown the poet adds,

> And alle that ufede clarioun,[4]
> In Cataloigne and Aragoun.

Cafteloigne is Catalonia in Spain.[5] The martial muficians of Englifh tournaments, fo celebrated in ftory, were a more natural and
obvious allufion for an Englifh poet.[6]

This poem contains great ftrokes of Gothic imagination, yet bor-
dering often on the moft ideal and capricious extravagance. The
poet, in a vifion, fees a temple of glafs:

> In whiche ther were moo ymages[7]
> Of golde, ftondynge in fondry ftages,
> And moo ryche tabernacles,

---

[1] [Book v. Profe 2-3, edit. Morris. See the extracts, *ibid.* vi-x.] Bradwardine,
a learned archbifhop and theologift, and nearly Chaucer's contemporary, [treated
this fubject] in his book, *De Caufa Dei*, edit. 1617. [Chaucer] touches on this
controverfy (*Nonnes Preefts Tale*, v. 1349. See alfo *Troilus and Creffeide*, lib. iv-v,
961 *et feq.*)

[2] [Morris's *Chaucer*, v. 75, ver. 1811.]

[3] [*Ibid.* v. 267, ver. 837. See *fupra*, p. 298, note 1.]   [4] [*Ibid.* v. 247, ver. 157.]

[5] See *Marchaunt's Tale*, ver. 1231. He mentions a rock higher than any in
Spain, B. iii. ver. 27. But this I believe was an Englifh proverb.

[6] He mentions a plate of gold, " As fine as *duckett* in *Venife*," B. iii. ver. 258.
But he fays that the Galaxy is called *Watlyng-ftrete*, B. ii. ver. 431. He fwears
by Thomas Becket, B. iii. ver. 41. In one place he is addreffed by the name of
Geoffrey, B. ii. ver. 221; but in two others by that of Peter, B. ii. ver. 526, B. iii.
ver. 909. Among the muficians he mentions " Pipirs of all the Duche tong," B.
iii. ver. 144.

[7] [Morris's *Chaucer*, v. 212, ver. 121.]

> And with perré [1] moo pynacles,
> And moo curioufe portreytures,
> And queynt maner of figures
> Of golde werke, then I fawgh ever.

On the walls of this temple were engraved ftories from Virgil's *Eneid* [2] and Ovid's *Epiftles*. [3] Leaving this temple, he fees an eagle with golden wings foaring near the fun :

> That fafte be the fonne, as hye [4]
> As kenne myght I with myn ye,
> Me thought I fawgh an egle fore,
> But that hit femede moche more [5]
> Then I had any egle feyne. [6]
>
> *   *   *   *   *
>
> Hyt was of golde, and fhone fo bryght,
> *That never fawgh men fuch a fyght.*

The eagle defcends, feizes the poet in his talons, and mounting again, conveys him to the Houfe of Fame, which is fituated, like that of Ovid, between earth and fea.   In their paffage thither they fly above the ftars, which our author leaves, with clouds, tempefts, hail, and fnow, far beneath him. This aerial journey is partly copied from Ovid's Phaeton in the chariot of the fun.   But the poet apolo-gifes for this extravagant fiction, and explains his meaning by alleging the authority of Boethius, who fays that Contemplation may foar on the wings of Philofophy above every element.   He likewife recol-lects, in the midft of his courfe, the defcription of the heavens given by Marcianus Capella in his book *De Nuptiis Philologiæ et Mercurii*, [7] and Alanus in his *Anticlaudian*. [8]   At his arrival in the confines of the Houfe of Fame, he is alarmed by confufed murmurs iffuing thence, like diftant thunders or billows.   This circumftance is alfo borrowed from Ovid's temple. [9] He is left by the eagle near the

---

[1] jewels.

[2] Where he mentions Virgil's hell, he likewife refers to Claudian *De Raptu Pro-ferpinæ* and Dante's *Inferno*, ver. 450.   There is a tranflation of a few lines from Dante, whom he calls "the wife poet of Florence," in the *Wife of Bath's Tale*, ver. 1125.   The ftory of Count Ugolino, a fubject which Sir Jofhua Reynolds has lately painted in a capital ftyle, is tranflated from Dante, "the grete poete of Italie that hight Dante," in the *Monkes Tale*, ver. 877.   A fentence from Dante is cited in the *Legend of Good Women*, ver. 360.   In the *Freeres Tale*, Dante is compared with Virgil, ver. 256.

[3] It was not only in the fairy palaces of the poets and romance-writers of the middle-ages that Ovid's ftories adorned the walls.   In one of the courts of the palace of Nonefuch, all Ovid's *Metamorphofes* were cut in ftone under the windows. Hearne, Coll. MSS. 55, p. 64.   But the *Epiftles* feem to have been the favourite work, the fubject of which coincided with the gallantry of the times.

[4] [Morris's *Chaucer*, v. 224, ver. 497.]   [5] greater.

[6] The eagle fays to the poet, that this houfe ftands

> "Right fo as *thine owne boke* tellith."

B. ii. ver. 204.   That is, Ovid's *Metamorphofes*.   See *Met.* l. xii. ver. 40, &c.

[7] See the *Marchaunt's Tale*, v. 1248, and Lidg. *Stor. Theb.* fol. 357.

[8] A famous book in the middle ages.   There is an old French tranflation of it. Bibl. Reg. Paris, MSS. Cod. 7632.

[9] See *Met.* xii. 39, and Virg. *Æn.* iv. 173 ; Val. Flacc. ii. 117 ; Lucan. 1. 469.

houſe, which is built of materials bright as poliſhed glaſs, and ſtands on a rock of ice of exceſſive height, and almoſt inacceſſible. All the ſouthern ſide of this rock was covered with engravings of the names of famous men, which were perpetually melting away by the heat of the ſun. The northern ſide of the rock was alike covered with names, but being here ſhaded from the warmth of the ſun, the cha-racters remained unmelted and uneffaced. The ſtructure of the houſe is thus imagined.

> me thought*e*, by ſeynte Gyle,[1]
> Alle was of ſtone of beryle,
> Both*e* caſtel and the toure,
> And eke the halle, and every boure,
> Wythouten peces or joynynges.
> But many ſubtile compaſſinges,
> As rabewyures and pynacles,
> Ymageries and tabernacles,
> I ſay ; and ful eke of wyndowes,
> As flakes falle in grete ſnowes.

In theſe lines, and in ſome others which occur hereafter, the poet perhaps alludes to the many new decorations in architecture which began to prevail about his time, and gave riſe to the florid Gothic ſtyle. There are inſtances of this in other poems [aſcribed to him.] In [the poem called *Chaucer's Dreme*,

> And of a ſute were all the toures,[2]
> Subtily corven after floures,
> *   *   *   *
> With many a ſmall turret hie.

And in the deſcription of the palace of Pleaſant Regard, in the Aſſembly of Ladies :

> Fairir is none, though it were for a king,[3]
> Deviſid wel and that in every thing ;
> The towris hie, ful pleſante ſhal ye finde,
> With fannis freſh, turning with everie winde.
> The chambris, and the parlirs of a ſorte,
> With bay windows, goodlie as may be thought :
> As for daunſing or othir wiſe diſporte,
> The galeries be al right wel ywrought.

In Chaucer's Life by William Thomas,[4] it is not mentioned that he was appointed clerk of the king's works in the palace of Weſt-minſter, in the royal manors of Shene, Kennington, Byfleet, and Clapton, and in the Mews at Charing.[5] Again in 1380, of the works of St. George's Chapel at Windſor, then ruinous.[6] But to return.

Within the niches formed in the pinnacles ſtood all round the caſtle,

---

[1] [Morris's *Chaucer*, v. 245, lib. iii. ver. 93.]   [2] [*Ibid.* v. 88, ver. 81.]

[3] Chaucer's Works, ed. Urry, p. 434, col. 2, lines 158-165.

[4] Chaucer's Life in Urry's edition. William Thomas digeſted this Life from collections by Dart. His brother, Dr. Timothy Thomas, wrote or compiled the Gloſſary and Preface to that edition. See Dart's *Weſtminſt. Abbey*, i. 80. Timothy Thomas was of Chriſt Church, Oxford, and died in 1757.

[5] Claus. 8, Ric. II.

[6] Pat. 14, Ric. II. *apud* Tanner, *Bibl.* p. 166, note e.

> al maner of mynftralles,[1]
> And geftiours, that tellen tales
> Bothe of wepinge and of game.

That is, thofe who fang or recited adventures either tragic or comic, which excited either compaffion or laughter. They were accompanied by the moft renowned harpers, among which were Orpheus, Arion, Chiron, and the Briton Glafkerion.[2] Behind thefe were placed, " by many a thoufand time twelve," players on various inftruments of mufic. Among the trumpeters are named Joab, Virgil's Mifenus, and Theodamas.[3] About thefe pinnacles were alfo marfhalled the moft famous magicians, jugglers, witches, propheteffes, forcereffes, and profeffors of natural magic,[4] which ever exifted in ancient or modern times: fuch as Medea, Circe, Calliope, Hermes,[5] Limotheus, and Simon Magus.[6] At entering the hall he fees an infinite multitude of heralds, on the furcoats of whom were richly embroidered the armorial enfigns of the moft redoubted champions that ever tourneyed in Africa, Europe, or

---

[1] [Morris's *Chaucer*, v. 245, ver. 107.]

[2] Concerning this harper, fee Percy's Ballads.

[3] See alfo the *Marchaunt's Tale*, v. 1236, *feq.*

[4] See the *Frankelein's Tale*, where feveral feats are defcribed, as exhibited at a feaft, done by natural magic, a favourite fcience of the Arabians. Chaucer there calls it " An art which fotill tragetoris plaie," v. 2696. Of this more will be faid hereafter.

[5] None of the works of the firft Hermes Trifmegiftus now remain[s]. S.e Cornel. Agrip. *De Van. Scient.* cap. xlviii. The aftrological and other philofophical pieces under that name are fuppofititious. See Fabr. *Biblioth. Gr.* xii. 708. And *Chan. Yem. Tale*, v. 1455. Some of thefe pieces were publifhed under the fictitious names of Abel, Enoch, Abraham, Solomon, Saint Paul, and of many of the patriarchs and fathers. Cornel. Agripp. *De Van. Scient.* cap. xlv. who adds, that thefe *trifles* were followed by Alphonfus, king of Caftile, Robert Groffetefte, Bacon, and Apponus. He mentions Zabulus and Barnabas of Cyprus as famous writers in magic. See alfo Gower's *Confefs. Amant.* p. 134, b; 149, b; edit. 1554. In fpeaking of ancient authors who were known or celebrated in the middle ages, it may be remarked, that Macrobius was one. He is mentioned by Guill. de Lorris in the *Roman de la Rofe*, v. 9. " Ung aucteur qui ot nom *Macrobe*." A line literally tranflated by Chaucer, " An author that hight *Macrobes*," v. 7. Chaucer quotes him in his *Dreme*, v. 284. In the *Nonnes Prieft's Tale*, v. 1238. In the *Affemblie of Foules*, v. 111, fee alfo *ibid.* v. 31. He wrote a comment on Tully's *Somnium Scipionis*, and in thefe paffages he is referred to on account of that piece. Petrarch, in a letter to Nicolas Sigeros, a learned Greek of Conftantinople, quotes Macrobius, as a Latin author of all others the moft familiar to Nicolas. It is to prove that Homer is the fountain of all invention. This is in 1354. *Famil. Let.* ix. 2. There is a manufcript of the firft and part of the fecond book of Macrobius, elegantly written, as it feems, in France, about the year 800. .*MSS. Cotton. Vitell.* C. iii. fol. 138. M. Planudes, a Conftantinopolitan monk of the fourteenth century, is faid to have tranflated Macrobius into Greek. But fee Fabric. *Bibl. Gr.* x. 534. It is remarkable that in the above letter, Petrarch apologifes for calling Plato the Prince of Philofophers, after Cicero, Seneca, Apuleius, Plotinus, Saint Ambrofe, and Saint Auftin.

[6] Among thefe he mentions *Jugglers*, that is, in the prefent fenfe of the word, thofe who practifed legerdemain: a popular fcience in Chaucer's time. Thus in *Squ. T.* v. 239:

> " As jogelours pleyen at this feftes grete."

It was an appendage of the occult fciences ftudied and introduced into Europe by the Arabians.

Aſia. The floor and roof of the hall were covered with thick plates of gold ſtudded with the coſtlieſt gems. At the upper end, on a lofty ſhrine made of carbuncle, ſat Fame. Her figure is like thoſe in Virgil and Ovid. Above her, as if ſuſtained on her ſhoulders, ſat Alexander and Hercules. From the throne to the gates of the hall, ran a range of pillars with reſpective inſcriptions. On the firſt pillar made of lead and iron,[1] ſtood Joſephus, the Jewiſh hiſtorian, "That of the Jewis geſtis told," with ſeven other writers on the ſame ſubject. On the ſecond pillar, made of iron, and painted all over with the blood of tigers, ſtood Statius. On another higher than the reſt ſtood Homer, Dares Phrygius, Livy,[2] Lollius, Guido di Columna, and Geoffrey of Monmouth, writers of the Trojan ſtory. On a pillar of " tinnid iron clere," ſtood Virgil : and next him on a pillar of copper, appeared Ovid. The figure of Lucan was placed on a pillar of iron " wroght full ſternly," accompanied by many Roman hiſtorians.[3] On a pillar of ſulphur ſtood Claudian, ſo ſymboliſed, becauſe he wrote of Pluto and Proſerpine :

> That bare up *than* the fame of helle ;[4]
> Of Pluto, and of Proſerpyne,
> That quene ys of the derke pyne.

The hall was filled with the writers of ancient tales and romances, whoſe ſubjects and names were too numerous to be recounted. In the mean time crowds from every nation and of every condition filled the hall, and each preſented his claim to the queen. A meſſenger is diſpatched to ſummon Eolus from his cave in Thrace ; who is ordered to bring his two clarions called *Slander* and *Praiſe*, and his trumpeter Triton. The praiſes of each petitioner are then reſounded, according to the partial or capricious appointment of Fame ; and equal merits obtain very different ſucceſs. There is much ſatire and humour in theſe requeſts and rewards, and in the diſgraces and honours which are indiſcriminately diſtributed by the queen, without diſcernment and by chance. The poet then enters the houſe or labyrinth of Rumour. It was built of ſallow twigs, like a cage, and therefore admitted every ſound. Its doors were alſo more numerous than leaves on the trees, and always ſtood open. Theſe are romantic exaggerations of Ovid's inventions on the ſame ſubject. It was moreover ſixty miles in length, and perpetually turning round. From this houſe, ſays the poet, iſſued tidings of

---

[1] In the compoſition of theſe pillars, Chaucer diſplays his chemical knowledge.

[2] Dares Phrygius and Livy are both cited in Chaucer's *Dreme*, v. 1070, 1084. Chaucer is fond of quoting Livy. He was alſo much admired by Petrarch, who, while at Paris, aſſiſted in tranſlating him into French. This circumſtance might make Livy a favourite with Chaucer. See *Vie de Petrarque*, iii. p. 547.

[3] Was not this intended to characteriſe Lucan ? Quintillian ſays of Lucan, " *Oratoribus* magis quam *poetis* annumerandus." *Inſtit. Orat.* L. x. c. 1.

[4] [Morris's *Chaucer*, v. 255, ver. 420.] Chaucer alludes to this poem of Claudian in the *Marchaunt's Tale*, where he calls Pluto, the king of " fayrie," ver. 1744.

every kind, like fountains and rivers from the sea. Its inhabitants, who were eternally employed in hearing or telling news, together with the rise of reports, and the formation of lies, are then humorously described : the company is chiefly composed of sailors, pilgrims, and pardoners. At length our author is awakened at seeing a venerable personage of great authority: and thus the Vision abruptly concludes.

Pope has imitated this piece with his usual elegance of diction and harmony of versification. But in the mean time, he has not only misrepresented the story, but marred the character of the poem. He has endeavoured to correct its extravagances by new refinements and additions of another cast : but he did not consider, that extravagances are essential to a poem of such a structure, and even constitute its beauties. An attempt to unite order and exactness of imagery with a subject formed on principles so professedly romantic and anomalous, is like giving Corinthian pillars to a Gothic palace. When I read Pope's elegant imitation of this piece, I think I am walking among the modern monuments unsuitably placed in Westminster Abbey.

SECTION XV.

NOTHING can be more ingeniously contrived than the occasion on which Chaucer's *Canterbury Tales* are supposed to be recited. A company of pilgrims, on their journey to visit the shrine of Thomas Becket at Canterbury, lodge at the Tabard Inn in Southwark. Although strangers to each other, they are assembled in one room at supper, as was then the custom ; and agree, not only to travel together the next morning, but to relieve the fatigue of the journey by telling each a story.[1] Chaucer undoubtedly intended to imitate Boccaccio, whose *Decameron* was then the most popular of books, in writing a set of tales. But the circumstance invented by Boccaccio, as the cause which gave rise to his *Decameron*, or the relation of his hundred stories,[2] is by no means so happily conceived as that of Chaucer for a similar purpose. Boccaccio supposes, that when the plague began to abate at Florence, ten young persons of both sexes retired to a country house, two miles from the city, with a design of

---

[1] There is an inn at Burford in Oxfordshire, which accommodated pilgrims on their road to Saint Edward's shrine in the abbey of Gloucester. A long room, with a series of Gothic windows, still remains, which was their refectory. Leland mentions such another, *Itin.* ii. 70.

[2] It is remarkable that Boccaccio chose a Greek title, that is, Δεκαμερον, for his *Tales.* He has also given Greek names to the ladies and gentlemen who recite the tales. His *Eclogues* are full of Greek words. This was natural at the revival of the Greek language.

enjoying frefh air, and paffing ten days agreeably. Their principal and eftablifhed amufement, inftead of playing at chefs after dinner, was for each to tell a tale. One fuperiority which, among others, Chaucer's plan afforded above that of Boccaccio, was the opportunity of difplaying a variety of ftriking and dramatic charaĉters, which would not have eafily met but on fuch an expedition ;—a circum-ftance which alfo contributed to give a variety to the ftories. And for a number of perfons in their fituation, fo natural, fo praĉticable, fo pleafant, I add fo rational, a mode of entertainment could not have been imagined.

The *Canterbury Tales* are unequal, and of various merit. Few perhaps, if any, of the ftories are the invention of Chaucer. I have already fpoken at large of the *Knight's Tale*, one of our author's nobleft compofitions.[1] That of the *Canterbury Tales*, which deferves the next place, as written in the higher ftrain of poetry, and the poem by which Milton defcribes and charaĉterifes Chaucer, is the *Squire's Tale*.[2] The imagination of this ftory confifts in Arabian fiĉtion engrafted on Gothic chivalry. Nor is this Arabian fiĉtion purely the fport of arbitrary fancy : it is in great meafure founded on Arabian learning. Cambufcan, a king of Tartary, celebrates his birth-day feftival in the hall of his palace at Sarra with the moft royal magnificence. In the midft of the folemnity, the guefts are alarmed by a miraculous and unexpeĉted fpeĉtacle : the minftrels ceafe on a fudden, and all the affembly is hufhed in filence, furprife, and fufpenfe.

> Whil that the kyng fit thus in his nobleye,[3]
> Herkyng his mynftrales her thinges pleye
> Byforn him atte boord delicioufly,
> In atte halle dore al fodeynly
> Ther com a knight upon a fteed of bras,
> And in his hond a brod myrour of glas ;
> Upon his thomb he had of gold a ryng,
> And by his fide a naked fwerd hangyng :
> And up he rideth to the heyghe bord.
> In al the halle ne was ther fpoke a word,
> For mervayl of this knight ; him to byholde
> Ful befily they wayten yong and olde.

---

[1] The reader will excufe my irregularity in not confidering it under the *Canterbury Tales*. I have here given the reafon, which is my apology, in the text.

[2] [Le Chevalier de Chatelain finds the original of this tale in the old French romance of *Cléomadès*, in 19,000 lines, printed in 1866 by the Belgian Academy, written from Spanifh and Moorifh fources by Adam or Adénès Le Roy, King of the Minftrels of the Duke of Brabant, in the thirteenth century. The Chevalier printed a modern French verfe fketch of the ftory of Cléomadès in 1858, and re-iffued it in 1869 with a frefh preface, as a fecond edition. The French Romance has a wooden horfe with fprings in it, which is managed by " tournant les chevilles," (pegs, pins), and Chaucer's brafs one is managed thus too : " Yͤ moote trille a pyn, ftant in his ere." But here, and in the faĉt that the common people are, in both tales, aftonifhed at the horfes, ends the likenefs of *Cléomadès* and the *Squire's Tale*.—F.]

[3] [Morris's Chaucer, ii. 357, ver. 69.] See a fine romantic ftory of a Comte de Macon who, while revelling in his hall with many knights, is fuddenly alarmed by the entrance of a gigantic figure of a black man, mounted on a black fteed. This

These presents were sent by the king of Arabia and India to Cambuscan in honour of his feast. The horse of brass, on the skilful movement and management of certain secret springs, transported his rider into the most diftant region of the world in the space of twenty-four hours; for, as the rider chose, he could fly in the air with the swiftness of an eagle: and again, as occafion required, he could stand motionless in oppofition to the strongest force, vanish on a sudden at command, and return at his master's call. The Mirror of Glass was endued with the power of shewing any future disasters which might happen to Cambuscan's kingdom, and difcovered the most hidden machinations of treason. The Naked Sword could pierce armour deemed impenetrable,

> Were it as thikke as is a braunched ook.

And he who was wounded with it could never be healed, unless its possessor could be entreated to stroke the wound with its edge. The Ring was intended for Canace, Cambuscan's daughter, and while she bore it in her purse, or wore it on her thumb, enabled her to understand the language of every species of birds, and the virtues of every plant:

> And whan this knight thus had*de* his tale told,[1]
> He rit out of the halle, and doun he light.
> His steede, which that schon as sonne bright,
> Stant in the court as stille as eny stoon.
> This knight is to his chambre lad anoon,
> And is unarmed, and to mete i-sett.
> This presentz ben ful richely i-fett,
> This is to sayn, the swerd and the myrrour,
> And born anon unto the highe tour,
> With certein officers ordeynd therfore;
> And unto Canace the ryng is bore
> Solempnely, ther sche syt atte table.

I have mentioned, in another place, the favourite philofophical studies of the Arabians.[2] In this poem the nature of those studies is difplayed, and their operations exemplified: and this confideration, added to the circumstances of Tartary being the scene of action, and Arabia the country from which these extraordinary presents are brought, induces me to believe this story to be [identical with one which was current at a very ancient date among] the Arabians. At least it is formed on their principles. Their sciences were tinctured with the warmth of their imaginations, and confifted in wonderful difcoveries and mysterious inventions.

This idea of a horse of brass took its rife from their chemical knowledge and experiments in metals. The treatife of Jeber, a famous Arab chemist of the middle ages, called *Lapis Philofophorum*, contains many curious and useful procefses concerning the nature of

---

terrible ftranger, without receiving any obftruction from guards or gates, rides directly forward to the high table; and, with an imperious tone, orders the count to follow him, &c. Nic. Gillos, *Chron.* ann. 1120. See alfo *Obs. Fair Qu.* § v. p. 146.
[1] [Morris's *Chaucer*, ii. 360, ver. 160.]   [2] Difs. i. ii.

metals, their fufion, purification, and malleability, which ftill main-
tain a place in modern fyftems of that fcience.[1] The poets of romance, who deal in Arabian ideas, defcribe the Trojan horfe as made
of brafs.[2] Thefe fages pretended the power of giving life or fpeech
to fome of their compofitions in metal. Bifhop Groffetefte's fpeaking
brazen head, fometimes attributed to [Roger] Bacon, has its foundation in Arabian philofophy.[3] In the romance of *Valentine and Orfon,*
a brazen head fabricated by a necromancer in a magnificent chamber
of the caftle of Clerimond, declares to thofe two princes their royal
parentage.[4] We are told by William of Malmefbury that Pope
Sylvefter II. a profound mathematician who lived in the eleventh
century, made a brazen head, which would fpeak when fpoken to,
and oracularly refolved many difficult queftions.[5] Albertus Magnus,
who was alfo a profound adept in thofe fciences which were taught by
the Arabian fchools, is faid to have framed a man of brafs, which not
only anfwered queftions readily and truly, but was fo loquacious, that
Thomas Aquinas while a pupil of Albertus Magnus, and afterwards
an Angelic doctor, knocked it in pieces as the difturber of his abftrufe
fpeculations. This was about the year 1240.[6] Much in the fame
manner, the notion of our knight's horfe being moved by means of
a concealed engine correfponds with their pretences of producing
preternatural effects, and their love of furprifing by geometrical
powers. Exactly in this notion, Rocail, a giant in fome of the
Arabian romances, is faid to have built a palace, together with his
own fepulchre, of moft magnificent architecture and with fingular
artifice : in both of thefe he placed a great number of gigantic ftatues
or images, figured of different metals by talifmanic fkill, which, in
confequence of fome occult machinery, performed actions of real life,
and looked like living men.[7] We muft add that aftronomy, which
the Arabian philofophers ftudied with a fingular enthufiafm, had no
fmall fhare in the compofition of this miraculous fteed. For, fays
the poet,

---

[1] The Arabians call chemiftry, as treating of minerals and metals, Simia ; from
Sim, a word fignifying the veins of gold and filver in the mines. Herbelot, *Bibl.
Orient.* p. 810, b. Hither, among many other things, we might refer Merlin's two
dragons of gold finifhed with moft exquifite workmanfhip, in Geoffrey of Monmouth, l. viii. c. 17. See alfo *ibid.* vii. c. 3, where Merlin prophefies that a brazen
man on a brazen horfe fhall guard the gates of London.

[2] See Lydgate's *Troye Boke,* B. iv. c. 35. And Gower's *Conf. Amant.* B. i. f.
13, b. edit. 1554. " A horfe of braffe thei lette do forge."

[3] Gower, *Confefs. Amant.* [ed. 1857, ii. 9.] L. iv. fol. lxiiii. a, edit. 1554.

> " For of the grete clerk Grofteft
> I rede how bufy that he was
> Upon the clergie an heved of bras
> To forge and make it for to telle
> Of fuche thinges as befelle—"

[4] Ch. xxviii. *feq.*

[5] *De Geft. Reg. Angl.* lib. ii. cap. 10. Compare *Maj. Symbolor. Aureæ Menfæ,*
lib. x. p. 453.

[6] Delrio, *Difquis. Magic.* lib. i. cap. 4.

[7] Herbelot, *Bibl. Orient.* v. *Rocail,* p. 717, a.

He that it wrought cowthe *ful* many a gyn;[1]
He wayted*e* many a conſtellacioun,
Er he hadd*e* do this operacioun.

Thus the buckler of the Arabian giant Ben Gian, as famous among the Orientals as that of Achilles among the Greeks, was fabricated by the powers of aſtronomy;[2] and Pope Sylveſter's brazen head, juſt mentioned, was prepared under the influence of certain conſtellations.

Natural magic, improperly ſo called, was likewiſe a favourite purſuit of the Arabians, by which they impoſed falſe appearances on the ſpectator. This was blended with their aſtrology. Our author's *Frankelein's Tale* is entirely founded on the miracles of this art.

For I am ſiker that ther ben ſciences,[3]
By whiche men maken dyverſe apparences,
Which as the ſubtile tregetoures[4] pleyen.
For ofte at feſtes ha*v*e I herd ſeyen,
That ɔregettoures, withinne an halle large,
Han made in come water and a barge,
And in the halle rowen up and doun.
Som tyme hath ſemed *come* a grym leoun;
Some tyme a caſtel al of lym and ſton.

Afterwards a magician in the ſame poem ſhews various ſpecimens of his art in raiſing ſuch illuſions: and by way of diverting King Aurelius before ſupper, preſents before him parks and foreſts filled with deer of vaſt proportion, ſome of which are killed with hounds and others with arrows. He then ſhews the king a beautiful lady in a dance. At the clapping of the magician's hands all theſe deceptions diſappear.[5] Theſe feats are ſaid to be performed by conſultation of

---

[1] [Morris's Chaucer, ii. 358, ver. 120.] I do not preciſely underſtand the line immediately following.

"And knew ful many a ſeal and many a bond."

Seal may mean a taliſmanic ſigil uſed in aſtrology. Or the Hermetic ſeal uſed in chemiſtry. Or, connected with *Bond,* may ſignify contracts made with ſpirits in chemical operations. But all theſe belong to the Arabian philoſophy, and are alike to our purpoſe. In the Arabian books now extant, are the alphabets out of which they formed Taliſmans to draw down ſpirits or angels. The Arabian word *Kimia* not only ſignifies chemiſtry, but a magical and ſuperſtitious ſcience, by which they bound ſpirits to their will and drew from them the information required. See Herbelot, *Dict. Orient.* p. 810, 1005. The curious and more inquiſitive reader may conſult Cornelius Agrippa, *De Vanit. Scient.* c. xliv.-vi.

[2] Many myſteries were concealed in the compoſition of this ſhield. It deſtroyed all the charms and enchantments which either demons or giants could make by *goetic* or magic art. Herbelot, *ubi ſupr.* v. *Gian.* p. 396, a.

[3] [Morris's *Chaucer*, iii. 14, ver. 411.]   [4] jugglers.

[5] But his moſt capital performance is to remove an immenſe chain of rocks from the ſea-ſhore: this is done in ſuch a manner, that for the ſpace of one week "it ſemed*e* that the rockes were aweye." *Ibid.* ver. 560. By the way, this tale appears to be a tranſlation. He ſays, "As theſe bokes me remembre." v. 507. And "From Gerour ay to the mouth of Sayne." v. 486. The Garoune and Seine are rivers in France.

the ftars.[1] We frequently read in romances of illufive appearances
framed by magicians,[2] which by the fame powers are made fuddenly
to vanifh. To trace the matter home to its true fource, thefe
fictions have their origin in a fcience which profeffedly made a confiderable part of the Arabian learning.[3] In the twelfth century the
number of magical and aftrological Arabic books tranflated into
Latin was prodigious.[4] Chaucer, in the fiction before us, fuppofes
that fome of the guefts in Cambufcan's hall believed the Trojan
horfe to be a temporary illufion, effected by the power of magic.[5]

> An apparence maad by fom magik,[6]
> As jogelours pleyen at this feftes grete.

In fpeaking of the metallurgy of the Arabians, I muft not omit the
fublime imagination of Spenfer, or rather fome Britifh bard, who feigns
that the magician Merlin intended to build a wall of brafs about Cair-
mardin (Carmarthen) ; but that being haftily called away by the Lady
of the Lake, and flain by her perfidy, he has left his fiends ftill at
work on this mighty ftructure round their brazen cauldrons, under a
rock among the neighbouring woody cliffs of Dynevor, who dare not
defift till their mafter returns. At this day, fays the poet, if you
liften at a chink or cleft of the rock :

> Such ghaftly noyfe of yron chaines[7]
> And brafen Caudrons thou fhalt rombling heare,
> Which thoufand fprights with long enduring paines
> Doe toffe, that it will ftonn thy feeble braines ;

---

[1] See *Frankel. Tale.* The Chriftians called this one of the diabolical arts
of the Saracens or Arabians. And many of their own philofophers, who afterwards wrote on the fubject or performed experiments on its principles, were faid
to deal with the devil. Witnefs our Bacon, &c. From Sir John Mandeville's
Travels it appears, that thefe fciences were in high requeft in the court of the Cham
of Tartary about the year 1340. He fays, that, at a great feftival, on one fide of
the Emperor's table, he faw placed many philofophers fkilled in various fciences,
fuch as aftronomy, necromancy, geometry, and pyromancy : that fome of thefe had
before them aftrolabes of gold and precious ftones, others had horologes richly
furnifhed with many other mathematical inftruments, &c. chap. lxxi. Sir John Mandeville began his travels into the Eaft, in 1322, and finifhed his book in 1364, chap.
cix. See Johannes Sarifb. *Polycrat.* l. i. cap. xi. fol. 10, b.

[2] See what is faid of Spenfer's *Falfe Florimel, Obs. Spens.* § xi. p. 123.

[3] Herbelot mentions many oriental pieces, " Qui traittent de cette art pernicieux
et defendu." *Dict. Orient.* v. Schr. Compare Agrippa, *ubi fupr.* cap. xlii. *feq.*

[4] " Irrepfit hac ætate etiam turba aftrologorum et magorum, ejus farinæ libris
una cum aliis de Arabico in Latinum converfis." Conring. *Script Comment.*
Sæc. xiii. cap. 3, p. 125. See alfo Herbelot. *Bibl. Orient.* v. *Ketab,* paffim.

[5] John of Salifbury fays, that magicians are thofe who, among other deceptions,
" Rebus adimunt fpecies fuas." *Polycrat.* i. 10, fol. 10, b. Agrippa mentions one
Pafetes a juggler, who " was wont to fhewe to ftrangers a very fumptuoufe banket,
and when it pleafed him, to caufe it vanifhe awaye, al they which fate at the table
being difapointed both of meate and drinke," &c. *Van. Scient.* cap. xlviii. p. 62,
b. Engl. Tranfl. *ut. infr.* Du Halde mentions a Chinefe enchanter, who, when the
Emperor was inconfolable for the lofs of his deceafed queen, caufed her image
to appear before him. *Hift. Chin.* iii. § iv. See the deceptions of Hakem an
Arabian juggler in Herbelot, in v. p. 412. See *fupr.* p. 229, 230.

[6] [Morris's *Chaucer,* ii. 361, ver. 210.]

[7] *Fairy Queen,* [lib. iii. c. 3, ft. 9-11, edit. Morris, p. 169.]

> And oftentimes great grones, and grievous ftownds,
> When too huge toile and labour them conftraines,
> And oftentimes loud ftrokes and ringing fowndes
> From under that deepe Rock moft horribly rebowndes.

> The caufe, fome fay, is this : A litle whyle
> Before that Merlin dyde, he did intend
> A BRASEN WALL in compas to compyle
> About Cairmardin, and did it commend
> Unto thefe Sprights to bring to perfeȼt end :
> During which worke the Lady of the Lake,
> Whom long he lov'd, for him in hafte did fend ;
> Who, thereby forft his workemen to forfake,
> Them bownd till his retourne their labour not to flake.

> In the meane time, through that falfe Ladies traine,
> He was furprifd, and buried under beare,
> Ne ever to his worke returnd againe ;
> Nath'leffe thofe feends may not their work forbeare,
> So greatly his commandement they feare,
> But there doe toyle and traveile day and night,
> Untill that brafen wall they up doe reare—

This ftory Spenfer borrowed from Giraldus Cambrenfis who, during his progrefs through Wales in the twelfth century, picked it up among other romantic traditions propagated by the Britifh bards.[1] I have before pointed out the fource from which the Britifh bards received moft of their extravagant fiȼtions.

Optics were likewife a branch of ftudy which fuited the natural genius of the Arabian philofophers, and which they purfued with incredible delight. This fcience was a part of the Ariftotelic philofophy which, as I have before obferved, they refined and filled with a thoufand extravagances. Hence our ftrange knight's *Mirror of Glafs,* prepared on the moft profound principles of art, and endued with preternatural qualities.

> And fom of hem wondred on the mirrour,[2]
> That born was up into the maifter tour,
> How men might in hit fuche thinges fe.
> Another anfwerd, and fayd, it mighte wel be
> Naturelly by compoficiouns
> Of angels, and of heigh reflexiouns ;
> And fayde that in Rome was fuch oon.
> They fpeeke of Alhazen and Vitilyon,
> *And* Ariftotle, that writen in her lyves
> Of queynte myrrours and profpeȼtyves.

And again,

> This mirour eek, that I have in myn hond,[3]
> Hath fuch a mighte, that men may in it fee
> When ther fchal falle eny adverfité
> Unto your regne," &c.

Alcen, or Alhazen, mentioned in thefe lines, an Arabic philofopher, wrote feven books of perfpeȼtive, and flourifhed about the

---

[1] See Girald: Cambrens. *Itin. Cambr.* i. c. 6 ; Holinfh. *Hift.* i. 129 ; and Camden's *Brit.* p. 734. Drayton has this fiȼtion, which he relates fomewhat differently : *Polyolb.* lib. iv. p. 62, edit. 1613. Hence Bacon's wall of brafs about England.
[2] [Morris's *Chaucer,* ii. 361, ver. 217.]   [3] [*Ibid.* p. 359, ver. 124.]

eleventh century. Vitellio, formed on the fame fchool, was likewife
an eminent mathematician of the middle ages, and wrote ten books
on *Perfpective.* The Roman mirror here mentioned by Chaucer,
as fimilar to this of the ftrange knight, is thus defcribed by Gower:

> Whan Rome ftood in noble plite,
> Virgile, which was tho parfite,
> A mirrour made of his clergie,[1]
> And fette it in the townes eye
> Of marbre on a piller without,
> That they by thritty mile about
> By day and eke alfo by night
> In that mirrour beholde might
> Her ennemies if any were.[2]

The Oriental writers relate that Giamfchid, one of their kings,
the Solomon of the Perfians and their Alexander the Great, poffeffed
among his ineftimable treafures cups, globes, and mirrors, of metal,
glafs, and cryftal, by means of which he and his people knew all
natural as well as fupernatural things. The title of an Arabian book,
tranflated from the Perfian, is, *The Mirrour which reflects the World.*
There is this paffage in an ancient Turkifh poet: " When I am
purified by the light of heaven my foul will become the mirror of
the world, in which I fhall difcern all abftrufe fecrets." Monfieur
Herbelot is of opinion, that the Orientals took thefe notions from
the patriarch Jofeph's cup of divination and Neftor's cup in Homer,
on which all nature was fymbolically reprefented.[3] Our great
countryman Roger Bacon, in his *Opus Majus,* a work entirely
formed on the Ariftotelic and Arabian philofophy, defcribes a variety
of Specula, and explains their conftruction and ufes.[4] This is the
moft curious and extraordinary part of Bacon's book, which was
written about the year 1270. Bacon's optic tube, with which he
pretended to fee future events, was famous in his age, and long afterwards, and chiefly contributed to give him the name of a magician.[5]
This art, with others of the experimental kind, the philofophers of

---

[1] learning; philofophy. The fame fiction is in Caxton's *Troye boke.* " Upon
the pinnacle or top of the towre he made an ymage of copper and gave hym in his
hande a looking-glaffe, having fuch vertue, that if it happened that any fhippes
came to harme the citie fuddenly, their army and their coming fhould appear in
the faid looking-glaffe." B. ii. ch. xxii.

[2] *Confefs. Amant.* l. v. [edit. 1857, ii. 195].

[3] Herbelot, *Dict. Oriental.* v. *Giam.* p. 392, col. 2. John of Salifbury mentions
a fpecies of diviners called Specularii, who predicted future events, and told various
fecrets, by confulting mirrors, and the furfaces of other polifhed reflecting fub-
ftances. *Polycrat.* i. 12, p. 32, edit. 1595.

[4] Edit. Jebb, p. 253. Bacon, in one of his MSS. complains, that no perfon
read lectures in Oxford *De Perfpectivâ* before the year 1267. He adds that in the
Univerfity of Paris, this fcience was quite unknown. *Epift. ad Opus Minus Cle-
menti IV.* Et ibid. *Op. Min.* cap. ii. MSS. Bibl. Coll. Univ. Oxon. c. 20. In
another he affirms that Julius Cæfar, before he invaded Britain, viewed our harbours
and fhores with a telefcope from the Gallic coaft. MSS. *Lib. De Perfpectivis.* He
accurately defcribes reading-glaffes or fpectacles, *Op. Maj.* p. 236. The
Camera Obfcura, I believe, is one of his difcoveries.

[5] Wood, *Hift. Antiquit. Univ. Oxon.* i. 122.

thofe times were fond of adapting to the purpofes of thaumaturgy; and there is much occult and chimerical fpeculation in the difcoveries which Bacon affects to have made from optical experiments. He afferts (and I am obliged to cite the paffage in his own myfterious expreffions): "Omnia fciri per Perfpectivam, quoniam omnes actiones rerum fiunt fecundum fpecierum et virtutum multiplicationem ab agentibus hujus mundi in materias patientes," &c.[1] Spenfer feigns, that the magician Merlin made a glaffy globe, and prefented it to King Ryence, which fhowed the approach of enemies, and difcovered treafons.[2] This fiction, which exactly correfponds with Chaucer's Mirror, Spenfer borrowed from fome romance, perhaps of King Arthur, fraught with Oriental fancy. From the fame fources came a like fiction of Camoens in the *Lufiad*,[3] where a globe is fhown to Vafco de Gama, reprefenting the univerfal fabric or fyftem of the world, in which he fees future kingdoms and future events. The Spanifh hiftorians report an American tradition, but more probably invented by themfelves, and built on the Saracen fables, in which they were fo converfant. They pretend that fome years before the Spaniards entered Mexico, the inhabitants caught a monftrous fowl, of unufual magnitude and fhape, on the lake of Mexico. In the crown of the head of this wonderful bird, there was a mirror or plate of glafs, in which the Mexicans faw their future invaders the Spaniards, and all the difafters which afterwards happened to their kingdom. Thefe fuperftitions remained, even in the doctrines of philofophers, long after the darker ages. Cornelius Agrippa, a learned phyfician of Cologne about the year 1520, and author of a famous book on the Vanity of the Sciences, mentions a fpecies of mirror which exhibited the form of perfons abfent, at command.[4] In one of thefe he is faid to have fhown to the poetical Earl of Surrey the image of his miftrefs, the beautiful Geraldine, fick and repofing on a couch.[5] Nearly allied to this was the infatuation of feeing things in a beryl, which was very popular in the reign of James I., and is alluded to by Shakefpeare. [Aubrey, in his *Mifcellanies*, defcribes the beryl, and a drawing of one accompanies the text. This ftill remains an article of practice and belief.]

The Arabians were alfo famous for other machineries of glafs, in which their chemiftry was more immediately concerned. The philofophers of their fchool invented a ftory of a magical fteel-glafs, placed by Ptolemy on the fummit of a lofty pillar near the city of

---

[1] *Op. Min.* MSS. *ut fupr.*   [2] *Fairy Queen*, iii. ii. 21.   [3] Cant. x.

[4] It is diverting in this book to obferve the infancy of experimental philofophy, and their want of knowing how to ufe or apply the mechanical arts which they were even actually poffeffed of. Agrippa calls the inventor of magnifying glaffes, "without doubte the beginner of all difhoneftie." He mentions various forts of diminifhing, burning, reflecting, and multiplying glaffes, with fome others. At length this profound thinker clofes the chapter with this fage reflection, "All thefe thinges are vaine and fuperfluous, and invented to no other end but for pompe and idle pleafure!" Chap. xxvi. p. 36. A tranflation by James Sandford [appeared in 1569].

[5] Drayton's *Heroical Epift.* p. 87, b. edit. 1598.

Alexandria, for burning ſhips at a diſtance. The Arabians called this pillar *Hemadeſlaeor*, or the Pillar of the Arabians.[1] I think it is mentioned by Sandys. Roger Bacon has left a tract on the formation of burning-glaſſes :[2] and he relates that the firſt burning-glaſs which he conſtructed coſt him ſixty pounds of Pariſian money.[3] Ptolemy, who ſeems to have been confounded with Ptolemy the Egyptian aſtrologer and geographer, was famous among the Eaſtern writers and their followers for his ſkill in operations of glaſs. Spenſer mentions a miraculous tower of glaſs built by Ptolemy, which concealed his miſtreſs the Egyptian Phao, while the inviſible inhabitant viewed all the world from every part of it.

> Great Ptolmœe it for his lemans ſake[4]
> Ybuilded all of glaſſe by Magicke powre,
> And alſo it impregnable did make.

But this magical fortreſs, although impregnable, was eaſily broken in pieces at one ſtroke by the builder, when his miſtreſs ceaſed to love. One of Boiardo's extravagances is a prodigious wall of glaſs built by ſome magician in Africa, which obviouſly betrays its foundation in Arabian fable and Arabian philoſophy.[5]

The Naked Sword, another of the gifts preſented by the ſtrange knight to Cambuſcan, endued with medical virtues, and ſo hard as to pierce the moſt ſolid armour, is likewiſe an Arabian idea. It was ſuggeſted by their ſkill in medicine, by which they affected to communicate healing qualities to various ſubſtances,[6] and by their knowledge of tempering iron and hardening all kinds of metal.[7] It

---

[1] The ſame fablers have adapted a ſimilar fiction to Hercules : that he erected pillars at Cape Finiſterre, on which he raiſed magical looking-glaſſes. In the *Seven Wiſe Maſters*, at the ſiege of Hur in Perſia, certain philoſophers terrified the enemy by a device of placing a habit (ſays an old Engliſh tranſlation) " of a giant-like proportion on a tower, and covering it with burning-glaſſes, looking-glaſſes of criſtall, and other glaſſes of ſeveral colours, wrought together in a marvellous order," &c. ch. xvii. p. 182, edit. 1674. The Conſtantinopolitan Greeks poſſeſſed theſe arts in common with the Arabians. See Moriſotus, ii. 3, who ſays that, in the year 751, they ſet fire to the Saracen fleet before Conſtantinople by means of burning-glaſſes.

[2] MSS. Bibl. Bodl. Digb. 183, and Arch. A. 149. But I think it was printed at Frankfort, 1614, 4to.

[3] Twenty pounds ſterling. *Compend. Stud. Theol.* c. i. p. 5, MS.

[4] *Fairy Queen*, iii. [c. 2, ſt. 20, edit. Morris].

[5] Hither we might alſo refer Chaucer's *Houſe of Fame*, which is built of glaſs, and Lydgate's *Temple of Glaſs*. It is ſaid in ſome romances written about the time of the Cruſades, that the city of Damaſcus was walled with glaſs. See Hall's *Satires*, &c. b. iv. s. 6, written [before] 1597 :

> " Or of Damaſcus magicke wall of glaſſe,
> Or Solomon his ſweating piles of braſſe," &c.

[6] The notion, mentioned before, that every ſtone of Stone-henge was waſhed with juices of herbs in Africa, and tinctured with healing powers, is a piece of the ſame philoſophy.

[7] Montfaucon cites a Greek chemiſt of the dark ages, " Chriſtiani Labyrinthus Salomonis, de temperando ferro, conficiendo cryſtallo, et de aliis naturæ arcanis." *Palæogr. Gr.* p. 375.

is the claffical fpear of Peleus, perhaps originally fabricated in the fame regions of fancy :

> And other folk have wondred on the fwerd,[1]
> That wolde paffe thorughout every thing ;
> And fel in fpeche of Thelophus the kyng,
> And of Achilles for his queynte fpere,
> For he couthe with hit bothe hele and dere,[2]
> Right in fuch wyfe as men maye with the fwerd,
> Of which right now ye have your-felven herd.
> They fpeken of fondry hardyng of metal,
> And fpeken of medicines therwithal,
> And how and whan it fchulde harded be, &c.

The fword which Berni, in the *Orlando Innamorato*, gives to the hero Ruggiero is tempered by much the fame fort of magic :

> Quel brando con tal tempra fabbricato,
> Che taglia incanto, ed ogni fatatura.[3]

So alfo his continuator Ariofto :

> Non vale incanto, ov'elle mette il taglio.[4]

And the notion that this weapon could refift all incantations is like the fiction above mentioned of the buckler of the Arabian giant Ben Gian, which baffled the force of charms and enchantments made by giants or demons.[5] Spenfer has a fword endued with the fame efficacy, the metal of which the magician Merlin mixed with the juice of meadow-wort, that it might be proof againft enchantment ; and afterwards, having forged the blade in the flames of Etna, he gave it hidden virtue by dipping it feven times in the bitter waters of Styx.[6] From the fame origin is alfo the golden lance of Berni, which Galafron, King of Cathaia, father of the beautiful Angelica and the invincible champion Argalia, procured for his fon by the help of a magician. This lance was of fuch irrefiftible power, that it unhorfed a knight the inftant he was touched with its point.

> e una lancia d'oro
> Fatto con arte, e con fottil lavoro.
>   E quella lancia di natura tale,
> Che refifter non puoffi alla fua fpinta ;
> Forza, o deftrezza contra lei non vale,
> Convien che l'una, e l'altra refti vinta :
> Incanto, a cui non è nel Mondo eguale,
> L'ha di tanta poffanza intorno cinta,
> Che nè il Conte di Brava, nè Rinaldo,
> Nè il Mondo al colpo fuo ftarebbe faldo.[7]

Britomart in Spenfer is armed with the fame enchanted fpear, which was made by Bladud, an ancient Britifh king fkilled in magic.[8]

---

[1] [Morris's *Chaucer*, ii. 362, ver. 228.]
[2] hurt; wound.   [3] *Orl. Innam.* ii. 17, ft. 13.   [4] *Orl. Fur.* xii. 83.
[5] [In 1694 was printed the *Hiftory of Amadis of Greece, fon of Lifwart of Greece, and the fair Onoloria of Trebifond.* This worthy is called the Knight of the Burning Sword.] See *Don Quixote*, B. iii. ch. iv.
[6] *Fairy Queen*, ii. viii. 20. See alfo Arioft. xix. 84.
[7] [Berni's] *Orl. Innam.* i. i. [43-4]. See alfo i. ii. ft. 20, &c. And Ariofto, viii. 17, xviii. 118, xxiii. 15.
[8] *Fairy Queen*, iii. 3, 60, iv. 6, 6, iii. 1, 4.

The ring, a gift to the king's daughter Canace, which taught the language of birds, is alſo quite in the ſtyle of ſome others of the occult ſciences of theſe inventive philoſophers;[1] and it is the faſhion of the Oriental fabuliſts to give language to brutes in general. But to underſtand the language of birds was peculiarly one of the boaſted ſciences of the Arabians, who pretend that many of their country-men have been ſkilled in the knowledge of the language of birds ever ſince the time of King Solomon. Their writers relate that Balkis, the Queen of Sheba or Saba, had a bird called *Hudhud,* that is, a lapwing, which ſhe diſpatched to King Solomon on various occaſions, and that this truſty bird was the meſſenger of their amours. We are told that Solomon having been ſecretly informed by this winged confidant that Balkis intended to honour him with a grand embaſſy, encloſed a ſpacious ſquare with a wall of gold and ſilver bricks, in which he ranged his numerous troops and attendants in order to receive the ambaſſadors, who were aſtoniſhed at the ſuddenneſs of theſe ſplendid and unexpected preparations.[2] Herbelot tells a curious ſtory of an Arab feeding his camels in a ſolitary wilderneſs, who was accoſted for a draught of water by Alhejaj, a famous Arabian commander, who had been ſeparated from his retinue in hunting. While they were talking together, a bird flew over their heads, making at the ſame time an unuſual ſort of noiſe, which the camel-feeder hearing, looked ſteadfaſtly on Alhejaj, and demanded who he was. Alhejaj, not chooſing to return him a direct anſwer, deſired to know the reaſon of that queſtion. " Becauſe," replied the camel-feeder, " this bird aſſured me that a company of people is coming this way, and that you are the chief of them." While he was ſpeak-ing, Alhejaj's attendants arrived.[3]

This wonderful ring alſo imparted to the wearer a knowledge of the qualities of plants, which formed an important part of the Arabian philoſophy.[4]

> The vertu of this ryng, if ye wol heere,[5]
> Is this, that who-ſo luſt it for to were
> Upon hir thomb, or in hir purs to bere,
> Ther is no foul that fleeth under the heven,
> That ſche ne ſchal underſtonden his ſteven,[6]
> And know his menyng openly and pleyn,
> And anſwer him in his langage ayeyn ;
> And every gras that groweth upon roote

---

[1] Rings are a frequent implement in romantic enchantment. Among a thouſand inſtances, ſee *Orland. Innam.* i. 14, where the palace and gardens of Dragontina vaniſh at Angelica's ring of virtue.

[2] *Dict. Oriental.* v. Balkis, p. 182. Mahomet believed this fooliſh ſtory, at leaſt thought it fit for a popular book, and has therefore inſerted it in the Alcoran. See Grey's note in *Hudibras,* part i. cant. i. v. 547.

[3] Herbel. *ubi ſupr.* v. *Hegiage Ebn Yuſef Al Thakeſi.* p. 442. This Arabian commander was of the eighth century. In the *Seven Wiſe Maſters* one of the tales is founded on the language of birds, ch. xvi.

[4] See what is ſaid of this in the *Diſſertations.*

[5] [Morris's *Chaucer,* ii. 359, ver. 138.]   [6] [voice.]

Sche ſchal eek knowe, to whom it wol do boote,
Al be his woundes never ſo deep and wyde.

Every reader of taſte and imagination muſt regret that, inſtead of our author's tedious detail of the quaint effeҫts of Canace's ring, in which a falcon relates her amours, and talks familiarly of Troilus, Paris, and Jaſon, the notable achievements we may ſuppoſe to have been performed by the aſſiſtance of the horſe of braſs are either loſt, or that this part of the ſtory, by far the moſt intereſting, was never written. After the ſtrange knight has explained to Cambuſcan the management of this magical courſer, he vaniſhes on a ſudden, and we hear no more of him.

And after ſouper goth this noble kyng [1]
To ſee this hors of bras, with al his route
Of lordes and of ladyes him aboute.
Swich wondryng was ther on this hors of bras,[2]
That ſethen this grete ſiege of Troye was,
Ther as men wondred on an hors alſo,
Ne was ther ſuch a wondryng as was tho.
But fynally the kyng aſkede the knight
The vertu of this courſer, and the might,
And prayd him tellen of his governaunce.
The hors anoon gan for to trippe and daunce,
Whan *that* the knight leyd hand upon his rayne,
*   *   *   *
Enformed when the kyng was of the knight,
And hadde conceyved in his wit aright
The maner and the forme *of* al this thing,
Ful glad and blith, this noble doughty kyng
Repeyryng to his revel, as biforn,
The bridel is unto the tour i-born,[3]
And kept among his jewels leef and deere;
The hors vanyſcht, I not in what manere.

---

[1] [Morris's *Chaucer*, ii. 364, ver. 294.]

[2] Cervantes mentions a horſe of wood which, like this of Chaucer, on turning a pin in his forehead, carried his rider through the air. [A ſimilar fiҫtion occurs in the *Arabian Nights' Entertainments*, and muſt be in the recolleҫtion of every reader.] This horſe, Cervantes adds, was made by Merlin for Peter of Provence; with it that valorous knight carried off the fair Magalona. The reader ſees the correſpondence with the fiҫtion of Chaucer's horſe, and will refer it to the ſame original. See *Don Quixote*, B. iii. ch. 8. We have the ſame thing in *Valentine and Orſon*, ch. xxxi. [The romance alluded to by Cervantes is entitled " La Hiſtoria de la linda Magalona hija del rey de Napoles y de Pierres de Provença," printed at Seville 1533, and is a tranſlation from a much more ancient and very celebrated French romance under a ſimilar title.—*Ritſon*. The French romance is confeſſedly but a tranſlation : "Ordonnée en ceſtui languaige . . . et fut mis en ceſtui languaige l'an mil cccclvii." A Provençal romance on this ſubjeҫt, doubtleſſly the original, was written by Bernard de Treviez, a canon of Maguelone, before the cloſe of the twelfth century. See Raynouard, *Poeſies des Troubadours*, vol. ii. p. 317. On the authority of Gariel, *Idee de la ville de Montpelier*, Petrarch is ſtated to have correҫted and embelliſhed this romance.—*Price*. Of this extremely popular book there were numerous editions in French and Spaniſh, and there is one in German. See Brunet, laſt edit. iv. 643-8.]

[3] The bridel of the enchanted horſe is carried into the tower, which was the treaſury of Cambuſcan's caſtle, to be kept among the jewels. Thus when King Richard I. in a cruſade, took Cyprus, among the treaſures in the caſtles are recited

By such inventions we are willing to be deceived. These are the triumphs of deception over truth :

> Magnanima menſogna, hor quando è al vero
> Si bello, che ſi poſſa à te preporre ?

The *Clerke of Oxenfordes Tale*, or the ſtory of Patient Griſelda, is the next of Chaucer's Tales in the ſerious ſtyle, which deſerves mention. The Clerk declares in his Prologue, that he learned this tale of Petrarch[1] at Padua. But it was the invention of Boccaccio, and is the laſt in his *Decameron*.[2] Petrarch, although moſt intimately connected with Boccaccio for near thirty years, never had ſeen the *Decameron*, till juſt before his death. It accidentally fell into his hands, while he reſided at Arqua, between Venice and Padua, in 1374. The tale of Griſelda ſtruck him more than any:—ſo much, that he got it by heart to relate it to his friends at Padua. Finding that it was the moſt popular of all Boccaccio's tales, for the benefit of thoſe who did not underſtand Italian, and to ſpread its circulation, he tranſlated it into Latin with ſome alterations. Petrarch relates this in a letter to Boccaccio: and adds that, on ſhowing the tranſlation to one of his Paduan friends, the latter, touched with the tenderneſs of the ſtory, burſt into ſuch frequent and violent fits of tears, that he could not read to the end. In the ſame letter he ſays that a Veroneſe, having heard of the Paduan's exquiſiteneſs of feeling on this occaſion, reſolved to try the experiment. He read the whole aloud from the beginning to the end, without the leaſt change of voice or countenance; but on returning the book to Petrarch con-feſſed that it was an affecting ſtory: " I ſhould have wept," added he, " like the Paduan, had I thought the ſtory true. But the whole is a manifeſt fiction. There never was, nor ever will be, ſuch a wife as Griſelda."[3] Chaucer, as our Clerk's declaration in the Prologue ſeems to imply, received this tale from Petrarch, and not from Boccaccio: and I am inclined to think, that he did not take it from Petrarch's Latin tranſlation, but that he was one of thoſe friends to whom Petrarch uſed to relate it at Padua. This too ſeems ſuffi-ciently pointed out in the words of the Prologue :

---

precious ſtones and golden cups, together with " *Sellis aureis* frenis *et calcaribus.*" Vineſauf, *Iter. Hieroſol.* cap. xli. p. 328. *Vet. Script. Angl.* tom. ii.

[1] [Morris's *Chaucer*, ii. 279. Mr. Thomas Wright ſtates in his ed. of the *Cant. Tales*, that Chaucer tranſlates his *Clerk's Tale* " cloſely from Petrarch's Latin Romance *De Obedientiâ et fide Uxoriâ Mythologia.*"—F.]

[2] Giorn. x. Nov. 10. Dryden, in the ſuperficial but lively Preface to his *Fables* ſays, " The Tale of Griſilde was the invention of Petrarch : by him ſent to Boccace, from whom it came to Chaucer."

It may be doubted whether Boccaccio invented the ſtory of Griſelda. For, as Tyrwhitt obſerves, it appears by a Letter of Petrarch to Boccaccio, pp. 540-7, edit. Baſil. 1581, *Opp. Petrarch*, ſent with his Latin tranſlation, in 1373, that Petrarch had heard the ſtory with pleaſure, many years before he ſaw the *Decameron*, vol. iv. p. 157.

[3] *Vie de Petrarque*, iii. 797.

I wil yow telle a tale, which that I[1]
Lerned at Padowe of a worthy clerk,

* * * * *

Fraunces Petrark, the laureat poete,
Highte this clerk, whos rethorique fwete
Enlumynd al Ytail of poetrie.

Chaucer's tale is alfo much longer, and more circumftantial, than Boccaccio's. Petrarch's Latin tranflation from Boccaccio [has been printed more than once].[2] It is in the royal library at Paris, in that of Magdalen College at Oxford, [among Laud's MSS. in the Bodleian],[3] and in Bennet College library.[4]

The ftory foon became fo popular in France, that the comedians of Paris reprefented a myftery in French verfe entitled *Le Myftere de Grifelidis Marquis de Saluces*, in the year 1393.[5] [Before, or in the fame year, the French profe verfion in *Le Ménagier de Paris* was compofed, and there is an entirely different verfion in the Imperial Library.[6]] Lydgate, almoft Chaucer's cotemporary, in his poem entitled the *Temple of Glafs*,[7] among the celebrated lovers painted on the walls of the temple,[8] mentions Dido, Medea and Jafon,

---

[1] [Morris's Chaucer, ii. 278, ver. 26]. Afterwards Petrarch is mentioned as dead. He died of an apoplexy, Jul. 18, 1374. See ver. 36.

[2] [See Brunet, laft edit. iv. 569-71, for a tolerably copious account of the editions of this tract in Latin, French, and German. Alfo for the *Epiftola in Waltherum*.] Among the royal MSS. in the Britifh Mufeum, there is, "Fr. Petrarchæ fuper Hiftoriam Walterii Marchionis et Grifeldis uxoris ejus." 8. B. vi. 17.

[3] MS. 177, 10, fol. 76; 275, 14, fol. 163. Again, ibid. 458, 3, with the date 1476, I fuppofe, from the fcribe.

[4] MSS. Laud, G. 80.

[5] [This piece was printed at Paris about 1550; it has been reprinted in facfimile from the (fuppofed unique) copy in the Bibl. Imperiale. See Brunet, iii. 1968-9 (laft edit.) The earlieft French] theatre is that of Saint Maur, and its commencement is placed in the year 1398. Afterwards Apoftolo Zeno wrote a theatrical piece on this fubject in Italy. I need not mention that it is to this day reprefented in England, on a ftage of the loweft fpecies, and of the higheft antiquity : I mean at a puppet-fhow. The French have this ftory in their *Parement des dames*. See *Mem. Lit.* tom. ii. p. 743, 4to.

[6] [Catal. No. 7999, edit. Paulin Paris.]

[7] And in a Balade, tranflated by Lydgate from the Latin, "Grifildes humble patience" is recorded. Urr. Ch. p. 550, ver. 108.

[8] There is a more curious mixture in [Gower's] *Balade to king Henry IV.*, where Alexander, Hector, Julius Cæfar, Judas Maccabeus, David, Jofhua, Charlemagne, Godfrey of Boulogne, and King Arthur, are [affociated as the Nine Worthies]. Ver. 281, *feq.* But it is to be obferved, that the French had a metrical romance called *Judas Macchabée*, begun by Gualtier de Belleperche, before 1240. It was finifhed a few years afterwards by Pierros du Reiz. Fauch. p. 197. See alfo Lydgate, [*apud*] Urr. Chauc. p. 550, ver. 89. Sainte Palaye has given us an extract of an old Provençal poem in which, among heroes of love and gallantry, are enumerated Paris, Sir Triftram, Ivaine the inventor of gloves and other articles of elegance in drefs, Apollonius of Tyre, and King Arthur. *Mem. Chev.* (Extr. de Poes. Prov.) ii. p. 154. In a French romance, *Le livre de cuer d'amour efpris*, written 1457, the author introduces the blazoning of the arms of feveral celebrated lovers : among which are King David, Nero, Mark Antony, Thefeus, Hercules, Eneas, Sir Lancelot, Sir Triftram, Arthur duke of Brittany, Gafton de Foix, many French dukes, &c. *Mem. Lit.* viii. p. 592, edit. 4to. The Chevalier Bayard, who

Penelope, Alceſtis, Patient Griſelda, Bel Iſoulde and Sir Triſtram,[1] Pyramus and Thiſbe, Theſeus, Lucretia, Canace, Palamon and Emilia.[2]

The pathos of this poem, which is indeed exquiſite, chiefly conſiſts in invention of incidents and the contrivance of the ſtory, which cannot conveniently be developed in this place ; and it will be im-poſſible to give any idea of its eſſential excellence by exhibiting detached parts. The verſification is equal to the reſt of our author's poetry.

SECTION XVI.

THE *Tale of the Nonnes Prieſt* is perhaps a ſtory of Engliſh growth. The ſtory of the cock and the fox is evidently borrowed from a collection of Æſopean and other fables, written by Marie [de France[3]], whoſe *Lays* [have been publiſhed.] Beſide the abſolute reſemblance, it appears ſtill more probable that Chaucer copied from Marie, becauſe no ſuch fable is to be found either in the Greek *Æſop*, or in any of the Latin Æſopean compilations of the dark ages.[4] All the manuſcripts of Marie's fables in the Britiſh Muſeum prove, that ſhe tranſlated her work " *de l'Anglois en Roman.*" Probably her Engliſh original was Alfred's Anglo-Saxon verſion of Æſop moderniſed, and ſtill bearing his name. She profeſſes to follow the verſion of a king who, in the beſt of the Harleian copies, is called *Li reis Alured.*[5] She appears, from paſſages in her *Lais*, to have underſtood Engliſh.[6] I will give her Epilogue to the Fables :[7]

> Al finement de ceſt eſcrit
> Qu'en romanz ai treite e dit
> Me numerai pour remembraunce
> Marie ai nun ſui de France
> Pur cel eſtre que clerc pluſur
> Prendreient ſur eus mun labeur
> Ne voit que nul ſur li ſa die
> Eil feit que fol que ſei ublie
> Pur amur le cunte Wllame

---

died about the year 1524, is compared to Scipio, Hannibal, Theſeus, King David, Samſon, Judas Maccabeus, Orlando, Godfrey of Boulogne, and Monſieur de Paliſſe, marſhal of France. [*Les geſtes enſemble la vie du preulx cheualier Bayard,* &c., printed in 1525.]

[1] From *Mort d'Arthur.* They are mentioned in Chaucer's *Aſſemble of Fowles,* ver. 290. See alſo *Compl. Bl. Kn.* ver. 367.

[2] MSS. Bibl. Bodl. (Fairfax 16).

[3] [By M. Roquefort, 1820, 2 vols. 8vo. Dr. Mall is preparing a new edition of Marie's *Lais* for 1871, with a much improved text.]

[4] [See MSS. Harl. 978, f. 76.]   [5] [*Ibid.* 978, *ſupr. citat.*]

[6] See Chaucer's *Canterb. Tales,* vol. iv. p. 179 [edit. Tyrwhitt].

[7] MSS. James, viii. p. 23, Bibl. Bod.

Le plus vaillant de nul realme
M'entremis de cefte livre feire
E des Engleis en romanz treire
Efop apelum ceft livre
Quil tranflata e fift efcrire
Del Gru en Latin le turna
Le Reiz Alurez que mut lama
Le tranflata puis en Engleis
E jeo lai rimee en Franceis
Si cum jeo poi plus proprement
Ore pri a dieu omnipotent, &c.

The figment of Dan Burnell's Afs is taken from a Latin poem entitled *Speculum Stultorum*,[1] written by Nigellus Wirecker [or Willhelmus Vigellus], monk and precentor of Canterbury cathedral and a profound theologift, who flourifhed about the year 1200.[2] The narrative of the two pilgrims is borrowed from Valerius Maximus.[3] It is alfo related by Cicero, a lefs known and a lefs favourite author.[4] There is much humour in the defcription of the prodigious confufion which happened in the farm-yard after the fox had conveyed away the cock :

> and after him thay ranne,[5]
> And eek with ftaves many another manne ;
> Ran Colle our dogge, and Talbot, and Garlond,[6]
> And Malkyn, with a diftaf in hir hond ;
> Ran cow and calf, and eek the verray hogges
> * * * *
> The dokes criden as men wold hem quelle ;[7]
> The gees for fere flowen over the trees ;
> Out of the hyves cam the fwarm of bees.

Even Jack Straw's infurrection, a recent tranfaction, was not attended with fo much noife and difturbance :

> So hidous was the noyfe, a *benedicite !*[8]
> Certes *he* Jakke Straw, and his meyné,
> Ne maden fchoutes never half fo fchrille, &c.

The importance and affectation of fagacity with which Dame Partlett communicates her medical advice, and difplays her knowledge in phyfic, is a ridicule on the ftate of medicine and its profeffors.

In another ftrain, the cock is thus beautifully defcribed, and not without fome ftriking and picturefque allufions to the manners of the times :

---

[1] ver. 1427.

[2] [The name of the author is varioufly given, and in fome of the later impreffions the title of the work is : *Liber qui intitulatur Brunellus in fpeculo Stultorum,* &c. See Brunet, laft edit. v. 1215. The earlieft edition appears to be that *fine ullâ notâ,* folio (Cologne, between 1471 and 1478).] It is a common MS. Burnell is a nick-name for Balaam's afs in the *Chefter Whitfun Plays.* MSS. Harl. 2013.

[3] ver. 1100. [4] See *Val. Max.* i. 7. And *Cic. de Divinat.* i. 27.

[5] [Morris's *Chaucer,* iii. 246, ver. 561.] [6] names of dogs. [7] kill.

[8] *Ibid.* This is a proof that the *Canterbury Tales* were not written till after the year 1381.

> a cok, hight Chaunteclere,[1]
> In al the lond of crowyng was noon his peere.
> His vois was merier than the mery orgon,[2]
> On maſſe dayes that in the chirche goon ;
> Wel ſikerer[3] was his crowyng in his logge,[4]
> Than is a clok, or an abbay orologge.
> *   *   *   *
> His comb was redder than the fyne coral,
> And batayld,[5] as it were a caſtel wal.
> His bile was blak, and as the geet it ſchon ;
> Lik aſur were his legges, and his ton ;[6]
> His nayles whitter than the lily flour,
> And lik the burniſcht gold was his colour.

In this poem the fox is compared to the three arch-traitors Judas Iſcariot, Virgil's Sinon, and Ganilion who betrayed the Chriſtian army under Charlemagne to the Saracens, and is mentioned by Archbiſhop Turpin.[7] Here alſo are cited, as writers of high note or authority, Cato, Phyſiologus or [Florinus] the elder, Boethius on muſic, the author of the legend of the life of Saint Kenelm, Joſephus, the hiſtorian of Sir Lancelot du Lak, Saint Auſtin, [Arch]biſhop Bradwardine, Geoffrey Vineſauf (who wrote a monody in Latin verſe on the death of King Richard I.), Eccleſiaſtes, Virgil and Macrobius.

Our author's *January and May,* or the *Merchant's Tale,* ſeems to be an old Lombard ſtory. But many paſſages in it are evidently taken from the *Polycraticon* of John of Saliſbury ;[8] and by the way, about forty verſes belonging to this argument are tranſlated from the ſame chapter of the *Polycraticon,* in the *Wife of Bath's Prologue.*[9] In the mean time it is not improbable, that this tale might have originally been Oriental. A Perſian tale has been publiſhed which it extremely

---

[1] [Morris's *Chaucer,* iii. 230, ver. 29.]   [2] organ.   [3] [ſurer.—*Ritſon.*]
[4] pen ; yard.   [5] embattelled.   [6] toes.
[7] ver. 407. See alſo *Monk. T.* ver. 399.
[8] " De moleſtiis et oneribus conjugiorum ſecundum Hieronymum et alios phi-loſophos. Et de pernicie libidinis. Et de mulieris Epheſinæ et ſimilium fide." L. iii. c. 11, fol. 193, b. edit. 1513.
[9] Mention is made in this Prologue of St. Jerom and Theophraſt, on that ſub-ject, ver. 671, 674. The author of the *Polycraticon* quotes Theophraſtus from Jerom, viz. " Fertur auctore *Hieronimo* aureolus *Theophraſti* libellus de non ducenda uxore," fol. 194, a. Chaucer likewiſe, on this occaſion, cites *Valerie,* ver. 671. This is not the favorite hiſtorian of the middle ages, Valerius Maximus. It is a book written under the aſſumed name of Valerius, entitled *Valerius ad Rufinum de non ducenda uxore.* This piece is in the Bodleian library with a large gloſs. MSS. Digb. 166, ii. 147. [It is a common MS. and is one of the productions aſcribed to Walter Mapes. See Wright's edit. of Mapes, 1841. The author] perhaps adopted this name, becauſe one Valerius had written a treatiſe on the ſame ſubject, inſerted in St. Jerom's works. Some copies of this Prologue, inſtead of " Valerie and *Theophraſt,*" read *Paraphraſt.* If that be the true reading, which I do not believe, Chaucer alludes to the gloſs above mentioned. *Helowis,* cited juſt after-wards, is the celebrated Eloiſa. Trottula is mentioned, ver. 677. Among the MSS. of Merton College in Oxford, is, " Trottula Mulier Salernitana de paſſionibus mulierum." There is alſo extant, " Trottula, ſeu potius Erotis medici muliebrium liber." Baſil. 1586, 4to. See alſo Montfauc. *Catal. MSS.* p. 385. And Fabric. *Bibl. Gr.* xiii. p. 439.

refembles;[1] and it has much of the allegory of an Eaftern apologue.

The following defcription of the wedding-feaft of January and May is conceived and expreffed with a diftinguifhed degree of poetical elegance :

> Thus ben thay weddid with folempnité ;[2]
> And atte feft fittith he and fche
> With othir worthy folk upon the deys.[3]
> Al ful of joy and blis is that paleys,
> And ful of inftrumentz, and of vitaile,
> The mofte deintevous of al Ytaile.
> Biforn hem ftood fuch inftruments of foun,
> That Orpheus, ne of Thebes Amphioun,
> Ne maden never fuch a melodye.
> At every cours ther cam loud menftralcye,
> That never tromped[4] Joab for to heere,
> Ne he Theodomas yit half fo cleere
> At Thebes, whan the cite was in doute.[5]
> Bachus the wyn hem fchenchith[6] al aboute,
> And Venus laughith upon every wight,
> (For January was bycome hir knight,
> And wolde bothe affayen his corrage
> In liberté and eek in mariage)
> And with hir fuyrbrond in hir hond aboute
> Daunceth bifore the bryde and al the route.

---

[1] [Tales tranflated from the Perfian (by Alex. Dow), 1768,] ch. xv. p. 252.

The ludicrous adventure of the Pear Tree, in *January and May*, is taken from a colle&tion of Fables in Latin elegiacs, written by one Adolphus in the year 1315. Leyfer. *Hift. Poet. Med. Ævi*, p. 2008. [They are printed entire in Wright's *Latin Stories*, &c. 1842, 174-91.] The fame fable is in Caxton's *Æfop*. [Adolphus took many of his ftories from Alfonfus.]

[2] [Morris's *Chaucer*, ii. 332, ver. 465.]

[3] I have explained this word, but will here add fome new illuftrations of it. Undoubtedly the high table in a public refe&tory, as appears from thefe words in Matthew Paris, " Priore prandente ad magnam menfam quam Dais vulgo appellamus." *Vit. Abbat. S. Albani*, p. 92. And again the fame writer fays, that a cup, with a foot or ftand, was not permitted in the hall of the monaftery, " Nifi tantum in majori menfa quam Dais appellamus." *Additam.* p. 148. There is an old French word, Dais, which fignifies a throne or canopy, ufually placed over the head of the principal perfon at a magnificent feaft. Hence it was transferred to the *table* at which he fat. In the ancient French *Roman de Garin :*

" Au plus haut dais fift roy Anfeis."

Either at the firft table, or, which is much the fame thing, under the higheft canopy.

[I apprehend that [dais] originally fignified the wooden floor : [*d'ais*] Fr. *de affibus*, Lat.] which was laid at the upper end of the hall, as we ftill fee it in college halls, &c. That part of the room therefore which was floored with planks, was called the *dais* (the reft being either the bare ground, or at beft paved with ftone) ; and being raifed above the level of the other parts, it was often called the *high dais*. As the principal table was always placed upon a dais, it began very foon, by a natural abufe of words, to be called itfelf *a dais* ; and people were faid to fit at the *dais*, inftead of at the table upon the *dais*. Menage, whofe authority feems to have led later antiquaries to interpret *dais* a *canopy*, has evidently confounded *deis* with *ders*, [which] as he obferves, meant properly the hangings at the back of the company. But as the fame hangings were often drawn over, fo as to form a kind of canopy over their heads, the whole was called a *ders.—Tyrwhitt.*]

[4] " fuch as Joab never," &c.   [5] danger.   [6] fill, pour.

And certeynly I dar right wel faye this,
Imeneus, that god of weddyng is,
Seigh never his lif fo mery a weddid man.
Holde thy pees, thow poete Marcian,
That writeſt us that ilke weddyng merye
Of hir Philologie and him Mercurie,
And of the fonges that the Mufes fonge;
To fmal is bothe thy penne and eek thy tonge
For to defcrive of this mariage.
Whan tender youthe hath weddid ftoupyng age.

* * * *

Mayus, that fit with fo benigne a cheere,
Hir to bihold it femede fayerye;[1]
Queen Efther lokede never with fuch an ye
On Affuere, fo meke a look hath fche;
I may not yow devyfe al hir beauté;
But thus moche of hir beauté telle I may,
That fche was lyk the brighte morw of May,
Fulfild of alle beauté and plefaunce.
   This January is ravyfcht in a traunce,
At every tyme he lokith in hir face,
But in his hert he gan hir to manace.

Dryden and Pope have modernifed the two laft-mentioned poems. Dryden the tale of the *Nonnes Prieſt*, and Pope that of *January and May:* intending perhaps to give patterns of the beft of Chaucer's Tales in the comic fpecies. But I am of opinion that the *Miller's Tale* has more true humour than either. Not that I mean to palliate the levity of the ftory, which was moft probably chofen by Chaucer in compliance with the prevailing manners of an unpoliſhed age, and agreeably to ideas of feftivity not always the moft delicate and refined. Chaucer abounds in liberties of this kind, and this muft be his apology. So does Boccaccio, and perhaps much more, but from a different caufe. The licentioufnefs of Boccaccio's tales, which he compofed *per cacciar la malincolia delle femine,* to amufe the ladies, is to be vindicated, at leaft accounted for, on other principles: it was not fo much the confequence of popular incivility, as it was owing to a particular event of the writer's age. Juft before Boccaccio wrote, the plague at Florence had totally changed the cuftoms and manners of the people. Only a few of the women had furvived this fatal malady; and thefe, having loft their hufbands, parents, or friends, gradually grew regardlefs of thofe conftraints and cuftomary formalities which before of courfe influenced their behaviour. For want of female attendants, they were obliged often to take men only into their fervice: and this circumftance greatly contributed to deftroy their habits of delicacy, and gave an opening to various freedoms and indecencies unfuitable to the fex, and frequently productive of very ferious confequences. As to the monafteries, it is not furprifing that Boccaccio fhould have made them the fcenes of his moft libertine ftories. The plague had thrown open their gates. The monks and nuns wandered abroad, and partaking of the common

---

[1] A phantafy, enchantment.

liberties of life and the levities of the world, forgot the rigour of their inftitutions and the feverity of their ecclefiaftical characters. At the ceafing of the plague, when the religious were compelled to return to their cloifters, they could not forfake their attachment to thefe fecular indulgences; they continued to practife the fame free courfe of life, and would not fubmit to the difagreeable and unfocial injunctions of their refpective orders. Cotemporary hiftorians give a fhocking reprefentation of the unbounded debaucheries of the Florentines on this occafion : and ecclefiaftical writers mention this period as the grand epoch of the relaxation of monaftic difcipline. Boccaccio did not efcape the cenfure of the Church for thefe compofitions. His converfion was a point much laboured; and in expiation of his follies he was almoft perfuaded to renounce poetry and the heathen authors, and to turn Carthufian. But, to fay the truth, Boccaccio's life was almoft as loofe as his writings; till he was in great meafure reclaimed by the powerful remonftrances of his mafter Petrarch, who talked much more to the purpofe than his confeffor. This Boccaccio himfelf acknowledges in the fifth of his eclogues, entitled *Philofotrophos*, which like thofe of Petrarch are enigmatical and obfcure.

But to return to the *Miller's Tale*. The character of the Clerk of Oxford, who ftudied aftrology, a fcience then in high repute, but, under the fpecious appearance of decorum and the mafk of the ferious philofopher, carried on intrigues, is painted with thefe lively circumftances : [1]

> This clerk was cleped heende Nicholas ; [2]
> Of derne[3] love he cowde and of folas;
> And therwith he was fleigh and ful privé,
> And lik *to* a mayden meke for to fe.
> A chambir had he in that hoftillerye[4]
> Alone, withouten eny compaignye,
> Ful fetifly i-dight with herbes foote,
> And he himfelf as fwete as is the roote
> Of lokorys, or eny cetewale.[5]
> His almageft,[6] and bookes gret and fmale,
> His aftrylabe,[7] longyng *to* his art,
> His augrym ftoones,[8] leyen faire apart

---

[1] [Morris's *Chaucer*, ii. 99, ver. 13.]   [2] the gentle Nicholas.   [3] fecret.
[4] Hofpitium, one of the old hoftels at Oxford, which were very numerous before the foundation of the colleges. This is one of the citizens' houfes; a circumftance which gave rife to the ftory.
[5] the herb Valerian.
[6] A book of aftronomy written by Ptolemy. It was in thirteen books. He wrote alfo four books of judicial aftrology. He was an Egyptian aftrologift, and flourifhed under Marcus Antoninus. He is mentioned in the *Sompnour's Tale*, v. 1025, and the *Wife of Bath's Prologue*, v. 324.
[7] aftrylabe ; an aftrolabe.
[8] ftones for computation. Augrim is Algorithm, the fum of the principal rules of common arithmetic. Chaucer was himfelf an adept in this fort of knowledge. The learned Selden is of opinion, that his Aftrolabe was compiled from the Arabian aftronomers and mathematicians. See his pref. to *Notes on Drayt. Polyolb.* p. 4, where the word Dulcarnon (*Troil. Cr.* ii. vol. iv. 933, 935,) is explained to be an

On fchelves couched at his beddes heed,
His preffe[1] i-covered with a faldyng reed.
And al above ther lay a gay fawtrye,
On which he made a-nightes melodye,
So fwetely, that al the chambur rang;
And *Angelus ad virginem* he fang.

In the defcription of the young wife of our philofopher's hoft, there is great elegance with a mixture of burlefque allufions. Not to mention the curiofity of a female portrait, drawn with fo much exactnefs at fuch a diftance of time.

Fair was the yonge wyf, and therwithal[2]
As eny wefil hir body gent and final.
A feynt fche were*de*, barred al of filk ;[3]
A barm-cloth eek as whit as morne mylk
Upon hir lendes, ful of many a gore.
Whit was hir fmok, and browdid al byfore
And eek byhynde on hir coler aboute,
Of cole-blak filk, withinne and eek withoute.
The tapes of hir white voluper
Weren of the fame fute of hire coler ;
Hir filet brood of filk y-fet ful heye.
And certeynly fche hadd a licorous eyghe ;
Ful fmal y-pulled weren hir browes two,
And tho were bent, as blak as a*n*y flo.
Sche was wel more blisful on to fee
Than is the newe perjonette tree ;
And fofter than the wol is of a wethir.
And by hir gurdil hyng a purs of lethir,
Taffid[4] with filk, and perled[5] with latoun.[6]
In al this world to feken up and doun

Arabic term for a root in calculation. His *Chanon Yeman's Tale* proves his intimate acquaintance with the Hermetic philofophy, then much in vogue. There is a ftatute of Henry V. againft the tranfmutation of metals in Stat. an. 4, Hen. V. cap. iv. [1416-17]. Chaucer, in the Aftrolabe, refers to two famous mathematicians and aftronomers of his time, John Some and Nicholas Lynne, both Carmelite friars of Oxford, and perhaps his friends, whom he calls " reverent clerkes." *Aftrolabe*, p. 440, col. i. Urr. They both wrote calendars which, like Chaucer's *Aftrolabe*, were conftructed for the meridian of Oxford. Chaucer mentions Alcabucius, an aftronomer, that is, Abdilazi Alchabitius, whofe [*Introductorium ad fcientiam judicialem aftronomiæ* was printed in 1473 and afterwards.] Compare Herbelot, *Bibl. Oriental.* p. 963, b. Ketab. *Alafthorlab.* p. 141, a. Nicholas Lynne above mentioned is faid to have made feveral voyages to the moft northerly parts of the world, charts of which he prefented to Edward III. Perhaps to Iceland, and the coafts of Norway, for aftronomical obfervations. Thefe charts are loft. Hakluyt apud Anderfon, *Hift. Com.* i. p. 191, *fub. ann.* 1360. (See Hakl. *Voy.* i. 121, *feq.* ed. 1598.)

[1] prefs.   [2] [Morris's *Chaucer*, ii. 100, ver. 47.]
[3] " A girdle [ftriped] with filk." The *Doctor of Phific* is " girt with a feint of filk with barris fmale." Prol. v. 138. See [Halliwell's *Arch. Dict.* in v.]
[4] taffeled ; fringed.
[5] [I believe ornamented with latoun in the fhape of pearls.—*Tyrwhitt.* An expreffion ufed by Francis Thynne in his letter to Speght will explain this term : " and Orfrayes being compounded of the French *or* and *frays*, (or *fryfe* Englifh,) is that which to this daye (being now made all of one ftuffe or fubftance) is called frifed or perled cloth of gold."—*Price.*]
[6] latoun, or chekelaton, is cloth of gold.

There nys no man fo wys, that couthe thenche
So gay a popillot,[1] or fuch a wenche.
For brighter was the *fchynyng* of hir hewe,
Than in the Tour the noble[2] i-forged newe.
But of hir fong, it was as lowde and yerne[3]
As eny fwalwe chiteryng on a berne.
Therto fche cowde fkippe, and make *a* game,
As eny kyde or calf folwyng his dame.
Hir mouth was fweete as bragat[4] is or meth,
Or hoord of apples, layd in hay or heth.
Wynfyng fche was, as is a joly colt ;
Long as a maft, and upright as a bolt.[5]
A broch[6] fche bar upon hir loue coleer,
As brod as is the bos of a bocleer.[7]
Hir fchos were laced on hir legges heyghe.

Nicholas, as we may fuppofe, was not proof againft the charms of
his blooming hoftefs. He has frequent opportunities of converfing
with her ; for her hufband is the carpenter of Ofeney Abbey near
Oxford, and often abfent in the woods belonging to the monaftery.[8]
His rival is Abfalom, a parifh-clerk, the gayeft of his calling, who
being amoroufly inclined, very naturally avails himfelf of a circumftance belonging to his profeffion : on holidays it was his bufinefs to
carry the cenfer about the church, and he takes this opportunity of
cafting unlawful glances on the handfomeft dames of the parifh. His
gallantry, agility, affectation of drefs and perfonal elegance, fkill in
fhaving and furgery, fmattering in the law, tafte for mufic, and many
other accomplifhments, are thus inimitably reprefented by Chaucer,
who muft have much relifhed fo ridiculous a character :

Now þer was of that chirche a parifch clerk,[9]
The which that was i-cleped Abfolon.
Crulle was his heer, and as the gold it fchon,
And ftrowted as a fan right large and brood ;
Ful ftreyt and evene lay his joly fchood.[10]
His rode[11] was reed, his eyghen gray as goos,
With Powles wyndowes corven in his fchoos.[12]

---

[1] " fo pretty a puppet." [This may either be confidered as a diminutive from
poupée a puppet, or as a corruption of *papillot*, a young butterfly.—*Tyrwhitt.*]
[2] a piece of money.
[3] [brifk, eager.—*Tyrwhitt.*]
[4] bragget. A drink made of honey, fpices, &c.
[5] " ftraight as an arrow."
[6] a jewel. [It feems to have fignified originally the tongue of a buckle or clafp,
and from thence the buckle or clafp itfelf. It probably came by degrees to fignify
any kind of jewel.—*Tyrwhitt.*]
[7] buckler.   [8] [See Morris's *Chaucer*, ii. 113, ver. 479.]

" I trow that he be went
For tymber, ther our abbot hath him fent :
For he is wont for timber for to go,
And dwellen at the Graunge a day or tuo."

[9] [Morris's *Chaucer*, vol. ii. p. 102, ver. 126.]   [10] hair.
[11] complexion.
[12] *Calcei feneftrati* occur in ancient Injunctions to the clergy. In Eton College
ftatutes, given in 1446, the fellows are forbidden to wear *fotularia roftrata*, as alfo
caligæ, white, red, or green, cap. xix. In a chantry, or chapel founded at Win-

In his hofes reed he went*e* fetufly.
I-clad he was ful fmal and propurly,
Al in a kirtel [1] of a fyn wachet,
Schapen with goores in the newe get.
And therupon he had a gay furplys,
As whyt as is the blofme upon the rys.[2]
A mery child he was, fo God me fave ;
Wel couthe he lete blood, and clippe and fchave,
And make a chartre of lond and acquitaunce.
In twenty maners he coude fkip*pe* and daunce,
After the fcole of Oxenforde tho,
And with his legges caften to and fro ;
And pleyen fonges on a fmal rubible ; [3]
Ther-to he fang fom tyme a lowde quynyble.[4]

His manner of making love muft not be omitted. He ferenades
her with his guittar :

He waketh al the night and al the day,[5]
To kembe his lokkes brode and made him gay.
He woweth hire by mene and by brocage,[6]
And fwor he wolde ben hir owne page.
He fyngeth crowyng [7] as a nightyngale ;
And fent hire pyment, meth, and fpiced ale,
And wafres pypyng hoot out of the gleede ; [8]
And for fche was of toune, he profred*e* meede.[9]

* * * * *

---

chefter in the year 1318, within the cemetery of the Nuns of the Bleffed Virgin,
by Roger Inkpenne, the members, that is, a warden, chaplain and clerk, are ordered to go "in meris caligis, et fotularibus non roftratis, nifi forfitan *botis* uti
voluerint." And it is added, "Veftes deferant non *fibulatas*, fed defuper claufas,
vel *brevitate* non notandas." *Regiftr. Priorat. S. Swithini Winton.* MS. *fupr. citat.*
quatern. 6. Compare Wilkins's *Concil.* iii. 670, ii. 4.

[1] jacket. [2] [branch.]
[3] A fpecies of guitar. Lydgate, MSS. Bibl. Bodl. Fairf. 16. In a poem
called *Reafon and Senfuallite, compiled by Jhon Lydgate :*

> "Lutys, rubibis (l. ribibles), and geternes,
> More for eftatys than tavernes."

[4] treble. [5] [Morris's *Chaucer*, ii. 104, ver. 187.]
[6] by offering money : or a fettlement. [7] quavering. [8] the [fire].
[9] See *Rime of Sir Thopas*, ver. 3357. Mr. Walpole has mentioned fome curious
particulars concerning the liquors which anciently prevailed in England. *Anecd.
Paint.* i. p. 11. I will add, that cider was very early a common liquor among our
anceftors. In the year 129[4-]5, an. 23 Edw. I. the king orders the fheriff of
Southampton [Hampfhire] to provide with all fpeed four hundred quarters of
wheat, to be collected in parts of his bailiwick nearest the fea, and to convey the
fame, being well winnowed, in good fhips from Portfmouth to Winchelfea. Alfo
to put on board the faid fhips, at the fame time, two hundred tons of cider. The
coft to be paid immediately from the king's wardrobe. This precept is in old
French. *Regiftr. Joh. Pontiffar. Epifc. Winton.* fol. 172. It is remarkable that
Wickliffe tranflates, Luc. i. 21, "He fchal not dryncke wyn & *cyfer*" [edit. 1848].
This tranflation was made about A.D. 1380. At a vifitation of St. Swithin's priory
at Winchefter, by the faid bifhop, it appears that the monks claimed to have, among
other articles of luxury, on many feftivals, "Vinum, tam album quam rubeum,
claretum medonem, burgaraftrum," &c. This was fo early as the year 1285.
Regiftr. Priorat. S. Swith. Winton. MS. *fupr. citat.* quatern. 5. It appears alfo,
that the *Hordarius* and *Camerarius* claimed every year of the prior ten *dolia vini,*
or twenty pounds in money, A.D. 1337. *Ibid.* quatern. 5. A benefactor grants to
the faid convent on the day of his anniverfary, "unam pipam vini pret. xx. *s.*" for

Som tyme, to fchewe his lightnes and maiftrye,
He pleyeth Herodz on a fcaffold hye.

Again:

Whan that the firfte cok hath crowe, anoon [1]
Up ryft this jolyf lover Abfolon,
And him arrayeth gay, at poynt devys.
But firft he cheweth greyn [2] and lycoris,
To fmellen fwete, or he hadde kempt his heere.
Under his tunge a trewe love he beere,
For therby wende he to be gracious.
He rometh to the carpenteres hous. [3]

In the mean time the fcholar, intent on accomplifhing his intrigue, locks himfelf up in his chamber for the fpace of two days. The carpenter, alarmed at this long feclufion, and fuppofing that his gueft might be fick or dead, tries to gain admittance, but in vain. He peeps through a crevice of the door, and at length difcovers the fcholar, who is confcious that he was feen, in an affected trance of abftracted meditation. On this our carpenter, reflecting on the danger of being wife, and exulting in the fecurity of his own ignorance, exclaims:

A man woot litel what him fchal betyde. [4]
This man is falle with his aftronomye

their refection, A.D. 1286. *Ibid.* quatern. 10. Before the year 1200, "Vina et medones" are mentioned as not uncommon in the abbey of Evefham in Worcefter-fhire. Dugdale, *Monaft.* [edit. Stevens,] Append. p. 138. The ufe of mead, *medo,* feems to have been very ancient in England. See *Mon. Angl.* i. 26. Thorne, *Chron.* fub ann. 1114. Compare *Differtat.* i. It is not my intention to enter into the controverfy concerning the cultivation of vines, for making wine, in England. I fhall only bring to light the following remarkable paffage on that fubject from an old Englifh writer on gardening and farming: " We might have a reafonable good wine growyng in many places of this realme: as undoubtedly wee had immediately after the Conqueft; tyll partly by flouthfulneffe, not liking any thing long that is painefull, partly by civill difcord long continuyng, it was left, and fo with tyme loft, as appeareth by a number of places in this realme that keepe ftill the name of Vineyardes: and uppon many cliffes and hilles, are yet to be feene the rootes and olde remaynes of Vines. There is befides Nottingham, an auncient houfe called Chilwell, in which houfe remayneth yet, as an auncient monument, in a Great Wyndowe of Glaffe, the whole Order of planting, pruyning, [pruning,] ftamping, and preffing of vines. Befide, there [at that place] is yet alfo growing an old vine, that yields a grape fufficient to make a right good wine, as was lately proved. There hath, moreover, good experience of late years been made, by two noble and honourable barons of this realme, the lorde Cobham and the lorde Wylliams of Tame, who had both growyng about their houfes, as good wines as are in many parts of Fraunce," &c. [Herefbachius] *Foure bookes of Hufbandry,* [tranflated by B. Googe,] 1578. *To the Reader.*

[1] [Morris's *Chaucer,* ii. 114, ver. 501.]

[2] Greyns, or grains, of Paris or Paradife occurs in the *Romaunt of the Rofe,* ver. 1369. A rent of herring pies is an old payment from the city of Norwich to the king, feafoned among other fpices with half an ounce of grains of Paradife. Blomf. *Norf.* ii. 264.

[3] It is to be remarked, that in this tale the carpenter fwears, with great propriety, by the patronefs faint of Oxford, faint Fridefwide, [Morris's *Chaucer,* ii. 106, ver. 262]:

" This carpenter to bleffen him bygan,
And feyde, Now help us, feynte Fridefwyde."

[4] *Ibid.* ver. 264.

In fom woodneffe, or in fom agonye.
I thought ay wel how that it fchulde be.
Men fchulde nought knowe [1] of Goddes pryvyté.
Ye ! bleffed be alwey a lewed man, [2]
That nat but oonly his bileeve can. [3]
So ferde another clerk with aftronomye ;
He walked in the feeldes for to prye
Upon the fterres, what ther fchulde bifalle,
Til he was in a marle pit i-falle.
He faugh nat that. But yet, by feint Thomas !
Me reweth fore for heende Nicholas ;
He fchal be ratyd of his ftudyyng.

But the fcholar has ample gratification for this ridicule. The carpenter is at length admitted ; and the fcholar continuing the farce, gravely acquaints the former that he has been all this while making a moft important difcovery by means of aftrological calculations. He is foon perfuaded to believe the prediction : and in the fequel, which cannot be repeated here, this humorous contrivance crowns the fcholar's fchemes with fuccefs, and proves the caufe of the carpenter's difgrace. In this piece the reader obferves that the humour of the characters is made fubfervient to the plot.

I have before hinted, that Chaucer's obfcenity is in great meafure to be imputed to his age. We are apt to form romantic and exaggerated notions about the moral innocence of our anceftors. Ages of ignorance and fimplicity are thought to be ages of purity. The direct contrary, I believe, is the cafe. Rude periods have that groffnefs of manners which is not lefs friendly to virtue than luxury itfelf. In the middle ages, not only the moft flagrant violations of modefty were frequently practifed and permitted, but the moft infamous vices. Men are lefs afhamed as they are lefs polifhed. Great refinement multiplies criminal pleafures, but at the fame time prevents the actual commiffion of many enormities : at leaft it preferves public decency, and fuppreffes public licentioufnefs.

The *Reve's Tale*, or the *Miller of Trompington*, is much in the fame ftyle, but with lefs humour. [4] This ftory was enlarged by Chaucer from Boccaccio. [5] There is an old Englifh poem on the fame plan, entitled : *A ryght pleafaunt and merye Hiftorie of the Mylner of Abyngdon,*

---

[1] " pry into the fecrets of nature."   [2] unlearned.
[3] Who knows only his Creed.
[4] See alfo *The Shipman's Tale*, which was originally taken from fome comic French trouvere. But Chaucer had it from Boccaccio. The ftory of Zenobia, in the *Monkes Tale*, is from Boccaccio's *Cas. Vir. Illuftr.* (fee *Lydg. Boch.* viii. 7). That of Count Ugolins in the fame tale, from Dante. That of Pedro of Spain, from Archbifhop Turpin, *ibid.* Of Julius Cæfar, from Lucan, Suetonius, and Valerius Maximus, *ibid.* The idea of this tale was fuggefted by Boccaccio's book on the fame fubject.
[5] *Decamer.* Giorn. ix. Nov. 6. But both Boccaccio and Chaucer probably borrowed from an old Conte or Fabliau by an anonymous French rhymer, *De Gombert, et de deux Clers.* See [Le Grand,] *Fabliaux et Contes*, Paris, 1756, tom. ii. p. 115 —124. The *Shipman's Tale*, as I have hinted, originally came from fome fuch French Conteur, through the medium of Boccaccio.

with his wife and his fayre daughter, and of two poore fchollers of Cambridge.[1] It begins with thefe lines:

> Fayre lordings, if you lift to heere
> A mery jeft your minds to cheere.

This piece is fuppofed by Wood [without much foundation, perhaps] to have been written by Andrew Borde.[2] It was at leaft evidently written after the time of Chaucer. It is the work of fome taftelefs imitator, who has fufficiently difguifed his original, by retaining none of its fpirit. I mention thefe circumftances, left it fhould be thought that this frigid abridgment was the ground-work of Chaucer's poem on the fame fubject. In the clafs of humorous or fatirical tales, the *Sompnour's Tale*, which expofes the tricks and extortions of the mendicant friars, has alfo diftinguifhed merit. This piece has incidentally been mentioned above with the *Plowman's Tale* and Pierce Plowman.

Genuine humour, the concomitant of true tafte, confifts in difcerning improprieties in books as well as characters. We therefore muft remark under this clafs another tale of Chaucer, which till lately has been looked upon as a grave heroic narrative. I mean the *Rime of Sir Thopas*. Chaucer, at a period which almoft realifed the manners of romantic chivalry, difcerned the leading abfurdities of the old romances: and in this poem, which may be juftly called a prelude to Don Quixote, has burlefqued them with exquifite ridicule. That this was the poet's aim, appears from many paffages. But, to put the matter beyond a doubt, take the words of an ingenious critic. "We are to obferve," fays he, "that this was Chaucer's own Tale: and that, when in the progrefs of it, the good

---

[1] [Abingdon is fituated on a mill-ftream, feven miles from Cambridge. See *Remains of the Early Popular Poetry of England*, iii. 98, *et. feqq.* The fcene of Chaucer's ftory is called *The Old Mill.* See Wright's *Anecdota Literaria*, 1844, where the fabliau, above referred to, will be found printed.]

Bibl. Bodl. Selden, C. 39, 4to. This book was given to that library, with many other petty black-letter hiftories, in profe and verfe, of a fimilar caft, by Robert Burton, author of the *Anatomy of Melancholy*, who was a great collector of fuch pieces. One of his books, now in the Bodleian, is the *Hiftory of Tom Thumb* [1630, 8vo,] whom a learned antiquary [Tho. Hearne], while he laments that ancient hiftory has been much difguifed by romantic narratives, pronounces to have been no lefs important a perfonage than King [Edgar's] dwarf.

[2] See Wood's *Athen. Oxon.* v. *Borde*, and [*Reliq. Hearn.* 1857, 822.] I am of opinion that Solere Hall, in Cambridge, mentioned in this poem, was Aula Solarii,—the hall with the upper ftory, at that time a fufficient circumftance to diftinguifh and denominate one of the academical hofpitia. Although Chaucer calls it, "a grete college," ver. 881. Thus in Oxford we had Chimney Hall, Aula cum Camino, an almoft parallel proof of the fimplicity of their ancient houfes of learning. Twyne alfo mentions Solere Hall, at Oxford. Alfo Aula Salarii, which I doubt not is properly Solarii. Compare Wood, *Ath. Oxon.* ii. 11, col. i. 13, col. i. 12, col. ii. Caius will have it to be Clare Hall.—*Hift. Acad.* p. 57. Thofe who read Scholars Hall (of Edw. III.) may confult Wacht. *v.* Soller. In the mean time, for the reafons affigned, one of thefe two halls or colleges at Cambridge might at firft have been commonly called Soler Hall. A hall near Brazenofe College, Oxford, was called Glazen Hall, having glafs windows, anciently not common. See Twyne, *Mifcel. Quædam*, &c. ad calc. *Apol. Antiq. Acad. Oxon.* [1608].

fenfe of the hoft is made to break in upon him, and interrupt him, Chaucer approves his difguft, and changing his note, tells the fimple inftructive tale of *Meliboeus—a moral tale vertuous*, as he terms it; to fhow what fort of fictions were moft expreffive of real life, and moft proper to be put into the hands of the people. It is further to be noted, that the *Boke* of *The Giant Olyphant and Chylde Thopas*, was not a fiction of his own, but a ftory of antique fame, and very celebrated in the days of chivalry; fo that nothing could better fuit the poet's defign of difcrediting the old romances, than the choice of this venerable legend for the vehicle of his ridicule upon them.[1]" But it is to be remembered, that Chaucer's defign was intended to ridicule the frivolous defcriptions and other tedious impertinences, fo common in the volumes of chivalry with which his age was overwhelmed, not to degrade in general or expofe a mode of fabling, whofe fublime extravagances conftitute the marvellous graces of his own Cambufcan; a compofition which at the fame time abundantly demonftrates, that the manners of romance are better calculated to anfwer the purpofes of pure poetry, to captivate the imagination, and to produce furprife, than the fictions of claffical antiquity.

SECTION XVII.

BUT Chaucer's vein of humour, although confpicuous in the *Canterbury Tales*, is chiefly difplayed in the characters with which they are introduced. In thefe his knowledge of the world availed him in a peculiar degree, and enabled him to give fuch an accurate picture of ancient manners, as no contemporary nation has tranfmitted to pofterity. It is here that we view the purfuits and employments, the cuftoms and diverfions of our anceftors, copied from the life, and reprefented with equal truth and fpirit, by a judge of mankind whofe penetration qualified him to difcern their foibles or difcriminating peculiarities, and by an artift, who underftood that proper felection of circumftances and thofe predominant characteriftics, which form a finifhed portrait.[2] We are furprifed to find, in fo grofs and ignorant an age, fuch talents for fatire and for obfervation

---

[1] [Warton feems to have been writing at random, when he defcribed *Sir Thopas* as "a ftory of antique fame." It is, on the contrary, a broad burlefque of Chaucer's own invention, as the whole context appears clearly to fhow. Tyrwhitt gravely obferves, as Price notes: "I can only fay, that I have not been fo fortunate as to meet with any traces of fuch a ftory of an earlier date than the Canterbury Tales,"—nor has any one elfe!]

[2] [Compare with Chaucer's fketches of 1380-90 with that of A.D. 1592, by Greene, in his *Quip for an Upftart Courtier*, copied and enlarged from Thynne's *Pride and Lowlines*, written before 1570. See *Temporary Preface to Six-Text Chaucer*, pp. 101-2.—F.]

on life ; qualities which ufually exert themfelves at more civilifed
periods, when the improved ftate of fociety, by fubtilifing our fpeculations, and eftablifhing uniform modes of behaviour, difpofes mankind to ftudy themfelves, and renders deviations of conduct and
fingularities of character more immediately and neceffarily the objects
of cenfure and ridicule. Thefe curious and valuable remains are
fpecimens of Chaucer's native genius, unaffifted and unalloyed. The
figures are all Britifh, and bear [comparatively faint marks] of Claffical,
Italian, or French imitation. The characters of Theophraftus are
not fo lively, particular, and appropriated. A few traits from this
celebrated part of our author, yet too little tafted and underftood,
may be fufficient to prove and illuftrate what is here advanced.

The character of the Priorefs is chiefly diftinguifhed by an excefs
of delicacy and decorum, and an affectation of courtly accomplifhments. [French of Stratford-at-Bow appears, in our poet's time, to
have been a, fort of bye-word] :

> Ther was alfo a Nonne, a Priorefle,[1]
> That of hire fmylyng was ful fymple and coy;
> Hire gretteft ooth nas but by feynt Loy ;[2]
> ⁕　　　⁕　　　⁕
> And Frenfch fche fpak ful faire and fetyfly,
> Aftur the fcole of Stratford atte Bowe,
> For Frenfch of Parys was to hire unknowe.
> At mete[3] wel i-taught was fche withalle ;
> Sche leet no morfel from hire lippes falle,

---

[1] [Morris's *Chaucer*, ii. 5, ver. 118.]
[2] *Saint Loy*, i.e. [Sanctus Eligius. T. This faint is mentioned by Lyndfay in his *Monarche*.] The fame oath occurs in the *Frere's Tale*, v. 300.
[3] dinner. [The Priorefs's exact behaviour at table is copied from *Rom. Rofe*, 14178—14199.

"Et bien fe garde," &c.

To fpeak French is mentioned above among her accomplifhments. There is a
letter in old French from Queen Philippa and her daughter Ifabel to the Prior of
Saint Swithin's at Winchefter, to admit one Agnes Patfhull into an eleemofynary
fifterhood belonging to his convent. The Prior is requefted to grant her, "Une
Lyvere en votre Maifon dieu de Wynceftere et eftre un des foers," for her life.
Written at *Windefor*, Apr. 25. The year muft have been about 1350. *Regiftr.
Priorat. MS.* fupr. citat. quatern. xix. fol. 4. I do not fo much cite this inftance
to prove that the Prior muft be fuppofed to underftand French, as to fhew that it
was now the court language ; and even on a matter of bufinefs there was at leaft
a great propriety that the queen and princefs fhould write in this language,
although to an ecclefiaftic of dignity. In the fame Regifter, there is a letter in old
French from the Queen Dowager Ifabel to the Prior and Convent of Winchefter ;
to fhew, that it was at her requeft, that King Edward III. her fon had granted a
church in Winchefter diocefe, to the monaftery of Leeds in Yorkfhire, for their
better fupport, "a trouver fis chagnoignes chantans tous les jours en la chapele du
Chaftel de Ledes, pour laime madame Alianore reyne d'Angleterre," &c. A.D.
1341, quatern. vi.

The Priorefs's *greateft* oath is by Saint Eloy. I will here throw together fome
of the moft remarkable oaths in the Canterbury Tales. The Hoft fwears by *my
father's foule.* Urr. p. 7, 783. Sir Thopas, by *ale and breade*, p. 146, 3377.
Arcite, by *my pan*, i.e. *head.* p. 10, 1167. Thefeus, by *mightie Mars the red*, p.
14, 1749. Again, *as he was a trew knight*, p. 9, 961. The Carpenter's wife, by
faint Thomas of Kent, p. 26, 183. The Smith, by *Chriftes foote*, p. 29, 674. The

Ne wette hire fyngres in hire fauce deepe.
Wel cowde fche carie a morfel, and wel keepe,
That no drope *ne* fil uppon hire brefte.
In curtefie was fett al hire lefte.[1]
Hire overlippe wypud*e* fche fo clene,
That in hire cuppe *ther* was no ferthing fene
Of grees, whan fche dronken hadde hire draught.
Ful femely aftur hire mete fche raught.[2]

*   *   *   *

And peyned hire to counterfete cheere
Of court, and ben eftatlich of manere.

She has even the falfe pity and fentimentality of many modern ladies :

Sche was fo charitable and fo pitous,[3]
Sche wolde weepe if that fche fawe a mous
Caught in a trappe, if it were deed or bledde.
Of fmale houndes hadde fche, that fche fedde
With roftud fleifsh, and mylk, and waftel breed.[4]
But fore wepte fche if oon of hem were deed,
Or if men fmot it with a yerde[5] fmerte :
And al was confcience and tendre herte.

The *Wife of Bath* is more amiable for her plain and ufeful qualifications. She is a refpectable dame, and her chief pride confifts in being a confpicuous and fignificant character at church on a Sunday.

Of cloth-makyng[6] fhe hadde fuch an haunt,[7]
Sche paffed hem of Ypris and of Gaunt.
In al the parifshe wyf ne was ther noon
That to the offryng byforn hire fchulde goon,
And if ther dide, certeyn fo wroth was fche,
That fche was thanne out of alle charité.
Hire keverchefs[8] weren ful fyne of grounde ;
I durfte fwere they weyghede ten pounde.

Cambridge Scholar, by *my father's kinn*, p. 31, 930. Again, by *my croune*, ib. 933. Again, for *godes benes*, or *benifon*, p. 32, 965. Again, by *feint Cuthberde.* ib. 1019. Sir Johan of Boundis, by *feint Martyne*, p. 37, 107. Gamelyn, by *goddis hoke*, p. 38, 181. Gamelyn's brother, by *faint Richere*, ibid. 273. Again, by *Criftis ore*, ib. 279. A Franklen, by *faint Jame that in Galis is*, i.e. Saint James of Galicia, p. 40, 549, 1514. A Porter, by *Goddis berde*, ib. 581. Gamelyn, by *my hals*, or neck, p. 42, 773. The Mafter Outlaw, by the *gode rode*, p. 45, 1265. The Hoft, by the *precious corpus Madrian*, p. 160, 4. Again, by *faint Paulis bell*, p. 168, 893. The Man of Law, *Depardeux*, p. 49, 39. The Marchaunt, by *faint Thomas of Inde*, p. 66, 745, The Sompnour, by *goddis armis two*, p. 82, 833. The Hoft, by *cockis bonis*, p. 106, 2235. Again, by *naylis* and by *blode*, i.e. of Chrift, p. 130, 1802. Again, by *faint Damian*, p. 131, 1824. Again, by *faint Runion*, ib. 1834. Again, by *Corpus domini*, ib. 1838. The Riotter, by *Goddis digne bones*, p. 135, 2211. The Hoft, to the Monk, by *your father kin*, p. 160, 43. The Monk, by his *porthofe*, or breviary, p. 139, 2639. Again, by *God and faint Martin*, ib. 2656. The Hoft, by *armis blode and bonis*, p. 24, 17. [See *Popular Antiquities of Great Britain*, 1870, ii. 248-50.]

[1] pleafure, defire.   [2] [reached].
[3] [Morris's *Chaucer*, ii. 5, ver. 143.]
[4] bread of a finer fort.   [5] ftick.
[6] It is to be obferved, that fhe lived in the neighbourhood of Bath ; a country famous for clothing [at that] day.
[7] [Morris's *Chaucer*, ii. 15, ver. 447.]   [8] head-drefs.

That on a Sonday were upon hire heed.
Hir hofen were of fyn fcarlett reed,
Ful ftreyte y-teyed, and fchoos ful moyfte and newe
Bold was hir face, and fair, and reed of hewe.
Sche was a worthy womman al hire lyfe,
Houfbondes atte chirche dore[1] hadde fche fyfe.

The *Franklin* is a country gentleman, whofe eftate confifted in
free land, and was not fubject to feudal fervices or payments. He
is ambitious of fhewing his riches by the plenty of his table : but his
hofpitality, a virtue much more practicable among our anceftors than
at prefent, often degenerates into luxurious excefs. His impatience,
if his fauces were not fufficiently poignant, and every article of his
dinner in due form and readinefs, is touched with the hand of Pope
or Boileau. He had been a prefident at the feffions, knight of the
fhire, a fheriff, and a coroner :[2]

An houfehaldere, and that a gret, was he ;[3]
Seynt Julian he was in his countré.[4]
His breed, his ale, was alway after oon ;
A bettre envyned[5] man was nowher noon.
Withoute bake mete was never his hous,
Of fleiffch and fiffch, and that fo plentyvous,
It fnewed[6] in his hous of mete and drynk*e*,
Of alle deyntees that men cowde thynk*e*.
Aftur the fondry fefouns of the yeer,
He chaunged hem at mete[7] and at foper.
Ful many a fat partrich had he in mewe,
And many a brem and many a luce[8] in ftewe.
Woo was his cook, but if his fauce were
Poynant and fcharp, and redy al his ger*e*.
His table dormant[9] in his halle alway
Stood redy covered al the longe day.

The character of the *Doctor of Phific* preferves to us the ftate of
medical knowledge and the courfe of medical erudition then in
fafhion. He treats his patients according to rules of aftronomy :
a fcience which the Arabians engrafted on medicine.

For he was groundud in aftronomye.[10]
He kepte his pacient wondurly wel
In houres by his magik naturel.

---

[1] At the fouthern entrance of Norwich cathedral, a reprefentation of the
Efpoufals, or facrament of marriage, is carved in ftone ; for here the hands of the
couple were joined by the prieft, and great part of the fervice performed. Here
alfo the bride was endowed with what was called *Dos ad oftium ecclefiæ*. This
ceremony is exhibited in a curious old picture engraved by Mr. Walpole, *Anecd.
Paint.* i. 31, [reprefenting a *Spofalizio*, but fuppofed by him to reprefent the marriage of Henry VII. Refpecting thefe alleged hiftorical paintings, fee fome
valuable remarks by Mr. John Gough Nichols in *Notes and Queries*, 3d S. x. 61,
131.] Compare Marten. *Rit. Eccl. Anecdot.* ii. p. 630. And Hearne's *Antiquit.
Glaftonb.* Append. p. 310.
[2] An office anciently executed by gentlemen of the greateft refpect and property.
[3] [Morris's *Chaucer*, ii. 11, ver. 339.]
[4] See [*Popular Antiquities of Great Britain*, 1870, i. 303.]
[5] [ftored with wine.—*Tyrwhitt*.]   [6] fnowed.   [7] dinner.
[8] pike.   [9] never removed.
[10] [Morris's *Chaucer*, ii. 14, ver. 414.]

Petrarch leaves a legacy to his physician John de Dondi of Padua,
who was likewise a great aftronomer, in the year 1370.[1] It was a
long time before the medical profeffion was purged from thefe fuperftitions. Hugo de Evefham, born in Worcefterfhire, one of the
moft famous phyficians in Europe, about the year 1280, educated in
both the univerfities of England, and at others in France and Italy,
was eminently fkilled in mathematics and aftronomy.[2] Pierre
d'Apono, a celebrated profeffor of medicine and aftronomy at Padua,
wrote commentaries on the problems of Ariftotle, in the year 1310.
Roger Bacon fays, " aftronomiæ pars melior medicina."[3] In the
ftatutes of New-College at Oxford, given in 1387, medicine and
aftronomy are mentioned as one and the fame fcience. Charles V.
of France, who was governed entirely by aftrologers, and who commanded all the Latin treatifes which could be found relating to the
ftars to be tranflated into French, eftablifhed a college in the univerfity of Paris for the ftudy of medicine and aftrology.[4] There is
a fcarce and very curious book, entitled : " *Novæ medicinæ methodus
curandi morbos ex mathematica fcientia deprompta, nunc denuo revifa,*
&c. Joanne Hasfurto Virdungo, medico et aftrologo doctiffimo,
auctore. 1518."[5] Hence magic made a part of medicine. In the
Marchaunts Second Tale, or *Hiftory of Beryn,* falfely afcribed to
Chaucer, a furgical operation of changing eyes is partly performed
by the affiftance of the occult fciences :

> The whole fcience of all furgery,[6]
> Was unyd, or the chaunge was made of both eye,
> With many fotill enchantours, and eke nygrymauncers,
> That fent wer for the nonis, maiftris, and fcoleris.

Leland mentions one William Glatifaunt, an aftrologer and phyfician, a fellow of Merton College in Oxford, who wrote a medical
tract, which, fays he, " nefcio quid Magiæ fpirabat.[7] " I could add
many other proofs.[8]

The books which our phyfician ftudied are then enumerated :

> Wel knew he the olde Efculapius,[9]
> And Deifcorides, and eeke Rufus;
> Old Ypocras, Haly, and Galien ;
> Serapyon, Razis, and Avycen ;
> Averrois, Damafcen, and Conftantyn ;
> Bernard, and Gatifden, and Gilbertyn.

Rufus, a phyfician of Ephefus, wrote in Greek, about the time of
Trajan. Some fragments of his works ftill remain.[10] Haly was a
famous Arabian aftronomer, and a commentator on Galen, in the
eleventh century, which produced fo many famous Arabian phyfi-

---

[1] See *Acad. Infcript.* xx. 443.   [2] Pits, p. 370. Bale, iv. 50, xiii. 86.
[3] Bacon, *Op. Maj.* edit. Jebb, p. 158. See alfo pp. 240, 247.
[4] Montfaucon, *Bibl. MSS.* tom. ii. p. 791, b.   [5] In quarto.
[6] v. 2989, Urr. Ch.
[7] Lel. apud Tann. *Bibl.* p. 262, and Lel. *Script. Brit.* p. 400.
[8] See Ames's *Hift. Print.* p. 147.   [9] [Morris's *Chaucer,* ii. 14, ver. 429.]
[10] Conring. *Script. Com.* Sæc. i. cap. 4, pp. 66, 67. The Arabians have tranflations of him. Herbel. *Bibl. Orient.* p. 972, b; 977, b.

cians.[1] John Serapion, of the fame age and country, wrote on the practice of physic.[2] Avicen, the most eminent physician of the Arabian school, flourished in the fame century.[3] Rhafis, an Afiatic physician, practifed at Cordova in Spain, where he died in the tenth century.[4] Averroes, as the Afiatic schools decayed by the indolence of the Caliphs, was one of those philofophers who adorned the Moorish schools erected in Africa and Spain. He was a profeffor in the university of Morocco. He wrote a commentary on all Ariftotle's works, and died about the year 1160. He was ftyled the moft peripatetic of all the Arabian writers. He was born at Cordova of an ancient Arabic family.[5] John Damafcene, fecretary to one of the Caliphs, wrote in various fciences, before the Arabians had entered Europe, and had feen the Grecian philofophers.[6] Conftantinus Afer, a monk of Caffino in Italy, was one of the Saracen physicians who brought medicine into Europe, and formed the Salernitan school, chiefly by tranflating various Arabian and Grecian medical books into Latin.[7] He was born at Carthage, and learned grammar, logic, geometry, arithmetic, aftronomy, and natural philofophy, of the Chaldees, Arabians, Perfians, Saracens, Egyptians, and Indians, in the fchools of Bagdat. Being thus completely accomplifhed in thefe fciences, after thirty-nine years' ftudy, he returned into Africa, where an attempt was formed againft his life. Conftantine, having fortunately difcovered this defign, privately took fhip and came to Salerno in Italy, where he lurked fome time in difguife. But he was recognized by the Caliph's brother then at Salerno, who recommended him as a fcholar univerfally fkilled in the learning of all nations, to the notice of Robert, Duke of Normandy. Robert entertained him with the higheft marks of refpect; and Conftantine, by the advice of his patron, retired to the monaftery of Caffino where, being kindly received by the abbot Defiderius, he tranflated in that learned fociety the books above mentioned, moft of which he firft imported into Europe. Thefe verfions are faid to

---

[1] *Id. ibid.* Sæc. xi. cap. 5, p. 114. Haly, called Abbas, was likewife an eminent phyfician of this period. He was called *Simia Galeni. Id. ibid.*

[2] *Id. ibid.* pp. 113, 114.

[3] *Id. ibid.* See Pard. T. v. 2407. Urr. p. 136.

[4] Conring. *ut fupr.* Sæc. x. cap. 4, p. 110. He wrote a large and famous work, called *Continens.* Rhafis and Almafor (f. Albumafar, a great Arabian aftrologer) occur in the library of Peterborough Abbey, Matric. *Libr. Monaft. Burgi S. Petri.* Gunton, *Peterb.* p. 187. See Hearne, *Ben. Abb. Præf.* lix.

[5] Conring. *ut fupr.* Sæc. xii. cap. 2, p. 118.

[6] Vofs. *Hift. Gr. L.* ii. c. 24.

[7] Petr. Diacon. *de Vir. illuftr. Monaft. Caffin.* cap. xxiii. See the *Differtations.* He is again mentioned by our author in the *Marchaunt's Tale*, ver. 565.

> " And many a letuary had he ful fyn,
> Such as the curfed monk daun Conftantin
> Hath writen in his book *de Coitu.*"

The title of this book is " De Coitu, quibus profit aut obfit, quibus medicaminibus et alimentis acuatur impediatur-ve." *Opera,* 1536.

be ftill extant. He flourifhed about the year 1086.[1] Bernard, or Bernardus Gordonius, appears to have been Chaucer's contemporary. He was a profeffor of medicine at Montpelier, and wrote many treatifes in that faculty.[2] John Gatifden was a fellow of Merton College, where Chaucer was educated, about the year 1320.[3] Pits fays that he was profeffor of phyfic in Oxford.[4] He was the moft celebrated phyfician of his age in England; and his principal work is entitled *Rofa Medica*, divided into five books, and printed at Paris in 1492.[5] Gilbertine, I fuppofe, is Gilbertus Anglicus, who flourifhed in the thirteenth century, and wrote a popular compendium of the medical art.[6] About the fame time, not many years before Chaucer wrote, the works of the moft famous Arabian authors, and among the reft thofe of Avicen, Averroes, Serapion,

---

[1] See Leo Oftienfis, or P. Diac. Auctar. ad Leon. *Chron. Mon. Caffin.* lib. iii. c. 35, p. 445. *Rerum Italic. Script.* edit. Muratori, iv. In his book *de Incantationibus*, one of his inquiries is, "An invenerim in libris Græcorum hoc qualiter in Indorum libris eft invenire," &c. *Op.* tom. i. *ut fupr.*

[2] Petr. Lambec. *Prodrom.* Sæc. xiv. p. 274, edit. *ut fupr.*

[3] It has been before obferved, that at the introduction of philofophy into Europe by the Saracens, the clergy only ftudied and practifed the medical art. This fafhion prevailed a long while afterwards. The Prior and Convent of S. Swithin's at Winchefter granted to Thomas of Shaftefbury, clerk, a corrody, confifting of two difhes daily from the prior's kitchen, bread, drink, robes, and a competent chamber in the monaftery, for the term of his life. In confideration of all which conceffions the faid Thomas paid them fifty marcs; and moreover is obliged, "defervire nobis *in Arte medicinæ.* Dat. in dom. Capitul. Feb. 15. A.D. 1319." Regiftr. Priorat. S. Swithin. Winton. MS. *fupra citat.* The moft learned and accurate Fabricius has a feparate article on Theologi Medici. *Bibl. Gr.* xii. 739, *feq.* See alfo Giannon. *Iftor. Napol.* l. x. ch. xi. § 491. In the romance of *Sir Guy,* a monk heals the knight's wounds. Signat. G. iiii.:

"There was a *monke* beheld him well
That could of *leach crafte* fome dell."

In Geoffrey of Monmouth, who wrote in 1128, Eopa, intending to poifon Ambrofius, introduces himfelf as a phyfician. But in order to fuftain this character with due propriety, he firft fhaves his head, and affumes the habit of a monk. Lib. viii. c. 14. John Arundel, afterwards bifhop of Chichefter, was chaplain and firft phyfician to Henry VI. in 1458. Wharton, *Angl. Sacr.* i. 777. Faricius, abbot of Abingdon, about 1110, was eminent for his fkill in medicine, and a great cure performed by him is recorded in the regifter of the abbey. Hearne's *Bened. Abb.* Præf. xlvii. King John, while fick at Newark, made ufe of William de Wodeftoke, abbot of the neighbouring monaftery of Croxton, as his phyfician. Bever, *Chron.* MSS. Harl. *apud* Hearne, Præf. *ut fupr.* p. xlix. Many other inftances may be added. The phyficians of the univerfity cf Paris were not allowed to marry till the year 1452. *Menagian.* p. 333. In the fame univerfity anciently, at the admiffion to the degree of doctor in phyfic, they took an oath that they were not married. MSS. Br. Twyne, 8, p. 249. See Freind's *Hift. of Phyfick,* ii. 257.

[4] p. 414.

[5] Tanner, *Bibl.* p. 312. Leland ftyles this work "opus luculentum juxta ac eruditum." *Script. Brit.* p. 355.

[6] Conring. *ut fupr.* Sæc. xiii. cap. 4, p. 127; and Leland, *Script. Brit.* p. 291, who fays that Gilbert's *Practica et Compendium Medicinæ* was moft carefully ftudied by many "ad quæftum properantes." He adds that it was common about this time for Englifh ftudents abroad to affume the furname *Anglicus,* as a plaufible recommendation. [See Wright's *Biog. Brit. Liter.* 1846, A-N. Period, 461-3.]

and Rhafis, above mentioned, were tranflated into Latin.[1] Thefe were our phyfician's library. But having mentioned his books, Chaucer could not forbear to add a ftroke of fatire fo naturally introduced :

His ftudie was but litel on the Bible.[2]

The following anecdotes and obfervations may ferve to throw general light on the learning of the authors who compofe this curious library. The Ariftotelic or Arabian philofophy continued to be communicated from Spain and Africa to the reft of Europe chiefly by means of the Jews : particularly to France and Italy, which were overrun with Jews about the tenth and eleventh centuries. About thefe periods, not only the courts of the Mahometan princes, but even that of the pope himfelf, were filled with Jews. Here they principally gained an eftablifhment by the profeffion of phyfic ; an art then but imperfectly known and practifed in moft parts of Europe. Being well verfed in the Arabic tongue, from their commerce with Africa and Egypt, they had ftudied the Arabic tranflations of Galen and Hippocrates; which had become ftill more familiar to the great numbers of their brethren who refided in Spain. From this fource alfo the Jews learned philofophy ; and Hebrew verfions, made about this period from the Arabic, of Ariftotle and the Greek phyficians and mathematicians, are ftill extant in fome libraries.[3] Here was a beneficial effect of the difperfion and vagabond condition of the Jews : I mean the diffufion of knowledge. One of the moft eminent of thefe learned Jews was Mofes Maimonides, a phyfician, philofopher, aftrologer, and theologift, educated at Cordova in Spain under Averroes. He died about the year 1208. Averroes, being accufed of heretical opinions, was fentenced to live with the Jews in the ftreet of the Jews at Cordova. Some of thefe learned Jews began to flourifh in the Arabian fchools in Spain, as early as the beginning of the ninth century. Many of the treatifes of Averroes were tranflated by the Spanifh Jews into Hebrew : and the Latin pieces of Averroes now extant were tranflated into Latin from thefe Hebrew verfions. I have already mentioned the fchool or univerfity of Cordova. Leo Africanus fpeaks of " Platea bibliothecariorum Cordovæ." This, from what follows, appears to be a ftreet of bookfellers. It was in the time of Averroes, and about the year 1220. One of our Jew philofophers, having fallen in love, turned poet, and his verfes were publicly fold in this ftreet.[4] My author fays that, renouncing the dignity of the Jewifh doctor, he took to writing verfes.[5]

---

[1] Conring. *ut fupr.* Sæc. xiii. cap. 4, p. 126. About the fame time the works of Galen and Hippocrates were firft tranflated from Greek into Latin, but in a moft barbarous ftyle. *Id. ibid.* p. 127.

[2] [Morris's *Chaucer,* ii. 14, ver. 438.]

[3] Eufeb. Renaudot. apud Fabric. *Bibl. Gr.* xii. 254.

[4] Leo African. *De Med. et Philofoph. Hebr.* c. xxviii. xxix.

[5] *Id. ibid.* " Amore capitur, et dignitate doctorum pofthabita cœpit edere carmina." See alfo Simon. in Suppl. ad Leon. Mutinens. *De Ritib. Hebr.* p. 104.

The Sumner or Summoner, whose office it was to summon un-canonical offenders into the archdeacon's court, where they were very rigorously punished, is humorously drawn as counteracting his pro-fession by his example : he is libidinous and voluptuous, and his rosy countenance belies his occupation. This is an indirect satire on the ecclesiastical proceedings of those times. His affectation of Latin terms, which he had picked up from the decrees and pleadings of the court, must have formed a character highly ridiculous :

> And whan that he wel dronken hadde the wyn,[1]
> Than wolde he speke no word but Latyn.
> A fewe termes hadde he, tuo or thre,
> That he hadde lerned out of som decree ;
> No wondur is, he herde it al the day ;
> And eek ye knowe wel, how that a jay
> Can clepe Watte,[2] as wel as can the pope.
> But who-so wolde in othur thing him grope,[3]
> Thanne hadde he spent al his philosophie,
> Ay, *Questio quid juris*, wolde he crye.

He is with great propriety made the friend and companion of the Pardoner, or dispenser of indulgences, who is just arrived from the pope, "brimful of pardons come from Rome al hote;" and who carries in his wallet, among other holy curiosities, the Virgin Mary's veil, and part of the sail of Saint Peter's ship.[4]

The Monk is represented as more attentive to horses and hounds than to the rigorous and obsolete ordinances of Saint Benedict. Such are his ideas of secular pomp and pleasure, that he is even qualified to be an abbot :[5]

> An out-rydere, that lovede venerye ;[6]
> A manly man, to ben an abbot able.
> Ful many a deynté hors hadde he in stable :
>
> *　　*　　*　　*　　*
>
> This ilke[7] monk leet forby hem pace,
> And helde aftur the newe world the space.
> He yaf nat of that text a pulled hen,[8]
> That seith, that hunters been noon holy men.

---

[1] [Morris's *Chaucer*, ii. 20, ver. 637.]
[2] So edit. 1561. See Johnson's *Dictionary*, in Magpie.
[3] examine.   [4] ver. 694, *seq.*
[5] There is great humour in the circumstances which qualify our monk to be an abbot. Some time in the thirteenth century, the prior and convent of Saint Swithin's at Winchester appear to have recommended one of their brethren to the convent of Hyde as a proper person to be preferred to the abbacy of that convent, then vacant. These are his merits. "Est enim confrater ille noster in glosanda sacra pagina bene callens, in scriptura [transcribing] peritus, in capitalibus literis appingendis bonus artifex, in regula S. Benedicti instructissimus, psallendi doctissi. mus," &c. *MS. Registr.* ut supr. p. 277. These were the ostensible qualities of the master of a capital monastery. But Chaucer, in the verses before us, seems to have told the real truth, and to have given the real character as it actually existed in life. I believe that our industrious *confrere*, with all his knowledge of glossing, writing, illuminating, chanting, and Benedict's rules, would in fact have been less likely to succeed to a vacant abbey, than one of the genial complexion and popular accomplishments here inimitably described.
[6] hunting. [Morris's *Chaucer*, ii. 6, ver. 166.]   [7] fame.
[8] "He did not care a straw for the text," &c.

He is ambitious of appearing a conspicuous and stately figure on horseback. A circumstance represented with great elegance :

> And whan he rood, men might his bridel heere [1]
> Gyngle in a whistlyng wynd so cleere,
> And eek as lowde as doth the chapel belle.

The gallantry of his riding-dress and his genial aspect are painted in lively colours :

> I saugh his sleves purfiled [2] atte hond [3]
> With grys, [4] and that the fyneft of a lond.
> And for to feftne his hood undur his chyn
> He hadde of gold y-wrought a curious pyn :
> A love-knotte in the gretter ende ther was.
> His heed was ballid, and schon as eny glas,
> And eek his face as he hadde be anoynt.
> He was a lord ful fat and in good poynt ;
> His eyen fteep, and rollyng in his heed,
> That ftemed as a forneys of a leed ;
> His bootes souple, his hors in gret eftat.
> Now certeinly he was a fair prelat ;
> He was not pale as a for-pyned gooft.
> A fat swan loved he beft of eny rooft.
> His palfray was as broun as eny berye.

The Frere, or friar, is equally fond of diversion and good living ; but the poverty of his establishment obliges him to travel about the country, and to practise various artifices to provide money for his convent, under the sacred character of a confessor.

> A frere ther was, a wantoun and a merye, [5]
> A lymytour, [6] a ful folempne man.
> In alle the ordres foure [7] is noon that can
> So moche of daliaunce and fair langage.
> *   *   *
> Ful sweetly herde he confessioun,
> And plesaunt was his absolucioun ;
> *   *   *
> His typet was ay farfud ful of knyfes
> And pynnes, for to yive faire wyfes.
> And certaynli he hadde a mery noote.
> Wel couthe he synge and pleye on a rote. [8]

---

[1] [Morris's *Chaucer*, ii. 6, ver. 169.]
[2] fringed.   [3] [Morris's *Chaucer*, ii. 7, ver. 193.]   [4] fur.
[5] [Morris's *Chaucer*, ii. 7, ver. 208.]
[6] A friar that had a particular grant for begging or hearing confessions within certain limits.
[7] of Mendicants.
[8] A rote is a musical instrument.   Lydgate, MSS. Fairfax, Bibl. Bodl. 16.

> " For ther was Rotys of Almayne,
>   And eke of Arragon and Spayne."

Again, in the same manuscript,

> " Harpys, fitheles, and eke rotys,
>   Wel according to ther notys."

Where *fitheles* is *fiddles*, as in the *Prol. Cl. Oxenf.* v. 298.   So in the *Roman d' Alexandre*, MSS. Bibl. Bodl. *ut supr.* fol. i. b, col. 2.

> " *Rote*, harpe, viole, et gigne, et siphonie."

I cannot help mentioning in this place, a pleasant mistake of Bishop Morgan, in

Of yeddynges[1] he bar utterly the prys.[2]
*   *   *   *   *   *

Ther was no man nowher so vertuous.
He was the befte begger in al his hous,[3]
*   *   *   *   *   *

Somwhat he lipfede, for wantounesse,
To make his Englisfch swete upon his tunge ;
And in his harpyng, whan that he hadde sunge,
His eyghen twynkeled in his heed aright,
As don the sterres in the frofty night.

With these unhallowed and untrue sons of the church is contrasted
the parson or parish-priest : in describing whose fanctity, simplicity,
sincerity, patience, industry, courage, and conscientious impartiality,
Chaucer shews his good sense and good heart. Dryden imitated this
character of the Good Parson, and is said to have applied it to
Bishop Ken. [The *Perfones Tale*, as Dr. Morris has pointed out,
was partly borrowed by Chaucer, with large variations, from the
French treatise, *La Somme de Vices et de Vertus*, by Frere Lorens,
of which there are versions in English, both prose and metrical.][4]

The character of the Squire teaches us the education and requisite
accomplishments of young gentlemen in the gallant reign of Edward III. But it is to be remembered, that our squire is the son of
a knight, who has performed feats of chivalry in every part of the
world ; which the poet thus enumerates with great dignity and simplicity :

At Alifandre he was whan it was wonne,[5]
Ful ofte tyme he hadde the bord bygonne[6]
Aboven alle naciouns in Pruce.
In Lettowe[7] hadde reyced and in Ruce
No criften man so ofte of his degré.
In Gernade atte siege hadde he be

---

his translation of the New Testament into Welsh, printed 1567. He translates the
Vials of wrath, in the Revelation, by *Crythan*, i. e. *Crouds* or Fiddles, Rev. v. 8.
The Greek is φιαλαι. Now it is probable that the bishop translated only from the
English, where he found vials, which he took for viols.

[1] [The *Prompt. Parv.* makes yedding to be the same as geste which it explains
thus : geeft or romaunce, geftio. So that yeddinges may perhaps mean of ftory-
telling.—*Tyrwhitt.*]

[2] [Morris's *Chaucer*, ii. 8, ver. 237.]

[3] convent.   [4] [*Ayenbite of Inwyt*, ed. 1866, Introd.]

[5] [Morris's *Chaucer*, ii. 3, ver. 51.]

[6] See this phrase explained above, p. 354, note 3. I will here add a similar expression from Gower, *Conf. Amant.* lib. viii. [iii. 299, edit. 1857.]

" Bad his marefhall of his halle
To fetten him in fuch degre,
That he upon him myghte fe.
The king was fone fette and ferved,
And he which had his prife deferved,
After the kings owne worde,
Was made begin a middel borde."

That is, " he was seated in the middle of the table, a place of diftinction and
dignity." [See the Forewords to *The Babees Book*, E. E. T. Soc. 1868. — F.]

[7] Lithuania.

Of Algefir,[1] and riden in Belmarie.[2]
At Lieys[3] was he, and at Satalie,[4]
Whan they were wonne ; and in the Greete fee
At many a noble arive hadde he be.
At mortal batailles hadde he ben fiftene,
And foughten for oure feith at Tramaffene[5]
In lyftes thries, and ay flayn his foo.
This ilke worthi knight hadde ben alfo
Somtyme with the lord of Palatye,[6]
Ayeyn[7] another hethene in Turkye :
And everemore he hadde a fovereyn prys.
And though that he was worthy he was wys.

The poet in fome of thefe lines implies, that after the Chriftians
were driven out of Paleftine, the Englifh knights of his days joined
the knights of Livonia and Pruffia, and attacked the pagans of
Lithuania and its adjacent territories. Lithuania was not converted
to Chriftianity till towards the clofe of the fourteenth century.
Pruffian targets are mentioned, as we have before feen, in the *Knight's
Tale*. Thomas, Duke of Gloucefter, youngeft fon of King Edward III.
and Henry Earl of Derby, afterwards Henry IV. travelled into
Pruffia : and in conjunction with the grand mafters and knights of
Pruffia and Livonia, fought the infidels of Lithuania. The Earl of
Derby was greatly inftrumental in taking Vilna, the capital of that

---

[1] [Algefiras ; a Spanifh town on the oppofite fide of the bay of Gibraltar.—*Price*.]
[2] Speght fuppofes it to be that country in Barbary which is called Benamarin.
It is mentioned again in the *Knight's Tale*, v. 1772.

" Ne in Belmary ther is no fel lyoun,
   That hunted is," &c.

By which at leaft we may conjecture it to be fome country in Africa. [Froiffart
reckons it among the kingdoms of Africa : Thunes, Bovgie, Maroch, Belle-
marine, Tremeffen. The battle of Benamarin is faid by a late author of Viage
de Efpanna, p. 73, n. 1, to have been fo called : " por haber quedallo en ella
Albohacen, Rey de Marruccos del linage de Aben Marin." Perhaps therefore the
dominions of that family in Africa might be called abufively Benamarin, and by a
further corruption Belmarie.—*Tyrwhitt*.]
[3] Some fuppofe it to be Laviffa, a city on the continent, near Rhodes. Others,
Lybiffa, a city of Bithynia.
[4] A city in Anatolia, called Atalia. Many of thefe places are mentioned in the
hiftory of the Crufades. The gulf and caftle of Satalia are mentioned by Benedictus Abbas, in the Crufade under the year 1191, " Et cum rex Franciæ receffiffet
ab Antiocheo, ftatim intravit gulfum Sathallæ.—Sathallæ Caftellum eft optimum,
unde gulfus ille nomen accepit ; et fuper gulfum illum funt duo Caftella et Villæ,
et utrumque dicitur Satalia. Sed unum illorum eft defertum, et dicitur Vetus
Satalia quod piratæ deftruxerunt, et alterum Nova Satalia dicitur, quod Manuel
imperator Conftantinopolis firmavit." *Vit. et Geft. Henr. et Ric. ii.* p. 680. Afterwards he mentions *Mare Græcum*, p. 683. That is, the Mediterranean from Sicily
to Cyprus. I am inclined, in the fecond verfe following, to read " Greke fea."
[" Probably the part of the Mediterranean, which wafhes the fhores of Paleftine in
oppofition to the fmall inland Sea or Lake of Gennefaret and the Dead Sea."—*Bell*.]
Leyis is the town of Layas in Armenia.
[5] " In the holy war at Thrafimene, a city in Barbary."
[6] Palathia, a city in Anatolia. See Froiffart, iii. 40.
[7] againft

country, in 1390.[1] Here is a seeming compliment to some of these
expeditions. This invincible and accomplished champion afterwards
tells the heroic tale of *Palamon and Arcite*. His son the *Squire*, a
youth of twenty years, is thus delineated :

> And he hadde ben somtyme in chivachie,[2]
> In Flaundres, in Artoys, and in Picardie,
> And born him wel, as in so litel space,
> In hope to stonden in his lady grace.
> Embrowdid was he, as it were a mede
> Al ful of fresshe floures, white and reede.
> Syngynge he was, or flowtynge, al the day ;
> He was as fresh as is the moneth of May.
> Schort was his goune, with sleeves long and wyde.
> Wel cowde he sitte on hors, and *faire* ryde.
> He cowde songes wel make and endite,
> Justne and eek daunce, and wel purtray and write.

To this young man the poet, with great observance of decorum,
gives the tale of Cambuscan, the next in knightly dignity to that of
Palamon and Arcite. He is attended by a yeoman, whose figure
revives the ideas of the forest laws :

> And he was clad in coote and hood of grene.[3]
> A shef of pocok arwes bright and kene[4]
> Under his belte he bar ful thriftily.
> Wel cowde he dresse his takel yomanly ;
> His arwes drowpud nought with fetheres lowe.
> And in his hond he bar a mighty bowe.
>
> *   *   *   *   *
>
> Upon his arme he bar a gay bracer,[5]

---

[1] See Hakluyt's *Voyages*, i. 122, *seq.* edit. 1598. See also Hakluyt's account of
the conquest of Prussia by the Dutch Knights Hospitallers of Jerusalem, *ibid.* [The
original documents relating to this expedition, and also to these knights' expedition
to the Holy Land, are now in the Record Office in London, and ought certainly to
be printed by some learned Society.—F.]

[2] Chivalry, riding, exercises of horsemanship, *Compl. Mar. Ven.* v. 144.

> " Ciclinius ryding in his chevaché
> Fro Venus."

[Morris's *Chaucer*, ii. 4, ver. 85.]

[3] *Ibid.* ver. 103.

[4] Comp. Gul. Waynflete, episc. Winton. an. 1471, (*supr. citat.*) Among the
stores of the bishop's castle of Farnham. "*Arcus cum chordis.* Et red. comp. de xxiv.
arcubus cum xxiv. chordis de remanentia —*Sagittæ magnæ.* Et de cxliv. sagittis
magnis barbatis cum pennis pavonum." In a *Computus* of Bishop Gerways, episc.
Winton. an. 1266, (*supr. citat*) among the stores of the bishop's castle of Taunton,
one of the heads or styles is, *Caudæ pavonum,* which I suppose were used for fea-
thering arrows. In the articles of *Arma,* which are part of the episcopal stores of
the said castle, I find enumerated one thousand four hundred and twenty-one great
arrows for cross-bows, remaining over and above three hundred and seventy-one
delivered to the bishop's vassals *tempore guerre.* Under the same title occur cross-
bows made of horn. Arrows with feathers of the peacock occur in Lydgate's
Siege of Troy, B. iii. cap. 22, sign. O iii. edit. 1555.

> " Many good archers
> Of Boeme, which with their arrows kene,
> And with fethirs of pecocke freshe and shene," &c.

[5] armour for the arms.

> And by his fide a fwerd and a bokeler,
> * * * *
> A Criftofre[1] on his breft of filver fchene.
> An hórn he bar, the bawdrik was of grene.

The character of the Reeve (or Steward), an officer of much greater truft and authority during the feudal conftitution than at prefent, is happily pictured.[2] His attention to the care and cuftody of the manors. the produce of which was then kept in hand for furnifhing his lord's table, perpetually employs his time, preys upon his thoughts, and makes him lean and choleric. He is the terror of bailiffs and hinds : and is remarkable for his circumfpection, vigilance, and fubtlety. He is never in arrears, and no auditor is able to over-reach or detect him in his accounts : yet he makes more commodious purchafes for himfelf than for his mafter, without forfeiting the goodwill or bounty of the latter. Amidft thefe ftrokes of fatire, Chaucer's genius for defcriptive painting breaks forth in this fimple and beautiful defcription of the Reeve's rural habitation :

> His wonyng[3] was ful fair upon an heth,[4]
> With grene trees i-fchadewed was his place.

In the Clerk of Oxford[5] our author glances at the inattention paid to literature, and the unprofitablenefs of philofophy. He is emaciated with ftudy, clad in a thread-bare cloak, and rides a fteed lean as a rake :

> For he hadde nought geten him yit a benefice,[6]
> Ne was not worthy to haven an office.
> For him was lever[7] have at his beddes heed
> Twenty bookes, clothed in blak and reed,
> Of Ariftotil, and of his philofophie,
> Then robus riche, or fithul,[8] or fawtrie.
> But although he were a philofophre,
> Yet hadde he but litul gold in cofre.[9]

His unwearied attention to logic had tinctured his converfation with much pedantic formality, and taught him to fpeak on all fubjects in a precife and fententious ftyle.[10] Yet his converfation was

---

[1] A faint who prefided over the weather. The patron of field fports.
[2] [See the Ballad of John de Reeve in the *Percy Folio Ballads and Romances*, ii. 550.]
[3] dwelling. [4] [Morris's *Chaucer*, ii. 19, ver. 606.]
[5] [For the early Oxford Life and Studies, fee Mr. Anfty's *Munimenta Academica*, Rolls Series, 1868.]
[6] [Morris's *Chaucer*, ii. 10, ver. 291.] [7] rather. [8] fiddle.
[9] Or it may be explained, "Yet he could not find the philofopher's ftone."
[10] [This opinion is founded on the following paffage :

> "Not oo word fpak he more than was neede ;
> Al that he fpak it was of heye prudence,
> And fchort, and quyk, and ful of gret fentence."
> Morris's *Chaucer*, ii. 10, 304.

Mr. Tyrwhitt has given a happier and unqueftionably a correcter interpretation of thefe lines : "'In forme and reverence,' with propriety and modefty. In the next line, 'ful of high fentence' means only, I apprehend, full of high or excellent fenfe. Mr. Warton will excufe me for fuggefting thefe explanations of this paffage in lieu of thofe which he has given. The credit of good letters is concerned that

inſtructive : and he was no leſs willing to ſubmit than to communicate his opinion to others :

> Sownynge in moral manere was his ſpeche,[1]
> And gladly wolde he lerne, and gladly teche.

The perpetual importance of the Serjeant of Law, who by habit
or by affectation has the faculty of appearing buſy when he has
nothing to do, is ſketched with the ſpirit and conciſeneſs of Horace:

> Nowher ſo beſy a man as he ther nas,[2]
> And yit he ſemede beſier than he was.[3]

There is ſome humour in making our lawyer introduce the
language of his pleadings into common converſation. He addreſſes
the hoſt :

> Hoſt, quod he, *De par Dieux I aſſente.*[4]

The affectation of talking French was indeed general, but it is
here appropriate and in character.

Among the reſt, the character of the Hoſt, or maſter of the
Tabard inn where the pilgrims are aſſembled, is conſpicuous. He
has much good ſenſe, and diſcovers great talent for managing and

---

Chaucer ſhould not be ſuppoſed to have made a pedantic formality and a preciſe
ſententious ſtyle on all ſubjects the characteriſtics of a ſcholar."—*Tyrwhitt.*]
[1] [Morris's *Chaucer*, ii. 10, ver. 307.]   [2] [*Ibid.* ii. 11, ver. 321.]
[3] [*Ibid.* ii. 171, ver. 39.] He is ſaid to have "oftin yben at the parviſe," ver. 312.
It is not my deſign to enter into the diſputes concerning the meaning or etymology
of parvis : from which parviſia, the name for the public ſchools in Oxford, is derived.
But I will obſerve, that parvis is mentioned as a court or portico before the church
of Notre Dame at Paris, in John de Meun's part of the *Roman de la Roſe*, ver.
12529 :

> " A Paris n'euſt hommes ne femme
> Au parvis devant Noſtre Dame."

The paſſage is thus tranſlated by Chaucer, or the writer of the *Rom. R. v.* 7109 :

> " Ther nas no wight in alle Parys
> Biforne oure lady at parvys."

The word is ſuppoſed to be contracted from Paradiſe. This perhaps ſignified an
ambulatory. Many of our old religious houſes had a place called Paradiſe. In
the year 1300, children were taught to read and ſing in the Parvis of St. Martin's
church at Norwich. Blomf. *Norf.* ii. 748. Our Serjeant is afterwards ſaid to have
received many fees and robes, v. 319. The ſerjeants and all the officers of the
ſuperior courts of law, anciently received winter and ſummer robes, from the king's
wardrobe. He is likewiſe ſaid to cite caſes and deciſions, " that from the time of
king William were full," v. 326. For this line ſee the very learned and ingenious
Mr. Barrington's *Obſervations on the antient Statutes.* [This ſubject is better diſcuſſed (ſays Mr. Douce) in Staveley's *Hiſtory of Churches*, p. 157. He thinks the
term is from *parvis pueris*, i. e. the children who were taught in a certain part of
the church ſo appropriated ; as appears from the quotation above cited in the note
from Blomefield. Herbert the preſs-hiſtorian adds, that Minſter-church in the iſle
of Thanet and St. Dunſtan's in the Eaſt, London, have portions of them aſſigned
for ſchools ; and no doubt but there are ſeveral others which have the ſame.—I can
add from my own knowledge, that the chapel at Hughington in the county of
Lincoln was appropriated to the purpoſes of a ſchool, and that King Street chapel,
Weſtminſter, has a portion of its ſtructure ſet apart for ſuch purpoſe : for I received
the greater ſhare of my education in both thoſe places.—*Park.*]
[4] [Morris's *Chaucer*, ii. 171, ver. 39.]

regulating a large company; and to him we are indebted for the
happy propofal of obliging every pilgrim to tell a ftory during their
journey to Canterbury. . His interpofitions between the tales are
very ufeful and enlivening; and he is fomething like the chorus on
the Grecian ftage. He is of great fervice in encouraging each perfon to begin his part, in conducting the fcheme with fpirit, in making
proper obfervations on the merit or tendency of the feveral ftories,
in fettling difputes which muft naturally arife in the courfe of fuch
an entertainment, and in connecting all the narratives into one continued fyftem. His love of good cheer, experience in marfhalling
guefts, addrefs, authoritative deportment, and facetious difpofition,
are thus expreffively difplayed by Chaucer:

> Greet cheere made oure oft us everichon,[1]
> And to the fouper fette he us anon;
> And ferved us with vitaille atte befte.
> Strong was the wyn, and wel to drynke us lefte.[2]
> A femely man oure oofte was withalle
> For to han been a marchal in an halle;
> A large man was he with eyghen ftepe,
> A fairere burgeys is ther noon in Chepe[3]
> Bold of his fpeche, and wys, and wel i-taught,
> And of manhede lakkede he right naught.
> Eke therto he was right a mery man.

Chaucer's fcheme of the *Canterbury Tales* was evidently left un-
finifhed. It was intended by our author, that every pilgrim fhould
likewife tell a Tale on the return from Canterbury.[4] A poet, who
lived foon after the *Canterbury Tales* made their appearance, feems to
have defigned a fupplement to this deficiency, and with this view to
have written a tale called the *Merchant's Second Tale*, or the *Hiftory
of Beryn*.[5] It was firft printed by Urry, who fuppofed it to be
Chaucer's.[6] In the Prologue, which is of confiderable length, there
is fome humour and contrivance: the author, happily enough,
continues to characterize the pilgrims, by imagining what each

---

[1] [Morris's *Chaucer*, ii. 24, ver. 747.]
[2] we liked.   [3] Cheapfide.
[4] Or rather, two on their way thither, and two on their return. Only Chaucer
himfelf tells two tales. The poet fays that there were twenty-nine pilgrims in
company: but in the Characters he defcribes more. Among the Tales which
remain, there are none of the Priorefs's Chaplains, the Haberdafher, Carpenter,
Webfter, Dyer, Tapifer, and Hoft. The Canon's Yeoman has a Tale, but no
Character. The *Plowman's Tale* is certainly fuppofititious. See *fupr.* and *Obs.
Spens.* ii. 217. It is omitted in the copy of the *Canterbury Tales*, MSS. Harl. 1758.
Thefe Tales were fuppofed to be fpoken, not written. But we have in the
Ploughman's, "For my writing me allow." And in other places, "For my
writing if I have blame."—"Of my writing have me excus'd," &c. See a note at
the beginning of the *Cant. Tales*, MSS. Laud, K. 50, Bibl. Bodl. written by John
Barcham. But the difcuffion of thefe points properly belongs to an editor of
Chaucer. [See Mr. Tyrwhitt's *Introductory Difcourfe to the Canterbury Tales.—
Price.*]
[5] [Lydgate alfo wrote his *Sege of Thebes* as a fupplementary Canterbury Tale.
—F.]
[6] Urr. *Chauc.* p. 595.

did, and how each behaved, when they all arrived at Canterbury. After dinner was ordered at their inn, they all proceed to the
cathedral. At entering the church one of the monks sprinkles them
with holy water. The Knight with the better sort of the company
goes in great order to the shrine of Thomas a Becket. The Miller
and his companions run staring about the church : they pretend to
blazon the arms painted in the glass windows, and enter into a dispute
in heraldry : but the host of the Tabard reproves them for their improper behaviour and impertinent discourse, and directs them to the
martyr's shrine. When all had finished their devotions, they return
to the inn. In the way thither they purchase toys for which that
city was famous, called *Canterbury brochis*, and here much facetious-
ness passes betwixt the Friar and the Sumner, in which the latter
vows revenge on the former, for telling a tale so palpably levelled at
his profession, and protests he will retaliate on their return by a more
severe story. When dinner is ended, the host of the Tabard thanks
all the company in form for their several tales. The party then
separate till supper-time by agreement. The Knight goes to survey
the walls and bulwarks of the city, and explains to his son the Squire
the nature and strength of them. Mention is here made of great
guns. The Wife of Bath is too weary to walk far ; she proposes to
the Prioress to divert themselves in the garden, which abounds with
herbs proper for making salves. Others wander about the streets.
The Pardoner has a low adventure, which ends much to his disgrace.
The next morning they proceed on their return to Southwark : and
our genial master of the Tabard, just as they leave Canterbury, by
way of putting the company into good humour, begins a panegyric
on the morning and the month of April, some lines of which I shall
quote, as a specimen of our author's abilities in poetical description :[1]

> Lo ! how the seson of the yere, and Averell[2] shouris,
> Doith[3] the bushis burgyn[4] out blossomes and flouris.
> Lo ! the prymerosys of the yere, how fresh they bene to sene,
> And many othir flouris among the grassis grene.
> Lo ! how they springe and sprede, and of divers hue,
> Beholdith and seith, both white, red, and blue.
> That lusty bin and comfortabyll for mannis sight,
> For I say for myself it makith my hert to light.

On casting lots, it falls to the Merchant to tell the first tale, which
then follows. I cannot [of course] allow that this Prologue and Tale
were written by Chaucer. Yet I believe them to be nearly coeval,
[within, perhaps, fifty years of the poet's death.]

[APPENDIX TO SECTION IX.

In connection with the *Canterbury Tales*,[5] it will be well to say
something of the MSS. of them, the classes of those MSS., the groups
and order of the Tales, the stages of the journey, Chaucer's use of

---

[1] There is a good description of a magical palace, v. 1973—2076.
[2] April.   [3] make.   [4] shoot.
[5] [The following paragraphs on Chaucer are by Mr. Furnivall.]

the final *e*, and the genuinenefs of fome of the poems attributed to him.

Of MSS. of the Tales we know at leaft forty-eight; and of thefe forty-two have been lately examined in order, 1. to choofe the beft fix un printed for the Chaucer Society to print, 2. to find ou. in what fragments and groups the Tales were left by Chaucer at his death, and 3. what great differences the MSS. fhow between themfelves. Lord Afhburnham, who has three MSS. of the Tales, has declined to allow the examination of his MSS. for the purpofes above ftated, but the remaining forty-two MSS. fhow that they may be ranged under two types, if we claffify by *readings*, namely that of the Harleian MS. 7334 (printed by Mr. Thomas Wright and Dr. Richard Morris) and that of the Ellefmere MS. (one of the type that Tyrwhitt printed). But if we claffify by *ftructure*,—by the order of the fragments of the Tales, and the changes made in the text by the changes of that order,—which plan beft exhibits the differences of the MSS., we muft range our MSS. under three main types.

Text A. Gamelyn in (generally); Man of Law's end-link changed to ferve as a Prologue to the Squire's Tale, which is mifplaced, to follow the Man of Law, as the Merchant's Tale is, to follow the Squire. Confequently, the ftanzas of the Clerk's end-link or envoy are mifplaced, fo as to break the join between it and the Merchant's Tale made by the lines

And let hem care and wepe, and wyng and wayle.[1]

Wepyng and wailyng, care and other forwe.[2]

No Hoft-ftanza between the Clerk's and Merchant's Tales; Squire's end-link (or Franklin's Prologue) ufed as the Merchant's Prologue. Generally, fpurious Prologues to Shipman and Franklin. Second Nun and Canon's Yeoman kept up high in the order of tales. Modern inftances in the Monk's Tale in their right places, after Zenobia.[3]

---

[1] End of Clerk, l. 9088, Wright.   [2] Line 1 of Merchant, l. 9089, Wright.

[3] The following are MSS. of the A type, though fome vary from it in certain points:

Lanfdowne, 851.	Trin. Coll. Cambr. R. 3. 15.
Lichfield Cathedral.	Trin. Coll. Cambr. R. 3. 3.
Harleian, 7333.	Barlow, 20.
Harleian, 1758.	Laud, 739.
Sloane, 1685.	New Coll. Oxf.
Royal, 17 D xv.	Corpus Chr. Coll. Oxf. 198.
Royal, 18 C ii.	Hatton, 1.
Camb. Univ. Ii 3. 26.	Rawl. MS. Poet. 149.
Sloane, 1686.	Rawl. Mifc. 1133.
Petworth.	(All the early printed editions.)
Camb. Univ. Mm. 2. 5.	

Other MSS. varying much in the order of Tales, or being incomplete, are

Harl., 1239.	Arch. Seld., B 14, (the only MS. that
Sion Coll.	rightly joins the Man of Law's and
Brit. Mus. Addit. 25, 718.	Shipman's Tales.)
Hengwrt.	Holkham.
Rawl. MS. Poet. 141.	Chrift Church, Oxf. 152.
Laud, 600.	

Text B. Harleian, 7334. Gamelyn in; Man of Law's end-link left, but with nothing to join into it. Clerk and Merchant kept together (no Hoſt-ſtanza between). Second Nun and Canon's Yeoman kept up. Modern inſtances in Monk's Tale in their right places (that is, the 2 Peters, Barnabo, and Hugilin, come after Zenobia, and before Nero).

Text C, or Edited Texts.[1] Gamelyn cut out. Man of Law's end-link cut out. Hoſt-ſtanza inſerted between Clerk and Merchant. Second Nun and Canon's Yeoman placed late. Modern inſtances in Monk's Tale put at the end, thus breaking the join made by

> But for that *fortune* wil alway aſſayle, 16249.
>
> And cover hir brighte face with a *clowde,* 16252.[2]
>
> He ſpak, how *fortune* was clipped with a *clowde,* 16268.[3]

It is ſomewhat curious that not one of the MSS. yet examined exhibits the Tales in the order in which Chaucer himſelf muſt have arranged or meant to arrange them, as ſhown by the ſtate he left them in at his death. That order is the following, which falls in well with a three-and-a-half days' journey of the pilgrims to Canterbury, allowing about ſixteen miles a day,—enough for the women to ride along the bad miry roads of thoſe early times:

Groups.	Frag-ments.	Tales and Links.	Allusions to Places, Times, Prior Tales, &c. (Wright's 2-col. ed.)	Diſtances and Stages.
		1 GENERAL PRO-LOGUE	In Southwerk at the Tabbard as I lay. (l. 20).	
		2 KNIGHT		
		3 Link		
A.	I	4 MILLER		
		5 Link	Lo heer is Deptford, and it is paſſed prime ; Lo Grenewich, ther many a ſchrewe is inne. (l. 3906-7).	
		6 REVE		
		7 Link		
		8 COOK		[? Dartford
		• • •	[? End of the Firſt Day's Journey.]	15 miles.]
	II.	1 Prologue		
		2 MAN OF LAW	It was ten of the clokke, he gan conclude (l. 4434).	
		3 Link		
		4 SHIPMAN		
B.		5 Link		
		6 PRIORESS		
		7 Link		
		8 SIR THOPAS		
	III.	9 L nk		
		10 MELIBE		
		11 Link		
		12 MONK	Lo, Rowcheſtre ſtant hee.-faſte by (l. 15412).	
		13 Link		
		14 NUN'S PRIEST		
		15 Link		[? Rocheſter
		• • •	[? End of the Second Day's Journey.]	30 miles.]

[1] MSS. of the C type, *Edited Texts,* are:

Elleſmere.
Camb. Univ. Gg. 4. 27.
Camb. Univ. Dd. 4. 24.
Harl. 7335.
Addit. Brit. Mus. 5140, (or Aſkew, 2.)

Duke of Devonſhire.
Helmingham.
Bodley, 686.
Haiſtwell MS. (or Aſkew, 1.)

[2] End of Monkes Tale, ed. Wright, from Harl. 7334.

[3] 6th line of Prologue of Nonne Preſtes Tale.

Groups.	Frag-ments.	Tales and Links.	Allusions to Places, Times, Prior Tales, &c. (Wright's 2-col. ed.)	Distances and Stages.
C.	IV.†	1 DOCTOR 2 Link and Prologue 3 PARDONER		
		* * *		
D.	V.	1 Prologue	Quod this Sompnour, " And I byfchrewe me But if I telle tales tuo or thre Of freres, er I come to Sydingborne. l. 6427-9).	
		2 WIFE OF BATH. 3 Link 4 FRIAR 5 Link 6 SOMPNOUR	My tale is dor, we ben almoft at toune. (l. 7876). [? Sittingbourne [? Halt in the Third Day's Journey for Dinner.] 40 miles.]	
		* * *		

† This group may go on any morning. It is put here to make the Tales of the Third Day not
lefs than thofe of the Second.

Groups.	Frag-ments.	Tales and Links.		Distances and Stages.
E.	VI.	1 Prologue 2 CLERK 3 Link 4 Link	For which heer, for the wyves love of Bathe (l. 9046).	
		5 MERCHANT	The wif of Bathe, if ye han underftonde, Of mariage, which ye han now in honde Declared hath ful wel in litel fpace (l. 9559-61)	
		6 Link	To tellen al ; wherfor my tale is do (l. 10314). [? Ofpringe [? End of the Third Day's Journey.] 46 miles.]	
		* * *		
F.	VII.	1 Link (l. 10315) 2 SQUIRE 3 Link 4 FRANKLIN	I wol not tarien you, for it is pryme (l. 10387).	
		* * *		
G.	VIII.	1 SECOND NUN 2 Link & Prologue 3 CANON'S YEOMAN	Er we fully had riden fyve myle, (l. 12483) At Boughton under Blee us gan atake A man, that clothed was in clothes blake. . It femed he hadde priked myles thre (l. 12489) His yeman eek was ful of curtefye, And feid, " Sires, now in the morwe tyde (l. 12516) Out of your oftelry I faugh you ryde . . . . . . al this ground on which we ben ridynge Til that we comen to Caunterbury toun (l. 12552). [Paufe. Go up Blean Hill, and through the Foreft.]	
		* * *		
H.	IX.	1 Prologue 2 MANCIPLE	Wot ye not wher ther ftont a litel toun, Which that cleped is Bob-up-and-doun, Under the Ble, in Caunterbury way ? (l. 16935) . . . Is ther no man, for prayer ne for hyre (l. 16938) That wol awake our felawe al byhynde ? A theef mighte [him] ful lightly robbe and bynde . . . Awake thou cook, fit up, God gif the forwe ! What eyleth the, to flepe by the morwe ? Haft thou had fleen al night, or artow dronke? Or haftow with fom quen al night i-fwonke, So that thou maift not holden up thyn heed ? (l. 16951).	
			By that the Maunciple [?] had his tale endid (l. 17295)	
I.	X.	1 Link & Prologue 2 PARSON	The fonne fro the fouth line is defcendid So lowe, that it nas nought to my fight Degrees nyne and twentye as in hight [Four] on the clokke it was, as I geffe . . As we were entryng at a townes end (l. 17306) Now lakketh us no moo tales than oon (l. 17310) I wol yow telle a mery tale in profe, (l. 17340) To knyt up all this feft, and make an ende; But hafteth yow, the fonne wol adoun (l. 17366). [End of the Fourth Day's Journey. Reach Canterbury] [56 miles]	

For a juftification of the conclufions here given, I muft refer to
my Temporary Preface to the Six Text edition of *Chaucer's Canterbury Tales*, Part I. 1868; and to Part I. of the Six-Text itfelf
for fpecimens of the changed Man of Law's and Squire's end-links,
the fpurious Prologues, &c., as well as tables fhowing the order of
the tales in thirty-fix MSS. and five old printed editions.

The language of Chaucer—efpecially his ufe of the final *e*—and by
it the fettlement of what works attributed to him are genuine and
what not, is a queftion of the higheft importance. The ufe of *e* final

by Chaucer, in the excellent, though flightly provincial MS. of *Canterbury Tales*, Harl. MS. 7334, as printed by Mr. Thomas Wright,
and by Gower in his *Confeffio Amantis*, as reprefented by Dr. Pauli's
edition, has been inveftigated with the greateft care by Prof. F. J.
Child, of Harvard Univerfity, Maffachufetts. His refults have been
incorporated by Mr. Alexander J. Ellis in his important work on
*Early Englifh Pronunciation, with fpecial reference to Chaucer and
Shakefpeare*, publifhed jointly by the Philological, Early Englifh
Text, and Chaucer Societies. Dr. Richard Morris in his admirable
Selections from Chaucer, has alfo ftated the main refults of Prof.
Child's and his own inveftigations into the ufe of the final *e* by
Chaucer ; and as both the two laft-named works are fo eafily to
be had, and fhould be in the poffeffion of every ftudent, a reference
to them is all that is needed here.

Mr. H. Bradfhaw, Librarian of the Univerfity of Cambridge, the
moft Chaucer-learned ftudent in England, ftated fome years back,
that having put in one clafs the works undoubtedly Chaucer's,—thofe
named as his by himfelf, or attributed to him by his cotemporaries,
or good MSS.,—and having put into a fecond clafs the other works
attributed to Chaucer on authorities other than thofe above fpecified,
he found on tefting them by the *ye-y* rhyme teft, that all the works of
the firft clafs ftood the teft and proved genuine, while all the works
of the fecond clafs failed under the teft, and proved (in his opinion)
fpurious. Having thus (as he fays) both external and internal evidence againft this fecond clafs, Mr. Bradfhaw rejects as Chaucer's
works, the following poems contained in Dr. R. Morris's Aldine
edition of the poet's Poetical Works, and *à fortiori*, all the fpurious
matter introduced into *Chaucer's Works* by former editors :

Court of Love, iv. 1.	Romaunt of the Rofe, vi. 1.
Boke of Cupide, or Cuckow and	Compleynte of a Loveres Lyfe, or
Nightingale, iv. 51.	Black Knyght, vi. 235.
Flower and Leaf, iv. 87.	Goodly Ballade of Chaucer, vi. 275.
Chaucer's Dream, v. 86.	Praife of Women, vi. 278.
Proverbs of Chaucer, vi. 303.	Leaulte vault Richeffe, vi. 302.
World fo wyde, *ib.*	Virelai, vi. 305.
Roundel, vi. 304.	Chaucer's Prophecy, vi. 307.

Mr. Bradfhaw's refults have fince been confirmed by a wholly independent inveftigator, Prof. Bernhard Ten Brink of Marburg, in
Caffel, whofe Chaucer *Studien*,[1] Part I. 1870, is at prefent the only
book worthy of notice on the fubject. But Prof. Ten Brink does not
agree with Mr. Bradfhaw in rejecting the *Romaunt of the Rofe* as
Chaucer's, on the ground of its *ye-y* rhymes, &c. as he thinks that in
this, the poet's earlieft work, he may have worked on lefs ftrict rules
of rhyme than he did in his later works. I ftrengthened this fuppofition by fhewing that at leaft three of Chaucer's immediate pre-
deceffors, Minot, William of Shoreham, and Robert of Brunne,

---

[1] Chaucer : *Studien zur Gefchichte feiner Entwicklung, und zur Chronologie feiner
Schriften*, A Ruffell, Münfter.

rhymed *ye* with *y*; and Mr. Jofeph Payne has now fhown[1] reafons for fuppofing that neither in Norman-French nor Early Englifh was the final *e* generally a feparate fyllable; and that Chaucer is no exception to the rule.   Mr. Payne's conclufion is, that on the ground of the *ye-y* rhyme, no work attributed to Chaucer can be declared fpurious. *Adhuc fub judice lis eft.*

Herr Ten Brink divides Chaucer's life into three periods, I. Up to the time of his Italian travels, 1372, when he was under French influence,[2] and produced the *Romaunt* in 1366, the *Boke of the Ducheffe* in 1369; II. After his Italian travels to 1384, his works being [the *Complaynt upon Pite*], the *Life of St. Cecile*, 1373, the *Parlement of Foules*, [the *Compleynt of Mars*], and *Palamon and Arcite*, *Boece*, *Troylus*, [the *Former Age*,[3] *Lines to Adam Scrivener*], with the *Houfe of Fame*, in 1384; III. Thence to the poet's death in 1400, comprifing the *Legende of Good Women*, the *Aftrolabe*, *Anelida and Arcite*, *Canterbury Tales*, *Complaynt of Venus*, with a few minor poems. Herr Ten Brink's *Studien* have been tranflated for, and will be publifhed by, the Chaucer Society.

Early in Chaucer's third period I fhould put his *Gentilneffe* (the firfte Fadir, &c.), *A B C*, and *Moder of God*.   His touching ballad of *Truth* (Flee fro the preefe) I fuppofe to have been written about the time of his loffes in 1388; and perhaps the *A B C* and *Moder of God* may go with it.   The fhort poems of Chaucer's old age are, the *Complaynt of Venus*, from the French of Sir Otes de Graunfon, a knight of Savoy, who became liegeman to Richard II., *Lenvoy to Bukton*, *Balade to King Richard*, *Lenvoy to Scogan* (written after Michaelmas in a year of "deluge of peftilence," which Mr. Brad-fhaw thinks was 1393), *Compleint ageins Fortune*, and his *Compleynte to his Purfe*, addreffed to Henry IV. in Sept. 1399, for which Henry probably granted him forty marks yearly on Oct. 3, 1399.   See further in the Trial-Forewords to my parallel-text edition of Chaucer's Minor Poems, Part I. Chaucer Soc. 1871.]

---

[1] [In the laft feftion of his valuable paper on the Norman element in the written and fpoken Englifh of the 12th, 13th, and 14th centuries, *Phil. Soc. Trans.* 1868-9, pp. 428-448, but written in 1870.]

[2] [See M. Sandras's *Etudes fur Chaucer*, Paris, 1859.]

[3] [A beautiful verfe tranflation of the fifth metre of the fecond book of Boethius, firft found by Mr. Bradfhaw in two MSS. in the Cambridge Univ. Libr., and printed in Dr. Morris's *Chaucer*, vi. 300, and at the end of his Chaucer's *Boethius*, p. 180 (E. E. T. Soc. 1868).]